1995

International Travel Health Guide

SIXTH ANNUAL EDITION 6

D1368958

STUART R. ROSE, M.D.

Travel Medicine, Inc. 1-800-872-8633
351 Pleasant St., Suite 312, Northampton, MA 01060

IMPORTANT NOTICE

Information in the *1995 International Travel HealthGuide* is not intended to replace professional medical advice or treatment. If such advice or treatment is required or recommended, either before, during, or after travel, the reader is advised to consult his or her own physician or other competent licensed health professionals, agencies, or facilities.

The author and publisher disclaim any liability, personal or otherwise, resulting from the advice or information contained in this book.

International Travel HealthGuide
1995 Edition

Published by:
Travel Medicine, Inc.
351 Pleasant Street, Suite 312
Northampton, MA 01060
413-584-0381

Printed in the United States of America by McNaughton and Gunn

ISBN 0–923947–05-1

PREFACE

Dear Traveler:

You are probably wondering as you plan your trip overseas, "How do I stay healthy abroad? And what do I do if I get sick or injured far from home?" You might be worrying about which diseases could be lurking in the exotic locales you're planning to visit—or perhaps you want to know which antibiotic is now considered the best treatment for travelers' diarrhea. And what about that new strain of cholera that has recently appeared? Is it really a threat to worry about?

Like many people, you probably crave new travel experiences, but you don't want a nasty surprise that could affect your health or comfort—especially if you find out later that information was readily available that could have prevented unnecessary illness, inconvenience, or expense.

The *1995 International Travel HealthGuide* was written with you in mind. The sixth edition contains over 450 pages of information (updated through October 1994) to help you avoid diseases such as malaria, meningitis, cholera, hepatitis, typhoid, travelers' diarrhea, dengue, yellow fever, and many others. Utilizing data from the World Health Organization, the Centers for Disease Control and Prevention, dozens of medical journals and publications, and travel medicine experts worldwide, the *1995 International Travel HealthGuide* also provides the following:

- Regional Disease Risk Summaries. These summaries cover 11 regions worldwide (Europe, sub-Saharan Africa, SE Asia, etc.) and tell you which common, and not-so-common, tropical and infectious diseases may be encountered.

- Country-by-country health advisories. These updated advisories tell you which diseases are most active in each country, and where the most important diseases (e.g., malaria, schistosomiasis, leishmaniasis, etc.) are transmitted.

- An expanded listing of air ambulance companies worldwide.

- A listing of over 600 travelers' clinics in the United States and Canada.

I am sure you will find the *1995 International Travel HealthGuide* an invaluable companion to help you plan a safe trip and, should problems occur, an informative, easy-to-understand source of advice about what to do.

Sincerely,

Stuart R Rose

Stuart R. Rose, MD

CONSULTING EDITOR

Harold C. Neu, MD, FACP, Professor of Medicine and Pharmacology, College of Physicians & Surgeons, Columbia University; Chief, Division of Infectious Diseases, Department of Medicine, Columbia Presbyterian Medical Center, New York, New York.

DEDICATION

The 1995 Edition of the International Travel HealthGuide is dedicated to Dr. Harold C. Neu for his many contributions to the study of infectious diseases, research, and teaching.

ACKNOWLEDGMENT

I would like to express my thanks to the following physicians who have offered helpful advice: Ronald Behrens, Jane Zucker, Charles Houston, Jay Levy, Leonard Marcus, Harold Neu, Karl Neumann, and Allen C. Steere.

Chris Page Consulting of Amherst, Massachusetts, provided assistance with software, text layout, and map design. I am also grateful to Laura Simmons, my editor, for her meticulous review of the entire manuscript and for her many helpful suggestions.

Cover: Adkins, Balchunas Design, Pawtucket, Rhode Island

ABOUT THE AUTHOR

Stuart Ramage Rose, MD, is an emergency physician in Massachusetts. A graduate of Amherst College and Columbia University, College of Physicians and Surgeons, he is board certified in both internal medicine and emergency medicine. As a result of his long-time interest in providing health care to travelers, Dr. Rose, a licensed pilot, previously owned and operated an air ambulance company providing worldwide transport and started a hospital travelers' clinic before founding Travel Medicine, Inc.

Dr. Rose is a member of the American Medical Association and the American Society of Tropical Medicine and Hygiene.

Contents

INTRODUCTION
Travel Abroad: What are the risks?

How risky is foreign travel? People tend to exaggerate unlikely dangers such as terrorism and disregard or minimize more common perils such as motor vehicle accidents or malaria.

The chances of encountering certain diseases depends largely on where you travel. Out of 30 million Americans who go abroad each year, about eight million will be traveling to lesser-developed countries where the incidence of tropical and infectious diseases is high. Almost seven million U.S. citizens travel to countries where there is risk of malaria.

The Risk of Illness While Traveling
If you are traveling to a country in Asia, Africa, or Latin America for a one-month period, there's a 60%–75% chance that you will have some type of illness or physical symptom. Your illness, however, will probably be minor, since there is only a 5% chance you will need to see a doctor for your symptoms. Your chance of being hospitalized will be less than 1%. Exact numbers, however, can't be assigned to specific health risks because multiple factors will determine your individual degree of risk. These factors include (1) the countries or regions you will visit, (2) the duration of your trip, (3) your use (or nonuse) of prophylactic antimalarial drugs, (4) your use of personal protection measures against insect bites, (5) which vaccinations you received, (6) your personal risk-taking behavior, and (7) your own health status.

Prevention of Illness
Most travel-related diseases can be prevented or, if properly diagnosed, readily treated. Diarrheal diseases, schistosomiasis, sexually transmitted diseases, and AIDS can be prevented with personal avoidance behavior. Diseases such as hepatitis, rabies, yellow fever, and meningitis can be prevented with vaccination; chemoprophylaxis, combined with protective measures against mosquito bites, prevents most cases of malaria.

Causes of Illness
• **Diarrhea (Chapter 4)**—This is the most common malady affecting travelers. There's a 35%–60% chance that you will get a bout of travelers' diarrhea during a month-long trip to a lesser-developed country. Pay careful attention to safe food and drink guidelines—this will reduce your risk. Prompt treatment with antibiotics and loperamide stops most cases of diarrhea.
• **Malaria (Chapter 5)**—This mosquito-transmitted illness, which can be fatal, is the most important parasitic disease to avoid overseas. Malaria is a serious health

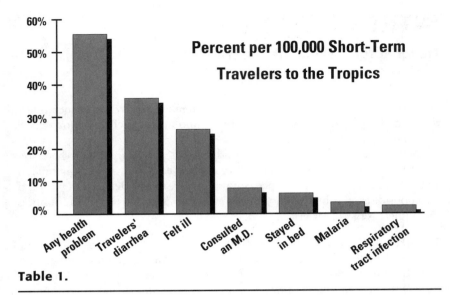

Table 1.

problem in many tropical and subtropical countries. Check your itinerary carefully to assess your risk of exposure.

• **Hepatitis (Chapter 10)**—This is the most important viral illness you need to avoid. Although rarely fatal, hepatitis A can ruin a carefully planned vacation and result in weeks or months lost from work. Prevent it with immune globulin prophylaxis and safe dietary practices. A hepatitis A vaccine will soon be available in the United States. You can prevent hepatitis B, a potentially more serious illness, with vaccination and/or personal avoidance behavior.

• **Other illnesses**—The graph above illustrates the frequency of various symptoms and illnesses you may encounter.[1] Viral diseases and colds, respiratory infections, constipation, skin rashes, ear infections and sunburn (very common among swimmers and divers in the tropics), sprains, contusions, and superficial injuries account for the majority of less-serious illnesses.

FATALITIES DURING TRAVEL

While it's quite possible you will have some type of symptom or minor illness while abroad, the chance that your illness will be fatal is reassuringly small. In 1984, out of 30 million travelers, just 1,298 deaths were recorded overseas.[2] Mortality abroad is due mainly to heart attacks and accidents. Infections cause relatively few deaths. Although heart attacks are the greatest overall cause, almost all of these deaths occur in older travelers who already have preexisting cardiovascular disease. Accidental deaths, however, unlike heart attacks, are directly travel related—and often preventable.

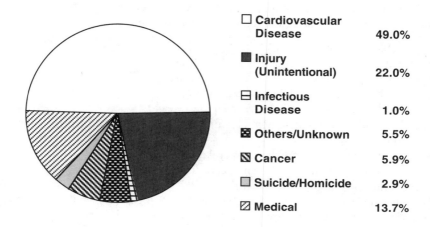

☐ Cardiovascular Disease	49.0%	
■ Injury (Unintentional)	22.0%	
⊟ Infectious Disease	1.0%	
▨ Others/Unknown	5.5%	
▨ Cancer	5.9%	
☐ Suicide/Homicide	2.9%	
▨ Medical	13.7%	

Table 2. Causes of Death While Traveling (all ages)

Overseas Fatalities of U.S. Travelers–an Overview

- Fatalities abroad are due mainly to heart attacks and accidental injuries.
- Heart attacks are the most common cause of death in older travelers—both males and females. Cardiovascular death rates, however, are not increased by travel.
- Injuries are the most common cause of death in younger travelers. The number of accidental deaths in 15- to 44-year-old travelers is higher by a factor of two to three as compared with rates among the same age group back home.
- "Excess mortality" abroad is mainly due to injuries—not heart attacks.
- Fatal injuries are mostly due to motor vehicle crashes or drownings.
- Infections cause only 1% of deaths among travelers.

HEART DISEASE AND TRAVEL

If you have a history of heart disease (e.g., heart attack, angina), you may be wondering "Should I travel?" If your medical condition is stable, travel should not represent any significant additional risk unless (1) you will be going to a remote location where the medical care that you might ordinarily receive in an emergency is not available, and/or (2) you will be subjecting yourself to unusual physical stress, (e.g., trekking at high altitudes). Under these circumstances you should have a medical consultation and pretravel testing to assess your exercise capacity. Testing may include a treadmill test, ambulatory heart monitoring, exercise thallium imaging, echocardiography, and coronary angiography.

Travelers without known heart diseases— If you are a man over the age of 40 and have one or more cardiac risk factors, or if you are a woman over 50 with two or more risk factors, you should review, with your physician, your fitness for safe travel. Risk factors for heart attack include the following:

- High blood pressure
- Diabetes
- Elevated total cholesterol—greater than 240 mg/dl
- Low HDL cholesterol—HDL less than 35 mg/dl
- Obesity (severe)—more than 30% over ideal weight
- Sedentary lifestyle—increases risk of heart attack triggered by physical exertion
- Cigarette smoking—more than 10 per day
- Family history of known coronary heart disease—definite heart attack before age 55 in a parent, brother, or sister
- Being a male—coronary heart disease is 3–4 times higher in men than women during middle age, and twice as high in elderly men as elderly women
- Prior history of heart attack, stroke, blocked blood vessel

Depending upon your medical history, your symptoms (if any), your lifestyle, number of risk factors, and also your itinerary, your doctor may advise a stress test.

NOTE: If you have no symptoms of heart disease, and have no risk factors, a treadmill test is usually not indicated.

Pretravel Cardiovascular Screening of Younger Travelers

Sudden exercise-related cardiac death in young people is very rare and mass screening is not practical or cost effective. The most common causes of sudden cardiac death in people under age 35, in decreasing order, are hypertrophic cardiomyopathy, focal cardiomyopathy, idiopathic left ventricular hypertrophy, coronary artery anomalies, familial coronary artery disease, ruptured aorta (associated with Marfan's syndrome), and mitral valve prolapse. The most efficient way to screen for these disorders is to complete a questionnaire that asks the following:

- Do you have a history of an unexplained heart murmur or chest pain?
- Have you ever suddenly felt weak enough to fall down, ever suddenly fainted, or ever fainted while exercising?
- Have you or anyone in your family ever been diagnosed with an abnormally thickened heart muscle or with Marfan's syndrome?
- Has anyone in your family died suddenly at a young age (under 35) from unknown causes, or from "heart problems"?

ACCIDENTS AND TRAVEL

Accidents are the leading cause of death among travelers under the age of 55. Deaths rates from motor vehicle accidents, for example, are much higher in some countries than in the United States (Table 3), illustrating one reason why "excess mortality" abroad is primarily injury-related.

Table 3
Motor Vehicle Fatalities

Country	Deaths per Million Registered Vehicles
Portugal	1,008
Greece	771
Spain	624
Ireland	496
Belgium	460
Luxembourg	348
Denmark	332
Italy	255
Germany	239
Netherlands	223
Great Britain	207
United States	257

A study of Peace Corps volunteers (PCV) also confirmed that motor vehicle accidents are the number one killer of younger people, followed by motorcycle accidents, drownings, and suicides.[3] Another study revealed an interesting fact: many road accidents involving tourists do not involve a collision between two vehicles, but are often due to loss of driver control caused by fatigue, alcohol, unfamiliar road conditions, or other factors.

Preventing Traffic Accidents and Injury

If you follow the recommendations below, you will decrease your chances of having an accident or being injured while driving overseas.

- Drive defensively. Don't rush.
- Don't drink and drive. Don't let friends drive drunk.
- Drive only when you are in good mental and physical condition. Don't drive when you are tired, stressed out, or hung over.
- Consider hiring a qualified guide or driver.
- Rent a larger rather than a smaller vehicle.
- Always wear your seat belt. Provide a car seat for infants.
- Know the meaning of all foreign road sign symbols.
- In most countries, a driver approaching a traffic circle must yield the right of way to those already in the circle. Although you supposedly have the right of way once in the circle, be careful not to cut anyone off exiting the circle.
- Know your route to your destination. Study road maps thoroughly.
- Try not to drive at night since there may be inadequate lighting and directional signs. Not all roads may be well marked. Also, emergency assistance will be more difficult to obtain.

- Be sure you are covered by collision and liability insurance.
- Drive a rented motorcycle and moped with extreme caution. Make sure the brakes and other equipment are in good working order.
- Wear a helmet if you do rent a motorcycle or moped.
  NOTE: If you do rent a moped, be sure you receive sufficient operating instructions from the rental agency.

Personal Safety Guidelines

Although you can't escape from the remote possibility that some nasty, unlucky incident might happen, you can take steps to lessen that possibility: plan your trip carefully, be reasonably cautious, obey common sense rules of behavior, and don't panic! Remember that the vast majority of travelers arrive home unscathed.

The following guidelines will be helpful in ensuring your travel safety.

- Carefully select swimming areas. Don't swim alone or while intoxicated.
- Avoid small, nonscheduled airlines in lesser-developed countries.
- Don't travel at night outside urban areas. If you are out at night, stay in a group.
- Don't go out on beaches at night.
- Don't hitchhike or pick up hitchhikers.
- Don't sleep in your car or RV by the road at night.
- Camp only in legal campsites.
- If you are drinking alcohol, don't relax by sitting on the railing of your hotel balcony. Falls and serious injuries often occur this way.
- Review hotel fire safety rules. Locate nearest exits.
- If possible, book a room between the second and seventh floors—high enough to prevent easy entrance by an intruder and low enough for fire equipment to reach.
- Lock your hotel room at all times.
- Keep valuables and travel documents in your room or hotel safe.
- Avoid politically unstable regions where there is civil violence.
- Avoid countries or regions where there is drug-related violence and drug trafficking. Avoid excursions into certain remote areas of countries such as Mexico, Colombia, or Peru, where you might be mistaken for a drug agent or drug dealer.
- Never purchase or use illegal drugs.

TRAVELERS' CLINICS

Before you depart you'll want to consult with a physician if you have chronic medical problems or cardiac risk factors, take medication, or are traveling to a lesser-developed country. Depending upon the complexity and length of your trip, you may need to visit a travelers' clinic. Although your own doctor may be able to administer basic immunizations and booster shots, the average physician's office doesn't stock the specialized vaccines that the overseas traveler often needs. Also, most practicing physicians in the United States have rarely, if ever, diagnosed or treated tropical diseases such as malaria, nor may they be qualified to advise travelers about health conditions overseas. Advising travelers can be quite time consuming, and many physicians, unfortunately, are not prepared to give this type of consultation. Fortunately, the specialty of travel medicine is rapidly growing and there are many doctors who either specialize in this field or who have developed a professional interest in it. These physicians are often those who are also authorized to administer the yellow fever vaccine, so visiting a physician's office that has been designated as a "Yellow Fever Vaccination Center, " or visiting an established travelers' clinic, will usually be a better source of help and advice. To help you gain access to this expertise, the *HealthGuide* contains a listing (see Appendix) of over 500 centers and travel medicine specialists.

Travelers' clinics vary in their capabilities and range of services. Some clinics only administer pretravel vaccinations and give basic travel-health advice. Many travelers need only this level of service. Other clinics are staffed by physicians who have received advanced training in tropical medicine and infectious diseases, and these clinics can provide a greater range of services, such as diagnosis and treatment of exotic tropical and infectious diseases. These clinics are often, but not invariably, associated with a university hospital or a medical school. If you need an in-depth predeparture consultation, or you suspect that you have acquired an exotic illness abroad, check on the capabilities of the clinic when you make the appointment. What is the training and experience of the staff? Are any of the clinic physicians members of the American Society of Tropical Medicine & Hygiene? Can the clinic perform laboratory testing for tropical diseases?

NOTE: Clinics listed in the Appendix that have an asterisk next to the name are staffed by one or more physicians with advanced training.

Travel Health Information

Knowledge is the key to successful travel. Knowing beforehand what hazards and hassles you may encounter—and how to deal with them—will make your trip not only more rewarding but also safer and less intimidating.

Good trip preparation involves a variable amount of "required" reading and data gathering, but a single source may not give you all the necessary health information you will need for your trip. Multiple sources may be necessary, and the *HealthGuide* lists many of these. For example, to find specific information, you can (1) consult the **World Medical Guide** section of this book, (2) go to a travelers' clinic, (3) call the CDC's hotline listed in the next chapter, (4) call one of the "900" numbers listed, (5) call a Public Health Service Quarantine Station for an advisory, and/or (6) read one or more of the publications listed below.

In addition to health matters, you will want to learn about the political, geographic, economic, and cultural environments of the countries you'll be visiting. A guidebook is a helpful starting point, and the *Frommer's* and *Lonely Planet* series are particularly informative and readable.

PUBLICATIONS

Travel Medicine

Traveller's Health—How to Stay Healthy Abroad by Dr. Richard Dawood (Oxford University Press, 1992; Third Edition). A comprehensive source of travel health information compiled by British experts. Highly recommended.

Travel Medicine Advisor. A comprehensive source of travel health information for physicians, travel clinics, corporations, health departments, and others who counsel travelers. Covers the entire spectrum of travel medicine. Includes bi-monthly updates, prepared by recognized travel medicine experts. $328 annual subscription. American Health Consultants, P.O. Box 740060, Atlanta, GA 30374; 800-688-2421.

Travelers' Medical Resource by William W. Forgey, M.D. (ICS Books, Inc., 1990; 800-541-7323; $19.95 plus $1.50 shipping). This is a comprehensive (894-page) paperback on travelers' health that also includes extensive first-aid information.

Health Hints for the Tropics published by the American Society of Tropical Medicine & Hygiene. Contact: Karl A. Western, M.D., ASTMH, 6436 31st Street N.W., Washington, D.C. 20015-2342; $5.

The Travel and Tropical Medicine Manual by Elaine C. Jong, M.D. (W.B. Saunders, 1987). An excellent source of information on travel-related infectious diseases.

Travel Medicine International, edited by Dr. Hugh L'Etang (Mark Allen Publishing Ltd., London). A quarterly journal of travel medicine topics. Recommended for travel clinics, travel medicine physicians, corporate medical directors, public health departments, etc. Write: Travel Medicine International, Croxted Mews, 288 Croxted Road, London SE24 9DA England. International phone from USA: 44 (country code)-81-671-7521.

Health Information for International Travel from Superintendent of Documents Government Printing Office, Washington, D.C. 20402. Call 202-783-3238 to order. $5. Stock number: 017-023-00189-2. Published annually. Vaccination requirements and recommendations.

The International Health Guide for Senior Citizen Travelers by W. Robert Lange, M.D. (Pilot Books, 103 Cooper Street, Babylon, NY 11702; 70 pages; $4.95). Many useful tips such as restaurant safety, how to exercise to help arthritis symptoms, a list of resource organizations, and more.

Wilderness Medicine

Medicine for the Outdoors by Paul S. Auerbach, M.D. (Little, Brown and Company, 1991). A comprehensive guide to first aid and emergency care for the traveler and outdoorsman.

Caring for Children in the Outdoors by Barbara Kennedy, M.D. (Adventure Medical Kits Publishing, 1994). Very informative 50 page booklet covering prevention and treatment of illness and injuries in infants, toddlers, and children during travel, plus much practical information on childcare in an out-doors environment.

Management of Wilderness & Environmental Emergencies, edited by Paul S. Auerbach, M.D., and Edward C. Geehr, M.D. (The C.V. Mosby Company, 1989; 1,067 pages; $110). The best book on the subject. A complete reference for out-door and wilderness medicine.

Going Higher: The Story of Man and Altitude by Charles S. Houston, M.D. (Little, Brown and Company). Written by the foremost expert on altitude-related illness. Highly recommended for hikers and climbers.

Underwater Medicine/Decompression Chambers

For a guide to hyperbaric and decompression chamber facilities worldwide, con-tact the Undersea and Hyperbaric Medical Society, 9650 Rockville Pike, Bethesda, MD; 301-571-1817.

First Aid

Emergency Medical Procedures, Revised Edition by the Deltakron Institute (Prentice Hall Press, 1987; 57 pages; $7.95). Medically accurate, concise. Written by emer-gency physician specialists. Gives easy-to-follow advice on emergency treatment of common illnesses and injuries.

Travelers' Self Care Manual by William W. Forget, M.D. (ICS Books, Inc., 1990; 800-541-7323; $6.95 plus $1.50 shipping).

Travel Medicine Data Bases

IMMUNIZATION ALERT! P.O. Box 406, Storrs, CT 06268; 203-487-0002. A PC data base of health information for international travel.

TRAVAX (Travel Health Information Service), 5827 West Washington Blvd., Milwaukee, WI 53208-1652; 414-774-4600. Data base available on disk or hardcopy. Extensive travel health information on 206 countries.

TRAVEL CARE, Inc., 9559 Poole Street, La Jola, CA 92037; 619-455-1484. Travel health information software for the Macintosh.

INTERNATIONAL ALERT! Herchmer Medical Consultants, 109 E. 89th Av-enue, Merrillville, IN 46410; 800-336-8334. A bimonthly newsletter giving up-dates of U.S. Department of State travel advisories and immunization require-ments. Six issues are $12.95. Individual country advisories can also be purchased.

Newsletters and Periodicals

Traveling Healthy and Comfortably, edited by Karl Neumann, M.D. (Traveling Healthy, 108-48 70th Road, Forest Hills, NY 11375; $24.95 per year). A bimonthly newsletter recommended especially for travel agencies, travelers' clinics, corpora-tions, and public health agencies.

The Diabetic Traveler Newsletter (Box 8223 RW, Stamford, CT 06905); 6-page quarterly; annual subscription $19.95.

Consumer Reports TRAVEL LETTER (800-525-0643 for subscription information).

The *New York Times* Sunday Travel section. The Travel section, especially the Practical Traveler column. The best weekly newspaper source of travel/health topics.

Physicians Overseas

The International Association for Medical Assistance to Travellers (IAMAT) publishes a booklet listing English-speaking physicians and health clinics worldwide. The participating physicians and clinics have agreed to a standard fee schedule for IAMAT members. IAMAT also sends members climate charts and detailed information on tropical diseases such as malaria and schistosomiasis. IAMAT is a tax-free foundation, and officially there is no charge for their publications; however, the *HealthGuide* suggests a $15 membership donation. In the United States, contact 417 Center Street, Lewiston, NY 14092; 716-754-4883. In Canada (main office): 40 Regal Road, Guelph, Ontario, N1K 1B5; 519-836-0102.

Kidney Dialysis Abroad

International Directory of Dialysis Centers (Creative Age Publications, 6728 Densmore Avenue, Van Nuys, CA 91406; 800-442-5667 or 818-782-7328; $6). Lists clinics worldwide where travelers can get kidney dialysis.

Dialysis Worldwide for the Traveling Patient (American Association of Kidney Patients, 1 Davis Blvd., Suite LL1, Tampa, FL; 813-251-0725). Information may also be available from your local dialysis center.

Business Travel and Health

The Traveller's Handbook, edited by Melissa Shales (Globe Pequot, 1988). A myriad of useful information on every aspect of travel; includes weather charts, immunization schedules, driving requirements, typical business hours, and much more.

World Business Travel Guide (Summerhill Press, Ltd., Toronto, 1987). Useful statistics on demographics, weather, hotels, airlines, and medical facilities in over 200 countries.

PERSONAL SAFETY AND TRAVEL

Security problems in certain countries of Latin America, Africa, the Middle East, and Asia mandate that you take precautions to reduce your risk of being involved in a terrorist act or a political kidnapping. When traveling to a politically unstable country, you should read publications that provide specific advice on how to reduce these risks. Some of the more useful publications are listed below. If you are a corporate traveler, chances are your company has also subscribed to a political-risk data base that offers additional information. Check this source also.

Personal Safety and Anti-Terrorism

TRAVEL SAFETY: Don't Be A Target! (published by Uniquest Publications. Available from Magellan's, Box 5485, Santa Barbara, CA 93150; 805-568-5400 or 800-962-4943; item #BB654: $7.95). A 75-page pocket manual with precautions, helpful hints, strategies, and tactics (1150 solid tips in all) on how to make your trip a safe one.

The Safe Travel Book, a Guide for the International Traveler by Peter Savage (MacMillan Publishing Co., 100 Front Street, Box 500, Riverside, NJ 08075–7500; 800-257-5755; $12.95). Covers every possibility from plane hijacking, kidnapping, and terrorism to how to prevent your passport from being stolen. Extensive pretravel checklists and information sources.

Executive Safety and International Terrorism: A Guide for Travellers by Anthony J. Scotti (Prentice-Hall, Englewood Cliffs, NJ 07632; $32.00).

The Complete Security Guide for Executives by Neil C. Livingston (Lexington Books, D.C. Heath & Company, 125 Spring St., Lexington, MA 02173; 800-235-3565; about $35).

Security and Anti-Terrorism Data Bases

Overseas Security Advisory Council (U.S. Department of State) provides security information to U.S. corporations doing business overseas. Services include an on-line computer data base, information sharing, and various publications. For additional information, see Chapter 16.

RISKNET™ provides corporate and other travelers with access to a data base analyzing terrorism, crime, and political-stability risks in 75 countries. Clients also receive in-depth written summaries and a guide to which air carriers are under greatest terrorist threat. Contact The Ackerman Group, 1666 Kennedy Causeway, Miami Beach, FL 33141; 305-865-0072.

How the U.S. Government Can Help

The U.S. government won't pay to fly you home if you get sick or injured overseas, but assistance to American citizens is available through U.S. embassies and consulates and also the **Citizens Emergency Center**, which is located in Washington, D.C.

The Citizens Emergency Center works with embassies to keep you (or your family) informed and advised when hospitalization occurs overseas. If emergency medical transport is needed, they will refer you (or the people helping you) to an assistance company; in some cases, the Emergency Center (working with the embassy or consulate) will coordinate stretcher transport on a commercial airliner to bring a sick traveler home to the States.

In event of death, they will assist with returning the remains. They will also give assistance with legal problems or missing persons.

To contact the Citizens Emergency Center, call 202-647-5225 from 8:15 A.M. to 10 P.M. during the week and 9:00 A.M. to 3:00 P.M. on Saturday. After these hours, if it's an extreme emergency, call the State Department at 202-634-3600 and request that the operator put you in touch with the Citizens Emergency Center's duty officer.

U.S. Department of State Travel Advisories

You can obtain these recorded advisories by calling the Citizens Emergency Center in Washington, D.C., at 202-647-5225.

State Department Travel Advisories and Other Information
Fax: 202-647-3000
Telephone: 202-647-5225
The U.S. State Department, Bureau of Consular Affairs, issues warnings about travel to certain countries, which may be obtained by **telephone or fax**—as may consular information sheets on any of 196 countries. With the fax service, you can get detailed information on conditions in countries you plan to visit without having to call and take notes from recorded information, as you would when calling the 202-647-5225 number. The fax service is also more flexible than the telephone service because it can print out the material in State Department leaflets, such as "Your Trip Abroad," that are usually sold by the Government Printing Office for $1. Other essential information available from the Bureau of Consular Affairs includes advisories on visa requirements, HIV testing requirements, and passport renewals.

Country Information Notices and Other Publications
The U.S. State Department also provides information through their **Country Information Notices**, which include topics such as currency and customs regulations, entry requirements, dual nationality, import and export controls, and drug warnings.

Single copies of the available publications are available for $1 by sending a stamped, self-addressed envelope to Bureau of Consular Affairs, Public Affairs Staff, Room 5807, Department of State, Washington, D.C. 20520.

The following publications are available:

- *A Safe Trip Abroad* • *Travel Warning on Drugs Abroad*
- *Your Trip Abroad* • *Travel Tips for Senior Citizens* • *International Adoptions*
- *Pets, Wildlife (U.S. Customs)* • *Tips for Travelers to the Caribbean*
- *Tips for Travelers to South Asia* • *Tips for Travelers to Cuba*
- *Tips for Travelers to Mexico* • *Tips for Travelers to Central & South America*
- *Tips for Travelers to Guatemala* • *Tips for Travelers to E. Europe*
- *Tips for Travelers to Russia* • *Tips for Travelers to Saudi Arabia*
- *Tips for Travelers to the Middle East and N. Africa*
- *Tips for Travelers to Sub-Saharan Africa*
- *Tips for Travelers to the People's Republic of China*

Notes:
1. Steffen, R, Conference on International Travel Medicine. Zurich, Switzerland, 1988.
2. Hargarten, S, M.D., et al. Conference on International Travel Medicine, Zurich, Switzerland, April, 1988.
3. Hargarten, S, Baker SP, Fatalities in the Peace Corps. *JAMA*. 1985; 254:1326-29.

1 Trip Preparation

When preparing for your trip, list the countries you will be visiting (in order) and the length of time you plan to spend in each of these countries. There are then four categories of questions you need to answer about your trip. Your answers will determine how carefully you must plan ahead to avoid illness and injury.

Where Am I Going?

You should ask yourself the following questions: What illnesses are prevalent in the region I will be visiting? What is the general level of sanitation? How competent, and close by, is medical care? How harsh is the climate? How safe are the roads? Is the country politically stable?

Also, remember that a trip to Europe, for example, doesn't require as much preparation as an extended stay in a remote village in a lesser-developed country. Because some countries and cities are much safer than others, be careful not to overdo precautions. You don't need an immune globulin shot against hepatitis if you are going to London or Tokyo, nor do you necessarily need a lot of shots if you're taking a brief trip to a lesser-developed country but staying exclusively in a first-class hotel in a large city. For updated information on country-by-country disease risks, see the **World Medical Guide** section of this book.

What Will I Be Doing?

Visiting rural areas of lesser-developed countries puts you at greater risk of contact with unsanitary food and drink and usually brings greater exposure to disease-carrying insects. You should answer these questions: Will I be traveling on a tour and staying only in air-conditioned, mosquito-free hotels, or traveling in rural areas where insects are more prevalent? Planning an adventure or wilderness itinerary and exposed to extremes of heat, cold, or altitude? Trekking or camping in a remote area, far from medical care? Driving a car, motorcycle, or moped in a lesser-developed country? *(Be aware that motor vehicle accidents account for most reported accidental fatalities among travelers.)* Swimming in unfamiliar waters or having contact with freshwater ponds, lakes, or streams? Having sexual or close physical contact with the indigenous population? A close analysis of your potential activities is critical to helping you avoid illness and injury.

How Long Will I Be There?

A brief trip means less exposure to various diseases and less opportunity for an accident. Longer trips increase the likelihood of spur-of-the-moment side trips that may place you at an unforeseen risk, perhaps for a mosquito-transmitted disease such as malaria or viral encephalitis. Longer travel may also cause you to discontinue prophylactic antimalarial medication, abandon safe food and drink practices, or neglect anti-insect measures. Before departing on a lengthy trip, you should also consider what psychological stresses (culture shock) you, and your family, will experience while adjusting to life abroad.

What Should I Bring?

Your itinerary, the climatic conditions you expect to encounter, the duration of your trip, and the disease risks in the countries you will be visiting all influence what you should bring. Your personal health status may also require you to take additional precautions.

Many travelers to tropical and subtropical regions neglect to take adequate anti-insect precautions necessary to prevent malaria and other insect-transmitted diseases. Be sure you have the necessary supplies. These include the following:

- A DEET-containing insect repellent
- Permethrin clothing spray or solution
- A mosquito bed net (often advisable)

When traveling overseas, take an ample supply of any medication that you use regularly. Don't carry a mixture of pills in unmarked vials. To avoid problems with customs officers who might suspect your pills are narcotic, keep each medication in its labeled original container.

Carry legally prescribed narcotics and controlled drugs (tranquilizers, sleeping pills, etc.) only if medically necessary. Get a letter from your doctor certifying the need for these medications. If you are an insulin-dependent diabetic carrying needles and syringes, you may arouse suspicion at customs checkpoints. Also get a letter from your doctor certifying your diagnosis and treatment. The same applies if you will be carrying needles and syringes in an AIDS/hepatitis prevention kit.

Preparation Checklists

Use the following checklists as general guidelines and modify them according to your itinerary and specific travel and health needs. A small nylon or canvas pack, or a first-aid kit with extra mesh pockets, can be used to carry many of the items below. If you need to take medication enroute, be sure you have it in your carry-on bag.

Medical and Personal Care Items

❏ Adequate supply of your prescription medications. How much of each medication will you need for the duration of your trip? If you will be living abroad, or traveling extensively, can you buy additional medication locally? Check availability. Make arrangements, if necessary, to have additional medical supplies shipped to you. Carry copies of your prescriptions by generic names.

❏ First-aid kit—all travelers should carry at least a basic kit that has a thermometer, wound dressings, bandages, an antibiotic ointment, tape, and other supplies to treat an abrasion, minor laceration, minor burn, etc.

❏ Analgesics—such as Advil, Tylenol

❏ Antacids—such as Maalox or Mylanta

❏ Antibiotics for treating travelers' diarrhea—the best choice is one of the quinolone antibiotics, either ofloxacin (Floxin) or ciprofloxacin (Cipro). Furazolidone (Furoxone) is a good alternative, and it can be used by children. Ofloxacin is also an excellent general purpose antibiotic for treating other infections (e.g., urinary tract, skin and soft tissue, and respiratory).

❏ Loperamide (Imodium)—for the treatment of travelers' diarrhea. Loperamide is more effective when it is used in combination with an antibiotic.

❏ Antimalarial drugs (depending on itinerary)—chloroquine, mefloquine, or doxycycline

❏ Pepto-Bismol—tablets are useful for the prevention of travelers' diarrhea; Pepto-Bismol liquid (not tablets) can be used for treatment of mild diarrhea.

❏ Motion/sea sickness drugs—Dramamine, Bucladin-S, or Transderm-Scōp

❏ Nasal decongestant spray—Afrin or Neo-Synephrine

❏ Antihistamine tablets—for allergic reactions and rhinitis (hay fever). Consider Hismanal or Claritan—they are long-acting and nonsedating.

❏ Vōsol solution—to prevent, or treat, swimmer's ear

❏ Topical corticosteroid cream—such as Cortaid or Topicort (by prescription)

❏ Antifungal foot powder, cream, or solution—such as Tinactin or Micatin, to prevent/treat athlete's foot

❏ Antifungal skin cream—Lotrisone or Nizoral are good choices. Fungal skin infections (not just athlete's foot) are among the most common skin disorders afflicting travelers to the tropics.

❏ Syrup of Ipecac, if traveling with young children. Use in case of accidental ingestion of poisonous substances. No prescription needed

❏ Extra pair of prescription glasses or contact lenses. Copy of lens prescription

❏ Tweezers for tick removal, small knife, scissors (or Swiss Army knife)

❏ Soap and detergents—An antibacterial soap such as Dial is good for personal use and also for disinfecting animal bites.

- Sterile needle/syringe pack—for travel to areas where hepatitis and HIV transmission are potential threats and where local medical care and supplies are substandard.
- 1-liter Nalgene water bottle—for preparing and storing safe drinking water. Also useful for mixing oral rehydration solutions
- Water filtration/disinfection supplies—Katadyn, PŪR or PentaPure filters, Potable Aqua iodine tablets, Polar Pure iodine crystals, or AquaCure.
- Oral rehydration salts to treat dehydration caused by severe diarrhea

For Rain, Sun, Altitude, Heat, and Insects

- Hat, sunglasses
- Sunscreens. Use minimum SPF 15. SPF 29/30 or higher is recommended for greater protection against deep ultraviolet damage
- DEET-containing insect repellent—such as Ultrathon, DEET-PLUS, or Repel; Skedaddle! is recommended for young children, infants.
- Permethrin clothing aerosol (Permanone, Duranon) or permethrin solution to protect against mosquitoes and ticks
- Mosquito bed net
- Insecticide spray (e.g., Raid Flying Insect Spray) to rid sleeping quarters of night-biting insects

Sources of supplies include **Travel Medicine, Inc.**, 351 Pleasant St., Suite 312, Northampton, MA 01060; 800-TRAV-MED (800-872-8633), and **Chinook Medical Gear**, 2805 Wilderness Place, Boulder, CO 80301; 800-766-1365.

Additional Supplies

- Electrical adaptor plugs and current converters; hotel door alarms; emergency smoke hoods; an inflatable pillow for airline travel; a 7-band, pocket-size, shortwave radio; a five-language electronic translator; and more are available from **Magellan's International Travel Corporation**. Their free 48-page catalogue, *Essentials for the International Traveler*, lists over 500 travel-related items. Box 5485, Santa Barbara, CA 93150-5485; 800-962-4943.

Checking the Weather—and More

There are useful sources available for checking the weather and more in countries worldwide.

The *World Weather Guide* by E.A. Pearce and Gordon Smith (Times Books) is available at bookstores or directly from Random House Inc., 401 Hahn Rd., Westminster, MD 21157; 800-733-3000; $17.95 plus $2.50 shipping.

You can also call one of the 900 numbers below to get up-to-the-minute weather forecasts and travel advisory information for hundreds of cities worldwide. Cost: 95 cents a minute. Use a touch-tone phone.

USA TODAY Weather Report 1-900-555-5555

- Weather in 650 U.S. and foreign cities: local time, temperature, daily temperature range; next day's forecast; four- and ten-day forecasts; hurricane and tropical storm warning advisories
- Foreign country entry requirements (visa, passport, AIDS testing, vaccinations)
- Malaria risk advisory
- U.S. dollar exchange rates
- Voltage requirements for appliances

American Express 1-900-WEATHER (1-900-932-8437)

- Local time, current weather, and 3-day forecast
- Passport and visa entry requirements
- Restaurant and hotel information

Wilderness Travel

If you're on an adventure itinerary, determine what exposure you will have to heat, cold, or altitude. This may require complex pretrip planning. Most tour organizers will advise you of what to bring, but you may need to consult experts in outdoor/wilderness travel to determine if it's adequate. Your equipment lists and preparation may be more extensive than those outlined below.

Checklist for campers, hikers, and trekkers—You need to anticipate sudden changes in weather, in particular, high winds, rain, and temperature drops. For your comfort and safety, be sure always to carry a windbreaker or parka (Gore-Tex preferred), wool cap or balaclava, and gloves. Review the checklist for additional items your trip may require.

- ❑ Sleeping bag and pad
- ❑ Bivouac bag
- ❑ Ground cloth and pad
- ❑ Vapor barrier
- ❑ Tent
- ❑ Thermal blanket
- ❑ Radiant heat barrier
- ❑ Fuel, firestarter
- ❑ Fire and camping permits
- ❑ Stove
- ❑ Matches
- ❑ First-aid kit

- ❑ Cooking supplies, dehydrated food
- ❑ Candle and candle lantern
- ❑ Maps and guides
- ❑ Compass
- ❑ Binoculars
- ❑ Altimeter
- ❑ Flashlight
- ❑ Extra batteries and bulbs
- ❑ Rope
- ❑ Trowel and shovel
- ❑ Chemical hand and feet warmers
- ❑ Washcloth, soap, toilet kit

Mail order sources—You can purchase equipment for wilderness travel from the following mail order companies:

- Recreational Equipment Incorporated (R.E.I.), P.O. Box 88125, Seattle, WA 98138-2125; 206-323-8333 or 800-426-4840

- L.L. Bean, Freeport, ME 04033-0001; 800-221-4221
- Eddie Bauer, 5th and Union Streets, Seattle, WA 98124-3700; 800-426-8020
- Outdoor Research, Inc., 1000 First Ave. S., Seattle, WA 98134; 206-467-8197 or 800-421-2421. Backcountry and mountaineering equipment checklist available on request.

Travel Documents You May Need

❑ **U.S. passport**—If you are a first-time applicant, you must apply in person at a passport agency, authorized clerk of court, or post office to fill out an application (Form DSP-11). At this time, you will be charged $55 for a 10-year adult passport, plus a $10 execution fee if you submit an application in person. Children under 18 receive a 5-year passport and are charged $30, plus a $10 execution fee, if applicable. You will need the following documents:

1. Proof of U.S. citizenship, e.g., a certified copy of your birth certificate (original with raised seal), or a certificate of naturalization or citizenship
2. Two identical, recent 2" x 2" black-and-white or color photographs
3. Proof of identity, such as a valid driver's license with photo

Passport renewal—If you have a passport issued within the past 10 years (and after your 18th birthday), you can apply by mail. Pick up Form DSP-82, available at most courthouses, post offices, and travel agencies. Send your old passport, the $55 application fee, and all the required documents, not to a regional address printed on the application, but to the new address, which will appear on future applications: **National Passport Center**, P. O. Box 371971, Pittsburgh, PA 15250.

Mail renewals consume about three weeks in the slow season and four weeks in the travel season. Holders of youth passports cannot renew them when the five years run out but must start at the beginning again.

Passport information—U.S. Passport Agency offices provide basic information about applying for or renewing a passport. Here is where to call for information:

Boston: (617) 565-6998; Chicago: (312) 353-7155; Honolulu: (808) 541-1919; Houston: (713) 653-3153; Los Angeles ((310) 575-7070; Miami: (305) 536-4681; New Orleans: (504) 589-6728; New York: (212) 399-5290; Philadelphia: (215) 597-7480; San Francisco: (415) 744-4444; Seattle: (206) 553-7941; Stamford, CT: (203) 325-4401; Washington, DC: (202) 647-0518. If you need a passport in a hurry, go directly to the nearest passport office and bring the necessary documents.

Lost passport overseas—Go to the nearest American consulate and bring the following:

- A police report that documents the loss or theft
- Four passport-size photos (must be 2" x 2" size)
- $55 in U.S. currency, traveler's checks, or local currency. Bring the exact change.

If you have a photocopy of the lost passport showing the passport number and the date and place of issue, it will expedite the process. With the right information, a replacement passport can often be obtained in 20 minutes. Otherwise, you might wait up to two days.

Passport and visa services—A travel service company can do the necessary legwork to obtain your passport and/or visa(s) if you provide them with the necessary documents. A service company can obtain your passport in 1–4 working days. Contact: **Passport Plus**, 677 Fifth Avenue, 5th floor, New York, NY 10022; 212-759-5540 or 800-367-1818; **Travisa**, 2122 P Street, N.W., Washington, D.C. 10037; 202-463-6166 or 800-222-2589, or **Passport & Visa Expeditors,** Washington, DC; 800-237-3270.

❑ **Visas**—Many countries require a visa, an official authorization stamped within the passport that permits travel within a country for a specified purpose (tourism, business, or immigration) and for a limited time.

Country visa requirements can be quickly checked in the **World Medical Guide** section of this book. You can also call either the USA TODAY or American Express weather phone (see above) for a quick check of visa requirements. An official pamphlet Foreign Visa Requirements, publication number 9517, is available for $0.50 from the Consumer Information Center, Department 438T, Pueblo, CO 81009.

After verifying the need for a visa, contact the embassy or consulate of the country(s) of destination for the most up-to-date information regarding the documents you will need and processing time required. Is an AIDS antibody test required for entry? What test is acceptable?

❑ **Extra photos**—Get at least eight (8) additional 2" x 2" photos when applying for your passport or visa(s). These extra photos will come in handy if you need additional visas, an international driver's permit, or need to replace a lost passport or other document.

❑ **Personal health records**—Consider carrying photocopies of your health and hospital records, cardiograms, test results, list of current medications, etc. You may wish to subscribe to a service that can assemble all of your medical records, store them in a computer, and fax them anywhere in the world within minutes. **Life-Fax** (800-487-0329) is an Atlanta-based company that will store your health information and insurance coverage details on a computer and can fax your medical history worldwide. A subscription costs $29. **Global Emergency Medical Services** (404-992-4427) and **Micro-Med Medical I.D. Card** (803-370-1768) are other services to consider.

❑ **Travel health insurance**—Consult Chapters 14 and 15 for a listing of companies that specialize in travel health insurance and other forms of travel assistance, such as medical evacuation. If you don't buy separate travel health insurance, check your existing health insurance policy to see what benefits are provided in case of illness overseas. Medicare does not pay for out-of-country illnesses or accidents. If you are over 65, you should purchase medi-gap coverage or a travel health insurance policy.

❑ **Doctors and hospitals abroad**—The International Association for Assistance to Travelers (**IAMAT**) publishes a booklet listing hospitals and English-speaking physicians who have agreed to adhere to a standard schedule of fees. Physicians are not listed by specialty. Contact IAMAT, 417 Center Street, Lewiston, NY 14092; 716-754-4883. Or in Canada, 40 Regal Road, Guelph, Ontario, N1K 1B5; 519-836-0102. No charge, but a donation is encouraged.

❑ **Medic Alert bracelet**—If you have a serious or chronic medical condition, a history of severe drug allergy, etc., you should consider wearing a Medic Alert–type bracelet. Call 1-800-ID-ALERT to order.

❑ **Divers' Alert Network (DAN)**—Scuba divers can call 919-684-2406 for general information. For medical information, call 919-684-2948. For emergency information, call 919-684-8111. Callers need not be members of DAN to receive telephone assistance.

❑ **Telephone number of your doctor or clinic in the USA**

❑ **Foreign language telephone assistance**—When dealing with medical problems long distance, there may be language barriers. Call **AT&T's Language Line** at 1-800-628-8486 for assistance. The service costs $3.50 per minute.

❑ **Traveler's checks**—Be sure to make a photocopy of the numbers. Leave the photocopy at home but carry the list of numbers with you that you get with the checks. Be sure you also copy the date and place of purchase. A comparative survey (*The New York Times*) found that lost or stolen American Express traveler's checks were replaced the quickest. To replace lost traveler's checks, call collect to the following numbers in the United States from abroad:

- American Express: 801-968-8300
- VISA: 415-574-7111
- MasterCard: 212-974-5696
- Bank of America: 415-622-3800
- Citibank: 813-879-7701
- Thomas Cook: 212-974-5696

❑ **Credit cards**—Know your charge card credit limits. U.S. citizens have been arrested in some countries for exceeding credit limits. Keep a copy of your credit card numbers in case they are lost or stolen. Report the loss immediately.

❑ **Money**—To have emergency funds sent overseas, call the **American Express MoneyGram** (800-926-9400) or the **Western Union Money Transfer** service (800-325-6000). The State Department's **Overseas Citizens Service** (202-647-5225) can also arrange money transfers abroad. Don't rely upon your ATM card in other countries if you lose all your money overseas.

❑ **Birth certificate and photo ID**—These documents can sometimes be used in lieu of a passport for entry into certain countries. They're also useful to have if you lose your passport. If you are living overseas or getting married in a foreign country, be sure to have these documents with you.

❑ **Green card for resident aliens**—Don't leave home without it.

❑ **International Certificate of Vaccination**—A validated certificate of vaccination (yellow card) is needed when yellow fever and/or cholera immunizations are required to enter a country. This document is obtained at an authorized Yellow Fever Vaccination Center, usually a traveler's clinic or a Health Department immunization clinic. You should carry the yellow card with your passport, and like your passport, you should also photocopy it. Without this important document, you could be denied entry into certain countries, be quarantined, or forced to receive an immunization, possibly with a nonsterile needle and syringe. The yellow card has useful sections where you can list all of your other immunizations, list what medications you take regularly, and also record your eyeglass prescription. There is a section that your doctor can fill out if you are unable to receive any required vaccinations because of a medical reason. If you want a doctor's exemption from vaccination, you should also inquire at the embassy or consulate of the country of destination to find out whether you will also need a written exemption from vaccination from that country's embassy or consulate.

❑ **AIDS virus antibody (anti-HIV) test certificate**—Check requirements in the **World Medical Guide** section or contact the State Department, Bureau of Consular Affairs (fax no. 202-647-3000). Usually required only for those applying for a foreign work permit, prolonged residence, or immigration—not for tourist visits of less than one month.

❑ **Doctor's letter**—You may want a doctor's letter describing the prescription medications you will be taking on your trip. This letter should contain the name of the medication, its generic name, and the dosage.

❑ **International driver's permit**—Call **AAA** (407-444-7000) or the nearest AAA listed in your telephone book. You don't need to be a member to get a permit. When applying you'll need two passport-size photos, your driver's license, and $10 for the fee. Permits can also be obtained through **Passport Plus, Inc.**, 677 Fifth Ave. (5th floor), New York, NY 10022; 800-367-1818 or 212-759-5540. Passport Plus provides nationwide service. The international driver's permit is printed in 9 languages and serves as a translation for your license, which is valid in many countries. Some countries, however, require the international permit. A few countries (China, Egypt, Nepal) don't allow tourists to drive.

❏ **Notarized parental consent**—Necessary when a minor child is traveling with the noncustodial parent. You may not be able to board the aircraft or enter a country (e.g., Mexico) without this document.

NOTE: Make two photocopies of your passport and visa pages. Also copy your airline ticket, traveler's checks, vaccination certificate, and any other important documents. Leave one copy at home and take one copy with you.

Vaccinations for Yellow Fever and Cholera

Yellow fever—Review and verify entry requirements for the countries on your itinerary. There are currently 17 countries in sub-Saharan Africa that require vaccination (immunization, inoculation) against yellow fever even if you arrive directly from the United States or Canada. Other countries worldwide may require yellow fever vaccination if you arrive from or have transited through an actively infected country or region. Some countries in Africa require a yellow fever shot if you are arriving from *any* country in the Yellow Fever Endemic Zones.

To be on the safe side, and to avoid hassles when crossing borders, you should get a yellow fever shot, if you will visit, or transit through, any of the countries in the Yellow Fever Endemic Zones, and then go on to another country in Central America, South America, the Middle East, Africa, Asia, or Oceania that has an entry requirement regarding yellow fever vaccination.

Cholera vaccination—Regarding cholera, the situation is less clear cut. The recent cholera epidemic (62 countries are officially reporting cases) has made it more likely that border officials in third world countries may require this vaccination, even though it is the official policy of the World Health Organization that cholera vaccination should no longer be required for foreign travel. If you travel from the United States or Canada to a country where cholera is active and then proceed to another country in Central America, South America, the Middle East, Africa, Asia, or Oceania, you may find yourself needing a valid cholera vaccination certificate to avoid denial of entry, quarantine, or an enforced vaccination (possibly with an unclean needle). Recommendation: Get a cholera vaccination prior to departure, or a doctor's letter of exemption from vaccination.

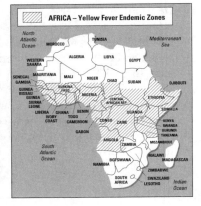

How to Find a Travelers' Clinic

Is your itinerary taking you to high-risk areas? Does your own doctor not give shots or provide travel advice? The *International Travel HealthGuide* lists over 500 travelers' clinics that can help you. See the Appendix for a listing of American and Canadian travelers' clinics and travel medicine specialists. State health departments are also included.

CDC Travelers' Health Hotline

404-332-4559—automated voice line
404-332-4565—fax line

The U.S. Public Health Service **Centers for Disease Control (CDC)** has greatly expanded its telephone and fax information system. The 24-hour hotline provides malaria advisories, immunization schedules, disease risk and prevention information by region of the world, and bulletins on disease outbreaks. With the fax line you get a hard copy of this information, and the cost of the fax is paid by the CDC. First call the fax line to get a directory sheet. The directory shows a six-digit number for each document. You then call back and order by number, as many as five documents at once.

NOTE: Physicians and other medical personnel can consult directly with a CDC medical advisor if they need information on the clinical management of a patient with a tropical or infectious disease. A CDC consultant can always be reached from 8:00 A.M. to 4:30 P.M. eastern time. If a malaria consultation only is needed, call the malaria information service directly at 404-488-4046 or 404-639-2888 (eve./nights).

Public Health Service Hotlines

There is an advantage in calling the **Public Health Service**. Unlike the CDC hotline, these numbers provide person-to-person consultation with a Public Health Service travel advisor. The *International Travel HealthGuide* recommends calling both hotlines to get the best advice. All times are local.

- Chicago: 312-686-2150 (noon to 8 P.M.)
- Honolulu: 808-541-2552 (6 A.M. to 3 P.M.)
- Los Angeles: 213-215-2365 (8 A.M. to 5 P.M.)
- Miami: 305-526-2910 (8 A.M. to 5 P.M.)
- New York: 718-917-1685 (8 A.M. to 10 P.M.)
- San Francisco: 415-876-2872 (8 A.M. to 4:30 P.M.)
- Seattle: 206-442-4519 (8 A.M. to 5 P.M.)

Immunizations for Travel

Ten to 12 weeks prior to departure, review your itinerary and check the **World Medical Guide** section to see which immunizations (vaccinations), if any, are required and/or recommended. Also review your current immunization status to see if you'll need boosters for tetanus/diphtheria, polio, or measles. Consider a flu shot, even if under age 65. If you are a pregnant woman, or a woman of childbearing age, you may want to verify your rubella immunity status prior to travel.

- Tetanus/diphtheria: Booster indicated every 5 years. Diphtheria protection is important, even for adults.
- Measles: A one-time measles vaccine booster is recommended if you were born between 1956 and 1987.
- Polio: Immunized travelers should receive a one-time polio booster prior to international travel.
- Hepatitis A: Immune globulin (or hepatitis A vaccine) is recommended for susceptible travelers going to any country with substandard sanitation.
- Hepatitis B, meningitis, rabies, yellow fever, cholera, and Japanese encephalitis: Review with your doctor the possible need for these immunizations.

Suggested Scheduling of Predeparture Vaccinations

Weeks to Departure	Immunization
12 weeks (or before)	Update all routine immunizations, as necessary (tetanus, diphtheria, polio, measles).
8–10 weeks	First hepatitis B (Engerix-B), first typhoid (if receiving the injectable vaccine), first Japanese encephalitis (JE)
6–8 weeks	Yellow fever, first rabies, second JE
5–6 weeks	Second rabies, meningitis, cholera
3–4 weeks	Second typhoid, second hepatitis B, third JE, hepatitis A, oral typhoid series (if injectable vaccine not used)
1–2 weeks	Immune globulin (IG), third rabies, third hepatitis B

- If time is short, immune globulin (IG), as well as most vaccines, can be given simultaneously, or over a period of a few days.
- Live virus vaccines (MMR, OPV, yellow fever) should be given either on the same day, or separated by at least 1 month.
- Immune globulin should be given at least 2 weeks after MMR.
- Separate yellow fever and cholera by three weeks—or administer on same day.
- Don't get injectable typhoid and cholera shots on the same day, or in the same arm.
- Oral polio vaccine (OPV) should not be taken on the same day as oral typhoid vaccine (OTV). OPV can be given 7–10 days before or 10–14 days after OTV.
- If necessary, rabies and JE can be given on an accelerated schedule of 2 im doses, given 1 week apart.
- Wait 3 weeks after intradermally administered rabies vaccine to start chloroquine. Get IM rabies vaccine if 3-week interval not possible.

Immunization Record

Vaccine \ Date	Dose #1	Dose #2	Dose #3	Booster Dose
Yellow Fever				
Cholera				
Hepatitis A				
Hepatitis B				
Immune Globulin				
Tetanus/Diphtheria				
Typhoid Fever				
Meningitis (Meningococcal)				
Japanese Encephalitis				
Polio				
Measles (or MMR)				
Rabies				
Tuberculin Skin Test (PPD)				
Tuberculosis (BCG)				
Tick Encephalitis				
Plague				
Influenza/Pneumococcal				

Childhood Immunization Checklist by Age

2 months	4 months	6 months	15 months	4-6 years	7-14 years
DTP-1	DTP-2	DTP-3	DTP-4	DTP-5	Td
OPV-1	OPV-2	HIB-3	OPV-3	OPV-4	
HIB-1	HIB-2		MMR-1	MMR-1	
			HIB-4		

- Recommended ages should not be construed as absolute. Td = tetanus/diphtheria.
- HIB=*hemophilus influenza* type b conjugate vaccine (4 types are available).
- DPT (diphtheria/pertussis/tetanus) and OPV can be initiated as early as 4 weeks after birth.
- Acellular pertussis vaccine (DTaP vaccine) is preferred for the fourth and fifth DTP vaccinations.
- The third dose of OPV (oral polio vaccine) can be given at 6 months if there is to be travel to a polio endemic area before 15 months.
- MMR (measles/mumps/rubella vaccine) can be given at 12 months in areas of measles transmission. If given earlier than 12 months, it should be repeated at 15 months, and again at entry to school.
- Hepatitis B vaccine is recommended at 1–2 mo., 4 mo. and 6–12 mo.
- The MMR #2 can be given upon entry to middle school or high school.

THE PRETRAVEL MEDICAL CHECKLIST

The following checklist will help you and your doctor avoid travel-related medical problems. Women travelers who are pregnant should also consult Chapter 17.

The Pretravel Medical Consultation

Before you leave, your doctor should do the following:

❑ Review your travel itinerary to plan for prevention of medical problems.

❑ Give specialized recommendations if you will be staying in areas where exposure to malaria, typhoid, hepatitis, yellow fever, rabies, plague, meningitis, and other infectious and tropical diseases can occur.

❑ Review your medical history and current medications.

❑ Alter current therapy when necessary for travel.

❑ Administer immunizations, as necessary.

❑ Review measures to prevent travelers' diarrhea, hepatitis, motion sickness, mountain sickness, and diseases caused by mosquito and insect bites.

❑ Review methods to prevent insect bites, emphasizing the use of DEET repellents, permethrin, mosquito bednets, and insecticide room sprays.

❑ Prescribe drugs for malaria prophylaxis, particularly if you will be exposed to chloroquine-resistant falciparum malaria.

❑ Review the symptoms of malaria.

❑ Prescribe, if appropriate, drugs for the emergency self-treatment of malaria.

❑ Prescribe medication to treat travelers' diarrhea, motion sickness, mountain sickness, jet lag, and other possible illnesses. Treat ear or sinus problems prior to air flight.

❑ Perform a physical examination, if necessary. Evaluate cardiac risk factors. Perform stress testing, if indicated.

❑ Advise you about traveling if you are pregnant or traveling with small children.

❑ Agree to provide telephone consultation from the United States if illness occurs overseas. Help with referral to foreign physicians.

❑ Screen for exposure to tuberculosis by administering a PPD skin test.

❑ Help arrange transport if you are physically challenged or chronically ill. The following companies can assist:

➤ **MedEscort International** provides medically trained health professionals to accompany disabled travelers worldwide. Contact: ABE International Airport, P.O. Box 8766, Allentown, PA 18105; 800-255-7182. Worldwide call collect at 215-791-3111.

➤ **Traveling Nurses' Network** provides registered nurses for worldwide escort. Contact Helen Hecker, RN, P.O. Box 129, Vancouver, WA 98666; 206-694-2462.

Travel and Heart Disease

During your trip you should have the following with you:

- An adequate supply of your current medications
- A copy of your most recent ECG
- A list of your medications and drug allergies (if any)
- The telephone numbers of your personal physician and nearest relative

If you have had a heart attack, or coronary artery bypass grafting surgery, a convalescence of 2–6 weeks prior to travel is usually adequate, but your case should be considered individually. A submaximal ECG stress test, combined with thallium perfusion imaging, can be administered as early as six to seven days after a heart attack to evaluate your cardiovascular status and to help determine if you are at increased risk for angina or arrhythmia.

Defer travel if you have any of the following problems: poorly controlled angina (i.e., angina at rest or at low levels of effort), symptomatic congestive heart failure, or ventricular arrhythmias.

If you've had a heart attack, there is a lower risk of subsequent cardiac arrest (and possibly safer travel) if you have the following:

- Well-preserved left ventricular function (ejection fraction >40%)
- Well-maintained exercise capacity. No fall in systolic blood pressure during exercise testing
- No significant ventricular arrhythmias
- Little or no ST-segment depression on exercise testing
- Normal signal-averaged ECG

Your chances of recurrent heart attack can be reduced by taking daily doses of aspirin (80 mg–160 mg) and a beta blocker drug (e.g., Lopressor, Tenormin). Other drugs associated with reduced mortality after a heart attack include Coumadin and the ACE inhibitors (e.g., Capoten).

Travel after angioplasty—Following coronary artery angioplasty, there is a 6- to 12-month period when there is about a 30% chance of restenosis. During this 6- to 12-month period, it is not advisable to travel to areas where expert cardiac care is not readily available. However, if you do well for 12 months after angioplasty, there is much less chance of artery closure (restenosis), and travel restrictions, in most cases, can be relaxed.

Having a pacemaker or an implanted defibrillator is not a contraindication to air travel, and these devices are not affected by airport security magnetometers.

Bear in mind that the risk of pulmonary embolism is increased within the first two weeks following a heart attack or surgery and that prolonged immobilization in the sitting position during long distance air travel will increase this risk.

Lung Disease and Air Travel

If you have emphysema, air travel is considered safe if you can walk a block or climb a flight of stairs without becoming breathless. In-flight oxygen is indicated if your sea level arterial oxygen level (PaO_2) is 70 mmHg or less. If your doctor advises oxygen, contact the airline medical department at least 48–72 hours prior to departure. There is a $50 charge for oxygen for each flight/plane change. The airline will request a physician's letter stating your medical condition and a prescription for the oxygen. Be sure to carry copies of these documents with you. A booklet **"Requirements for Traveling with Oxygen,"** published by the American Association for Respiratory Care, also gives the requirements of the various airline and cruise ships and is available from Travel Medicine, Inc. Send $1.00 and a self-addressed stamped envelope to 351 Pleasant St., Suite 312, Northampton, MA 01060.

Unlike foreign airlines, U.S. carriers must legally supply all in-flight oxygen. You will not be allowed to use your personal oxygen supply enroute, and if you have a portable unit, it must be empty when checked in. Unfortunately, on-board oxygen delivery systems (mask or nasal cannulae) are not standardized, and you may need to use a system other than your own. In addition, the airline won't provide oxygen for ground use. You'll need to make arrangements yourself if you'll need ground oxygen between flights.

Peptic Ulcer, Gastrointestinal Disease

If you are taking an antiulcer drug, such as Zantac or Tagamet, your risk of travelers' diarrhea may be increased. You might consider switching to the antiulcer drug Carafate (sucralfate) during your trip. This drug does not decrease the stomach's protective acid secretion and, in fact, may even reduce your chance of travelers' diarrhea due to its activity against bacteria in your stomach.

If you have had stomach or intestinal surgery, defer travel until after the tenth postoperative day in order to avoid excessive intestinal gas expansion.

Allergies

If you have a history of severe bee sting reactions or severe food or drug allergies, you should consider carrying an emergency kit (e.g., EpiPen, Ana-Guard), containing self-injectable epinephrine (adrenaline). These kits are available by prescription for about $30.

Medications

Some drugs that are prescribed for travel may interact with some commonly prescribed medications.

- Mefloquine (Lariam) should not be taken together with beta blocker drugs.
- Ciprofloxacin (Cipro) may prolong the action of the blood thinner warfarin

Insulin Adjustment During Jet Travel Across Multiple Time Zones*

East Bound

Daily insulin regimen	Day of departure	First morning at destination	10 hours after morning dose	Second day at destination
Single dose schedule	Usual dose	2/3 usual dose	If blood sugar over 240, take remaining 1/3 of AM dose	Usual dose
Two dose schedule	Usual morning and evening doses	2/3 usual dose	Usual evening dose. If blood sugar over 240, take remaining 1/3 of AM dose	Usual two doses

West Bound

Daily insulin regimen	Day of departure	18 hours after AM dose	First day at destination
Single dose schedule	Usual dose	If blood sugar over 240, take 1/3 usual AM dose, followed by snack	Usual dose
Two dose schedule	Usual morning and evening doses	If blood sugar over 240, take 1/3 usual AM dose, followed by snack	Usual two doses

*Reprinted with permission from Edward A. Benson, MD (Virginia Mason Clinic, Seattle, WA)

(Coumadin) and the asthma drug theophylline. Ofloxacin (Floxin) does not have this disadvantage.

- Phototoxicity is caused when sunlight interacts with certain medications to produce a sunburn-like rash. Drugs predisposing to phototoxicity include tetracyclines, phenothiazines, thiazide diuretics, sulfonamides, oral hypoglycemic agents, and griseofulvin. If you will be exposed to sunlight during your trip, review your medications with your physician.
- Antacids, Pepto-Bismol, and Carafate (sucralfate) may block the absorption of quinolone antibiotics such as Cipro and Floxin, the drugs of choice for treating travelers' diarrhea.

Diabetes

- If you take pills to control blood sugar, no time zone adjustment of dosage is necessary when flying. Take your medication according to the local time.
- If you are an insulin dependent diabetic, take enough insulin and U-100 syringes to last the entire trip. (Many countries still use U-80 syringes.)
- If traveling by airliner, call 72 hours before departure to order a diabetic menu.
- Hand carry your insulin at airport security checkpoints.
- Keep your insulin in your carry-on baggage to protect it from temperature extremes. Insulin will keep its full potency for several months even if its not refrigerated, but its temperature should be kept below 86°F.
- Leave your wristwatch unadjusted during flight so that it corresponds to the time of departure.
- Carry blood glucose testing strips or glucometer. Test blood glucose at six-hour intervals or before each meal during the flight.
- Carry sugar cubes or a snack in case meals are delayed, or you feel an insulin reaction (hypoglycemia) setting in.
- Consider carrying all your diabetic supplies in a specially designed case. A popular model, the DIA-PAK, is available from **Mercury Marketing**, P.O. Box 8223 - RW, Stamford, CT 06905; 203-327-5832; $19.95 plus shipping.

Teeth, Eyes, and Feet

- Schedule a dental checkup—Allow enough time for corrective work. Avoid dental work and injections in countries where AIDS and hepatitis B are threats. Consider carrying an emergency dental kit to treat broken or lost fillings.
- Schedule an eye examination if required—Obtain extra prescription eyeglasses. Make a copy of your eyeglass prescription.
- Check your feet—Proper foot care is essential, especially for diabetics. Carefully trim nails, corns, and calluses. Use foot powder to keep feet dry. Be sure shoes and hiking boots are broken in and fit properly. Thin liner socks should be worn by hikers. Don't let a painful, infected blister or other preventable foot problems ruin your trip or jeopardize your health.

AFTER YOU RETURN

If you have traveled to lesser-developed countries (especially for an extended period of time), traveled extensively in rural areas, had intimate contact with the indigenous population, or were exposed to mosquito and insect bites, you may be at higher risk for illness or for harboring an organism in your system that could continue to cause medical problems and possibly infect others close to you. If you have any of the following posttravel symptoms, you should consult your physician.

• Abdominal pain • diarrhea • fever • weight loss • fatigue • cough • skin rash

Of all the symptoms that you may develop, fever is the most important. The table below is helpful in diagnosing the cause of fever in returning travelers.

Differential Diagnosis of Fever in Returning Travelers

(Source: Wiselka MJ, et al. *Travel Medicine International*, October 1992.)

	Acute (0–14 days)	Subacute (2 weeks–6 mo.)	Chronic (Over 6 months)
Protozoa	Malaria Trypanosomiasis Amebic colitis	Malaria Amebic abscess Leishmaniasis	Malaria Amebic abscess Leishmaniasis
Bacteria	Typhoid fever Leptospirosis Meningitis Legionellosis	Brucellosis Tuberculosis	Brucellosis Tuberculosis
Rickettsial	Boutonneuse fever* Rocky Mt. spotted fever Typhus group		

	Acute	Subacute	Chronic
Viral	Dengue Other arboviruses Viral hemorrhagic fever	Hepatitis A, B, E HIV seroconversion	Hepatitis B HIV
Parasitic	Schistosomiasis Tropical eosinophilia	Schistosomiasis Filariasis	Filariasis

*Also known as Mediterranean spotted fever and African tick typhus. Other tick-borne rickettsial diseases include North Asian tick-borne rickettsiosis and Queensland tick typhus.

```
┌─────────────────── Important Malaria Note ───────────────────┐
│ Malaria is the most important illness to consider if you develop a │
│ fever after having been in a malaria endemic area. Undiagnosed or │
│ misdiagnosed cases of malaria, some fatal, have occurred in travelers │
│ after they have returned home, usually after a trip to sub-Saharan │
│ Africa. If you develop a fever after returning home, be sure to tell your │
│ doctor that you have traveled abroad—a tropical illness, especially │
│ malaria—must be considered. │
└──────────────────────────────────────────────────────────┘
```

Posttravel Medical Consultation

A routine posttravel medical consultation and testing is generally not needed if you were a short-term traveler and remained healthy during and after your trip. However, if you developed symptoms during or after your trip, or if you were a long-term traveler (more than 3 months abroad), you should undergo a posttravel check-up. The scope of this check-up will depend upon your itinerary, your potential exposure to tropical diseases, the length of your trip, and the nature, duration, and severity of any symptoms you may have developed.

The Basic Posttravel Medical Exam Includes

➤ History and physical examination which should include the following key points:

- Which pretravel vaccinations you received
- The dates of your departure and return
- Your itinerary: Did you travel to rural areas of tropical or subtropical countries?
- Onset of your symptoms (days? weeks? months?) after possible expo sure to infectious disease
- Adherence to malaria prophylaxis (if prescribed); adherence to mea sures preventing mosquito and insect bites
- Illnesses you had while traveling and the medications taken, including any injections or transfusions received abroad
- Your exposure to (1) unsafe food and drink; (2) insect or animal bites; (3) walking barefoot outdoors; (4) freshwater swimming, bathing, wading; (5) high-risk sexual partners; and (6) drugs

➤ Laboratory examination

- Complete blood count with smear; screen for parasites, anemia, eosinophilia
- Microscopic stool examination to screen for ova and parasites; stool immunoassay to test for giardia (GiardEIA™ assay)
- Stool culture to test for diarrhea-causing bacteria

Diagnostic Pearl

Hookworm disease, schistosomiasis, and strongyloidiasis are the most common causes of eosinophilia in long-term travelers.

The Comprehensive Posttravel Exam May Include

- Basic posttravel history, physical, and laboratory testing, as above
- Blood chemistry profile. Liver function tests. Serum folic acid level if macrocytic anemia is present
- Urinalysis to check for schistosome eggs
- Serologic tests for hepatitis, HIV, and sexually transmitted diseases
- PPD skin test (exposure to tuberculosis)
- Chest x-ray (check for active tuberculosis, Legionnaires's disease, melioidosis, Q fever, tropical eosinophilia)
- Blood smear for malaria parasites, microfilariae, and trypanosomes
- Serologic tests or skin tests to aid in the diagnosis of amebiasis, Chagas' disease, cysticercosis, echinococcosis, fascioliasis, filariasis, leishmaniasis, schistosomiasis, strongyloidiasis, toxoplasmosis, trichinosis, and arbovirus-caused illness (e.g., dengue fever)
- Febrile agglutinins (screen for brucellosis, tularemia, leptospirosis)
- Blood, bone marrow cultures (typhoid fever, salmonellosis, brucellosis, leptospirosis)
- Weil-Felix and/or indirect fluorescent antibody tests for suspected rickettsial diseases (e.g., Rocky Mountain spotted fever, Mediterranean spotted fever, typhus, scrub typhus, Q fever)
- Biopsies of the skin, muscle, liver, or bone marrow (to diagnose leishmaniasis and trichinosis)
- Sigmoidoscopy and rectal biopsy (for schistosomiasis); small intestine endoscopy, aspiration, or biopsy to test for giardia parasites; small intestine endoscopy and biopsy to diagose tropical sprue and coeliac disease, causes of chronic diarrhea and malabsorption
- Ultrasound or CT of liver (for suspected amebic liver abscess, hydatid cysts, toxocariasis, or fascioliasis)
- Lumbar puncture, CSF serology, CT or MRI scan (if schistosomiasis involving the spinal cord, or neurocysticercosis, is suspected)

NOTE: For some parasitic infections e.g., toxoplasmosis, trichinosis, echinococcosis, amebic liver abscess, Chagas' disease, leishmaniasis, and occult filarial infections, serologic tests are very useful. Specific diagnosis, however, is made by finding eggs, or life-cycle stages of the parasite, in the stool, urine, skin or other tissues, or body fluids.

Diagnosis of ascariasis (roundworm infection), cryptosporidiosis, amebiasis, hookworm disease, and overt malaria should be made by microscopic examination of the stool or blood.

2 Jet Lag

Motion Sickness
Medical Problems During Flight
Travelers' Thrombosis

Many travelers have experienced jet lag. The common symptoms—insomnia, fatigue, change in appetite, irritability—are due in part to your body's cyclical hormone production being temporarily out of synch with your activities. After several days at your destination, your body's biological clock (circadian rhythm) becomes reset, and the symptoms subside.

Like many disorders that have no cure, there are lots of proposed jet lag remedies and preventatives. Numerous travelers have tried the Argonne jet lag diet[1]. More recently, exposure to artificial light sources has been touted as being effective in resetting the body's clock.

Jet Lag Diets

Despite their apparent popularity, there is no scientific evidence that jet lag diets do any good. Many travelers find these diets too complex and tedious to follow. Any claimed benefits may be purely psychological, due to placebo effect.

A study conducted by the U.S. Army showed that test subjects who followed the Argonne jet lag diet felt no better after a seven-hour simulated flight than the control group. The diet group, in fact, probably fared worse: they did not sleep as well, possibly due to the caffeine they drank as part of their anti–jet lag diet.

Light Exposure

In contrast to jet lag diets, light exposure seems to play a role in resetting circadian rhythms. The mechanism involves suppression of the hormone melatonin, which is secreted by the brain's pineal gland. What's not clear, though, is what time of day is best to receive light exposure, how you should receive it (sunlight? artificial light?), and for how long.

One group of army test subjects was given four-hour light treatments the morning after a simulated seven-hour flight and on three more consecutive mornings. They felt more alert and happier than those who followed the anti–jet lag diet or who underwent no treatment.

And a recent jet lag "breakthrough" announced by Harvard researchers involved resetting the internal clock by exposing test subjects to three daily five-hour light exposure treatments. These researchers recommend avoiding morning light and maximizing exposure to afternoon light—regardless of the direction of travel. However, the researchers say that light exposure must be carefully timed, cautioning that incorrect timing "would make jet lag twice as bad."[2]

A Jet Lag Pill?

Research is now being done to see if hormone supplements can "internally" correct circadian rhythms. Travelers in one study were given 5 mg of melatonin at the "destination nighttime" for three days before travel, then for three days after arrival. They experienced less fatigue, required less time to normalize their sleep patterns, and scored better on a visual analog scale. But should millions of travelers take a hormone each time they travel long distance?

Before you are "treated" for jet lag, consider the following:

- Is the treatment safe? Are there side effects?
- Is the treatment effective?
- Is the treatment practical and cost-effective?

By these criteria, it's difficult to be enthusiastic about the jet lag treatments mentioned above. The oft-recommended Argonne diet is probably ineffective, but it seems to cause no harm.

Light research is still in its infancy, and researchers presently don't agree when it's best for you to get this exposure. Manufacturers are jumping on the bandwagon to sell travelers artificial light sources, some that you wear on your head for hours at a time. Assuming these devices are safe, and possibly even effective, would you want to do this? Should you force yourself to go outdoors to get sunlight when you would rather be doing something else? (What if you're in Scandinavia in December, and there's hardly any sunlight anyway?) Finally, should you make special, prolonged, unnatural efforts to alter your daily activity in an obsessive desire to avoid or treat jet lag?

And what about a miracle hormone pill to prevent jet lag? As of now, the jury is still out while further research is underway.

What Really Causes Jet Lag Anyway?

Feeling tired and irritable after a long trip is not due entirely to changes in your circadian rhythms. The issue is more complex. Consider the typical scenario:

For several days prior to departure, you are frantically taking care of what seems like a thousand and one last minute errands and details • You are probably too keyed up to get enough sleep • Your normal eating and drinking patterns are disrupted • You are somewhat apprehensive about flying • You are anxious about leaving home and/or your family • You fight heavy traffic getting to the airport • You park your car, but wonder if it will be safe • You carry a heavy suitcase half a mile to check in and hope it won't get lost • You catch a connecting flight • You stand in line again at check-in • You clear security checkpoints • Then you wait in a crowded, smoky airport lounge because your overseas flight is delayed three hours.

It's no surprise that you're feeling stressed out even before takeoff. Add to this a lack of sleep enroute, cramped seating, further dehydration—even constipation.

Then, after arrival in a foreign country, you face still more hassles simply getting to your hotel. No wonder you've got jet lag.

The *HealthGuide* takes the following view—Jet lag is not a single entity that will ever be completely prevented or cured by some diet, magical treatment, or miracle drug. The symptoms you experience are a combination of travel-related physical and emotional stress, sleep deprivation, plus the biological effect of your circadian biorhythms being out of synch.

Strategies to Reduce Jet Lag

You can lessen the effects of jet lag by being physically fit, a nonsmoker, and diet-conscious. Good physical health helps you deal with any type of stress. Some other tips are as follows:

- Don't drink too much alcohol—There's no reason not to have a cocktail or two, but anything more may cause problems. Alcohol is a depressant drug, and larger doses can cause rebound nervous stimulation and restlessness, interfering with your sleep and well-being. Contrary to popular belief, having a few drinks won't dehydrate you during a flight.
- Don't drink too much coffee—Excess caffeine may cause overstimulation, nervousness, anxiety, tremors, and insomnia. Possible side effects also include excess stomach acidity and sometimes diarrhea. However, if you habitually drink many cups of coffee each day, missing your "caffeine fix" during a long flight may not be a good idea—you might get symptoms of caffeine withdrawal, and feel even worse!
- Do drink water—lots of it. You may be dehydrated at the beginning of the flight due to disrupted eating and drinking habits prior to departure. Breathing dry cabin air promotes dehydration unless you take steps to correct it.

Dehydration diminishes blood flow to your muscles and reduces kidney function, causing fatigue and listlessness. To combat this effect, you should drink extra fluids before and during your trip; otherwise, a long trip could leave you dehydrated, and your jet lag will be even more pronounced.

Water: Still the Best Anti–Jet Lag Diet

Recent studies suggest that jet travel doesn't necessarily cause dehydration; in fact, the stress of travel stimulates your kidneys to retain salt and water, counteracting dehydration. The retained water, however, due to prolonged sitting, is mostly sequestered in your extremities as edema fluid and does not contribute significantly to circulating blood volume. (You have probably noticed swollen feet and ankles after a long flight.) For this reason, you should still maintain a high fluid intake during travel to help maintain blood volume.

Before and during your trip, drink extra fluids. The best fluid is water. Don't rely solely on fruit juices or soft drinks—their sugar content is too high. Drink two 8-oz. glasses of water before departure. Drink one liter or more during a six- to seven-hour flight, in addition to whatever other liquid you take with your meals. Drink on a regular basis even though you are not thirsty. After arrival, continue a high water intake for several days.

Jet Lag Tactics

If possible, schedule a flight that departs in the morning. If you're flying from the East Coast to Europe, you'll be arriving in the evening, local time. Your body's internal clock, however, will say it's still mid-afternoon. Have a late dinner and go to bed. Take a sleeping pill if you have insomnia. The next day try to eat and sleep according to local time. If possible, don't nap during the daytime, but do so if you become tired. Keep your nap under 45 minutes to avoid Stage IV (REM) sleep. If you stay active and outside, exposed to natural light, it may help you adjust more rapidly. Continue to drink extra fluids, but limit alcohol and caffeine consumption.

The same general advice applies if you have a night departure and arrive at your destination in the morning. Chances are you'll be very tired. After getting to your hotel, take a short nap if you feel like it. This will help restore you. Pay no attention to those who advise forcing yourself to stay awake. Afterwards, go outside to get some exercise and sunlight, if this is what you feel like doing. At bedtime, take a sleeping pill if insomnia is a problem. The next morning, start to eat and sleep according to local time. Discontinue sleeping medication after two to three nights.

Business travelers—When traveling long distances, consider reserving a sleeperette (reclining airline seat). Arriving a day or two early will help you adjust to your new schedule and improve your performance.

Sleeping Pills

Insomnia is one of the most troublesome symptoms of jet lag and is related to your altered biorhythms. You're trying to sleep while your internal clock is saying "wake up." Your response to insomnia, however, is an individual matter. How much do you mind being awake?

If you need to adapt more rapidly to the new time zone, and insomnia is a significant problem for you, ask your doctor to prescribe a short-acting sleeping pill.

Halcion (triazolam) is a drug that acts rapidly, is quickly eliminated from the body, and is only rarely associated with next-day sedation. There have been reports, however, of next-day memory impairment/amnesia following the use of Halcion, especially when it was taken in higher doses (0.5 mg) during flight. To help avoid the possibility of this side effect, don't exceed the recommended dose of 0.25 mg (elderly travelers should not exceed a dose of 0.125 mg). In addition, you should (1) not take Halcion during your flight, but reserve it for bedtime use after arrival, and (2) not drink alcohol when taking Halcion.

Although recently banned in Great Britain, Finland, and Norway, because of reputed adverse side effects, Halcion is, nevertheless, a safe, effective drug if used properly. Most adverse side effects seem to occur after prolonged use; therefore, limit your use of Halcion to a few nights only.

Because of the adverse publicity, some travelers have decided to avoid Halcion. Two other efficacious sleep inducers to consider are the following:

- Restoril (temazepam). The recommended dosage is 15 to 30 mg for adults. Follow the same precautions as for Halcion.
- Pro-Som (estazolam). The recommended dosage is 1 to 2 mg for adults. Follow the same precautions as for Halcion.

Both Restoril and Pro-Som belong to the same chemical class of drugs as Halcion (the benzodiazepines), but there are fewer reports of adverse side effects associated with their use. However, if you use one of these drugs, take the lowest effective dose and discontinue the medication after 3–5 nights.

Are sleeping pills safe? Generally yes, if they are used for only a short time and in the lowest effective dose. According to the *Harvard Medical School Health Letter* (May 1990), "Taking sleeping pills for a short period—perhaps a few days—can be quite helpful . . . and there is little controversy about prescribing them to help people through a crisis."

Jet Lag Formulas

These vitamin–amino acid formulas supposedly help reset your biorhythms, but no scientific studies have been done. Jet lag formulas previously contained the amino acid L-tryptophan, which has mild sedative qualities, but the purified substance is now banned. Other amino acids have been substituted, but may be less effective. If you do take a formula, they are safe. The only harmful side effects will be to your wallet.

Keep the Problem of Jet Lag in Perspective

Enjoying your vacation is more important than fighting jet lag. Don't waste your time following complex jet lag diets and cures that don't work. Try not to worry too much about jet lag. Less than one-half of travelers report significant symptoms. If you are a business traveler, though, you probably have more need than others to reduce the symptoms of jet lag so you should budget, if possible, one or two extra days after arrival to rest and recuperate prior to business activities.

MOTION SICKNESS

Strictly speaking, motion sickness is neither an illness nor "sickness" but a normal, albeit exaggerated, response to unfamiliar motion of increased intensity and duration. Nausea, sweating, salivation, and vomiting are the usual symptoms. If vomiting does occur, it is frequently followed by drowsiness and lethargy.

Risk Factors

- Sea > Air > Car > Train
- Women > Men
- Inexperienced travelers > Experienced travelers
- Passengers > Driver

Motion sickness occurs in about 1% of airline passengers. Symptoms are rare below age 2 and peak between the ages of 3 and 12. The elderly are less susceptible.

Preventing/Treating Motion Sickness

Don't travel on an empty stomach; this seems to promote symptoms. If you feel yourself becoming nauseated, keep your head stationary. Don't read, but do listen to music if you have a walkman or airline headset. A stable head position is very important in controlling motion sickness because your inner ears contain the balance "gyroscopes" that monitor and coordinate motion and body position.

Body position—On boats, try to stay amidships. Lie supine with your head supported on pillows. Keep your head still and your eyes closed. If on deck, look out at the horizon. One trick: pretend you are "dancing with the ship." On airliners, either (1) press your head against the seat in front of you, or (2) lean back in the seat, keep your head still, and look straight ahead. In cars, sit in the front seat. Look forward at the horizon, rather than out the side windows.

Acupressure bands (Sea-Bands)—Some people swear by these wrist bands with the plastic beads, but a study conducted by *Conde Nast Traveler* magazine (October 1991) found no effect on seasickness.

Drugs

Antihistamine-type medications are useful in reducing or preventing the symptoms of motion sickness. Drowsiness is the main side effect, which can be troublesome if you are driving a car. Drowsiness otherwise can help you lie quietly and thus may be beneficial. The following drugs are commonly used to combat motion sickness.

Antivert (meclizine)—The initial adult dose is 25 to 50 mg. Take one hour prior to embarkation. Repeat every 12–24 hours, as needed, for the duration of the journey. Available by prescription only.

Bucladin-S SOFTABS—Take one tablet one-half hour before departure. A second tablet can be taken in 4 to 8 hours, if necessary. You can take Bucladin-S without swallowing water by allowing the tablet to dissolve in your mouth. This is especially useful if you are nauseated and don't feel like drinking fluids. One tablet usually suffices to relieve symptoms. If nausea persists, you can take one tablet every 8 hours. Available by prescription only. Contraindicated during pregnancy.

Dramamine (dimenhydrinate)—Available without prescription. This drug has a rapid onset of action, and you can use it for either prevention or treatment of symptoms. Adults and children over 12 should take one or two tablets every four to six hours, as needed. Start one hour before embarkation. Follow package instructions for younger children.

Phenergan (promethazine)—The average adult dose is 25 mg taken twice daily. Take the first dose one-half to one hour prior to embarkation and repeat in 8–12 hours, as necessary. For children: Phenergan tablets, syrup, or rectal suppositories, 12.5 to 25 mg, twice daily may be administered. Available by prescription.

Combination therapy—If motion sickness is a serious problem for you, try a combination therapy, using Phenergan and ephedrine. British travel experts often prescribe drugs together. The adult dosage is Phenergan 25 mg, plus ephedrine 50 mg, every 12 hours.

Transderm-Scōp—This is an effective drug whose long action (72 hours) makes it well suited for preventing seasickness on a long cruise. The skin patch contains the drug scopolamine and is meant to *prevent*, not treat, motion sickness. You apply the patch behind your ear, where skin permeability to the drug is highest (Figure 2.1). Be sure to apply the patch at least eight hours prior to exposure to motion and don't let any of the drug get in your eye while applying the patch.

Mildly unpleasant side effects may include blurred vision, drowsiness, or dry mouth. Side effects may be increased in the elderly. More serious side effects, including hallucinations, disorientation, and confusion, have rarely been reported.

MEDICAL PROBLEMS DURING FLIGHT[3]

Sinuses and Ears

When traveling by commercial airliner, you will be cruising at an altitude of 30,000 to 40,000 feet above sea level. Your cabin will be pressurized to an altitude of 6,000 to 8,000 feet above sea level. The air contained within your middle ear and sinuses will expand by about 25% and will usually escape without causing any symptoms. During descent, however, cabin air pressure starts to increase and exceeds the pressure within the middle ear. To allow equalization of pressure on either side of the eardrum, the eustachian tube must open to allow air to enter from the back of your nose. If necessary, clearing the tube can usually be accomplished by yawning or swallowing. Pinching your nostrils closed and gently forcing air from your lungs into the nasopharynx can assist this process. Chewing gum can also help contract the muscles at the end of the tube to allow passage of air up into the middle ear.

Figure 2.1 The small patch placed behind the ear releases minute amounts of scopolamine that permeate the intact skin at a preprogrammed rate over a 72-hour period. The scopolamine is directly absorbed into the bloodstream.

Scopolamine then acts on the nerve fibers of the inner ear and brainstem to reduce nausea and vomiting.

The transdermal patch should be used with caution in travelers with glaucoma and prostate enlargement. Blurred vision and urinary retention may occur. Don't rub your eyes after touching the patch; you may get a dilated pupil and blurred vision.

If the pressure difference between your middle ear and the nasopharynx becomes too great during descent, the end of the eustachian tube might collapse completely, making further ventilation of the middle ear impossible (Figure 2.2). If this occurs, pressure will continue to rise outside the eardrum (tympanic membrane), causing painful stretching and inward bulging of this structure. You might experience dizziness, vertigo, and decreased hearing. There could be bleeding into the middle ear from ruptured blood vessels. More commonly, you might experience several hours, rarely days, of pain and pressure in the ear. During this period of inadequate middle ear ventilation, an acute middle ear infection requiring antibiotics might develop.

If your sinus openings are blocked, pressure symptoms will develop over that particular sinus which air is trying to enter. You may feel a headache over the lower forehead or eyebrows, or over your cheek and around your eyes.

Prevention and treatment—Your ear structure may be such that you cannot adapt to the pressure changes described. (You would probably also note similar symptoms when scuba diving, traveling in high speed elevators, or even driving in the mountains.) If so, recognize your limitations and plan an alternative to air travel.

If you are suffering from an acute ear infection, sinusitis, hay fever, or an upper respiratory infection, you might have too much swelling and edema of the nasal mucous membranes to allow equalization of pressure during air travel. You should not fly under these conditions. If in doubt, consult with your physician or an ear-nose-throat specialist.

Here are some steps you can take to reduce the chances of middle ear and sinus problems when traveling by air:

- If you are suffering from hay fever with nasal congestion (allergic rhinitis), ask your doctor to prescribe a cortisone-type nasal spray such as Vancenase or Beconase plus a nonsedating antihistamine such as Seldane or Hismanal. For increased effectiveness, also take a non-antihistamine-containing decongestant

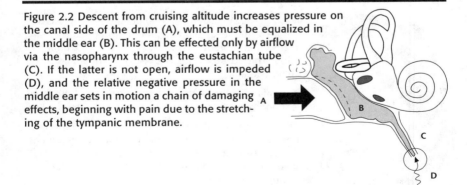

Figure 2.2 Descent from cruising altitude increases pressure on the canal side of the drum (A), which must be equalized in the middle ear (B). This can be effected only by airflow via the nasopharynx through the eustachian tube (C). If the latter is not open, airflow is impeded (D), and the relative negative pressure in the middle ear sets in motion a chain of damaging effects, beginning with pain due to the stretching of the tympanic membrane.

such as Sudafed or Entex-LA. If there is suspicion of a bacterial sinus infection, you will also need an antibiotic. Start medications several days prior to departure.

- If you have a regular head cold with nasal congestion, take a nonprescription decongestant such as Sudafed, Actifed, or Drixoral.
- Topical decongestants: Two hours prior to descent of the aircraft, use Afrin or Neosynephrine spray to open your nasal passages further and unblock the eustachian tube.
- Blow your nose frequently to remove mucous.
- Remain awake during descent in order to keep up with pressure changes as they occur.
- Infants: During descent, they should be only in a sitting position when given their bottles, which should contain only water. This precaution prevents aspiration of milk or formula into the middle ear (via the eustachian tube).

TRAVELERS' THROMBOSIS

An overseas airline flight subjects you to prolonged sitting, usually in a seat where you can't extend your legs. This may result in a condition known as the "travelers' thrombosis."

A prolonged sitting position with the seat cushion pressing against the back of your legs creates conditions that can cause blood clots to form in the deep veins of your legs (deep vein thrombosis—DVT). The clots that form are potentially life-threatening because they can break off and lodge in the lungs (pulmonary embolism). Physicians writing in the British journal Lancet[4] report that journeys as short as three to four hours can cause these clots to form. The chances of this happening, however, are not exactly known.

There are some reports of travelers in good health who have developed DVT, but those at greatest risk are people with varicose veins; people with a history of deep venous thrombosis, especially with chronic venous stasis; patients with cancer, especially adenocarcinoma; pregnant women, or women in the first month postpartum; persons using estrogen products, especially the elderly; travelers with chronic edema of the legs; and those with a past history of pulmonary embolism. Another risk group are patients who had "same day surgery" and then travel within the following 48-72 hours.

To prevent DVT, travelers, especially those at risk, should do the following:

- Avoid dehydration. Drink extra fluids before and during the flight.
- Take frequent walks in the aisles.
- Do isometric exercises while seated.
- Wear support stockings.
- Consider low dose aspirin.

According to the authors of the Lancet article, "Frequent leg and body exercises are advised and regular walks from the aisle seat (avoiding the inside seat, if possible) should be taken, particularly by passengers in the more cramped economy class." They advise both avoiding dehydration, which can promote clotting, and drinking nonalcoholic beverages regularly.

Another useful measure to help prevent clots is to reserve a seat at a bulkhead so that you can fully extend your legs. You may even need to fly in a first-class sleeperette if full extension and elevation of your legs is medically required. If you are on anticoagulants, be sure your physician has your medication dosage properly adjusted prior to departure. If you have severe varicose veins, have your doctor order you some graduated compression stockings.

If you get DVT, you may notice swelling and tenderness of the calf of your leg. If DVT causes a pulmonary embolus, you'll notice abrupt shortness of breath and chest pain. An embolus can strike (sometimes fatally) right after the flight, or many days later.

Notes:

1. See *Overcoming Jet Lag* by Dr. Charles F. Ehret and Lynne Waller Scanlon. Berkley Books, New York.
2. *Conde Nast Traveler*, September 1989: p. 35.
3. Adapted from Schley, WS: Airflight and the middle ear. *HOSPITAL MEDICINE,* March 1988, pp. 85, 86, and 95. Copyright Hospital Publications, Inc. Used with permission of the author and the publisher.
4. Cruikshank J, Gorlin R, Jennett B, Air Travel and Thrombotic Episodes: The Economy Class Syndrome. *Lancet,* Aug. 27th, 1988: pp. 497–498.

3 Food & Drink Safety

Most Americans take for granted the safety of their food and water. If we do worry, we usually focus on sugar, salt, cholesterol, saturated fat—and food additives. We forget that our modern methods of food preparation, packaging and refrigeration, and the use of preservatives—combined with efficient municipal water purification and sanitation—have resulted in the United States and the Western world having unparalleled safety and freedom from infectious diseases transmitted by contaminated food and water. Probably the main health hazard we face from food in this country is its abundance. We eat *too much*. Obesity, not travelers' diarrhea, is rampant.

Food and Drink in the United States and Canada

Despite our excellent safety record, 400–600 outbreaks of food- and water-borne illness are officially reported each year in the United States. The consumption of undercooked bacteria-contaminated eggs, meat, and chicken is responsible for most cases of disease. Salmonellosis, campylobacteriosis, and hepatitis are the most common illnesses, often affecting institutionalized people such as hospital patients, nursing home residents, or school children. Recently, cases of hemolytic-uremic syndrome (HUS), caused by undercooked hamburger meat containing *E. coli* bacteria, have received extensive publicity, but cases of HUS have also been associated with the consumption of raw cider as well as person-to-person contact. Gastroenteritis caused by various Vibrio species of bacteria is occasionally reported from the Gulf of Mexico; most cases are related to the consumption of raw shellfish. Botulism, caused by improperly canned food, is sporadically reported nationwide, and giardiasis, a water-borne parasitic illness, sometimes afflicts hikers and wilderness campers who drink from contaminated ponds, lakes, or streams. Giardiasis and cryptosporidiosis outbreaks have also been traced to chlorinated but inadequately filtered municipal water supplies.

Food and Drink Overseas

Outside of the USA, Canada, Europe, Australia, and parts of Asia, the situation is far more serious. Most third world countries don't have our standard of living, our sanitation technology, nor our cultural attitudes toward the disposal of human fecal material. Toilets may drain into the sources of drinking water, and agricultural fields may be contaminated with various bacteria, viruses, and parasites because human feces (night soil) are often used as fertilizer.

Many countries have only rudimentary water treatment facilities and water distribution systems, and where these facilities do exist there are often breakdowns in the system. Public health regulations and inspections may be unenforced or nonexistent. The hygiene of restaurant personnel is usually below Western standards. The importance of handwashing may not be emphasized to kitchen workers. Refrigeration of food in restaurants may be inadequate, or totally lacking, and countertops and cutting surfaces may not be cleaned as required.

Such practices not only promote the transmission of diarrheal diseases caused by bacteria and viruses, but also help spread hepatitis A, typhoid, poliomyelitis, trichinosis, tapeworm, and other bacterial and parasitic diseases rarely found in this country.

> In lesser-developed tropical countries where food- and water-borne diseases and diarrhea are day-to-day facts of life, diarrhea is the number one killer of infants and young children.

FOOD

When you choose foods to eat, evaluate each item in terms of its ability to harbor dangerous organisms or harmful toxins. Eating undercooked, raw, or unpasteurized products is especially hazardous. Remember that thorough cooking will destroy harmful bacteria, parasites, and viruses. Food contamination can result from any of the following:

(1) Contamination at the source: Shellfish, for example, may be harvested from polluted water containing hepatitis A virus or cholera bacteria; chicken and beef can be fecally contaminated during slaughter, picking up salmonella or E. coli bacteria; lettuce and other uncooked vegetables may be contaminated in the field from contact with night soil, and transmit a variety of bacteria and parasites; unpasteurized dairy products, made from milk produced by sick cattle, can cause brucellosis, listeriosis, and tuberculosis.

(2) Contamination from handling: Foods that require a lot of touching during preparation and that are not cooked afterwards, especially vegetables and salads, are risky. Salads may have also been washed with contaminated water during preparation.

(3) Contamination from bacterial growth: Foods that are wet and warm and allowed to sit around under these conditions are risky because bacterial growth is stimulated. Reheated foods are particularly dangerous.

(4) Contamination from parasitic larvae: Beef, pork, fish, and shellfish may contain parasitic larvae encysted in their flesh. Aquatic plants (watercress, water chestnuts) may have parasitic cysts attached to their shoots. Examples of illness transmitted by encysted parasites include trichinosis, beef and pork tapeworm disease, anisakiasis, and clonorchiasis, paragonimiasis, and fascioliasis (liver fluke and lung fluke diseases).

No matter where you decide to eat, if you follow the guidelines below, you'll improve your chances of staying healthy.

- Eat only meat and fish that is thoroughly and recently cooked, not rewarmed. Beef and pork should be well done without any pink areas.
  CAUTION: Microwaving may not completely destroy surface bacteria. Microwave thoroughly.
- Eat only thoroughly cooked fruits and vegetables and fruits that can be peeled by you.
- Wash the surface of melons before slicing. Bacteria can otherwise be carried onto the cut surface.
- Foods that require little handling are safer.
- Order hard-boiled eggs served in the shell because they are safer than those served out of it.
- Choose dairy products from large, commercial dairies. Boiled milk is safe.
- Milk and dairy products in Canada, Western Europe, and Australia are considered safe. Canned milk is safe.

Foods to Avoid
- Rare or raw meat; raw fish, shellfish, crayfish, and sushi. (Japan and Scandinavia have higher safe food standards regarding sushi and raw fish.)
- Raw vegetables, especially leafy salads served in restaurants.
- Fruits not peeled by you and fruits with punctured skins. Watermelons should be suspect because they are often injected with tap water to increase their market weight.
- Aquatic plants in the Orient (e.g., watercress, water chestnuts).
- Raw eggs, undercooked eggs, unpasteurized milk and cheese. Some cooking techniques (e.g., sunny-side up, "soft" scrambled) won't kill salmonella bacteria.
- Street vendor food unless it is hot and well cooked.
- All food that has been left out in the sun, especially dairy products.
- Buffet food that has been rewarmed or recycled (e.g., the same cheeses brought out at each meal).
- Airline food in lesser-developed countries.

Street Vendor Guidelines
You should be suspicious of all food sold by street vendors. Follow these rules.

- Choose food that is cooked, boiled, steamed, or grilled directly in front of you. These items are safe if served fresh and hot.
- Avoid food handled excessively by the vendor after cooking.
- Avoid juices and other drinks unless they are commercially bottled.
- Eat only food that is served in a clean container.

Wash Your Hands

If possible, wash your hands before you eat. You could have picked up diarrhea-causing germs from touching objects or shaking hands. These germs can then be transferred directly to your mouth or to the food that you touch and then eat.

If you have travelers' diarrhea, or if you are caring for someone with this problem, be sure to wash your hands with soap and water after using the toilet, or after having personal contact with the patient. Shigellosis and giardiasis, in particular, can be spread directly between people, and personal hygiene is important to prevent such person-to-person spread.

Safe Restaurants

Appearances can be deceiving. It's not always possible to tell if a particular restaurant serves safe food. While the big, established restaurants and hotels may have better safety records, even their kitchens can have lapses in sanitation. As for eating in local restaurants, ask for a recommendation from business contacts, hotel managers, tour guides, etc. When in doubt, don't hesitate to eat in a deluxe hotel restaurant. Some travelers say that Chinese restaurants are often the safest. These restaurants use fresher ingredients, cooked at high temperature (not reheated), which are served immediately. Mexican-style restaurants are riskier because many dishes require more handling to prepare and contain eggs, lettuce, and uncooked vegetables.

The following checklist will also help you decide which restaurants may be safer than others.

- Are the silverware, tablecloths, glasses, and plates clean?
- Are the toilets clean? Are soap and hot water provided for hand washing?
- Are there many flies inside? (Flies can carry disease germs.)
- Is there adequate screening to keep out flies and other insects?
- Is there excess/uncovered garbage outside?
- Are the waiters well groomed?
- Is the restaurant recommended by knowledgeable people?

Remember that the enjoyment of eating is partly what travel is all about. Eating well will also help you stay well, provided you use common sense. Be sure you have enough to eat and drink to avoid fatigue and dehydration. Within reason, you can often eat what the locals eat. For example, if you're traveling in Europe, choose a tasty but well-cooked specialty such as Wiener schnitzel and pass up the risky, uncooked, steak tartare. In the Orient, enjoy the Peking duck but skip the raw sushi.

WATER AND BEVERAGES

In all lesser-developed countries, water from streams, ponds, wells, and irrigated areas should be considered unsafe. Tap water, however, is sometimes unfairly maligned. Properly filtered and chlorinated tap water is perfectly safe and is available in many cities, hotels, and resorts worldwide. Drink it, however, only if you're sure it has been reliably treated. When in doubt, treat the water as outlined below.

Safe Beverages
- Boiled water.
- Chemically treated water.
- Filtered water is generally safe for older children and adults in most countries. It should be avoided by infants, children, and pregnant women in lesser-developed countries unless the water filter also employs a virus-killing iodine resin (see discussion below about filters and viruses).
- Hot beverages such as tea or coffee are generally safe. Even if the water was never actually boiled during preparation, heating water over a period of time is similar to pasteurizing it, and most, if not all, harmful bacteria, parasites, and viruses will be eliminated. Be sure the cup you drink from is clean.
- Commercially bottled or canned beverages, carbonated water, soft drinks, fruit juices, beer, and wine.

Beverages to Avoid
- Untreated tap water by the glass, in mixed drinks, or in the form of ice cubes. Commercial ice in blocks should be suspect.
- Locally bottled water. Be suspicious. These bottles are sometimes refilled with local tap water.
- Uncapped bottled water. These bottles may also have been refilled locally. Use your judgment about when to refuse it.
- Sea water is always unfit to drink because of the salt content, but it can be used for cooking.
- Pristine-looking water in wilderness lakes and streams in the United States and Canada may be contaminated with giardia parasites or campylobacter.

Planning Your Water Needs
Review your itinerary to determine what your water needs and sources will be. Will you be vagabond traveling, wilderness trekking, living in tropical countries, touring the third world? All present different problems and require different strategies. You may be faced with preparing quantities of safe drinking water from polluted sources or simply disinfecting small amounts of tap water in your hotel room. When planning your water needs, consider the following:

- Will you be in an urban, rural, desert, mountain, or jungle environment?
- For how long will you be there?

- Will you be hiking or trekking? Need to disinfect water enroute?
- Will you be staying at a fixed base camp?
- Will you be storing drinking water on a boat or vehicle?
- How many people are in your group?
- How much water (maximum amount) will you need to disinfect at one time?
- How close will you be to rivers, lakes, streams? Will you be using this water to drink? How safe is this water to drink?
- What illnesses are common at your destination?
- What type of disinfection equipment or chemicals are you planning to take on your trip?
- What type and how many water containers will you carry?

Wilderness hiking and camping in the USA and Canada expose you mainly to giardia, whereas drinking water in lesser-developed countries is potentially more dangerous—especially near population centers where raw sewage may contaminate the drinking water. In lesser-developed countries, additional protection against bacteria is essential. Protection against viruses should be considered for certain groups (see "Recommendations" below).

Except in resorts, first-class hotels, and cities that properly filter and chlorinate their water, you should disinfect tap water. Use a polyethylene Nalgene bottle (available at camping outlets) to store the treated water. Also use this disinfected water for brushing your teeth.

Transporting Water

The traditional container for carrying water is a plastic water bottle or canteen. Many hikers/trekkers use the standard 1-liter, widemouthed Nalgene bottle because it is easy to fill, especially if dipped in a stream. A newer alternative is the Coldbuster Waistbelt Thermos (**Upstream Products**, 24991 Skyland Road, Los Gatos, CA 95030; 415-655-3466; $39.95). This is a vinyl-lined fanny pack with a 2.5-quart capacity. It is designed with filtering in mind since it can be filled directly with a Katadyn, PŪR, or First Need filter, using an adaptor.

Whichever container you use, fill it at every opportunity. Carrying two bottles, or a waistbelt thermos and one bottle, will allow you to keep one in reserve, filled with filtered or chemically treated water, while drinking from the other container.

Drink sufficient water—Dehydration is fatiguing. Drink at least 2–3 liters of water daily under usual conditions.

What About Viruses?

In wilderness areas in the USA and Canada, where giardiasis is the main threat, water filters alone can be used. They are an acceptable alternative to iodine, chlorine, or boiling water for ridding water of parasites. When traveling or trekking overseas, however, you may be advised not to rely upon filters because they may not trap viruses. The Wilderness Medical Society states, "Filtration may be used for giardia and . . . bacteria, but for field use, filtration is not practical for viruses (although many are removed by adhering to larger particles)."

Should everyone drinking unsafe water in third world countries use iodine, chlorine, or boiling to guarantee protection against viruses? Or rely on bottled water? Just what illnesses do viruses cause that we must guard against? Consider:

➤ The most dangerous water-borne virus to avoid is polio, but this disease is effectively prevented by immunization. Hepatitis A, also caused by a virus, can be prevented by passive immunization with immune globulin (IG) or the new hepatitis A vaccine.

➤ The most common illness-causing viruses are the Norwalk and Rotaviruses. These cause vomiting and watery diarrhea, but except for dehydration in children, and sometimes the elderly, viral gastroenteritis is usually not considered a serious problem.

➤ Water-borne viral hepatitis E is common in southern Asia, but severe illness occurs only in pregnant women. In all others, hepatitis E is self-limited and appears to be nonlethal. It is not prevented by immune globulin prophylaxis.

Recommendations

The considerations above lead the *HealthGuide* to recommend the following:

1. **All travelers** should be fully immunized against polio and hepatitis A if they are going to be in an area of substandard sanitation.
2. **Pregnant women** in high-risk, third world regions (especially India, Nepal, and Pakistan) need to avoid hepatitis E and should drink only bottled or boiled water, or water treated with chlorine or iodine (short-term iodine use suggested). A PentaPure Cup or one of the PŪR filters is a good choice since they utilize an iodine resin to eliminate viruses.
3. **Infants, young children, and the elderly** should take the above precautions in order to avoid intestinal viral infections that cause dehydration.
4. **For immunized adults,** the Katadyn, PŪR, or First Need filters (see "Water Filtration and Purification Devices" below) or the PentaPure Cup are excellent choices. Many travelers, in fact, rely upon these devices and have little or no diarrheal illness.

In reality, many travelers may want to have *both* a water filter and a chemical disinfectant to use as local sanitary conditions, itinerary, length of stay, convenience, and personal preference dictate. One technology doesn't necessarily exclude the other. Each method has advantages and disadvantages. You may not have your filter with you at all times. It may clog or break, or you may not have a replacement filter element. Likewise, you may lose your taste for iodine, or perhaps you may run out of chlorine or iodine. Whatever the scenario, you may need a backup method of water disinfection.

Remember that no matter what system you use to disinfect water, intestinal illness is still possible because it is also caused by contaminated food and sometimes from microorganisms that are spread directly from person to person. Water disinfection only reduces your risk of illness; it doesn't eliminate it entirely.

WATER DISINFECTION

Obtaining Clear Water

If you are drawing water from a polluted source, it may be grossly contaminated with organic material. For aesthetic reasons alone, you wouldn't want to drink cloudy, scummy water. Furthermore, cloudy water requires more time and bigger doses of chemicals to disinfect, especially if it is cold. Chlorine, in particular, reacts with, and is neutralized by, organic material such as rotting vegetation. Unless you are literally dying of thirst, you should take enough time to clarify your drinking water before it is treated. Here are some techniques:

Sedimentation—Let the turbid water stand undisturbed for several hours, then pour off the upper, clear portion. This works best if the cloudiness is due to sand, silt, or other inorganic material.

Flocculation—Organic impurities may not sediment out with gravity alone. Add a pinch of alum (available over the counter in drug stores) and mix. Flocculation (clumping) of suspended organic impurities will occur, and these clumped particles will settle to the bottom of the container. Pour off the clarified water. To save time, you can pour the water through a coffee filter, commercial filter paper, fine cloth, or a canvas filter bag to remove the flocculated sediment more rapidly.

Filtering—Most filters readily remove bacteria but their main advantage is the removal of parasites, especially giardia and cryptosporidia, which are often resistant to chlorination. Adding a carbon filter attachment removes also chemicals and improves taste.

Methods of Disinfecting Water

Boiling water—Water that is brought just to a boil and then allowed to cool is safe to consume. Boiling water for 10 to 20 minutes, even at high altitudes, is unnecessary and wastes time and fuel. Some people even question the need to boil water at all—they just "pasteurize" it by heating it for a period of time at a sub-boiling temperature. To kill cholera germs, for example, boiling is not necessary. Heating contaminated water to 144°F (62°C) for 10 minutes is sufficient to eliminate completely all strains of this bacterium.

NOTE: Boiling water at 10,000 feet raises its temperature to an adequate 194°F (90°C).

Advantages of boiling—Boiling water completely eliminates bacteria, cysts of parasites (amoebic, giardia, cryptosporidia), worm larvae that cause schistosomiasis, and viruses (the cause of hepatitis, polio, and viral gastroenteritis). Briefly boiling water won't eliminate the spores of certain bacteria; hence, the water can't be considered absolutely sterile. However, bacterial spores, should they be in the water, don't cause intestinal illness and can be consumed without harm.

Disadvantages of boiling—It is easier said than done. Heating the water is time-consuming, often inconvenient, and may require you to carry a source of fuel with you. Boiling is usually most easily done at a base camp, not on the trail. Other technologies of water disinfection now make boiling water seem tedious and old-fashioned.

Iodine and chlorine (halogens)—Under proper conditions, both iodine and chlorine (chemically known as halogens) are excellent water disinfectants, especially for removing bacteria and viruses. You will get the best results by obtaining clear or clarified water (see above) and allowing extra time for the halogen to work.

U.S. Army studies have previously demonstrated that iodine, under field conditions (dirty, cold water; short contact time), is superior to low doses of chlorine. With a ten-minute contact time at room temperature, iodine completely kills bacteria, parasites, viruses, and worm larvae. Iodine tablets are the choice of the U.S. Army for soldiers in the field.

CAUTION: If you are pregnant, medical authorities advise not drinking iodine-treated water for more than three to four weeks, but careful studies have never been done.

Iodine tablets—Potable Aqua is the most popular brand. Dissolve one tablet in a liter of water and wait 20–30 minutes. If the water is cold and cloudy, use two tablets and wait at least 30 minutes.

Advantages—Tablets usually have a long shelf life, even under adverse conditions, and they won't stain your pack or clothing if spilled. Tablets are also convenient and quite safe even if swallowed. Potable Aqua tablets are widely sold through camping stores. They are also available by mail order from **R.E.I. Outfitters**, P.O. Box 88125, Seattle, WA 98138; 800-426-4840; item #407071; about $5.50 for 50 tablets.

Saturated iodine solution—Polar Pure sells a 3-oz. bottle containing 8 gm of iodine crystals to which you add water to make a saturated iodine solution. You can disinfect up to 2,000 quarts (500 gallons) of water with a single bottle.

Advantages—It is economical, has a long shelf life, and is compact. Polar Pure is available at camping outlets and also from R.E.I. Outfitters; 800-426-4840; item #A407-150. Bulk quantities (> 24 bottles) are available from **Polar Equipment**, 12881 Foothill Lane, Saratoga, CA 95070; 408-867-4576; $9.95 a bottle retail.

Liquid chlorine bleach (4% to 6% Clorox)—Household bleach is easily available and cheap, but is not guaranteed to kill giardia or cryptosporidia cysts, especially if the water is cloudy or cold. Add two drops of chlorine bleach to each quart of water if it is clear and from the tap; add four drops if the water is cloudy or not from the tap. Wait at least 30 minutes before drinking.

AquaCure—Chlorine tablets make a commercial reappearance with this new product that is registered under the new EPA guidelines to kill bacteria, parasites, and viruses. Box of 30 tablets sells for about $8.

PentaPure Purification Cup—Water is poured through the disinfecting unit, which contains the patented PentaPure iodine resin, into the drinking cup as shown below.

This economical purifier cup, made by **Water Technologies, Inc.**, is lightweight and well-suited for short-term travel where smaller quantities of water (e.g., hotel tap water) need to be treated. Wt. 13 oz. Retail price $29.95.

How PentaPure™ works: PentaPure is a purification technology based on electrostatic chemical forces. Through a patented process, iodide ions are bound to an anion exchange resin, creating an electrically charged structure. When negatively charged contaminants contact the resin, iodine is instantly released, penetrating the microorganism. By this process, bacteria, viruses, and parasites are killed, without large amounts of iodine actually being in solution. Using this patented process, Water Technologies, Inc., has developed a large number of purification products.

Water Filtration and Purification Devices

The principle of filtering bacteria-containing solutions is well established. Filters are effective. Bacteriology laboratories and pharmaceutical plants routinely use special filters made of glass, cellulose, or ceramic to remove bacteria from serums and antibiotic solutions that would otherwise be damaged by heat processing. More recently, filter technology has been adapted for the outdoors. Some filters for campers are designed to filter out only larger organisms such as parasites (e.g., giardia) and worm larvae, whereas others are fine enough to also trap bacteria. By adding an iodine resin matrix after the filter element, viruses can also be eliminated, and the unit then becomes a true purification device. Units that employ an activated charcoal filter can trap chemical contaminants, improving odor, taste, and safety.

Katadyn PF Pocket Filter—This high-quality, Swiss-made filter removes bacteria and parasites from even grossly contaminated water. Heavily silted water may cause the ceramic filter to clog, but it can be brushed-cleaned up to 300 times. Although the Katadyn has a high initial cost, the ability to clean the filter eliminates the expense and inconvenience of replacement filters. The 0.2-micron ceramic filter element is impregnated with silver quartz to prevent bacteria growth within its pores. The 28-inch intake hose has a strainer to eliminate coarse debris. The Katadyn will mate with the Coldbuster fanny pack thermos (adaptor costs $1.95). Flow rate: 3/4 liters per minute. Retail price $250.

PŪR Portable—This compact unit (formerly called the Traveler) combines a 1.0-micron filter with a tri-iodine resin matrix to eliminate bacteria, parasites, and viruses. The filter cartridge has a 100-gallon service life. The big advantages of this filter are its small size (12 oz.) and ability to eliminate viruses. The Portable is especially convenient for disinfecting glass-size amounts of water in hotels and restaurants. Minimal iodine taste remains in the water. Retail price $69.95.

PŪR Scout—This economical hand pump filter is well-suited for campers and backpackers. All microorganisms, parasites, and viruses are eliminated. Unit comes with long intake and output hoses. An optional carbon cartridge can be attached to remove chemicals, pesticides, and herbicides and improve taste. Retail price $59.95. Replacement filter $19.95.

First Need filter—The First Need filter comprises a pump, purifying cartridge, and a prefilter to prevent inadvertent clogging of the purification cartridge. The 10-micron prefilter is backwashable and inexpensive.

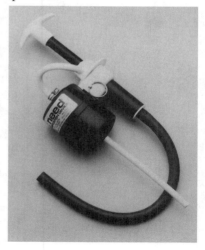

Inside the purification unit there is a 0.4-micron retention filter that extracts bacteria, parasites, and other particles. Chemical contaminants, odors, and tastes are removed by an absorption matrix. Electrostatic charges in the matrix remove viruses and other ultrasmall particles, binding them to the matrix without affecting the "pass-through" of water. The manufacturer claims the canister filters about 100 gallons before replacement is required. Registered by the EPA. About $55.

Timberline filter—The Timberline is a lightweight, economical filter that is used primarily by campers and backpackers to eliminate giardia parasites from drinking water obtained from backcountry lakes, ponds, and streams. The Timberline has a 2.0 micron filter, sufficient for the removal of parasites, but not small enough to remove bacteria, which may be a threat in wilderness areas due to human and animal fecal contamination of water sources. For further product information, contact Timberline Filters, Inc., P.O. Box 12007, Boulder, CO 80303; 303-972-0737. About $30.

4 Travelers' Diarrhea

Diarrhea is by far the most common medical problem among people traveling to lesser-developed tropical and semitropical countries. Travelers' diarrhea, however, is not a specific disease. The term describes the symptoms of an intestinal infection caused by certain bacteria, parasites, or viruses that are transmitted by the consumption of contaminated food or water. The severity and duration of symptoms depend upon which microorganism is causing the illness. There are three main types of travelers' diarrhea, classified according to symptoms.

Type I. Watery Diarrhea

Up to 60% of short-term travelers are affected by this type of diarrhea. Most cases of watery diarrhea, worldwide, are caused by a bacterium called enterotoxigenic (toxin-producing) *E. coli*. Other causes of Type I diarrhea include salmonella, shigella, and vibrio bacteria. About 10% of cases are caused by intestinal viruses.

The symptoms of Type I travelers' diarrhea range from several loose or watery stools per day to a more explosive illness with profuse, but nonbloody, diarrhea. Associated symptoms often include nausea, vomiting, abdominal cramps, and a low-grade fever. These symptoms, if untreated, usually last three to five days. For some travelers, Type I diarrhea is a major cause of inconvenience and discomfort, potentially ruining a carefully planned vacation or business trip.

The main medical danger from profuse Type I diarrhea is dehydration, especially in children and the elderly. Early treatment of Type I diarrhea with fluids and antibiotics is usually successful.

Type II. Dysentery (Bloody Diarrhea)

Up to 15% of travelers are affected by dysentery. Dysentery results from a more serious intestinal infection caused by certain bacteria (and sometimes parasites) that invade and inflame the intestinal wall. The most common type of dysentery is bacillary dysentery, also called shigellosis, which is caused by certain species of shigella bacteria. Other bacterial microorganisms that can cause dysentery include salmonella, campylobacter *(C. jejuni)*, yersinia, and entero-invasive *E. coli*. A less common form of dysentery is amebic dysentery (amebiasis), caused by *E. histolytica* parasites invading the colon.

Dysentery is typically recognized by the presence of bloody diarrhea (or bloody stools mixed with mucus), fever, abdominal pain and tenderness, and prostration.

If you get the symptoms of dysentery, you should start antibiotic treatment (as described below), drink sufficient fluids to prevent dehydration, and seek medical attention. If your symptoms are severe, or if you don't improve with antibiotics, you should see a doctor immediately—you may need to be hospitalized.

Type III. Chronic Diarrhea

Less than 2% of travelers develop chronic diarrhea. Occasionally, travelers develop diarrhea that lasts for several weeks, or more, and which is associated with vague abdominal pain, bloating, nausea, loss of appetite, fatigue, weight loss, and low-grade fever.

Chronic travelers' diarrhea is usually due to giardiasis, a parasitic disease discussed in Chapter 8. Other diseases causing chronic diarrhea include amebiasis, cryptosporidiosis, schistosomiasis, and cyclosporidiosis, caused by a recently discovered parasite, *Cyclospora cayetanensis.*

If you develop chronic diarrhea, consult with your physician or an infectious disease specialist. Testing should be done to establish a precise diagnosis. However, if you are overseas in a remote area, and medical consultation is not available, assume that you have giardiasis and start self-treatment with metronidazole (Flagyl) or tinidazole (Fasigyn), and be sure to seek follow-up medical care as soon as possible.

NOTE: Distinguishing giardiasis from amebiasis symptoms is not always easy. Giardiasis, however, unlike amebiasis, does not cause bloody diarrhea.

Travelers' Diarrhea Facts

- Bacteria cause about 80% of travelers' diarrhea.
- The most common source of travelers' diarrhea is contaminated food and, to a lesser degree, contaminated water.

Your Risk of Getting Travelers' Diarrhea

This is related to which countries you visit and the precautions you take. There is little risk (attack rate about 8%) when visiting North America, northern and central Europe, Australia, and New Zealand. Intermediate attack rates (8%–20%) are found in travelers to most destinations in the Caribbean, southern Europe, Israel, Japan, and South Africa. High-risk destinations (attack rates up to 60% during first two weeks) include Mexico and the developing countries of Africa, South and Central America, the Middle East, and Asia.

Your first attack of travelers' diarrhea won't "immunize" you against further episodes, and second attacks are frequent. Most long-term travelers, however, notice a decrease in diarrheal episodes after residing several months in a foreign country.

Causes and Geographic Variations of Travelers' Diarrhea

The four principal bacterial microorganisms causing travelers' diarrhea in most high-risk areas are *E. coli*, shigella species, salmonella species, and campylobacter.

Temperature, annual rainfall, presence or absence of rivers, lakes, or seacoasts, dry and rainy seasons, monsoons, and other geographic and climatic factors will determine which diarrhea-causing bacteria are most common in any particular region. For example, in Thailand, after *E. coli*, salmonella and vibrio bacteria are most commonly found; in Nepal, after *E. coli*, shigella and campylobacter are the most common diarrhea-causing bacteria. In Mexico, *E. coli*, salmonella, and shigella predominate in the rainy summer season, whereas campylobacter is more common in the drier winter season.

These studies show that globally the causes of infectious diarrhea are not fixed and that each region has a unique pattern of disease.

PREVENTING TRAVELERS' DIARRHEA

Diet

The risk of travelers' diarrhea can be significantly reduced by following the old adage "boil it, cook it, peel it, or forget it." In reality, most travelers won't adhere to such strict dietary guidelines. Many people can't resist salads, they eat fruit that can't be peeled, and they still put ice cubes in their drinks. While it may be unrealistic to expect you to avoid completely any dietary indiscretion, studies do show that fewer lapses will result in less illness. Pay careful attention to what you eat and drink and try to follow the safe food and drink guidelines spelled out in Chapter 3.

Handwashing

Always wash your hands with soap and water before eating. This prevents transferring diarrhea-causing bacteria or parasites to your food or mouth.

If you have diarrhea, be sure to wash your hands after using the toilet. You can easily spread diseases such as giardiasis, amebiasis, and shigellosis to others through person-to-person contact, or through food that you have touched during preparation. For the same reasons, you should always wash your hands after changing a child's diaper.

Drug Prophylaxis for Travelers' Diarrhea

You should consider prophylaxis with either Pepto-Bismol or antibiotics if you will be traveling short-term (less than three weeks) and cannot afford to have your trip interrupted, or travel plans altered, because of illness. You might be, for example, a businessperson, musician, or athlete who can't afford to miss an important meeting or event.

Or, you might have a medical condition that would be adversely affected by any additional illness. This would also be an indication for prophylaxis. Specific medical conditions sometimes warranting prophylaxis include inflammatory bowel disease (colitis), insulin-dependent diabetes, or heart disease, especially if you are an elderly person. People who have had peptic ulcer surgery, or who take stomach acid-reducing drugs (e.g., Zantac, Tagamet, Pepcid), are also at increased risk of travelers' diarrhea and should consider prophylaxis.

NOTE: Travelers who take the antiulcer drug Carafate (sucralfate) may actually reduce their risk of diarrhea because this drug has antibacterial properties.

Prophylaxis with Pepto-Bismol

Taking Pepto-Bismol (bismuth subsalicylate) can reduce your chances of getting travelers' diarrhea by about 65%. This is a good prophylactic drug for adult travelers and older children because it is quite effective and there is minimal chance of an allergic or toxic reaction, as may be caused by antibiotics.

How does it work? Medical studies indicate that Pepto-Bismol actually eliminates harmful bacteria from the stomach. This antibacterial action is due to the bismuth component of the medication. The salicylate in Pepto-Bismol has an antisecretory and antiinflammatory effect on the bowel wall, reducing the output of diarrheal fluid.

Dosage: 2 tablets (or 2 oz. of the liquid), 4 times daily. Take with meals and at bedtime. The tablet form of Pepto-Bismol is as effective as the liquid preparation, and the tablets easier to carry.

Children's dosage: Pepto-Bismol can be used by children older than three years. They should use one-half the adult dose. For using Pepto-Bismol in a child under age three, consult with your pediatrician.

NOTE: 2 tablespoons or tablets of Pepto-Bismol has the salicylate content of about one adult aspirin tablet.

Pepto-Bismol is most effective when taken with meals because if the food is contaminated the drug comes into immediate contact with the microorganisms.

Contraindications: Pepto-Bismol should be avoided by people who (1) are allergic to, or intolerant of, aspirin, (2) have any type of bleeding disorder, (3) are taking an anticoagulant (warfarin, Coumadin), or (4) have a history of peptic ulcer disease or gastrointestinal bleeding.

Side effects: Pepto-Bismol causes darkening of the tongue and stool, but this is not harmful. Excessive use can cause ringing in the ears (tinnitus), due to salicylate toxicity. Don't take aspirin and Pepto-Bismol simultaneously—the risk of salicylate toxicity (tinnitus, easy bruising) will be increased. If you are on a warfarin anticoagulant (e.g., Coumadin), you should not take Pepto-Bismol because the chance of bleeding will be increased.

Check with your doctor about the safety of Pepto-Bismol if you have any chronic medical condition for which you are taking medication. Pepto-Bismol should not be taken with doxycycline since it can prevent the absorption of the latter. Pepto-Bismol may also inhibit the absorption of other antibiotics but the extent of this interaction has not been well studied.

Prophylactic Antibiotics

Taking an antibiotic (especially one of the quinolones) can significantly reduce your risk of travelers' diarrhea. However, since all antibiotics have potential side effects, physicians are hesitant to prescribe them routinely to healthy travelers. Also, if diarrhea occurs while taking the antibiotic, then what should you do? It can be argued that an antibiotic, such as a quinolone, should not be used for prophylaxis when it is also the treatment of choice, and therefore should be reserved for that purpose.

Prophylactic antibiotics are not generally recommended for young children; Pepto-Bismol is safer for them.

Pepto-Bismol Combined with Standby Antibiotics— The Best Prophylactic Option?

Before insisting on prophylactic antibiotics be aware that the quinolone antibiotics (below) are rapidly effective in the treatment of most cases of diarrhea. In fact, a quinolone usually stops diarrhea within 10 hours or less. Therefore, if you take Pepto-Bismol prophylactically, and carry the antibiotic in reserve, you can significantly reduce your chance of travelers' diarrhea and at the same time preserve the therapeutic option of an antibiotic. Pepto-Bismol prophylaxis, combined with quick antibiotic treatment, as needed, is probably the best choice for most travelers requesting prophylaxis.

NOTE: Don't take Pepto-Bismol and an antibiotic simultaneously—the absorption of the antibiotic may be impaired.

Antibiotics Used to Prevent Travelers' Diarrhea

Norfloxacin (Noroxin)	400 mg daily
Ciprofloxacin (Cipro)	500 mg daily
Ofloxacin (Floxin)	400 mg daily
TMP/SMX (Bactrim, Septra)	1 tablet daily
Doxycycline (Vibramycin)	100 mg daily

TREATMENT OF TRAVELERS' DIARRHEA

The treatment of travelers' diarrhea (depending upon the severity) employs one or more of the following:

- Fluids
- Pepto-Bismol (bismuth subsalicylate)
- Loperamide (Imodium)
- Antibiotics

Fluids

If you are having frequent, copious diarrhea (especially diarrhea caused by cholera), dehydration is a potential threat and you may need treatment with an oral rehydration solution, as described below in the section "Oral Hydration Therapy." If your diarrhea is not particularly severe, then follow these guidelines:

Mild/moderate diarrhea: Adults— If your diarrhea is less than 5–8 episodes daily, you're at little risk for becoming dehydrated. Continue with your regular diet (soup and salted crackers are good additions) and drink at least 2–3 liters of fluid (mostly water) daily—or more if you are in a hot climate. Avoid dairy products (milk and cheese) during the acute phase of diarrhea.

Mild diarrhea: Infants—They should continue to receive their regular formula or food and whatever liquids they normally consume. Pedialyte, Ricelyte, or their equivalents (described below) are useful fluid supplements for mild to moderate diarrhea in infants and younger children.

Pepto-Bismol

In addition to its role in prophylaxis, Pepto-Bismol can also be used for the treatment of travelers' diarrhea. Pepto-Bismol reduces the number of unformed stools by 50% through its antimicrobial, antisecretory, and antiinflammatory actions. Bloody diarrhea (dysentery) is not a contraindication to the use of Pepto-Bismol, but dysentery, if present, should also be treated with an antibiotic.

Dosage: 2 tablespoons (1 oz.) immediately and then 1 oz. every 1/2 hour to 1 hour. Don't exceed 8 oz. in any 24-hour period.

Children's dosage: Children over age three can be given one-half the adult dosage.

You can consume an entire 8-oz. bottle over 4–8 hours to treat an episode of diarrhea. Don't use the tablets for treating diarrhea since the liquid form is much more effective. Don't take aspirin at the same time you are taking Pepto-Bismol since salicylate toxicity could occur. Use Tylenol (acetaminophen) if you need medication for pain or fever.

If your diarrhea is not adequately controlled with 8 oz. of Pepto-Bismol given over a short period of time, you should start antibiotic treatment. Stop Pepto-Bismol at this point since it may inhibit antibiotic absorption.

Loperamide

Loperamide (Imodium) reduces diarrhea (both the frequency of passage of stools and the duration of illness) by up to 80%. Compared to Pepto-Bismol, loperamide is more effective in reducing the number of unformed stools passed during the first four hours of treatment. Loperamide has a rapid and direct effect on the bowel and has few side effects. Its action is due to its antimotility effect (reducing peristalsis) as well as its antisecretory effect (blocking the bowel's output of salt and water).

Dosage: 2 capsules (4 mg) immediately, then 1 capsule after each loose or watery stool. Don't take more than 8 capsules over any 24-hour period. Don't take loperamide if you have bloody diarrhea or a fever (see below). Loperamide can be given to children between the ages of two and five, but is available only by prescription for children in this age range. Do not give loperamide to children less than two years old unless you have consulted previously with your pediatrician.

Side effects: These are usually mild. Overuse can cause constipation and occasional dizziness and drowsiness.

NOTE: A theoretic concern about antimotility drugs is that they may prolong illness by interfering with the body's natural "flushing" mechanism. In reality, when travelers have used loperamide to treat watery diarrhea, no significant prolongation of illness has been observed, even when stool cultures have later shown the presence of an invasive microorganism, e.g., shigella. Nevertheless, medical experts say some caution is necessary. Don't take loperamide if you have bloody diarrhea or a fever greater than 101° F. Bloody diarrhea and fever may indicate a more severe invasive infection of the gut wall, and slowing down intestinal motion with an antimotility drug can theoretically result in exacerbation or prolongation of illness.

Loperamide Plus Antibiotics

The problem with loperamide, used alone, is that it does not treat the cause of the diarrhea—only the symptoms. Some people don't respond to treatment, and others have a relapse when the drug is stopped.

Recent studies indicate that combining loperamide with an antibiotic is better therapy for diarrhea because it combines the antimotility action of the former with the curative effects of the latter. Studies conducted in Mexico, for example, showed that when travelers took only loperamide for watery diarrhea, their immediate symptoms did improve but their diarrhea also lasted an average of 50 hours; when they took an antibiotic (TMP/SMX) alone, their diarrhea lasted an average of 27 hours; but when they took both loperamide and TMP/SMX, their diarrhea lasted an average of only 4.5 hours.

In Egypt, when the U.S. Navy treated military personnel with ciprofloxacin, they also found that additional improvement occurred when loperamide was used. (This study, however, also demonstrated that ciprofloxacin, used alone, was extremely effective. The addition of loperamide reduced symptoms somewhat during the first 24 hours, but not dramatically.)

Antibiotics

The discovery of the fluroquinolone (quinolone) antibiotics has revolutionized the treatment of travelers' diarrhea. These antibiotics are especially effective in eradicating those bacteria (*E. coli*, shigella, salmonella, and campylobacter) responsible for the majority of cases of watery diarrhea and dysentery. Often, just one or two doses of a quinolone are curative. So far little antimicrobial resistance worldwide to the quinolones has developed.

Which Quinolone to Use?

Two quinolone antibiotics, ciprofloxacin (Cipro) and ofloxacin (Floxin), are commonly used for the treatment of travelers' diarrhea.

1. **Cipro (ciprofloxacin)**—Cipro was the first quinolone to receive FDA approval for treating infectious diarrhea. Cipro has excellent activity against the common dysentery-causing bacteria (shigella, salmonella, and campylobacter) which have become increasingly resistant to other antibiotics, especially TMP/ SMX (trimethoprim/sulfamethoxazole) and doxycycline.
   Dosage: 500 mg twice daily for 1 to 3 days.
   Alternate dosage: 1,000 mg as a single dose given daily for 1–2 days.
2. **Floxin (ofloxacin)**—Floxin is not only as effective as Cipro against diarrhea-causing bacteria, but it has better activity against pneumococcal, streptococcal, and staphylococcal bacteria. Floxin, unlike Cipro, is also effective against chlamydia.
   Dosage: 400 mg twice daily for 1 to 3 days.

NOTE: Although just one or two doses of a quinolone are usually needed to stop most cases of travelers' diarrhea, this is not always the case. When illness is caused by *Shigella dysenteriae* (a more virulent strain of shigella), a 7–10 day course of treatment is necessary.

Cipro and Floxin are also commonly prescribed for the treatment of skin, bone, soft tissue, and urinary tract infections, as well as gonorrhea, PID, bronchitis, and pneumonia. This wide range of antimicrobial activity makes these drugs useful for a traveler to carry for self-treatment of a variety of infections, particularly in areas where medical care is not close by. Floxin may be preferred because of its somewhat better activity against gram-positive bacteria.

Alternative Drugs Used to Treat Travelers' Diarrhea

Furazolidone (Furoxone)—Although not as rapidly effective as the quinolones, furazolidone has excellent activity against the majority of gastrointestinal pathogens, including *E. coli*, salmonella, shigella, campylobacter, and the vibrio species (which cause cholera). Furazolidone, in fact, was found to be the most effective antibiotic against cholera in Rwanda. One distinct advantage of furazolidone is that it is also effective against giardia. Furazolidone can also be used with Pepto-Bismol without a decrease in absorption.

Adult dosage: 100 mg (1 tablet) 4 times daily for 1 to 3 days. For giardiasis, the drug should be given for 7–10 days.

Children's dosage: Children 5 years and older should receive 25 to 50 mg (1/4 to 1/2 tablet) four times daily.

Liquid furazolidone contains 15 mg per tablespoonful. The drug should not be administered to infants under 1 month of age.

5 years and older—1/2 to 1 tablespoonful four times daily.

1 to 4 years—1 to 1-1/2 teaspoonfuls four times daily.

1 month to 1 year—1/2 to 1 teaspoonful four times daily.

Side effects: Occasional nausea and vomiting. The drug should not be taken with alcohol. Probably safe for use in pregnancy; no reports of adverse effects have been reported from animal studies or in the fetus or newborn.

Trimethoprim/sulfamethoxazole (TMP/SMX) —This sulfa-containing drug (Bactrim-DS, Septra-DS) has until recently been recommended as primary treatment of travelers' diarrhea but resistant strains of shigella and salmonella are increasingly common in all developing countries. In addition, TMP/SMX is not effective against campylobacter or giardia. TMP/SMX is said to be still effective against shigella in inland (noncoastal) areas of Mexico, but elsewhere TMP/SMX is now considered a second-line drug, to be used only by travelers who can't take the quinolones or furazolidone.

NOTE: TMP/SMX is also effective treatment for diarrhea caused by cyclospora parasites.

Dosage: 2 double-strength (DS) tablets immediately followed by 1 double-strength tablet twice daily for 3 days. Combining TMP/SMX with loperamide increases effectiveness.

Side effects: GI upset, rash.

TMP/SMX is safe for children over age 2 months and can be considered for use by pregnant women. Its use during pregnancy, especially during the first and third trimesters, should be discussed with a physician.

Metronidazole (Flagyl)—This drug is used for the presumptive treatment of giardiasis. If you have diarrhea that persists longer than two weeks, you could be harboring giardia parasites. Start self-treatment for giardiasis if you are in a remote area and you will be unable to get timely medical consultation.

Adult dosage: 500 mg, three times daily for 5 to 7 days.

Do not drink alcohol when taking Flagyl—side effects are enhanced.

Treatment of Children and Pregnant Women

Furazolidone and TMP/SMX can be used in children over age two months, but replacement of fluids is considered the primary treatment of diarrhea in infants and children. When using TMP/SMX, combine it with erythromycin in order to provide coverage against campylobacter.

The quinolones should not be used routinely by children or pregnant women. Worries about harmful effects in children, however, may be exaggerated since children with cystic fibrosis are often treated with quinolones, without apparent harm. The *HealthGuide* believes you should not arbitrarily withhold quinolones if a child has bloody diarrhea and high fever because the benefits of treatment most likely will outweigh the risks. The same is true for pregnant women. If the mother's health is in jeopardy, treatment with a quinolone should not be withheld out of a theoretical concern about the effect of the drug on the fetus.

Summary of Treatment of Travelers' Diarrhea

- Treatment options for travelers' diarrhea include Pepto-Bismol (bismuth subsalicylate), loperamide (Imodium), antibiotics, or antibiotics combined with loperamide. If you decide initially to treat symptoms only with loperamide or Pepto-Bismol, and your symptoms are not improved after 4 to 6 hours, start antibiotics, preferably a quinolone (e.g., Floxin).
- If you do start antibiotics, stop Pepto-Bismol—it may interfere with the absorption of the antibiotic.
- If your symptoms are primarily vomiting, with minimal diarrhea, you probably have an intestinal virus; sipping plenty of slightly salty fluids and taking Pepto Bismol is the best treatment.
- If you have copious or explosive diarrhea, take an antibiotic and loperamide immediately. Continue the antibiotic for 1 to 3 days, as necessary, but stop loperamide after 12–24 hours. Don't take loperamide if you have bloody diarrhea or fever greater than 101°F.
- Dysentery (bloody diarrhea, high fever) always requires antibiotic treatment and medical follow-up.
- Furazolidone (Furoxone) is an underrated drug for the treatment of travelers' diarrhea. Although its action against intestinal bacteria is somewhat slower than seen by the quinolones, it has a broader spectrum—due to its effectiveness against giardia parasites. Furazolidone is also effective against cholera. Furazolidone, unlike the quinolones, comes in a liquid form and is suitable for infants and children.
- Drink extra fluids to prevent dehydration. The addition of soup or broth, salted crackers, and extra water to your diet will maintain hydration while also providing nutrients. If you have copious diarrhea causing dehydration, follow the instructions in this chapter for preparing and administering oral rehydration solutions. Maintaining hydration is especially important for infants and children.
- Chronic diarrhea is usually caused by a parasitic disease such as giardiasis or amebiasis. Treat with metronidazole (Flagyl), furazolidone (Furazone), or tinidazole and seek follow-up medical care. Trimethoprim/sulfameth-oxazole (Bactrim) is effective against cyclosporidiosis.
- Diarrhea danger signs include continued bloody diarrhea, high fever, vomiting, severe abdominal pain, prostration, and dehydration. Consult a physician if your symptoms are severe, if you are not improved after 24 hours of antibiotic treatment, or if you have continued vomiting.
- If you had diarrhea on your trip, get a posttravel checkup, including a stool examination and a stool culture to test for pathogenic microorganisms. You could be harboring an organism (e.g., giardia, *E. histolytica*, shigella, salmonella, cryptosporidia, or cyclospora) that you can pass to others.

ORAL HYDRATION THERAPY

The initial treatment of moderate to severe travelers' diarrhea begins by replacing the salt and water lost through your intestinal tract. Severe watery diarrhea (as seen with cholera, for example) can cause life-threatening fluid losses from the intestine of one liter or more per hour. Treating dehydration of this magnitude is an urgent priority, especially in infants, young children, and the elderly. Early, vigorous treatment is even more important in hot, tropical climates where fluid requirements are higher. Hospitalization and intravenous fluid therapy is required if oral intake cannot keep up with fluid losses.

The first mistake that most people make when treating copious diarrhea is that they don't drink enough fluids. The second mistake they make is using the wrong fluids. They may drink salt-free, high-sugar beverages or a too-salty beverage without the correct glucose concentration necessary to optimize salt and water absorption. Not drinking enough, or using too much of the wrong fluids to treat severe diarrhea, can make matters worse, especially in infants.

On the other hand, you may be in a location (e.g., a hotel room in Khartoum at 3:00 a.m.) where you can't get the right fluids or the necessary ingredients (sodium and potassium-containing salts, a source of glucose or carbohydrate) to prepare a balanced solution. Under these circumstances, just about any kind of beverage (disinfected tap water, bottled water, tea, coffee, dilute soda pop, etc.) is better than no fluid replacement at all. This will buy enough time to procure the necessary ingredients and prepare a proper solution—or get to a medical treatment facility if you don't improve. First, though, review these basic facts about how the body absorbs salt and water.

Facts About Sugar, Salt, and Water

- Glucose promotes water absorption. Your intestine first absorbs glucose by the process of active intestinal transport.
- Sodium absorption is coupled with glucose. One sodium molecule travels with each absorbed glucose molecule in an obligatory, linked fashion. The co-transport of sodium with glucose forms the basis for oral rehydration therapy.
- The absorbed glucose and sodium create an osmotic force that pulls water through the intestinal wall. The movement of water into the body is entirely passive.
- Maximum absorption of water occurs when the glucose concentration in a solution is about 2.5%.
- A high-sugar concentration in the intestine inhibits the absorption of water. Highly sweetened drinks, in fact, can increase intestinal fluid loss by causing osmotic diarrhea. Apple juice, Gatorade, nondiet cola drinks, and Jell-O have high glucose concentrations of 6% or more.
- Starchy foods (e.g., rice cereal, potatoes) also supply glucose, but in a form that enhances the absorption of water. The lower intestinal osmotic pressure of a

starch solution increases salt and water absorption, and decreases diarrheal volume as well as the duration of symptoms.

- Even in the presence of most diarrheal diseases, your intestine is still able to absorb glucose, salt, water, and other nutrients.

Oral Rehydration Solution (ORS)

Quick ORS formula #1—You can prepare a basic emergency oral rehydration solution by adding one teaspoon of salt and 2–3 tablespoons of sugar or honey to a liter of water. Although lacking bicarbonate and potassium, the solution is easy to prepare and will effectively maintain blood volume and tissue hydration.

Quick ORS formula #2—Mix one 8-oz. cup of orange juice (or other fruit juice) with three cups of water and add one teaspoon of salt.

WHO formula—Packets of World Health Organization (WHO) rehydration formula are ideal for the emergency treatment of dehydration, especially in infants and children. Just add the contents of a packet to a liter (or 4 cups) of potable water. The packets (see photo) contain the right balance of sodium, potassium, bicarbonate, and glucose and are favored by many travelers who want a quick, convenient source of full-strength ORS.

Homemade ORS—If you don't have packets of ORS salts, or your supply has run out, you can prepare a balanced ORS from commonly available ingredients. Mix together:

1 liter clean water (boiled, bottled, or chemically treated)
1/2 tsp. table salt
1/4 tsp. salt substitute (provides potassium chloride)
1/2 tsp. baking soda (provides bicarbonate)
2–3 tbsp. of table sugar, or 2 tbsp. of honey or Karo syrup

If you can't obtain baking soda or a salt substitute, use one teaspoon (1 tsp.) of table salt per liter of solution.

Limitations of Glucose-Based ORS

The glucose-based ORS solutions described above can keep you hydrated, but they do not decrease stool volume or shorten the duration of acute diarrhea. Cereal- and food-based ORS do both. They also supply up to four times more calories during a time when appetite may be suppressed. With cereal-based ORS, partially-hydrolyzed cooked starches act as effective sodium cotransporters, providing water and electrolyte absorption without added osmotic penalty.

Ricelyte—Ricelyte contains rice starch in solution. Glucose in polymer form (starch) presents the intestine with a much lower "osmotic load," and water absorption is greatly enhanced. Ricelyte is available in the United States in 8- and 32-oz. bottles.

Gerber Rice Cereal—It's not just for kids! This is probably the best product for preparing your own ORS, but its utility in this matter is largely unrecognized. Gerber Rice Cereal contains fully cooked rice starch, is tasty, and inexpensive.

1 to 2 cups of Gerber Rice Cereal

4 cups water

1/2 tsp. table salt

Using a measuring spoon, accurately measure salt. Dissolve in the water.

Gradually add cereal to the salty water until the mixture is as thick as is drinkable.

Food-based oral rehydration—If you don't have Ricelyte or Gerber Rice Cereal, you can prepare a solution with these ingredients:

One liter of water

8 oz. mashed-up potato (about 1/2 pound). Cook the potato in the water and allow to cool. Then add:

1/2 tsp. table salt

1/4 tsp. baking soda (provides bicarbonate)

1/4 tsp. salt substitute (provides potassium)

If you can't obtain baking soda or salt substitute, use one teaspoon of table salt per liter/quart of solution.

Treatment Technique for Older Children and Adults

Step 1. Vigorously treat dehydration. Drink 3–6 liters, or more, of full-strength oral rehydration solution over 2–4 hours. Don't stop ORS as soon as your thirst is quenched—drink enough to restore urine output.

Step 2. Diet and maintenance fluids—After rehydration, your energy and sense of well-being will improve. If you are not vomiting, start to eat (see below) and continue to drink fluids to maintain hydration. The best fluids are dilute fruit juices and water. If you are not eating, however, use half-strength ORS as a maintenance fluid.

Step 3. If watery diarrhea continues after rehydration, prevent recurrent dehydration by drinking 8–12 oz. of full-strength ORS each time you have a watery stool. Continue to eat and also consume water as thirst dictates.

Start antibiotics—If you start early treatment with a quinolone antibiotic, or furazolidone, you will shorten your illness significantly.

Diet

Your intestine continues to absorb water and nutrients despite diarrhea. Food promotes the absorption of water and also stimulates intestinal enzyme activity. Remember that food, especially easy-to-digest starches, reduces the volume of diarrhea. Food enhances water absorption and is a source of sodium and energy-providing calories.

Soup or broth, plus toast and/or salted crackers, is an excellent starting diet. (The best soups are lightly salted rice and noodle soups.) Also good are lightly salted oatmeal, cream of wheat, and Gerber Rice Cereal. The BRAT diet (bananas, rice, applesauce, toast) is easily remembered and well-tolerated. With improvement, you can advance to skinless chicken, cooked carrots, and other cooked vegetables. A regular diet can be resumed as soon as your appetite allows.

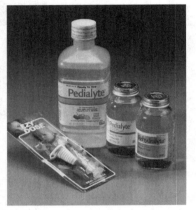

What Not to Eat and Drink

Omit dairy products (lactose may aggravate diarrhea). Avoid highly sugared drinks as the only fluid source. Gatorade, for example, contains too much sugar and too little sodium, potassium, and bicarbonate. Gatorade is designed to replace fluid losses from sweat, not diarrhea. Also avoid other highly sweetened drinks (see below), coffee, alcoholic drinks, and high-fat foods.

Commercial rehydration solutions such as Pedialyte or Ricelyte are widely available in the United States. The EZY DOSE syringe, av-ailable in most pharmacies, is a convenient way to give fluid to an infant.

Treatment Technique for Infants and Young Children

You should know when a child has the potential to become dehydrated. The history is critical: How long has the child been having diarrhea, and what is the frequency and volume? Has he or she also been unable to take oral fluids because of vomiting?

Signs of dehydration: Observe the child for increased thirst, lethargy, decreased urine output, and dry mucous membranes. Severe dehydration requires hospitalization and intravenous fluid therapy. Early, vigorous administration of ORS usually keeps a child from reaching this stage.

How much fluid to give? You should give a dehydrated infant or child 1 to 1-1/2 oz. (30–45 ml) of ORS per pound of body weight. Administer this over 2–4 hours. A dehydrated 22-lb. infant, for example, might require as much as a quart of ORS during the first 2–4 hours of treatment. If the child is not vomiting, give

ORS as rapidly as the infant or child will accept it. Use a spoon, dropper, or a baby bottle for infants. Some parents squirt the solution into the child's mouth with a small syringe (ask your doctor for one before leaving or purchase the EZY DOSE syringe shown in picture). Watch for the return of urine output and improvement in the child's appearance.

Vomiting—Don't let it deter you from giving ORS! Give 1 teaspoon (5 ml) of ORS every minute, even if the child is vomiting. If available, use a 5-ml syringe, a graduated infant bottle, or a medicine cup. Giving just a teaspoon of ORS every minute avoids stomach distention caused from too-rapid fluid administration, but can provide an hourly intake of 10 oz. (300 ml). This process often requires time and patience and it may take you 4–6 hours to rehydrate a sick child. Seek medical care if vomiting continues to interfere with oral feedings and rehydration.

- Ricelyte and Pedialyte. These rehydration solutions are widely used in the United States and Canada for treating dehydration in infants and young children. Ricelyte is preferred, if available.
- Breast-feeding—You should continue if your child will accept the feedings. For every one feeding of breast milk, give two feedings of ORS.

CAUTION: Don't give full-strength soft drinks or fruit juice to dehydrated infants or children as their only source of fluid replacement. The high sugar content of these solutions will draw water out of the intestine, increase diarrhea, worsen dehydration, and possibly lead to a condition called hypernatremia, where the blood sodium concentration is dangerously high. Typical drinks NOT to give include the following:

Apple juice	Grape juice
Cola (Coke, Pepsi, etc.)	Jello
Gatorade	Orange juice
Ginger ale	7-Up

If you do give a dehydrated child a sugar-containing soft drink, be sure to dilute it 3:1 with water.

Refeeding Infants and Children

After rehydration is complete, give breast milk or formula (dilute formula 1:1 with water). Cow's milk, if given, should be diluted 1:1 with water. **Early feeding is important**—the intestine continues to absorb water and nutrients despite diarrhea. The World Health Organization, in fact, advises parents *not* to stop giving infants with diarrhea their regular formula or food. Starving an infant (or yourself) to rest the intestine will only make matters worse.

Older infants and children—Restore a child's regular diet as soon as possible. After rehydration and cessation of vomiting, start the BRAT diet, mentioned earlier. Children, like adults, recover more quickly when fed.

5 Malaria

Malaria is the most important parasitic disease that you will face in most tropical and subtropical countries. A delay in diagnosis and treatment can have serious or fatal consequences. If you travel to a malarious region, there are five things you must do:

1. Become informed about your risk of acquiring malaria in that particular region.
2. Take measures to prevent mosquito bites. (This very important malaria-prevention measure is usually underutilized.)
3. Take a prophylactic drug (e.g., chloroquine, mefloquine, or doxycycline), if necessary. Don't skip prescribed doses.
4. Know the symptoms of malaria.
5. Seek immediate medical treatment if symptoms of malaria occur, especially if you are in, or have returned from, a country where falciparum malaria is endemic. Always consider malaria if you develop a fever after returning from a malarious area because symptoms can be delayed for weeks or months, sometimes years, after exposure—even if you took a prophylactic drug.

Malaria Statistics

- Malaria-transmitting mosquitoes are currently found in 102 countries, and the disease threatens over 40% of the world's population.
- Over 200 million clinical cases occur every year. Over 270 million people are chronically infected with malaria parasites.
- One to two million people die annually of malaria.
- Eight hundred thousand of these victims are children.
- Ninety percent of all malaria infections in the world occur in sub-Saharan Africa.
- Seven million Americans each year travel to countries where malaria occurs.
- Over 30,000 American and European travelers contract malaria each year.

Your Risk of Getting Malaria

It depends upon where you travel and can vary markedly from country to country. The risk of malaria can also vary within any particular destination because the disease may be transmitted only in certain locations within a country, during certain seasons, or below certain altitudes.

Various categories of travelers are also at different risk. Tourists staying in air-conditioned, mosquito-free hotels, for example, will be at less risk than travelers venturing into low-lying rural areas during the rainy season.

Table 5.1 shows disease rates worldwide and demonstrates an important fact. Travel to sub-Saharan Africa carries not only the greatest risk for contracting malaria, but most fatal cases of malaria also originate in this region. (Although not shown, the risk of malaria in Oceania is equally high.) By contrast, travel to Asia and Latin America is much safer in terms of malaria risk.

Table 5.1   Estimated Monthly Incidence Rate of Malaria Without Chemoprophylaxis (per 100,000 travelers, including fatalities)[1]

Destination	Number of Cases	Percentage of Cases Due to *P. falciparum*	Number of Fatal Cases
West Africa	2,400	90%	42
East Africa	1,500	90%	27
Indian Sub-Continent	350	20%	1.0
Far East	100	30%	0.6
South America	50	15%	0.2
Central America and Mexico	<10	<10%	0.02

Tropical Africa is a high-risk destination compared to Latin America and Asia for the following reasons.

- Tourists in Africa spend considerable time in rural areas such as game parks, where mosquito activity is high.
- Tourists in Latin America and Asia, however, spend more time in urban or resort areas, where there is little, if any, risk of exposure, and they usually travel to rural areas only during daytime hours when there is little malaria-transmitting mosquito activity.
- In Latin America and Asia, malaria transmission is more seasonal, or focally

distributed in rural areas away from the usual tourist routes. For example, 52% of the 1.1 million malaria cases reported from the Americas in 1989 were from Brazil, but 97% of these cases were reported from three gold-mining areas rarely visited by tourists. And in Asia (e.g., Thailand) most malaria occurs in remote forested areas—also places where fewer tourists go.

- Malaria is transmitted in many large cities in sub-Saharan Africa, whereas almost all large cities in Asia and Latin America (with the exception of Guayaquil, Ecuador and urban areas of Papua New Guinea) are malaria free. There is no malaria in Bangkok, Kuala Lumpur, Jakarta, Singapore, Rangoon, Phnom-Penh, central Manila, and most other major urban areas.
- Mosquitoes in Africa are more apt to be carrying malaria parasites. For example, the mean rate of infective anopheles mosquitoes in western Kenya may exceed 20%, whereas in Latin America and Asia less than 1% of anopheles mosquitoes are infective.

— Malaria Fact —

In countries where malaria occurs, the highest rates of transmission occur in low-lying rural areas during, and just after, the rainy season. In parts of Africa and Oceania, however, malaria transmission may be high year-round, even in urban areas.

The Cause of Malaria

Malaria is caused by a single-cell protozoan of the genus Plasmodium. There are four different species of Plasmodium parasites that infect humans: (1) *Plasmodium falciparum*, which accounts for 40%–60% of malaria cases worldwide and 95% of all malaria deaths, (2) *Plasmodium vivax*, which causes 30%–40% of malaria cases worldwide, (3) the less frequently encountered *Plasmodium ovale*, and (4) *Plasmodium malariae*.

Worldwide Distribution of Malaria Species

The occurrence of each plasmodium species varies from region to region.

P. falciparum causes 80%–95% of malaria in sub-Saharan Africa. It is also the most common species in Haiti and the Dominican Republic, the Amazon Basin, and parts of Oceania. In South America, outside the Amazon Basin, *P. falciparum* accounts for 10%–50% of cases. *P. falciparum* is also common on the Indian subcontinent, SE Asia, and Oceania.

P. vivax causes about 95% of malaria in Mexico and Central America, and is also common in South America, North Africa, the Middle East, the Indian subcontinent, China, Asia, and Oceania. It is very rarely encountered in sub-Saharan Africa (except for Somalia and Ethiopia) because most blacks are inherently resistant to this species of plasmodium.

P. malariae causes up to 10%–15% of malaria in sub-Saharan Africa and 1%-5% of cases elsewhere, worldwide.

Figure 5.1. The Cycle of Malaria Transmission[2]

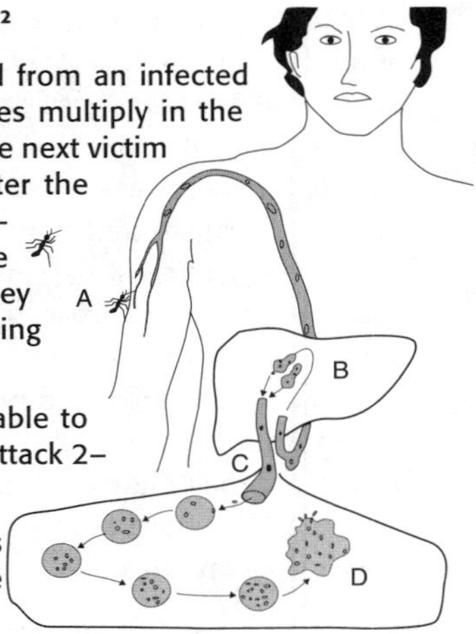

When the female anopheles mosquito draws blood from an infected person, it picks up malaria parasites. These parasites multiply in the mosquito for 1-2 weeks. When the mosquito bites the next victim (A) it infects that person with parasites, which enter the bloodstream and travel to the liver, where they multiply (B). Five to fourteen days later, the parasites leave the liver and invade red blood cells (C), where they multiply again, rupturing the red cells (D), and triggering an attack of malaria.

The parasites released from the red cells are each able to infect new red blood cells, causing another malaria attack 2–3 days later.

Infections with *P. vivax* and *P. ovale*: Some parasites remain behind in the host liver cells and can cause delayed attacks of malaria.

Note: Prophylactic drugs don't prevent parasites from invading the liver, and, with the exception of proguanil, don't prevent multiplication of parasites within liver cells. Most prophylactic drugs eliminate malaria parasites only in the blood, at stages C and D.

P. ovale is rare. It exists primarily in West Africa where it causes up to 5% of malaria, and it also occurs sporadically in Oceania and SE Asia.

Malaria is uncommon at high altitudes because reproduction of the parasites within the anopheles mosquito is temperature sensitive. For this reason, falciparum malaria rarely occurs over 1,000 meters elevation. Vivax parasites, which are hardier, can reproduce at altitudes as high as 2,000 meters (6,500) feet.

Malaria in the United States—A few cases of locally acquired vivax malaria have been reported from New Jersey and New York, raising the possibility of malaria regaining a foothold in this country. Theory: *P. vivax* parasites are imported by immigrants and are transmitted to local anopheles mosquitoes.

How Malaria Is Transmitted

Malaria is transmitted by female anopheles mosquitoes. These mosquitoes require a blood meal every 3–4 days to promote the fertilization and growth of their eggs. There are over 400 anopheles species worldwide, of which 60 are known to transmit malaria.

Anopheles mosquitoes feed from dusk to dawn, so when evening comes you need to take extra measures to prevent bites. Not every mosquito transmits malaria, but it takes just one bite from an infective insect to give you the disease; therefore, even a brief trip to a malarious area can put you at risk.

How Malaria Infects the Body

After they are injected into the body by a feeding mosquito, malaria parasites first invade the liver, then the red blood cells (Figure 5.1), where they again multiply. When the parasite-filled red cells rupture, an attack of malaria occurs.

Falciparum malaria is the most serious and sometimes fatal form of malaria. The severity of *P. falciparum* infections is due to the high percentage of red blood cells that can be parasitized by this particular plasmodium. In extreme infections, up to 80% of red blood cells can be parasitized and destroyed. This massive red cell destruction triggers fatal clogging of the circulation to vital organs, especially the brain and kidneys.

In contrast, the three other forms of malaria are usually nonlethal. In malaria caused by *P. vivax*, *P. ovale*, and *P. malariae*, only about 1%–2% of red blood cells become parasitized, and fatalities are rare.

Severe malaria occurs, by definition, when more than 3%–5% of red blood cells are parasitized. Other criteria defining severe malaria include decreased consciousness (indicates cerebral malaria), severe anemia, hypoglycemia (low blood sugar), kidney/liver failure, pulmonary edema, prolonged hyperthermia, and persistent vomiting and diarrhea.

If you are treated appropriately for malaria, your illness should improve within 48–72 hours. Indications of successful treatment include (1) lysis of fever and (2) at least a 75% reduction in the number of red blood cells that are parasitized.

Delayed Attacks of Malaria

If you have been bitten by mosquitoes transmitting *P. vivax* or *P. ovale*, you can get a delayed attack of malaria. The reason? Some of these parasites, after reaching the liver, can remain dormant for many months—even years.

Prophylactic drugs, unfortunately, don't eradicate parasites in the liver. Prophylactic drugs usually only work in the blood to suppress the multiplication of plasmodia in red cells. You're safe from an attack of malaria only as long as you take the suppressive (prophylactic) drug. To get rid of dormant liver parasites, you'll need to take another drug, primaquine, discussed later.

Fortunately, *P. falciparum* and *P. malariae* parasites don't have a dormant liver phase, so prophylaxis continued for four weeks after exposure usually gives your body enough time to eliminate them. However, untreated or inadequately treated *P. falciparum* or *P. malariae* can sometimes result in low-grade blood stream infections, leading to recrudescent symptoms. Untreated *P. malariae*, in fact, can cause chronic infections lasting 25 years or more.

Symptoms of Malaria

Getting malaria makes you feel like you have the flu—only worse. Before an attack of malaria begins, you may have one or two days of "not feeling well" and during this time notice headache, fatigue, loss of appetite, and a low-grade fever. The acute attack starts abruptly with chills (the cold stage), soon followed by a high fever (the hot stage), lasting 2–6 hours. During this time you may also notice pains in your chest, stomach, joints, and muscles. The attack ends with 2–3 hours of heavy sweating. If you are not treated promptly, symptoms will recur and complications may develop, especially if the attack is caused by *P. falciparum*.

NOTE: Malaria can occur as soon as seven days after an infective bite, and almost all cases occur within 30 days after an infective bite in people not taking a prophylactic drug.

Illnesses sometimes confused with malaria include typhoid fever, dengue, brucellosis, hepatitis, urinary tract infections, relapsing fever, and amebic liver abscess.

Although a blood smear is required to make the diagnosis, the most important aspect of diagnosis is always *to think of malaria as a possible cause of your illness.* This is especially important because not every case of malaria presents with the typical progression of symptoms. If you are in a malarious area and you get a fever, and medical care is not immediately available, it may be advisable for you to start self-treatment before a diagnosis is established. Self-treatment is discussed later.

Malaria Caution

When in, or recently returned from, a malarious area, consider any illness with fever to be malaria until proven otherwise.

MALARIA PREVENTION

Virtually all cases of malaria can be prevented. Several studies show that a high proportion of travelers who acquire malaria simply did not receive information on, or did not comply with, malaria prevention measures.

Avoiding malaria requires that you (1) know where it exists, (2) prevent mosquito bites, and (3) take a prophylactic drug.

Read Chapter 6 (Insect Protection) to acquaint yourself with the best methods of insect-bite prevention.

Preventing Mosquito Bites

No drug is 100% effective against all strains of plasmodium. Therefore, it is imperative to prevent as many mosquito bites as possible by following these guidelines:

- Eliminate mosquitoes from your living and sleeping quarters. Measures include screening doors and windows and spraying rooms with a pyrethrum-containing insecticide (e.g., RAID Flying Insect Spray™, Doom™, etc.).
- Wear trousers and long-sleeved shirts in the evening.
- Apply a DEET-containing insect repellent to exposed skin.
- Apply permethrin to your clothing.
- Sleep under a mosquito bednet, preferably one treated with permethrin.

Chemoprophylaxis

Before departing for a malarious area, you and your doctor should decide if prophylaxis is indicated and which drug, if any, you should take. Current malaria prophylaxis recommendations are summarized in Table 5.2. In general, if your risk of exposure will be moderate to high, prophylaxis is necessary and the drug you will use, depending on your itinerary and other factors, will be chloroquine, mefloquine, or doxycycline.

If the risk of malaria is low, the benefits of prophylaxis have to be more carefully assessed. In low-risk situations where prompt medical care is available, it may be acceptable not to take a prophylactic drug, but to rely instead on immediate treatment.

Factors determining your need for, and choice of, prophylaxis include (1) your itinerary, (2) the intensity and duration of your exposure to mosquito bites, especially those transmitting *P. falciparum*, (3) your ability to obtain quick, qualified medical care should symptoms occur, (4) your own knowledge of malaria and its symptoms, (5) your medical history and personal health status, (6) your history

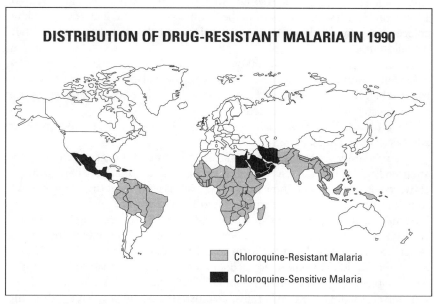

The map shows those areas where malaria caused by chloroquine-resistant *P. falciparum* is reported. In East Africa, virtually 100% of *P. falciparum* infections are chloroquine-resistant. In West Africa, chloroquine resistance has increased to about 50%. Chloroquine-resistant *P. falciparum* is also common in the Amazon Basin, southern China, Northeast India, SE Asia, and Oceania (the Solomon Islands, Papua New Guinea, and Vanuatu). NOTE: Chloroquine-resistant *P. vivax* is now reported in Papua New Guinea and Irian Jaya.

of known drug allergies or known ability (or inability) to tolerate certain prophylactic drugs, (7) your use of other medications that may be incompatible with prophylactic drugs, (8) your age, and (9) your pregnancy status, if applicable.

The complexity of the situation is one reason why seeing a travel medicine specialist is often advisable when exposure to malaria is likely. In all cases, however, remember that the best prophylaxis is mosquito-bite prevention. If you don't get bitten, you can't get malaria.

Chloroquine

Chloroquine phosphate is a synthetic 4-aminoquinolone that is the drug of choice to prevent *P. vivax*, *P. ovale*, and *P. malariae*, as well as susceptible strains of *P. falciparum*. The drug is used when prophylaxis is needed in malarious areas of the Caribbean (Dominican Republic, Haiti, and parts of Trinidad), Mexico and Central America, temperate South America, North Africa, and the Middle East.

Even in areas of the world where chloroquine-resistant *P. falciparum* is found, chloroquine is not necessarily useless. It can still provide protection against *P. vivax*, as well as strains of *P. falciparum* that remain chloroquine-sensitive. Also, chloroquine probably provides some partial protection against resistant strains of *P. falciparum*. A research study from the Netherlands showed that travelers taking chloroquine who developed falciparum malaria were less sick than those not taking chloroquine.

Adult dosage—500 mg salt (300 mg base) once weekly, beginning one week before and continuing four weeks after leaving the malarious area. Starting chloroquine before you leave gives you a protective blood level and also lets you know if any unusual side effects will occur.

Child dosage—8.3 mg/kg salt (5 mg/kg base) once weekly, up to maximum adult dose of 500 mg salt/week.

It is needlessly confusing, but the tablet strength and dosages of chloroquine are usually given two ways: as the salt form of the drug and as the base form. To convert: 500 mg of chloroquine phosphate (salt) is equivalent to 300 mg of chloroquine base; 250 mg of salt is equivalent to 150 mg of base.

Generic chloroquine tablets are sold in the United States in strengths of 250 mg and 500 mg. Brand name chloroquine (Aralen™) is available only in the 500 mg tablet strength. Only the tablet form of chloroquine is available in the United States, but liquid chloroquine for pediatric use is readily available overseas. The Aralen tablet is difficult to crush up for children. The generic tablets are easier to split and crush, but are bitter. Parents can crush tablets into powder, divide it, and then mask flavor with syrup, jam, etc. Another strategy is to have a pharmacist pulverize the tablets and prepare gelatin capsules with the proper weekly dose. Mixing the powder from the capsule with food or drink will make the bitter taste more palatable.

Side effects—Chloroquine is generally well tolerated and serious side effects rarely occur. Nausea, however, is not uncommon. Gastrointestinal side effects can

Table 5.2   Malaria Prophylaxis According to Geographic Area[1]

Chloroquine Sensitive Areas	Drug of Choice	Alternative Drug(s)
Central America Caribbean Middle East, N. Africa	chloroquine " "	mefloquine or proguanil[2]

Chloroquine Resistant Areas	Drug of Choice	Alternative Drug(s)
S. America[3]	mefloquine	chloroquine + Fansidar standby
Amazon basin	mefloquine	doxycycline
Africa (sub-Saharan)	mefloquine	doxycycline chloroquine + proguanil[4]
Far East & Indian subcontinent	mefloquine	doxycycline chloroquine + Fansidar standby
SE Asia	mefloquine	doxycycline
Oceania	mefloquine	doxycycline
Thailand	doxycycline	mefloquine proguanil + sulfonamide[5]

1. In Central and South America and SE Asia, travelers are generally at risk only in rural areas during evening and nighttime hours. In sub-Saharan Africa and Oceania, malaria is often transmitted in both urban and rural areas.
2. Some strains of *P. vivax* and *P. malariae* are resistant to proguanil, but remain sensitive to chloroquine.
3. Chloroquine, with Fansidar standby, can be used in rural northern Argentina and considered in temperate areas outside the Amazon Basin.
4. Fansidar or halofantrine can be carried for use as emergency treatment in remote areas if malaria is suspected in travelers taking chloroquine and/or proguanil.
5. Combination of proguanil and a sulfa is an alternative for travelers in Thailand unable to take either doxycycline or mefloquine, e.g., pregnant women and children. (Dosage: proguanil, 200 mg daily, plus either sulfisoxazole, 75 mg/kg daily, or sulfamethoxazole, 1,500 mg daily.)

usually be controlled by taking chloroquine with meals. Dizziness, headache, blurred vision, and itching may also occur, but these symptoms will rarely require you to stop taking the drug. Fears about long-term prophylaxis causing degenerative eye (retinal) changes are unfounded. Chloroquine can safely be taken by pregnant women and children, including infants.

CAUTION: An overdose of chloroquine can be fatal. The drug should be kept in a child-safe container out of reach of children.

NOTE: Chloroquine interferes with the antibody response to rabies vaccine when the vaccine is administered intradermally. If you are taking chloroquine prophylaxis and need rabies vaccination, the vaccine must be given intramuscularly.

Hydroxychloroquine

An alternative to chloroquine phosphate is hydroxychloroquine (Plaquenil). It has the same action as chloroquine, but causes fewer gastrointestinal side effects. (Hydroxychloroquine can also be used to treat chloroquine-sensitive malaria.)

Adult prophylactic dosage—400 mg salt (310 mg base) weekly.

Child dosage—6.5 mg/kg salt (5.0 mg base) weekly, up to the adult dosage.

Mefloquine

Mefloquine (Lariam) is currently the recommended drug for malaria prophylaxis in almost all countries where there is chloroquine-resistant *P. falciparum*. The drug is also effective against *P. vivax*, *P. ovale*, and *P. malariae*. In forested areas of Thailand, however, the incidence of mefloquine-resistant *P. falciparum* is as high as 50%, and prophylaxis with doxycycline is recommended. Reports also indicate increasing mefloquine resistance in West Africa.

Adult dosage—250 mg (one tablet) once a week. Mefloquine should be started two weeks prior to departure to see if bothersome side effects will occur, necessitating a switch to another prophylactic drug. Mefloquine should be taken once weekly during travel in malarious areas and for 4 weeks after leaving such areas.

Child dosage—Children over 15 kg (30 lb.) only: 15–19 kg, 1/4 tablet weekly; 20–30 kg, 1/2 tablet weekly; 31–45 kg, 3/4 tablet weekly; and > 45 kg, 1 tablet weekly.

NOTE: If a person is taking quinine or quinidine, 12 hours should elapse before mefloquine is administered.

Side effects—Mefloquine in prophylactic doses is generally well tolerated, but 20% to 25% of users report side effects—strange dreams, nightmares, insomnia, nausea, dizziness, weakness, changes in sensation, and visual difficulties. Serious neuropsychiatric side effects (confusion, seizures, and psychosis) have occurred, but are very rare with prophylactic dosages—about 1 in 12,000 users.

Despite the apparent low incidence of significant side effects, sporadic reports of disabling side effects, especially insomnia and nightmares, continue to surface. If these adverse effects are severe, another prophylactic, e.g., doxycycline, should be substituted for mefloquine.

CAUTIONS: Mefloquine should never be used by people who have a known hypersensitivity or allergy to the drug. The CDC and the manufacturer recommend that mefloquine not be used by children under 30 pounds or travelers with a history of epilepsy or severe psychiatric disorders. Cautions are also listed by the manufacturer and others for use by drivers of vehicles, pilots, operators of machinery and heavy equipment, scuba divers, mountain climbers, and people on drugs affecting cardiac conduction (beta-adrenergic blockers, quinine, and quinidine). These cautions, however, are based on limited data or theoretical concerns only and should not in all cases be considered as absolute contraindications to the use of mefloquine.

The proscription against mefloquine during pregnancy has been modified; the drug is no longer contraindicated for women during their second and third trimester, especially if they will be exposed to the dangerous *P. falciparum* variety.

Doxycycline

Doxycycline (Vibramycin) is a tetracycline-related drug that is more than 90% effective against multidrug-resistant *P. falciparum*. You can use doxycycline as an alternative to mefloquine. The drug is also effective against *P. vivax*, *P. ovale*, and *P. malariae*. Doxycycline is the prophylactic of choice in forested border areas in Thailand, where there is a high incidence of malaria due to chloroquine- and mefloquine-resistant *P. falciparum*.

An advantage of doxycycline is its price. Generic doxycycline costs 10 to 20 cents a tablet, versus $6–$8/tablet for mefloquine.

A disadvantage of doxycycline is that it must be taken every day. This may reduce compliance with taking the drug as prescribed.

Adult dosage—100 mg daily. Doxycycline should be started 1 to 2 days prior to travel. It should be continued daily in malarious areas and for 4 weeks after departure from the area.

Child dosage (for children older than 8 years of age)—2 mg per kg of body weight per day up to the adult dose of 100 mg daily.

Side effects—Most travelers tolerate doxycycline well, but nausea and vomiting can occur. Doxycycline should be taken with meals to reduce the chance of GI upset. In addition, doxycycline can cause phototoxicity (an exaggerated sunburn reaction to strong sunlight). Risk is minimized by avoiding prolonged, direct exposure to the sun, using a sunscreen containing a UVA-blocker (e.g., Photoplex with Parsol, or one of the newer titanium dioxide-containing sunscreens), and taking the drug in the evening. Women taking doxycycline may develop a vaginal yeast infection.

Doxycycline is contraindicated for pregnant women and children under the age of 8.

Proguanil

Proguanil (Paludrine) is an inhibitor of the dihydrofolate reductase enzyme system. In sub-Saharan Africa proguanil is a widely used prophylactic, but its effectiveness is only about 70% against *P. falciparum*. Proguanil is active against most strains of *P. vivax*, and in chloroquine-sensitive areas, proguanil can be used as an alternative to chloroquine.

Adult dosage—200 mg daily, and continue for 4 weeks after leaving the area. Proguanil is not available in the United States, but is available over the counter in many countries. It is not available in liquid form.

Child dosage—Less than 2 years, 50 mg daily; 2–6 years, 100 mg daily; 7–10 years, 150 mg daily; over 10 years, 200 mg daily.

Side effects—Toxicity is very low. Nausea, vomiting, and mouth ulcers have been reported. Serious reactions (such as neuropsychiatric events) are not reported. Proguanil is safe to take during pregnancy.

Chloroquine & Proguanil

Chloroquine, combined with proguanil, is recommended by some European physicians as first-line prophylaxis for travelers to sub-Saharan Africa. This combination, however, is only 72% effective against chloroquine-resistant *P. falciparum* in East Africa and is recommended only when a traveler to Africa is unable to take either mefloquine or doxycycline. This combination is not recommended for prophylaxis against chloroquine-resistant *P. falciparum* in geographic regions outside of Africa.

Dosage (adults)—chloroquine, 500 mg weekly, plus proguanil, 200 mg daily. Continue prophylaxis for 4 weeks after exposure.

Side effects—Mainly nausea and mouth ulcers. The relatively high incidence of side effects from the combination (about 30%) is said to cause some travelers to discontinue prophylaxis. This failure to continue prophylaxis may contribute to the lesser effectiveness of this drug combination.

Proguanil & sulfonamide—Combining proguanil with a sulfonamide, such as sulfisoxazole or sulfamethoxazole, may dramatically increase prophylactic effectiveness, especially against chloroquine-resistant *P. falciparum*. Studies done in Thailand with this combination have shown over 90% protection.

Experimental studies conducted by the Walter Reed Army Institute of Research have shown that the antibiotic **azithromycin** (Zithromax) has causal prophylactic activity against a chloroquine-resistant strain of *P. falciparum* in non-immune individuals. If confirmed, azithromycin may offer significant advantages over both doxycycline and mefloquine.

S.R.

Prompt Treatment/Self-Treatment Strategies

Self-treatment for malaria is not a new concept. For centuries, people in tropical countries, as well as many of the early explorers, used naturally occurring antimalarial substances to treat a fever. These early "drugs" included the bark from the cinchona tree and the Chinese herb *Artemisia annua.*

In 1985 the CDC advised American travelers to take weekly chloroquine and carry a self-treatment dose of pyrimethamine/sulfadoxine (Fansidar) when going to areas where chloroquine-resistant *P. falciparum* is endemic.

In 1991 safe, effective prophylaxis with mefloquine became widely available and the prophylactic use of Fansidar was phased out. However, not every traveler at risk of exposure to chloroquine-resistant falciparum malaria is necessarily able to take mefloquine (or doxycycline). And other travelers may be at sufficiently low risk that the benefits of prophylaxis must be weighed against potential drug side effects, cost, and convenience. Alternative strategies must therefore be devised. The following scenarios illustrate some of these strategies.

Scenario #1—Standby prompt treatment: You're going on a three-day business trip to West Africa, and will be returning directly to New York City where your personal physician is associated with a travelers' clinic at a major teaching hospital. While in Africa you will have some rural and evening exposure to mosquitoes, but are well prepared to prevent bites with repellents, permethrin-treated clothing, a permethrin-impregnated bednet, and an insecticide bedroom spray. You feel that your short exposure time, combined with careful mosquito-bite prevention measures, puts you at low risk. Under these circumstances, you would prefer not to take a prophylactic drug for the six weeks required, but will immediately see your own physician, an expert in malaria treatment, if you develop a fever after returning home.

Comment: Your decision to forego prophylaxis is reasonable. Exposure is low, due primarily to the brevity of your trip and your conscientious antimosquito measures, but should symptoms occur you can get immediate evaluation and treatment by your physician. Very importantly, you know that the symptoms of malaria can be delayed, and you will be watching for them after you have left the malarious area. Because the incubation period of *P. falciparum* is at least 7–10 days, and your trip is for 3 days, you'll be back home and close to qualified medical care, should malaria develop.

This scenario is best suited for travelers in good basic health whose medical conditions could tolerate some malarial symptoms, should they occur.

Scenario #2—Self-treatment: You're going to live and work in rural Central America for six months. You have previously taken chloroquine for malaria prophylaxis but you had unpleasant side effects (headache and dizziness) and you don't want to take it again on a regular basis. You are basically healthy and have no underlying diseases, such as diabetes, that could complicate an attack of malaria. You do agree, however, to carry a treatment dose of chloroquine to take if you get a fever, and you also will take measures to prevent insect bites.

Comment: You are going to a low-risk area where virtually 100% of malaria is due to the more benign *P. vivax* species. Since you are in good underlying health, your risk of complications if you do get malaria is low. Treating yourself with chloroquine should be effective, but you realize that fever can be caused by other diseases, and if your symptoms don't improve with chloroquine, you'll need to see a doctor for reevaluation. Also, if you do get vivax malaria, you will also need subsequent treatment with primaquine to prevent recurrent attacks of malaria caused by parasites sequestered in the liver, unaffected by chloroquine.

Alternative actions in this case would be to take proguanil for prophylaxis, or to carry a treatment dose of halofantrine to use instead of chloroquine.

Prompt treatment by a physician, as in scenario #1, is usually preferable to self-treatment. Self-treatment should be considered primarily when you are in a remote or medically underserved area and will be unable to obtain qualified medical care quickly.

Problems associated with self-treatment include the following:

- Diagnosing another disease as malaria and delaying appropriate treatment.
- Risking side effects from inappropriately administered antimalarial drugs.
- Delaying the use of, or not even using, the self-treatment drugs you are carrying because of uncertainty, lack of sufficient information, poor advice, etc. One survey showed, for example, that only one-third of those who carried self-treatment for malaria in East Africa used the drugs appropriately when fever occurred.

Scenario #3—Postexposure treatment/prophylaxis with halofantrine: Here's an innovative possibility for travelers who are exposed to *P. falciparum* during a short trip (10 days or less) and who are reluctant to take standard postexposure prophylaxis (mefloquine or doxycycline) for four weeks or more. Take halofantrine, 500 mg daily for 3 days, on departure from the malarious area and repeat the treatment 7 days later. Any parasites inoculated during exposure should be released from your liver within 10 days, and these parasites will be eradicated by halofantrine.

Scenario #4—Prophylaxis plus standby self-treatment: You're traveling to sub-Saharan Africa and will have strong exposure to mosquitoes in a remote location where medical care is not available. You are allergic to tetracycline-type drugs and have a history of epilepsy. Fearing side effects, your doctor doesn't want to prescribe either doxycycline or mefloquine. What should you do?

Comment: Prophylaxis with chloroquine/proguanil is indicated. This combination is somewhat less effective than mefloquine or doxycycline, and since you are going to a remote area, you should carry standby self-treatment doses of an effective antimalarial, e.g., quinine plus clindamycin, or halofantrine.

Scenario #5—Intermittent prophylaxis: You are an expatriate living in Nairobi, Kenya. Although Kenya is a high-risk country, Nairobi itself is malaria-free. Your work, however, takes you to western Kenya, a high-risk area, several times a year and each time you remain there for several weeks. What should you do?

Table 5.3   Self-Treatment Options[1]

Drug	Dose
chloroquine[2]	500 mg initially, followed by 250 mg 6, 24, and 48 hours later
Fansidar	3 tablets at once
mefloquine[3]	3–5 tablets (750 mg–1,250 mg)
quinine	650 mg every 8 hours for 3 to 7 days
quinine + tetracycline[4]	650 mg every 8 hrs for 3 to 7 days 250 mg 4 times daily for 7 days
quinine + clindamycin[4]	650 mg every 8 hrs for 3 to 7 days 900 mg 3 times daily for 7 days
halofantrine[5]	500 mg every 6 hours for 3 doses Treatment repeated in 7 days

1. Travelers should be aware that self-treatment should be followed as soon as possible by medical evaluation and further treatment, if required. Self-treatment is usually not recommended or necessary in countries or regions where good medical care is available.
2. Chloroquine-resistant *P. vivax* is reported in Papua New Guinea and Irian Jaya.
3. Treatment with mefloquine is associated with a high incidence of side effects.
4. Doxycycline, 100 mg twice daily, can be used in place of tetracycline or clindamycin.
5. Halofantrine (in standard doses) is not recommended in Thailand, due to cross resistance with mefloquine. Elsewhere, halofantrine is the self-treatment drug of choice.

Comment: Short-term prophylaxis is indicated. Malaria risk varies by microlocation, so merely being in East Africa doesn't necessarily mandate year-round prophylaxis. Prophylaxis is indicated, however, when you visit a high-risk area, especially during and just after the rainy season, when mosquito activity is high. Since mefloquine is not available in East Africa, you should use doxycycline. If this is not feasible, then take chloroquine and proguanil, and seek immediate treatment if you develop a fever. Self-treatment is not routinely indicated in Kenya since qualified medical care is available in-country. (If you are in a remote location, however, consider self-treatment with halofantrine, a drug that is available in Kenya.)

These scenarios demonstrate how prophylaxis/treatment can be individualized, especially if you are exposed to chloroquine-resistant *P. falciparum* and can't take mefloquine or doxycycline. Recommendations, of course, will change as new drug-resistance patterns emerge and as new prophylactic drugs are developed.

MALARIA TREATMENT

If you suspect you are having an attack of malaria, urgently seek medical care. If medical care is not readily available, don't wait—if you are carrying standby anti-malarial drugs, start self-treatment immediately.

Chloroquine

In areas where chloroquine-resistant *P. falciparum* is not reported, start treatment on the following schedule:

- Day 1. Chloroquine 500 mg (salt) by mouth immediately, then chloroquine, 250 mg (salt), six hours later.
- Day 2. Chloroquine 250 mg orally.
- Day 3. Chloroquine 250 mg orally.

Severe chloroquine-sensitive malaria requires an intravenous infusion of chloroquine, 0.83 mg/kg/hr (base) for 30 hours, or intramuscular chloroquine, 3.5 mg/kg (base) repeated every 6 hours for 36 hours (6 doses). Oral chloroquine can be started as soon as tolerated, for a total dose of 25 mg/kg (base).

Mefloquine

This drug, which is chemically similar to quinine, is highly active against all malaria strains, except in Thailand, where cure rates against *P. falciparum* have fallen to 50%–70%. Mefloquine-resistant *P. falciparum* is also increasingly reported in other parts of SE Asia and in West Africa.

Dosage: 1,250 mg (or 25 mg/kg) best given as a divided dose of 750 mg (or 15 mg/kg) followed by 500 mg (or 10 mg/kg) 6 hours later.

Side effects—Adverse side effects are much more frequent with treatment dosages of mefloquine than with prophylactic doses. Reports of severe neuropsychiatric side effects, in fact, have tempered the enthusiasm for using mefloquine in the treatment of malaria. The frequency of severe neuropsychiatric symptoms (hallucinations, seizures, delirium, acute psychosis) is estimated at about 1 in 250 treatment doses.

Other adverse reactions include nausea and vomiting, loss of balance and coordination, dizziness, inability to concentrate, headache, and insomnia. Side effects can last as long as 14 days.

Mefloquine should be administered cautiously when the patient has previously received, or is receiving, chloroquine, quinine, quinidine, or procainamide (a cardiac drug). If these drugs are being used, mefloquine administration should be delayed at least 12 hours after the last dose. Recent reports (see "Halofantrine Caution") indicate cardiac side effects may occur when halofantrine is administered following mefloquine treatment. Mefloquine has no adverse cardiac effects when given by itself.

Mefloquine is currently the recommended prophylactic drug for people traveling to areas of the world (Thailand excepted) where chloroquine-resistant malaria occurs. However, mefloquine-resistant falciparum malaria is increasing in Africa and SE Asia, and possibly elsewhere. Any traveler who develops a fever during mefloquine prophylaxis, or shortly afterwards, should be evaluated for possible mefloquine-resistant *P. falciparum*.

Fansidar (pyrimethamine/sulfadoxine)

Each tablet of Fansidar contains pyrimethamine, 25 mg, and sulfadoxine, 500 mg. Travelers who use a 3-tablet self-treatment dose of Fansidar for a presumptive *P. falciparum* infection should seek follow-up medical care as soon as possible.

Fansidar is an alternative drug that can be used for self-treatment in Africa or southern Asia when halofantrine (below) is not available.

P. falciparum resistance to Fansidar is low in Africa, South America outside the Amazon Basin, and southern Asia, outside of Thailand.

Fansidar is slower in action than chloroquine or quinine and should not be used alone for the treatment of a severe infection. Nor should Fansidar be used as sole treatment chloroquine-resistant falciparum malaria, even though the infection may be uncomplicated. Fansidar can be used to treat vivax malaria, but *P. vivax* infections clear more slowly after treatment with Fansidar than after treatment with other drugs (chloroquine, quinine, or mefloquine).

Adult dosage—3 tablets, taken at once.

Child dosage—Less than 1 year, 1/4 tablet; 1 to 3 years, 1/2 tablet; 4 to 8 years, 1 tablet; 9 to 14 years, 2 tablets.

Side effects: Minor side effects can include headache, nausea, vomiting, and skin rash. The risk of a life-threatening cutaneous reaction (e.g., exfoliative dermatitis) from a single treatment dose of Fansidar is estimated to be 0.1 per million.

Contraindications include people who are allergic to sulfa drugs and infants less than one month of age. Fansidar has been used to treat malarial infection in large numbers of pregnant women without apparent harmful effects on the fetus.

Halofantrine, because of its increased effectiveness and lower risk of side effects, should soon supplant Fansidar for self-treatment.

Halofantrine

Halofantrine (Halfan) is a phenanthrene-methanol chemically similar to mefloquine. It is highly effective against all four plasmodium species, including *P. falciparum*. The cure rate is generally more than 90% with a 1-day course of treatment and 100% effective when two courses of treatment are administered.

In Thailand, however, where there is a high incidence of multidrug-resistant falciparum malaria, the standard 1-day treatment course of halofantrine is only about 65% effective. High-dose halofantrine (3-day treatment) is 90% curative but cardiac side effects are increased, raising questions about the safety of high-dose halofantrine for general use.

Halofantrine has recently been licensed in the United States and will soon be available. It is already available in many countries in Africa and Europe. Because of its effectiveness and low incidence of side effects, it soon may become the treatment drug of choice, especially for people who work or travel in areas where professional medical care is not readily available and where self-treatment may be necessary.

Standard dose: 500 mg (or 8 mg/kg) every 6 hours for 3 doses. A second 3-dose treatment should be administered 7 days later.

Halofantrine should be taken either on an empty stomach or with a fatty meal. Because of its erratic absorption and short half-life, halofantrine is not used for chemoprophylaxis. The drug is available in 250 mg tablets and in a pediatric suspension of 100 mg/5 ml.

Side effects: Side effects are usually minor and may consist of GI upset (diarrhea, nausea, abdominal pain), pruritus (itching), skin rash, and a slight elevation of liver transaminase enzymes. Unlike mefloquine, no serious central nervous system side effects (e.g., seizures, psychosis) occur, and there is less dizziness.

Cardiac side effects include dose-related delay of AV conduction (first-degree block) and prolongation of the Q-T interval. These effects are magnified in patients who have been given mefloquine, since both mefloquine and halofantrine are structurally related. Mobitz type I and II blocks have been observed with high-dose halofantrine. Patients on quinidine should not use halofantrine unless the quinidine has been discontinued for 12 hours.

CAUTION: The effects of halofantrine (even in standard doses) on cardiac conduction may increase the risk of ventricular tachyarrhythmias and cardiac arrest in people with a prolonged Q-T interval (Romano-Ward syndrome). Because of these concerns, a pre-treatment ECG to screen for a prolonged Q-T interval, although not recommended by the manufacturer, is probably a good idea for any traveler who may be using this drug.

Halofantrine is embryotoxic and is excreted in breast milk; it is therefore not recommended during pregnancy or breast feeding.

Quinine

This drug is active against all four species of plasmodium. Quinine is also the most rapidly acting drug for treatment of severe malaria caused by *P. falciparum*. In the United States intravenous quinine (quinine dihydrochloride, quinine) is available only at certain military facilities and is not available to the general public. Oral quinine is available as quinine sulfate in tablet and capsule form.

Resistance to quinine is appearing (West Africa, Brazil, Burma, Thailand). Although quinine rapidly reduces parasite counts and is the drug of choice in severe

P. falciparum infections, quinine by itself may not be adequate for eliminating all parasites permanently from the blood, and recrudescent infections can occur. Therefore a second drug, such as doxycycline or tetracycline, Fansidar, or clindamycin, should also be used in conjunction with quinine treatment.

Dosage for severe (complicated) malaria—Quinine dihydrochloride by intravenous infusion, 20 mg/kg loading dose over 4 hours, followed by 10 mg/kg every 8 hours given over 2-4 hours. Oral therapy with quinine sulfate, combined with tetracycline, doxycycline, or clindamycin, should be substituted as soon as possible.

Dosage for uncomplicated malaria—Quinine sulfate, 650 mg (or 10 mg/kg) orally every 8 hours for 3 to 7 days. Combine quinine with one of the following: 1) Doxycycline, 100 mg twice daily, or 2) tetracycline, 250 mg four times daily, or 3) clindamycin, 450-900 mg three times daily. In SE Asia, drugs should be administered for 7 days, 3 days elsewhere.

Side effects—Headache and tinnitus (ringing in the ears) are the most common side effects of quinine. Cinchonism—nausea, vomiting, abdominal pain, blurred vision, vertigo, and tremors—are common during the first several days of treatment. Serious, occasionally fatal side effects (hypotension, convulsions, heart block, ventricular fibrillation) can occur with too rapid intravenous injection of the drug. Slow IV administration, or oral administration, is usually safe but can cause minor ECG changes (prolongation of the Q-T interval and T wave flattening).

Quinine can be used, if necessary, during pregnancy. Although quinine has been considered an abortifacient, its use in the treatment of malaria is not associated with drug-induced abortion.

Quinidine

Quinidine, a chemical isomer of quinine, is a commonly used cardiac drug. It can also be used either intravenously or orally to treat chloroquine-resistant falciparum malaria. It is particularly useful in Thailand for the treatment of multidrug-resistant malaria.

Dosage—A loading dose of quinidine gluconate, 10 mg/kg, in normal saline is given intravenously over a 2- to 4-hour period, followed by a constant infusion at 0.02 mg/kg min (1.0–1.5 mg/kg/hour) for 3 to 7 days. Oral quinine sulfate plus doxycycline, tetracycline, or clindamycin should be started as soon as tolerated.

Side effects—Intravenous quinidine therapy should be administered in an intensive care unit. ECG monitoring is essential. Cardiac effects are similar to those caused by quinine, dose-related Q-T interval prolongation, and QRS widening.

Artemisinin (qinghaosu) and Derivatives

Artemisinin (qinghaosu) is a potent antimalarial drug extracted from the medicinal herb *Artemeisia annua* (sweet wormwood), a plant used by traditional Chinese practioners since A.D. 341. Isolated in 1972, Artemisinin is a sesquiterpene lactone peroxide and is chemically unrelated to other currently used antimalarials. Artemisinin is effective against *P. vivax* as well as chloroquine-resistant strains of *P. falciparum*, but recurrence of infection is common. To prevent recrudescent infections, artemisinin is best given in conjunction with another antimalarial, such as doxycycline, tetracycline, or mefloquine. Artemisinin is produced for clinical use in China and Vietnam and is presently not available outside these countries.

Oral dosage—3 gm (or 50 mg/kg) given over 3 to 5 days.

Intramuscular dosage—1.0 to 1.2 gm (adult dose) over 3 to 5 days.

Several derivatives of artemisinin are currently being evaluated. These include artemether and artesunate.

Artemether is an oil-soluble derivative of artemisinin and is effective in both mild and severe malaria. Oral artemether given over 5 days was found to have a higher cure rate, with fewer side effects, than mefloquine against multidrug-resistant *P. falciparum* in Thailand. In studies done in Malawi, intramuscular artemether acted more rapidly than intravenous quinine in clearing coma and reducing parasite counts in children with cerebral malaria, but overall mortality rates were not improved.

Oral dosage—700 mg given over 5 days.

Intramuscular dosage—3.2–4 mg/kg, then 1.6–2 mg/kg every 24 hrs for three to six days. Artemether, dissolved in oil, is supplied in 1.0-ml ampoules containing 80 mg of the drug for intramuscular injection. The average treatment for adults is six ampoules.

Side effects—No significant side effects are reported.

Artensunate, which is an oral, water-soluble derivative of artemisinin, has been combined successfully with mefloquine to treat drug-resistant *P. falciparum* in Thailand.

Dosage (Oral, IV, IM)—100 mg, then 50 mg every 12 hours for three to six days.

RADICAL CURE

Primaquine

If you have traveled to a region where vivax malaria predominates, and are no longer taking prophylaxis, you may be at risk for a delayed malaria attack, caused by dormant *P. vivax* (or the rare *P. ovale*) parasites residing in your liver. Your risk of malaria is proportional to your degree of exposure to mosquito bites, and primaquine treatment (called "radical cure") may be advised if you spent prolonged time in a rural malarious area or experienced a large number of mosquito bites. You have two options:

1. Take primaquine to eliminate any incubating *P. vivax* parasites, as outlined below. If your exposure to mosquitoes was of long duration (more than 3 months), then your chance of harboring dormant parasites is probably high enough to justify treatment. Start the 2-week course of primaquine after finishing prophylaxis. OR

2. Wait: If your exposure was low to moderate, the chance of dormant infection is less. Defer primaquine and watch for symptoms. Get treated for malaria if it occurs—and then follow antimalaria treatment with primaquine. Another reason for waiting is that primaquine is occasionally toxic and also usually requires that you get a pretreatment blood test to screen for G-6-PD enzyme deficiency. This enzyme deficiency is most common in blacks, Asians, and people of Mediterranean descent. If primaquine is administered to a person with G-6-PD deficiency, hemolytic anemia will occur.

Adult dosage—15 mg base (26.3 mg salt) daily for 14 days.

Child dosage—0.3 mg base per kg (0.5 mg/kg salt) daily for 14 days.

NOTE: The U.S. Army does not routinely screen for G-6-PD enzyme deficiency since the extent of hemolysis, even in persons with severe deficiency, is not clinically important when primaquine is used at a dosage of 15 mg per day, given for 14 days, and patients are warned to discontinue primaquine should they have jaundice (scleral icterus) or dark urine.

Primaquine-Resistant *P. vivax*

Primaquine-resistant strains of *Plasmodium vivax* are found in SE Asia and Oceania (Papua New Guinea, Indonesia, the Solomon Islands) and travelers exposed in these regions should be treated with a higher dose of primaquine (6 mg base per kg of body weight, given in daily doses of 15 mg to 30 mg per kg). For adults, this higher dose of primaquine is usually given as 30 mg per day for 14 days.

Notes:

1. Adapted from Phillips-Howard PA, Travel Medicine 2. Proceedings of the Second Conference on International Travel Medicine, Atlanta, GA, USA, May 9–12, 1991; pp. 82. Published by the International Society of Travel Medicine, P.O. Box 15060, Atlanta, GA, 30333-0060.
2. Reprinted with permission from *Professional Guide to Drugs*. Copyright 1982, Springhouse Corporation. All rights reserved.

General References:

Wyler DJ. Malaria Chemoprophylaxis for the Traveler. *N Engl J Med* 1993; 329: 31–37.

Lobel HO, Steffen R, Kozarsky PE. Travel Medicine 2. Proceedings of the Second Conference on International Travel Medicine, Atlanta, GA, USA, May 9–12, 1991; pp. 10–14 and 81–116. Published by the International Society of Travel Medicine, P.O. Box 15060, Atlanta, GA, 30333-0060.

Keystone JS. Prevention and Self-Treatment of Malaria. Travel Medicine Advisor Update July/August 1993; pp. 21–22, 3.1–3.10. Published by American Health Consultants, Atlanta, GA.

Lackritz EM, Lobel HO, et al. Imported *Plasmodium falciparum* Malaria in American Travelers to Africa. JAMA. January 16, 1991; pp. 383–85.

Hoffman SL. Diagnosis, Treatment, and Prevention of Malaria. Med Clinics of N America. November 1992; pp. 1327–1355.

Schwartz IK. Prevention of Malaria. Inf Disease Clinics of N America. June 1992; pp. 313-331.

6 Insect Protection

Mosquitoes

Mosquitoes are ubiquitous insects. They can be found in nearly every climatic region of the world from the arctic to the tropics. Such is their adaptability that, depending on the species, they can be found breeding in all types of water from heavily polluted to clean, from small collections of water in tin cans to pools, lakes, and streams.

Both male and female mosquitoes feed on nectar or fruits for sustenance but female mosquitoes require a blood meal every three to four days for the protein necessary to produce eggs.

Mosquitoes can be divided generally into two types: daytime and nighttime biters. Those mosquitoes that transmit malaria and Japanese encephalitis (anopheles and culex mosquitoes) bite most intensively after sunset, whereas *Aedes aegypti* mosquitoes, which transmit dengue and yellow fever, are predominantly daytime biters. Mosquitoes also bite indoors, so you need to prevent mosquitoes from gaining entry into living and sleeping quarters, and to eliminate those that might already be there.

The most common mosquito-transmitted diseases that you need to protect yourself from in tropical and subtropical climates are

- malaria and
- dengue

Less common mosquito-transmitted diseases include

- yellow fever
- filariasis
- viral encephalitis (e.g., Japanese encephalitis, Venezuelan equine encephalitis), and
- miscellaneous viral illnesses. In addition to Rift Valley fever, West Nile fever, Chikungunya fever, and Sindbis fever, there are about 30 rarely diagnosed viral fevers that are also mosquito transmitted.

Ticks and Biting Flies

The same personal protection measures that you use against mosquitoes will also protect you against ticks and biting flies—insects that transmit Lyme disease, tick-borne encephalitis, relapsing fever, typhus, leishmaniasis, onchocerciasis, trypanosomiasis, and several other tropical and infectious diseases. Of these diseases, leishmaniasis, transmitted by sand flies, is the most common.

You will want to avoid mosquitoes and biting flies for another reason: intense insect activity, even without the risk of disease, can make you miserable. Bites usually cause unpleasant swelling and itching as well as mental aggravation, and they sometimes become infected.

Mosquito and insect protection entails more than just applying an insect repellent to your skin. *A multipronged approach is essential.* Using the personal protection methods described in this chapter, you can achieve 99%–100% protection against mosquito and other insect bites.

Carefully read this chapter before you depart. Not every mosquito or insect carries disease, but just *one* bite from an infected mosquito or insect can make you sick.

INSECT REPELLENTS

DEET

The first line of defense against insect bites consists of applying an insect repellent to your skin. Commercial repellents containing DEET (acronym for the chemical N, N-diethyl-meta-toluamide) are the most effective and widely used. DEET was developed in the 1930s and U.S. government-certified in 1954 as a repellent. It is primarily effective against mosquitoes and ticks, less so against gnats, blackflies, biting flies, fleas, and mites. DEET works by masking the insect-attracting odor of carbon dioxide given off by the human body. In the United States at least 16 brand-name repellents are available, with DEET concentration ranging from 6.5% to 100%. All U.S. repellents must be labeled with their DEET content.

DEET provides effective protection when applied to skin. It is effective in relatively small amounts provided it is spread evenly and completely over all exposed areas. DEET, however, has little "spatial activity," meaning that nearby, untreated skin is vulnerable.

Most insect repellents typically work for about three to four hours but need to be reapplied more frequently if the wearer sweats heavily or gets wet from rain. More frequent application may also be necessary if the local mosquito density is high. Also, the effectiveness of any particular product may vary with the individual. Some people's body chemistry attracts insects more than others.

Adults should use a repellent that contains at least 15% DEET. Repellents with DEET concentrations of 55%–100% are available, but these higher concentrations are probably unnecessary and may possibly cause toxicity.

DEET Toxicity

DEET has been marketed in the United States since 1956 and is used by an estimated 50–100 million persons each year. Since some DEET is absorbed into the bloodstream through the skin, there is the potential for toxic reactions, especially in children. The safety concerns about DEET stem from reports of allergic reactions (urticaria) and skin irritation (dermatitis) to, in extreme cases, neurological harm.

Dermatological side effects—Skin reactions to DEET are infrequent but can include itching, swelling, blistering, or redness of the skin and burning or stinging of the lips, tongue, and mouth. These side effects occur more frequently with exposure to the higher concentrations of DEET.

Neurological side effect—Between 1961 and 1988, the scientific literature documented at least six children, all girls from one to eight years of age, who were reported to have possible toxic neurological reactions to DEET. Exposure to the repellent in these cases ranged from several days to three months. Symptoms in the patients included slurred speech, staggering gait (ataxia), lethargy, seizures and/or coma; three died. In August 1989 the N.Y. State Department of Health investigated five reports of seizures associated with (but not necessarily caused by) the use of DEET. The patients were four boys aged 3–7 and one 29-year-old man. All patients recovered quickly. They all had applied varying concentrations of DEET to their skin; four had fewer than three applications. The interval between the last use of DEET and the onset of seizures ranged from 8 to 48 hours. In another study, episodes of confusion and insomnia have been reported by Everglades National Park employees following repeated and prolonged use of DEET.

These anecdotal reports of seizures and other symptoms are difficult to interpret. Not all can be clearly established as DEET toxicity, and it may be only coincidental that the dramatic increase in DEET use to prevent Lyme disease in New York and Connecticut was associated with the seizures reported in 1989. Nevertheless, DEET use should be considered as a possible cause of seizures, especially in children, unless another cause, such as epilepsy, is clearly to blame. It must be borne in mind, however, that millions of people use DEET without any apparent problems.

To minimize the possible adverse reactions to DEET, you should take the following common-sense precautions:

- Don't apply high concentration products to the skin of children.
- Do not inhale or ingest (drink) repellents or get them in your eyes.
- Wear long sleeves and long pants, when possible, to reduce the skin surface area that needs to be treated with DEET.
- Avoid applying repellents to portions of children's hands that are likely to have contact with their eyes or mouth.
- Never use repellents on wounds or inflamed or irritated skin.
- Use repellent sparingly; one application usually lasts 3–4 hours; some products last 8–12 hours. Saturation does not increase efficacy.
- Wash repellent-treated skin after coming indoors, provided there are no mosquitoes inside.
- If a suspected reaction to the repellent occurs, wash treated skin immediately and contact a physician.

The highly concentrated products should not be used on infants and children because their thinner skin and greater surface-area-to-body-weight ratio places them at increased risk of DEET absorption. Repellents containing 10% to 20% DEET, such as DEET PLUS and Skedaddle!, or the polymer-containing Ultrathon, are safer for them, provided the repellent is used as directed. Natrapel, containing citronella oil, is also an option for many children, but the presumed safety of citronella must be weighed against its decreased efficacy in preventing bites; this could be of critical importance in a malarious area.

How Safe Then Is DEET?

It's not known exactly how many serious toxic reactions are possibly caused by DEET-containing repellents each year (estimated at less than 10), but millions of people use the products, even the 100% DEET brands, without apparent problems. According to the EPA, which has done extensive testing, when properly used "DEET is the safest and most effective repellent available."

It's also clear that DEET shouldn't be misused. Misuse includes repeated and heavy coatings beyond the manufacturers' recommendations, and the use of high-concentration DEET on infants and children. Although neurological toxicity doesn't seem to be a significant problem for adults, they shouldn't expose themselves to prolonged and excessive use of high-concentration products. Although there is no good argument for the use of 100% DEET, limited use by adults is considered safe.

How Low Should You Go?

Because of the fear of toxic reactions, particularly in children, several companies are marketing low-concentration DEET repellents. Skintastic (7.5% DEET), sold by S.C. Johnson, and Skedaddle! (10% DEET), by Littlepoint Corp., are two examples. The problem with the low-concentration products, however, is that extensive tests haven't been done to confirm their effectiveness against a wide range of insects. We currently don't know, for example, if using a low concentration DEET repellent would protect against all species of malaria-transmitting mosquitoes.

Natural Repellents

Since long before the advent of synthetic chemicals, people have been using plant-derived substances to try to kill and repel mosquitoes. The essential oils of a multitude of plants have been shown to have mosquito-repellent properties. Examples include camphor, citronella, lemongrass, clove, eucalyptus, and others. Citronella oil is the most popular and effective extract and is one of the few natural products that is still used in natural repellents in Europe and North America. When compared to DEET, however, citronella oil is much less effective and has a shorter duration of action.

Figure 6.1 Technique for Impregnating Clothing or Mosquito Netting with Permethrin Solution.

1. Pour 4 to 8 oz. of 13.3% permethrin solution into the plastic bag or a small basin.

2. Add 2 to 4 quarts of water. Mix. Solution will turn milky white.

3. Place mosquito net or 1-2 garments in bag or basin. (Tie bag shut.)

4. Submerge fabric in solution to impregnate. Let rest 10 minutes.

5. Remove items from solution. Wring out excess solution.

6. Hang up clothing or netting for 2-3 hours to dry. You can also lay out fabric to dry on a clean surface.

Directions for Spraying with Permethrin Aerosol

One 6 oz. aerosol will treat 1-2 sets of clothing (shirt & trousers = 1 set) or 2 nets.

1. Place the clothing or mosquito net on a plastic sheet.
2. Spray, using a slow, circular motion, holding the can 8"–12" above the fabric. Moisten all areas. Fabric will temporarily darken when moist.
3. Shirts: Spray each side 30 seconds. Trousers: Spray each side 30–45 seconds. Jackets: Spray each side 30–45 seconds.
4. Mosquito nets: Partially unroll the net onto the plastic sheet. Spray 30 seconds. Turn net, and spray another 30 seconds. Keep turning and spraying the net until you have used about one-half the contents of the can.
8. Hang up, or lay out, clothing or net to dry. Allow 2–3 hours for complete drying. Effective for 2-6 weeks. Permethrin, when applied, is odorless and nonstaining.

Natural repellents, however, have become more popular as consumers have begun to worry about DEET toxicity, and companies have rushed to exploit "DEET anxiety." Natrapel, which contains citronella oil, is the most popular brand in the United States. *Skin-So-Soft,* a bath oil made by Avon, contains no known repellent but is popular with some travelers, although its reputed effectiveness lasts only one-half hour or less. It may work better for some people because something in their skin chemistry combines with the bath oil to prevent bites.

The Bottom Line
The main point to remember is that prudent application of DEET is an essential step in preventing insect bites that can transmit serious, even fatal, disease. Be sure you don't avoid—or underuse—DEET repellents that are effective in safeguarding your health.

PROTECTIVE CLOTHING

Clothing provides a physical barrier to biting insects, provided it is sufficiently thick or tightly woven. For increased protection, especially when there is more intense mosquito activity (e.g., in the evening), you should wear long-sleeved shirts and avoid shorts. Tucking your pant leg into your socks or boots is a good idea because mosquitoes often bite around the lower leg and ankles.

Chemically Treated Clothing
Clothing protection is dramatically increased when the fabric is sprayed or impregnated with a chemical that will either repel or directly kill any insect that alights on the fabric. Both DEET and permethrin (below) are effective clothing treatments, but DEET has now been largely superseded for this purpose by permethrin.

PERMETHRIN

Unlike DEET, which is used primarily as a skin repellent, permethrin is an insecticide that is applied only to fabric, such as clothing or mosquito nets. Permethrin, however, is far more than a repellent—it is an insecticide that knocks down, or kills, insects that come in contact with it. Consider the following:

- Permethrin kills insects that alight on treated fabric.
- Permethrin is safe; human toxicity does not occur except for occasional skin irritation.
- Permethrin adheres tightly to fabric and will last through multiple washings. It will not harm or stain fabric, even silk.
- Unlike DEET, permethrin will not soften or melt plastic or synthetic material.
- It is effective against mosquitoes, ticks, flies, and other insects.
- It is biodegradable. Permethrin does not accumulate in the environment.
- Permethrin is EPA-labeled for use on clothing.

Permethrin is a synthetic chemical analogue of the naturally occurring plant insecticide pyrethrum, and it acts as a neurotoxin. The repellent ("excito-repellency") effect and direct killing effect of permethrin are due to its blockage of sodium ion transport in insect nerve fibers.

Although highly toxic to insects, permethrin is not hazardous to humans; skin absorption of the chemical is extremely low, and any absorbed permethrin is rapidly metabolized by the liver. To date, no cases of toxicity, carcinogenicity, or mutagenicity have been reported in human subjects. In fact, in FDA-approved products such as 1% NIX® head lice cream and 5% ELIMITE® antiscabies cream, permethrin is safe enough to be applied directly to scalp and skin.

Permethrin and DEET—The Miracle Combination?

The best way to avoid insect bites—and the diseases insects transmit—is to apply DEET to your skin and permethrin to your clothing. The effectiveness of this combination is confirmed by many studies, such as the one reported by the *Medical Letter* (May 1989) that demonstrated 100% protection against mosquito bites when test subjects wore permethrin-treated clothing and applied a DEET repellent to their skin. In a similar study done by the U.S. Army in Alaska, 99.9% protection was achieved.

How to Use Permethrin

Spraying—Lay out the clothing to be sprayed. For shirts and trousers, spray the front of each garment for 1 to 2 minutes. For socks and bandanas, spray for 30 seconds per side. Use a slow sweeping motion, holding the can about 12 inches from the fabric. Spray inside cuffs. Turn the garment(s) over and repeat. The fabric should be slightly damp. Hang up to dry. You should use about two-thirds of a can to treat a shirt and trousers. The treated garments, even after several launderings, will kill mosquitoes and ticks for about six weeks.

Impregnating—Treating clothing in a permethrin solution will give longer protection. The U.S. Army uses this method on jungle and desert uniforms. Al-

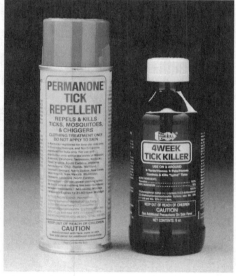

Figure 6.2. Permanone or Duranon spray is an important adjunct in insect-borne disease prevention. PermaKill 4Week 13.3% solution (right) can also be used safely to treat clothing and mosquito netting. Follow instructions in Figure 6.1.

though permethrin solutions are not toxic to humans and are considered safe, they have not yet been approved by the EPA for use on clothing. For this reason, commercially impregnated clothing is not available; travelers who want to use this technique can follow the directions shown in Figure 6.1.

In the United States, permethrin is commercially available in a 0.5% aerosol spray (Duranon or Permanone) or in a 13.3% solution (PermaKill 4Week Tick Killer). See Figure 6.2.

Preventing Tick Bites

The measures described above are also dramatically effective against ticks. In all studies, 100% protection against tick attachment has been shown when using a combination of DEET-containing repellent on exposed skin and permethrin-treated clothing. The treated clothing not only is a physical barrier but knocks down or kills any ticks that touch it. If you are not wearing much protective clothing, you need to rely more on an insect repellent and vigilant self-inspection for ticks, especially about the legs, thighs, neck, and waist, the regions where ticks like to migrate. Tip: wear a bandana treated with permethrin. This will deter ticks from attaching about the head and neck.

Mosquito Nets

Mosquito nets play an underutilized role in preventing malaria and other insect-borne illnesses such as Japanese encephalitis, leishmaniasis, and filariasis. (Nets are less important in preventing dengue since the aedes mosquitoes that transmit dengue are primarily daytime biters.) The use of bed nets and other personal protection measures against bites is increasing as more travelers are being exposed to multidrug-resistant malaria, for which no prophylactic drug regimen is completely effective. The prevention of mosquito bites, in fact, is the best defense against malaria and other insect-transmitted illnesses.

Bed nets, however, have certain problems. They are often not well-fitted and can be easily torn, and mosquitoes can feed through a net if part of the body touches it during the night. These factors provide a rationale for treating nets with permethrin; the insecticide repels and/or kills mosquitoes that always land on the net before they have a chance to find a hole to enter or to feed.

The first treatment of nets with insecticidal or repellent compounds began in the 1930s in the USSR, using lysol, and in the American and German armies during World War II, using DDT. In 1973 photostable insecticidal pyrethroids, developed as molecular analogues of the natural plant insecticide pyrethrum, were synthesized and found to be highly effective against mosquitoes when applied to fabric.

In 1984 field trials of permethrin-impregnated nets were first carried out. These and subsequent trials demonstrated that (1) permethrin binds tightly to nylon, polyester, and cotton; (2) insecticidal fabric levels can be maintained for 6 to 12 months; (3) permethrin-treated fabric directly kills insects that land on it; (4) treated nets also repel insects; and (5) treated nets reduce mosquito counts within dwellings.

Many tropical countries now have public health programs that supply permethrin-impregnated nets to villages in malaria-endemic areas. More and more travelers to these countries are now also beginning to use similar permethrin-treated nets.

Types of Nets

One problem with the use of bed nets in a hot climate is lack of adequate ventilation. Because some nets have a tightly woven mesh, airflow through the bed net is reduced. This problem can be overcome by using a permethrin-bed net with a larger mesh. Since insects always stop first on the fabric before going through an opening, a permethrin-treated net, even with a large mesh, will kill or repel any insect that tries to get through, and also provide better ventilation.

The type of mosquito net you should purchase depends upon several factors. If you are traveling solo from location to location, you'll want something light and not too big. On the other hand, if there are two people residing in a fixed location for an extended period of time, then a larger, roomier model is preferred.

The Spider. This bell-shaped net has a fairly large mesh to provide good ventilation and is large enough to cover a king-size bed, but is also lightweight and portable. Contact Travel Medicine, Inc., 1-800 TRAV-MED. $69.95 plus shipping. Includes attachment kit.

La Mosquette. This net is of a classic rectangular design and is supported by lightweight aluminum poles. The net will cover either a single or a double bed and is well suited for travelers who will be staying in a fixed location for a longer period of time. Contact IAMAT, 417 Center Street, Lewiston, NY 14092; 716-754-4883. Or in Canada, 40 Regal Road, Guelph, Ontario, N1K 1B5; 519-836-0102. About $90 plus shipping.

SleepScreen I. The single-model net accommodates one person in a sleeping bag or bed. It comes with 5-piece shock-corded poles and nylon stuff sack. Compacts to size of folding umbrella. Wt: 10 oz.

SleepScreenII. The double-wide SleepScreen accommodates two people in sleeping bags or double (or wider) bed. Comes with 5-piece shock-corded poles and nylon stuff sack. Total weight: 23 oz. Size: 55" wide x 28" high. $39.95

TropicScreen. A lightweight, very portable bed net. Comes with 9-piece shock-corded poles and nylon carry bag. This net completely encloses two people on the ground or one sleeper on a cot. Weight: 37 oz. Size: 93" x 54" x 36" high.

Insect-Proofing Your Sleeping Quarters

Even if you are staying in an air-conditioned hotel or a well-screened house, you should use an insecticide aerosol to rid your sleeping quarters of mosquitoes and other biting insects that might have gotten into your room. Several brands are effective and widely available in the United States. RAID® Flying Insect Spray and Green Thumb® Flying Insect Killer (available at True Value and other hardware stores) contain permethrin-type insecticides. In East Africa, Doom® Insect Spray, which contains permethrin and pyrethrum, is locally available. Spray your sleeping quarters with one of these aerosols one hour before bedtime to help guarantee an insect-free indoor environment.

7 Insect-Borne Diseases

YELLOW FEVER

In 1900 Dr. Walter Reed demonstrated that yellow fever is a viral illness transmitted by mosquitoes. The disease is so named because jaundice, the result of liver damage, is a common sign of this illness.

There are two distinct cycles of transmission, but the resulting disease is the same. Urban yellow fever is transmitted by a mosquito from an infected person to another person (Figure 7.1). In jungle (sylvatic) yellow fever, mosquitoes transmit the infection between monkeys and humans or vice versa (Figure 7.2).

Yellow fever occurs in tropical areas of certain countries in Africa, the Caribbean, and Latin America (see Chapter 1). These countries comprise the yellow fever endemic zones. Interestingly, there is no yellow fever in the Middle East or Asia, despite the presence of the aedes mosquitoes, which transmit the virus.

Many yellow fever infections are mild and go unrecognized, but severe life-threatening illness is not uncommon. Symptoms include headache, abdominal pain, and vomiting, followed by liver and kidney failure. Liver failure is the result of severe viral hepatitis which often causes jaundice, a characteristic yellowing of the skin and eyes. In nonvaccinated persons, mortality is as high as 50%.

Fortunately, a vaccine is available that effectively prevents this disease. A single injection of the live, attenuated vaccine every 10 years affords almost 100% protection. All travelers to rural areas of endemic zone countries should be vaccinated.

NOTE: Seroconversion rates during pregnancy may be as low as 38%, suggesting that pregnant women may not be adequately protected by the yellow fever vaccine.

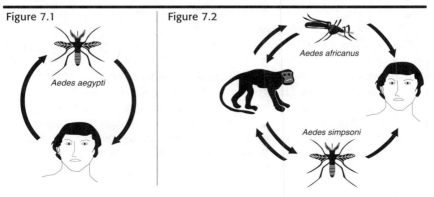

Figure 7.1

Aedes aegypti

Figure 7.2

Aedes africanus

Aedes simpsoni

DENGUE

This viral illness is distributed worldwide, with over half the population of the globe at risk for infection. Dengue (pronounced DENG-ee) is prevalent in many Caribbean countries, Central and South America (including Mexico), the Pacific islands, the tropical countries of Asia, and parts of tropical Africa. Since 1985, major epidemics in the Western Hemisphere have occurred in Mexico, Guatemala, El Salvador, Nicaragua, Colombia, Bolivia, Brazil, Aruba, Barbados, St. Lucia, and Puerto Rico. In the United States, the majority of dengue occurs in tourists who have just returned from Puerto Rico or the Virgin Islands.

Dengue is spread by the female *Aedes aegypti* mosquito, which is the same mosquito that transmits yellow fever. (The dengue and yellow fever viruses, incidentally, belong to the same family of viruses and have very similar molecular structures.) Aedes mosquitoes like to feed during the day, with most biting activity in the morning and again at twilight (unlike the malaria-spreading anopheles mosquito, which feeds in the evening and at night). The aedes mosquito is found mostly in urban areas where they breed in stagnant pools of water found in water entrapment receptacles such as cisterns, discarded tires, buckets, cans, bottles, and barrels; it's therefore not surprising that urbanization has increased the spread of dengue fever in many tropical third world countries.

There are four types (serotypes) of dengue viruses, designated dengue types 1, 2, 3, and 4. If you are infected with one type of virus, you will gain lifelong immunity against that particular serotype, but unfortunately there is little "crossover" protection, and you will still be susceptible to disease caused by the other serotypes.

Symptoms and Treatment of Dengue

Classic dengue—Infection with any of the four virus types causes flulike symptoms: sudden high fever, severe headache, muscle and joint pain, and fatigue (these initial symptoms can mimic an attack of malaria). After three to four days a rash appears, which may spread from the torso to the arms, legs, and face (at this stage the disease can be confused with measles). Most cases of dengue fever are over in about a week, although recovery may be prolonged. Symptoms resolve without specific treatment (antibiotics do not help). Treatment consists of supportive care involving rest, fluid replacement, and analgesics.

Dengue hemorrhagic fever (DHF)—This is a severe, sometimes fatal form of dengue fever that rarely strikes Western tourists. DHF affects predominantly two types of persons: (1) any person with a second dengue infection, and (2) infants with a primary infection. The theory explaining the severity of the infection is that dengue antibodies already present—either from a previous infection, or acquired by an infant from its mother—interact with an infecting dengue virus, producing an "enhanced" infection.[1] Symptoms of DHF occur around the fifth day of illness when bleeding, usually in the form of skin hemorrhages, may be noted. Severe cases can progress to a shock-like state with a mortality of 2%–10%. Most cases of DHF are reported from Southeast Asia, especially among children.

Is it dengue or malaria? If you are traveling in a malarious area and develop a fever, you should seek immediate medical attention. Even though your symptoms might be caused by the dengue virus, it's important first to make sure that you don't have malaria. You should see a doctor right away for tests, and if malaria is the culprit, start appropriate treatment, especially if you are in an area where there is chloroquine-resistant falciparum malaria. If you can't be seen by a physician right away, you should start self-treatment for malaria with an appropriate drug (e.g., quinine plus tetracycline, halofantrine, or mefloquine). Continue to seek medical consultation as soon as possible. If the diagnosis of malaria can be excluded, you can assume that dengue is a likely diagnosis and that supportive care is all that is probably necessary.

Preventing Dengue

The aedes mosquitoes, which transmit dengue, bite primarily during the daytime and are present in populous urban areas as well as resort and rural areas. You can reduce or eliminate your risk of acquiring dengue by avoiding mosquito bites. Follow the guidelines in Chapter 6. Apply a DEET-containing insect repellent to your skin and wear clothing that has been treated with permethrin. Although you are most concerned with daytime bites, a permethrin-treated mosquito net is still a good idea because treated indoor nets decrease the number of mosquitoes within a household.

The risk of dengue infection for the international traveler appears to be small, unless an epidemic is in progress. Nevertheless, travelers returning to the United States should report to their physician any illness with fever occurring within two weeks after leaving an endemic or epidemic area.

World Distribution of Dengue–1992

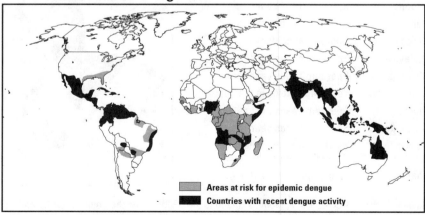

Source: Division of Vector-Bourne Infectious Diseases, National Center for Infectious Diseases, Centers for Disease Control and Prevention

JAPANESE ENCEPHALITIS (JE)

This mosquito-transmitted viral illness is the number one cause of encephalitis in Asia. Over 50,000 cases of JE are reported annually from China, Korea, Japan, Southeast Asia, and the Indian subcontinent. (Encephalitis means "inflammation of the brain." Less frequently, encephalitis is also caused by the herpes simplex and measles viruses.)

How, Where, and When JE Is Transmitted

See Table 7.1, below. Japanese encephalitis occurs in rural-agricultural areas throughout Asia. In temperate regions such as the People's Republic of China, Japan, Korea, and the northern areas of Southeast Asia, JE transmission is highest from April to September. In northern India and Nepal, peak transmission is from June to November. In the tropical regions of Asia, JE occurs year-round.

The virus of Japanese encephalitis is transmitted by culex mosquitoes. These mosquitoes breed where there is abundant water, such as in rice paddies, and feed primarily on local domestic animals, usually pigs. Visiting a rural-agricultural rice-growing, pig-farming region, therefore, can put you at risk. About 1%–3% of the culex mosquitoes in endemic areas are infective. Since these mosquitoes are night feeders, there is less risk of JE transmission during the day.

Table 7.1 Geographical Distribution of Japanese Encephalitis

Country	Prevalence
Bangladesh	Yearly epidemics with sporadic cases year-round
China	Disease is present everywhere except in Tibet and Xinaginag
India	Yearly epidemics and sporadic cases in the south
Indonesia	Rare sporadic cases
Japan	Rare seasonal cases
Cambodia	Sporadic cases year-round
Korea	Occasional epidemics
Malaysia	Sporadic cases year-round
Myanmar	Sporadic cases year-round
Nepal	Yearly epidemics in the south
Philippines	Sporadic cases occur
Sri Lanka	Sporadic cases year-round
Taiwan	Yearly epidemics in the north Sporadic cases in the south
Thailand	Yearly epidemics in the north Sporadic cases in the south
Russia	Occasional epidemics limited to the SE, between the Chinese border and the Sea of Japan
Vietnam	Sporadic cases year-round

Symptoms of JE

Watch for nausea, vomiting, headache, and fever. A severe attack will cause lethargy and coma. Fortunately, most JE infections are very mild or inapparent—only 1 in 200–300 infected individuals becomes sick. Unfortunately, if you do develop symptoms, the resulting illness can be severe, with a mortality as high as 10%–25%, with the chance of residual neurological damage being 50%.

Treatment

There is no drug treatment for JE. Good nursing care is essential in more severe cases.

Risk to Tourists

The average tourist is not at risk. If you are a short-term traveler, and if you are visiting only urban areas, your risk of getting JE is very low—approximately one in one million.[1] You will be at greater risk if living in rural agricultural (rice-growing, pig-farming) areas during the season of peak transmission. Your risk then rises to approximately 1 in 5,000 per month of exposure.

Preventing JE

Mosquito protection measure—All travelers should take measures to prevent mosquito bites. These measures include applying a DEET-containing skin repellent, wearing permethrin-treated clothing, eliminating indoor mosquitoes through screening and spraying, and sleeping under a permethrin-treated bed net.

Vaccination—Three doses of JE vaccine, administered over a 30-day period, are recommended for travelers at risk. An abbreviated 3-dose, 2-week schedule can be used when the 30-day schedule is impractical. If you find that neither schedule is possible, 80%–90% protection can be achieved with two doses of vaccine, administered one week apart. You should receive your shots a minimum of 10 days prior to departure to (1) allow time for immunity to develop, and (2) see if any side effects occur. Serious side effects consist of urticaria (hives) or angioedema (facial swelling) that can occur within minutes following vaccination, or during the 10 days following vaccination. (Most serious vaccine reactions will occur within the first 48 hours.) Rates of serious reactions are low (approximately 1–104 per 10,000). Despite this low incidence you should not embark upon international travel within 10 days of JE vaccination because of the possibility of delayed allergic reactions. If you have a history of allergies, the risk of side effects is increased.

Who Should Be Vaccinated

Vaccination against JE is recommended for anyone who will be spending 30 days or more in a rural-agricultural endemic area during the transmission season.

Short-term tourist/business travel—Vaccination is not routinely recommended for travel of less than 30 days unless intense exposure to mosquitoes in a rural-agricultural area is anticipated during the peak transmission period.

The JE vaccine is now available again at travel clinics in the United States. It is also available in Canada, most European countries, Japan, Hong Kong, and Bangkok. In Great Britain, you can get the JE vaccine at any British Airways travel clinic (there are 36 BA clinics countrywide). Most Asian countries also have the vaccine. If you're not sure where to go for vaccination overseas, contact the nearest U.S. consulate for information.

SLEEPING SICKNESS
(African Trypanosomiasis)

The Gambian variety of sleeping sickness is found in Central and West Africa and is spread by the bite of the tsetse fly. Most cases occur in travelers who have visited game parks. The illness starts with an ulcer at the site of the fly bite, followed by fever, lymph node swelling, and headache. Without treatment the infection spreads to the central nervous system. The sleeping sickness phase of the illness, however, does not occur for many months or years after infection first occurs.

The best prevention is to avoid the bite of the tsetse fly by following the guidelines in Chapter 6.

In 1990 a new drug, Ornidyl, was approved for the treatment of sleeping sickness. Ornidyl is extremely effective, even against advanced cases of the disease. Unlike its predecessor, melarsoprol, Ornidyl is virtually nontoxic. The drug can be taken orally, but is most effective if given intravenously over a two-week period.

The Rhodesian form of sleeping sickness is found along the savanna and woodlands of eastern equatorial Africa. This illness occurs two to 21 days after the tsetse fly bite. Signs and symptoms include high fever, headache, rash, and slight lymph node swelling. Rapid progression of the illness may occur, and medical care is then urgently required. Ornidyl is less effective for Rhodesian sleeping sickness and may have to be combined with other medication.

CHAGAS' DISEASE

This disease is caused by a small single-cell protozoan parasite called *Trypanosoma cruzi* (*T. cruzi*) which, when injected into the body, causes an acute but often asymptomatic illness followed in some cases (usually years later) by damage to the heart, gastrointestinal tract, and nervous system

How the Disease Is Spread

T. cruzi is transmitted by species of ruduviid or triatomid bugs, commonly called assassin, or kissing, bugs because of their predilection for biting the face while the victim is sleeping. Chagas' disease can also be transmitted by unscreened blood transfusions. (Up to 1.9%–6.5% of blood in some blood banks in Latin America is contaminated by *T. cruzi* parasites.)

Where Chagas' Disease Occurs

Chagas' disease occurs in Latin America in rural areas extending north from Chile and Argentina to Mexico. Most risk occurs in Brazil. A few cases have been reported in the southern United States (Texas and Oklahoma). Transmission occurs primarily in areas where there are poorly constructed adobe-style native huts. The assassin bugs (not all are infective) live in the thatch roofs and mud walls of these huts and come out at night to feed on the blood of sleeping humans, usually biting the exposed face near the eye or the corner of the mouth.

People staying in tourist accommodations are rarely infected. If you are traveling only to large cities, or to remote jungle sites, you are not at risk. If, however, you are a traveler staying in villages with adobe-style huts, you should take the precautions listed below.

Symptoms of Chagas' Disease

Only about one-third of infected persons develop symptoms of acute Chagas' disease. Local symptoms: The first symptom may be confused with a simple "bedbug bite," usually on the face. One to three weeks after exposure there may be a swollen nodule or pimple at the site of the bite, followed by fever and localized lymph node enlargement. If you were bitten near the eye, you may develop swelling of your face and eyelid, and conjunctivitis (reddening of the eye). These localized symptoms may last 1–2 months, then disappear. Generalized symptoms: Two weeks after the initial bite, parasites can spread throughout the body, infecting many tissues, particularly the heart, skeletal muscles, and the nervous system. At this stage you may develop fever, generalized lymph node enlargement, a rash, liver and spleen enlargement, and a gelatinous edema of your face and/or torso. In severe cases a condition called myocarditis (inflammation of the heart) can occur and you would notice rapid heart rate, shortness of breath, and other symptoms of cardiac arrhythmia and heart failure.

Acute Chagas' disease can be confused with malaria, mumps, eye infections, sinusitis, and cellulitis of the skin.

The most serious aspect of Chagas' disease is the delayed damage it can inflict on the heart and intestinal tract. About 10% of infected people go on to develop heart block and chronic heart failure. Chagas' disease, in fact, is the leading cause of heart disease in endemic areas of Latin America and is responsible for one-quarter of all deaths in the 25- to 44-year age group in these endemic areas. Chronic enlargement of the esophagus and colon (megacolon) can also occur.

Diagnosis and Treatment of Chagas' Disease

A microscopic examination of your blood in the acute phase of illness may demonstrate *T. cruzi* parasites. Blood cultures and/or lymph node aspiration can also be diagnostic. Serologic screening tests (fluorescent antibody, complement fixation, or agglutination) may be useful. An ELISA assay using purified antigen is available and is specific and more accurate.

There is no treatment of chronic Chagas' disease. Acute illness can be shortened with nifurtimox, but side effects may be severe. Treatment with ketoconazole has been effective experimentally, but it has not been tested extensively in humans.

Preventing Chagas' Disease

Preventing Chagas' disease means avoiding the assassin bug. If you are camping in an endemic area, stay some distance away from adobe hut–type structures. If you are sleeping indoors, take the following precautions:

- Search your sleeping quarters and bed for hidden insects.
- Spray an insecticide in your living and sleeping quarters. RAID Formula II Crack and Crevice Spray is a good choice.
- Fumigant canisters can prevent reinfestation.
- Sleep under a well-tucked-in mosquito net.
- Sleep in the middle of the room, away from the walls.
- Apply insect repellent to your face and neck at bedtime.
- Use a residual insecticide on the walls and roofs of houses, if living in the region in an adobe structure.
- Do not use old rugs, blankets, or sheets from the hut.

Chagas' disease can also be spread by unscreened blood transfusions, so these should be avoided.

FILARIASIS

Filariasis is prevalent throughout the tropics and is a group of diseases caused by threadlike roundworms, called filaria, which are transmitted by various mosquitoes, flies, and biting midges. Filariasis includes the more common lymphatic filariasis (Bancroftian and Malayan filariasis), and subcutaneous filariasis—onchocerciasis ("river blindness") and loiasis.

Bancroftian and Malayan Filariasis

These illnesses are transmitted by aedes, culex, Mansonia, or anopheles mosquitoes found in tropical regions of Central and South America, the Caribbean, Africa, China, India, Southeast Asia, and Oceania. Infective larvae (microfilariae) are injected into the skin by the bite of the mosquito. The larvae migrate through the lymphatic channels of the skin and become trapped in lymph nodes, where the adult worms develop. The offspring of these adult worms (microfilariae) then migrate farther in the tissues and also circulate in the blood. During this phase there may be redness of the skin and swelling of lymph nodes of the arms and legs, headache, weakness, muscle pain, coughing, wheezing, and fever.

If you have sustained only a few infective insect bites and have only a light infection, you may be completely without symptoms. If you depart the infected area, and thus limit your exposure, no treatment is usually needed. Heavier exposure (many bites over three to six months) is generally necessary to cause symptomatic disease. Thousands of mosquito bites may be required, in fact, before microfilariae are evident in the blood. Continued exposure, which is unlikely to occur in tourists, may result in permanent lymphatic inflammation and obstruction. Progression of the disease, usually observed only in the indigenous population of the endemic area, can cause the grotesque swelling of the legs known as elephantiasis. Treatment of filariasis with diethylcarbamazine (Hetrazan) is effective. Recently, high-dose ivermectin (200 micrograms/kg) has shown to be effective and also has fewer side effects. Prevention of insect bites is the first line of defense.

To check for exposure to filariasis, your doctor can examine your blood for eosinophilia and microfilaria. ELISA-based serological tests can further pinpoint the diagnosis.

Onchocerciasis

One type of subcutaneous filariasis that is particularly devastating is onchocerciasis, or river blindness, common in equatorial Africa, the Sahara, Yemen, and parts of Latin America (Mexico, Guatemala, Venezuela, Ecuador, Colombia, and Brazil). The disease is transmitted by black flies that breed in vegetation along fastflowing rivers in these regions. Usual symptoms include a rash with itching (pruritus), skin nodules, swollen lymph nodes, and inflammation of the eye.

If you have been exposed to onchocerciasis, your blood eosinophil count will usually be elevated, and therefore a simple blood count (CBC) is a good screening test for exposure. Blood serology tests, including a specific enzyme-linked immunosorbent assay, can help diagnose early exposure to onchocerciasis. To make a definite diagnosis, a skin biopsy is done to identify filariae. Treatment is with ivermectin.

Loiasis

This form of subcutaneous filariasis is common to the rain forests of West and Central Africa. Loiasis is also the most frequently diagnosed blood filaria infection in travelers returning to North America and the United Kingdom from Africa. The tiny *Loa loa* worms (microfilariae) are transmitted by the bite of an infective Chrysops biting fly, also known in Africa as the red fly. This is a day-biting fly that breeds in wet mud on the edge of shaded streams in the rain forests. After the microfilariae enter the body they develop into adult worms in the subcutaneous tissues. The adult worms can survive for up to 17 years.

Symptoms of loiasis are due to migration of the adult *Loa loa* worms through the skin. Symptoms, which take 12 months or more to develop, include fever, itching, and skin swelling (Calabar swelling), usually involving the hands, wrists, forearms, or face. Adult worms can also be observed migrating on the surface of the eye, beneath the conjunctiva.

If you have been lightly exposed to *Loa loa*, you probably will have few if any symptoms. A blood test for eosinophilia and an ELISA screening test can be done to check for exposure. If you have a heavier infection, you'll need drug treatment.

The treatment currently available, diethylcarbamazine (DEC), requires a 20- to 30-day regimen and causes frequent side effects. It is poorly active against adult worms. Experimental treatment with a single dose of ivermectin, 400 µg/kg, has shown good results (microfilaremia reduced to less than 10% of pretreatment levels) with fewer side effects.

Preventing Filariasis
No vaccine or prophylactic drugs are available. You should take personal protection measures to prevent insect bites. These measures include using a deet-containing skin repellent, wearing permethrin-treated clothing, and using a mosquito bed net.

LEISHMANIASIS

Leishmaniasis is one of the most common parasitic diseases in the world. The disease is found on all continents except Australia and Antartica. It is an important public health problem in Mexico, Central and South America, North Africa, sub-Saharan Africa, the Middle East, central Asia, southern Russia, northern China, and India. Scattered areas of disease activity occur in southern Europe, mainly Portugal, southern France, Italy, the Greek Isles, the Costa del Sol, and Majorca. In the United States, cases of the disease have been reported in Texas and Oklahoma.

What Causes Leishmaniasis?
Leishmania are single-cell organisms (protozoa) just a bit smaller than a red blood cell. Infection occurs when these tiny parasites are injected into the body by the bite of an infective sand fly and then invade lymphoid cells (called macrophages) located in the liver, spleen, bone marrow, skin, and mucus membranes. Which form of leishmaniasis (cutaneous, mucocutaneous, or visceral) that you develop depends upon (1) which species of Leishmania (there are about 20) causes the disease, (2) which organs and cells are predominantly infected, and (3) your state of immunity (many cases of leishmaniasis are self-healing).

Sand flies are usually found on the edge of forested areas. They feed from dusk to dawn and have a limited flight range.

Three Types of Leishmaniasis
1. Visceral leishmaniasis (kala azar)—This disease affects primarily the internal organs and bone marrow. Hallmarks of the disease are enlargement of the liver and spleen, and anemia.

Symptoms include fatigue, muscle aches (myalgia), chills and fever, weight loss, cough, and diarrhea. Warty skin nodules or skin ulcers may also occur. Some kala azar infections are self-limited, and never progress to cause illness. More commonly, however, treatment is first sought two to six months after infection.

To diagnose kala azar, your doctor will run blood tests and do a bone marrow examination. (A monoclonal fluorescent antibody test of the bone marrow is also available.) If these tests are inconclusive, your doctor may need to have tissue cultures done.

Diseases that can be confused with kala azar include malaria, typhoid fever, brucellosis, Chagas' disease, schistosomiasis, tuberculosis (miliary variety), and amoebic liver abscess. Since massive enlargement of the spleen sometimes occurs, kala azar can also mimic leukemia or lymphoma.

Untreated, fulminate kala azar is usually fatal. However, prompt treatment with the drug sodium stibogluconate (Pentostam) is usually curative. Pentostam is given in an intravenous dose of 20 mg/kg daily for 30–40 days. Pentostam is available from the Parasitic Disease Drug Service Branch of the Centers for Disease Control in Atlanta, Georgia. An alternative first-line treatment is amphotericin. It is administered in 14 doses on alternate days in a dose of 0.5 mg/kg, infused in 5% dextrose over 6–8 hours. With amphotericin there is quicker abatement of fever and more complete spleen regression without serious adverse effects. Another, but somewhat less effective, drug against leishmaniasis is pentamidine. It is given as 20 intramuscular injections of 4 mg/kg, administered on alternate days. For further information about drug treatment and the serological diagnosis of leishmaniasis, physicians should contact the **Parasitic Disease Drug Service of the CDC** at 404-488-4050, 404-488-4414, or 404-639-3670.

2. Cutaneous leishmaniasis (Old World variety)—This infection is characterized by nodular and ulcerative skin lesions caused by one of several species of Leishmania. Local names for this disease include Oriental sore, Baghdad boil, Delhi boil, and Biskra button.

Risk areas include the Mediterranean Basin, the Middle East, Africa (stretching from Senegal to Sudan, Ethiopia, and Kenya), southern Russia, central Asia, and northwestern India.

Symptoms: As the name implies, cutaneous leishmaniasis affects the skin. A variety of lesions can occur. Watch for self-healing skin nodules or ulcers, chronic mutilating or nonhealing sores or ulcers, or nonulcerating, warty skin nodules.

The skin sites involved are those areas usually not covered by protective clothing, that is, the face, forearms, back of hands, and legs. The number of lesions is proportional to the number of infective sand fly bites that you sustain. Symptoms usually occur 2–8 weeks after a bite. The lesions may ulcerate and discharge pus, or they may remain dry. Healing tends to occur over a period of several months to two years.

Cutaneous leishmaniasis (New World variety)—Two species complexes of leishmania (*Leishmania mexicana* and *L. braziliensis*) are responsible for most of the cutaneous leishmaniasis occurring in Mexico and in Central and South America. The majority of cases are reported from Brazil and Peru.

Symptoms: Skin nodules and/or ulcers are found on exposed skin areas, usually the face and ear. These lesions appear 2–8 weeks after exposure. Spontaneous healing may take 6 to 18 months, or longer.

3. Mucocutaneous leishmaniasis (espundia)—If parasites spread from the skin to the mucus membranes of the mouth, nose, and throat, a more destructive form of leishmaniasis occurs. This illness is usually preceded by a simple skin ulcer, which may heal. Then one month to several years after the initial exposure, destructive ulcerations of the nose and mouth occur. Severe disease with disfigurement (espundia) results if treatment is delayed.

To diagnose all types of cutaneous leishmaniasis, your doctor needs to obtain tissue samples from your skin for examination under the microscope, or for culture. Blood tests (immunofluorescent antibody, complement fixation, enzyme-linked immunosorbent assay, Western blot) are also helpful. The Parasitic Disease Branch of the Centers for Disease Control can run immuno-diagnostic tests for physicians who submit samples.

The treatment of choice for large or multiple cutaneous lesions is intravenous sodium stibogluconate (Pentostam) in a dose of 20 mg/kg daily for 30–40 days. Recently, treatment of cutaneous leishmaniasis with dapsone, 100 mg twice daily for six weeks, has shown good results. Ketoconazole, 600 mg daily for 28 days, has also been used with success in cutaneous leishmaniasis.

Preventing Leishmaniasis

This illness in its various forms is transmitted by the bite of an infective sand fly, and to prevent leishmaniasis you need to take personal protection measures against insect bites. (You may be doing this anyway to prevent diseases such as malaria or dengue.) Use a deet-containing insect repellent, treat your clothing with permethrin, and, if necessary, sleep under a mosquito net.

Sand flies bite from dusk to dawn so nighttime protection is important. If you are using a mosquito bed net and it has a standard mesh size, be sure it has been sprayed or impregnated with permethrin in order to prevent the tiny sand flies from coming through. (The sand fly is smaller than a mosquito). Mosquito nets with very fine (no-see-um size) mesh (e.g., the SleepScreen and Long Road models) don't require treatment with permethrin, but their tight weave also cuts down on ventilation.

RELAPSING FEVER

This is an acute bacterial infection that can be transmitted to humans by ticks or lice. The cause is a spirochete (*Borrelia recurrentis*). Tick-borne relapsing fever is found in Asia, Africa. Europe, and the Americas, including mountainous areas of the western United States. Louse-borne relapsing fever is found in Asia, Africa, and Europe.

Symptoms include chills, fever, nausea, vomiting, severe headache, and a variety of rashes. Without treatment, the attack terminates in 3–10 days but may recur in a milder form 1–2 weeks later. The most effective treatment is tetracycline, erythromycin, or penicillin.

Prevention of relapsing fever consists of tick- or louse-bite prevention.

RIFT VALLEY FEVER

This is a viral disease of sheep, cattle, monkeys, and rodents and is transmitted to humans by mosquito bites. Rift Valley fever is not contagious and occurs primarily in sub-Saharan Africa. The symptoms are similar to dengue with headache, fever, weakness, nausea, and vomiting. No specific treatment is available, but the illness is usually brief and complete recovery is the rule.

SANDFLY FEVER

Sandfly fever is a viral disease transmitted by the bite of an infective sand fly and occurs in parts of Europe, Asia, Africa, and Latin America. It occurs primarily in tropical and subtropical areas with hot, dry weather. The vector of the causative virus is the common sand fly, which bites at night.

Symptoms appear 3 to 6 days after the sand fly bite and consist of fever, headache, nausea, weakness, and myalgia. These symptoms may be severe but are rarely, if ever, fatal, and treatment with fluids and analgesics is usually sufficient. Prevention of sand fly fever consists of nighttime protection against insect bites.

MEDITERRANEAN SPOTTED FEVER

This tick-borne rickettsial disease is also known as boutonneuse fever in North Africa, African or Kenyan tick typhus in sub-Saharan Africa, and Indian tick typhus in southern Asia. The disease is caused by *Rickettsia conorii* and is transmitted by ixodid ticks, the same tick responsible for spreading Lyme disease. Exposure to the ticks usually results from close contact with tick-carrying dogs or rodents.

Symptoms include chills, fever, headache, and a rash. An ulcer with a black crust may be noted at the site of the tick bite. Treatment with tetracycline or doxycycline is effective.

TICK-BORNE ENCEPHALITIS (TBE)

This viral disease occurs primarily in forested areas of the former Soviet Union, eastern and central Europe, and Scandinavia. It is transmitted by ixodes ticks and is a risk to campers and hikers who visit forested areas, or the fringes of forests, where shrubs and undergrowth can brush against a person's body, allowing contact with infective ticks. Tick-borne encephalitis can also be transmitted by drinking unpasteurized milk. Individuals at high risk can be protected with a vaccine against TBE.

SCRUB TYPHUS

This is a mite-transmitted disease found in Southeast Asia, the western Pacific, and Australia. (Scrub typhus is endemic in a triangular area between northern Japan and southeast Siberia to the north, Queensland, Australia, to the south and Pakistan to the west.) The cause is a rickettsial organism *Rickettsia tsutsuga-*

mushi. The disease is transmitted in scrub lands and forest clearings where mites abound on the vegetation. Humans who come in contact with infected vegetation can be bitten by the larval form of mites, called chiggers. One to three weeks after the mite bite, symptoms occur, and consist of chills, fever, rash, and prostration. A blister, followed by a black scab, occurs at the site of the mite bite.

Treatment of scrub typhus with tetracycline or doxycycline is effective. Prevention consists of using personal protection measures against mite bites. Prophylaxis with 200 mg of doxycycline weekly is effective.

CRIMEAN-CONGO HEMORRHAGIC FEVER

This is a tick-borne viral disease found in eastern Europe, the former Soviet Union, Asia, the Middle East, and all of Africa. Humans may be infected through the bite of an ixodid tick, by handling infected domestic animals, or by person-to-person spread. Symptoms include the rapid onset of severe headache, fever, chills, and muscle and joint pain. In 3 to 5 days bleeding from the gums, nose, and elsewhere can occur. Treatment with ribivirin may be effective. Prevention consists in avoiding tick bites by using personal prevention measures.

HEMORRHAGIC FEVER WITH RENAL SYNDROME

Hemorrhagic fever with renal syndrome refers to a viral disease characterized by fever and renal failure, with or without hemorrhagic manifestations. The causative viruses are known as Hantaviruses. These viruses have a worldwide distribution and are harbored primarily by rodents. Human infection results from inhalation or contact with virus-infected rodent urine, saliva, or feces. Severe disease caused by Hantaan virus occurs in Korea, China, eastern Russia, and in Eastern Europe, including the Balkan countries. A milder form of the disease occurs in Scandinavia and other European countries.

PLAGUE

NOTE: Plague is a disease of extreme poverty. The risk of tourists contracting plague is extremely low.

Plague is caused by infection with the bacterium *Yersinia pestis,* that is carried by rats, other rodents, and their fleas. Cats can also acquire plague and transmit the disease directly to humans. Most cases result from the bites of infected fleas, but can also result from handling infected animals or inhaling infectious airborne droplets from persons with plague pneumonia (pneumonic plague), who may spread the disease by coughing.

The disease occurs rarely and sporadically in the southwest United States, and from 1979 to 1994 it was reported from 22 countries in Africa, Asia, Asia Minor, Europe, and South America. Currently, an epidemic of primarily pneumonic plague is occurring in India, north of Bombay, with some cases also reported in Calcutta and New Delhi.

Symptoms of plague start 2 to 7 days after exposure with rapid onset of fever, chills, headache, generalized aches and pain, and exhaustion. Patients with the bubonic form develop painful swelling of the lymph glands (buboes) in the groin, armpit, or neck; those with the pneumonic form develop cough and difficulty breathing.

Untreated, plague is fatal in 50–60% of cases. Early treatment with antibiotics, however, is effective, especially if started within a few hours of the onset of symptoms. Preferred drugs include streptomycin, chloramphenicol, and intravenous tetracycline.

Prevention: The plague vaccine is not available in the United States and is of unproven effectiveness. Prophylactic antibiotics can prevent plague; they should be taken by certain individuals (e.g., medical personnel, relief workers, etc.) when face-to-face transmission of bacteria has potentially occurred or is anticipated. Adults should take doxycycline or tetracycline; children 9 years of age, or under, sulfonamides.

The most important measure to prevent bubonic plague is to avoid fleas and rodents such as rats, rabbits, squirrels, and chipmunks in endemic areas. These animals are the primary reservoir of plague bacteria. Sick or dead animals should also not be handled. Regular use of flea powders on domestic pets (dogs and cats) having access to both human and rodent habitats is strongly advised in plague-active areas. The application of DEET-containing repellents on exposed skin and permethrin on clothing will reduce the chance of flea bites. People at high risk of exposure to infected fleas should also consider prophylactic antibiotics.

8 Travel-Related Diseases

Giardia
lamblia

GIARDIASIS

Giardia lamblia (shown above), the parasite that causes giardiasis, is found in contaminated water worldwide as a result of fecal contamination from humans or animals (mostly dogs, beavers, and cattle). Giardiasis is also known as backpacker's diarrhea or beaver fever because the parasites are often found in ponds and streams in rural or mountainous areas, posing a risk to campers and hikers. Giardia cysts are very infectious and can easily be spread person-to-person. Homosexuals are particularly prone to pick up this illness through oral-anal contact. The infection can also be spread within households and day care centers through poor personal hygiene, lack of handwashing, and close physical contact.

Giardiasis occurs worldwide, but a high incidence has been reported in travelers returning from Russia. Up to 80% of travelers visiting St. Petersburg have had symptoms and positive stool tests for giardia. Contaminated municipal tap water appears to have been the source of illness. While travelers to Mexico and countries in Asia, Africa, and Latin America may also risk infection, fewer than 3% of travelers returning from these areas have been found to harbor giardia.

Symptoms of Giardiasis

Symptoms can be sudden and severe or occur gradually. Some travelers may have no complaints except one large, loose bowel movement daily. Nausea, fatigue, weight loss, abdominal cramps, foul-smelling stools, nonbloody diarrhea, and excessive gas and abdominal bloating can also occur to varying degrees. Fever is rare. When the illness is chronic, symptoms may last for weeks or months and be passed off as indigestion, simple gastroenteritis, or irritable bowel syndrome. Some cases of chronic fatigue syndrome may be due to giardiasis.

Diagnosis and Treatment

If you have diarrhea lasting more than two to three weeks, you should suspect giardiasis and be tested for the presence of intestinal parasites. Most likely, your doctor will ask you to submit several stool samples to a qualified laboratory for microscopic examination. Detecting giardia parasites can be difficult, however, since organisms are not constantly present in your stool; therefore, if the microscopic examination is negative, more sophisticated methods, such as endoscopy, or a string test, may be required. Recently, an immunoassay screening test has been introduced that simplifies diagnosis. The GiardEIA® test takes only 10 minutes and can be done in a physician's office. It is a fast, accurate, inexpensive alternative to direct microscopic examination. (GiardEIA is available from **Antibodies Incorporated,** Davis, California; 916-758-4400.) If the enzyme immunoassay test is negative, then giardiasis is unlikely and you should consider other parasitic diseases, such as amebiasis. Less common intestinal parasites that can also cause chronic diarrhea include *D. fragilis, Isospora belli,* cryptosporidia, and cyclospora. Some cases of undiagnosed, mysterious, chronic diarrhea may be caused by these parasites.

Treatment

Metronidazole (Flagyl), 500 mg, three times daily for 7 days, is 90% effective. Quinacrine, 100 mg, three times daily is also very effective and has fewer side effects than metronidazole, but quinacrine (Atabrine) is no longer available in the United States. Overseas, the drug tinidazole (Fasigyn) is available and is extremely effective against giardia. Dose: 2 gm daily for 1 to 3 days.

Furazolidone (Furoxone), 100 mg four times daily for 7 to 10 days, is a good alternative for several reasons: (1) it is available in a liquid preparation (useful for children), and (2) the drug is also effective against most bacterial causes of travelers' diarrhea, making furazolidone useful as broad spectrum treatment when the cause of the diarrhea is not known.

If you are in a remote area and testing is not available, start treatment with one of the drugs above on the assumption that giardiasis is the probable cause of your diarrhea. Improvement in your symptoms indicates a likely diagnosis of giardiasis. If no improvement occurs, get medical consultation as soon as possible.

Prevention

There is presently no prophylactic drug or vaccine to prevent giardiasis. Follow the food, drink, and water disinfection guidelines as outlined in Chapter 3. Hand washing and good personal hygiene are important measures.

AMEBIASIS

This potentially serious illness is caused by parasites that invade the wall of the large intestine, causing either acute dysentery or chronic diarrhea of variable severity. The parasites can also infect the liver, causing inflammation and liver abscess. In the carrier state, which is common, parasites live in the intestine without causing symptoms.

Transmission occurs through ingestion of fecally contaminated food or water. Flies can serve as carriers of the amebic cysts. Infected food handlers can spread the disease. Person-to-person contact is important in transmission; household members and sexual partners can easily become infected.

High-risk areas (where up to 50% of the population carry the parasite) are Mexico, South America, India, and West and Southern Africa.

Symptoms of Amebiasis

The symptoms of amebiasis are variable. You may be carrying the parasites and have no symptoms whatsoever. Mild illness causes crampy abdominal pain, little or no fever, and semiformed, fetid-smelling stools. Mucus may be present but usually without blood. Soft stools or diarrhea may alternate with constipation. You may experience fatigue, loss of appetite, and some weight loss. The symptoms at this stage are similar to those of giardiasis.

More severe illness (amebic dysentery) is characterized by fever, bloody diarrhea, generalized abdominal tenderness, vomiting, and much greater toxicity. Illness at this stage represents a medical emergency and requires urgent care.

Travelers who develop an amebic liver abscess usually don't have diarrhea or other intestinal symptoms. Instead, they may note fever, upper abdominal pain, and an enlarged, tender liver. Sweating, chills, weight loss, and fatigue may also be present.

Diagnosis

A stool examination to identify trophozoites or amebic cysts will confirm the diagnosis. Blood serology tests are useful, especially if an amebic liver abscess is suspected. Amebic dysentery must be distinguished from other infections causing bloody diarrhea (e.g., enterocolitis caused by shigella, campylobacter, yersinia, or *Clostridium difficile*). Regional enteritis and ulcerative colitis can mimic amebiasis and must be considered in the younger patient. In older persons, conditions such as diverticulitis can simulate amebiasis.

Treatment

Amebiasis is treated with Flagyl (metronidazole), 750 mg, three times daily for 10 days, followed by iodoquinol, 650 mg, three times daily for 20 days. Treatment eliminates cysts from the stool, thus preventing transmission of the disease to close contacts such as family members.

CHOLERA

This disease is caused by toxin-producing *Vibrio cholerae* bacteria which are transmitted by contaminated food and water. Cholera bacteria can sometimes cause severe, life-threatening diarrhea, but the disease is highly preventable and responds well to treatment with fluids and antibiotics.

Cholera occurs both sporadically and in worldwide epidemics. As of November 1994, 66 countries were officially reporting cases. The most recent epidemic started in Peru in December 1990 and has spread throughout Central and South America. An increasing number of cases are also being reported in Africa, which has long had cholera in many countries.

If you're the average traveler, you don't need to worry too much about this disease, especially if you're on a tourist itinerary. Very few Western travelers ever get seriously ill from cholera. In fact, the disease is officially reported in only 1 in

A new strain of cholera (*V. cholerae* 0139) has recently appeared in Bangladesh and India (Bay of Bengal) and has spread to Thailand and Nepal. This so-called Bengal strain threatens to cause the world's next global cholera epidemic. The current vaccine, prepared against *V. cholerae* 01, is not protective against the Bengal strain.

The Bengal strain of cholera is sensitive to tetracycline, doxycycline, the quinolones, ampicillin, chloramphenicol, and erythromycin, but may be resistant to co-trimoxazole (trimethoprim/sulfamethoxazole) and furazolidone.

500,000 returning travelers. Cholera is basically a disease of poverty, and most illness occurs among people in third world countries who ingest the bacteria from heavily contaminated water or food.

Unlike some germs, cholera bacteria are easily killed by stomach acid. However, if you do ingest a large dose of bacteria from heavily contaminated water— or if you are taking antacids or antiulcer drugs—bacteria can get past the stomach and enter your small intestine. Cholera enterotoxin then act on the intestinal wall to cause an outpouring of water and salt into the gut.

Symptoms of Cholera
In healthy tourists the illness is usually mild because (1) they rarely eat or drink enough heavily contaminated food or water necessary to trigger severe disease, and/or (2) their immune system limits infection.

The clinical picture of cholera varies widely. Seventy-five percent of infections are mild or without any symptoms. Only 2%–5% of infections cause severe symptoms.

Cholera in its most severe form is characterized by massive watery diarrhea, vomiting, and muscle cramps. Vomiting is common and may be severe. The frequent, watery stools soon lose all fecal appearance ("rice water stools") and practically all odor. Loss of fluids and electrolytes can cause vascular collapse and death in hours if fluid replacement treatment is not provided.

Milder cases of cholera can mimic travelers' diarrhea caused by *E. coli*, shigella, salmonella, intestinal viruses, and parasites. The lack of blood, mucus, or pus in the stools is a distinguishing feature of cholera.

Treatment
Cholera kills solely by dehydration. If you develop severe watery diarrhea, you should start immediate rehydration treatment.

Fluids—Drinking an oral rehydration solution (ORS) is essential and its prompt use has saved many lives. ORS prepared from packets of WHO rehydration salts (or its equivalent) is the best fluid to use for immediate treatment (see

Chapter 4). After rehydration with ORS you should drink 8 to 12 ounces, or more, of full-strength rehydration solution after every loose stool. If your diarrhea is very profuse and exceeds what you can drink, or if you are vomiting and can't retain fluids, you will need to be hospitalized and be treated with intravenous fluids.

NOTE: Don't underestimate fluid requirements—some patients with severe watery diarrhea require 10–12 liters of fluid replacement daily.

Antibiotics—Antibiotics will shorten the duration of illness and are an important adjunct to fluid therapy. The best antibiotic for treating cholera is either tetracycline or doxycycline but the quinolones are also effective. Other antibiotics used for treating cholera include co-trimoxazole (trimethoprim/sulfamethoxazole), erythromycin, and furazolidone (Furoxone). However, cholera serogroup 0139 (the Bengal strain) is reported to be resistant to co-trimoxazole and furazolidone.

Prevention of Cholera

Food and drink precautions—The best prevention against cholera is to pay careful attention to what you eat and drink (Chapter 3). It is particularly important to (1) avoid raw or undercooked food and seafood, and (2) drink only bottled, boiled, filtered, or chemically disinfected water, without ice. Cold seafood salad (called ceviche in Latin America) may be particularly risky.

Vaccination—The cholera vaccine is about 50% effective against the cholera 01 strain; it is ineffective against the Bengal strain (*Vibrio cholerae* 01). The World Health Organization does not recommend vaccination because the vaccine, besides not being very effective, does not halt the spread of epidemics. Some individual travelers, however, may benefit from vaccination. These include (1) people taking anti-ulcer drugs, such as Zantac or Tagamet, which decrease protective levels of cholera-killing gastric acid, and (2) people on long-term assignment in areas of poor sanitation where there is increased exposure to heavily contaminated food and water.

A third indication for vaccination is to satisfy the entry requirements of certain countries. Because the health administrations of some countries continue to demand proof of cholera vaccination (despite WHO recommendations), some travelers without proof of vaccination may be refused entry or given the option of on-the-spot vaccination, often with needles and syringes of dubious sterility. The price to the traveler may be infection with HIV or hepatitis B virus.

Therefore, check your itinerary carefully. If you will be traveling to, or passing through, a country where cholera is active, vaccination may be advisable.

TYPHOID FEVER

Typhoid fever (sometimes called enteric fever) is a serious, sometimes life-threatening disease caused by one particular species of salmonella bacteria (*Salmonella typhi*) and is contracted by the consumption of contaminated food or water, or by contact with an infected person. Although typhoid fever is found in all countries in the developing world where there is substandard sanitation, the highest disease rates are reported from Peru, Chile, Nigeria, India, Pakistan, and Indonesia.

Symptoms and Diagnosis

The early symptoms of typhoid fever are flu-like and consist of chills and fever, headache, weakness, loss of appetite, abdominal pain, and body aches (myalgia). A rash, with pink spots measuring 2–4 mm, may appear on the chest and abdomen. There is a 50% occurrence of diarrhea, which is sometimes bloody, but constipation also occurs. In fact, if your doctor considers diarrhea a prerequisite for the diagnosis of this disease, the diagnosis may be missed.

The best test for diagnosing typhoid fever is a culture of a bone marrow aspirate (80%–95% positive), or a blood culture combined with a stool culture (40%–80% positive).

Treatment

Untreated, typhoid fever lasts 2–6 weeks and has a mortality as high as 30%. Antibiotics used for treating typhoid fever include ampicillin, trimethoprim/sulfamethoxazole, chloramphenicol, ceftriaxone (Rocephin), and the quinolones. Chloramphenicol-resistant strains are reported from Mexico, Southeast Asia, and India. The best choice for a traveler with suspected typhoid is a quinolone. Travelers should start self-treatment either with Cipro or Floxin and seek medical consultation. Even after antibiotic treatment, however, it is possible to harbor typhoid bacteria in your intestinal tract. These bacteria can be passed to close contacts such as family members. Therefore, be sure to tell your doctor if you were treated for this illness while traveling. A follow-up stool culture is needed to see if you are a carrier and require additional treatment.

Severe typhoid fever should be treated with intravenous chloramphenicol, ceftriaxone, or a quinolone. The addition of high-dose dexamethasone (given as 3 mg/kg IV initial dose followed by 8 doses of 1 mg/kg every 6 hours) markedly improves the prognosis in patients with the symptoms of delirium, stupor, coma, or shock.

Prevention

Salmonella typhi bacteria are transmitted by human carriers of the organisms, and in all countries with substandard sanitation, there is risk of typhoid transmission. Pay close attention to dietary safety. Especially avoid raw vegetables and salads because these items are often grown in contaminated irrigation water. All food should be well cooked. You should drink only bottled, boiled, or treated water, or commercial beverages. Flavored ices sold by street vendors are especially risky.

Vaccination—Several vaccines are available which provide up to 70% protection. The older injectable vaccine (prepared from heat-inactivated bacterial components) should be avoided due to a high incidence of side effects (fever, pain at injection site). The oral typhoid vaccine, which is preferred, is prepared from an attenuated strain (Ty21A) of live *S. typhi* bacteria and has few side effects. The problem with the oral vaccine, however, is that it is complicated to administer. It must be kept refrigerated at all times and is administered in four doses given as one capsule every other day. These requirements decrease effectiveness due to improper handling and compliance. A new, one-dose injectable vaccine (Typhim Vi) is soon to be marketed and should replace the oral vaccine due to its simplicity of administration.

Typhoid vaccine is routinely recommended for travelers going to high-risk areas, but how good is it? Manufacturers claim about 70% effectiveness, but travelers from developed countries can still acquire typhoid if exposed to a dose of salmonella bacteria heavy enough to overwhelm their vaccine-conferred immunity. This means that your main defense against typhoid must still be dietary discretion. Don't rely entirely on vaccination for protection!

SALMONELLA ENTEROCOLITIS (SALMONELLOSIS)

Other species of salmonella bacteria (*Salmonella enteritidis, Salmonella cholerae-suis,*) can cause an intestinal illness termed enterocolitis. Typical symptoms include nausea, vomiting, crampy abdominal pain, and diarrhea. Occasionally, salmonella bacteria break out into the bloodstream and cause a severe, life-threatening illness termed salmonella bacteremia. Symptoms of bacteremia include chills, high fever, and prostration. Fatalities from bacteremia occur most often in infants, the elderly, the chronically ill, and those with immune deficiencies. In cases of bacteremia, *Salmonella typhimurium* is the most common salmonella serotype isolated from blood.

Unlike *Salmonella typhi* bacteria, which are harbored only by humans, the other salmonella species are primarily harbored by a variety of animals. Animal reservoirs include poultry (especially chickens), turkeys, ducks, livestock (pigs, horses, sheep), dogs, cats, rodents, and reptiles (snakes, lizards, turtles).

Infection is transmitted by direct contact with the flesh of an infected animal (e.g., during butchering or food preparation) or by the consumption of undercooked, contaminated food. Undercooked chicken eggs and unpasteurized dairy products are also common sources of illness. Poultry products account for over half the cases of salmonellosis. Pork, beef, and lamb are implicated in 13% of salmonellosis epidemics.

Prevention and Treatment

The typhoid fever vaccine is not effective against the bacteria that cause salmonella enterocolitis. Prevention of salmonellosis is entirely dependent upon eating well-cooked food.

Salmonella enterocolitis responds to fluid replacement and a 3- to 5-day course of a quinolone antibiotic. Salmonella bacteremia requires intravenous antibiotic treatment with a quinolone, ceftriaxone, or chloramphenicol.

SHIGELLOSIS (BACILLARY DYSENTERY)

The most common type of bacterial dysentery is called shigellosis, after the shigella bacteria that cause it. Shigellosis accounts for 10% to 40% of diarrhea worldwide. Very small numbers of bacteria are needed to transmit this disease. You can easily pick up the infection from contaminated food or from person-to-person contact with people who may be carriers of the bacteria. In the United States, unsanitary conditions in day care centers, with person-to-person spread of germs, cause most outbreaks. Overseas, contaminated food and water are responsible for most cases of shigellosis occurring in travelers. Flies can also carry and transmit shigella.

Diagnosis

Although a stool culture is needed for exact diagnosis, shigellosis can be suspected on the basis of your symptoms. In the classic case, you would develop voluminous watery diarrhea, usually with fever and abdominal cramps, followed by the passage of many small-volume stools containing blood and mucus. Other bacteria that can cause similar symptoms include campylobacter, salmonella, *Vibrio parahemolyticus*, yersinia, and enteroinvasive *E. coli*, but since these microorganisms, like shigella, can all be treated with a quinolone antibiotic, it is not necessary to know the exact bacterial diagnosis before starting treatment.

Treatment

As with diarrhea from any cause, you should drink extra fluids to prevent dehydration. Shigellosis responds best to treatment with a quinolone antibiotic (Cipro or Floxin) because bacterial resistance to doxycycline, tetracycline, and trimethoprim/sulfamethoxazole has increased worldwide. If your initial symptoms are severe with high fever and dehydration, hospitalization is imperative. One species of shigella (*S. dysenteriae*) is more resistant to antibiotics and 10 days of quinolone treatment is usually required.

MENINGOCOCCAL MENINGITIS

This illness is caused by bacteria (*Neisseria meningitidis*) that infect the membranes lining the brain and spinal cord. Untreated, meningococcal meningitis is almost always fatal.

Meningococcal meningitis is primarily a disease of children and adolescents. Military recruits are also particularly susceptible. Most adults have developed some immunity to meningococcal bacteria. Nevertheless, serious outbreaks of meningitis can occur; for example, in Sao Paulo, Brazil, in 1974, an urban epidemic of meningococcal meningitis resulted in 13,000 cases. Recent outbreaks of meningitis have been reported in the following areas: Nepal, Kenya and northern Tanzania, the Delhi region of India, and Saudi Arabia (Mecca). You should be vaccinated if planning travel to these countries or

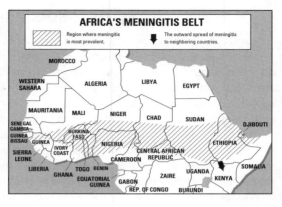

regions. You should also be vaccination if planning extended travel to the "meningitis belt" of Africa, shown in the map.

The neisseria bacteria are normally carried harmlessly in the nasal passages of a small percentage of healthy people, resulting in only sporadic cases of the disease. The bacteria are spread person-to-person by coughing and sneezing. Crowded living conditions will increase the number of carriers and the incidence of meningitis.

Symptoms

Fever, vomiting, headache, and confusion or lethargy are the most common symptoms. The illness may begin abruptly or develop over several days.

Treatment

Immediate treatment is usually lifesaving and requires large intravenous doses of penicillin, chloramphenicol, or ceftriaxone (Rocephin). Treatment should be started even though an early diagnosis may not be possible.

Prevention

The meningococcal meningitis vaccine is usually given to Peace Corps volunteers, missionaries, teachers, and others planning to live in close contact with the indigenous population of a third world country (especially in sub-Saharan Africa) for a prolonged period of time (more than 4 weeks).

The meningococcal vaccine has a clinical efficacy of 85% to 95% for at least three years, with protection being achieved one to two weeks following vaccination.

If you will be traveling or living in a meningitis risk area, also get a flu shot before you depart. Medical researchers say that having influenza makes it easier for meningococci bacteria to gain entrance to the body by way of nasal tissues inflamed by the influenza virus.

SCHISTOSOMIASIS

Schistosomiasis (blood fluke disease) is a parasitic disease caused by schistosomes, or blood flukes. The disease affects over 200 million people in 75 countries. The disease is endemic in Africa (most countries), South America (Brazil, Venezuela, Suriname), and parts of the Middle East and Asia (see map). In the Caribbean, schistosomiasis has been reported to occur sporadically in Puerto Rico, Antigua, Dominica, Guadeloupe, Martinique, Montserrat, and Saint Lucia.

The three most common schistosome species are *Schistosoma mansoni* (the cause of intestinal schistosomiasis), *Schistosoma hematobium* (the cause of urinary schistosomiasis), and *Schistosoma japonicum* (Far Eastern schistosomiasis). A fourth species, *Schistosoma mekongi*, found in Southeast Asia, is less common. Infection takes place when schistosome cercariae (larvae), shed into fresh water by snail intermediate hosts, penetrate the skin of an individual exposed to contaminated water. Exposure usually occurs during washing, bathing, or swimming in ponds, lakes, streams, or irrigation ditches in endemic areas. After skin penetration, there follows a four- to six-week incubation period during which time the young schistosome worms migrate to the liver and to the veins draining the intestine and the bladder. The fully grown worms live in the veins of the urinary bladder or the wall of the intestine where they produce large numbers of eggs that cause inflammation and progressive tissue damage. The adult worms can persist for decades, producing various, often puzzling, symptoms.

Symptoms

Light infections from a brief immersion in contaminated water may be completely asymptomatic. If you are exposed, you should towel off vigorously and wash your skin with rubbing alcohol. This may prevent penetration of the cercariae.

Dermatitis—When schistosome cercariae penetrate the skin, there may be brief tingling and a slight rash. Corticosteroid creams and antihistamines can help control symptoms.

Schistosomiasis Facts

- Always assume that bodies of fresh water in endemic areas are contaminated by schistosomes. Even deep water, far offshore, may be infective. Salt and brackish water, however, are safe.
- Water sports are risky because of the degree of exposure.
- A history of exposure to contaminated water is one of the most important elements in the diagnosis of schistosomiasis. The FAST-ELISA assay should be done when stool or urine tests are negative for eggs.
- High-risk areas for schistosomiasis include the Nile River, Lake Victoria, the Tigris and Euphrates rivers, Lake Malawi, Lake Kariba in Zimbabwe, and Lake Volta in Ghana.

Acute schistosomiasis (Katayama fever)—Four to six weeks after a heavy exposure, you may develop additional symptoms. Migrating worms can cause an acute illness called Katayama fever. Symptoms include fever, headache, cough, a rash (urticaria), fatigue, abdominal pain, tender enlargement of the liver and spleen, weight loss, and muscle aches. These symptoms are thought to represent an allergic hypersensitivity reaction to the invading parasites. Katayama fever can be confused with malaria or typhoid fever but a blood count will show eosinophilia, suggesting the correct diagnosis.

NOTE: Not all persons will develop Katayama fever during the acute infection; sometimes just a feeling of fatigue or ill health occurs.

Dysentery—Eggs deposited by the migrating worms can work their way through the bowel wall, causing crampy abdominal pain and bloody diarrhea. Schistosomiasis, therefore, should always be considered when a traveler develops dysentery.

Central nervous system (CNS) schistosomiasis—Migrating eggs or adult worms can invade the central nervous system and CNS symptoms are sometimes the initial complaint. Symptoms of cerebral schistosomiasis include headaches, visual loss, and seizures. Symptoms of spinal cord schistosomiasis include urinary incontinence, leg pain, and difficulty walking.

Chronic schistosomiasis—Heavy infections (rarely seen in travelers) can last for years and can damage the liver, bladder, and/or nervous system. *S. mansoni*, *S. japonicum*, and *S. mekongi* parasites primarily affect the biliary tract and liver; chronic infections can lead to enlargement of the liver and spleen, followed by cirrhosis of the liver and gastrointestinal bleeding from esophageal varices. *S. hematobium* primarily affects the genitourinary tract; chronic infections can lead to persistent cystitis, pyelonephritis, obstructive renal disease, and an increased incidence of bladder cancer.

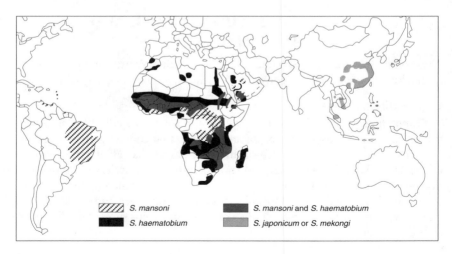

▨ *S. mansoni*	▰ *S. mansoni* and *S. haematobium*
▰ *S. haematobium*	▨ *S. japonicum* or *S. mekongi*

Diagnosis, Treatment, and Prevention

One of the most important elements in diagnosing schistosomiasis is obtaining a history of freshwater exposure in an endemic area. A white blood cell count will usually show eosinophilia, but this finding is not specific for schistosomiasis. The most reliable diagnostic test is an examination of stool and urine for schistosome eggs. In some cases, a bowel or bladder biopsy will demonstrate eggs; schistosome eggs, however, do not appear for at least 40 days following the initial exposure. In suspected early schistosomiasis, a highly accurate serology test using the Falcon assay screening test–enzyme-linked immunosorbent assay (FAST-ELISA) may be diagnostic. Contact the CDC's **Parasitic Disease Branch (404-488-4050)** for information about the FAST-ELISA assay.

Neuroschistosomiasis causes variable neurological symptoms. The blood eosinophil count can be normal, and the stool and urine egg examination can be negative. Diagnosis is made with the FAST-ELISA assay combined with an MRI examination of the central nervous system.

Treatment—For *S. mansoni* and *S. hematobium*, the drug praziquantil (Biltricide) is curative in a single dose of 40 mg per kg body weight. For the treatment of *S. japonicum* and *S. mekongi*, praziquantel, 60 mg/kg, is given in three divided doses six hours apart. Dexamethasone, a corticosteroid, is a useful adjunct in the treatment of acute neuroschistosomiasis.

Prevention—There is no vaccine; therefore, avoiding contact with contaminated water is the most important preventive measure. Do not swim in fresh water unless a reliable source assures you that it is safe. (Chlorinated swimming pools and sea water are safe.) Water for bathing is considered safe if it has been heated to above 50°C (122°F) for more than five minutes, if it has stood more than 48 hours in a tub or container, or if it has been chemically treated (e.g., chlorinated) like drinking water.

LIVER FLUKES, LUNG FLUKES, AND INTESTINAL FLUKES

These other flukes, unlike the blood flukes (which cause schistosomiasis), are acquired by eating raw or undercooked fish, shellfish, or raw water vegetables.

Liver Fluke Diseases

Clonorchiasis—Infection with *Clonorchis sinensis* occurs after the consumption of raw, undercooked, pickled, or smoked fish that contain parasites (metacercariae). Clonorchiasis is common in Laos, Cambodia, Thailand, southern China, Hong Kong, Korea, Japan, and far eastern Russia. Travelers can avoid this disease by eating only well-cooked fish. Symptoms relate to inflammation and obstruction of the bile ducts and include abdominal pain, fever, and jaundice. It is treated with praziquantel, 75 mg/kg in 3 divided doses, plus surgery if biliary obstruction occurs.

Opisthorchiasis—This disease is caused by Opisthorchis species of flukes. Symptoms are similar to clonorchiasis.

Fascioliasis—Infection with *Fasciola hepatica* parasites is acquired by ingesting parasitic cysts attached to aquatic plants, usually watercress. Human infection is quite widespread, occurring in Europe, Latin America, Africa, and China.

Lung Fluke Disease

Paragonimiasis—Humans develop paragonimiasis after consuming raw, salted, or wine-soaked crustacea (freshwater crabs, crayfish, and shrimp). The species *Paragonimus westermani* is prevalent in parts of China, Korea, Japan, the Philippines, and Taiwan. Other paragonimus species infect humans in West Africa and Central and South America. Travelers can avoid lung fluke disease by not eating raw or undercooked shellfish. Symptoms include coughing up blood and chest pain. It is treated with praziquantel, 75 mg/kg in 3 divided doses on 2 consecutive days.

Intestinal Fluke Disease

Fasciolopsiasis—Giant intestinal fluke disease is common in the Far East and is acquired through the ingestion of parasitic cysts attached to aquatic plants such as water chestnuts, which have been contaminated by sewage from mammals (pigs, humans). The causative parasite is *Fasciolopsis buski*. Symptoms of heavy infections include abdominal pain, chronic diarrhea, loss of appetite, and weight loss. Treatment is with praziquantel.

OTHER HELMINTHIC (WORM) INFECTIONS

Intestinal Roundworm Diseases

Whipworm disease (trichuriasis)—*Trichuris trichuria* is one of the most prevalent helminths in the world. The adult worms can live for many years in the intestinal tract, producing thousands of eggs that are passed in the stool. Heavy infections can cause abdominal pain and chronic diarrhea. Treatment with mebendazole, 100 mg twice a day for 3 days, is recommended. Travelers can prevent infection by eating only cooked food and rinsing vegetables in hot water (65°C or above) or an iodine solution.

Intestinal capillariasis—This is a serious infection that occurs in the Philippines, Thailand, and occasionally in other countries in SE Asia. The infection is acquired by the ingestion of raw freshwater fish that harbor infective worm larvae. The parasitic worms, *Capillaria philippinensis*, invade the small intestine and can cause chronic diarrhea, malnutrition, and wasting.

The diagnosis of capillariasis is made by finding characteristic eggs in the stool or by examining tissue obtained from a biopsy of the small intestine. An blood serolgy (ELISA) test is available in certain research laboratories. Eosinophilia occurs but is a nonspecific finding. Treatment with mebendazole, 200 mg twice daily for 20 days, is curative. Albendazole is also effective. Avoiding raw fish prevents this infection.

Ascariasis—This is the most common helminth infection in the world. The cause of ascariasis is the roundworm *Ascaris lumbricoides*, which lives in the intestine and produces eggs that are passed in human feces. When these eggs are ingested through fecally contaminated food or water, they enter the intestinal tract and hatch into larvae that penetrate the gut wall, are carried to the lung, coughed up, and swallowed. The larvae develop into adult worms and start producing eggs, starting the cycle over again.

Symptoms of ascariasis are produced by migration of larvae through lung tissue and also by their presence in the intestinal tract. Symptoms include cough, fever, chest pain, and eosinophilic inflammation of lung tissue. Intestinal symptoms from heavy infection include nausea, loss of appetite, diarrhea, and malabsorption. Intestinal perforation, bile duct obstruction, appendicitis, and pancreatitis can be caused by migrating worms.

Treatment is with Albendazole given as a single 400 mg dose. It cures 100% of infections but is not licensed in the United States. Mebendazole, 100 mg twice daily for 3 days, is also effective.

Hookworm disease (ancylostomiasis)—This disease is picked up by walking barefoot in areas where there is fecally contaminated soil harboring hookworm larvae. The larvae enter the body by penetrating the skin of the foot, pass through the lungs, and end up in the intestine, where they develop into adult worms. Symptoms of hookworm disease include coughing and wheezing, abdominal pain, diarrhea (sometimes bloody), and weakness from anemia. Treatment is with mebendazole, 100 mg twice daily for 3 days.

Strongyloidiasis—Like hookworm, strongyloides larvae also enter the body through skin penetration, pass through the lungs, and enter the intestine. Classical symptoms include urticaria, abdominal pain, and diarrhea. Treatment is with thiabendazole, 25 mg/kg twice daily for 3 days.

Anisakiasis—This is a parasitic disease transmitted by eating raw, undercooked, or lightly pickled saltwater fish, especially salmon, herring, mackerel, whitefish, cod, pollock, bonito, and sole. The parasite is the larval form of a marine roundworm belonging to the family Anisikadae. These larvae may be present in the muscles and organs of the fish mentioned above. Symptoms include nausea and vomiting, or abdominal pain that mimics appendicitis. The treatment is surgical excision of the worm from the intestinal tract.

Intestinal Tapeworm Diseases

Diphyllobothriasis (fish tapeworm disease)—This is a disease caused by a fish tapeworm called *Diphyllobothrium latum* and occurs among people who eat raw, smoked, pickled, or undercooked fish. These include Eskimos, fishermen, and devotees of sushi bars. Symptoms include crampy abdominal pain and diarrhea. Treatment (adults) is with a single 2-gm dose of niclosamide.

Beef tapeworm disease—This is a disease acquired through eating raw or undercooked beef and is caused by the beef tapeworm *Taenia saginata*. People with this infection may notice a segment or longer "tape" of the worm passed in their stool during a bowel movement. Symptoms may include nausea and crampy abdominal pain, but macrocytic anemia due to vitamin B_{12} deficiency can also occur because tapeworms in the human intestine can consume this essential vitamin.

Pork tapeworm disease—This infection is caused by pork tapeworm *Taenia solium* and is acquired through eating undercooked pork that contains the encysted larvae of the tapeworms. This is a potentially more serious infection than beef tapeworm disease because pork tapeworms can cause another disease called cysticercosis. **Cysticercosis** occurs when a person ingests pork tapeworm eggs, usually by eating contaminated food. The eggs hatch within the intestine and develop into larvae that penetrate the intestinal wall and invade various organs and tissues of the body. The most serious illness that results, **neurocysticercosis**, occurs when tapeworm larvae invade the brain and form cysts, causing seizures and other neurological symptoms. Cysticercosis is common in Mexico, Central and South America, Africa, India, China, Eastern Europe, and Indonesia.

Both praziquantel and albendazole are effective drugs, but the latter is preferred for the treatment of subarachnoid cysts. Corticosteroids should be prescribed as adjunctive treatment.

Trichinosis—This disease (also called trichinellosis) occurs worldwide, except in Australia, and is most often acquired when people eat raw or undercooked pork containing the larval cysts of the parasite *Trichinella spiralis*. Trichinosis, however, can also be transmitted by the ingestion of undercooked meat of other carnivorous animals and wild game such as black bear, polar bear, walrus, wild boar, bush pigs, and wart hogs.

During the first week after ingestion, the larvae in the intestine develop into adult worms, causing abdominal pain, diarrhea, nausea, vomiting, and prostration. Next, there is tissue invasion by newly produced larvae, bringing fever, headache, swelling of the eyelids and face, conjunctivitis, muscle pain, weakness, and an urticarial rash. Symptoms caused by larval invasion of the heart and central nervous system include cardiac arrhythmias and seizures.

Treatment with Prednisone (60 mg/day) is used in acute trichinosis to reduce inflammation and alleviate symptoms. Mebendazole (200 mg/day for 4 days) is used to remove adult worms from the intestine, and then is administered at a dose of 5 mg/kg/day until a satisfactory response is obtained.

Adequate cooking, freezing, smoking, or pickling of pork will prevent this disease.

BRUCELLOSIS

This is a bacterial disease contracted through (1) the consumption of contaminated dairy products, particularly unpasteurized soft cheeses and milk, or (2) by exposure to the flesh of infected animals, particularly that of cattle, hogs, or goats. In this regard, farmers, herdsmen, veterinarians, and slaughterhouse workers are at particular risk.

The highest incidence of brucellosis occurs in Middle Eastern countries such as Saudi Arabia, Kuwait, and Lebanon, but the incidence is also high in Central and South America, sub-Saharan Africa, India, Greece, France, and Spain.

Brucellosis should be suspected in travelers who have visited these areas and then develop a prolonged illness with fever.

The Brucella bacteria may incubate in the body for a month or more before causing symptoms and the diagnosis, initially, may not be suspected. The most common symptoms include fever, chills, sweating, muscle and joint aches, abdominal pain, weakness, weight loss, and headache. The physical examination often demonstrates enlargement of the spleen and liver and swelling of the lymph nodes. Other infectious diseases to be considered in the diagnosis include typhoid fever, malaria, leishmaniasis, and tuberculosis.

Early diagnosis of brucellosis hinges upon suspecting the illness and in this regard knowing the travel history is very important. A positive serology test (febrile agglutination titer over 1/160) and positive blood or bone marrow cultures will confirm the diagnosis.

Brucellosis is a difficult disease to treat because the bacteria often persist inside white blood cells despite antibiotic treatment. Treatment with two antibiotics for at least six weeks is therefore required. Doxycycline, 100 mg twice daily, is usually given for 45 days, while a second agent (e.g., rifampin) is given in conjunction for at least several weeks. The quinolones and co-trimoxazole are also effective.

Brucellosis can be prevented by the destruction of infected dairy animals, immunization of susceptible animals, and pasteurization of milk and milk products. Travelers should avoid consuming unpasteurized milk and other dairy products in risk countries.

9 Lyme Disease
and other tick-borne illnesses

Lyme disease is a potentially serious illness that occurs worldwide. The disease was first recognized in the United States in 1975, following an investigation of a group of children with arthritis in Lyme, Connecticut. Lyme disease is now the most common tick-transmitted illness in the United States.

The most serious aspect of Lyme disease is not knowing you have it. Early signs and symptoms may not be noticed or may be misdiagnosed. Untreated illness can cause serious problems.

Where Lyme Disease Commonly Occurs

United States—Lyme disease occurs over wide areas of the United States (see map), but is most frequently found in the Northeast, the Mid-Atlantic states, the upper Midwest (Minnesota, Wisconsin), and the Pacific Coast. Ninety percent of all known cases have occurred in nine states: California, Connecticut, Massachusetts, Minnesota, New Jersey, New York, Pennsylvania, Rhode Island, and Wisconsin. Alaska and Hawaii are low-risk areas.

Overseas—Most cases overseas are reported from Europe (especially Germany's Black Forest region, southern Sweden, eastern Austria, and the northern Swiss plateau), the former Soviet Union (from the Baltics to the Pacific), China, Japan, and Australia. Only South America and Antarctica are allegedly free of the disease. In Africa, cases have recently been reported from Nigeria, Angola, Kenya, Tanzania, and Zambia.

Variation of risk—In any region where Lyme disease occurs, the risk will not be evenly spread. For a particular area within an endemic region to support Lyme disease, there must be the right ecological mix of woods, deer, rodents (e.g., white-footed mice), and, of course, enough Ixodes ticks. You can be in one area where every house has a backyard with infective ticks, and five miles away there might be none.

The Cause

Lyme disease is caused by a screw-shaped bacterium known as a spirochete and is transmitted by the bite of various species of Ixodes ticks—*Ixodes dammini* in the East and Midwest, *Ixodes scapularis* in the Southeast, *Ixodes pacificus* in the Pacific Coast and Northwest, *Ixodes ricinus* in Europe, and *Ixodes persulcatus* in Asia. The spirochete (scientific name: *Borrelia burgdorferi*) can infect many animals (called hosts), but the preferred host in much of the United States is the white-footed mouse and the white-tailed deer. People become infected when larval ticks feed on the host animal, become infected, and then, following a period of further growth, feed on humans. This rather complex cycle is illustrated in Figure 9.1

During the two-year life cycle of the tick, the tiny larvae develop into nymphs, and then into adults. Ixodes ticks are very small and hence difficult to notice (Figure 9.2). The ticks feed most actively from spring until late summer—the time of greatest risk. The nymphs are your chief threat because they are the most active feeders, and their small size makes casual detection very difficult.

How Humans Get Infected

Ticks like to live in grassy or wooded areas, but can also be found in your backyard. They are not found on sand dunes, where there is no grass. Ticks don't fly, jump up from the ground, or drop from trees. Instead, they climb to the tips of vegetation and wait for you to brush by. Since the deer ticks are so small, and their bite is painless, you will probably be unaware when a tick attaches itself to your clothing or skin.

Lyme disease from pets—Dogs and cats can get Lyme disease but there is no evidence that your pet can transmit the disease to you. Ticks carried into your house by a pet won't drop off and then attach to you.

People at risk—People most at risk are those engaged in outdoor activities—campers, hikers, hunters, fishermen, farmers, backyard gardeners, telephone line-workers, foresters, and military personnel on training maneuvers.

Figure 9.1 Life Cycle of Ixodes Tick[1]

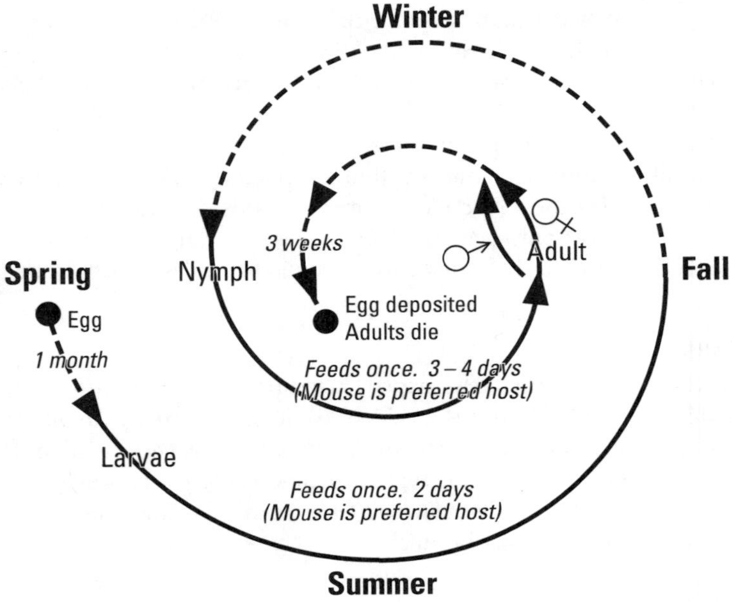

Are All Ticks a Threat?

Not every tick carries the Lyme disease spirochete. On the West Coast, only 1% to 3% of *Ixodes pacificus* ticks (western black-legged ticks) are infected, so Lyme disease occurs only sporadically. In some areas of the Northeast, however, more than 50% of *Ixodes dammini* ticks (deer ticks) are infected. Community attack rates as high as 35% have been reported in some coastal areas of Massachusetts.

Other Ticks and Other Tick-borne Diseases

Two major families of ticks transmit disease: *Ixodidae* (hard ticks) and *Argasidae* (soft ticks). Most tick-borne illnesses, however (except for relapsing fever and some cases of tick paralysis), are transmitted by various species of Ixodes (hard) ticks.

In the USA—Lyme disease is not the only illness in the United States transmitted by ticks. Ixodes ticks can also transmit babesiosis, a disease similar to malaria. The cause of babesiosis is a parasite, *Babesia microti*. Babesiosis occurs primarily in the northeastern coastal United States, particularly the islands off the southern New England coast (including Nantucket, Martha's Vineyard, Block Island, Shelter Island, and Long Island), as well as mainland southeastern Connecticut. Infections have been reported from as far south as Maryland and Virginia, as well as the Midwest and the West Coast.

Diagnosis of babesiosis is through direct observation under the microscope of parasites (trophozoites or merozoites) in red blood cells. Treatment of babesiosis is with quinine and clindamycin.

The American dog tick, the Lone Star tick, the Rocky Mountain wood tick, and other hard ticks sometimes carry the Lyme spirochete, but they are not effective transmitters of Lyme disease. These ticks, however, can transmit serious diseases such as Rocky Mountain spotted fever, tularemia, Colorado tick fever, erlichiosis, tick-borne viral encephalitis, and tick paralysis. Soft ticks, especially *Ornithodoros,* transmit relapsing fever.

Overseas—Serious diseases transmitted by Ixodes and other ticks (soft ticks) include Central European tick-borne viral encephalitis, Far Eastern tick-borne viral encephalitis, Crimean-Congo hemorrhagic fever, Omsk hemorrhagic fever, relapsing fever, North Asian tick typhus, Queensland tick typhus, and Mediterranean spotted fever (also known variously as Mediterranean tick typhus, boutonneuse fever, African tick typhus, Kenya tick typhus, South African tick bite fever or India tick typhus).

Protective Measures

Much advice is given about how to prevent Lyme disease, but is it practical? For example, wearing protective clothing from head to toe can certainly prevent tick bites, but how many people will actually do this during hot weather? And inspect-

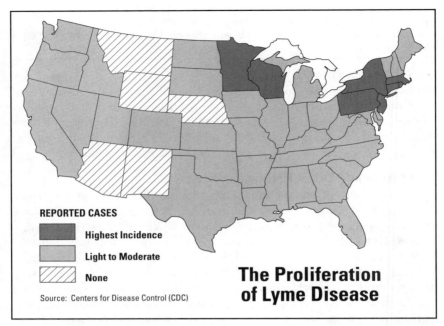

REPORTED CASES

	Highest Incidence
	Light to Moderate
	None

Source: Centers for Disease Control (CDC)

The Proliferation of Lyme Disease

ing your entire body for ticks sounds like a sensible thing to do, but most people won't bother. And how can a single person do a complete inspection?

The best way to prevent tick bites is to combine appropriate clothing with "chemical warfare." Use an insect repellent on your exposed skin and treat your clothing with the insecticide permethrin (see Chapter 6). These measures, when properly applied, are extremely effective, as well as being easy to implement.

Tick Removal

All ticks should be promptly removed. The correct technique is important. Don't squeeze or crush the tick because disease organisms can be transmitted.

Some anecdotal methods for making a tick detach may not be successful. Applying substances such as petroleum jelly, fingernail polish, or rubbing alcohol usually will not cause the tick to back out. You could burn yourself trying to touch a hot match to the tick, and this technique frightens children. The best method involves using tweezers to exert upward traction on the tick. Here's the technique:

1. Use tweezers, curved forceps, or a small alligator clamp to grasp the tick. If you use your fingers, cover the tick with plastic wrap, tissue or toilet paper, or paper toweling.
2. Grasp the tick with the instrument as close to the skin as possible.
3. Pull upward with a steady, even pressure, trying not to squeeze, crush, or puncture the tick. Don't try to twist or jerk it out.

4. After removing the tick, wipe off the attachment site with disinfectant (such as alcohol or Betadine). Wash your hands with soap and water.
5. If the tick won't release with the above technique, apply a small amount of permethrin spray to the tick. Wait ten minutes and try the removal technique again.
6. Dispose of the tick carefully to avoid contamination. Flush it down the toilet, or cover the tick with disinfectant and bundle it in tissue paper before throwing it away. You may also consider showing the tick to a physician for examination. If so, save the tick in a bottle with moist paper.

After removing the tick, observe the bite area for any sign of a rash. The typical Lyme disease rash, if it's going to occur, appears from 3 to 30 days after the bite. If you get a rash immediately, or within 24 hours after being bitten, it is not a Lyme disease rash—it is an allergic (hypersensitivity) reaction to the bite. (These allergic rashes are usually itchy.)

Wood ticks, dog ticks, and Lone Star ticks should also be removed in the same manner as described above.

Symptoms of Lyme Disease

Because you may not have noticed the tick bite and because the symptoms of Lyme disease are sometimes passed off as "the flu," illness can be overlooked or misdiagnosed. Ten to 20% of infected people may not even develop early symptoms. Up to 40% of victims may not develop the typical rash.

Stage I (days to weeks)—A spreading, circular, pink or red rash (erythema migrans) is the hallmark of early Lyme disease. This rash, which originates at the site of the tick bite, is caused by organisms (spirochetes) migrating in an expanding fashion from the central point of inoculation. The rash can become quite large—5 to 10 inches, or more, in diameter. The appearance of the rash is somewhat variable. In some cases it is halo-shaped with an almost clear central area surrounded by a pink or red outer ring (bull's-eye rash). Other rashes have a deep red center with secondary rings and a red outer border. The red areas may be slightly raised and warm to the touch.

With the rash, you may also develop flu-like symptoms: low-grade fever, headache, muscle and joint aches, swollen glands, fatigue, nausea, and loss of appetite. Absence of respiratory symptoms (e.g., cough, runny nose) helps distinguish Lyme "flu" from that caused by a cold virus. There's a 15% – 20% chance you won't have the characteristic rash. This makes early diagnosis more difficult. Antibiotic treatment shortens Stage I illness and prevents progression to Stage II.

Stage II (weeks to months)—If Stage I goes untreated, the spirochetes become entrenched in tissues throughout the body. Symptoms of Stage II Lyme disease include multiple skin rashes, more severe headache, arthritis (usually affecting only one knee), increased pains in the muscles, bones, joints, and tendons. Signs of meningitis or encephalitis (headache with stiff neck, irritability, poor memory), or facial or other nerve paralysis may occur. Cardiac problems include heart block, myopericarditis, and left ventricular dysfunction.

In Europe, there is a higher incidence of facial nerve palsy and encephalitis, and less arthritis than experienced by people with the United States version. Some victims of European Lyme disease also suffer a darkening and tightening of the skin of their hands, symptoms rarely seen in the United States.

Stage III (months to years)—If untreated, you can develop prolonged arthritis attacks in one or multiple joints, chronic fatigue, polyneuritis, paralysis, encephalopathy (symptoms include mental changes and memory lapses), and a variety of rashes with inflammation and thinning of the skin. Mental symptoms may include forgetting names, misplacing objects, or missing appointments. There may be problems speaking and trouble finding words. Neuritis symptoms include backache with shooting pains and lack of feeling in the hands and feet.

Diagnosis of Lyme Disease

Early diagnosis is important because prompt treatment will prevent complications. The early diagnosis of Lyme disease should be based on a history of possible exposure and on the presence of tell-tale symptoms. If you live in, or have visited an area where the disease is endemic, and then develop the typical erythema migrans rash, you should consider the diagnosis established. Don't rely on a blood test to verify the diagnosis because serological testing has poor sensitivity in early Lyme disease. The current tests are unreliable during the first two to three weeks after exposure.

Laboratory tests—Testing for Lyme disease usually begins with a test called an enzyme-linked immunosorbent assay (ELISA). After several weeks of infection, the ELISA will detect elevated serum levels of antibodies in people who have—or previously had—Lyme disease. If the ELISA is negative several weeks after exposure, Lyme disease can usually be excluded. Problems with serological tests include the following:

1. Serological assays are not standardized nationwide. Results often vary from laboratory to laboratory.
2. A positive test may indicate previous exposure—not acute disease.
3. False-positive tests can be caused by diseases such as syphilis, rheumatoid arthritis, lupus, and others.
4. Inadequate early antibiotic treatment can interfere with test accuracy in Stage II and Stage III disease.
5. False negative tests occur, but are rare. If necessary, a Western blot test can be done to clarify the diagnosis.

Treatment of Lyme Disease

If the diagnosis seems clear cut on the basis of your exposure and symptoms, you should receive immediate antibiotic treatment. Don't let your doctor withhold treatment just to see if your blood test will turn positive.

On the other hand, if your symptoms are not typical, you should defer treatment and have a serological assay done in two weeks time. If the test is negative, treatment is not necessary.

Lyme Disease Fact

Tests for Lyme disease are not accurate or helpful in early disease. Therefore, prompt, aggressive antibiotic treatment can be started solely on the basis of clinical findings.

Treating Lyme disease anxiety—Some people, of course, are so convinced about possibly having Lyme disease that their anxiety level alone sometimes requires treatment. In situations where there is perhaps some minimal chance of disease, plus extreme anxiety, oral therapy may not be unreasonable.

All stages of Lyme disease should be treated, but early treatment is the most effective and will usually prevent complications. Oral antibiotics can be used to treat early (Stage I) Lyme disease, but intravenous antibiotics should generally be used to treat most cardiac and neurological symptoms. Lyme arthritis may respond to 30 days of oral antibiotics.

Early Lyme disease with typical erythema migrans rash and/or "flu" symptoms should be treated with doxycycline, 100 mg twice daily for 10 to 30 days, or amoxicillin, 500 mg three times daily for 10 to 30 days.

Some authors favor treating erythema migrans with higher drug doses, using doxycycline, 100 mg three times daily for 21 to 30 days, or amoxicillin, 1 gm three times daily for 21 to 30 days.

Alternative treatment drugs include azithromycin (Zithromax), 500 mg daily for 10 days, or cefuroxime (Ceftin), 500 mg twice daily for 21 to 30 days.

Amoxicillin is the drug of choice for pregnant women and children under eight years of age. Pregnant women who are allergic to penicillin should receive erythromycin base, 250 mg–500 mg, four times daily for 10 to 30 days.

Lyme arthritis should be treated with doxycycline, 100 mg twice daily, for 30 days, or amoxicillin, 500 mg–1 gm three times daily for 30 days, or ceftriaxone (Rocephin), 2 gm daily for 14 days to 30 days.

Cardiac and neurological symptoms may also occur. Facial nerve palsy (Bell's palsy) can be treated with high-dose oral doxycycline or amoxicillin according to the following schedule: doxycycline, 100 mg three times daily for 21 to 30 days, or amoxicillin, 1 gm three times daily for 21 to 30 days.

First-degree heart block (PR-interval less than 0.3 seconds) can also be treated with doxycycline or amoxicillin with the higher doses used for Bell's palsy. All other neurological or cardiac complications should be treated intravenously with ceftriaxone (Rocephin), 2 gm daily for 14–30 days, or aqueous penicillin G, 20 million units daily for 14 to 30 days.

A 2-week course of ceftriaxone improves symptoms of polyneuritis and encephalopathy; however, one out of three patients will relapse after six months because either the treatment has not killed all spirochetes, or permanent nervous system damage has already occurred.

Should You Take Antibiotics After a Tick Bite?

Finding a tick attached to you doesn't automatically mean you will get Lyme disease because (1) the tick may not be infective, or (2) the tick may not have been attached long enough to transmit spirochetes. (Transmission of *Borrelia burgdorferi* spirochetes is estimated to take at least 18–24 hours.) Nevertheless, a deer tick bite signifies potential risk, especially in areas with a high incidence of Lyme disease. This is especially true if the tick has had time to become engorged with blood.

In geographic areas where a high percentage of ticks are known to be infective, a case can sometimes be made for taking prophylactic antibiotics after a bite. You should consider the following:

- Are you sure you were bitten by a tick?
- Can you identify the tick? Is it the Ixodes type?
- Was the tick engorged with blood? This increases the risk of transmission.
- How prevalent is Lyme disease in the area?
- Do you have drug allergies?
- What degree of anxiety do you have about possible illness?

These factors play a role in the decision whether to take prophylactic antibiotics. There's no question that it is advantageous to treat Lyme disease at the earliest possible time, before the spirochete has spread. Once the spirochete has become entrenched in body tissues, treatment becomes more difficult. Secondly, your level of anxiety about the disease cannot be ignored. If your anxiety level is high, then you probably should be treated. Finally, if you are a female and are pregnant, and you discover a blood-engorged tick, you certainly should be treated.

Note:

1. Adapted from *What You Should Know About Lyme Disease.* Copyright 1989, S.C. Johnson & Son, Inc.

General References:

1. Steere, AC. Lyme disease. *N Engl J Med.* Aug. 31, 1989: 586–596.
2. Johnson, RA. Lyme Borreliosis: A New Great Imitator. Current Challenges in Dermatology. Spring 1989. Copyright 1989, The Upjohn Co.

10   Hepatitis

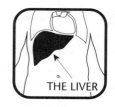

THE LIVER

Four Distinct Types

Hepatitis is an inflammation of the liver caused by one of several viruses. There are four types of hepatitis of which all travelers should be particularly aware: Types A, B, C, and E.* The means of transmission and long-term effects vary, depending upon which virus causes the disease.

Type A and type E hepatitis are transmitted primarily by contaminated food and water. High-risk areas are lesser-developed countries where poor sanitation results in fecal contamination of groundwater, tap water, and well water. Outbreaks of hepatitis A are also caused by food that has been contaminated by an infective foodhandler.

Type B and type C hepatitis are spread mainly through sexual contact (exchange of body fluids), unscreened blood transfusions, and contaminated needles and syringes.

Symptoms of Hepatitis

Your symptoms can be variable. Some cases of hepatitis, in fact, go completely unnoticed. In a textbook case, however, you would develop fatigue, loss of appetite, jaundice, dark urine, fever, abdominal pain, and aching joints.

Symptoms of hepatitis occur weeks to months after exposure and typically last from two to six weeks. Complete recovery occurs in virtually all cases of types A and E hepatitis, but 10% to 50% of types B and C may progress, causing chronic, sometimes fatal, liver disease.

Hepatitis A

This is the most common type of hepatitis worldwide. The virus is usually transmitted by food and water in areas where there is poor sanitation. Contaminated shellfish, harvested from polluted water, are often responsible for outbreaks. A less common means of transmission is through sexual contact. There seems to be little risk from heterosexual vaginal intercourse, but male homosexuals have a high incidence of the disease. Hepatitis A, in fact, is the most common form of hepatitis in homosexual males vaccinated against hepatitis B.

---

*A fifth virus, hepatitis D, is of little concern to the average traveler. It can occur only in people who are already carriers of the hepatitis B virus and is transmitted primarily through intravenous drug use or sexual contact with a carrier. Overseas, most hepatitis D is found in southern Italy, parts of North Africa adjacent to the Mediterranean, and the upper reaches of the Amazon Basin.

Risk to travelers—The risk of a nonimmunized traveler acquiring hepatitis A is estimated at 3–6 cases per 1,000 persons per month of stay in a developing country. For adventure travelers and rural travelers, the risk increases six-fold.

Symptoms of Hepatitis A

Symptoms usually appear 2–6 weeks after exposure. Most adults have textbook symptoms with jaundice, whereas young children often have mild, often asymptomatic, disease. The fatality rate of hepatitis A is less than 0.5%.

Treatment of Hepatitis A

If you do come down with hepatitis A, supportive care is all that is necessary. There is no specific treatment that will shorten your illness. Eat a nutritious diet and avoid alcohol. Limiting exercise has no effect on your rate of recovery. Hospitalization is rarely necessary. By the time symptoms appear, the virus is no longer in your stool or blood, and you are no longer infectious, so quarantine or isolation procedures are not really necessary. Nonimmune close contacts such as family members or companions should receive immune globulin.

Prevention of Hepatitis A

Hepatitis A vaccine—There is now a vaccine that provides active immunity against hepatitis A. Havrix (manufactured by Smith Klein Beecham) is presently available in Europe. Two doses are given 2–4 weeks apart, followed by a booster dose 6 months later. Two doses provide immunity for at least one year and the booster extends protection for 10 years. An American-made vaccine should soon be available in the United States. A single dose is reported to be highly protective. Both vaccines can be administered concomitantly with immune globulin.

Hepatitis A vaccination is recommended for (1) frequent travelers who want to avoid getting an injection of immune globulin prior to each trip to a risk area, and (2) persons planning extended travel or residence abroad, especially in a lesser-developed country.

NOTE: If you are over the age of 40, the chances are statistically higher that you may be naturally immune to hepatitis A. You might consider an antibody screening test prior to immunization to see if you really need to be vaccinated.

Immune globulin (IG)—You can get short-term protection against hepatitis A with an injection of immune globulin. The standard dose (usually 2 ml in an adult) contains enough hepatitis A antibodies to protect you for about 2 months. If you'll be overseas longer, have your doctor administer a 5 ml dose. This will protect you for about four months, possibly five. If you are on extended travel to high-risk countries, you will need regular booster shots of IG to maintain immunity against hepatitis A.

NOTE: HIV antibodies (but not the virus) may be present in pooled immune globulin, and the possibility for transient HIV seroconversion exists following administration of IG. Physicians and other caregivers should take this into account if an individual without HIV risk factors tests HIV positive.

Safe food and drink—Follow these rules to reduce your risk of hepatitis A:

1. Drink only boiled, bottled, carbonated, or chemically treated water, soft drinks, fruit juices, beer, or wine.
2. Avoid ice and ice cubes in your drinks.
3. Eat only well-cooked foods. Avoid raw or undercooked meat, fish and shell-fish, and raw fruits and vegetables, unless you peel them yourself. Stick to piping hot foods, if possible.
4. Avoid salads.

Hepatitis B

This is the most important type of hepatitis because of its potential severity and widespread occurrence worldwide. Although the hepatitis B virus is not as lethal as the AIDS virus, it is more infectious and is more easily spread by person-to-person contact.

Symptoms of Hepatitis B

In unvaccinated people, hepatitis B occurs from 40 to 180 days after exposure, with an average of 75 days. The most common response to the virus is asymptomatic infection, so you may not even be aware of the illness. (Your chance of developing jaundice during the infection is less than 50%.) Whether you are symptomatic or not, your illness may last for several weeks, or even months, but if you are an adult you have a 90% to 95% chance of recovering completely and having lifelong immunity against any further attacks. Hepatitis B, though, differs in an important respect from hepatitis A: there is a 0.1% to 1% risk of death with the acute infection and an overall fatality rate of 1%–3%. Five percent, or less, of infected adults (but up to 90% of infected newborns) become chronic carriers of the virus. If you do become a carrier of the virus, you can infect others, and you are also at risk for the development of chronic hepatitis, cirrhosis, and liver cancer. Therefore, you should take every precaution to protect yourself against this virus.

High-Risk Countries and Exposure to the Virus

Areas where up to 5% to 20% of the population are carriers of the hepatitis B virus include all of sub-Saharan Africa, the Balkans, the Middle East, China, Southeast Asia, including Korea and Indonesia, the South Pacific Islands (Oceania), the interior Amazon Basin, and Haiti and the Dominican Republic.

Travelers to these areas are at increased risk if they are exposed to the blood or body fluids of infected people. Sexual contact appears to be the most frequent cause of disease transmission, especially among expatriates staying long-term in a risk area. Virus transmission also occurs from intravenous drug use, medical injections or vaccinations with contaminated needles and/or syringes, receipt of unscreened blood transfusions, or skin-to-skin contact with carriers of the virus who have open sores due to tropical ulcers, impetigo, scabies, or infected insect bites. Fluid from these open sores can transmit the virus, and children especially may be at risk from playmates who have these open skin sores.

Prevention of Hepatitis B

Your risk of getting hepatitis B can be reduced or eliminated by practicing safe sex (or practicing abstinence), avoiding injectable drugs or fluids, and being vaccinated. Both active and passive immunization will protect you against hepatitis B. The vaccines available in the United States are Recombivax-HB and Engerix-B, both of which are genetically engineered vaccines derived from yeast. These vaccines are completely safe and virtually 100% effective after three doses have been administered.

Vaccination—If departing on short notice, consider Engerix-B. The three primary doses of vaccine can be given on an accelerated schedule over a two-month period. There is an optional booster at 12 months. Recombivax-HB vaccine is administered over a 6-month period.

Vaccination should be considered for the following groups: all persons, including children, living for prolonged periods (more than 3 months) in those high-risk areas listed above; health care workers; people who contemplate close contact, or sexual contact with the local populace; and drug users.

Prevention after exposure—If you are exposed to hepatitis B and have not been vaccinated, you should receive hepatitis B immune globulin (HBIG), as well as the vaccine. This should be done within 24–48 hours if you were exposed to blood. If you were sexually exposed, you should receive HBIG plus the vaccine within 14 days of sexual contact. If you have regular sex with a carrier of the virus, you should also be vaccinated. For simultaneous administration of HBIG and the hepatitis B vaccine, your doctor should use separate injection sites.

Hepatitis C

This disease was formerly called non-A, non-B hepatitis. Twenty to 40% of all hepatitis is caused by the hepatitis C virus. You can get the disease from the following:

- Intravenous drug use (40% of cases)
- Sexual contact (10%)
- Blood transfusion (5% to 10%)
- Work-related exposure (5%)
- Unidentified sources. In 35% to 40% of hepatitis C cases, there is no association with any identifiable risk factors such as transfusions, drugs, or multiple sex partners.

Like hepatitis B, hepatitis C is sometimes fatal in the early stages. If you recover from the immediate illness, you have about a 50% chance of continuing to carry the virus in your blood. This persistent viral infection, chronic hepatitis C, causes liver damage (cirrhosis) in about 20% of those infected, and it may also cause liver cancer.

Prevention of Hepatitis C

Hepatitis C, like HIV (the AIDS virus) and hepatitis B, can be transmitted by unsafe sex and intravenous drug use; therefore, avoid these practices. There is no vaccine to prevent hepatitis C, but large doses (5 to 10 cc, or more) of immune globulin may possibly give some protection following exposure to an accidental stab from a contaminated needle.

Historically, the hepatitis C virus caused most cases of hepatitis that followed blood transfusions. In 1990, testing of the blood supply for this virus became available in the United States. Many lesser-developed countries, however, lack the resources to screen blood completely, so travelers who require an emergency blood transfusion overseas may still be at risk of hepatitis C.

Blood transfusions abroad—Avoid blood transfusions in lesser-developed countries, or donate your own blood two weeks in advance if you are having elective surgery that may require a blood transfusion. If you're living abroad, find out if your spouse or healthy friends or colleagues in your expatriate community would be suitable donors in case of emergency surgery.

Since hepatitis C screening is now available in most developed countries, your only other prudent option, if you are having *elective* surgery requiring a possible blood transfusion, and if the test is not locally available, is to be treated in a country where hepatitis C blood screening is done.

Treatment of Hepatitis B and C

With either type of hepatitis, supportive treatment is indicated. Your diet can be unrestricted, except for alcohol; bed rest does more harm than good. About 10% of hepatitis B cases and 50% of hepatitis C cases become chronic. You should have serial blood tests to check your liver function to document recovery—or to see if you have become a carrier and predisposed to develop a progressive form of liver disease. If you develop chronic hepatitis B or C, the drug alpha interferon may be helpful. About one third of treated patients have had remission of their disease. The drug is now available commercially as Intron A from Schering-Plough Corporation.

Treatment of acute hepatitis C—Recently, Japanese researchers (*Lancet*, Oct. 12, 1991) treated acute hepatitis C with beta interferon and prevented progression of the disease to its chronic form. Discuss this experimental treatment with your physician if you are diagnosed with this illness.

Liver transplantation—Patients who have fulminate, life-threatening hepatitis, or whose hepatitis causes progressive, irreversible liver disease, may need liver transplantation. Improvements in antirejection drugs have made transplants increasingly successful.

Hepatitis E

The hepatitis E virus is usually transmitted by sewage-contaminated water. Transmission often increases following heavy rains where there is inadequate sewage disposal; surface water and wells then become contaminated. The virus can also be transmitted directly from person-to-person, through close contact. Like hepatitis A (and unlike hepatitis B and C), hepatitis E does not cause chronic liver disease, but occasional fatalities occur in pregnant women.

Hepatitis E occurs primarily in Asia, especially in Nepal, northern India, and Pakistan. The highest incidence occurs in Pakistan. More recently, there have been reports of hepatitis E from Africa, and outbreaks have also occurred in Mexico (south of Mexico City and near Tijuana).

The majority of patients will recover from hepatitis E without any problems whatsoever. The exception is pregnant women. For uncertain reasons, hepatitis E during pregnancy is more serious, with a mortality rate of about 20%.

Prevention of Hepatitis E

A vaccine is not currently available. If you are in a rural area with poor sanitation, drink only bottled, boiled, or chemically treated water. This advice is most important for pregnant women. Filtering may not remove the virus unless your filter has an iodine resin matrix incorporated into the unit. Especially avoid untreated well water or surface water in high-risk areas such as Algeria, Burma, the Indian subcontinent, Africa, the former Soviet Union, and rural Mexico. Immune globulin administered in the United States is probably not protective against hepatitis E since the product given in this country is not made from donors carrying sufficient antibodies to this virus.

11 AIDS & Sexually Transmitted Diseases

Travelers' Concerns about AIDS

More travelers are asking, "Is it safe to travel? What about the risk of AIDS?" These questions are understandable. There is an AIDS epidemic, and in many parts of the world, it's growing rapidly. Over one million cases of AIDS have now been reported. The World Health Organization estimates that the 1990s will bring 10 to 20 million new cases of infection with HIV (human immunodeficiency virus) and a tenfold or more increase in the cases of AIDS. These estimates could be low because (1) AIDS is often underreported, and (2) AIDS is starting to spread rapidly in Southeast Asia, West Africa, Latin America, and parts of Europe.

Sexual contact is the major route of spreading HIV worldwide. *This means that prevention of AIDS is largely under your control.* Don't be complacent. You need to know as much as possible about the HIV virus that causes AIDS and how it is and is not spread.

Knowing the causes and prevention of AIDS is no different than knowing about any other infectious disease; there are guidelines to protect you. This chapter will give you those specific guidelines. Don't let exaggerated or distorted information keep you at home.

What Is AIDS?

The Centers for Disease Control has issued the following advisory:

Acquired Immunodeficiency Syndrome (AIDS) is a consequence of infection by the human immunodeficiency virus (HIV). Other less severe illnesses, sometimes grouped under the term AIDS-related complex (ARC), as well as asymptomatic infection may also result from infection with HIV. The incubation period for AIDS may be long, ranging from a few months to several years. Some individuals infected with HIV remain asymptomatic for 5–10 years—sometimes longer. Currently, there is no vaccine to protect against infection with HIV, and there is no cure for AIDS.

AIDS has been reported from more than 130 nations, but adequate surveillance systems are lacking in many countries. Because HIV and AIDS are globally distributed, the risk to international travelers is determined less by their geographic destination than by their individual behavior.

HIV infection is preventable. There is no documented evidence of HIV transmission through casual contacts; air, food, or water routes; contact with inanimate objects; or through mosquitoes or other arthropod (insect) vectors. HIV is transmitted through sexual intercourse, blood or blood components, and perinatally (at birth) from an infected mother.

Travelers are at increased risk if they: have sexual intercourse (homosexual or heterosexual) with an infected person; use or allow the use of contaminated, unsterilized syringes or needles for any injections, e.g., illicit drugs, tattooing, acupuncture, or medical/dental procedures; or use infected blood, blood components, or clotting factor concentrates. This would be an extremely rare occurrence in those countries or cities where donated blood/plasma is screened for HIV antibody.

Travelers should avoid sexual encounters with all persons who are thought to be infected with HIV or whose HIV infection status is unknown. This will mean avoiding sexual activity with intravenous drug users and persons with multiple sexual partners, including male or female prostitutes. Condoms may reduce, but not entirely eliminate, transmission of HIV. Persons who engage in vaginal, anal, or oral-genital intercourse with anyone who is infected with HIV or whose infection status is unknown should use condoms.

In many countries, needle sharing by IV drug users is a major source of HIV transmission. Do not use drugs intravenously or share needles.

In the United States, Australia, Canada, Japan, and western European countries, the risk of infection of transfusion-associated HIV infection is greatly reduced through mandatory testing of all donated blood for the presence of antibodies to HIV.

If produced in the United States by manufacturers approved by the Food and Drug Administration, immune globulin preparations (such as those used to prevent hepatitis A and B) and hepatitis B virus vaccine are free of HIV and therefore are safe to use.

In other countries, especially lesser-developed nations, there may not be a formal program for testing blood or biological products for antibody to HIV. In these countries, use of locally-produced blood clotting factor concentrates should be avoided. If transfusion is necessary, the blood should be tested, if at all possible, for HIV antibodies by appropriately-trained technicians using a reliable test. All needles used to draw blood or administer injections should be sterile, preferably of the disposable type, and pre-packaged in a sealed, single-unit container. Diabetics or other persons who require frequent or routine injections, especially if they are traveling to sub-Saharan Africa, should carry a supply of syringes and needles sufficient to last their entire stay abroad.

Travel has contributed in a general way to the global spread of HIV, but fear of traveling because of AIDS is rarely justified. If you follow the guidelines in this chapter, your chance of contracting the virus is extremely remote, if not impossible. You may have heard stories of travelers getting AIDS from emergency transfusions of unsafe blood, but these situations are rare; "emergency injections" that might cause AIDS are almost never required.

AN OVERVIEW OF AIDS WORLDWIDE

AIDS in the USA, Canada, Europe, Australia, N. Zealand

In these countries, AIDS is still largely a disease of homosexual and bisexual males and urban intravenous drug users, infecting 11 males for every female. Because of greater awareness about AIDS, new cases among homosexuals, except for gay teenagers, are declining.

Only about 5% of AIDS is spread through heterosexual intercourse, but these cases are increasing, especially among the female sexual partners of intravenous drug users. More inner-city teenagers and homeless youths are also becoming infected. In the United States, the increase in syphilis in inner cities is also contributing to the spread of heterosexual AIDS. The syphilitic sores promote the transmission of the AIDS virus.

The risk of AIDS from blood transfusions is very low in the developed countries, where blood banks routinely screen for the HIV antibody.

AIDS in the Middle East, E. Europe, and Former Russian Republics

Only small numbers of cases are reported in the Middle East, usually among persons who have brought the disease back from infected areas. Recently, many more cases of AIDS have been reported from the former Soviet Union and Romania. Transmission of AIDS in these countries is primarily through HIV-contaminated blood and the use of unclean needles and syringes. Except for Romania, Eastern Europe is relatively AIDS-free.

AIDS in Africa

In sub-Saharan Africa, AIDS has become a devastating problem. In the "AIDS-belt" countries of central and east Africa (see the map below), the infection has broken out into the general population and is spread primarily by heterosexual intercourse, not homosexuality or IV drug use. Men and women are infected almost equally by the virus. Over 5% of the general population in most of these countries is infected with HIV. In the urban areas of AIDS-belt countries, however, up to 30% or more of sexually active people carry HIV; prostitutes in some cities are 90% infected.

In West Africa, another strain of the AIDS virus, HIV-2, is prevalent and causes a disease similar to AIDS.

Factors Causing the Epidemic

- Multiple sexual partners—There is widespread, culturally tolerated promiscuity in many sub-Saharan countries.
- Contact with prostitutes—This is a common social practice in the AIDS-belt countries. Many, if not most, prostitutes are infected with the AIDS virus.
- Widespread venereal diseases—These greatly enhance the spread of the virus. Diseases such as syphilis and chancroid cause open sores on the genitals, and

these sores allow easier transmission of the virus between partners. Gonorrhea also facilitates HIV transmission.

- Public health factors— Social resistance to the use of condoms, lack of education, and rudimentary public health programs against AIDS and venereal disease also stymie efforts to control the epidemic.
- Unclean needles and syringes—These are widely used for medical injections, and they help spread the disease. Few countries can afford sterile, disposable supplies for safe injections.
- Blood transfusions—The transmission of AIDS from contaminated blood and blood products is a serious problem in sub-Saharan Africa. Some countries don't screen blood for the AIDS virus. Unless your need is critical, don't receive any transfusions unless you know HIV-antibody screening has been done. Also check for screening against the hepatitis B and C viruses.
- Other factors—The degree of tourism, travel, and trade between various countries also affects the spread of the virus. For example, Nigeria, which at present has little AIDS, is an English-speaking country surrounded by four French-speaking countries. The language barrier, relative lack of tourism, and its distance from the AIDS-belt have limited the country's contact with HIV-positive

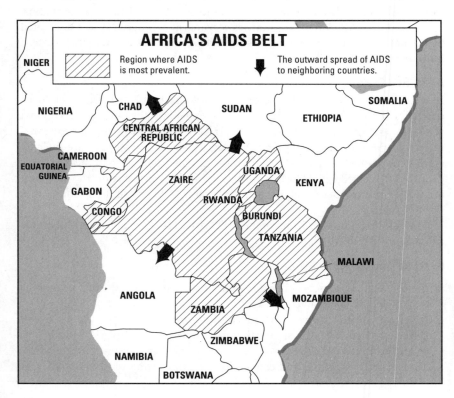

AFRICA'S AIDS BELT

Region where AIDS is most prevalent.

The outward spread of AIDS to neighboring countries.

NIGER
NIGERIA
CHAD
SUDAN
SOMALIA
CENTRAL AFRICAN REPUBLIC
ETHIOPIA
CAMEROON
EQUATORIAL GUINEA
ZAIRE
UGANDA
KENYA
GABON
RWANDA
CONGO
BURUNDI
TANZANIA
MALAWI
ANGOLA
MOZAMBIQUE
ZAMBIA
ZIMBABWE
NAMIBIA
BOTSWANA

outsiders. (Nigeria also has a lower incidence of venereal disease, and this factor also contributes to a lower AIDS rate.)

AIDS in Latin America and the Caribbean

AIDS is now spreading rapidly in Latin America, the Bahamas, and the Caribbean. The reason: AIDS is spilling over to women from infected bisexuals and intravenous drug abusers. The average ratio of infected men to women is 2.4:1—approaching the 1:1 ratio found in Africa.

AIDS in India, China, SE Asia, Japan, and the Pacific

The AIDS epidemic in India is rapidly expanding. Thirty percent, or more, of the prostitute population is infected. Poverty, prostitution, sexually transmitted diseases (which help spread AIDS), and the absence of circumcision in the Hindu population could herald a major AIDS epidemic in India in the near future. There is another focus of AIDS in India in IV drug users in Manipur, which borders the heroin-producing "Golden Triangle" of Asia. The epidemic in Manipur has spread into Myanmar (Burma), northern Thailand, and into China. No AIDS cases were reported in China until 1988, when an outbreak was reported among the tribesmen of the Yunnan Province in the western part of the country, bordering the "Golden Triangle." Sexually transmitted AIDS, however, is not expected to pose a major problem in China in the near future.

In Thailand rates of infection among drug users has increased from 1% to 43% between 1987 and 1988. Up to 70% of rural prostitutes in Thailand are now infected, and spillover into the heterosexual population is occurring rapidly, causing a serious public health problem.

In the Philippines, Indonesia, Malaysia, Sri Lanka, Taiwan, and Korea, the HIV rate among prostitutes still remains very low, although spread into the heterosexual population is a threat wherever commercial sex is widespread. At the present, the incidence of AIDS in Japan and Oceania also is very low.

CONTRACTING AND PREVENTING AIDS

Heterosexual Risk of Contracting AIDS

Surveys show that people continue to practice unsafe sex. Gallup poll results (*USA Today*, November 2, 1989) show that 20% of young, single women have had three or more sex partners during the past five years without using condoms, possibly placing them at "high risk" for AIDS. Twelve percent have had two partners without using condoms, placing them at "medium risk." The poll also concludes that "smart, rich women are fooling themselves into believing that AIDS is not an issue for them."

The *Travel Medicine Advisor* (March 1991) reports that sex tours remain popular with European travelers and that long-term travelers and overseas workers are very likely to engage in sexual contact involving some degree of risk. They also report that after six months abroad, 70% of men and 45% of women that were interviewed had high-risk sexual contact. Studies also revealed very low condom use among men over age 40 (only 27% used condoms) and women of all ages who were sexually active (zero percent used condoms).

Can You Quantify Your Risk?

Drs. Norman Hearst and Stephen Hulley, writing in the *Journal of the American Medical Association* (*JAMA*, April 22, 1988), have attempted to define the statistical chances of becoming HIV positive after sex with various partners.[1] Your risk of getting HIV, they say, depends primarily upon your partner's probability of being infected—and also whether you use a condom.

Their *JAMA* article confirms that your chance of contracting AIDS from a single act of intercourse can vary enormously. Their conclusion: *Choosing a "low-risk partner" is the most important strategy.*

Risk Category #1

If your partner is HIV positive, they estimate your chance of picking up the AIDS virus from one-time intercourse at 1 in 500. Receptive anal intercourse and the presence of genital ulcers and venereal warts will increase your risk *tenfold*, or more. Avoid sex with individuals from the groups below; they are more apt to be HIV positive.

- Homosexual or bisexual men
- Drug addicts
- Prostitutes—higher risk in sub-Saharan Africa, Latin America, the Bahamas, Haiti, and the Caribbean
- Residents of Central and East Africa
- Hemophiliacs—Hemophiliacs are often infected from having received contaminated blood products. One study (*AMA* News, April 14, 1989) also found that hemophiliac teenagers are not practicing safe sex, despite their awareness of the importance of abstinence and the use of condoms.
- Recipients of multiple blood transfusions—Blood before 1985 was not screened for the AIDS virus. Blood transfusions after 1985 in the USA, Europe, Japan, and other industrialized countries have generally been considered safe from HIV.
- People with venereal disease—You naturally don't want to pick up VD but you should avoid these individuals for another reason: they may have had many sex partners and thus are more likely to carry the AIDS virus. If they have active venereal disease, they can more easily transmit the AIDS virus to you. Likewise, if you have a venereal disease such as herpes, syphilis, chancroid, gonorrhea, or genital warts you are more susceptible to getting AIDS from an HIV-infected partner. If you are a woman and have vaginitis, you are more susceptible to HIV transmission.

Risk Category #2

If your partner is known to be HIV negative, the risk of contracting AIDS from such an HIV-negative partner (using a condom) is estimated at 1 in 5 billion. There's still a slight risk since people can be infectious before their test turns positive—and condoms can fail.

Risk Category #3

If your partner is not in a high-risk group (see above), but his/her HIV test status is unknown, your risk is 1 in 5 million for one-time sex (without a condom) with such a low-risk partner.

Can You Really Be Sure?

In theory, choosing a low-risk partner will protect you. But these statistics can also mislead you. It can be a potentially fatal mistake to assume or hope that your partner is in risk category #3.

Traveling may not give you sufficient time to know enough about the other person. Is he/she really low-risk? How do you know that your prospective partner wasn't unwittingly infected by someone else? Or maybe he or she has used IV drugs or is bisexual and wants to conceal this behavior from you. You certainly can't test your sexual partner for the AIDS virus.

Unfortunately, there are people who continue to have sex and don't tell the truth about their condition or background. They will even lie to you. Your intuitive sense about the safety of the relationship may be misleading. Asking your new-found acquaintance about his or her past sexual habits or drug use may not be enough.

Abstinence

A good case can be made for avoiding sexual contact with casual acquaintances. Indeed, abstinence probably is your safest course of action.

Condoms

You've decided you are going to be sexually active, but you're not sure about your partner's risk category; you think it's low. Then bear this in mind: *AIDS is possible after a single act of unprotected intercourse with an infected partner.* That's why it's imperative to take added precautions. Not many people, unfortunately, follow this advice.

Use of condoms is the best preventive measure short of abstinence. If you are a man, always use a condom; if you are a woman, insist on condom use. For added protection, use a diaphragm and spermicidal jelly (the jelly may inactivate the AIDS virus). Another benefit of condoms and diaphragms is that they help prevent venereal disease, hepatitis, and pregnancy.

NOTE: Women taking oral contraceptives have a lower risk of HIV transmission. Women using IUDs have a higher risk of HIV transmission.

Summary
Aids is not spread through:

- Casual contact at work or school
- Touching or hugging
- Handshaking
- Coughing or sneezing
- Insect or mosquito bites
- Food or water
- Eating utensils, cups, plates
- Toilets
- Swimming pools or baths

You can avoid contracting AIDS if you:

- Abstain from sex
- Have sex only with your spouse or a monogamous, noninfected partner
- Avoid contaminated blood, syringes, and needles

If you are otherwise sexually active, you should:

- Avoid sex with high-risk partners
- Always use a condom
- Avoid anal intercourse

AIDS TESTING AND FOREIGN TRAVEL

In most countries, tourists staying less than one month don't need to show evidence of an AIDS test. But dozens of countries—including the United States—do require an AIDS test for those coming to study, work, stay for long periods, or apply for immigrant status. Under those roles, people testing HIV-positive usually are denied entry, although sometimes a waiver may be issued. Countries that screen immigrants for AIDS include Argentina, China, Costa Rica, Cuba, Hungary, Iraq, Israel, Mongolia, Myanmar (Burma), the Philippines, Russia, South Africa, South Korea, Syria, Thailand, and the United States. Furthermore, several countries have policies of rejecting or expelling all foreigners with AIDS. Among those countries are Indonesia, Malaysia, Sri Lanka, and Thailand.

Sometimes visa forms ask whether a visitor has any infectious or communicable diseases, so if you are HIV positive, be prepared to face this question—and rejection if you answer truthfully. The World Health Organization regards HIV screening as discriminatory and unnecessary from a public health perspective.

For the most current list of HIV testing requirements for foreign travel, send a self-addressed, stamped envelope to the **Bureau of Consular Affairs, CA/PA, Room 5807, Department of State, Washington, DC 20520.** Country requirements are also found in the World Medical Guide section. If you need additional information, telephone that country's consulate in the United States.

Some of the countries requiring testing will accept a test done in the United States. If you need a test, contact the country's nearest consulate to find out which laboratories in the United States can run the test and how the results are authenticated and certified. You want to avoid, if possible, having your blood drawn overseas. Consider carrying sterile, disposable needles and syringes with you if you anticipate overseas testing. If you will be tested overseas, call the U.S. Embassy in the country of your destination to inquire about the safety of a test done locally and if sterile needles are used.

Be aware that a country's announced policy and what actually happens may differ. If you are black, you might be singled out for random testing, especially if you are of African nationality. Also, travelers found carrying an anti-AIDS drug, such as AZT, may be turned away.

SEXUALLY TRANSMITTED DISEASES

In addition to AIDS, you can acquire other sexually transmitted diseases (STDs), especially by having sex with a high-risk partner. STD risk factors also include the number of your sexual exposures, number of different partners, number of anonymous partners (including prostitutes), and use (or nonuse) of condoms.

Causes of STDs

Unlike AIDS, some STDs can be spread by kissing and mouth-to-genital contact. Sexually transmitted diseases include those caused by viruses, bacteria, and protozoa.

Virus-caused STDs

- AIDS • hepatitis B • hepatitis C
- Hepatitis A (oral-anal contact)
- Genital herpes • genital warts

Bacteria-caused STDs

- Gonorrhea • syphilis • chancroid • chlamydia infections
- Gay bowel syndrome in homosexual men, caused by shigella, salmonella, or other bacteria

Protozoa-caused STDs

- Gay bowel syndrome in homosexual men, caused by giardia, isospora, cryptosporidia, E. histolytica, or other parasites
- Vaginal or urethral infections due to yeast (Candida) or trichomonas

Symptoms of STDs

The most common STDs are infections caused by gonococcus and chlamydia bacteria. The symptoms in men are a heavy, yellow discharge of pus from the penis, or a whitish, watery discharge. Rectal pain or discharge may also indicate infection. If you have any of these symptoms, receive treatment and notify your partner.

PID—Women who develop lower abdominal pain, vaginal discharge, and fever should be examined for the possibility of pelvic inflammatory disease (PID), which is an infection of the uterus and/or fallopian tubes. This is usually a mixed infection, most often caused by gonococci and/or chlamydia. Bear in mind that appendicitis, an ovarian cyst, and even an ectopic pregnancy can mimic pelvic inflammatory disease, so a precise diagnosis is important.

If you notice any ulcers or sores on your genitals, examine them for the presence of herpes, syphilis, or chancroid. Check to see if there is any local swelling of the lymph nodes in your groin. A *painless* ulcer may indicate syphilis, while herpetic ulcers are usually shallow and quite painful. These lesions again require exact diagnosis and appropriate treatment. Be sure to seek qualified medical care.

Prevention of STDs

Practice abstinence or have sex only in a monogamous relationship. If you are, however, sexually adventurous, follow the same prevention guidelines as for AIDS.

Treatment

Several individual drugs, as well as some drug combinations, can be used to treat STDs. Uncomplicated pelvic inflammatory disease is effectively treated with a 250-mg injection of **ceftriaxone** (Rocephin) plus a 7-day course of **doxycycline**. A 7-day course of **ofloxacin** (Floxin) will eradicate both microorganisms. A single 1-gm dose of **azithromycin** (Zithromax) will eradicate chlamydia and will also cure uncomplicated PID due to gonorrhea.

For the treatment for gonorrhea in men, authorities recommend a single 250mg injection of **ceftriaxone (Rocephin)**. Because chlamydia bacteria are also present in up to 45% of women and 25% of heterosexual men with gonorrhea, a 7-day course of either **doxycycline** (100 mg, twice daily), **tetracycline** (500 mg, four times daily), or **azithromycin** (Zithromax), 1 gm orally, as a single dose, should also be administered. Ceftriaxone will also eradicate incubating syphilis, should that disease also be present.

If ceftriaxone is not available to treat gonorrhea, you can take a single dose of one of these alternative drugs:

- Ciprofloxacin (Cipro), 500 mg
- Ofloxacin (Floxin), 400 mg
- Cefixime (Suprax), 400 mg

Also take either doxycycline, tetracycline, or azithromycin to eliminate a possible associated chlamydia infection.

If neither ceftriaxone or any of the alternative drugs is available to treat gonorrhea, consider either (1) intramuscular procaine penicillin, 4.8 million units, plus Benemid, 1 gm orally, or (2) amoxicillin, 3 gm orally, plus Benemid, as a single dose. Doxycycline or tetracycline should also be administered for seven days to eliminate chlamydia.

Treatment during pregnancy—If you are pregnant and have gonorrhea, you can be treated with ceftriaxone, cefixime, or procaine penicillin plus Benemid. Avoid the quinolones (ciprofloxacin and ofloxacin) because they are contraindicated during pregnancy. For the treatment of chlamydia don't use doxycycline or tetracycline since these drugs are also contraindicated in pregnancy; instead, take erythromycin, 500 mg, 4 times daily for seven days.

Homosexually transmitted gonorrhea—Homosexually transmitted gonorrhea is less apt to be associated with chlamydia and can usually be treated with a single dose of ceftriaxone or one of the alternative drugs.

Posttreatment follow-up—If you were treated for gonorrhea or PID while traveling, you should contact your physician when you return home. Women should have follow-up cultures of the cervix to see if they are still carrying gonorrhea and/or chlamydia. Both men and women should have a blood test to check for syphilis and should consider screening for HIV infection. Screening tests may not be positive for 6 weeks or longer after exposure.

Note:

1. *Journal of the American Medical Assoc.*, April 22/29, 1988. pp. 2428-2432.

12 Altitude Sickness

Even if you are in perfect health you can develop altitude sickness if you ascend rapidly to elevations over 6,000 feet. More severe illness can occur if you travel above 8,000 feet without acclimatizing. The most common altitude-related disorder is called acute mountain sickness (AMS). The symptoms, in decreasing order of frequency, are headache, shortness of breath, light-headedness, fatigue, insomnia, loss of appetite, and nausea.

The headache is often throbbing, made worse by lying down, and aggravated by strenuous exercise. Some or all of these symptoms may develop within 4 to 12 hours of reaching high altitudes, attain maximum severity within 24 to 48 hours, then subside after two to three days. If you ignore these early symptoms—and some people do if they are determined climbers or skiers—AMS can progress to a severe, life-threatening illness: high altitude pulmonary edema (HAPE) and/or high altitude cerebral edema (HACE), described below.

What Causes Altitude Sickness?

Basically, altitude sickness is caused by lack of oxygen. As you climb higher, there is less oxygen in the air that you breathe; in fact, at 15,000 feet the pressure of oxygen in your blood is only half that at sea level. A low blood oxygen level triggers AMS, but there is a delay between attaining altitude and the onset of symptoms. Acute mountain sickness, in fact, occurs hours to days after climbers ascend to high elevation. The reason? Researchers say that an abnormal physiological response known as *sleep apnea* is largely to blame. Here's what happens: Decreased blood oxygen is a physiological stimulus that makes a person breathe faster. Some climbers, however, don't respond normally; while asleep, their breathing rate remains very low, apparently because of a genetic insensitivity of their brain's respiratory center to low oxygen levels. Climbers with sleep apnea can become severely hypoxic, and hypoxia (low tissue oxygen) causes leakage of water and plasma from capillaries, particularly in the lungs and the brain, causing the symptoms of AMS. The amount of fluid buildup in these organs determines whether you have mild, moderate, or severe AMS.

Hypoxia has another effect—it causes the blood pressure in your pulmonary arteries to rise, forcing more fluid to leak from the lung capillaries into the air spaces (alveoli). Excessive leakage results in high altitude pulmonary edema (HAPE), described below.

Risk Factors That Influence Your Chance of Getting AMS

Anyone going to high altitudes can get AMS. Check the risk factors below to assess your potential risk. Risk factors include the following:

- Fast ascent (more than 3,000 feet/day)
- Altitude above 6,000 feet. Risk increases as altitude increases.
- Strenuous activity at high altitudes
- Previous history of AMS
- Obesity
- Lack of acclimatization
- Female sex (slightly increased risk)
- Use of sedatives and sleeping pills

Factors Not Associated With, or Protective Against, AMS

- Previous altitude experience
- Smoking
- Pre-trek training
- Good physical condition

It may seem surprising that good physical condition does not prevent AMS, but young, fit climbers often climb higher and faster than others and they also engage in more strenuous activity at high altitudes. Women are affected by AMS slightly more often than men, but they are said to have a lower incidence of high altitude pulmonary edema. Although smoking is not a risk factor for AMS, smokers generally have less physical endurance than nonsmokers.

Susceptibility to AMS can vary over time. Previous ability to ascend to high altitudes without getting AMS is no guarantee you won't become afflicted in the future.

Incidence of AMS in trekkers—Depending upon the speed and steepness of your ascent, and your altitude, the chance of getting AMS can be quite high. One study of trekkers in Nepal showed an attack rate of 58%. These climbers were crossing a mountain pass at 16,000 feet and also sleeping at high altitudes. Among skiers visiting Colorado resorts at altitudes between 7,900 and 9,200 feet, 12% developed symptoms of altitude sickness. Another study in Colorado documented mild AMS in 42% of those attending a 4 day conference at an elevation of 9,800 feet (3,000 meters).

How to Prevent AMS

Eat a high carbohydrate diet—Eat a diet that is 70% to 80% carbohydrates. This type of diet generates more carbon dioxide in your body's tissues, which in turn stimulates respiration. Avoid high-protein diets. Compared to diets high in carbohydrates, a high-protein diet increases your body's water requirements and reduces cold tolerance.

Drink extra fluids—Dehydration is common at high altitudes and it may aggravate the symptoms of AMS. Maintain an adequate fluid intake by drinking enough water to keep your urine output copious and clear.

Reduce activity—If you travel rapidly to an elevation over 8,000 feet (2,500 meters), you can reduce your chance of illness by not engaging in strenuous activity for several days.

Climb high, sleep low—No matter how high you are climbing during the day, try to sleep at a lower altitude, if this is an option.

Acclimatize—You can avoid or lessen AMS by making a slow, gradual ascent. Slow ascent means not increasing your sleeping altitude by over 2,000 feet (600 meters) on successive nights, especially when climbing above 10,000 feet. An alternate strategy, called staging, is to spend two to three days at an intermediate altitude (e.g., 7,000 to 10,000 feet) before resuming ascent. Every 3,000–4,000 feet thereafter, you should stop for a day to acclimatize further.

Unfortunately, cautious guidelines on the rate of ascent are usually not followed by most climbers. This is because they are in a hurry to get to the top. "Slow ascent" is too slow and impractical. For example, if you were to ascend Mt. Kilimanjaro as part of a guided tour, you would find yourself on a climbing schedule that forces you to sleep at much higher altitudes on successive nights. You begin the ascent at 5,000 feet. The huts where you sleep are at 9,000, 12,000, and 14,500 feet. Only a single rest day is spent (sometimes) at the highest hut before the final ascent to the 19,000-foot summit the following morning. Needless to say, AMS frequently occurs among those climbing Mt. Kilimanjaro this rapidly.

Take a prophylactic drug—In situations where you are ascending rapidly to high altitudes without the opportunity to acclimatize, consider taking a drug that helps prevent AMS. This is especially important if you have previously experienced altitude sickness. There are three drugs available that will lessen the frequency and severity of AMS. These same drugs can also be used to treat AMS.

Acetazolamide (Diamox): It will lessen your chances of getting AMS by 30% to 50%. The drug speeds acclimatization by forcing your kidneys to excrete bicarbonate, causing your blood to be more acidic. Blood acidosis has two effects: (1) it stimulates respiration, so your breathing pattern during sleep is restored toward normal, and (2) the more acidic blood can more efficiently deliver oxygen to the tissues of your body. Acetazolamide also causes the kidneys to excrete extra salt and water, so you'll notice more frequent urination. Use acetazolamide with caution if you have allergies to sulfa drugs.

Dosage: 250 mg every 12 hours is the usual dose (some travel experts recommend 500 mg of Diamox-SR once daily). Start acetazolamide 1–2 days before you ascend to high altitudes, and take the drug for 2–3 days at the higher altitude. Side effects include frequent urination and a tingling sensation of the face and lips.

Dexamethasone (Decadron): Although not routinely recommended for the prevention of AMS because of possible side effects, dexamethasone is a useful drug for those who need to ascend abruptly to very high altitudes—for example, those going on a mountain rescue mission. For treating AMS most authorities recommend dexamethasone when symptoms are more pronounced or if descent must be delayed.

Prevention dosage: 2 to 4 mg every 6 hours, begun the day of ascent, continued for three days at the higher altitude, then tapered over five days.

Treatment dosage: 8 mg initially, then 4 mg every 6 hours for one to three days. For more severe illness, use IV dexamethasone, if available. The IV dose is 10 mg initially, then 6 mg every 6 hours.

Nifedipine (Procardia, Adalat): Nifedipine has been used experimentally in the prevention and treatment of high altitude pulmonary edema (HAPE). It is an antihypertensive drug that not only lowers pulmonary artery pressure, but also improves oxygenation by distributing blood flow more evenly throughout the lungs.

Dosage: 10–20 mg every 8 hours.

Altitude Sickness Fact

Acetazolamide, dexamethasone, and nifedipine have all been shown to be valuable for prophylaxis or treatment of AMS, but, if unremitting symptoms of AMS occur, descent is imperative.

Diagnosing AMS

Before treating AMS you need to be sure you have made the correct diagnosis. Here are some other conditions that can either mimic AMS or aggravate established AMS.

- Dehydration (can cause nausea, weakness, headache)
- Hypothermia (can cause loss of balance, staggering gait)
- Exhaustion (can cause loss of balance, staggering gait)
- Respiratory infection (causes coughing, shortness of breath)
- Carbon monoxide poisoning (causes rapid breathing)
- Hyperventilation (causes rapid breathing)
- Psychiatric problems (can cause hyperventilation)
- Trauma (can cause any of the symptoms above)

Mild AMS

Mild AMS is like a hangover: headache, fatigue, nausea, and loss of appetite. You'll also notice insomnia and increased breathlessness. If you stop your ascent and rest, symptoms should clear in two to three days. To help the headache, take aspirin, acetaminophen (Tylenol), or ibuprophen (Advil, Nuprin, etc.). Acetazolamide is effective for treating AMS. Take 250 mg every 8 hours for 3–5 days. Contrary to popular belief, drinking extra fluids doesn't help; this is because people who develop AMS already are retaining extra salt and water.

NOTE: Some authorities advise not taking aspirin or any nonsteroidal anti-inflammatory drug (e.g., ibuprophen) above 14,000 feet altitude. They feel these drugs increase the risk of retinal hemorrhage.

Moderate AMS

Moderate AMS is an extension of mild AMS. If your headache becomes severe and resistant to medication and you notice increased shortness of breath on exertion, you are developing moderate AMS. The most important symptom of moderate AMS, however, is ataxia (staggering gait). Stop your ascent immediately if these symptoms occur. Use oxygen (flow rate of 4L/min.), if it's available. Acetazolamide and/or dexamethasone may also help. *You must descend to a lower altitude if your symptoms do not improve.* Descent, in fact, is the most reliable treatment. Noticeable improvement may result if you descend as little as 1,500 feet (500 meters) but a descent of at least 1,000 meters is recommended. Further descent, however, may be necessary if you have ataxia or other symptoms that don't remit.

High Altitude Pulmonary Edema (HAPE)

The severity of altitude sickness is a continuum. What starts out as typical AMS can progress to a more serious and occasionally fatal disorder called high altitude pulmonary edema. HAPE kills more people each year than any other altitude-related condition. In this illness the capillaries of the lung leak even more fluid, causing fluid to fill the small air sacks (alveoli) that attach to the end of the bronchial tubes. This further chokes off the oxygen supply to the blood, and a vicious cycle results.

HAPE strikes an estimated 1% to 2% of those who climb above 12,000 feet. (Fatal cases, however, have occurred as low as 8,000 feet.) At increased risk are climbers who have previously experienced HAPE; they have a 60% chance of recurrence during another exposure to high altitudes.

HAPE usually occurs after a rapid, strenuous ascent to high altitude by a young, healthy climber. Early symptoms of HAPE begin 24–72 hours after arrival at the higher altitudes and consist of shortness of breath, rapid pulse, and persistent, dry cough. Stopping ascent may permit symptoms to subside over the next one to three days. If your symptoms don't improve, or if they worsen, you must descend immediately until symptoms improve. A descent of 1,000 meters may be sufficient. You should also start oxygen, if it's available, at a flow rate of 4–5 liters/minute. If your descent is delayed, take dexamethasone, 8 mg initially, then 4 mg every 6 hours. The drug nifedipine has recently been found to be rapidly effective for treating HAPE. The mechanism? Nifedipine reverses hypoxia-induced pulmonary hypertension. The dose is 20 mg every 8 hours.

Preventing HAPE

The best prevention against HAPE consists of acclimatization with gradual ascent over several days or more. Don't set climbing goals that exceed your physical capacity. Taking acetazolamide may help prevent HAPE, but don't let it give you a false sense of security because it's not 100% effective. Nifedipine has recently been shown to be an effective preventative, particularly in climbers with a previous history of HAPE. Dosage: 20 mg every 8 hours, beginning at the start of ascent. NOTE: Experience with nifedipine, while favorable, is still limited. At this time, prophylactic nifedipine should be used only by persons who will be climbing at elevations over 12–14,000 feet, and where oxygen is not available and/or rapid descent may not be possible.

Don't be a stoic climber and pass off the early symptoms of HAPE as simple exhaustion. Be aware of the earliest symptoms so that you can halt your ascent, start treatment, and plan for descent if symptoms progress.

High Altitude Cerebral Edema (HACE)

High altitude cerebral edema (edema means swelling) is a severe form of AMS that can develop after several days of high-altitude exposure. Mild symptoms of HACE can occur as low as 9,000 feet. HACE and HAPE can occur simultaneously, but HACE also occurs as a single entity without lung congestion. Watch for headache, mental confusion, drowsiness, staggering gait, and loss of balance (ataxia). Nausea and vomiting are often severe. Coma and death may ensue if treatment measures are not taken. The preferred measures are oxygen (if available) and an immediate descent of at least 3,000 feet of altitude. Give dexamethasone, 8–10 mg orally or intravenously, as soon as possible, then 4–6 mg every six hours. You can also use prednisone, 50 mg, followed by 25 mg orally every six hours.

The Gamow Bag

This device, which is a portable hyperbaric chamber, is an air-tight, 7-foot cylindrical bag, made of coated nylon, and it weighs less than 18 lbs with pump and/or rebreathing unit. It is best used for the temporary treatment of AMS when descent is unavoidably delayed. The Gamow bag apparently works by increasing blood oxygen saturation.

The stricken climber is placed inside the bag, which is then pressurized with a foot or hand pump to 140–220 mbars above ambient pressure. This amount of pressurization simulates a decrease of 1,500 to 2,500 meters in altitude and, depending upon the starting altitude, is usually sufficient to raise arterial oxygen saturation to over 90%. A one-hour treatment may provide relief from most symptoms of AMS, but the effect is temporary and for this reason the Gamow bag should be used to facilitate, but not delay, descent when illness occurs at high altitude.

The main advantage of the Gamow bag is its independence from consumable oxygen and the device is best suited for alpine expeditions and search and rescue teams that don't carry bottled oxygen. For further information contact **Portable Hyperbarics, Inc.**, P.O. Box 510, Ilion, NY 13357-0510; 315-895-7485.

Bottled Oxygen

This is usually supplied by "E" type cyclinders that weigh about 18 lbs. One full tank will last 2.5 hours at a flow rate of 4 L/min. Supplemental oxygen is slightly more effective than the Gamow bag in raising arterial oxygen saturation and its use does not restrict access to the victim.

Rapid Travel to High Altitudes

Not all travelers to high altitudes are climbers or skiers. You may be a businessperson or tourist flying directly to one of the many cities in the world where the altitude is greater than 6,000 feet (Table 12.1). Since you won't have a chance to acclimatize, consider starting Diamox the day of departure and avoid strenuous exertion for several days after arrival.

What about your heart? What are the risks at high altitudes? This issue is discussed below, but suffice it to say that there seems to be little risk, even for those with known cardiac conditions. For example, it takes only 3–5 hours to travel from Lima, Peru, near sea level, to La Oroya, elevation 12,400 feet, yet there are few, if any, reports of sudden heart attacks occurring in travelers shortly after they arrive. And in a survey of medical evacuations among 148,000 persons trekking in Nepal, medical researchers reported no cardiac causes of death.

THE HEART AT HIGH ALTITUDES

If you have a history of heart disease, there is good news: Altitude appears to have less effect on climbers with heart disease than previously believed. In fact, there is no evidence that exercise after acclimatization at a high altitude is of greater risk to your heart than similar exercise performed at sea level. Some physicians, however,

Table 12.1 Cities at Elevations Greater Than 6,000 Feet Above Sea Level	
Location	**Altitude**
Addis Ababa	7,900 feet
Aspen, Colorado	7,902–11,200 feet
Bogota, Colombia	8,393 feet
Cuzco, Peru	11,152 feet
Arequipa, Peru	7,559 feet
Cochabamba, Bolivia	8,393 feet
Darjeeling, India	7,431 feet
Guanajuato, Mexico	6,726 feet
Toluca, Mexico	8,793 feet
La Paz, Bolivia	11,736 feet
Pike's Peak, Colorado	14,000 feet
Lhasa, Tibet	12,002 feet
Quito, Ecuador	9,249 feet
Mexico City	7,546 feet

discourage their heart patients from going to altitude out of fear that the patient will have a cardiac arrest or will develop congestive heart failure. Therefore, what tests, if any, should you have to help assess your risk? And what precautions should you take to avoid problems? And who shouldn't engage in climbing or trekking? The following checklist will help you plan your high altitude activities.

Climbers without known heart disease—If you are age 40 or older and going on a trek or alpine climb where medical facilities are not available, consider having a stress test if you have one or more of the following cardiac risk factors: systolic blood pressure over 140, high cholesterol, diabetes, cigarette smoking, or a family history of early heart attack. A history of unexplained fainting or loss of consciousness also warrants stress testing. The rationale for screening asymptomatic persons before climbing is to deter those who may have silent coronary artery disease from starting an imprudent exercise program.

Climbers with a normal stress test—If your stress test is normal at a high workload, then further testing is not needed. Although a normal test does not always exclude silent coronary disease, your chance of having a heart attack is very low with a negative stress test and no symptoms.

NOTE: Recent studies have shown that the risk of an unexpected exercise-related heart attack is much less in people who exercise regularly. Sedentary people with silent coronary heart disease are at higher risk of a heart attack triggered by sudden physical exertion.

Climbers with an abnormal stress test—If you have a stress test where the results are borderline or abnormal, a thallium scan may help decide if you have significant coronary artery disease. If your stress test is markedly abnormal, you should have an angiogram. You may need coronary artery bypass surgery or angioplasty.

Climbers with known heart disease—If you have a history of angina, you should have a stress test before commencing vigorous exercise. This will help determine your exercise capacity as well any tendency to develop dangerous heart rhythms during exertion. If you have sustained a previous heart attack, there are two tests that will help predict your chance of sudden death.

Following coronary angioplasty, the risk of restenosis is increased between the 6th to the 12th week after the procedure and travel should be curtailed during this period. Six months after angioplasty, the risk of restenosis is minimal.

If you've had a heart attack, there is a lower risk of subsequent cardiac arrest (and possibly safer travel) if you have the following:

- Well-preserved left ventricular function (ejection fraction >40%)
- No significant ventricular arrhythmias or ST depression on exercise testing
- Normal signal-averaged ECG
- Well-maintained exercise capacity. No systolic BP drop during exercise testing.

Another test that can help determine the risk of serious or fatal cardiac arrhythmia is the induction of sustained ventricular tachycardia by programmed ventricular stimulation. Ask your doctor, or a cardiologist, whether you should have this type of testing prior to travel.

Climbing after coronary bypass surgery—If you have a normal stress test and no angina, you can safely go to altitude. In fact, trekkers have gone as high as 19,000 feet after bypass surgery. An abnormal test, however, should lead to repeat angiography to see if any of the grafts are blocked.

Climbing after coronary angioplasty—If you have had coronary angioplasty, you should wait six months before climbing. The reason? During the first six months after the procedure, there is a 30% risk of occlusion of the opened artery. After six months, the risk of thrombosis of the opened artery is reduced and is about the same as for patients who have had bypass surgery.

Facts About Heart Disease and Altitude

- High altitude increases cardiac work during the first few days. However, there is no evidence that cardiac work at altitude puts a greater stress on your heart than does similar cardiac work at sea level.
- If you have few or no symptoms at sea level while doing moderate to heavy exercise, you are probably at no greater risk of a heart attack at altitudes even as high as 19,000 feet.
- If you have heart disease with symptoms, you may notice an increase in your symptoms (e.g., angina, shortness of breath) while you are acclimatizing.
- While acclimatizing, you should reduce activity and increase your medications. Discuss your medication dosages with your doctor.
- If you have moderate to severe symptoms at sea level, you can expect a marked increase in your symptoms after arriving at altitude. Be prepared to descend immediately if rest and medication don't control symptoms.
- When angina drugs are required, nitrates and calcium channel blockers are preferable to beta blockers. Beta blockers slow down the heart and may impede acclimatization.
- Your maximal physical exertion at high altitude is determined more by your lung function than by your cardiac work capacity.
- If you have congestive heart failure, you probably should not travel above 8,000 feet. Altitude-induced fluid retention may cause problems.
- If you have a history of unstable arrhythmias or cardiac arrest, mountain travel is not advisable. If you do travel to altitude, a pacemaker or implantable defbrillator may be advisable.

How Two Physicians Advise Their Patients Who Climb

Dr. Drummond Rennie, a cardiologist in San Francisco, writing in the *Journal of the American Medical Association*, advises, "My own practice is to take a careful history from people who ask if they can go trekking at high altitudes. I explain that if they are able to carry out strenuous, long, continued exercise at sea level, they can probably expect to do so at high altitude. I suggest also that, if possible, they should give themselves a trial at moderate altitude, say 8,000 feet. If they have any symptoms, say angina, they should ascend even more slowly than usual so that they can acclimatize." And Dr. Charles Houston says, "Coronary artery disease, per se, is not an absolute contraindication to trekking at higher altitudes. If reserve circulation is sufficient, if the patient is wise in recognizing symptoms and accepting limits, if the anticipated stress of hiking and climbing does not produce signs and symptoms at sea level, then a person may go ahead, properly warned and prepared, because the emotional and psychological benefits are large."

Before You Travel to High Altitudes

If you have a history of heart disease, your "exercise prescription" has to be carefully individualized. Your physician should review your medications, if any, and present you with the possible risks and hazards based on your past history, symptoms, and test results. You should make your decision based on this advice, plus your own desire to go. Bear in mind that if problems occur, you will be far away from a hospital. See a cardiologist for a complete evaluation when the issue is not clear cut. Also bear in mind that many intelligent, well-informed people who understand the risks, and also their own capabilities and limitations, want to live life to the fullest. This is a reasonable desire and should not be unnecessarily infringed upon.

13 Medical Care Abroad

What do you do if you are suddenly taken ill or have a serious accident in a foreign country? How do you find an English-speaking physician? Or a reputable hospital? Where do you turn for help and advice?

The first step in avoiding disaster is prevention. This means careful pretrip planning as outlined in this *HealthGuide*. But what if an unexpected illness or accident occurs?

Statistics show that 25% of travelers develop some type of medical problem over a two-week period. Most accidents and cases of medical illness are relatively minor. The problem may be self-evident. Most conditions resolve by themselves or can be treated with simple first-aid measures or with the medication you have on hand.

But what if you need a physician's treatment or hospitalization? When an emergency happens far from home, even a seasoned traveler may have trouble coping—especially if medical care is urgently needed. What starts out as a routine vacation or business trip could end up as a real nightmare.

How to Cope When Illness or Injury Suddenly Strikes

Stay calm—You may be able to solve the problem yourself. You may already have medicine with you to treat a minor infection, a rash, a cut, a bruise, or a sprain. If diarrhea should occur, follow the treatment guidelines for travelers' diarrhea in Chapter 4. Check to see what's in your medical kit. Home health care guides and first-aid manuals are a source of useful advice, so you may wish to bring one of these with you.

Serious accidents or illness demand immediate attention—If you sustain a deep laceration, a fracture, a possible heart attack, or a stroke, or if you have bleeding, unremitting chest or abdominal pain, or trouble breathing, don't waste your time trying to find a local physician. Go immediately to the nearest hospital. If you are in a large city, go to a hospital associated with a medical school, if possible (these hospitals usually have English-speaking doctors as well as qualified specialists on their staff). You can ask for directions or assistance from your hotel, your tour guide, a taxi driver, or the police. A taxi or private car taken directly from your location may be faster than an ambulance, but call an ambulance if necessary and if one is available. Remember, in an emergency, minutes count. Don't delay!

NOTE: If you're having a possible heart attack, early diagnosis and treatment is critical. If the hospital can administer a clot-dissolving drug during the first four hours, your chance of recovery is greatly improved.

Less urgent illness—This can usually be treated during a daytime visit to a doctor's office, but some doctors will make an after hours hotel "house call." Your hotel can usually provide the names of one or more English-speaking physicians. Better yet, if you have friends, relatives, or business associates who are residents of the area, ask them for a referral to a doctor they know is qualified.

Colds, sore throats, earaches, bronchitis, diarrhea, most urinary infections, and the flu are some of the conditions usually not requiring emergency attention. You may have your own medication to relieve discomfort and tide you over until you can see a physician. However, if you have a fever and think you might have malaria, be sure you are examined and treated within 6 to 12 hours.

NOTE: Foreign brand names of drugs will vary. Insist that all medications that you receive from the doctor be identified or labeled with the generic or trade name. This is important if you have drug allergies and must avoid certain medications or develop a drug-related reaction or have to see another doctor for ongoing care. He or she will need to know what you are taking.

Carry a phrase book—A phrase book that provides medical words and phrases in various foreign languages can be invaluable when you need to describe your symptoms and an English-speaking physician is not immediately available. Try to find an interpreter as soon as possible.

Call your doctor in the States—If you are hospitalized, a consultation with your own physician can be invaluable. Hopefully your doctor, or an associate, will be available at the time you call. Leave your number if necessary. Describe the history of your illness, your symptoms, what the diagnosis is, and what treatment you are receiving. Let your doctor know if you are exposed to tropical diseases. Have your own doctor discuss your case with the local doctor caring for you. Obviously, for certain conditions, treatment is standard and straightforward—surgery for appendicitis, casting for fractures, etc.—and your treatment may have already been rendered. However, for more serious or life-threatening problems, this consultation is important. Your diagnosis may be in doubt, and the hospital and physician possibly may not have the expertise to provide adequate care. Your physician can help assess the situation and reassure you that you are receiving proper care and that there's no need to worry, or your physician may feel a second opinion is warranted or even that transfer to another facility is advisable.

Locating Physicians Abroad

You have many options when it comes to finding a physician to care for you. The **American and Canadian embassies and consulates** maintain referral lists from which you can choose. The embassy or consulate, however, won't recommend individual doctors on the list. Other options to consider include the following:

Hotel doctors—Most large hotels will refer you to a local doctor or to a doctor who will come to your room to render treatment. Be warned, however, that the main qualification some of these doctors have is a kickback arrangement with the hotel management.

The World Medical Guide section of the *International Travel HealthGuide*—This year's edition has an expanded listing of hospitals, clinics, and individual physicians, including specialists.

IAMAT—The International Association for Assistance to Travelers (IAMAT) is a Canadian foundation that publishes a booklet listing hospitals and English-speaking physicians who have agreed to adhere to a standard schedule of fees. Physicians are not listed by specialty. Contact IAMAT, 417 Center Street, Lewiston, NY 14092; 716-754-4883. Or in Canada, 40 Regal Road, Guelph, Ontario, N1K 1B5; 519-836-0102. No charge, but a donation is encouraged.

InterContinental Medical—A new service, available from InterContinental Medical, a company with a database of 5,000 physicians worldwide. For $28.50, ICM will mail you a list of hospitals and physicians in up to three countries. (Additional countries cost $3 each.) InterContinental indicates physicians' specialties and also indicates if the physicians accept credit cards. For information, call 800-ICM-8828.

Cardholder assistance—Credit-card companies provide 24-hour emergency medical hotlines available to many of their cardholders, usually those in the "Gold card" category. Typically, the hotlines can refer you to English-speaking doctors and dentists and to hospitals with English-speaking staff members, arrange for replacement of prescription medicines, and help you rent an air ambulance. If you are an American Express cardholder, call the Global Assist hotline at 800-554-AMEX (301-214-8228 collect from overseas). If you are an American Express Platinum cardholder, call your special assistance number, 800-345-2639 (202-331-1688 collect from overseas). Visa Gold and Classic cardholders can call 800-332-2484 (410-581-9994 collect from overseas). MasterCard cardholders can call 303-278-8000 (collect from overseas).

Travel insurance with assistance—If you have purchased a travel health policy with assistance, call the 24-hour hotline number and you'll be connected with an assistance center that can give a physician referral. See Chapter 14 for a listing of companies.

Personal recommendation—Probably the best method of locating a qualified English-speaking physician (assuming time allows it) is to find a satisfied English-speaking patient who lives in the area. Try contacting employees of American or Canadian multinational corporations, or any other expatriate (schoolteacher, relief worker, missionary, etc.). If you have no luck with these sources, you can call an embassy or consulate (American, Canadian, British, Australian, or New Zealand). Try to find a sympathetic staff member, or talk to the embassy nurse, for his or her personal recommendation.

Making International Calls for Assistance

In many countries it is possible to use an express call service such as AT&T's *USADirect* or MCI's Call USA. Calling their local access number connects you to an operator in the United States. You can now charge the call to your telephone credit card—or call collect. If you are calling the access number from your hotel room, you will avoid the hotel surcharge on overseas calls. Information on AT&T's USADirect can be obtained by calling 800-874-4000, ext. 359. For MCI, call 800-444-4444.

Foreign Physicians

Because of cultural differences, the attitude of physicians toward their patients in foreign countries is often different than in the United States. Physicians abroad are often perceived as being more autocratic and authoritarian. This can make patient-doctor communication difficult. The doctor caring for you may not want you to question his or her care and may not be available to answer your questions (to be fair, this can sometimes be said of American physicians also). This does not mean that your care is substandard. In fact, the doctor caring for you may have more knowledge of local diseases than your own physician and be perfectly well qualified to diagnose and treat your illness.

Foreign Hospitals

Keep in mind that foreign hospitals can range from the very primitive to the most modern, but the quality of your medical care shouldn't necessarily be judged by your surroundings. If you're hospitalized in a lesser-developed country, you might wonder if you should be moved to a "more modern" facility. This question faces hospitalized patients everywhere, not just travelers overseas. An analogy to being hospitalized in the United States might be appropriate. In the United States, the smaller community hospitals are adequate for almost all medical care. Occasionally, however, a patient requires transport to a specialty center for advanced, sometimes lifesaving treatment. The same is true overseas. You may be in a small, seemingly inadequate facility that may, in fact, be perfectly adequate for your medical needs. Having someone available, in serious situations, to assess your diagnosis and treatment will help you or your family know when transfer or medevac is indicated.

Assessing Foreign Hospitals

If you need emergency care and minutes count, go to the closest facility. However, if the situation is not immediately critical—and there's more than one hospital nearby—use the following checklist to get a basic idea of what level of care is available to you. The checklist will also help you tell your doctor at home what services can be provided.

- Does the hospital have a coronary care unit, ICU, recovery room, and advanced resuscitation and diagnostic equipment?
- What medical and surgical procedures can be performed locally? Is a neurosurgeon on staff? If not, where is the closest referral facility?
- Can they treat heart attacks with clot-dissolving drugs (e.g., t-PA or streptokinase)?

- Can the hospital render qualified obstetrical care?
- Is CT and MRI scanning available? Ultrasound?
- Does the hospital or clinic stock disposable supplies, especially needles and syringes?
- Does the blood bank test for the HIV antibody, hepatitis B surface antigen, and hepatitis C antibody?
- What vaccines are available (e.g., tetanus, immune globulin, rabies, rabies immune globulin, hepatitis B, hepatitis B immune globulin)?
- How clean is the hospital? Is it air-conditioned? Are there private rooms? What is the food like?
- Are special nurses available?
- Does the hospital have 24-hour receiving and admitting capability?
- Does the hospital receive ambulances and treat major trauma?
- Is there a list of on-call physicians? What specialists are available and what are their qualifications?
- Do most of the doctors speak English?
- What are the room rates and the charges for various medical and surgical procedures?
- How does the hospital want to be paid? Will they accept direct payments from your travel insurance company? Will they accept a major credit card?

Paying for Medical Care Abroad

Usually, foreign doctors, hospitals, and clinics like to be paid in cash when their services are rendered. Only a few accept Blue Cross/Blue Shield (The American Hospital in Paris, for example). Unless you have a direct-payment travel policy (see Chapter 14), expect to pay in full when leaving the hospital or doctor's office. Most foreign physicians and hospitals are familiar with health insurance forms and should be willing to complete these so you can be reimbursed later.

Have all your bills itemized in legible English, detailing all diagnostic and therapeutic procedures performed as well as the discharge diagnosis. When you return home, file your claim with your insurance company for reimbursement. Normally, there is no problem if you were treated for an emergency, but certain elective procedures, such as cosmetic surgery, won't be covered.

Be sure to keep copies of all bills and receipts, and have the physician prepare a complete summary of your treatment in case there is a dispute over your reimbursement.

If you are a member of an HMO, your coverage extends worldwide and all emergency care will be reimbursed. All other care will have to be authorized for payment by your HMO since you are "out of area." If you are hospitalized overseas, the HMO may find it medically advisable and sometimes cost-effective to evacuate you back home so that ongoing care will be provided by the HMO staff physicians. *It is best to check with your HMO prior to departure about what proce-*

dures to follow in event of illness or accident overseas. Ask if they will make direct payments for hospitalization and under what circumstances they will pay for medical evacuation or repatriation.

How One Traveler Coped with Sudden Illness

In a letter published in the Travel section of *The New York Times* in October 1987, Mr. Carlton Zucker describes the problems of getting sick in a foreign country.[1]

No one, I thought at the time, could prepare adequately for the kind of terror that grabbed me when I awoke abruptly at 5 A.M. in the Tel Aviv Sheraton to find that I was hemorrhaging internally.

Today I realize that with careful planning for a possible medical emergency, I might have avoided the panic.

If, before leaving home, I had asked my doctor for the names of doctors and hospitals in Israel, my wife Joan and I would have saved precious hours. And if we had remembered to call a toll-free number in Geneva set up by the insurance company whose medical policy I carried we might not have fumbled about. Instead, my wife's first action was to call the hotel operator for a doctor (he was to come an hour later) and mine was to call my doctor in Chicago (it was 10 P.M. there) to ask for help. My doctor gave me the name of a physician who, fortuitously, had just returned to Israel from Chicago. If I couldn't reach him, my doctor advised, I should get over to Hadassah Hospital.

We enlisted the operator's assistance. She could not find the physician, and there was no Hadassah Hospital in Tel Aviv. It was in Jerusalem, 40 miles away. My doctor phoned back from Chicago a moment later to confirm what the operator had just told us, and he ordered me to go to the nearest Tel Aviv hospital.

At that moment the hotel doctor arrived, examined me, said I had bleeding diverticulitis (the hemorrhaging in my intestines had stopped) and directed that I go immediately to Ichilov Hospital, a public hospital affiliated with Tel Aviv University. He also warned that I might not find the bedside manner expected in the United States because, he said, Israel has socialized medicine and there wasn't time for manners. He asked for 70,000 shekels, about $47 at that time, and packed his bag.

The hotel operator had called a cab, which whisked us to the emergency room of a sprawling hospital compound. The emergency room had about two dozen empty beds and three nurses who struggled to understand English. I know that I should have been prepared with a phrase book to describe my symptoms quickly and precisely.

The doctor arrived, examined me, and ordered me up to Surgery No. 1, complete with intravenous and stomach tubes. I was wheeled to the fourth floor where I found myself in an ugly, dirty, crowded nine-bed ward.

My experiences over the next three days were a curious mixture of revulsion at the hospital's physical condition and awesome respect for an overworked medical staff. My condition and treatment were, fortunately, simple—no food, just intravenous fluids and bed rest for at least two days, to be followed by tests to determine whether the bleeding had really stopped. Only then would I be discharged. Certainly I would not board the plane for home, as planned, the following morning.

My greatest fear, as I look back, was not that I couldn't leave for Chicago the following day—it was that I might never leave because I would contract some horrible disease from the hospital conditions. The dining alcove outside my ward, I learned when I could get up to eat the third day, included two picnic benches to seat about twenty, hundreds of ants and one visible cockroach. And, in all fairness, a vat of very good chicken soup. The corridors were filled with cigarette smoke—from the doctors, nurses, patients, visitors, orderlies. Israelis, I was told, have more to worry about than cigarettes.

And yet the medical care was superb. From the professor who headed the surgery to the Arab aides who worked on Shabbat (Saturday, the day of rest for Israel's Jews), everyone on the staff displayed the kind of professionalism one could hope to get in the finest hospital in the States. The deputy director, the resident, the intern and the medical students, whom I saw at least twice daily, spent more time meticulously monitoring my condition than I ever expected.

Behind the dirty corridors lay some surprisingly modern equipment, like the elaborate sigmoidoscope machine with which I became intimately acquainted. It had been donated by a Hadassah chapter in an upstate New York hospital. And where else in the world would one find the nurses offering their patients a choice of sleeping tablets?

With few exceptions, these patients accepted without complaint the hospital conditions. After all, this was a paradise compared to what most of them had been through in their battles for survival both before and after the formation of Israel in 1948.

My wife, struggling with her own problems, was aided by some good planning. One thing we had done right before leaving home was to invest in a comprehensive travel insurance policy offered through American Express. For thirty days we were to be protected against losses due to changes in flight plans, medical emergency and missing baggage. I had become ill on the 29th day. Joan called a toll-free number in Geneva to report this emergency (after I entered the hospital) and was told to call New York. It was by then 2 A.M. New York time, and no one was standing by the phone.

Later, though, we learned that the insurance company would honor the medical expenses, to the tune of $860. Medicare would pay no part of medical costs outside the United States. The policy would also cover the cost of arranging another flight home. Joan cancelled our original airline tickets. We were in Israel on a TWA senior pass plan, almost as rigid as for charter flights. She wouldn't know for at least three more days when we would leave.

Another thing we had done right beforehand was to book into hotels where English is easily understood and where hotel employees can take care of emergencies in the appropriate language.

The day I entered Ichilov Joan had met with the chief cashier to discuss payments. Be ready, he told her, to pay 325,600 shekels ($220) a day. Only shekels, he warned.

Joan cashed all our remaining traveler's checks. The Sheraton's Bank Leumi office gave her a fistful of shekels.

On the morning of my discharge, Joan and I hustled down to the cashier to seek my release. The bill produced two immediate reactions. The first: how could the hospital afford to provide medical services at such low prices—electrocardiogram, $10; urinalysis, $6; endoscopy, $34? The second: we were short $71.

Joan counted out the shekels, then offered to pay the balance in dollars, in cash, by check or by credit card. The cashier refused. After 15 minutes of argument, Joan broke into tears. The cashier responded with "Have a cup of tea." Twenty minutes later he agreed to accept dollars for the missing shekels, provided we would accept a receipt that read shekels, not dollars.

We left Ichilov in a taxi, went to a travel agency, booked two seats on a Swissair flight to Chicago the next morning, then strolled back to the hotel. Free at last. Of course, it wasn't until the plane landed at O'Hare, the next evening, that we really felt free.

It's apparent that these travelers did several things right. They had trip interruption insurance. They had the telephone number of their private physician. They had medical insurance; however, it did not provide telephone access to a physician-directed assistance center, nor did it pay their medical bills directly. Luckily, they raised enough currency to pay the hospital bill.

This account also illustrates a little-known fact: medical costs overseas are sometimes far lower than in the United States. A daily rate of $220 is very inexpensive compared to this country. Even so, be aware that in some countries, especially in Europe, hospital and physician's fees may be just as high as in the United States.

Note:
1. Copyright 1988 by *The New York Times*. Reprinted by permission.

14 Travel Insurance

Health insurance in the United States, unlike many countries, is characterized by its diversity. There are dozens of Blue Cross/Blue Shield plans, hundreds of commercial insurers, and a multiplicity of managed care plans involving HMOs, IPAs, and PPGs. For some, there is Medicaid, and for those over 65, there is Medicare. All these various types of plans have different benefits, costs, deductibles, exclusions, and restrictions.

Before you travel, check your existing health policy to see what it pays for. It will probably reimburse you for 80% to 100% of the cost of emergency medical care abroad, excluding any deductible or co-payment. For nonemergency care overseas, you may be covered, but you will probably have to call your insurance company or HMO in the United States for authorization of treatment. Check with your health plan about this before you leave home. Failure to get authorization may mean denial of reimbursement if you later file a claim.

If your current health insurance policy doesn't cover medical care abroad, or you are without any coverage whatsoever, you should consider purchasing a travel health-specific insurance policy (see below). And even if your present insurance will pay doctor and hospital bills abroad, you may want to purchase a travel policy to get some important additional benefits, such as coverage for air ambulance transport and on-site payment of medical expenses.

Medicare and Travel

If you're over 65, be aware that Medicare does not cover health care costs outside the United States except in limited circumstances in Canada and Mexico. Fortunately, there are "Medigap policies" that offer protection against foreign illness. Eight Medigap plans (Plans C through J) include some coverage for foreign travel and many organizations and insurance companies offer these Medigap policies. The policies offered through the **American Association of Retired Persons** (800-523-5800) and underwritten by Prudential are typical; the least expensive policy that covers care in foreign countries is Plan D, at $65.00 a month. There's a $250 deductible, and then the plan covers 80% of charges for up to 60 days of treatment. More comprehensive plans range up to $140 a month.

Another sponsor of Medigap insurance that covers foreign travel is the **National Council of Senior Citizens** (800-596-6272). Commercial insurance agents, too, offer various Medigap policies, and the limitations and deductibles may vary from insurer to insurer.

Before shopping around for a Medigap policy, find out if you already are covered for foreign travel through an existing policy. Such a policy might be one you have under, for example, a corporate retirement medical plan.

Medical Care Abroad

Foreign doctors and hospitals won't bill your insurance company. They usually want you to pay them with cash or a credit card (not always possible) at the time of treatment or admission to a hospital. You then must submit your claim (with all necessary bills in English and any necessary documentation) to your insurance company when you return home. You'll be reimbursed only after the claim has been processed and the trip long over.

Another factor complicating reimbursement for overseas medical care is that most insurance companies, HMOs, and managed care plans now require you to notify their review panel that you have been, or plan to be, admitted to a hospital for treatment. Most private insurers also require a second opinion before they will pay for certain types of treatment. In an emergency, the requirements are relaxed, but nevertheless, getting reimbursed will be more complicated if your medical care was rendered abroad. You may not be able to notify your carrier within the 24-hour time limit for emergency admissions, and if the medical record and copies of your bill are in a foreign language, there may be a delay in payment. Incomplete records, or bills that are not itemized, may not be acceptable. For these, and other reasons, travelers often decide to purchase a separate travel health insurance policy that will make on-site payments, or payment guarantees, to the overseas provider.

In addition to guaranteeing payment to the doctor and hospital, travel health insurance policies provide another very important benefit—they usually pay for medical evacuation, by air ambulance if necessary, to the nearest adequate medical facility. Most policies will also pay to transport you home if further treatment is required after your condition has stabilized—a benefit known as repatriation.

There are two major types of travel insurance policies: (1) policies that can make direct payments for medical care and which also provide "assistance," and (2) reimbursement policies that cover medical expenses, but not up front—you must pay these yourself and then file a claim when you return home.

Travel Insurance with Assistance

Imagine the following scenario: You find yourself hospitalized with a serious illness in a foreign country and the doctor caring for you speaks hardly any English. He's treating you with an unfamiliar drug, and you are worried about an allergic reaction or a serious side effect. The doctor then says you may need surgery, but you're not sure of the diagnosis. The situation is becoming more and more like a nightmare. Where do you turn for help and advice?

If you find yourself in this situation, then having travel insurance with assistance can be a godsend. Here are some of the reasons:

Medical monitoring—Travel insurance with assistance gives you the 24-hour telephone number of an assistance center where multilingual personnel, backed up by physician specialists, are available round-the-clock to evaluate your treatment and to monitor your medical care.

Emergency medical transport/repatriation—If you need immediate air ambulance or another form of emergency medical transportation to a better-qualified medical facility, the assistance center will arrange for it and pay the costs, up to the policy limit. And if you're unable to return home unassisted after your condition has stabilized, the insurer, working through the assistance center, will arrange and pay for stretcher transport with a qualified medical attendant so that you can recover closer to home and family.

Emergency medical payments—The assistance center can also guarantee payment to those providing your medical care or, when necessary, can advance money for on-site payment. This means that, aside from possibly paying a small deductible, you will not have to make cash payments yourself, providing the policy covers the illness and the doctor and/or hospital will accept the insurance (which they often will).

Traveler's assistance—Assistance centers can also help with a variety of other problems, including replacement of lost prescriptions, physician referral, or finding you a local dentist. Nonmedical assistance includes travel document and ticket replacement, emergency cash transfer, emergency message center, legal assistance (e.g., lending you bail money, locating a lawyer), helping to replace a lost prescription, or helping replace a lost passport or other document.

What Else Do These Policies Cover?

Accidental death and disability—For an additional fee, most policies will also cover accidental death and disability (AD&D), lost luggage, and trip interruption or cancellation insurance. You may not need extra coverage for AD&D if you already have enough of your own life insurance, and your lost luggage may be covered by your homeowner's policy.

Trip interruption insurance—This can be an important money saver if illness or other problems force you to miss your scheduled flight. Some medical emergency policies offer this benefit in the basic package or as an optional benefit available for an additional fee. A trip interruption policy should cover the following:

➢ Interruption due to sickness, injury, or death to you, members of your immediate family, your traveling companion, or your business partner.

➢ An accident or emergency that causes you to miss a scheduled departure (or connection) when you're traveling to the departure point.

➢ Travel delays due to an unannounced strike, bad weather, or a hijacking.

➢ Destination-area terrorism that causes trip cancellation.

How Much Travel Insurance Do You Need?

Some travel insurance policies pay medical benefits as low as $2,500 while others pay up to $100,000. How should you choose? The answer depends on (1) whether your existing health insurance covers foreign travel, and how high the benefits, deductibles, and co-payments are, and (2) how much evacuation insurance you might need.

If you don't have a health insurance policy that covers overseas travel, then buy a travel policy with a high dollar benefit, such as **TravMed** or **Health Care Abroad** ($100,000 coverage). If you do have major medical or Medigap coverage, then a $2,500 to $5,000 medical reimbursement benefit is probably sufficient since this amount should be enough to cover any deductible or co-payments.

Be sure, however, that the policy's evacuation benefit is adequate for your needs. A long-range chartered air ambulance flight can cost $75,000, or more. For trips to Europe an evacuation benefit of $20,000 to $25,000 is probably sufficient, but if you are going on a trip to a remote area half way around the world, you want a policy that will pay unlimited evacuation costs, or a high dollar amount, for example, $100,000.

Exclusions—Read Carefully

Read the policy carefully to see what is *not* covered. Exclusions and restrictions vary among the policies. For example, some policies won't pay for complications of pregnancy while other policies do provide this coverage. Sports activities such as scuba diving, sky diving, and mountain climbing are usually not covered, but some policies will cover scuba diving for a supplemental fee.

Probably the exclusion of greatest significance to many travelers—particularly the elderly—is the exclusion for preexisting medical conditions. This exclusion could prove disastrous if a condition becomes active during travel and requires emergency treatment or medical evacuation. A typical exclusion states that coverage is excluded for "any injury or sickness (or complications arising therefrom) which manifests itself, or for which treatment or medication was prescribed or taken in the 180 days immediately prior to the period of insurance." However, other policies (e.g., Travel Guard International) are mush less restrictive, excluding only "any condition that has required treatment in the past 60 days, unless the condition is controlled through the taking of prescription drugs or medication and remains controlled throughout the 60-day period."

Two companies, **Lifespan International Association** and **International SOS Assistance**, provide members with an unlimited medical evacuation benefit without any exclusion for preexisting conditions. If you do have an active medical condition, consider one of these policies. If you get sick overseas, your regular health insurance should reimburse you later for doctor and hospital costs, but you won't have to worry about the costs of medical evacuation, should it be necessary. These costs, which are potentially much higher, would be paid entirely by Lifespan or SOS Assistance.

Travel Insurance with Assistance

Worldwide Assistance Services, Inc.
1133 15th Street, N.W., Suite 400
Washington, DC 20005
800-821-2828 or 202-331-1609
This company is a member of the French-owned Europe Assistance Group, the oldest and largest travelers' support system in the world. Their Travel Assistance International Plan provides a $15,000 medical benefit plus unlimited expenses for emergency evacuation. Policy covers medical complications of pregnancy through the third trimester. $75 deductible applies. Pre-existing conditions: 180 days.

TravMed
Box 10623, Baltimore, MD 21285-0623
800-732-5309 or 410-296-5225
$100,000 medical and air ambulance coverage for $3.50 a day. Age 71 and older, $5 a day. $25 deductible. SCUBA coverage, $1.00 a day extra. $25,000 student-abroad coverage available at $2.50 per day. Pre-existing conditions: 90 days.

HealthCare Abroad
243 Church Street N.W., Suite 100-D
Vienna, VA 22180
800-237-6615 or 703-281-9500
$100,000 coverage available up to age 76 with $100 deductible. $25,000 coverage ages 76–84 with $250 deductible. No coverage for medical complications of pregnancy. Pre-existing conditions: 180 days.

Travel Guard International
1100 Center Point Drive
Stevens Point, MI 54481–9970
800-782-5151 or 715-345-0505
$15,000 medical and $20,000 emergency evacuation benefit. No deductible. Pays for scuba diving injuries. Pre-existing conditions: 60 days, but covers "controlled" pre-existing conditions.

Mutual of Omaha
3201 Farnam St.
P.O. Box 31685
Omaha, NE 68131-0618
The Travel Assure plan pays $10,000 medical and $25,000 evacuation benefit on deluxe plan. Pre-existing conditions: 90 days.

WorldCare Travel Assistance
1150 South Olive St.
Los Angeles, CA 90015
800-253-1877 or 213-749-1358
Policy will cover medical complications of pregnancy through the third trimester.

Carefree Travel Insurance
P.O. Box 247
Providence, RI 02901-0247
800-323-3149
$5,000 medical and $25,000 evacuation benefit on deluxe plan. Pre-existing conditions: 60 days, but covers "controlled" pre-existing conditions.

International SOS Assistance
Box 11568
Philadelphia, PA 31685
800-523-8930 or 215-244-1500
SOS membership provides assistance (e.g., medical monitoring) as well as worldwide emergency medical transport. There is no cost limit on the evacuation benefit and no pre-existing condition exclusion. SOS also offers an optional insurance policy to cover hospital and doctor costs.

Access America International
P.O. Box 90315
Richmond, VA 23286-4991
800-284-8300
$10,000 emergency medical and $50,000 evacuation benefits. Pre-existing conditions: 60 days, but covers "controlled" pre-existing conditions. Covers complications of pregnancy and scuba diving.

American Express
P.O. Box 919010
San Diego, CA 92191-9970
800-234-0375
Travel Protection Plan benefits include $100,000 for medical evacuation and $10,000 for medical illness or accident. Covers scuba diving injuries. Pre-existing conditions: 60 days, but covers "controlled" pre-existing conditions.

Travelers Insurance Company
800-243-3174 or 203-277-2318
The Travel Pak Policy pays up to $25,000 for emergency medical evacuation, depending upon how much trip cancellation insurance you purchase. Medical policy covers complications of pregnancy.

Credit-Card Assistance
The American Express Platinum Card will pay for emergency medical transport. Cardholders should contact Travel Emergency Assistance at 800-345-2639 or 202-331-1688 collect from overseas.

Scuba Diving Insurance
Divers Alert Network
800-446-2671 or 612-588-2731
For $40 members get $15,000 in coverage; this is increased to $30,000 for an additional payment of $5. Policy pays costs of emergency transport and decompression chamber treatment.

PADI Diver Accident Program
Minneapolis, MN 55440
800-223-9998 or 310-402-1882
$40,000 benefit for in-water diving accidents. Pays recompression and air ambulance expenses.

Diver Security Insurance
Boulder, CO 80301
800-288-4810
A comprehensive annual coverage of $40,000 costs $40.

Travel Membership Associations
Lifespan International Association, Inc.
1333 Corporate Drive, Suite 310
Irving, TX 75038
800-355-5742 or 214-580-0006
A membership organization providing emergency medical, travel, and legal assistance nationwide and worldwide, whenever members travel 150 miles or more away from home. Air ambulance evacuation and other benefits are covered worldwide with no pre-existing conditions exclusion. Members also have access to comprehensive pretravel health advisory information. Membership is purchased on an annual basis and is available to individuals, families, as well as groups.

Lifeguard Emergency Travel, Inc.
4201 N. Main Street
Fort Worth, TX 76106
817-740-1247
Working in conjunction with Worldwide Assistance Services, Inc., Lifeguard benefits include worldwide air ambulance evacuation and guarantee of insurance payments to overseas hospitals and doctors. Membership is sold on an annual basis

Insurance for Foreign Travelers
Worldwide Assistance Services, Inc.
1133 15th Street, N.W., Suite 400
Washington, DC 20005
800-821-2828 or 202-331-1609
The Travel Assistance U.S.A. plan is offered by Worldwide Assistance, Inc., a part of the Europe Assistance Group. A medical assistance package with emergency medical insurance of $50,000 to $100,000 is available for international visitors to the United States.

15 Emergency Medical Transport

Arranging Medical Transport

Should air evacuation be necessary, it's much easier to have an insurance company make these arrangements through an assistance company than for you to make them yourself. Suppose, though, you have purchased a policy that only reimburses you for these expenses, or perhaps you didn't purchase emergency medical insurance at all but are counting on your regular health insurance or HMO to reimburse you when you return home.

Without an assistance policy, you'll have to make all the transport arrangements yourself, pay up front, and hope your insurance policy or medical plan will reimburse you for costs up to the policy limit. Before paying you, the insurance company or your HMO will insist on knowing if the transport was "medically necessary," and for this you will need a letter or other documentation from your physician or treatment facility.

Unless it's an urgent situation, it's better to contact the insurance company or HMO before medical transport occurs, tell them why the medevac is necessary and what the cost is, and get the insurance company to preauthorize the cost of the transport. This way you will avoid problems when submitting the bills afterward.

Medical Transport by Commercial Airliner

Stretcher transport with a medical attendant is possible worldwide on many scheduled airlines. Your first step is to call the airline and ask for their medical department, special services department, or "stretcher desk." Explain the problem. (If you're sick abroad, somebody back home will probably do this for you.) Most major airlines are experienced in transporting stretcher patients, and they will explain what the procedures are. In most cases, a section of seats is curtained off and a stretcher unit and oxygen installed. Extra seats are allotted for a medical attendant and sometimes a family member. The airline's medical director must authorize the transport, and a medical attendant, either a nurse or a doctor, is contracted with to accompany the patient (sometimes a family member can be the attendant when medical treatment will not be needed enroute). Ground ambulance pickup must be arranged at either end and coordinated with departure and arrival. All these arrangements must flow smoothly, especially when the patient is seriously ill. Making these arrangements can be quite a feat, especially when you may be dealing with non-English-speaking people halfway around the world and many time zones away.

The cost of stretcher transport on a commercial airliner is usually nine to ten times the cost of a one-way economy seat (or four times the cost of a first-class seat). Oxygen, nurse's or doctor's fees, and ground transport will be extra. Scheduling normally takes 48 to 72 hours, or more, and is dependent upon seat availability as well as the airline's acceptance of the transport. Some airlines will not transport stretcher patients. In general, only patients with stable, noncritical medical conditions will be accepted by airlines that do provide stretcher transport.

Let's say you have arranged for stretcher transport of an injured relative back home. The airline probably serves only a limited number of major U.S. cities, which means that you will have to arrange ongoing transport within the United States, either by ground or air ambulance. This is another reason why you may need some type of assistance to coordinate what is sometimes a very complex undertaking. An air ambulance company may be your best bet.

Transport by Air Ambulance

If your medical condition requires immediate air ambulance evacuation, you must contact an air ambulance company that can provide a medically equipped and staffed air ambulance—often a Learjet or turboprop. Most of these companies provide an excellent response, but at a high cost (usually three times the cost of a comparable stretcher-equipped commercial flight). They will also require prepayment of the total fee or preauthorization of the full amount by an insurance company.

Some air ambulance companies will also make stretcher arrangements for you on a commercial airliner, and this can be very helpful, especially in complex cases where there is considerable legwork involved. They will provide medical attendants, obtain medical clearances and consultations, handle language problems, arrange for ground ambulance pickup, and arrange, as necessary, for ongoing air ambulance transport in the United States after arrival from overseas. The fees charged will vary from company to company, so it's best to get several price quotations.

Because of their geographic proximity, U.S. companies are best suited for air ambulance evacuation from Mexico, the Caribbean, Canada, and South America. They can usually arrange transport from Europe or the Pacific Basin to the United States.

When dealing with medical evacuation in other parts of the world, it is advisable, and in some cases necessary, to deal with a European-based company. This is true when charter aircraft must be flown to Africa, Asia, the Middle East, the former Soviet Union, or Eastern Europe. American companies are too remote to provide this service, and they do not have the necessary flight clearances to enter many third world countries.

In certain situations, an air ambulance can be used to provide immediate evacuation from a remote area to a more advanced medical facility. For example, a patient might be flown from Egypt to Geneva, Switzerland, on a Learjet ambulance to receive lifesaving care. After initial treatment and stabilization, the patient might be flown on a stretcher-equipped commercial airliner to the United States for ongoing treatment and convalescence, if required. This last leg of the trip, since it is being done on a scheduled airliner, would be much less expensive than if done by Learjet.

Companies Providing Air Ambulance Services

If you look in the Yellow Pages of any big-city telephone book, you'll find numerous private air ambulance companies listed. What you can't be sure of is their quality. The following companies are well-established in the air ambulance-medevac field. They provide aircraft, flight doctors and nurses, trip coordinators, and worldwide communication capabilities. They can also arrange stretcher transport on commercial airliners. If a particular transport is outside a company's normal service area, they can make arrangements with another company or airline to provide the service for you directly.

U.S.-Based Services

North American Air Ambulance
Blackwood, NJ
800-257-8180
800-322-8167 (New Jersey)

National Air Ambulance
Fort Lauderdale, FL
305-525-5538, 800-327-3710

Aero Ambulance International
Fort Lauderdale, FL
800-749-2376, 305-776-6877
Affiliates in Philadelphia, San Juan,
and Sao Paulo, Brazil
(Worldwide capabilities)

Air Ambulance Professionals
Ft. Lauderdale, FL
800-752-4195, 305-491-0555

Care Flight International
St. Petersburg/Clearwater, FL
800-282-6878, 813-530-7972
(Also provides worldwide medical
escorts)

MedJet International
Birmingham, AL
800-356-2161, 205-841-4460

Life Flight
Hermann Hospital
Houston, TX
800-231-4357

AAA Air Ambulance of America
Austin, TX
512-479-8000
(Has agreements with operators in
Mexico and Spain)

Kalita Flying Service
Ypsilanti, MI
800-521-1590, 313-484-0888
(Global capabilities)

Samaritan Air Evac
Phoenix, AZ
800-321-1823, 602-234-9444
(Also specializes in newborns)

Aeromedical Services International
Las Vegas, NV
800-222-9993, 702-798-4600

Air Ambulance Incorporated
San Carlos, CA
800-982-5806, 510-591-9589

Schaefer's Air Service
Van Nuys, CA
800-247-3355, 818-786-8713

Caribbean/Mexico/Latin America

I.C.A.R.E. Air Medical Services
Queen Juliana Airport
St. Maarten, Neth. Antilles
[599] (5)-70201
or direct dial from U.S.A. 1-809-497-5302 (Anguilla office)

Bohlke Aviation International
Alexander Hamilton Airport
St. Croix, U.S. Virgin Islands
809-778-9177

Emergencia Aera Nacional
Mexico City
[52] (5)-655-3644 or (5)-573-2100

Vuelo de Vida (Life Flight)
Caracas, Venezuela
[58] (2) 919-054 or (2) 351-143

United Kingdom/Europe

Trans Care International
London, England
[44] (81)-993-6151

Heathrow Air Ambulance Services
London, England
[44] (81)-897-6185
(Connecting Europe, the Middle East, North Africa, West Africa)

Swiss Air Ambulance
Zurich, Switzerland
[41] (1)-383-1111
(Extensive operations in Europe, the C.I.S., Africa, the Middle East, and globally)

German Air Rescue
Stuttgart, West Germany
[49] (711)-701-070

Compagnie Generale de Secours
Paris, France
[33] (1)-4747-6666

Euro-Flite O.Y., Ltd. (Finland)
Helsinki Int'l Airport
[358] (0)-174-655
(Service in Finland, the Baltics, the C.I.S.)

EMA Assistance, Ltd.
Helsinki, Finland
[358] (0)-448-557

Turkey

M.A.R.M.
Izmir (Smyrna)
[90] (51)-633-322 or (51)-219-556

Israel

Herzliya Medical Center
Tel Aviv
[972] (9)-592-555
Provides air ambulance evacuation for the Middle East, the former Soviet Union, Africa, and the Eastern Mediterranean. Highly trained medical staff provides evacuations.

East Africa

Flying Doctors Society
Nairobi, Kenya
World famous air ambulance service now offers evacuation services to tourists. Tourists can call about their insurance coverage.
[254] (2)-501-280 or (2)-336-886

Botswana/Zimbabwe/Zambia/Mozambique

Medical Air Rescue Service, Ltd.
Belgravia, Harare, Zimbabwe
[263] (0)-73-45-13/14/15

South Africa

Medical Rescue International
Johannesburg, SA
[27] (11)-403-7080
Extensive assistance network in sub-Saharan Africa. Has mobile decompression chamber for diver emergencies

India

East West Rescue
New Delhi, India
[91] (11)-698-865/623-738/698-554
Specializes in all of the Indian sub-continent & surrounding islands

S.E. Asia

Asia Emergency Assistance
Singapore
[65] 338-2311 or 440-0445
Specializes in evacuations from Hong Kong, China, Far-East Asia, Pacific Rim, and westernmost Pacific islands

Heng-Gref Medical Services
Singapore
[65] 272-6028
Covers S.E. Asia and Indonesia. Assistance office in Bali

Medical Transport of the Overseas Employee

If you are an overseas employee and are sick or injured, your company can help arrange medical transportation to a local hospital. If the local hospital is not adequate, you may need to be flown to another hospital, perhaps in the United States. The following checklist will help your company arrange this type of transportation. They can:

- Assess availability of local ground ambulance and rescue services.
- Establish ground ambulance access protocols. Determine if you will need a language interpreter in emergency situations. Suggestion: Contact the consular section of the U.S. Embassy, a United States consulate, or a corporate neighbor. Since they have already arranged emergency protocols for their own personnel, they can identify reliable English-speaking doctors, and also relate their experience with local hospitals, pharmacies, and ambulance services.
- Formulate medical evacuation protocols for emergencies that can't be handled locally, including planning for disasters as well as individual medevac cases.
- Check availability of stretcher transport on commercial airlines for nonemergency cases.

- Establish access and credit arrangements with an international air ambulance company such as Swiss Air Rescue, EuropAssistance, International SOS Assistance, or one of the other companies listed in this chapter. Commercial airliners will not transport emergency cases.
- Determine if exit visas or other formalities are required.
- Provide on-site employees with 24-hour telephone or telex number(s) of an assistance company, and/or the home office, in case of a medical emergency.

16 Business Travel & Health

Business travel is increasingly international in scope, and more companies are taking steps to protect the health and safety of their employees who are traveling or living abroad.

Business travel is different from tourism. Business travelers are under higher stress due to job performance requirements, tight schedules, sudden departures, separation from home and family—plus the increased fear of kidnapping and terrorism. If you are on a long-term assignment overseas, not only you but also your spouse must deal with culture shock and adapt to living abroad. This chapter will help you prepare for this type of travel.

MEDICAL PREPARATION

Vaccinations and a Travel Kit

Schedule a predeparture medical consultation with your company's medical department to receive any necessary vaccinations. Be sure you have a travel kit that contains basic first-aid supplies, plus analgesics, antacids, a quinolone antibiotic for treating travelers' diarrhea, antimalarial drugs (if needed), and a short-acting sleeping pill for jet lag. Pack mosquito repellents and permethrin clothing spray if you are traveling to a malarious area. Take a mosquito bed net if you will be exposed to mosquitoes or other biting insects at night.

If you work for a smaller company that does not have a medical department, then contact a travelers' clinic for your shots and predeparture health advice.

Start Medication

If you're going to a malarious area and your doctor has prescribed prophylactic mefloquine or chloroquine, start this medication two weeks prior to departure. Under certain circumstances, your doctor might also start you on short-term prophylactic antibiotics to prevent travelers' diarrhea. This might be justified if your project demands your complete availability and physical well-being. Alternatively, you could start prophylactic Pepto-Bismol (two tablets, four times daily) and, if diarrhea occurs, immediately start combination treatment with a quinolone antibiotic (either Cipro or Floxin), plus loperamide.

Keep Shots Up to Date

Between trips, keep your yellow fever and cholera vaccination certificates current if your job requires a possible *immediate departure* to countries requiring one or both of these vaccinations for entry. Remember that the certificate isn't valid until six to ten days after you get these shots. If time is short, have the certificate backdated, but some doctors may hesitate to do this. Not having a valid vaccination certificate could mean being quarantined, being denied entry to a country, or, even worse, being given a vaccination with an unsterile needle or syringe.

Avoid Unsafe Injections

It's virtually impossible to get infected with HIV or the hepatitis B virus if you avoid unsafe injection and unscreened blood transfusions—and don't have sexual contact with a high-risk person. Although getting an unsafe injection overseas is unlikely, such instances can occur when travelers receive emergency medical treatment in hospitals or clinics in lesser-developed countries. Many health care facilities abroad can't afford disposable needles and syringes, so these items are often used over and over, sometimes without adequate sterilization. Because of this situation, some employees of multinational corporations now carry kits stocked with sterile needles and syringes, suture supplies, and, in some cases, intravenous fluids, in case they need injections, wound repair, or IV fluids. For information on emergency medical kits, contact **Travel Medicine, Inc.,** 351 Pleasant St., Suite 312, Northampton, MA 01060; 800-872-8633.

Hepatitis B, the Real Risk

Although people usually focus on HIV, the virus that causes AIDS, sexually acquired hepatitis B is statistically a much greater threat to your health. A study in the *British Medical Journal* (February 1987) reported a 50% exposure to this virus over a five-year period in expatriate male company employees in Southeast Asia. Sexual contact with the local populace was the apparent mode of transmission. If you are a male traveling to either Asia or sub-Saharan Africa, where there is a high incidence of hepatitis B, and wish to avoid hepatitis B, you should (1) practice safe sex, (2) practice abstinence, and/or (3) get vaccinated against hepatitis B.

Travel Insurance

You should purchase travel insurance if your company does not have the resources to (1) pay your hospital bills on the spot or (2) evacuate you in event of serious illness or injury. The best travel policies also provide telephone access to an emergency assistance center through a 24-hour hotline. At the assistance center, multilingual personnel can monitor your medical condition and, if necessary, arrange emergency transportation if your treatment in a local hospital is inadequate. In Chapter 14, you'll find a list of companies that underwrite this type of insurance.

Medical Assistance

An alternative method of protecting a traveling employee is for a company to purchase travel assistance directly. Your firm sets up a credit account with an assistance company. They monitor your medical care, provide direct payments to overseas doctors and hospitals from your account, and arrange air ambulance evacuation, if necessary. Contact **Medex Assistance Corporation**, 1447 York Rd., Suite 410, Lutherville, MD 21093; 410-296-2530. Fax: 410-494-9036. Other companies that provide emergency assistance to corporate travelers include **Lifespan International Association** (800-355-5742), **USAssist** (800-756-5900), and **International SOS Assistance** (800-523-8930).

KIDNAPPING AND TERRORISM

You may be concerned not only about your health but also about your physical safety. What are the risks of being kidnapped, hijacked, or taken hostage? What's the best way to reduce these risks? How should you react in a terrorist incident? When traveling to a hostile or unstable country, what rules should you follow to maintain a low profile? These and many other questions increasingly concern today's business traveler, and rightly so. Multinational corporations and their employees are often the target of dissident groups who are trying to make a political statement or to extort money.

Preparing for a Safe Trip

If your company has a corporate security division, contact that office for a briefing. You also need to start some essential background reading. Suggested titles include *The Safe Travel Book—A Guide for the International Traveler* by Peter Savage (see Introduction) and *Managing Terrorism Risks*, available from The Ackerman Group (see next page).

Safe Travel Tips

Don't

- Dress like a high-profile businessperson.
- Carry expensive luggage.
- Display tickets from U.S. airlines.
- Wear shirts or hats with logos of U.S. corporations.
- Carry English-language publications.

Do

- Take a nonstop flight.
- Send sensitive documents separately.
- Leave detailed itinerary at the office.
- Carry medical evacuation insurance.
- Check U.S. State Department advisories (202-647-5225).

Risk Management

Risk management firms, usually run by former employees of the State Department or CIA, have sprung up to meet the security needs of multinational corporations and certain high-risk travelers. These firms do more than just arrange kidnap insurance. They can do the following:

- Train employees to reduce their risk of being taken hostage.
- Conduct counterterrorism-training seminars.
- Provide personal security training.
- Prepare a crisis management plan.
- Negotiate hostage release.
- Provide antikidnapping equipment (for example, armored cars).
- Alert you to which airlines are under increased terrorist threat (and advise appropriate travel alternatives).
- Provide detailed security advisory prior to travel to a high-risk country.

The best-known firms are listed below. Kidnap insurance is arranged through their affiliated underwriter.

➤ **The Ackerman Group, Inc.** (Chubb Insurance)
1666 Kennedy Causeway
Miami Beach, FL 33141
(305-865-0072)

➤ **Control Risks, Ltd.** (Lloyd's of London)
4350 East-West Highway, Suite 900
Bethesda, MD 20814
(301-654-2075)

➤ **Argen, Inc.** (AIG Insurance)
666 3rd Ave.
New York, NY 10017
(212-986-5151)

➤ **Paul Chamberlain International**
9701 Wilshire, Suite 1201
Beverly Hills, CA 90212
(213-276-2601)

The Overseas Security Advisory Council (OSAC)

This is a joint venture between the State Department and the private sector. OSAC provides corporations doing business overseas with access to an electronic bulletin board that provides information on overseas security conditions. Subscribers can also get further background security data through direct telephone consultation with an OSAC analyst. Criteria for access to the data base include the following:

- Any American-owned, not-for-profit organization or any enterprise incorporated in the United States (parent company, not subsidiaries or divisions) doing substantial business overseas.
- Consultants and private sector security firms sponsored by a U.S. corporation or other private sector enterprise with substantial business overseas but who do not intend to access the electronic data base.

Interested firms should send a letter of application to the following:

Executive Director
Overseas Security Advisory Council
DS/DSS/OSAC
P.O. Box 3590
Washington, D.C. 20007-0090
or call: 202-663-0002

BUSINESS TRAVEL AND STRESS

Your Health May Be at Risk

Business travel can be stimulating and rewarding, but it also can be stressful to the point of jeopardizing your health. In fact, a study by the Hyatt Hotels Corporation found that business travel lasting more than 5.2 days interfered significantly with a traveler's personal life.

The problem is more than just chronic jet lag. Frequent departures on short notice, high-pressure work schedules, job-performance anxiety, living in hotels and motels, traveling alone, eating calorie-dense restaurant and airline food, and not exercising all take their toll. Add to this being separated from your home, your family, and your usual routines. No wonder you feel depressed and lonely—even disoriented at times. You may start to smoke and drink too much— or overeat. You need a sleeping pill at night and then a tranquilizer in the morning. Fatigue mounts and performance suffers. Things spiral downward. The possible outcome? Burnout—or worse. You need a plan.

- Start with physical fitness. A regular exercise program promotes physical and mental health. Exercising also helps control your weight and combats insomnia. Not being fit can lower your self-esteem. What's the best exercise? It's the one you like doing, but experts often recommend either walking or jogging. You can do them almost anywhere, without charge, and they build aerobic stamina.
- Plan the exercise activities you want to pursue during your trip and pack the necessary equipment: footwear, gym gear, bathing suit, tennis racquet, etc.

Take into account the climate (how hot?) and the geography (seashore? mountains?) at your destination.

- Stay in hotels that cater to travelers interested in fitness. Ask about the facilities when you make your reservation. Are there Lifecycles? StairMasters? A swimming pool? Tennis courts? Most major hotels and resorts now have workout rooms and health clubs. The Hyatt, Hilton, and Marriott even provide guests with information on dealing with all types of stress.
- Use a guidebook to plan walking tours of local tourist attractions, museums, scenic areas, etc. If possible, walk to your business appointments. Wear walking shoes made by companies such as Rockport—many models are also formal enough for business dress.

Emotional needs of travelers—In addition to exercise and diet, you need to care for your emotional and psychological needs.

- Keep in close touch with your office and family. Carry some photos of your spouse and children, or close friend. Write postcards and letters. Keep a diary. Take pictures. Buy gifts and souvenirs to bring home.
- Carry playing cards, a board game, a walkman with your favorite cassettes (or foreign language tapes), and a shortwave radio to listen to music and news on the Voice of America or the BBC. The Grundig 7-band short wave radio ($99 from **Magellan's**; 800-962-4943) is a good choice.
- If you are a recovering alcoholic, find out if there is a local AA chapter or other self-help group in the area. For a directory of AA chapters overseas, contact: **AA World Services**, P.O. Box 459, Grand Central Station, New York, NY 10163; or call 212-686-1100. Price: 75 cents.
- Research your destination. Find out as much as possible about the country you're in, its history, and its culture. Make it a project to learn something specific about some aspect of the culture. If you can speak some of the language, do this as much as possible.
- Turn your trip into a psychic adventure. Stripped of your ordinary surroundings, your friends and family, and your usual routine, you are forced into a more direct experience with your new surroundings and yourself. This can be painful, but don't retreat. View your new surroundings not only in terms of work but as an opportunity to learn and grow.

Long-Term Assignments and Stress

If you are being assigned to an overseas post, and will be living abroad for many months, or even years, you and your family will encounter additional stresses. If your spouse and children are traveling with you, how will they adjust? Studies show that spouses (usually the wife of a busy executive) bear the greatest burden adapting to overseas living. Today, most companies anticipate these stresses and provide appropriate counseling. Predeparture orientation and counseling can have a dramatic effect on your psychological well-being and the success of your trip.

To better prepare for your trip also consider the following:

➤ Survival Kit for Overseas Living—Widely used guide for adapting to living abroad. $7.95 plus $2 shipping: Item #306.

➤ *Going International*—Videotape on crosscultural orientation and training. $12.95 plus $2 shipping: Item #535.

➤ Culture Shock—Explores the psychological consequences of exposure to unfamiliar environments. Includes a section on adjustment experiences of business executives. $15.95 plus $2 shipping: Item #578.

Contact the **Intercultural Press,** Inc., P.O. Box 700, Yarmouth, ME 04096, 207-846-5168, for their catalog or to order directly.

Stages of adjustment—What happens when you are uprooted and sent overseas to live and work? Research has delved into the lives of people stationed abroad in order to analyze their psychological reactions to their new environment. These studies show that adaptation will typically occur in three phases.

- Phase 1. You experience an initial period of excitement and well-being, usually lasting about a month. You then start to "come down" as the reality of life in a foreign country sets in.
- Phase 2. This is a period of disillusionment, usually lasting several months. The disillusionment may be with your host country, your work, or both. Instead of acknowledging your feelings, you may instead experience physical symptoms such as fatigue, headaches, and stomach problems, and pass these off as simple stress. You, or your spouse, may even become overtly depressed. In this case, you should seek psychological counseling. (Some employees, or their spouses, don't get over this phase. They can't adapt to their new environment, and consequently reconsider their decision to remain abroad.)
- Phase 3. After about six months, you will have adjusted to your new life in a foreign country. You will also have picked up some of the language, your children will have adjusted to school, your home will be established, and social connections made.

Stress Management: Role of the Medical Director

Culture shock, isolation, loneliness, drug and alcohol abuse—these factors often bring out a darker side to travel. Dr. Elmore Rigamer of the U.S. State Department, speaking at the First International Travel Conference in Zurich, Switzerland, in April 1988, noted an important role in travel for the corporate medical director. By becoming more aware of the common adjustment reactions to relocation and adaptation to other cultures, Dr. Rigamer states that the corporate medical director (or personal physician, for that matter) is in an ideal position to assist the employee in adjusting to overseas living.

According to Dr. Rigamer, treatment of these problems is usually very successful and "predeparture orientation programs that include culture familiarization and language training pay handsome rewards in the prevention area."

Recognizing symptoms for what they are and explaining their causes to the traveling or overseas employee are important aspects of this treatment.

17 Travel & Pregnancy

If you are a healthy woman, a normal pregnancy should not curtail reasonable travel. According to the American College of Obstetricians and Gynecologists, the best time for travel is during the fourth through the sixth months (second trimester) when your body has adjusted to the pregnancy, but you're not so bulky that moving about is difficult. This time is also safer because the probability of miscarriage is less. After the sixth month, the risk of premature labor and other complications increases.

Review your itinerary with your physician and read the trip preparation guidelines in Chapter 1. Because of your pregnancy, you need to follow even more closely those precautions that all travelers should take to prevent accident and illness. Remember, when traveling by automobile, always wear your seat belt. Studies have shown that in nearly 100% of motor vehicle crashes where direct trauma is sustained, the fetus recovers quickly from any pressure the seat belt exerts and suffers no lasting injury. Seat belts with both shoulder and lap restraints are better than lap restraints only because wearing only the lap belt allows forward flexion of your upper body, causing uterine compression. The lap belt should be worn low on your hips under the bulge of your abdomen, as shown below in Figure 17.1.

When to Limit Travel

Review your travel plans with your doctor. A brief trip to Canada or Europe during your second trimester represents a far safer scenario than an extended trip to a third world country where you might have limited access to advanced obstetrical/

Figure 17.1

Proper position of seat belt when pregnant.

Place the lap belt well below your abdomen as low as possible over the pelvic bones. Putting a thin blanket between the belt and your body may increase comfort.

Reprinted with permission from American College of Obstetricians and Gynecologists: *Car Safety for You and Your Baby* (ACOG Patient Education Pamphlet AP018). Washington, D.C., ACOG; 1988.

medical care. *If you will be far away from quick, expert medical care, and your exposure to other diseases is increased, then travel should be discouraged.*

After the 28th week—Most obstetricians advise their patients not to travel beyond a 100-mile radius after the 28th week. Problems after this time include premature labor, preterm rupture of membranes, development of hypertension, phlebitis, and increased risk of uterine and placental injury from motor vehicle accidents.

There are some absolute reasons to avoid overseas travel and many reasons to exercise caution. Your past obstetrical history is important. Having had any of the following conditions places you at higher risk for a possible complication.

- Miscarriage • ectopic (tubal) pregnancy • toxemia
- Premature labor • incompetent cervix • prolonged labor
- Caesarean section • premature ruptured membranes
- Uterine or placental abnormalities • hypertension
- Pelvic inflammatory disease (PID)

Pretravel Checklist

Focus on the following to help you and your doctor evaluate the advisability, and relative safety, of your travel.

- Your past obstetrical history—Have you had complicated pregnancies or difficult deliveries?
- Your present pregnancy—Are there problems?
- Personal comfort—Will it be manageable and acceptable?
- The duration of your trip—More than a few days?
- Your destination—More than 100 miles from home?
- The quality and availability of medical and obstetrical care in the country(s) of your destination.

Prenatal checkups—Don't let your travel plans interfere significantly with these important checkups. You should have your first prenatal appointment at ten weeks. The fetal heart tones are regularly heard by this time, and their presence is reassuring that your pregnancy is probably proceeding normally. Once fetal heart tones are heard, the chance of miscarriage is small. You should then have checkups every four weeks until week 30, then every two weeks until week 36, then weekly until delivery.

Pelvic ultrasound—Before you leave, consider an ultrasound examination to check for tubal pregnancy, twins, placental abnormalities, or other problems.

Your Medical History

- Are you diabetic? Do you take insulin?
- Are you taking medication for any other illness?
- Do you have congenital or acquired heart disease?
- Do you have severe anemia, lung disease, or asthma?
- Do you have other medical illnesses?
- Do you have a previous history of phlebitis?
- Are you very prone to motion sickness?

Have your doctor clear you medically for travel and prescribe any medications that you may need during your trip. This is a good time to start researching the availability of obstetrical and medical care in the cities on your itinerary. Think ahead. What will you do if an emergency arises?

Medical Care Abroad

Before you leave home, learn as much as possible about health care availability abroad. Unfortunately, your own doctor probably won't be of much help because few physicians or obstetricians are familiar with foreign doctors and hospitals. A travelers' clinic might better assist you. Give the nearest one a call. Some clinics maintain their own list of overseas physicians and specialists. Check country listings in the World Medical Guide section of this book. Many physicians are listed who can make a referral. When you arrive overseas, you can contact the nearest American Consulate. They maintain lists of local physicians.

IAMAT—Many travelers join the International Association for Medical Assistance to Travelers (IAMAT) to obtain a listing of qualified English-speaking doctors overseas. Call IAMAT at 519-836-0102 (their main office near Toronto) for membership information.

Travel insurance—If you are going to a lesser-developed country, consider purchasing a travel health insurance policy that provides assistance (see Chapter 14). Calling the assistance hotline number puts you in contact with medical personnel who can help arrange medical treatment, monitor your care, and provide emergency air transport, if needed.

NOTE: Travel insurance policies won't cover any medical expenses associated with a normal pregnancy, e.g., delivery. Some policies don't cover complications in the third trimester. Other policies don't cover miscarriage, which is usually a first trimester problem. Compare the various policies and read their exclusions before you buy.

Call your doctor—*The HealthGuide* suggests that you carry your doctor's telephone number with you. There's nothing wrong with a long distance call to the United States or Canada if you have any problems or questions during your trip.

See Chapter 13, Medical Care Abroad, for additional information about locating English-speaking physicians overseas.

Obstetrical Emergencies

Review with your doctor those signs and symptoms that indicate a possible obstetrical emergency. Seek immediate, *qualified* obstetrical care if you have any of the following:

- Vaginal bleeding
- Passing of tissue or blood clots
- Lower abdominal pain, cramps, or contractions
- Gush of watery fluid from vagina (indicates ruptured membranes)
- Headaches, blurred vision, ankle swelling, high blood pressure (severe toxemia)

Don't overlook other causes of illness. Abdominal pain, for example, does not necessarily indicate an obstetrical emergency. It could be due to appendicitis, a urinary tract infection, or merely simple indigestion. Diagnosing the cause of abdominal pain is usually more difficult during pregnancy. *Readily available, high-quality medical care is essential if you develop worrisome symptoms.* NOTE: Ultrasound is helpful in diagnosing appendicitis and other intra-abdominal disorders.

Normal symptoms that are generally no cause for concern include the following:

- Increased urination • fatigue • insomnia • heartburn • indigestion
- Constipation • slight increase in vaginal discharge
- Sore, bleeding gums • leg cramps • occasional mild dizziness
- Mild swelling around ankles • hemorrhoids

Trauma During Pregnancy

Women in their third trimester tend to have more falls. Eighty percent occur after the 32nd week and are mostly due to easy fatigability, a fainting spell, a protruberant abdomen, and/or looseness of the pelvic joints. Most of these falls are minor and may require only a brief period of observation and fetal monitoring.

A direct blow to your abdomen is more apt to injure the placenta than the fetus. Mild abdominal trauma may cause placental separation (*abruptio placentae*) in 1% to 5% of cases. Major blunt abdominal trauma causes separation in 20% to 50% of cases. Symptoms of *abruptio placentae* are cramping, bleeding, and leaking of amniotic fluid.

Early detection and treatment of *abruptio placentae* is critical in order to prevent fetal death and preserve the mother's health. If you sustain a more severe injury, or are in a motor vehicle accident, with or without direct abdominal trauma—and the fetus is viable (gestational age > 26 weeks)—experts recommend that you have continuous fetal monitoring for at least 24 hours.[1] A pelvic ultrasound study should also be done.

If you are discharged from the hospital soon after an injury, contact your physician immediately if you have any of the following warning symptoms: vaginal bleeding, leak of fluid from the vagina, decrease in or lack of fetal motion, severe abdominal pain around the uterus, rhythmic contractions that come and go, or fainting or dizziness. Rarely, abruption occurs several days after the accident. In most cases, however, symptoms occur in the first four hours following injury.

Immunization Guidelines

Discuss with your doctor which immunizations, if any, you should receive, but defer your shots, if possible, until after the first trimester. If you are traveling to a lesser-developed country, it is generally safer to be immunized against certain diseases than to run the risk of contracting a serious, possibly life-threatening infection.

- Have you been vaccinated against measles and rubella? These diseases can have a devastating effect upon the developing fetus, especially during the first trimester. Measles can also cause severe illness in the mother.
- If not sure about ever having had measles/rubella shots, you should be tested for immunity to these diseases.
- If you lack immunity to measles and/or rubella, you should defer travel to a lesser-developed country because the risk of disease is higher in these countries. Vaccination with measles and/or rubella vaccines during pregnancy is contraindicated because of theoretical harm to the fetus from a live viral vaccine. The vaccines have never caused documented harm when given inadvertently to a pregnant woman, but official policy still advises against their use.
- Tetanus: Get a booster shot if you have not had one within 5 years.
- Polio vaccine: Get a polio booster if traveling to a lesser-developed country. Either inactivated polio vaccine (eIPV) or live viral vaccine (OPV) can be used.
- Hepatitis: Do receive immune globulin or hepatitis B vaccine if you will be at risk for hepatitis A or hepatitis B.
- Oral or injectable typhoid vaccine: Either one can be given if risk of disease is substantial. Avoid during first trimester, if possible.
- Yellow fever: You should receive the yellow fever vaccine if traveling to a risk area in South America or Africa.
- Cholera vaccine: Safe, but should be used only for high-risk travel or to satisfy a country's entry requirements. It's unpredictable if a waiver for the shot will be accepted at a border crossing.
- Rabies, Japanese encephalitis, plague, and meningococcal vaccines can be safely administered, as needed.
- Influenza vaccine is advised if you suffer from heart or lung disease, or simply desire additional protection against this illness.

Antimalarial Drugs and Pregnancy

Avoiding malaria is very important if you are pregnant. Not only is the disease more severe, but there is a higher incidence of miscarriage and premature labor. If possible, you should avoid travel to malarious areas while you are pregnant. *This is especially true if you will be exposed to mosquitoes that transmit chloroquine-resistant falciparum malaria.*

If you do travel to malarious areas, it is important that you (1) avoid mosquitoes, and (2) take prophylactic drugs. Chloroquine and proguanil are safe to take during pregnancy. Mefloquine (Lariam) is not presently approved for use in pregnancy. Fansidar can be used for prophylaxis but only in extreme situations. A treatment dose of Fansidar can be taken for an attack of chloroquine-resistant falciparum malaria.

Do not take doxycycline for prophylaxis if you are pregnant. This drug can stain the teeth of the developing fetus and cause retardation of bone growth. However, doxycycline or tetracycline may have to be used when treating chloroquine-resistant malaria.

Primaquine should not be used during pregnancy because it may cause severe anemia in the fetus. If your doctor wants to treat you with primaquine, continue chloroquine until delivery, after which primaquine can be safely administered.

Other Drugs

As a general rule, avoid all drugs unless they are absolutely necessary for your health or comfort. This is especially true during the first trimester when certain drugs have the greatest potential for causing harm. Don't take drugs for trivial symptoms. Employ nondrug remedies when possible. For example, use warm compresses for muscle aches instead of an analgesic. Throat lozenges, nasal sprays, and cough drops, rather than a drug taken internally, can often be used to treat symptoms. Remember, though, that in cases of serious illness, such as an infection, drugs such as antibiotics should be used appropriately to safeguard your health as well as the baby's.

Many drugs are safe to take during pregnancy, and no specific warnings are issued against their use. But drug companies, partly because of liability worries, often hedge their bets by saying their product "has not been shown to be safe during pregnancy" even though the drug may have been taken thousands of times with no evidence of fetal injury. Other drugs may cause abnormalities in test animals but show no apparent harmful effects in humans. These drugs are often put on the "caution" list, usually to prevent a possible lawsuit. The net effect of this uncertainty is to make patients and physicians cautious about using almost any drug during pregnancy. The attitude is "better safe than sorry." This may be good advice in general, but don't let it prevent you from taking certain drugs, such as chloroquine, or an antibiotic, that may be essential to your health.

NOTE: If you are sexually active and not practicing birth control, or you are trying to become pregnant, then you should also avoid all drugs that are contraindicated during pregnancy; take other medication cautiously and only if necessary.

Drug Use Guidelines

Consult with your physician or obstetrician about any drugs you possibly may need to take while traveling. Avoid any drug to which you might be allergic. Take drugs only if the severity of your symptoms outweighs the risk of possible side effects.

Drugs for Pain and Arthritis

Acetaminophen (Tylenol)—Non-aspirin analgesics containing acetaminophen are safe.
Aspirin—Avoid (increases chance of bleeding).
Nonsteroidal antiinflammatories (ibuprophen, etc.)—Avoid.

Drugs for Diarrhea

Bismuth subsalicylate (Pepto-Bismol)—Avoid (contains salicylate).
Loperamide (Imodium)—Probably safe. Use only for watery diarrhea.
Lomotil*—Use only if diarrhea is a significant problem.
Furazolidone (Furoxone)—Safe.
Trimethoprim/sulfamethoxazole (Bactrim*)—Probably safe. Avoid at term.
Quinolones (Floxin, Cipro)—Avoid unless severity of infection warrants use.
Metronidazole (Flagyl*)—Use caution in first trimester. Avoid unless severity of infection justifies use.
Quinacrine—Probably safe.
Tetracycline, doxycycline—Avoid unless severity of infection warrants use.

Drugs for Altitude Sickness

Dexamethasone (Decadron)—Short-term use is safe.
Acetazolamide (Diamox)—Probably safe. Avoid at term.

Sleeping Pills & Tranquilizers

Halcion, Restoril, Valium—Avoid.
Alcohol—Avoid.

Drugs for Motion Sickness & Colds

Dramamine—Probably safe. Use only if motion sickness is a significant problem.
Meclizine (Antivert)—Probably safe. Use only if motion sickness is a significant problem.
Transderm Scōp—Probably safe. Use only if motion sickness is a significant problem.
Decongestants and cough remedies—Probably safe. Some obstetricians, however, prefer only topical decongestants such as Neo-Synephrine or Afrin nasal spray. Avoid combination cold remedies that contain aspirin, alcohol, or iodides.
Hismanal, Seldane—Avoid during first trimester.

Drugs for Malaria and Other Infections

Chloroquine (Aralen, Nivaquine)—Safe.

Proguanil (Paludrine)—Safe.

Fansidar*—Can be taken as a single dose for treatment of malaria.

Quinine—Indicated for treatment of chloroquine-resistant falciparum malaria. Otherwise avoid.

Quinidine—Probably safe. Can be used as an alternative to quinine.

Mefloquine (Lariam)—Probably safe but not currently recommended for prophylaxis unless alternate drugs not available.

Halofantrine (Halfan)—Safe for treatment of falciparum malaria.

Tetracycline, doxycycline—Avoid unless needed to treat chloroquine-resistant falciparum malaria or another life-threatening infectious illness.

Primaquine—Avoid until after delivery.

Penicillin, amoxicillin—Safe. Many urinary infections, however, are now resistant to ampicillin and amoxicillin.

Quinolones (Floxin, Cipro)—Avoid unless necessary to treat a severe infection.

Erythromycin—Safe.

Cephalosporins (e.g., Rocephin, Ceftin)—Safe.

Sulfisoxazole (Gantrisan)—Probably safe. Avoid near end of third trimester.

Macrodantin—Probably safe, but avoid at term. Selected by many obstetricians, due to its effectiveness, as the initial choice for most urinary tract infections.

Praziquantel (Biltricide)—Probably safe.

Paromomycin—Safe; an alternative drug to treat amebiasis.

Iodoquinol—Avoid.

Other Drugs

Iodine water purification tablets—Avoid prolonged use (more than 2–3 weeks).

*Use only in absence of suitable alternative.

Exercise and Pregnancy

Labor is aptly named. Childbearing takes a lot of stamina, and it's no surprise that moderate exercise is appropriate (and recommended) for healthy pregnant women. Today, many obstetricians and sports-medicine specialists say that more strenuous exercise, such as running or jogging, is not harmful to the fetus and may even help build stamina for labor and recovery afterward. But how much exercise is too much? And who should avoid exercise? The general guidelines set forth by the American College of Obstetricians and Gynecologists recommend the following:

- Maternal heart rates during exercise should not exceed 140 beats per minute.
- Strenuous activities should not exceed 15 minutes in duration.
- No exercise should be performed in the supine position after the fourth month.
- Maternal core temperature should not exceed 38°C (101.4°F).

Some authorities believe the 15-minute limitation is too restrictive. Researchers have studied women in good physical condition who were six months pregnant and who rode exercise bicycles to exhaustion. The women suffered no untoward effects from the exercise—nor did fetal heart rates slow during exercise, indicating that fetal blood flow was well maintained. Researchers, citing this and other studies, say that more vigorous exercise can be safe for mother and child, but advocate the following:

- Taylor exercise to your needs and abilities. If you are normally a sedentary person who has never exercised vigorously, low intensity workouts that involve walking, stationary cycling, and swimming are probably best.
- Exercise within a comfort zone—don't exhaust yourself, over heat, or become dehydrated. Be especially cautious when exercising in a hot, humid climate. Factors that affect heat tolerance include your body weight, your exercise intensity, and whether you're used to the heat. It usually takes about two weeks for your body to become acclimated, i.e., adjusted to the heat.[2]
- If you are a healthy person used to very vigorous exercise, there's probably no reason you can't exceed the ACOG guidelines as long as you do not become hyperthermic or dehydrated. Studies have shown that healthy women with normal pregnancies can safely exercise three times a week for 43 minutes at heart rates up to 144 beats per minute.
- After exercising do not abruptly stop—cool down slowly.
- Take into account your medical history and physician's advice. Absolute contraindications against exercising include a history of the following conditions: three or more spontaneous miscarriages, ruptured membranes, premature labor, diagnosed multiple gestations, an incompetent cervix, bleeding or a diagnosis of placenta previa, and a diagnosis of heart disease.
- Stop exercising if you experience pain, bleeding, dizziness, shortness of breath, or palpitations.
- Avoid extreme pursuits such as water skiing and downhill skiing after the first trimester. Avoid cross country skiing in the third trimester to lessen the chance of falls.
- Avoid high-altitude treks—You'll be far from medical care if an emergency occurs.
- Do not scuba dive at any depth.

Altitude and Pregnancy

There is no known fetal risk when pregnant women go to high altitudes for a few days.[3] Some authorities, however, advise against trekking in remote areas above 7,000 feet. Not only will you be exposed to acute altitude sickness, but emergency medical and obstetrical care will be far away.

Women who remain at high altitudes during their pregnancies have an altitude-associated increase in fetal growth retardation, high blood pressure, and premature delivery. Consult with your doctor if you are pregnant and will be traveling to, or plan to live at, altitudes greater than 6,000 feet.

Commercial Flying

Be aware that domestic airlines ordinarily won't allow travel after the 36th week of gestation and that the cutoff for foreign airlines is 35 weeks.

After 24 weeks—Get a letter from your doctor specifying details of your pregnancy and giving permission to travel. *This letter is mandatory if you must travel after week 35.* Call the particular airline that you will be using to verify their requirements.

Unless you have severe anemia or sickle cell disease/trait, the reduced cabin oxygen pressure will not harm you or the fetus. If your blood count is reduced more than 25% to 30%, you may require pretravel treatment of the anemia and/or supplemental oxygen en route.

Cosmic radiation is increased at the flight altitudes of commercial jets. Studies suggest that an exposure of 50 millirems of radiation per month (about 80 hours of flight) will not harm the fetus. This is the permissible monthly exposure allowed pregnant flight attendants.

NOTE: Airport metal detectors will not harm the fetus.

Varicose veins can be a problem during the third trimester. Request an aisle seat so that you can get up and walk around every 20 to 30 minutes and be sure to drink extra fluids en route. This will help prevent phlebitis. If possible, get a bulkhead seat so that you can extend and elevate your legs.

Breast-Feeding

If your child is born overseas, you definitely should breast-feed instead of bottle feed your baby. This is not only a question of convenience, but also of health. Breast-feeding is associated with a much lower incidence of infant diarrhea, especially in countries with hot climates.

Travelers' Diarrhea

It is not entirely clear how pregnant travelers should treat diarrhea. Some authorities, worried about the safety of the fetus, shy away from recommending practically any drug treatment.[4] You should discuss with your physician under what circumstances you might take a drug to relieve symptoms.

When diarrhea is more severe, be sure you drink enough fluids to prevent dehydration. Follow the instructions in Chapter 4 regarding oral rehydration and fluid maintenance therapy. Consider taking loperamide if your diarrhea is watery and frequent and you would experience undue inconvenience or embarrassment from not controlling symptoms.

Antibiotic treatment—A recent study carried out in Mexico showed that watery diarrhea often responds quickly (within 1–2 hours) to a combination of the antibiotic trimethoprim/sulfamethoxazole (Bactrim, Septra) and the antimotility drug loperamide (Imodium). Ask your doctor about the pros and cons of taking a short course (1–2 days) of treatment with these drugs to help control more severe symptoms. This treatment should be considered especially during the second or third trimester when exposure to drugs is generally safer for the fetus. Unfortunately, there is increasing resistance to trimethoprim/sulfamethoxazole by the bacteria that cause travelers" diarrhea. You should not use antibiotics such as doxycycline, tetracycline, or the quinolones to treat simple watery diarrhea.

Furazolidone (Furoxone) is probably the best antibiotic for treating diarrhea during pregnancy. It has a broad antimicrobial spectrum covering the majority of gastrointestinal tract pathogens including *E. coli*, salmonella, shigella, aerobacter, vibrio, and *Giardia lamblia*. According to the PDR (Physicians's Desk Reference), animal studies have demonstrated no evidence of teratogenicity (birth defects) following the administration of furazolidone over long periods of time and at doses far in excess of those recommended for humans.

If you develop Type II diarrhea (dysentery) with fever and bloody stools, you should seek immediate medical attention. Fluid replacement is still a priority, but you will probably need antibiotic treatment as well as diagnostic studies to test for salmonella, shigella, and other organisms. Check with your doctor prior to departure about what antibiotic you might take with you for the emergency treatment of dysentery. Starting self-treatment with trimethoprim/sulfamethoxazole is one option, but many strains of shigella and salmonella are now resistant to this antibiotic. This leaves two other choices: furazolidone or one of the quinolones. Although the quinolones are generally contraindicated during pregnancy, the severity of your illness should determine the appropriate choice of antibiotic since curing a severe infection is the first priority. Discuss appropriate antibiotic treatment with your physician, because effective treatment should not be withheld if your health (and your child's) is in jeopardy from a severe gastrointestinal infection.

Notes:

1. Trauma in Pregnancy. *Postgraduate Medicine*, Nov. 1, 1990. p. 89.
2. *University of California Wellness Letter*, Vol. 6, July 1990.
3. Barry M., Bia F. Pregnancy and Travel. *Journal of the American Medical Association*. Feb. 3, 1989. pp. 728-730.
4. Barry M., Bia F. Pregnancy and Travel. *Journal of the American Medical Association*. Feb. 3, 1989. pp. 728-730.

World Medical Guide

Yellow Fever Endemic Zones

The countries listed on the next page lie in the so-called Yellow Fever Endemic Zones. These are the regions in Central and South America and in Africa that harbor mosquitoes (mainly *Aedes aegypti* species) that can potentially transmit the yellow fever virus or where outbreaks of yellow fever are reported or have been reported previously. When cases of yellow fever are reported to the World Health Organization (WHO), yellow fever is then reported "active" in that country by the WHO in its periodic bulletins. Yellow fever activity, however, sometimes occurs without being officially reported. This fact has several implications: (1) if you travel to an Endemic Zone country not reporting yellow fever, and you visit certain rural areas, you still could be at risk of being bitten by an infective mosquito, and (2) after visiting an Endemic Zone country, you may need a yellow fever vaccination certificate to be allowed entry into other countries on your itinerary; border crossing authorities in certain countries may fear that anyone arriving from the Endemic Zone—even from a "disease-free" country—may potentially be infected and spread the yellow fever virus.

Who Needs Shots?

- Some countries in Africa and South America (they're identified by the ★) require a valid yellow fever vaccination certificate from ALL travelers, no matter where they are arriving from. If you are going to one of these countries, be sure you get inoculated at least 10 days prior to arrival so that your certificate will be valid and you will be allowed entry into that country.
- If you are traveling to a country where yellow fever is reported "active" but the vaccination is not REQUIRED for entry, then the yellow fever vaccination is RECOMMENDED.
- If you are traveling to an Endemic Zone country where no yellow fever activity is reported, and the vaccination is not required, you don't need to be vaccinated UNLESS (1) you anticipate travel to rural areas of that country (where yellow fever may be lurking), or (2) you will be traveling onwards to another country(s) in Central America, South America, the Middle East, Africa, Asia, Southeast Asia, or Oceania that require the yellow fever vaccine of Endemic Zone travelers. If no individual country on your on-going itinerary requires it, consider getting vaccinated anyway—you may have an itinerary change and yellow fever vaccination could unexpectedly be required.

Types of Vaccination Requirements You May Encounter

- A yellow fever (YF) vaccination certificate is required of ALL travelers arriving from ALL COUNTRIES. Countries with this requirement are listed below and are identified by an asterisk ★.
- A vaccination certificate is required of all travelers arriving from ANY COUNTRY IN THE ENDEMIC ZONES.
- A vaccination certificate is required of travelers arriving from YELLOW FEVER-INFECTED AREAS.
  In this situation, the *HealthGuide* recommends that you receive the YF vaccination if you will be arriving from *any* Endemic Zone country, even if you didn't visit an "infected area" within that particular country.
- A vaccination certificate is required of travelers arriving from a country ANY PART OF WHICH IS INFECTED.

YELLOW FEVER ENDEMIC ZONE COUNTRIES

Africa

Angola
Benin ★
Botswana
Burkina Fasso ★
Burundi
Cameroon ★
Central African Rep. ★
Chad
Congo ★
Cote d'Ivoire ★
Equatorial Guinea

Ethiopia
Gabon ★
Gambia
Ghana ★
Guinea-Bissau
Ivory Coast
Kenya
Liberia ★
Mali ★
Malawi
Mauritania★
Niger ★

Nigeria
Rwanda ★
Sao Tome & Principe ★
Senegal ★
Sierra Leone
Somalia
Sudan
Tanzania
Togo ★
Uganda
Zaire★
Zambia

Central/South America

Belize
Bolivia
Brazil
Colombia
Costa Rica

Ecuador
French Guiana ★
Guatemala
Guyana
Honduras
Nicaragua

Panama
Peru
Suriname
Venezuela
Trinidad & Tobago

Cholera Vaccination Requirements

There is no longer any official World Health Organization requirement for cholera vaccination. About 25 countries, however, have their own cholera vaccination requirements, and if you are a traveler visiting lesser-developed countries, you may suddenly be confronted by a border crossing official demanding to see a valid cholera vaccination certificate. Failure to have this document may cause you to be quarantined, denied entry, or possibly vaccinated against your will, perhaps with an unclean needle/syringe. Since it's not always possible to predict when this requirement will be enforced, it's a good idea to either 1) have at least one cholera shot to validate a certificate, or 2) have your doctor indicate on your "International Certificate of Vaccination" that you have a medical contraindication to the cholera vaccine. The certificate has a section for this purpose, and your doctor should fill it out, sign it, and affix the official stamp. This should be done if you are traveling to one of the countries below and then proceeding to other countries in Africa, the Middle East, or Asia.

CHOLERA-INFECTED COUNTRIES
(World Health Organization, November 1994)

Afghanistan	Ghana	Pakistan
Albania	Guatemala	Panama
Angola	Guinea	Peru
Argentina	Guyana	Philippines
Belize	Honduras	Russian Federation
Benin	India	Rwanda
Bhutan	Indonesia	Sao Tome & Principe
Bolivia	Iran	Sierra Leone
Brazil	Iraq	Sudan
Burkina Fasso	Kazakhstan	Suriname
Burundi	Kenya	Sri Lanka
Cambodia	Laos	Swaziland
Cameroom	Liberia	Tanzania
Chad	Malawi	Tajikistan
Chile	Malaysia	Togo
China	Mali	Tuvalu
Colombia	Mauritania	Uganda
Costa Rica	Mexico	Ukraine
Cote d'Ivoire	Mozambique	Venezuela
Djibouti	Nepal	Vietnam
Ecuador	Nicaragua	Zaire
El Salvador	Niger	Zambia
French Guiana	Nigeria	

USA

Washington, DC ... GMT -5 hrs, -4 hrs (Apr–Oct)

Entry Requirements
- Passport/Visa: A passport is required. Travelers should check visa requirements.
- AIDS test: Not required for tourists.
- Vaccinations: None required.

Telephone Country Code: 1

Canadian Embassy: 501 Pennsylvania Ave., N.W., Washington, D.C. 20001. Tel. (202)-682-1770.

Health Advisory

Health insurance: Medical care in the United States is expensive. Foreign travelers can purchase additional health insurance through Worldwide Assistance, Inc. (800-821-2828 or 202-331-1609). Their Travel Assistance U.S.A. plan pays up to $100,000 in medical expenses. Travel Insurance Services (800-937-1387 or 510-932-1387) is another broker offering health insurance for overseas travelers in the United States.

Travelers' diarrhea: Low risk. Tap water from municipal water systems is potable.

Food-borne disease: Low risk. Sporadic cases of food-borne illness, usually due to salmonella or campylobacter, are reported. Raw eggs and undercooked chicken are sometimes a source of salmonellosis outbreaks. Undercooked fast food hamburger meat caused a multistate outbreak in 1993 of bloody diarrhea caused by *E. coli* O157:H7. Cholera, transmitted by contaminated shellfish (crab, shrimp, raw oysters) occurs sporadically along the Gulf of Mexico (Texas, Louisiana). Gastroenteritis, due to *Vibrio* species, salmonella, or campylobacter, has been reported after the consumption of contaminated oysters in Louisiana, Maryland, North Carolina, Florida, and Mississippi. Ciguatera fish poisoning is occasionally reported from Hawaii and Florida.

Giardiasis: Occurs primarily in wilderness areas of the Rocky Mountains and the Pacific Northwest. Pockets of disease occur elsewhere. Nationwide distribution of risk, however, is not precisely delineated. Campers and hikers should always boil or filter drinking water obtained from streams, lakes, or ponds.

Tick-borne diseases: Lyme disease occurs in the Middle Atlantic states, the Northeast, the upper Midwest, and the northern Pacific Coast. Ehrlichiosis and Rocky Mountain spotted fever occur in the southcentral and southeastern United States. Travelers to rural or suburban areas of these regions should take anti-tick precautions, especially during the spring and summer.

Viral encephalitis: One hundred and twenty two cases of viral encephalitis were reported in 1991. More than one-half were cases of St. Louis encephalitis which occurred in Arkansas and Texas. Cases of eastern equine encephalitis (EEE) have been reported in Massachusetts, Florida, Georgia, and South Carolina. A cluster of 5 cases of EEE occurred in Florida in July 1991. Viral encephalitis is commonly spread by culex mosquitoes, but the *Aedes albopictus* mosquito (the "Asian tiger mosquito") is also known to transmit the virus. *A. albopictus* is an aggressive biter and is now widespread in the central and southeastern United States in both forest and suburban habitats. Travelers to these areas should avoid mosquito bites.

Rabies: Very low risk nationwide but the potential risk of transmission from raccoons to humans is increasing in the northeast. Raccoon rabies is endemic in the southeastern and Middle Atlantic states and is spreading rapidly in the northeastern United States. In northcentral and southcentral United States, and California, skunk rabies predominates. Along the Mexican border, dog-transmitted rabies is a threat to humans. In Alaska, the arctic and red fox are primarily infected. Bats anywhere in the United States should be considered potentially rabid. Travelers should seek immediate treatment for any unprovoked animal bite, particularly if from a raccoon, fox, skunk, or bat. Other wild animals that rarely transmit rabies include groundhogs, wolves, bobcats, and black bears. No cases of wild animal rabies have been reported from the states of Washington, Idaho, Utah, Nevada, or Colorado.

Hantavirus infections: An outbreak of respiratory illness caused by Hantavirus has recently been reported in the western and southwestern United States. Transmission is due to aerosolized rodent urine or secondary aerosolization of dried rodent excreta.

CANADA

Ottawa ... GMT -5 hrs, -4 hrs (Apr–Oct)

Entry Requirements
- Passport/Visa: Americans visiting Canada are required to carry proof of citizenship. Acceptable documents are (1) a passport; (2) an original birth certificate, or a notarized copy; (3) a voter's registration card; (4) a Selective Service card; (5) a naturalization certificate; or (6) a baptismal certificate, for infants. A driver's license is not accepted as proof of citizenship, but may be used to verify the other documents. Children under 16 must have written travel permission if not accompanied by parent or guardian. For further information, contact the Canadian embassy in Washington at (202) 682-1770.
- AIDS test: Not required.
- Vaccinations: None required.

Telephone Country Code: 1

American Express: 220 Laurier Avenue West, Ottawa; Tel. (613) 563-0231.

Embassies/Consulates: U.S. Embassy, Ottawa, 100 Wellington Street; Tel. (613) 238-5335. Canadian Embassy, 501 Pennsylvania Ave., N.W., Washington, D.C. 20001; Tel. (202) 682-1770.

Hospitals/Doctors in Canada
The Montreal General Hospital (Emergency Department); Tel: 937-6011
The Toronto Hospital (Emergency Department). Tel: 340-3946
L'Hotel Dieu de Quebec, Quebec City (Emergency Department); Tel: 691-5151
Metropolitan General Hospital, Windsor (Emergency Department); Tel: 254-1661

Travelers' Clinics in Canada

Tropical Disease Unit
The Toronto Hospital
200 Elizabeth Street
Toronto, Ontario M5G 2C4
Tel: 416-340-3671

Travel Counselling & Immunization Unit
St. Michael's Hospital
61 Queen St., 3rd floor
Toronto, Ontario
Tel: 416-864-6040

The Travel Clinic
Bishop's Cross Medical Centre
2300 John St.
Thornhill, Ontario L3T 6G7
Tel: 416-889-5777

Tropical Disease Clinic
Ottawa Civic Hospital
1053 Carling Ave.
Ottawa, Ontario K1Y 4E9
Tel: 613-761-4972

McGill University Centre
for Tropical Diseases
Montreal General Hospital
1650 Cedar Ave., Rm. 787
Montreal, Quebec H3G 1A4
Tel: 514-934-8049

For additional information on Canadian travelers' clinics, contact either IAMAT or the Canadian Society for International Health, Division of Tropical Medicine, 1565 Carling Avenue, Suite 400, Ottawa, Ontario K1Z 8R1; 613-725-3789.

Health Advisory for Canada
No unusual health risks are present. Degree of sanitation is comparable to the United States.
Health insurance: U.S. citizens visiting Canada should carry adequate health insurance coverage. Travelers over 65 are not covered by medicare in Canada, and supplemental travel insurance is recommended. See Chapter 14 for a listing of companies underwriting travel insurance.
Giardiasis: Occurs sporadically in wilderness areas. Rural streams, lakes and ponds may be contaminated with the parasite. Campers and hikers should follow safe water guidelines in risk areas. Water filtration is usually adequate to prevent transmission of disease. To help prevent the spread of giardiasis, all campers should dispose of fecal material in a safe fashion.
Insects: Black flies and mosquitoes can be a significant problem during the spring and summer months. Travelers to outdoor rural areas (especially campers, hikers, fishermen) are urged to have adequate protection against biting insects. Adequate protection consists of head nets, mosquito bed nets, a skin repellent containing deet, and permethrin-treated clothing.
Hepatitis B: There is a high carrier rate of the hepatitis B virus in the Inuit population in northern Canada. Hepatitis B vaccination is recommended for healthcare workers and others who will have close contact with this population.
Rabies: Very low risk to humans. Less than 5% of cases are transmitted by dogs. Most rabies in Canada is confined to animals, particularly arctic and red foxes. Travelers should seek immediate treatment for any unprovoked animal bite, particularly if from a fox, raccoon, skunk, or bat. Other wild animals in Canada that can potentially transmit rabies include groundhogs, wolves, bobcats, and black bears.

D I S E A S E   R I S K   S U M M A R Y
Mexico, Central America, and the Caribbean

Malaria: There is low risk of malaria in Mexico. Most cases are confined to rural areas of the West Coast. *P. vivax* accounts for 98% of malaria infections, the remainder are attributed to *P. falciparum*. Chloroquine prophylaxis is recommended when visiting malarious areas. Chloroquine-resistant falciparum malaria has not been reported. Drug prophylaxis is not necessary when visiting resort areas in Mexico, but personal protective measures against mosquito bites are recommended.

In Central America, there is risk of vivax malaria in rural areas. There is no malaria in the major cities of Central America. Chloroquine prophylaxis is recommended for travelers visiting rural areas. Travelers should consider mefloquine prophylaxis in malarious areas of Panama, where chloroquine-resistant *P. falciparum* may be present.

There is no risk of malaria in the Caribbean, except in Haiti, the Dominican Republic, and in southwestern Trinidad where an outbreak of vivax malaria has been recently reported in the town of Icacos.

All travelers to Mexico, Central America, and the Caribbean should take measures to prevent mosquito bites. These precautions include applying a deet-containing skin repellent, wearing permethrin-treated clothing, and, when appropriate, sleeping under a mosquito bed net.

Yellow fever: Yellow fever is reported active only in the remote jungle areas of Trinidad. Several countries in Central America are in the Yellow Fever Endemic Zone, where yellow fever is potentially active. Vaccination is recommended for persons who plan to travel to rural areas of these Endemic Zone countries.

Cholera: Mexico and the other countries in Central America are currently reporting cases of cholera. Although cholera vaccination is not required for entry to any country if arriving directly from the U.S. or Canada, one may be required if arriving from a cholera-infected area, or required for on-going travel to other countries in Latin America, Africa, the Middle East, or Asia. Travelers should consider vaccination or a doctor's letter of exemption from vaccination. The risk to travelers of acquiring cholera is considered low. Cholera occurs primarily in areas with inadequate sanitation and unsafe water supplies such as urban slums and rural areas. Prevention consists primarily in adhering to safe food and drink guidelines.

Travelers' diarrhea: High risk in Mexico and Central America, except for first-class hotels and major resort areas. Lower risk in Belize and Costa Rica, where sanitation is generally better. Medium risk in most Caribbean islands, except for Haiti, where the risk is high. Travelers should observe all food and drink safety precautions. A quinolone antibiotic is recommended for the treatment of acute diarrhea. Diarrhea not responding to treatment with an antibiotic, or chronic diarrhea, may be due to a parasitic disease such as giardiasis or amebiasis.

Hepatitis: All susceptible travelers should consider immune globulin prophylaxis or hepatitis A vaccine prior to travel to these regions. The hepatitis B carrier rate in the general population of these regions is generally less than 1%–2% and vaccination is not routinely recommended for tourist travel. Vaccination against hepatitis B is recommended for healthcare workers to this region.

Amebiasis: There is a high incidence of amebiasis in Mexico and Central America, where up to 50% of the high-risk population may be infected with *E. histolytica* parasites. To avoid amebiasis, travelers should drink only safe water and eat only well-cooked food. All fruit should be peeled before eating.

Typhoid fever: Typhoid vaccination is recommended for persons traveling for periods longer than 3–4 weeks in rural areas, and who will be staying in areas where there is substandard sanitation.

Dengue fever: Dengue is widespread throughout Central America and the islands of the Caribbean, including Puerto Rico and the U.S. Virgin Islands. In Mexico, dengue occurs primarily during July, August, and September. There is no dengue in Bermuda, the Cayman Islands, or Costa Rica. The Aedes mosquitoes, which transmit dengue, bite primarily during the daytime and are present in populous urban areas as well as resort and rural areas. Prevention of dengue consists of taking protective measures against mosquito bites.

Schistosomiasis: Risk, albeit low, is present in the Antigua, Dominican Republic, Guadeloupe, Martinique, Montserrat, Puerto Rico, and Saint Lucia. Travelers should avoid swimming or bathing in freshwater ponds or streams that may be snail infested.

Leishmaniasis: Cutaneous leishmaniasis (chicleros ulcer), mucocutaneous leishmaniasis (espundia), and visceral leishmaniasis (kala azar) occur in scattered areas of Mexico and Central America. These diseases are transmitted by sand flies (which bite from dusk to dawn). All travelers should take measures to prevent bites by these insects.

Filariasis (Bancroftian variety): This mosquito-transmitted disease occurs (rarely) in the Lesser Antilles from Trinidad north to Guadeloupe. Puerto Rico and the eastern coastal areas of Central America are also potential risk areas. Highest risk is presently in Haiti and the Dominican Republic. Travelers to these regions should take measures to prevent mosquito bites.

Onchocerciasis: This is a form of filariasis prevalent in southern Mexico and Guatemala. Travelers should take measures to prevent insect (black fly) bites.

Chagas' disease: Occurs in many areas of rural Central America. Risk occurs primarily in those rural-agricultural areas where there are adobe-style huts and houses that potentially harbor the night-biting triatomid (assassin) bugs. Travelers sleeping in such structures should take precautions against nighttime bites. Unscreened blood transfusions are also a source of infection and should be avoided.

Rabies: This disease is present in all Central American countries, but the risk is highest in Mexico, El Salvador, Guatemala, and Honduras. There is a lower risk of rabies in Costa Rica. Mongoose-borne rabies has been reported in Puerto Rico. There is no risk of rabies in the Caribbean, except for Haiti, the Dominican Republic, and Grenada. Travelers should avoid stray animals, especially dogs, and seek emergency treatment of any animal bite. Pre-exposure rabies vaccination is recommended for all persons planning a long stay (4 weeks or more), or extensive travel in rural areas of Mexico and Central America.

AIDS: In Mexico and Central America, homosexual and bisexual activity is the prevailing mode of transmission, but the heterosexual spread of AIDS is increasing. In the Caribbean, there are high rates of heterosexually transmitted AIDS, especially in the Bahamas, Haiti, and the Dominican Republic.

Helminthic diseases: Hookworm is common, especially in rural areas. Travelers should wear shoes to prevent transmission of this disease. Ascariasis and trichuriasis (roundworm and whipworm diseases), caused by the ingestion of food contaminated with the eggs of these worms, can be prevented by washing vegetables and adequately cooking all food. In Mexico and Central America, pork tapeworm disease (caused by the parasite *Taenia solium*) is common and can be prevented by thoroughly cooking food. Cysticercosis and neurocysticercosis, caused by the ingestion of pork tapeworm eggs, is prevalent. (Pork tapeworm eggs are transmitted by fecally contaminated food and/or water.)

Other illnesses: Anthrax, brucellosis (from consumption of raw dairy products or occupational contact with animals), coccidiomycosis, histoplasmosis, toxocariasis, toxoplasmosis, sexually transmitted diseases, and tuberculosis.

Animal hazards: Scorpions, black widow spiders, brown recluse spiders, and several species of tarantulas are common in many areas of Mexico and Central America. The beaded lizard, gila monster, and vampire bat occur in Mexico and elsewhere.

Marine hazards: The Portuguese man-o'-war, stingrays, several species of poisonous fish, stinging anemones, coral and hydroids, and jellyfish are present in coastal waters and are a potential hazard to unprotected swimmers.

Accidents: Drownings and motor vehicle accidents are the primary threats. There is a high risk of injury from motor vehicle, motorcycle, and moped accidents in all countries of Central America and the Caribbean.

MEXICO

Consulate: 202-736-1000   *Mexico City*   *GMT -6 hrs*

Entry Requirements

- Passport/Visa: Tourist card and proof of citizenship are required for American or Canadian citizens. A passport is the best document. Travelers can call the Mexican consulate in Washington to check requirements and obtain additional information.
- AIDS Test: Not required.
- Vaccinations: A yellow fever vaccination certificate is required from all travelers older than 9 months of age arriving from yellow fever infected areas.

Telephone Country Code: 52   **AT&T:** 95-800-462-4240   **MCI:** 95-800-674-7000

Electricity/Plugs: AC 60 Hz, 127/220 volts; frequency is not stable; plug Type A.

Mexican Government Tourist Office: Washington, DC. Tel. (202) 728-1750.

American Express: La Reforma 234, Mexico City; Tel. (5) 33-03-80.

Embassies/Consulates: U.S. Embassy, Mexico City. Paseo de la Reforma 305; Tel. (5) 211-00-42. U.S. Consulate, Ciudad Juarez; Tel. (16) 13-40-48. U.S. Consulate, Guadalajara; Tel. (36) 25-29-98, 25-27-00. U.S. Consulate, Mazatlan; Tel. (678) 5-22-07. U.S. Consulate, Merida; Tel. (992) 5-54-09. U.S. Consulate, Monterey; Tel. (83) 45-21-20. U.S. Consulate, Tijuana; Tel. (66) 81-77-00.

Canadian Embassy, Mexico City. Calle Schiller 529; Tel. (5) 254-32-88.

Doctors/Hospitals: In Mexico City: John F. Smyth, M.D., Campos Eliseos No. 81 Colonia Polanco; Tel. (5) 545-7861 (office) or (5) 250-0019 (home). The British-American Hospital (160 beds); private hospital; most of the staff are U.S. or British board-certified; specialties include cardiology, ob/gyn, emergency medicine, neurology; Tel. (5) 277-5000.

In Monterrey: Hospital Jose A. Muguerza (1154 beds); private hospital; most specialties, including cardiology, ob/gyn, kidney dialysis; Tel. 460-100.

Dr. Jose Gonzalez University Hospital (704 beds); public hospital; most specialties; Tel. 487-926.

In Guadalajara: Civil Hospital (1,000 beds); some specialties; English-speaking, U.S.-trained physicians.

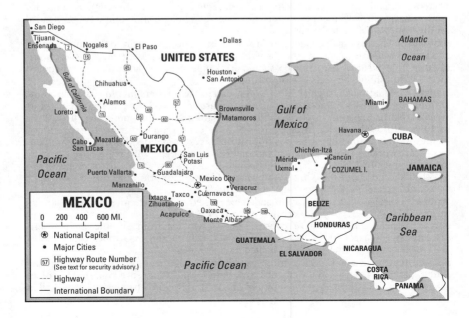

Health Advisory

Malaria: Malaria is present year-round, except for Sinaloa and Sonora States and in the central valleys, where the risk is from May to October. Malaria is endemic in rural areas under 1,000 meters elevation, southward from Guaymas on the Pacific coast, southward from Tampico on the Gulf coast, and in the valleys of central Mexico. There is no malaria risk in urban areas. *P. vivax* accounts for 98–99% of infections, the remainder attributed to *P. falciparum*. Although some treatment failures are alleged to have occurred in Chiapas, no drug-resistant cases of falciparum malaria have yet been reported from Mexico. The incidence of malaria is highest in the states of Chiapas, Oaxaca, Guerrero, Campeche, and Quintana Roo. Chloroquine prophylaxis is recommended only when visiting malarious rural areas and staying overnight. Campers and hikers on the coasts should take chloroquine. Persons staying overnight at the following archaeological sites should also take chloroquine: Palenque, Bonampak, Uxmal, Kabah, Labna, Sayil, Edzna, Coba, and Tulum. Chloroquine is not recommended when visiting resort areas on either the Pacific or Gulf coasts because the risk of malaria is deemed low. In resort areas, preventing mosquito bites is a reasonable measure.

Cholera: This disease is reported active in this country. Although cholera vaccination is not required for entry if arriving directly from the U.S. or Canada, it may be required if arriving from a cholera-infected area, or required for on-going travel to other countries in Latin America, Africa, the Middle East, or Asia. Depending upon their itinerary, travelers should consider vaccination or a doctor's letter of exemption from vaccination. The risk to travelers of acquiring cholera is low. Prevention consists primarily in strictly adhering to safe food and drink guidelines. It is particularly important to avoid raw or undercooked seafood, to avoid undercooked food from street vendors, to avoid uncooked vegetables and unpeeled fruits, and to drink only boiled, bottled, filtered, or chemically treated water.

Travelers' diarrhea: High risk, especially outside of resorts and first-class hotels. The risk of diarrhea is highest May through October, especially in Yucatan, in Mexico City, and in the northeastern border states. Limited and/or contaminated water supplies are a major problem throughout the country. Piped water is available in most large urban areas, but is almost always contaminated because of inadequate treatment and/or distribution systems. Rural areas must depend on wells, springs, and surface water sources (rivers, streams, lakes, and ponds), which frequently are contaminated at the source by human and animal waste. Bacterial organisms (*E. coli, Campylobacter, Salmonella,* and *Shigella*) account for approximately 80% of cases of travelers' diarrhea. A quinolone antibiotic is recommended for the treatment of acute diarrhea.

Amebiasis: There is a high incidence of amebiasis in Mexico, especially in the South Central and South Pacific areas where up to 9% of the population is seropositive for *E. histolytica* antibodies. To avoid amebiasis, travelers should drink only safe water and eat only well-cooked food. All fruit should be peeled before eating.

Hepatitis: Hepatitis A is highly endemic. All susceptible travelers should receive immune globulin or hepatitis A vaccine, especially if planning travel outside the usual resort areas. Hepatitis B: Estimates of the carrier rate in the adult population range from 0.3% to 1.6%, although carrier rates up to 4% have been reported from Chiapas State. Immunization against hepatitis B is not routinely recommended for tourist travel, but healthcare workers should consider vaccination. Hepatitis E: Outbreaks have occurred in the vicinity of Mexico City and Tijuana. To help prevent this form of hepatitis, travelers should avoid drinking unsafe water. The consumption of bottled, boiled, or chemically treated water is strongly recommended.

Typhoid fever: Vaccination is recommended for those traveling extensively outside of tourist areas. This disease is highly endemic and from 1975 to 1984, more cases of typhoid fever in North American travelers were reported from Mexico than from any other Latin American country. An increased risk of typhoid fever occurs from June to October, countrywide. Outbreaks are associated with contaminated food and water.

Dengue fever: Dengue occurs in most areas below 1,200 meters elevation, but recently dengue has been reported in the city of Taxco, elevation 1,700 meters elevation. The risk of dengue is currently greatest in the southern and central Pacific urban coastal areas and in extreme northeastern Mexico. Increased risk may occur during the rainy season, from July through October. This disease is transmitted by the *Aedes aegypti* mosquito, but the Asian "tiger mosquito" (*Aedes albopictus*) may also transmit the virus. All travelers to risk areas below 1,200 meters elevation are advised to take precautions against mosquito bites. A vaccine is not available.

Viral encephalitis: Rare cases of St. Louis encephalitis, Venezuelan equine encephalitis, and eastern and western encephalitis are reported.

Leishmaniasis: This disease is transmitted by sand flies, which are most active between sunset and dawn. Cutaneous leishmaniasis is endemic in rural areas in the southern territory of Quintana Roo, eastern Yucatan, Campeche, eastern Tabasco, Chiapas, Oaxaca, and eastern Veracruz. Mucocutaneous leishmaniasis (espundia) has occurred in Jalisco State, and visceral leishmaniasis (uncommon) has occurred in Guerrero and Morelos States. Diffuse cutaneous leishmaniasis occurs in both the northeast and southeast regions. Mucocutaneous leishmaniasis has occurred in Jalisco State. Travelers should take measures to protect themselves against insect (sandfly) bites.

Onchocerciasis: This black fly-transmitted disease is limited to areas along rivers between 600 and 1,500 meters elevation in Chiapas and Oaxaca States. Highest risk is from October through April. Travelers should take measures to prevent insect (black fly) bites.

Chagas' disease: Risk occurs below 1,500 meters elevation in the rural areas of the southern and western states. Most risk is found in those rural-agricultural areas where there are adobe-style huts and houses that potentially harbor the night-biting triatomid (assassin) bugs. Travelers sleeping in such structures should take precautions against nighttime bites. Unscreened blood transfusions are also a source of infection and should be avoided. (Up to 17% of blood donations tested have been seropositive.)

Rabies: About 70 human cases are reported annually. Ninety percent of cases are acquired from contact with rabid dogs, usually in urban areas. Rabid vampire bats reportedly are a problem in Sinaloa State. Travelers should especially avoid stray dogs, and seek immediate treatment of any wild animal bite. Rabies vaccination is indicated following the unprovoked bite of a dog, cat, vampire bat, or monkey.

Helminthic infections: Hookworm, roundworm, and whipworm infections, and also strongyloidiasis, are highly prevalent in most rural areas. (Hookworm disease infects up to 90% of some rural villagers). Travelers should wear shoes to prevent the hookworm and strongyloides larvae from penetrating the skin. All food should be thoroughly cooked to destroy roundworm, whipworm, and pork tapeworm eggs. Pork tapeworm disease is common and can be prevented by eating only thoroughly cooked pork.

Respiratory infections: Acute respiratory infections (e.g., bronchitis) are a common cause of illness in Mexico and can be exacerbated by air pollution in major metropolitan areas. Travelers should be warned that severe air pollution occurs year-round in Mexico City. Travelers with heart disease, emphysema, and asthma may need to limit or avoid travel to regions with poor air quality.

Tuberculosis: This disease is highly endemic, particularly among the native Indian populations in southern Mexico and Baja California; drug-resistant strains are common.

AIDS: Incidence appears to be increasing rapidly. In 1989, approximately 76% of adult cases were due to bisexual or homosexual contact, 11% to heterosexual contact, and almost 12% to intravenous drug use or blood products.

Other diseases/hazards: Anthrax (small outbreaks reported in Zacatecas, central Mexico), brucellosis (90% of cases associated with contact with goats; greatest risk occurs in the northern and central states), coccidiomycosis ("valley fever," endemic in the dry north of Baja California Norte, Sonora and Chihuahua States, and along the Pacific Coast), cysticercosis and neurocysticercosis (caused by the ingestion of pork tapeworm eggs; common, especially in Guanajuato and Michocan States), gnathstomiasis (acquired through ingestion of a parasite found in raw fish; occurs in areas along the Papaloapan River in southeastern Mexico), histoplasmosis (contact with bat guano transmits this fungal disease), tuberculosis (a serious public health problem, especially in native Indian populations of southern Mexico and Baja California), typhus (both louse- and flea-borne; reported in Chiapas State), and tick-borne rickettsioses (spotted fever group; reported in some rural areas).

BELIZE

Entry Requirements

- Passport/Visa: U.S. citizens need a valid passport, a return ticket, and proof of sufficient funds (either $50/day or a credit card). No visa necessary.
- AIDS Test: Testing required of travelers seeking employment, immigration, or staying longer than 3 months. Travelers should call the Belize Embassy in Washington (202-332-9636) for further information.
- Vaccinations: A yellow fever vaccination certificate is required of all travelers arriving from infected areas.

Telephone Country Code: 501   **AT&T:** 555

Electricity/Plugs: AC 60 Hz, 110/220 volts; plug types A and B.

American Express: Albert Street 41 Belize City. Tel. (2)77185.

Embassies/Consulates: U.S. Embassy, Belize City. Gabourel Lane and Hutson Street. Tel. (2)77161. Canadian Consulate, Belize City. Tel. (2)44700/44221.

Doctors/Hospitals: Manuel Lizama, MD. 13 Handy Side, Belize City. Tel. 45138. Manuel Cabrera, MD. Tel. (2) 44-368. General practitioner in Belize City. Can give referral to specialists, as needed. British Forces Belize Hospital (11 beds); the best hospital in Belize but will treat nonmilitary patients only in emergencies. Tel. (2)52-191. Belize City Hospital (75 beds); general medical/surgical; rudimentary x-ray/laboratory services.

Scuba diving emergencies: A decompression chamber is located in San Pedro.

Health Advisory

Cholera: This disease is active in this country. Although cholera vaccination is not required for entry if arriving directly from the U.S. or Canada, it may be required if arriving from a cholera-infected area, or required for on-going travel to other countries in Latin America, Africa, the Middle East, or Asia. Travelers should consider vaccination (one dose) or a doctor's letter of exemption from vaccination. The risk to travelers of acquiring cholera is low.

Malaria: Risk is present year-round in all rural areas of the country under 400 meters elevation. Elevated risk in the north. There is no risk of malaria in Belize City. *P. vivax* causes approximately 96% of cases, *P. falciparum* 3.6%. Occasional cases are due to *P. malariae*. Chloroquine-resistant falciparum malaria has not been reported. Chloroquine prophylaxis is currently recommended for overnight visits to rural areas, rain forests, or the offshore islands.

Travelers' diarrhea: Moderate risk except for tourist resorts, where the risk is low. Belize now provides treated water to 85% of urban population, 55% to rural areas. Raw sewage emptied into ocean may cause beach contamination. Travelers should follow safe food and drink precautions. A quinolone antibiotic is recommended for the treatment of acute diarrhea.

Hepatitis: Immune globulin or hepatitis A vaccine is recommended for all susceptible travelers. The hepatitis B carrier rate in the general population is estimated at 1.4%–3%. Hepatitis B vaccination should be considered by long-term visitors to this country.

Dengue fever: Moderate risk in both urban and rural areas. All travelers are advised to take measures to prevent mosquito bites.

Leishmaniasis: Greatest risk is May through December, especially in rural forested areas. Prevalence is highest in the central part of the country, lowest in the south. Cases of cutaneous leishmaniasis have been reported among tourists and field study participants. All travelers are advised to take measures to prevent insect (sandfly) bites.

Rabies: Low risk. One or two cases of human rabies are reported each year. Travelers should avoid contact with stray dogs and seek immediate treatment of any unprovoked animal bite.

Other diseases: Amebiasis and giardiasis (low incidence), brucellosis, Chagas' disease (endemic at low levels in Cayo District), cutaneous myiasis (caused by larvae of the human bot fly), histoplasmosis (outbreaks associated with guano in bat caves), leptospirosis, tuberculosis (low incidence), typhoid fever (few officially reported cases), and intestinal helminthic infections.

COSTA RICA
San Jose ... GMT -6 hrs

Entry Requirements
- Passport/Visa: Visa not required for travelers holding U.S. or Canadian passport.
- AIDS Test: Testing required of travelers staying more than 90 days. Travelers can contact the Costa Rican embassy in Washington (202-234-2945) for further information.
- Vaccinations: No vaccinations are required to enter this country.

Telephone Country Code: 506   **AT&T:** 114   **MCI:** 162

Electricity/Plugs: AC 60 Hz, 120/240 volts; plug types A, D, I, and J.

American Express: Tam Travel Agency. Avenida Central-Primera, 4th Floor, San Jose; Tel. 33-00-44.

Embassies/Consulates: U.S. Embassy, San Jose. Avenida 3 and Calle 1; Tel. 33-11-55. Canadian Embassy, Edificio Cronos, 4th Floor, Calle 3 and Avenida Central; Tel. 23-04-46.

Hospitals/Doctors: Hospital Clinica Biblica; private hospital with extensive medical/surgical capabilities, including cardiac surgery, 24-hour emergency room, and ambulance service. CT and MRI are now available. Hospital-based physician group is 90% English-speaking; many staff physicians have received advanced training in the United States. Hospital Clinica Biblica is used by embassy personnel, tourists and expatriates. Address: Calle Central and Ave. 14; Tel. 57-04-66.

Health Advisory

Yellow fever: No recent cases have been reported but vaccination is nonetheless recommended for all travelers going to rural areas. Because this country is in the Yellow Fever Endemic Zone, a valid certificate may be required for on-going travel to other countries that require a certificate of vaccination.

Cholera: This disease is reported active in this country but the risk to travelers of acquiring cholera is extremely low. Although cholera vaccination is not required for entry if arriving directly from the U.S. or Canada, a certificate of vaccination may be required for on-going travel to other countries in Latin America, Africa, the Middle East, or Asia that require a certificate.

Malaria: Risk occurs year-round in rural areas below 500 meters elevation. Risk is increased during, and just after, the rainy season, May through November, peaking during September-October. Risk is greatest in the coastal lowlands, especially on the Atlantic side near the Nicaraguan border. Seventy percent of malaria cases are reported from Limon Province. Vivax malaria accounts for over 97% of cases. No cases of drug-resistant falciparum malaria have been reported. Chloroquine prophylaxis is not routinely recommended for tourists going to Costa Rica but should be considered by anyone staying overnight near the border with Nicaragua.

Travelers' diarrhea: Low risk in most areas. Tap water in San Jose is potable. A quinolone antibiotic is recommended for the treatment of acute diarrhea.

Hepatitis: The risk of hepatitis A is low but immune globulin or hepatitis A vaccine is recommended for all susceptible travelers. The hepatitis B carrier rate in the general population is less than 1%. Vaccination against hepatitis B should be considered by healthcare workers or long-term visitors to this country.

Dengue fever: Low risk. Cases of dengue have recently been reported from Puntarenas and the Liberia region. To prevent dengue, travelers who visit the Pacific coastal areas, especially during the rainy season, should take measures to prevent mosquito bites.

Leishmaniasis: Potential for transmission occurs in most rural and jungle areas below 800 meters elevation, with the greatest risk occuring from May through July. Travelers take precautions against insect (sandfly) bites.

Other diseases: Brucellosis, Chagas' disease (occurs sporadically in rural areas of Alajuela, Guanacaste, Heredia, and San Jose Provinces at elevations below 1,300 meters, but is not considered a major public health problem), cysticercosis, filariasis (transmitted by black flies; endemic near Puerto Limon), leptospirosis, rabies (very low risk), tick-borne rickettsioses (Rocky Mountain spotted fever reported from Limon Province), and strongyloidiasis and other helminthic infections are reported.

GUATEMALA

Guatemala City ... GMT -6 hrs

Entry Requirements

- Passport/Visa: Passport and tourist card required for entry.
- AIDS Test: Not required.
- Vaccinations: A yellow fever vaccination certificate is required from travelers over 1 year of age coming from infected or endemic areas.

Telephone Country Code: 502   **AT&T:** 190   **MCI:**189

Electricity/Plugs: AC 60 Hz, 110/240 volts; plug types A and I.

American Express: Clark Tours. Edificio El Triangulo, 2nd Floor. 7A Avenida 6-53 Zona 4, Guatemala City; Tel. (2) 31-02-13.

Embassies/Consulates: U.S. Embassy, Guatemala City. 7-01 Avenida de la Reforma; Tel. (2) 31-15-41. After hours: 37-23-47. Canadian Embassy, Guatemala City. Edificio Galerias Espana, 6th Floor. Avenida 11-59; Tel. (2) 32-14-11.

Hospitals/Doctors: In Guatemala City: Rodolfo Herrera, M.D. Hospital Herrera Llerandi (68 beds); many specialties, including surgery, gynecology, and orthopedics; Tel. (2) 36-771 or 66-775. Hospital Centro Medico (76 beds); Tel. 365061.

Health Advisory

Yellow fever: A yellow fever vaccination is recommended for travel outside urban areas. Because this country is in the Yellow Fever Endemic Zone, a valid certificate may be required for ongoing travel to certain other countries.

Cholera: This disease is active in this country. Although cholera vaccination is not required for entry if arriving directly from the U.S. or Canada, it may be required if arriving from a cholera-infected area, or required for on-going travel to other countries in Latin America, Africa, the Middle East, or Asia. Travelers should consider vaccination (one dose) or a doctor's letter of exemption from vaccination.

Travelers' diarrhea: High risk. Travelers should drink only bottled, boiled, or treated water. All food should be thoroughly cooked. A quinolone antibiotic is recommended for the treatment of diarrhea. Diarrhea not responding to antibiotic treatment may be due to a parasitic disease such as giardiasis or amebiasis.

Malaria: Risk exists year-round, with peak transmission occurring from May through October. All areas below 1,500 meters elevation, except for Guatemala City and the central highland areas, are considered malarious. Risk is greatest in the Pacific lowlands, along the border with El Salvador, and in the north (Peten). *P. vivax* accounts for 97% of all cases. Chloroquine prophylaxis is recommended for travel to malarious areas.

Hepatitis: Immune globulin or hepatitis A vaccine is recommended for all susceptible travelers. The hepatitis B carrier rate in the general population is estimated at 1.4% to 3.0%. Hepatitis B vaccination is recommended for healthcare workers and should be considered by long-term travelers to this country.

Onchocerciasis: Risk occurs near fast-flowing rivers between 300 and 1,600 meters elevation in the Pacific coast foothills and along the border with Mexico in the south. Travelers to these areas should take measures to prevent insect (black fly) bites.

Leishmaniasis: Outbreaks of cutaneous leishmaniasis are reported occurring in forested areas in Peten Department. Limited risk of visceral leishmaniasis occurs in the semiarid valleys and the foothills of east-central Guatemala. Travelers to these areas should take measures to prevent sandfly bites.

Schistosomiasis: No cases have been reported since 1980. Risk appears negligible.

Rabies: Travelers should avoid stray animals, especially dogs, and seek emergency treatment of any animal bite. Pre-exposure rabies vaccination (3 doses) is recommended for all persons planning a long stay (4 weeks or more) or extensive travel in rural areas.

Other diseases: Anthrax, brucellosis, Chagas' disease (endemic in many rural areas), coccidiomycosis, dengue fever (risk occurs year-round in lowland urban areas; extensive outbreaks reported in 1991, 1992), measles, paralytic shellfish poisoning, relapsing fever (tickborne), syphilis, typhoid fever, tuberculosis, strongyloidiasis and other helminthic infections, and typhus are reported.

EL SALVADOR

San Salvador ... GMT -6 hrs

Entry Requirements

- Passport/Visa: Passport and visa required for all travelers.
- AIDS Test: Not required.
- Vaccinations: A yellow fever vaccination certificate is required from travelers over 6 months of age coming from infected or endemic areas.

Telephone Country Code: 503   **AT&T:** 190   **MCI:** 195

Electricity/Plugs: AC 60 Hz, 115/230 volts; plug types A, B, G, and J.

American Express: El Salvador Travel Service; Centro Comercial. La Mascota, San Salvador; Tel. 23-0177.

Embassies/Consulates: U.S. Embassy, San Salvador. 25 Avenida Norte, No. 1230; Tel. 26-7100.

Hospitals/Doctors: Policlinica Salvadorena Hospital (103 beds); some specialties; emergency services; ICU; CCU. Clinicas Medicas, San Salvador; Tel. 25-0277.

Health Advisory

Yellow fever: Yellow fever vaccination is recommended for travel outside urban areas. Because this country is in the Yellow Fever Endemic Zone, a valid certificate may be required for ongoing travel to certain other countries.

Cholera: This disease is active in this country. Although cholera vaccination is not required for entry if arriving directly from the U.S. or Canada, it may be required if arriving from a cholera-infected area, or required for on-going travel to other countries in Latin America, Africa, the Middle East, or Asia. Travelers should consider vaccination (one dose) or a doctor's letter of exemption from vaccination. Prevention consists primarily in adhering to safe food and drink guidelines.

Malaria: Risk is present rear-round in rural areas below 1,000 meters elevation. Greatest risk is in coastal areas below 600 meters elevation and is minimal in northern and central zones. There is no risk of malaria in urban areas. This disease is highly active. Vivax malaria accounts for 98% of cases. Chloroquine prophylaxis is recommended for travel in rural areas.

Travelers' diarrhea: Piped water supplies may be contaminated. Travelers should observe all food and drink safety precautions. A quinolone antibiotic (Cipro or Floxin) is recommended for the treatment of acute diarrhea. Diarrhea not responding to treatment with an antibiotic, or chronic diarrhea, may be due to a parasitic disease such as giardiasis or amebiasis.

Hepatitis: Immune globulin or hepatitis A vaccine advised for all susceptible travelers. The carrier rate of the hepatitis B virus is estimated at 1.2% in the general population.

Dengue fever: Variable incidence. Most cases occur June–December in the vicinity of San Salvador and in the eastern regions bordering Honduras. Travelers should take measures to prevent mosquito bites.

Leishmaniasis: Cutaneous leishmaniasis is reported from the Rio Lempa valley. Most risk occurs in forested rural areas. There is risk of visceral leishmaniasis in the warm, dry valleys near the Honduran border.

Chagas' disease: Occurs in all rural areas under 1,500 meters elevation where there are adobe-style dwellings that potentially harbor the night-biting triatomid (assassin) bugs. Travelers sleeping in such structures should take precautions against nighttime bites.

Rabies: About 10–12 human deaths annually are reported. Although rabid vampire bats are common, dogs are the primary source of human infection. Rabies vaccination is indicated following the unprovoked bite of a dog, cat, bat, monkey, or other animal. Vaccination against rabies is recommended for long-term travel to this country.

Other diseases: Anthrax, brucellosis, coccidiomycosis, cysticercosis, leptospirosis, measles, relapsing fever (tick-borne), syphilis, AIDS (low number of cases reported), tuberculosis (highly endemic), typhoid fever, strongyloidiasis and other helminthic infections, and typhus are reported.

HONDURAS

San Pedro Sula ... GMT -6 hrs

Entry Requirements

- Passport/Visa: A valid passport and visa required from all travelers.
- AIDS Test: Not required.
- Vaccinations: A yellow fever vaccination certificate is required from travelers coming from infected or endemic areas.

Telephone Country Code: 504   **AT&T:** 123   **MCI:** 001-800-674-7000

Electricity/Plugs: AC 60 Hz, 110/220 volts; plug types A and B.

American Express: Agencia De Viajes Trans. Mundo S. De R.I., 6 Avenida S.O., 15 San Pedro Sula; Tel. 54-1140.

Embassies/Consulates: U.S. Embassy, Tegucigalpa. Avenida La Paz; Tel. 32-3120.

Hospitals/Doctors: Hospital Escuela, Tegucigalpa (400 beds); government hospital; some specialties; Tel. 322-322. JTF-Bravo Medical Element (USA Field Hospital); Tel. 31-5300/72-0454, ext. 153. Eva de Gomez, M.D., Tel. 220-429 or 321-023. In Comayaguela: Marco Bogran, M.D.

In San Pedro Sula: Sergio Bendana, M.D., Tel. 543-454 or 543-147. Hospital Leonardo Martinez (286 beds); general medical/surgical facility; some specialties; Tel. 32-2322.

Health Advisory

Yellow fever: A yellow fever vaccination is recommended for travel outside urban areas. This country is in the Yellow Fever Endemic Zone.

Cholera: This disease is active in this country. Although cholera vaccination is not required for entry if arriving directly from the U.S. or Canada, it may be required if arriving from a cholera-infected area, or required for on-going travel to other countries in Latin America. Travelers should consider vaccination (one dose) or a doctor's letter of exemption from vaccination. Prevention consists primarily in adhering to safe food and drink guidelines.

Malaria: Risk occurs year-round in rural areas. Most cases occur in the coastal lowlands below 500 meters elevation and along the border with Nicaragua. *P. vivax* accounts for 98% of reported cases. Falciparum malaria is more common along the Nicaraguan border and in the Caribbean coastal region. In Gracias a Dios Dept. on the Caribbean coast, *P. falciparum* malaria accounts for 10% of cases. Chloroquine-resistant *P. falciparum* has not been reported. Chloroquine is the drug of choice for malaria prophylaxis. A weekly dose of chloroquine is also recommended for travelers who will visit Ceiba, Tela, or the Bay Islands.

Travelers' diarrhea: High risk. Treatment and distribution systems for piped water are inadequate and tap water is commonly contaminated. Treatment of diarrhea with a quinolone antibiotic (either Cipro or Floxin) is recommended.

Hepatitis: Immune globulin or hepatitis A vaccine is recommended for all susceptible travelers. The hepatitis B carrier rate in the general population is estimated at 3%. Vaccination against hepatitis B should be considered by long-term visitors to this country.

Dengue fever: Most outbreaks have occurred in southern Honduras, but risk of disease also occurs along the northern coast, particularly in the San Pedro Sula area. All travelers, especially to these higher risk areas, should take measures to prevent mosquito bites.

Leishmaniasis: Cutaneous leishmaniasis is widespread, with some mucocutaneous disease also reported. Foci of visceral leishmaniasis have been reported on Tigre Island and in the southern rural areas. Travelers should take measures to prevent sandfly bites.

Chagas' disease: Risk is present predominately in the southern half of the country, especially in the Tegucigalpa area. In endemic areas 23.5% of the population is seropositive. Blood transfusions are a significant means of transmission of Chagas' disease in Honduras.

Rabies: Higher risk of dog rabies than in all other countries of Latin America, except Mexico. Travelers should seek immediate medical evaluation/treatment of any animal bite.

Other diseases: Brucellosis (limited risk in cattle raising areas), coccidimycosis, leptospirosis, measles, myiasis (caused by human bot fly), syphilis, AIDS (relatively high incidence for Central America), typhoid fever, tuberculosis, strongyloidiasis and other helminthic infections, and typhus are reported.

NICARAGUA

Managua ... GMT -6 hrs

Entry Requirements

- Passport/Visa: A passport only is required for entry.
- AIDS Test: Not required.
- Vaccinations: A yellow fever vaccination certificate is required from travelers over 1 year of age coming from infected or endemic areas.

Telephone Country Code: 505   **AT&T:** 174 (02-174 outside Managua)

Electricity/Plugs: AC 60 Hz, 120, 120/240 volts; frequency is stable; plug type A.

Embassies/Consulates: U.S. Embassy, Managua; Carraterra Street; Tel. (2) 66-010/66-013.

Hospitals/Doctors: Hospital Manolo Morales, Managua (300 beds); general medical/surgical facility; emergency services; Tel. 70990 or 70828.

Jose Angel Montiel, M.D. Clinica Tiscapa; Tel. (2) 714-57 or (2) 666828. Clinica Tiscapa; Tel. (2) 71-300. Hospital Bautista (30 beds); private hospital; 24-hour emergency services; patients must arrange for their own physicians; Tel. 24154/23345.

Health Advisory

Yellow fever: Vaccination is recommended for travel outside urban areas. This country is in the Yellow Fever Endemic Zone. Although a vaccination certificate may not be required for entry to this country, one may be required for on-going travel to other countries in Africa, the Middle East, and Asia.

Cholera: This disease is active in this country. Although cholera vaccination is not required for entry if arriving directly from the U.S. or Canada, it may be required if arriving from a cholera-infected area, or required for on-going travel to other countries in Latin America, Africa, the Middle East, or Asia. Travelers should consider vaccination (one dose) or a doctor's letter of exemption from vaccination.

Malaria: Risk is present in rural areas below 1,000 meters elevation. There is minimal risk of malaria in suburban areas of Managua, Chinan, Granada, Nandaime, Leon, and Tipitapa. *P. vivax* accounts for 86%–90% of cases, *P. falciparum* for 8%. There are no reports of chloroquine-resistant *P. falciparum*. Chloroquine prophylaxis is recommended in all rural areas.

Travelers' diarrhea: Water supplies in Managua are tested regularly by the local water company and are considered potable. All travelers, however, are advised to consume bottled, boiled, or treated water unless they are assured of the safety of municipal water supplies. All other water should be considered contaminated. A quinolone antibiotic (Cipro or Floxin) is recommended for the treatment of acute diarrhea. Diarrhea not responding to treatment with an antibiotic, or chronic diarrhea, may be due to a parasitic disease such as giardiasis or amebiasis. (A high incidence of amebiasis is reported in Nicaragua. Infection rates of up to 23% have been reported for giardiasis.)

Hepatitis: Immune globulin or hepatitis A vaccine is recommended for all susceptible travelers. The hepatitis B carrier rate in the general population is estimated at 1.1%. Vaccination against hepatitis B is recommended for healthcare workers.

Dengue fever: A major outbreak occurred in Managua in 1985 with 500,000 cases unofficially reported. The *Aedes* mosquitoes which transmit dengue fever bite during the daytime and are present in populous urban areas as well as resort and rural areas.

Leishmaniasis: Cutaneous leishmaniasis is reported, primarily from the northern and eastern regions. Travelers should take measures to prevent insect (sandfly) bites.

Chagas' disease: Reported in Atlantic coastal, western, and central regions under 1,500 meters elevation. Chagas' disease occurs in rural areas where there are adobe-style huts and houses that potentially harbor the night-biting triatomid (assassin) bugs. Travelers sleeping in such structures should take precautions against nighttime bites.

Rabies: About 4 cases of human rabies per year are reported. Travelers should seek immediate evaluation and treatment of any animal bite.

Other diseases: Anthrax, brucellosis, coccidiomycosis, filariasis (possible risk near Lake Managua), leptospirosis, measles, syphilis, AIDS (low incidence), tuberculosis, and strongyloidiasis and other helminthic infections.

PANAMA

Panama City ... GMT -5 hrs

Entry Requirements
- Passport/Visa: Visa not required.
- AIDS Test: Not required.
- Vaccinations: None required.

Telephone Country Code: 507   **AT&T:** 109   **MCI:** 108

Electricity/Plugs: AC 60 Hz, 120/220 volts; frequency is stable; plug types A and B.

American Express: Sociedad Int'l. De Servicios Banco, Union Bldg., 12th floor. 5 Avenida Samuel Lewis, Panama City. Tel. 63-58-58.

Embassies/Consulates: U.S. Embassy/Panama City. 37th St. & Balboa Ave. Tel. 27-17-77.

Hospitals/Doctors: Gorgas Army Hospital, Panama City; Tel. (313) 382-5102. Carlos Garcia, M.D. Tel. 63-7977/26-1278. Centro Medico Paitilla (180 beds). Private hospital operated by the Hospital Corp. of America. General medical/surgical facility; CAT scan, emergency services. Tel. 63-6060. Clinica San Fernando (150 beds); private hospital; general medical/surgical facility; CAT scan, trauma unit. Tel. 61-6666. Hospital Samaritano, Colon; Tel. 47-1780.

Health Advisory

Yellow fever: Vaccination is recommended for travel outside urban areas. This country is in the Yellow Fever Endemic Zone. Although a vaccination certificate may not be required for entry to this country, one may be required for on-going travel to other countries in Africa, the Middle East, and Asia.

Cholera: This disease is active in this country. Although cholera vaccination is not required for entry if arriving directly from the U.S. or Canada, it may be required if arriving from a cholera-infected area, or required for on-going travel to other countries in Latin America, Africa, the Middle East, or Asia. Travelers should consider vaccination or a doctor's letter of exemption from vaccination.

Malaria: Risk exists year-round in rural areas of the eastern provinces (Darien and San Blas) and the northwestern provinces (Bocas Del Toro and Veraguas). Areas immediately adjacent to the Panama Canal and all main urban areas are malaria free. Vivax malaria predominates in Panama, with falciparum malaria accounting for 6% to 28% of all cases. Chloroquine-resistant *P. falciparum* may occur in all malarious areas east of the Canal and in the vicinity of Gatun Lake, west of the Canal, as well as in the extreme northwest, near the border with Costa Rica. Travelers to rural areas should take weekly chloroquine prophylaxis. Mefloquine or doxycycline prophylaxis is recommended when traveling to areas east of the Canal and in the vicinity of Gatun Lake, and the Costa Rican border.

Travelers' diarrhea: Variable risk. The water in Panama City, Colon, Santiago, and David is adequately treated, but may be subject to contamination in some parts of the distribution system. In all other parts of the country, all water sources should be considered potentially contaminated. A quinolone antibiotic is recommended for the treatment of diarrhea.

Hepatitis: Immune globulin or hepatitis A vaccine is recommended for all susceptible travelers. The hepatitis B carrier rate in the general population is estimated at 0.7%. Vaccination against hepatitis B is recommended for healthcare workers.

Dengue fever: Risk occurs, but no major outbreaks have occurred in Panama since 1942. All travelers, however, should take measures to prevent mosquito bites.

Leishmaniasis: Outbreaks occur in many rural areas of the country, but most cases are reported from the eastern and south-central regions. Ninety eight percent of cases are cutaneous, the remainder mucocutaneous. All travelers should take measures to prevent sandfly bites.

Chagas' disease: Twenty two percent of the population is reported seropositive. Chagas' disease occurs throughout most rural areas of this country, including the former Canal Zone.

Other diseases: Amebiasis, cysticercosis, filariasis , giardiasis (25% of food handlers are carriers), histoplasmosis (from exposure to bat guano), leptospirosis, measles, rabies (currently a minor threat to humans), AIDS (low incidence; sero-prevalence of 0.1% of blood donors reported), tick-borne rickettsioses (spotted fever group), tuberculosis (incidence declining), typhoid fever, viral encephalitis, strongyloidiasis and other helminthic infections are reported.

DISEASE RISK SUMMARY
THE CARIBBEAN

Yellow fever: Yellow fever activity is reported only in the remote forested areas of Trinidad. No human cases reported since 1980. Vaccination is recommended for persons who plan to travel to rural areas of this country.

Malaria: Malaria occurs in Haiti and the Dominican Republic, where falciparum malaria accounts for approximately 99% of all cases. Chloroquine-resistant *P. falciparum* is not reported. An outbreak of vivax malaria was reported in 1991 in southwestern Trinidad, in the town of Icacos. All other islands in the Caribbean are currently malaria-free. Chloroquine prophylaxis should be considered for travel to islands with malaria risk.

Diarrheal disease: Highly endemic in much of the region. Common pathogens include enterotoxigenic *E. coli*, shigella, and salmonella species. Rotavirus is the most common causative agent of nonspecific diarrhea in children in this region. Amebiasis and giardiasis presumably are moderately endemic in most Caribbean countries. Data for cryptosporidiosis are sparse.

Hepatitis: Immune globulin or hepatitis A vaccine is recommended for susceptible travelers. The hepatitis B carrier rate in the Caribbean varies from 0.8% to 4.1%. Vaccination against hepatitis B is recommended for healthcare workers and should be considered by long-term visitors to this region.

Dengue fever: This mosquito-transmitted viral disease is widespread throughout the Caribbean, including Puerto Rico and the Virgin Islands. Outbreaks reported on Guadeloupe and Trinidad. Only Bermuda and the Cayman Islands are reported dengue-free.

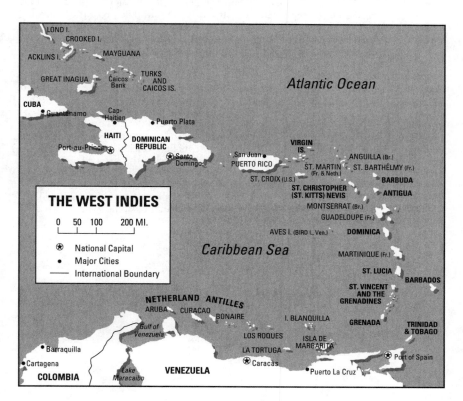

Arboviral fevers: Low risk. Mosquito-transmitted viral encephalitis is reported in the Caribbean. Venezuelan equine encephalitis is reported from Barbados, St. Vincent, and Trinidad and Tobago.

Leishmaniasis: Currently, cutaneous and mucocutaneous leishmaniasis occur only on the island of Hispaniola (Haiti and the Dominican Republic). Travelers to Hispaniola should take measures to prevent insect (sandfly) bites. Elsewhere, risk of leishmaniasis is low or absent. Members of the *Leishmania mexicana* complex have been historically identified in Trinidad and Tobago, Martinique, and Guadeloupe, as have parasites (presumably *L. chagasi*) of visceral leishmaniasis in Martinique and Guadeloupe.

Filariasis: Bancroftian variety; mosquito-transmitted. Highest risk is in Haiti and the Dominican Republic. Filariasis occurs (rarely) in the Lesser Antilles from Trinidad north to Guadeloupe. Puerto Rico is also a potential risk area. Travelers to these countries should take measures to prevent mosquito bites.

Schistosomiasis: Limited risk is present on Antigua, Guadeloupe, Martinique, Montserrat, Puerto Rico, and Saint Lucia. The disease may occur sporadically in the other islands. Travelers should avoid swimming, bathing, or wading in freshwater ponds or streams that may be snail infested.

Leptospirosis: A disease of considerable public health concern in the Caribbean. Transmission of disease is through skin contact with water or moist soil contaminated with the urine of infected animals. Highest risk occurs in Barbados, Jamaica, Saint Vincent, and Trinidad and Tobago.

Chagas' disease: This disease has been detected in Trinidad and Tobago. Potential vectors (triatomid bugs) occur on several other islands, including Antigua, Aruba, Curacao, Guadeloupe, Jamaica, and Martinique. Risk occurs in rural-agricultural areas where there are adobe-style huts and houses that potentially harbor the night-biting triatomid (assassin) bugs. Travelers sleeping in such structures should take precautions against nighttime bites.

Rabies: Low risk. Mongoose-borne rabies has been reported on Grenada. There is no risk of rabies in the Caribbean, except for Haiti, The Dominican Republic, and Grenada. Travelers should avoid stray animals, especially dogs, and seek emergency treatment of any animal bite.

AIDS: Reported from all Caribbean countries. HIV prevalence throughout the region, based on blood donor screening, is estimated at 0.5%. Most cases of AIDS in this region are transmitted through sexual contact. Highest HIV rates, as well as the highest rates of heterosexually transmitted AIDS, are found in Haiti, the Dominican Republic, and the Bahamas.

Other diseases/health threats: Brucellosis, histoplasmosis, leishmaniasis (not currently endemic, except possibly for the Dominican Republic), fascioliasis (confirmed on Guadeloupe), helminthic infections (ancylostomiasis, ascariasis, strongyloidiasis, and trichuriasis), syphilis (the Turks and Caicos, the Bahamas, the Cayman Islands, and the British Virgin Islands have the highest official rates), toxocariasis (reported from several islands; higher infection rates in children), tuberculosis (endemic throughout the Caribbean), typhoid fever, ciguatera fish toxin poisoning (outbreaks have occurred), and swimming related hazards (jellyfish, spiny sea urchins, and coral).

ANTIGUA & BARBUDA
St. John's ... GMT -4 hrs

Entry Requirements
- Passport/Visa: Visa not required.
- AIDS Test: HIV testing required of foreign university students and travelers suspected of being HIV infected.
- Vaccinations: A yellow fever vaccination certificate is required from travelers over 1 year of age coming from infected areas.

Telephone Area Code: 809
Electricity/Plugs: AC 60 Hz, 220 volts, plug types A, B, and G.
American Express: Antours. BWIA Sunjet House Long & Thames. St. John's. Tel. 462-4788.
Embassies/Consulates: U.S. Embassy, St. John's. Tel. 462-3505/06. Independent since 1981, these islands remain within the British Commonwealth.
Hospitals/Doctors: Holberton Hospital, St. John's (215 beds). Travelers should contact the U.S. Embassy for physician referrals.

Health Advisory

Malaria, yellow fever: No risk.
Travelers' diarrhea: Low to moderate risk. In urban and resort areas, the hotels and restaurants serve reliable food and potable water. Elsewhere, travelers should observe safety precautions. A quinolone antibiotic is recommended for the treatment of acute diarrhea.
Hepatitis: Low risk to tourists. Susceptible travelers should consider immune globulin prophylaxis or hepatitis A vaccination.
Dengue fever: This mosquito-transmitted viral disease is prevalent in the Caribbean. All travelers should take measures to prevent insect bites.
Schistosomiasis: Foci of potential infection are present on Antigua. Travelers should avoid swimming, bathing, or wading in freshwater ponds, lakes, or streams unless advised they are safe. Snail infested water areas are fairly well defined and usually can be avoided.
Other diseases/health threats: Leptospirosis, intestinal worms (helminths), rabies, syphilis, AIDS, tuberculosis, typhoid fever, ciguatera fish poisoning, and swimming related hazards (jellyfish, spiny sea urchins, and coral).

ARUBA
Oranjestad ... GMT -4 hrs

Entry Requirements
- Passport/Visa: Visa not required.
- AIDS Test: Not required.
- Vaccinations: None required.

Telephone Country Code: 297
Electricity/Plugs: AC 50, 60 Hz; 115/230 volts; plug types A,B, and F.
American Express: S. E. L. Maduro & Sons. Rockefellerstraat 1, Oranjestad. Tel. (8) 23888.
Hospitals/Doctors: Oduber Hospital, Oranjestad: (279 beds). This hospital is regarded as one of the better medical facilities in the West Indies. Tel. (8) 243-00.

Health Advisory

Malaria, yellow fever, cholera: No risk.
Travelers' diarrhea: Low to moderate risk. Food and water are generally safe on this island. Outside of resort and urban areas travelers are advised to follow safety precautions.
Hepatitis: Low risk to tourists. Travelers should consider immune globulin prophylaxis or vaccination against hepatitis A.
Dengue fever: Low degree of risk. Travelers should take protective measures against mosquito bites.
Other diseases/health threats: Typhoid fever, dengue hemorrhagic fever, Chagas' disease (potential threat), filariasis, leptospirosis, ciguatera fish poisoning, and swimming related hazards (jellyfish, spiny sea urchins, and coral).

BAHAMAS

Freeport ... GMT -5 hrs

Entry Requirements

- Passport/Visa: Visa not required.
- AIDS Test: Not required.
- Vaccinations: A yellow fever vaccination certificate is required from travelers over 1 year of age coming from infected or endemic areas.

Telephone Area Code: 809   **AT&T:** 1-800-872-2881   **MCI:** 1-800-624-1000

American Express: Mundy Tours. Regent Centre 4, Freeport. Tel. (809)-352-4444/-6641.

Embassies/Consulates: U.S. Embassy, Nassau. Mosmar Building, Queen Street. Tel. (809) 322-1181 or 328-2206. Canadian Consulate. Tel. 323-2124.

Hospitals/Doctors: J. Wavell Thompson, M.D., Nassau. Tel. 322-1357/1358 (office), 328-0292 (H). Princess Margaret Hospital, New Providence (478 beds); general medical/surgical facility; emergency room. Lucayan Medical Center, Freeport; Tel. 352-7288/373-4689. Rand Memorial Hospital, Freeport (74 beds); general medical/surgical services; emergency room.

Health Advisory

Malaria, yellow fever, cholera: No risk.

Travelers' diarrhea: Low to moderate risk. In urban and resort areas, the hotels and restaurants serve reliable food and potable water. Elsewhere, travelers should observe safety precautions. A quinolone antibiotic is recommended for the treatment of acute diarrhea.

Hepatitis: Low to medium risk to tourists. Travelers should consider immune globulin prophylaxis or vaccination against hepatitis A.

Dengue fever: Low degree of risk. All travelers, however, should take protective measures against mosquito bites.

Other diseases/health threats: Typhoid fever (low risk), syphilis, AIDS (among the highest incidence in the Caribbean), ciguatera fish poisoning, moped and motorcycle accidents, and swimming related hazards (jellyfish, spiny sea urchins, and coral).

BARBADOS

Bridgetown ... GMT -4 hrs

Entry Requirements

- Passport/Visa: Visa not required.
- AIDS Test: Not required.
- Vaccinations: A yellow fever vaccination certificate is required from travelers over 1 year of age coming from infected or endemic areas.

Telephone Area Code: 809

Electricity/Plugs: AC 50 Hz, 115/230 volts; plug types A, B.

American Express: Barbados International Travel Services, McGregor Street, Bridgetown; Tel. 431-2423.

Embassies/Consulates: U.S. Embassy, Bridgetown, Broad Street; Tel. 436-4950.

Hospitals/Doctors: Roger Goddard, M.D. Diagnostic Clinic & Hospital, St. Michael; Tel. 426-5051/436-3362. Queen Elizabeth's Hospital, Bridgetown (600 beds); all specialties, including hemodialysis; Tel. 436-6450. Westgate Clinic, Bridgetown; Tel. 436-6633/429-2978.

Health Advisory

Malaria, yellow fever, cholera: No risk.

Travelers' diarrhea: Low to moderate risk. In urban and resort areas, the hotels and restaurants serve reliable food and potable water. A quinolone antibiotic is recommended for the treatment of acute diarrhea.

Hepatitis: Low risk to tourists. Travelers should consider immune globulin prophylaxis or vaccination against hepatitis A.

Other diseases/health threats: Typhoid fever, dengue, leptospirosis, filariasis, ciguatera fish poisoning, and swimming related hazards (jellyfish, spiny sea urchins, and coral).

BONAIRE (NETH. ANTILLES)

GMT -4 hrs

Entry Requirements
- Passport/Visa: Visa not required.
- AIDS Test: Not required.
- Vaccinations: None required.

Telephone Country Code: 599 (7)

Health Advisory
Travelers should refer to health advisory for Aruba.

BRITISH VIRGIN ISLANDS
(ANEGADA, TORTOLA, VIRGIN GORDA)

Tortola ... GMT -4hrs

Entry Requirements
- Passport/Visa: Visa not required.
- AIDS Test: All immigrants and work permit applicants are required to have HIV testing. U.S. tests accepted.
- Vaccinations: None required.

Telephone Area Code: 809
American Express: Romney Associates Consultants, Waterfront Plaza, Tortola. Tel. 494-2872.
Doctors/Hospitals: Peebles Hospital, Tortola (50 beds); limited medical/surgical services.

Health Advisory

Malaria: No risk.
Travelers' diarrhea: Low to moderate risk. In resort areas, the hotels and restaurants serve reliable food and potable water. Elsewhere, travelers should observe safety precautions. A quinolone antibiotic (Floxin or Cipro) is recommended for the treatment of acute diarrhea.
Hepatitis: Low risk to tourists. Susceptible travelers should consider immune globulin prophylaxis or hepatitis A vaccination.
Dengue fever: This mosquito-transmitted viral disease is prevalent in the Caribbean. Travelers should take measures to prevent insect bites.
Other diseases/health threats: Typhoid fever, sexually transmitted diseases, ciguatera fish poisoning, and swimming related hazards (jellyfish, spiny sea urchins, and coral).

CAYMAN ISLANDS (BRITISH WEST INDIES)

Grand Cayman ... GMT -5 hrs

Entry Requirements
- Passport/Visa: Visa not required.
- AIDS Test: Not required.
- Vaccinations: None required.

Telephone Area Code: 809   **AT&T:** 1-800-872-2881   **MCI:** 1-800-624-1000
Electricity/Plugs: AC 50 Hz, 115/230 volts; plug types A, B.
American Express: Cayman Travel Services, Ltd., Grand Cayman. Tel. 949-8755.
Hospitals/Doctors: General Hospital, Georgetown (52 beds); general medical services; emergency room.
Scuba diving: A decompression chamber is located on Grand Cayman.

Health Advisory

Malaria: No risk.
Travelers' diarrhea: Low to medium risk. Hotel food and water is considered generally safe in this country.
Dengue fever: Low risk, but dengue fever is again being reported. (Until 1989, the Cayman Islands were disease free.) All travelers are advised to take measures to prevent mosquito bites.

CUBA

Havana ... GMT -5 hrs

Entry Requirements

- Passport/Visa: Required by all travelers.
  U.S. travelers should contact the State Department (202-376-0922) regarding travel restrictions applying to U.S. citizens.
- AIDS Test: Testing required for all travelers except tourists upon arrival in Cuba.
- Vaccinations: None required.

Electricity/Plugs: AC 60 Hz, 110 volts. Information on plug types not available.

Embassies/Consulates: U.S. Interest Section, Havana. Calzado, between Calles L and M, Vedado. Tel. 32-0551-59. The United States does not maintain formal diplomatic relations with Cuba.

Hospitals/Doctors: Hermanos Almajeiras Hospital, Havana (950 beds); full range of specialty services; nuclear medicine, CT scanner; burn unit. U.S. Navy Hospital, Guantanamo Bay; Tel. (5) 399-7230. Dr. Ernesto Guevara Hospital de la Serna General Hospital, Las Tunas (630 beds); emergency and intensive care services; burn unit.

Health Advisory

Malaria, yellow fever: No risk.

Travelers' diarrhea: Moderate to high risk. In large urban areas tap water frequently is contaminated due to the poor condition of the water distribution system. In resort areas, the hotels generally serve reliable food and potable water. Elsewhere, travelers should observe all safety precautions. Shigella infections outnumber salmonella 2:1. A quinolone antibiotic is recommended for the treatment of acute diarrhea. Diarrhea not responding to antibiotic treatment may be due to a parasitic disease such as giardiasis or amebiasis. (Nearly 50% of schoolchildren in a Havana suburb were found infected with giardia organisms. Recent data on amebiasis not available.)

Hepatitis: Low to moderate risk. All susceptible travelers should receive immune globulin or hepatitis A vaccine. The hepatitis B carrier rate in the general population is estimated at 0.8%. Vaccination against hepatitis B is recommended for healthcare workers and all long-term visitors to this country.

Dengue fever: This mosquito-transmitted viral disease is prevalent in the Caribbean. Dengue is not currently endemic in Cuba, but sporadic cases may occur. An epidemic occurred in 1981 in which over 300,000 people were affected. The *Aedes* mosquitoes, which transmit dengue, bite primarily during the daytime and are present in populous urban areas as well as resort and rural areas. All travelers are advised to take measures to prevent mosquito bites.

Typhoid fever: High incidence reported. Vaccination is recommended for those traveling extensively outside of tourist areas.

Leptospirosis: More than 300 cases are reported annually. Transmission of disease occurs primarily in low-lying, poorly drained areas where animal urine-infected water accumulates. Holguin Province is reportedly a high-risk area, especially September–October, during the rainy season.

Rabies: Low risk, but several human cases are reported annually. Travelers should seek immediate treatment of any animal bite. Rabies post-exposure vaccination is indicated following the unprovoked bite of a dog, cat, mongoose, bat, or monkey. Bites by other animals should be considered on an individual basis. Pre-exposure vaccination against rabies (3 doses) should be considered for long-term travel to this country. This is especially true for travelers going to remote rural areas if they will be unable to receive antirabies treatment within 24 hours of exposure to a potentially rabid animal.

Other diseases/health threats: Abdominal angiostrongyliasis, brucellosis, dengue hemorrhagic fever, eastern equine encephalitis, fascioliasis (more commonly reported than in any other Latin American country), toxocariasis, toxoplasmosis, tick-borne rickettsioses (may occur), ciguatera fish poisoning, and swimming related hazards (jellyfish, spiny sea urchins, and coral).

DOMINICA

Roseau ... GMT -4 hrs

Entry Requirements
- Passport/Visa: Visa not required. Dominica has been independent since 1978 and is a member of the British Commonwealth of Nations.
- AIDS Test: Not required.
- Vaccinations: A yellow fever vaccination certificate is required from travelers over 1 year of age coming from infected or endemic areas.

Telephone Area Code: 809

Electricity/Plugs: AC 50 Hz, 220 volts; plug type G. Adaptors and transformer necessary for U.S.-made appliances.

American Express: Whitchurch Travel. Old Street, Roseau; Tel. 448-2181.

Embassies/Consulates: Canadian High Commission (Barbados); Tel. (809) 429-3550.

Hospitals/Doctors: General Hospital, Portsmouth (50 beds); limited medical services. Princess Margaret Hospital, Roseau (247 beds); general medical/surgical facility; Tel. 448-2231.

Health Advisory

Malaria: No risk.

Travelers' diarrhea: Low-medium risk. Tap water is generally potable, but mineral water is advised. In urban and resort areas, the hotels and restaurants serve reliable food and potable water. Elsewhere, travelers should observe safety precautions. A quinolone antibiotic (Floxin or Cipro) is recommended for the treatment of acute diarrhea. Diarrhea not responding to antibiotic treatment may be due to a parasitic disease such as giardiasis or amebiasis.

Hepatitis: Low risk to tourists. Susceptible travelers should consider immune globulin prophylaxis or hepatitis A vaccination.

Schistosomiasis: Foci of infection are possibly present on this island. Travelers should avoid swimming, bathing, or wading in freshwater ponds, lakes, or streams unless advised they are safe. Schistosomiasis is of limited risk to nonindigenous personnel because the foci of snail-infested water are fairly well defined and can be avoided.

Dengue fever: Risk is present. The *Aedes* mosquitoes, which transmit dengue, bite primarily during the daytime and are present in populous urban areas as well as resort and rural areas. All travelers are advised to take measures to prevent mosquito bites.

Other diseases/health threats: Brucellosis, strongyloidiasis, toxoplasmosis, tuberculosis, typhoid fever, viral encephalitis, ciguatera fish poisoning (outbreaks have occurred), and swimming related hazards (jellyfish, spiny sea urchins, and coral).

DOMINICAN REPUBLIC

Santo Domingo ... GMT -4 hrs

Entry Requirements
- Passport/Visa: Passport and tourist card required.
- AIDS Test: Not required.
- Vaccinations: None required.

Telephone Area Code: 809   **MCI:** 1-800-751-6624

Electricity/Plugs: AC 60 Hz, 110/220 volts; plug types A and J.

American Express: Banco Del Progreso, Avenida J.F. Kennedy 3, Santo Domingo; Tel. 567-5832.

Embassies/Consulates: U.S. Embassy, Santo Domingo. Calle Cesar Nicolas Penson & Calle Leopoldo Navarro; Tel. (809) 541-2171. Canadian Consulate, Santo Domingo. Mahatma Ghandi 200; Tel. (809) 689-0002.

Hospitals/Doctors: Clinica Abreu (76 beds); general medical/surgical facility; emergency room; frequently used by embassy personnel; Tel. 688-4411.
Jordi Brossa, M.D. Tel. 682-2090 or 565-1167. Dr. Francisco Moscoso Puella Hospital (290 beds); general medical/surgical facility; blood bank; Tel. 682-8016. Centro Medico Universidad Hospital (200 beds); general medical/surgical facility; 4-bed ICU; Tel. 682. In Santiago: Clinica Corominas; Tel. 582-1171 or 582-3913.

Health Advisory

Malaria: There is year-round risk of malaria in rural areas under 400 meters elevation in the provinces of Dabajon, Estrelleta, Monte Cristi, and Pedernales along the border with Haiti. On the northern coast, an area of risk may be extending eastward. Almost 100% of malaria in the Dominican Republic is falciparum malaria, but no chloroquine-resistant cases have been reported. Chloroquine prophylaxis is recommended for all travelers going to rural malarious areas.

Travelers' diarrhea: Low to moderate risk in resort areas, first-class hotels and restaurants, which generally serve reliable food and potable water. Elsewhere, travelers should observe all safety precautions. High risk of bacterial-related illness occurs in rural areas. Tap water in cities may be contaminated. A quinolone antibiotic (Floxin or Cipro) is recommended for the treatment of acute diarrhea. Diarrhea not responding to antibiotic treatment may be due to a parasitic disease such as giardiasis or amebiasis.

Hepatitis: There is a high risk of hepatitis A in this country. All susceptible travelers should receive immune globulin or hepatitis A vaccine. The hepatitis B carrier rate in the general population is among the highest in the Americas and is estimated to exceed 4%. Vaccination against hepatitis B is recommended for healthcare workers and for those travelers planning an extended (more than 4 weeks) visit to this country.

Dengue fever: Sporadic cases occur year-round countrywide. The *Aedes* mosquitoes, which transmit dengue, bite primarily during the daytime and are present in populous urban areas as well as resort and rural areas. All travelers are advised to take precautions to prevent insect (mosquito) bites.

Schistosomiasis: Although relatively few cases are reported, an estimated 200,000 Dominicans are infected. Infection rates of up to 24% reported in one major focus. Year-round risk is present in several areas of the eastern lowlands. Potential for spread to other areas exists because the freshwater snail host is found on many parts of the island. Travelers should avoid swimming or bathing in freshwater ponds, lakes, or streams.

Rabies: Sporadic human cases (about 3 annually) are reported, most due to dog bites. Canine rabies increased during the 1980s. Travelers should seek immediate treatment of any animal bite. Rabies vaccination may be indicated, especially following the unprovoked bite of a dog, cat, bat, or monkey. Bites by other animals should be considered on an individual basis. Pre-exposure vaccination against rabies (3 doses) should be considered for long-term travel to this country. Pre-exposure vaccination does not preclude the need for post-exposure treatment.

AIDS: Incidence is reported to be increasing rapidly. The majority of cases have been attributed to homosexual or bisexual contact, but promiscuous heterosexual behavior is now a major risk factor. Intravenous drug abuse does not appear to be a significant factor in the spread of AIDS at this time. Estimates of overall HIV prevalence in 1990 were 2.6% in high-risk urban groups and 1.6% in low-risk urban groups. HIV rate in prostitutes as reported to be nearly 50%.

Other illnesses/health threats: Brucellosis, filariasis (limited to Santo Domingo area, the central valley, and the north coast), intestinal helminths (including ascariasis and trichuriasis), cutaneous and mucocutaneous leishmaniasis (undetermined risk; 1 small focus exists in eastern part of the country), leptospirosis (sporadic cases only), strongyloidiasis, tuberculosis (relatively high rates reported), typhoid fever (high incidence), viral encephalitis, ciguatera fish poisoning (outbreaks have occurred), and swimming related hazards (jellyfish, spiny sea urchins, and coral).

GRENADA
St. George's ... GMT -4 hrs

Entry Requirements
- Passport/Visa: Visa not required. Grenada has been independent from Britain since 1974.
- AIDS Test: Not required.
- Vaccinations: A yellow fever vaccination certificate is required from all travelers coming from infected areas.

Telephone Area Code: 809   **AT&T:** 1-800-872-2881   **MCI:** 1-800-624-8721

Electricity/Plugs: AC 50 Hz, 220 volts; plug types C, D, and G. AdAptors and transformer necessary for U.S.-made appliances.

American Express: Grenada International Travel Services. Church Street, St. George's; Tel. 440-2945.

Embassies/Consulates: U.S. Embassy, St. George's; Tel. (809) 440-1731.

Doctors/Hospitals: St. George's General Hospital (240 beds); general medical/surgical facility; Tel. 440-2051. Barry A. Rapier, MD. Tel. 440-2055 or 4531. Bernard Gittens, MD. Tel. 440-2769 or 4380.

Health Advisory

Malaria: No risk.

Travelers' diarrhea: Low to moderate risk. In urban and resort areas, the hotels and restaurants generally serve reliable food and potable water. Elsewhere, travelers should observe all food and drink safety precautions. A quinolone antibiotic (Floxin or Cipro) is recommended for the treatment of acute diarrhea. Diarrhea not responding to antibiotic treatment may be due to a parasitic disease such as giardiasis or amebiasis.

Hepatitis: Low overall risk to tourists. Susceptible travelers should consider immune globulin prophylaxis or hepatitis A vaccination.

Dengue fever: This mosquito-transmitted viral disease is prevalent in the Caribbean. Travelers should take measures to prevent insect bites.

Schistosomiasis: This disease is present, but is of limited risk. Most snail-infested freshwater foci have been identified and can be avoided.

Other diseases/health threats: Brucellosis, Bancroftian filariasis (mosquito-borne; may be a threat), histoplasmosis, intestinal helminthic infections (ancylostomiasis, ascariasis, strongyloidiasis, and trichuriasis), syphilis, AIDS, toxocariasis, toxoplasmosis, tuberculosis, typhoid fever, viral encephalitis, ciguatera fish toxin poisoning (outbreaks have occurred), and swimming related hazards (jellyfish, spiny sea urchins, and coral).

GUADELOUPE (FRENCH WEST INDIES)
Gosier ... GMT -4 hrs

Entry Requirements
- Passport/Visa: Visa not required. Guadeloupe is a French possession (French Overseas Department).
- AIDS Test: Not required.
- Vaccinations: A vaccination certificate is required of all travelers older than 1 year arriving from infected areas.

Telephone Country Code: 590

Electricity/Plugs: AC 50 Hz, 220 volts; plug types C, D, and E. Adaptors and transformer necessary for U.S.-made appliances.

American Express: Petrelluzzi Travel Agency. 2 Rue Henry IV, Pointe-A-Pitre; Tel. 830-399.

Embassies/Consulates: U.S. Embassy, French Caribbean Dept., 14 Rue Blenac, Martinique; Tel. (596) 631-303. Canadian High Commission (Trinidad); Tel. (809) 623-4787.

Hospitals/Doctors: Regional Hospital, Pointe-a-Pitre; general medical/surgical facility; numerous specialties; Tel. (8) 910-10. In Gosier: Nicole Duhamel, M.D. Tel. (84) 3562.

Health Advisory

Malaria: No risk.

Travelers' diarrhea: Low to moderate risk. In urban and resort areas, the hotels and restaurants generally serve reliable food and potable water. Elsewhere, travelers should observe all food and drink safety precautions. A quinolone antibiotic (Floxin or Cipro) is recommended for the treatment of acute diarrhea. Diarrhea not responding to antibiotic treatment may be due to a parasitic disease such as giardiasis or amebiasis.

Hepatitis: Low risk to tourists. Susceptible travelers should consider immune globulin prophylaxis or hepatitis A vaccination.

Dengue fever: This mosquito-transmitted viral disease is prevalent in the Caribbean. Travelers should take measures to prevent insect bites.

Leishmaniasis: Limited risk (historically) of cutaneous and visceral leishmaniasis. Travelers should take measures to prevent insect (sandfly) bites.

Schistosomiasis: This disease (*Schistosoma mansoni* variety) is present, but risk of transmission is deemed low. Most snail-infested freshwater foci have been identified and can be avoided.

Other diseases/health threats: Brucellosis, fascioliasis, filariasis (Bancroftian variety; mosquito-borne; may occur in the Lesser Antilles from Trinidad north to Guadeloupe), histoplasmosis, intestinal helminthic infections (ancylostomiasis, ascariasis, strongyloidiasis, and trichuriasis), leptospirosis, mansonellosis (vectored by *Culicoides* midges; may occur), sexually transmitted diseases, AIDS, tuberculosis, typhoid fever, viral encephalitis, ciguatera fish toxin poisoning, and swimming related hazards (jellyfish, spiny sea urchins, and coral).

HAITI

Port-au-Prince ... GMT -5 hrs

Entry Requirements

- Passport/Visa: Travelers should possess valid passport. A visa is not required.
- AIDS Test: Not required.
- Vaccinations: A yellow fever vaccination certificate is required from all travelers arriving from infected areas.

Telephone Country Code: 509   **AT&T:** 001-800-972-2883   **MCI:** 001-800-444-1234

American Express: Agence Citadelle S.A. 35 Place Du Marron Inconnu, Port-Au-Prince; Tel. (2) 25-900.

Embassies/Consulates: U.S. Embassy, Port-au-Prince. Harry Truman Blvd; Tel. (2) 20-200. After hours: 22-03-68. Canadian Embassy, Port-au-Prince. Edifice Banque Nova Scotia. Tel: 22-23-58.

Hospitals/Doctors: Rene Charles, M.D., Port-au-Prince. Bois Zerne, #15; Tel. 45-27-98 (office), 57-32-52 (home). Hospital du Canape Vert (46 beds); some specialty services; no physician on duty in emergency department; care must be pre-arranged; commonly used by U.S. Embassy personnel. Tel. 45-10-52. Hospital Adventiste de DiQuini (42 beds); private hospital; modern equipment; 24-hour emergency room physicians on duty; ambulance service. Tel. 34-20-00.

Health Advisory

Malaria: High risk year-round countrywide, including urban areas at elevations under 500 meters. Malaria is a major public health problem in this country. Falciparum malaria accounts for over 99% of cases, with other cases due to *P. malariae*. Chloroquine-resistant falciparum malaria has not been reported. Prophylaxis with chloroquine is currently recommended.

Travelers' diarrhea: All travelers should observe strict food and drink precautions, especially outside of resort areas. Tap water should be avoided. A quinolone antibiotic is recommended for the treatment of acute diarrhea. Diarrhea not responding to antibiotic treatment may be due to a parasitic disease such as giardiasis, amebiasis, or cryptosporidiosis

Hepatitis: All susceptible travelers should receive immune globulin or hepatitis A vaccine. The hepatitis B carrier rate in the general population is estimated at 1.7%– 13%. Vaccination against hepatitis B is recommended for healthcare workers and long-term visitors to this country.

Dengue fever: Year-round risk, elevated April through September. Dengue occurs primarily in the coastal-urban areas and is probably under-reported. To prevent dengue, travelers should take protective measures against mosquito bites.

Filariasis: Bancroftian filariasis occurs in coastal areas, primarily in the north and around the Gulf of La Gonave. To prevent filariasis, travelers to risk areas should take protective measures against mosquito bites.

Rabies: Low apparent risk, since only occasional human cases are reported. Any unprovoked animal bite, however, should be considered a medical emergency. Rabies vaccination is recommended for anyone planning an extended stay in this country.

AIDS: High incidence of HIV infection in the general population with heterosexual and bisexual contact, the predominate mode of transmission. There is also a high incidence of maternally transmitted HIV infections. HIV prevalence is estimated at 4.4%–5.8% of the general population. High-risk groups have a much higher prevalence of HIV infection, with HIV prevalence of female prostitutes estimated at over 40%. Tropical spastic paresis, due to the human T-lymphotropic virus, type 1 (HTLV-1), is endemic. All travelers are cautioned against unsafe sex, unsterile medical injections, IV drug use, and blood transfusions.

Tuberculosis: A major public health problem; all medical personnel, relief workers, and others having close contact with the Haitian population should be skin tested with PPD and consider BCG vaccination.

Other diseases/health threats: Brucellosis, helminthic infections (ancylostomiasis, ascariasis, strongyloidiasis, and trichuriasis), leptospirosis, mansonellosis, relapsing fever (louseborne), toxoplasmosis, typhoid fever (highly prevalent; vaccination recommended), viral encephalitis, and ciguatera fish toxin poisoning.

JAMAICA
Kingston ... GMT -5 hrs

Entry Requirements
- Passport/Visa: Visa not required.
- AIDS Test: Not required.
- Vaccinations: A yellow fever vaccination certificate is required from all travelers arriving from infected areas.

Telephone Area Code: 809   **AT&T:** 0-800-872-2883   **MCI:** 800-674-7000

Electricity/Plugs: AC 50 Hz, 110/220 volts, plug types A and B. Adaptors and transformer necessary for U.S.-made appliances.

American Express: Stuart's Travel Service, Ltd. 9 Cecelio Avenue, Kingston; Tel. 929-4329.

Embassies/Consulates: U.S. Embassy, Kingston. 2 Oxford Road; Tel. (809) 929-4850. Canadian High Commission Kingston. 30-36 Knutsford Boulevard; Tel. 962-1500.

Hospitals/Doctors: In Kingston: University Hospital (504 beds); general medical/surgical facility; ICU; burn unit; emergency services; Tel. 927-1620. Distir Misir, M.D., Medical Associates, 18 Tangerine Place; Tel. 926-0571. In Ochos Rios: Dr. Noel A. Black; Tel. 972-2296.

Health Advisory
Malaria: No risk.

Travelers' diarrhea: Low to moderate risk. In urban and resort areas, the hotels and restaurants generally serve reliable food and potable water. Elsewhere, travelers should observe all food and drink safety precautions. A quinolone antibiotic (Floxin or Cipro) is recommended for the treatment of acute diarrhea. Diarrhea not responding to antibiotic treatment may be due to a parasitic disease such as giardiasis or amebiasis.

Hepatitis: Low risk to tourists. Susceptible travelers should consider immune globulin prophylaxis or hepatitis A vaccination.

Dengue fever: This mosquito-transmitted viral disease is prevalent in the Caribbean. Travelers should take measures to prevent insect bites.

Leptospirosis: This spirochetal infection is reported from this country. The risk to tourists is deemed to be low. Travelers should avoid contact with animal urine or water potentially contaminated with animal urine.

Other diseases/health threats: Brucellosis, Chagas' disease (low apparent risk; reduviid bug vectors have been detected on several islands, including Jamaica), histoplasmosis, helminthic infections (ancylostomiasis, ascariasis, strongyloidiasis, and trichuriasis), sexually transmitted diseases, AIDS, tropical spastic paresis (due to HTLV-1; seroprevalence in adult blood donors estimated at 3.5%–5%), toxocariasis, tuberculosis, typhoid fever, viral encephalitis, ciguatera fish toxin poisoning (outbreaks have occurred), and swimming related hazards (jellyfish, spiny sea urchins, and coral).

MARTINIQUE (FRENCH WEST INDIES)
Fort-de-France ... GMT -4 hrs

Entry Requirements
- Passport/Visa: A valid passport is required. A visa is not required.
- AIDS Test: Not required.
- Vaccinations: Yellow fever: A vaccination certificate is required of all travelers older than 1 year arriving from infected areas.

Telephone Country Code: 596

Electricity/Plugs: AC 50 Hz, 220 volts, plug types C, D, and E. Adaptors and transformer necessary for U.S.-made appliances.

American Express: Roger Albert Vaoages, 7 Victor Hugo, Fort-de-France; Tel. 71-55-55.

Embassies/Consulates: U.S. Embassy, French Caribbean Dept. 14 Rue Blenac, Martinique; Tel. (596) 631-303. Canadian High Commission (Trinidad); Tel. (809) 623-4787.

Hospitals/Doctors: La Maynard Hospital, Fort-de-France Regional Hospital Center (764 beds); general medical/surgical facility; trauma and 24-hour emergency services. Yves Donatien, MD. Tel. 715-822.

Health Advisory

Malaria: No risk.

Travelers' diarrhea: Low to moderate risk. In urban and resort areas, the hotels and restaurants generally serve reliable food and potable water. Elsewhere, travelers should observe all food and drink safety precautions. A quinolone antibiotic (Floxin or Cipro) is recommended for the treatment of acute diarrhea. Diarrhea not responding to antibiotic treatment may be due to a parasitic disease such as giardiasis or amebiasis.

Hepatitis: Low risk to tourists. Susceptible travelers should consider immune globulin prophylaxis or hepatitis A vaccination.

Dengue fever: Risk is present. This mosquito-transmitted viral disease is prevalent in the Caribbean. Travelers should take measures to prevent insect bites.

Leishmaniasis: Limited risk. Cutaneous and visceral forms of leishmaniasis may be present. Travelers should take measures to avoid insect (sandfly) bites.

Schistosomiasis: Disease due to intestinal schistosomiasis (due to *S. mansoni*) is present on this island, but the risk is deemed to be low. Most snail-infested freshwater foci have been identified and can be avoided. Travelers should avoid swimming, bathing, or wading in freshwater ponds, lakes, or streams unless advised they are safe. Chlorinated swimming pools are considered safe.

Other diseases/health threats: Brucellosis, filariasis (Bancroftian variety; mosquito-borne; may occur in the Lesser Antilles from Trinidad north to Guadeloupe), histoplasmosis, intestinal helminthic infections (ancylostomiasis, ascariasis, strongyloidiasis, and trichuriasis), leptospirosis, sexually transmitted diseases, AIDS, toxocariasis, tuberculosis, typhoid fever, viral encephalitis, ciguatera fish toxin poisoning, and swimming related hazards (jellyfish, spiny sea urchins, and coral).

MONTSERRAT (BRITISH WEST INDIES)
GMT -4 hrs

Entry Requirements
- Passport/Visa: Visa not required. Montserrat is a French Dependent Territory.
- AIDS Test: Not required.
- Vaccinations: No vaccinations required.

Telephone Area Code: 809

Electricity/Plugs: AC 60 Hz, 220 volts; plug types A, B, and G.

American Express: Caribbean World Travel. Parliament Street, Plymouth; Tel. 491-2713.

Doctors/Hospitals: Glendon Hospital, Plymouth (67 beds); general medical/surgical facility; emergency services; Tel. 491-2552.

Health Advisory

Travelers' diarrhea: Low to moderate risk. In urban and resort areas, the hotels and restaurants generally serve reliable food and potable water. Elsewhere, travelers should observe all food and drink safety precautions. A quinolone antibiotic is recommended for the treatment of acute diarrhea.

Hepatitis: Low risk to tourists. Susceptible travelers should consider immune globulin or hepatitis A vaccination.

Dengue fever: Risk is present. This mosquito-transmitted viral disease is prevalent in the Caribbean. Travelers should take measures to prevent insect bites.

Schistosomiasis: This disease is present but the risk is low. Most snail-infested freshwater foci have been identified and can be avoided.

Other diseases/health threats: Intestinal helminthic infections, syphilis, AIDS, toxoplasmosis, tuberculosis, typhoid fever, viral encephalitis, ciguatera fish toxin poisoning (outbreaks have occurred), and swimming related hazards (jellyfish, spiny sea urchins, and coral).

PUERTO RICO AND U.S. VIRGIN ISLANDS
San Juan ... GMT -4 hrs

Entry Requirements
- Passport/Visa: Passport recommended.
- AIDS Test: Not required.
- Vaccinations: None required.

Telephone Area Code: 809

American Express: Travel Network. 1035 Ashford Avenue, Condado Area, San Juan; Tel. 725-0950.

Hospitals/Doctors: Ashford Presbyterian Hospital, San Juan; Tel. 721-2160.
Dwight Santiago, M.D. Ashford Medical Center; Tel. 722-5513 or 843-4588.

Health Advisory

Travelers' diarrhea: Low to moderate risk. In urban and resort areas, the hotels and restaurants generally serve reliable food and potable water.

Hepatitis: Low risk to tourists. Susceptible travelers should consider immune globulin prophylaxis or hepatitis A vaccination.

Dengue fever: This disease occurs in Puerto Rico and the Virgin Islands. All travelers should take measures to prevent insect (mosquito) bites.

Schistosomiasis: Risk is present, but is deemed low. Travelers should avoid swimming or wading in freshwater ponds, lakes, or streams. Chlorinated pools are safe.

Other diseases/health threats: Bancroftian filariasis (mosquito-borne; may be a threat; travelers should prevent insect bites), intestinal helminthic infections (ancylostomiasis, ascariasis, strongyloidiasis, and trichuriasis), sexually transmitted diseases, AIDS, typhoid fever, viral encephalitis, ciguatera fish toxin poisoning (outbreaks have occurred), and swimming related hazards (jellyfish, spiny sea urchins, and coral).

ST. BARTHELEMY (FRENCH WEST INDIES)

Gustavia ... GMT -4 hrs

Entry Requirements
- Passport/Visa: Visa not required. Visitors arriving by air are required to show return or ongoing ticket. This island, often called "St. Barts," is a dependency of Guadeloupe, which in turn is a Department of France.
- AIDS Test: Not required.
- Vaccinations: None required.

Telephone Country Code: 590

Electricity/Plugs: AC 50 Hz, 220 volt;, plug types D and G. Adaptors and transformer necessary for U.S.-made appliances.

Doctors/Hospitals: Gustavia Clinic (staffed by 5 physicians and 3 dentists); Tel. 27-60-35.

Health Advisory

Travelers' diarrhea: Low to moderate risk. In urban and resort areas, the hotels and restaurants generally serve reliable food and potable water. Elsewhere, travelers should observe all food and drink safety precautions. A quinolone antibiotic (Floxin or Cipro) is recommended for the treatment of acute diarrhea. Diarrhea not responding to antibiotic treatment may be due to a parasitic disease such as giardiasis or amebiasis.

Hepatitis: Low risk to tourists. Susceptible travelers should consider immune globulin prophylaxis or hepatitis A vaccination.

Dengue fever: This mosquito-transmitted viral disease is prevalent in the Caribbean. Travelers should take measures to prevent insect bites.

Other diseases/health threats: Typhoid fever, viral encephalitis, ciguatera fish toxin poisoning (outbreaks have occurred), and swimming related hazards (jellyfish, spiny sea urchins, and coral).

ST. KITTS & NEVIS

Basseterre ... GMT -4 hrs

Entry Requirements
- Passport/Visa: Visa not required. These islands have been independent of Britain since 1983.
- AIDS Test: Not required.
- Vaccinations: A yellow fever vaccination certificate is required from travelers over 6 months of age coming from infected or endemic areas.

Telephone Area Code: 80   **AT&T:** 1-800-872-2881

Electricity/Plugs: AC 60 Hz, 220 volts, plug types D and G. Adaptors and transformer necessary for U.S.-made appliances.

Doctors/Hospitals: Joseph N. France Hospital, Baseterre (164 beds); general medical/surgical facility; emergency room; Tel. 465-2551.

Health Advisory

Travelers' diarrhea: Low to moderate risk. In urban and resort areas, the hotels and restaurants generally serve reliable food and potable water. Elsewhere, travelers should observe all food and drink safety precautions. A quinolone antibiotic (Floxin or Cipro) is recommended for the treatment of acute diarrhea.

Hepatitis: Low risk to tourists. Susceptible travelers should consider immune globulin prophylaxis or hepatitis A vaccination.

Dengue fever: This mosquito-transmitted viral disease is prevalent in the Caribbean. Travelers should take measures to prevent insect bites.

Other diseases/health threats: Typhoid fever, viral encephalitis, ciguatera fish toxin poisoning (outbreaks have occurred), and swimming related hazards (jellyfish, spiny sea urchins, and coral).

SAINT MARTIN (FRENCH WEST INDIES)
Marigot ... GMT -4 hrs

Entry Requirements
- Passport/Visa: Visa not required. Saint Martin is a French Dependent Territory.
- AIDS Test: Not required.
- Vaccinations: None required.

Telephone Country Code: 590

Doctors/Hospitals: Hopital de Marigot (55 beds); general medical/surgical facility; physicians on call 24 hours; Tel. 87-50-07. Ambulance; Tel. 87-86-25.

Health Advisory

Malaria: No risk.

Travelers' diarrhea: Low to moderate risk. In urban and resort areas, the hotels and restaurants generally serve reliable food and potable water. Elsewhere, travelers should observe all food and drink safety precautions. A quinolone antibiotic (Floxin or Cipro) is recommended for the treatment of acute diarrhea. Diarrhea not responding to antibiotic treatment may be due to a parasitic disease such as giardiasis or amebiasis.

Hepatitis: Low risk to tourists. Susceptible travelers should consider immune globulin prophylaxis or hepatitis A vaccination.

Dengue fever: This mosquito-transmitted viral disease is prevalent in the Caribbean. Travelers should take measures to prevent insect bites.

Other diseases/health threats: Typhoid fever, viral encephalitis, ciguatera fish toxin poisoning (outbreaks have occurred), and swimming related hazards (jellyfish, spiny sea urchins, and coral).

SAINT MAARTEN (NETH. ANTILLES)
Philipsburg ... GMT -4 hrs

Entry Requirements
- Passport/Visa: Visa not required. Saint Maarten is part of the Netherland Antilles.
- AIDS Test: Not required.
- Vaccinations: None required.

Telephone Country Code: 599   **AT&T:** 001-800-872-2881   **MCI:** 001-800-950-1022

Electricity/Plugs: AC 60 Hz, 110 volts. Adaptors not necessary.

Doctors/Hospitals: St. Maarten Medical Center, Philipsburg (57 beds); new multispecialty clinic and hospital (opened in 1992); 24-hr. emergency coverage; 3-bed ICU; hemodialysis (2 units); Tel. (5) 31111. Ambulance; Tel. 22111. To call St. Martin Medical Center from French St. Martin, travelers should dial (93)-25685.

Health Advisory

Malaria: No risk.

Travelers' diarrhea: Low to moderate risk. In urban and resort areas, the hotels and restaurants generally serve reliable food and potable water. Elsewhere, travelers should observe all food and drink safety precautions. A quinolone antibiotic (Floxin or Cipro) is recommended for the treatment of acute diarrhea.

Hepatitis: Low risk to tourists. Susceptible travelers should consider immune globulin prophylaxis or hepatitis A vaccination.

Dengue fever: This mosquito-transmitted viral disease is prevalent in the Caribbean. Travelers should take measures to prevent insect bites.

Other diseases/health threats: Typhoid fever, viral encephalitis, ciguatera fish toxin poisoning (outbreaks have occurred), and swimming related hazards (jellyfish, spiny sea urchins, and coral).

SAINT LUCIA
Castries ... GMT -4 hrs

Entry Requirements
- Passport/Visa: A passport is required for entry.
- AIDS Test: Not required.
- Vaccinations: A vaccination certificate is required of all travelers older than 1 year arriving from infected areas.

Telephone Country Code: 809

Electricity/Plugs: AC 50 Hz, 220 volts; plug type G. Adaptors and transformer necessary for U.S.-made appliances.

American Express: Carib Travel Agency. 5 Jeremie Street, Castries; Tel. 452-2151.

Embassies/Consulates: Canadian High Commission (Barbados); Tel. (809) 429-3550.

Doctors/Hospitals: Victoria Hospital, Castries (211 beds); general medical/surgical facility; Tel. 452-2421.

Health Advisory

Malaria: No risk.

Travelers' diarrhea: Low to moderate risk. In urban and resort areas, the hotels and restaurants generally serve reliable food and potable water. Elsewhere, travelers should observe all food and drink safety precautions. A quinolone antibiotic (Floxin or Cipro) is recommended for the treatment of acute diarrhea. Diarrhea not responding to antibiotic treatment may be due to a parasitic disease such as giardiasis or amebiasis.

Hepatitis: Low risk to tourists. Susceptible travelers should consider immune globulin prophylaxis or hepatitis A vaccination.

Dengue fever: This mosquito-transmitted viral disease is prevalent in the Caribbean. Travelers should take measures to prevent insect bites.

Schistosomiasis: Disease due to intestinal schistosomiasis (caused by *S. mansoni*) is present on this island, but is of limited risk. Most snail-infested freshwater foci have been identified and can be avoided. Risk areas include Cul de Sac River Valley (south of Castries), the Roseau Valley, and around Soufriere and Riche Fond. Travelers should avoid swimming or wading in freshwater ponds, lakes, or streams in these areas.

Other diseases/health threats: Brucellosis, filariasis (mosquito-borne; low apparent risk; may occur in the Lesser Antilles from Trinidad north to Guadeloupe), Chagas' disease (low apparent risk; reduviid bug vectors have been detected on several other islands), histoplasmosis, helminthic infections (ancylostomiasis, ascariasis, strongyloidiasis, and trichuriasis), leptospirosis (skin contact with water or moist soil contaminated with the urine of infected animals), syphilis, AIDS, tuberculosis, typhoid fever (St. Lucia had the highest incidence reported in the Caribbean in 1987 (36 cases per 100,000 population), viral encephalitis, ciguatera fish toxin poisoning, and swimming related hazards (jellyfish, spiny sea urchins, and coral).

TURKS & CAICOS
GMT -5 hrs

Entry Requirements
- Passport/Visa: Visa not required. Turks & Caicos is a British Dependent Territory.
- AIDS Test: Not required.
- Vaccinations: None required.

Telephone Area Code: 809

Doctors/Hospitals: General Hospital, Cockburn Town (32 beds); limited medical and surgical services; Tel. 946-2040.

Health Advisory

Malaria: No risk.

Travelers' diarrhea: Low to medium risk. Travelers should drink bottled or treated water and carry a quinolone antibiotic for the treatment of more severe diarrhea.

Dengue fever: This mosquito-transmitted viral disease is prevalent in the Caribbean. Travelers should take measures to prevent insect bites.

SAINT VINCENT AND THE GRENADINES
(INCLUDES MUSTIQUE AND BEQUIA)
Kingstown ... GMT -4 hrs

Entry Requirements
- Passport/Visa: Visa not required.
- AIDS Test: Not required.
- Vaccinations: A vaccination certificate is required of all travelers older than 1 year arriving from infected areas.

Telephone Area Code: 809

Electricity/Plugs: AC 50 Hz, 220 volts; plug type B. Adaptors and transformer necessary for U.S.-made appliances.

American Express: Caribbean International Travel Service. Granby Street, Kingstown; Tel. 457-1841.

Doctors/Hospitals: General Hospital, Kingstown (204 beds); general medical/surgical facility; Tel. 456-1185.

Health Advisory

Malaria: No risk.

Travelers' diarrhea: Low to moderate risk. In urban and resort areas, the hotels and restaurants generally serve reliable food and potable water. Elsewhere, travelers should observe all food and drink safety precautions. A quinolone antibiotic (Floxin or Cipro) is recommended for the treatment of acute diarrhea. Diarrhea not responding to antibiotic treatment may be due to a parasitic disease such as giardiasis or amebiasis.

Hepatitis: Low risk to tourists. Susceptible travelers should consider immune globulin prophylaxis or hepatitis A vaccination.

Dengue fever: This mosquito-transmitted viral disease is prevalent in the Caribbean. Travelers should take measures to prevent insect bites.

Other diseases/health threats: Brucellosis, filariasis (Bancroftian variety; mosquito-borne; may occur in the Lesser Antilles from Trinidad north to Guadeloupe), histoplasmosis, intestinal helminthic infections (ancylostomiasis, ascariasis, strongyloidiasis, and trichuriasis), leptospirosis, sexually transmitted diseases, AIDS, tuberculosis, typhoid fever, viral encephalitis, ciguatera fish toxin poisoning, and swimming related hazards (jellyfish, spiny sea urchins, and coral).

TRINIDAD & TOBAGO

Port-of-Spain ... GMT -4 hrs

Entry Requirements

- Passport/Visa: A visa is not required.
- AIDS Test: Not required.
- Vaccinations: A yellow fever vaccination certificate is required from travelers over 6 months of age coming from infected or endemic areas.

Telephone Area Code: 809

Electricity/Plugs: AC 60 Hz, 115/230, 230/400 volts; plug type B.

American Express: The Travel Centre, Ltd. Uptown Mall, Level 2, Edward Street, Port-of-Spain; Tel. 625-1636.

Embassies/Consulates: U.S. Embassy, Port-of-Spain, 15 Queen's Park; Tel. 622-6371. Canadian High Commission, Port-of-Spain, 72 South Quay Street; Tel. 623-4787.

Hospitals/Doctors: In Port-of-Spain: Gordon A. Toby, M.D. Tel. 622-2544. General Hospital (882 beds); general medical and surgical facility; neurosurgery, orthopedics; Tel. 623-2951/7715.

Health Advisory

Malaria: An outbreak of vivax malaria has recently been reported in southwestern Trinidad, in the town of Icacos. Travelers to this region should use chlorquine prophylaxis, as well as measures to prevent mosquito bites.

Yellow fever: Yellow fever has been reported active in the jungle regions of Trinidad and vaccination is advised for all travelers older than 9 months of age who plan travel outside of urban areas. No human cases of yellow fever have been reported since 1980. This country is in the Yellow Fever Endemic Zone. Although a vaccination certificate may not be required for entry to this country, one may be required for on-going travel to other countries in Latin America, Africa, the Middle East, or Asia.

Travelers' diarrhea: Low to moderate risk. In urban and resort areas, the hotels and restaurants generally serve reliable food and potable water. Elsewhere, travelers should observe all food and drink safety precautions. A quinolone antibiotic (Floxin or Cipro) is recommended for the treatment of acute diarrhea. Diarrhea not responding to antibiotic treatment may be due to a parasitic disease such as giardiasis or amebiasis.

Hepatitis: Low risk to tourists. Susceptible travelers should consider immune globulin prophylaxis or hepatitis A vaccination.

Dengue fever: This mosquito-transmitted viral disease is prevalent in the Caribbean. Major outbreaks of dengue have previously occurred on Trinidad. Travelers should take measures to prevent insect (mosquito) bites. The *Aedes* mosquitoes, which transmit dengue, bite primarily during the daytime and are present in populous urban areas as well as resort and rural areas.

Leishmaniasis: Low apparent risk. The disease, however, has been reported historically. Travelers should take measures to prevent insect (sandfly) bites.

Chagas' disease: Low apparent risk. Disease may be transmitted in rural-agricultural areas where there are the adobe-style huts and houses that can potentially harbor the night-biting triatomid (assassin) bugs. Travelers sleeping in such structures should take precautions against nighttime bites.

Leptospirosis: This spirochetal infection is reported from this country. Travelers should avoid contact with animal urine or water potentially contaminated with animal urine.

Rabies: Animal rabies was reported in 1987. The potential of transmission to humans exists. Travelers should especially avoid stray dogs and seek immediate treatment of any wild animal bite. Rabies vaccination is indicated following the unprovoked bite of a dog, cat, vampire bat, monkey, or other animal.

Other diseases/health threats: Brucellosis, filariasis (Bancroftian variety; mosquito-borne; may occur in the Lesser Antilles from Trinidad north to Guadeloupe), histoplasmosis, intestinal helminthic infections (ancylostomiasis, ascariasis, strongyloidiasis, and trichuriasis), leptospirosis, sexually transmitted diseases, AIDS, tuberculosis, typhoid fever, viral encephalitis, ciguatera fish toxin poisoning, and swimming related hazards (jellyfish, spiny sea urchins, and coral).

DISEASE RISK SUMMARY
South America

Malaria: There is risk of malaria in most tropical regions of South America. There is increased risk in the Amazon Basin and along the coast of Ecuador. Chloroquine- and Fansidar-resistant falciparum malaria is an increasing problem, especially in the Amazon Basin. Chemoprophylaxis with either mefloquine or doxycycline is currently recommended for travel to these areas. Alternative malaria regimes (e.g., chloroquine alone, or chloroquine with Fansidar standby) should be discussed with a travel medicine or infectious disease specialist when traveling to lower-risk areas. All travelers should also take anti-insect precautions. These precautions include applying a deet-containing skin repellent, wearing permethrin-treated clothing, and sleeping under a mosquito net, preferably permethrin-treated.

Yellow fever: Risk is present in rural and jungle areas in all countries except Paraguay, Uruguay, Argentina, Falkland Islands, and Chile. Vaccination is recommended for travel to rural areas of all Endemic Zone countries.

Cholera: Disease activity is reported in Argentina, Bolivia, Brazil, Chile, Colombia, Ecuador, French Guiana, Guyana, Peru, Suriname, and Venezuela. Although cholera vaccination is not required for entry to any country in South America if arriving directly from the U.S. or Canada, it may be required if arriving from a cholera-infected area, or required for ongoing travel to other countries in Latin America, Africa, the Middle East, or Asia. Travelers should consider vaccination (one dose) or a doctor's letter of exemption from vaccination. The risk to travelers of acquiring cholera is considered low. Prevention consists primarily in adhering to safe food and drink guidelines.

Travelers' diarrhea: High risk outside of first-class hotels and resort areas. Lower risk occurs in Argentina and the Falkland Islands, where sanitation is generally better. Travelers should observe all food and drink safety precautions. A quinolone antibiotic (Cipro or Floxin) is recommended for the treatment of acute diarrhea. Diarrhea not responding to treatment with an antibiotic, or chronic diarrhea, may be due to a parasitic disease such as giardiasis or amebiasis, and treatment with metronidazole (Flagyl) or tinidazole (Fasigyn) should be considered. All cases of diarrhea should be treated with adequate fluid replacement.

Hepatitis A: All susceptible travelers should receive immune globulin or hepatitis A vaccine prior to travel to South America.

Hepatitis B: The hepatitis B carrier rate in the Amazon Basin of Brazil is as high as 20%. High rates also reported among aboriginal tribes in Venezuela and French Guiana. Most other countries have hepatitis B carrier rates in the general population of 1%–3%. Hepatitis B vaccination recommended for healthcare workers and those travelers expecting to have close, prolonged contact with the indigenous population of these countries, especially in Brazil.

Typhoid fever: The highest rates of typhoid fever in South America occur in Peru and Chile. Typhoid vaccination is recommended for persons traveling longer than 2–4 weeks in areas with substandard sanitation. The best prevention against typhoid fever is avoiding unsafe food and drink.

Amebiasis: There is a high incidence of amebiasis in South America, where up to 50% of the high-risk population may be infected with *E. histolytica* parasites. To avoid amebiasis, travelers should drink only safe water and eat only well-cooked food. All fruit should be peeled before eating.

Dengue fever: Outbreaks and epidemics are reported from Ecuador, Colombia, Peru, Venezuela. *Aedes aegypti* mosquitoes, which transmit dengue, bite during the daytime and are present in populous urban areas as well as resort and rural areas. Prevention of dengue consists of taking protective measures against mosquito bites, especially during the daytime when the *Aedes* mosquitoes are most active.

Schistosomiasis: Risk is present in Brazil, Suriname, and north-central Venezuela. Travelers should avoid swimming, wading, or bathing in freshwater lakes, ponds, or streams that are possibly infested with schistosome-carrying snail larvae.

Leishmaniasis: Risk is present in most countries of tropical South America. Cutaneous, mucocutaneous, and visceral leishmaniasis (kala azar) occur in many countries. Travelers to rural areas should take measures to prevent insect (sandfly) bites. Sand flies bite most actively between dusk and dawn and are found in greatest number on the periphery of rural forested areas.

Filariasis: Mosquito-borne; risk is present in parts of Brazil, French Guiana, Guyana, Suriname, and Venezuela. Travelers to risk areas should take measures to prevent insect (mosquito) bites.

Onchocerciasis: This form of filariasis is transmitted by blackflies of the Simulian species. These flies are found near rivers, where they breed in surrounding vegetation. Disease is prevalent in Venezuela, Colombia, Ecuador, and northern Brazil. Travelers to these regions should take personal protective measures against insect (black fly) bites.

Chagas' disease: Occurs in all tropical areas of South America. Chagas' disease is transmitted primarily in rural areas where there are adobe-style huts and houses that often harbor the night-biting triatomid (assassin) bugs. Travelers sleeping in such structures should take precautions against nighttime bites. These precautions include spraying sleeping quarters with an insecticide (such as Raid), sleeping away from walls, or sleeping under a mosquito net. Unscreened blood transfusions are also a source of infection and should be avoided.

Bartonellosis (Oroya fever): This is a sandfly-transmitted illness found in arid river valleys on the northern slopes of the Andes (Peru, Ecuador, and Colombia) up to 3,000 meters elevation. Prevention consists of preventing insect bites.

Rabies: Animal rabies has been reported from many countries, especially Argentina, Brazil, Colombia, and Ecuador. Human rabies in South America is usually transmitted by infected dogs, but an outbreak of vampire bat-transmitted rabies has been reported in the Amazon jungle of Peru. Rabies vaccination is indicated following the unprovoked bite of a dog, cat, bat, or monkey. Bites by other animals should be evaluated on an individual basis. Pre-exposure vaccination against rabies (3 doses) is recommended for long-term travel to remote rural areas.

AIDS: Homosexuality and bisexuality remain the prevailing mode of HIV transmission in South America, but there is a trend towards greater heterosexual transmission, especially in major cities in Brazil and Chile. HIV-1 prevalence estimated at less than 1% of the general population of the countries of Latin America, but in some urban areas (e.g., Rio de Janeiro), up to 28% of female prostitutes and 80% of IV drug users are HIV positive. HIV-2 is reported to occur in South America.

Helminthic infections: Hookworm and whipworm are common, especially in rural areas. Travelers should wear shoes to prevent transmission of these diseases. Ascariasis, caused by the ingestion of food contaminated with the eggs of roundworms, can be prevented by adequate cooking. Pork and beef tapeworm disease is prevalent and can be avoided by thorough cooking of meat.

Other diseases/health threats: Brucellosis, echinococcosis (occurs in sheep raising regions), coccidiomycosis, cysticercosis and neurocysticercosis (very high incidence in Colombia), histoplasmosis, leptospirosis, plague, sexually transmitted diseases, toxocariasis, trichinosis, tuberculosis (often a serious public health problem), typhoid fever, louse- and flea-borne typhus, and viral encephalitis. Portuguese man-of-war, sea wasps, jellyfish, spiny sea urchins, stinging anemones, and sharp corals may occur in the coastal waters of these countries and pose a potential threat to swimmers. Carnivorous fish (including the piranha) may be found in freshwater bodies of some countries. Animal hazards include snakes (coral snakes, vipers), scorpions, black widow spiders, and large animals of the cat family, especially jaguars.

Accidents: There is a high risk of injury from motor vehicle, motorcycle, and moped accidents in the developing countries due to poor road conditions, chaotic traffic, lack of driver training, and poor vehicle maintenance. Rental vehicles and taxis may not be equipped with seat belts. All travelers should drive with extreme caution.

Caribbean Sea

Cristobal De Colon 18,950 ft. ▲

ARUBA CURACAO BONAIRE

I. DE MARGARITA

TRINIDAD & TOBAGO

L. Maracaibo

⊛ Caracas

VENEZUELA

PANAMA

Medellin •

Orinico R.

GUYANA

Georgetown
⊛ Paramaribo

SURINAME

Cayene •

FRENCH GUIANA (Fr.)

⊛ Bogata

COLOMBIA

Angel Falls

Huila ▲
18,865 ft.

⊛ Quito

ECUADOR

Manaus •

Amazon R.

Belem •

Equator

Fortaleza •

PERU

Porto Velho •

BRAZIL

Recife •

Chimbote •

⊛ Lima

• Cusco

El Misti (vol.)
19,145 ▲

Lake Titicaca

⊛ La Paz

BOLIVIA

Brasilia ⊛

Pico Da Bandeira
9,452 ft. ▲

Parana R.

PARA-GUAY

Asuncion ⊛

Rio de Janeiro •

Sao Paulo •

Atacama Desert

Salado del Norte R.

Parana R.

Tropic of Capricorn

CHILE

Santiago ⊛

Buenos Aires ⊛

URUGUAY

Montevideo •

Concepcion •

ARGENTINA

South Atlantic Ocean

North Atlantic Ocean

South Pacific Ocean

Puerto Deseado •

Santa Cruz •

FALKLAND ISLANDS (Br.)

• Stanley

Tierra del Fuego

Strait of Magellan

SOUTH AMERICA

0   200   400   600 MI.

⊛   National Capital
•   Major Cities
—   International Boundary
—   Major Rivers
▲   Mountain Peaks

ARGENTINA

Embassy: 202-939-6400   *Buenos Aires*   *GMT -3 hrs*

Entry Requirements

- Passport/Visa: A valid passport and visa are required.
- AIDS Test: Not required.
- Vaccinations: None required.

Telephone Country Code: 54   **AT&T:** 001-800-200-1111   **MCI:** 001-800-333-1111

Electricity/Plugs: AC 50 Hz, 220 volts; plug types C and I. Adaptors and transformer necessary for U.S.-made appliances.

American Express: American Express Travel Service & Business Center. Hotel Plaza Florida 1005, Buenos Aires. Tel. (1) 312-0900.

Embassies/Consulates: U.S. Embassy, Buenos Aires. 4300 Columbia, 1425; Tel. (1) 774-7611/8811/9911. Canadian Embassy, Buenos Aires. Brunetta Building, Suipacha & Santa Fe; Tel. (1) 312-9081/88.

Doctors/Hospitals: The British Hospital, Buenos Aires (400 beds); general medical/surgical facility; used by the American community. Mater Dei Hospital, Buenos Aires (100 beds); most specialty services; used by the American community. Goodman Mercer, M.D.; Tel. (1) 790-1656 or 799-6497. In San Lorenzo, Santa Fe, Rogelio Beltramone, M.D. Tel. (42) 22061 (office); in Tucuman, Juan Carlos Farhat, M.D.; Tel. (81) 21851 (office); in Parana-Entre Rio Adolfo Thevenin, M.D.; Tel. (21) 5184 (office).

Health Advisory

Yellow fever: Vaccination is recommended for all travelers who visit rural forested areas in the northeastern part of the country.

Cholera: This disease is active in this country. Although cholera vaccination is not required for entry if arriving directly from the U.S. or Canada, it may be required if arriving from a cholera-infected area, or required for on-going travel to other countries in Latin America, Africa, the Middle East, or Asia. Travelers should consider vaccination (one dose) or a doctor's letter of exemption from vaccination. The risk to travelers of acquiring cholera is considered low. Prevention of cholera consists primarily in adhering to safe food and drink guidelines.

Malaria: Malaria occurs below 1,200 meters elevation in the rural areas of Salta and Jujuy Provinces in northwest Argentina near the Bolivian border. Occasional cases have been reported in Corrientes and Misiones Provinces. Risk is increased December through May. *P. vivax* accounts for virtually 100% of cases. Chloroquine prophylaxis is recommended for travel in rural malarious areas.

Travelers' diarrhea: Water supplies in Buenos Aires are considered potable. Higher risk occurs countrywide outside of Buenos Aires. In urban and resort areas, the hotels and restaurants generally serve reliable food and potable water. Elsewhere, travelers should observe all food and drink safety precautions. A quinolone antibiotic (Floxin or Cipro) is recommended for the treatment of acute diarrhea. Diarrhea not responding to antibiotic treatment may be due to a parasitic disease such as giardiasis or amebiasis.

Hepatitis: All susceptible travelers should receive immune globulin prophylaxis or hepatitis A vaccine. The hepatitis B carrier rate in the general population is estimated at 1.1%. Vaccination against hepatitis B is recommended for all healthcare workers and should be considered by all long-term visitors to this country.

Dengue fever: Low overall risk. Dengue may occur in northeast regions bordering Paraguay. Travelers to the northeast regions should take precautions against insect bites.

Leishmaniasis: Risk of cutaneous and mucocutaneous leishmaniasis is limited to the northern one-third of the country, with the majority of cases reported from Salta, Jujuy, Catamarca, and Santiago del Estero Provinces. Occasional cases of visceral leishmaniasis have been reported from Salta and Chaco Provinces. Travelers to these areas should take measures to prevent sandfly bites.

Chagas' disease: High occurrence in rural areas, particularly in the north central regions of this country. There may be some risk in Buenos Aires. Risk of transmission, however, occurs primarily in those rural-agricultural areas where there are adobe-style huts and houses that potentially harbor the night-biting triatomid (assassin) bugs. Travelers sleeping in such structures should take precautions against nighttime bites. Unscreened blood transfusions are also a potential source of infection and should be avoided.

Echinococcosis: High incidence reported in southern cattle/sheep rearing regions. Human prevalence is among the highest reported worldwide. Travelers to these regions should avoid contact with dogs in order to prevent accidental ingestion of infective eggs which are passed in dog feces. Strict personal hygiene, especially handwashing, is important and all travelers should pay close attention to food and drink guidelines in order to avoid ingestion of potentially contaminated food.

Rabies: Relatively low risk; 18 to 20 human cases are reported annually from both urban and rural areas. Travelers, especially children, should avoid stray dogs and seek immediate treatment of any animal bite. Rabies vaccination is indicated following the unprovoked bite of a dog, cat, or other animal. Pre-exposure vaccination against rabies should be considered by long-term travelers to this country, especially if they will be unable to receive antirabies treatment within 24 hours of exposure to a potentially rabid animal.

Other diseases: Anthrax, arboviral fevers (mosquito-transmitted; eastern equine encephalitis, St. Louis encephalitis, Venezuelan encephalitis are reported), brucellosis (high incidence), fascioliasis (from consumption of wild watercress), hemorrhagic fever with renal syndrome (transmitted by infective rodent urine or feces), plague, syphilis, AIDS, trachoma (occurs in NE areas), trichinellosis, tuberculosis, typhoid fever, strongyloidiasis and other intestinal helminthic infections are reported.

BOLIVIA

Consulate: 202-232-4828   *La Paz*   *GMT -4 hrs*

Entry Requirements

- Passport/Visa: A valid passport and visa are required.
- AIDS Test: Not required.
- Vaccinations: A yellow fever vaccination certificate is required from all travelers arriving from infected areas.

Telephone Country Code: 591   **AT&T:** 0-800-1112   **MCI:** 0-800-2222

Electricity/Plugs: AC 50 Hz, 220 volts; plug types A, B, C, and F. Adaptors and transformer necessary for U.S.-made appliances.

American Express: Magri Turismo, Ltd., Ave. 16 De Julio 1490, 5th Floor, La Paz; Tel. (2) 341201.

Embassies/Consulates: U.S. Embassy, La Paz. Banco Popular Del Peru Building. Calle Mercado & Calle Colon; Tel. (2) 350-251. Canadian Consulate, La Paz. Avenido Arce. 2342; Tel. (2) 375224.

Hospitals/Doctors: Methodist Hospital, La Paz (113 beds); private hospital; limited emergency services; Tel. (2) 78-3509. Hugo Palazzi, M.D.; Tel. (2) 78-43-71; Clinica del Sur; Tel. 78-40-01/02/02. In Cochabamba: Centro de Salud; Tel. (42) 21-887. In Santa Cruz; Clinica Angel Foianini. Tel. (33) 42-211.

Health Advisory

Yellow fever: This disease is active in jungle areas east of the Andean highlands. A yellow fever vaccination is recommended for all travelers who are destined for risk areas such as the Departments of Beni, Chuquisaca, Cochabamba, Pando, Santa Cruz, Tarija, and part of La Paz Department. This country is in the Yellow Fever Endemic Zone. A yellow fever vaccination is required from travelers arriving from infected areas and may be required for ongoing travel to other countries in Latin America, Africa, the Middle East, and Asia.

Cholera: This disease is active in this country, especially in Cochabamba and Tarija Departments. Although cholera vaccination is not required for entry if arriving directly from the U.S. or Canada, it may be required if arriving from infected areas, or for on-going travel to other countries in Latin America, Africa, the Middle East, or Asia. Travelers should consider vaccination (one dose) or a doctor's letter of exemption. The risk to U.S. and Canadian travelers of acquiring cholera is considered low.

Malaria: There is no risk of malaria in the highlands of La Paz, the provinces of Oruro and Potosi (southwestern portions of the country), and the cities of Cochabamba and Sucre. All other rural areas of the country below 1,000 meters elevation should be considered risk areas, especially the lowlands east of the Andean Cordillera and Pando Department. Limited risk may extend up to 2,500 meters elevation in some rural areas. Vivax malaria accounts for over 90% of all cases, while falciparum malaria accounts for approximately 5.8% of cases. Chloroquine-resistant falciparum malaria is becoming more prevalent in the north and along the Brazilian border. Prophylaxis with mefloquine or doxycycline is recommended when traveling to northern risk areas near the Brazilian border; elsewhere, antimalarial prophylaxis with chloroquine is recommended.

Travelers' diarrhea: High risk outside of first-class hotels and tourist resorts. Contamination of water sources is common throughout the year in many areas of the country. Travelers should follow all food and drink precautions. A quinolone antibiotic is recommended for the treatment of acute diarrhea. Diarrhea not responding to antibiotic treatment may be due to a parasitic disease such as giardiasis or amebiasis.

Hepatitis: Immune globulin or hepatitis A vaccine is recommended for all susceptible travelers. The hepatitis B carrier rate in the general population is estimated at under 2%. Vaccination against hepatitis B is recommended for healthcare workers. Hepatitis E may occur but has not been reported.

Dengue fever: Risk occurs primarily in urban areas below 1,200 meters elevation. The most recent large outbreak of dengue (7,000 cases reported) occurred in and around Santa Cruz in 1988. To prevent dengue travelers to all regions should take measures to prevent mosquito bites.

Leishmaniasis: Cutaneous and mucocutaneous leishmaniasis occurs year-round below 2,000 meters elevation. Risk is elevated in the Yungas region, the forested foothill valleys at 1,000 to 2,000 meters elevation east of the Andean Cordillera. A few cases of visceral leishmaniasis have been reported from the Yungas region, which is northeast of La Paz. All travelers to rural areas should take measures to prevent insect (sandfly) bites.

Plague: Low risk. Plague occurs only in very limited areas. Recent outbreaks of flea-borne plague occurred in Santa Cruz Department near the Cochabamba-Chuquisaca border and north of Lake Titicaca, along the border with Peru. Travelers should avoid close contact with rodents (which may be carrying infective fleas). Travelers at risk of possible exposure should consider either vaccination or tetracycline/doxycycline prophylaxis.

Chagas' disease: Widely distributed in rural areas at elevations up to 3,600 meters, including portions of the Altiplano. In southcentral Cochabamba, up to 100% of villagers are seropositive. Risk occurs especially in those rural-agricultural areas where there are the adobe-style huts and houses that can harbor the night-biting triatomid (assassin) bugs. Travelers sleeping in such structures should take precautions against nighttime bites. Unscreened blood transfusions are also a source of infection and should be avoided.

Altitude sickness (AMS): Risk is present for those arriving in La Paz (altitude 3,500 meters) and/or traveling to the Altiplano zone in southwestern Bolivia where the altitude lies between 3,350 and 4,265 meters elevation. Travelers should consider starting acetazolamide (Diamox) prophylaxis before traveling to high altitudes and should also follow standard medical advice meant to reduce symptoms of AMS. Descent to lower altitude is the best treatment for moderate to severe AMS.

Rabies: Incidence of human rabies increased to over 30 cases annually in the late 1980s. Dogs are the primary source of human infection. Rabies vaccination is indicated following the unprovoked bite of a dog, cat, vampire bat, monkey or other animal. Pre-exposure vaccination against rabies is recommended for long-term travelers to this country and for travelers going to remote rural areas.

Other diseases: Bolivian hemorrhagic fever (low risk), brucellosis, coccidiomycosis (endemic near border with Paraguay), echinococcosis (occurs primarily in sheep-raising regions of the Altiplano), fascioliasis (liver fluke disease; high incidence in northwest Altiplano), AIDS (low incidence), tuberculosis (a serious public health problem; highest incidence in South America), strongyloidiasis and other helminthic infections, toxoplasmosis, typhoid fever, and typhus (louse-borne).

BRAZIL

Brasilia ... GMT -3 hrs

Entry Requirements

- Passport/Visa: A valid passport and visa are required.
- AIDS Test: Not required.
- Vaccinations: A yellow fever vaccination certificate is required from travelers over 6 months of age arriving from infected areas. A certificate is also required from travelers arriving from Africa: Angola, Cameroon, Gambia, Ghana, Guinea, Kenya, Mali, Nigeria, Sudan, and Zaire.

  Americas: Bolivia, Ecuador, Colombia, Peru.

Telephone Country Code: 55   **AT&T:** 000-8010   **MCI:** 000-8012

Electricity/Plugs: Wide range of voltages and plug types exist.

American Express: Kontik-Franstur S.A., S.C.S. Ed. Central, S1001/1008, Brasilia; Tel. (61) 224-9783.

Embassies/Consulates: U.S. Embassy, Brasilia. Avenida das Nocoes, Lote 3; Tel. (61) 321-7272. U.S. Consulate, Rio de Janeiro. Avenida Presidente Wilson, No. 147; Tel. (21) 292-7117. U.S. Consulate, Sao Paulo. Rue Padre Joao Manoel, No. 933; Tel. (11) 881-6511. Canadian Embassy, Brasilia. Avenida das Nocoes, Lote 16; Tel. (61) 223-7515.

Hospitals/Doctors: In Brasilia: Hospital de Base (600 beds); most specialty services including trauma; 24-hour emergency room. In Sao Paulo: Hospital Samaritano (160 beds); 24-hour emergency services; Tel. 825-1122. Ernesto Azevado, M.D. Tel. (11) 215-7368, 62-9947 (home). In Rio de Janeiro: Hospital Miguel Couto (117 beds); some specialty services including trauma and emergency; Tel. 274-6050, 274-9097. Hospital Souza Aguiar (480 beds); most specialty services including orthopedics, trauma, and emergency; Tel. 221-2121, 296-4114. Roberto Laura Lana, M.D. Tel. (21) 247-2473. In Brasilia: Casa de Saude Santa Lucia; some specialty and emergency services; Tel. 245-3344. Evaldo Leal, M.D. Tel. 245-3344.

Health Advisory

Yellow fever: This disease is active in this country in widely scattered foci, primarily in the Amazon Basin. Yellow fever vaccination is recommended for travel to rural areas in the States of Acre, Amazonas, Goias, Mato Grosso, Mato Grosso do Sul, Para, Rondonia, and the territories of Amapa and Roraima. This country is in the Yellow Fever Endemic Zone. Although yellow fever vaccination is not required for entry into this country if arriving directly from the U.S. or Canada, it may be required for on-going travel to other countries in Latin America, Africa, the Middle East, or Asia.

Cholera: This disease is active in this country. Although cholera vaccination is not required for entry if arriving directly from the U.S. or Canada, it may be required if arriving from a cholera-infected area, or required for on-going travel to other countries in Latin America, Africa, the Middle East, or Asia. Travelers should consider vaccination (one dose) or a doctor's letter of exemption from vaccination. The risk to travelers of acquiring cholera is considered low. Prevention consists primarily in adhering to safe food and drink guidelines.

Malaria: Risk is present year-round in all areas of Acre, Amapa, Rondonia, and Roriama States, and in all rural areas of Amazonas, Bahia, Espirito Santo, Goias, Maranhao, Mato Grosso, Mato Grosso do Sul, Minas Gerais, Para, Parana, Piaui, and Santa Caterina States. There is no malaria risk in Iguassu Falls, and the cities of Manaus, Santarem, or Belem. Most malaria occurs in the Amazon Basin. Over 60% of cases are reported from the states of Maranhao, Para, and Rondonia. Falciparum malaria (caused by *P. falciparum*) accounts for 55% of malaria cases from the Amazon region and 22%–42% of cases elsewhere. Nearly all malaria cases not due to *P. falciparum* are due to the *P. vivax*. Multidrug-resistant falciparum malaria is a major problem, particularly in the Amazon region where *P. falciparum* resistant to chloroquine and Fansidar, and to a lesser extent, mefloquine (Lariam) and quinine, has been reported. At the present time, chemoprophylaxis with mefloquine or doxycycline is recommended when traveling to risk areas. All travelers planning an Amazon River cruise should take prophylactic antimalarial medication. Travelers should remember that prevention of mosquito bites is also essential.

Travelers' diarrhea: High risk outside of resorts and first-class hotels. Travelers should follow all food and drink precautions. A quinolone antibiotic is recommended for the treatment of diarrhea. Diarrhea not responding to antibiotic treatment may be due to a parasitic disease such as giardiasis or amebiasis.

Hepatitis: Immune globulin or hepatitis A vaccine is recommended for all susceptible travelers. The hepatitis B carrier rate may approach 20% in some areas of this country, especially in the Amazon Basin. Vaccination against hepatitis B is recommended for healthcare workers and should be considered by long-term visitors to this country. Hepatitis E accounts for 12%–25% of acute viral hepatitis in this country.

Dengue fever: Risk is present year-round, especially in the coastal areas, primarily Rio de Janeiro State and Sao Paulo and Ceara States. To prevent dengue, travelers should take measures to prevent daytime mosquito bites, especially in urban areas.

Leishmaniasis: Risk occurs year-round, but is elevated May–August. Cutaneous, mucocutaneous, and visceral leishmaniasis occur in rural and periurban areas. Cutaneous leishmaniasis and mucocutaneous leishmaniasis occur nearly countrywide except for the extreme south, with risk increased in the northern and central states. Outbreaks of cutaneous leishmaniasis have occurred in periurban slum areas of Rio de Janeiro. Most cases of visceral leishmaniasis are reported from the northeastern states, with one focus reported in extreme western Mato Grosso do Sul State. All travelers to these regions should take protective measures to prevent insect (sandfly) bites.

Onchocerciasis: Found near swift-flowing streams in the north near the border with Venezuela. Travelers to this area should take measures to prevent insect (black fly) bites.

Filariasis: Risk of Bancroftian filariasis occurs in two areas: the metropolitan areas of Recife (State of Perambuco) and in Belem (State of Para), in the northeastern and northern regions. Travelers to these regions should take measures to prevent insect (mosquito) bites.

Schistosomiasis: Intestinal schistosomiasis is a major public health problem. Risk is present in northern and eastern states from Maranhao to Parana. Most cases are reported from Minas Gerais and Bahia States. Travelers to these areas should avoid swimming, wading, or bathing in freshwater ponds, lakes, or streams. There is no apparent risk of schistosomiasis in the Amazon Basin.

Chagas' disease: Risk is present in most rural areas of eastern and southern Brazil. An estimated 6 million Brazilians are infected, among the highest rates in Latin America. Risk occurs primarily in well-populated rural-agricultural areas where there are adobe-style huts and houses that often harbor the night-biting triatomid (assassin) bugs. Travelers sleeping in such structures should take measures to prevent nighttime bites. Unscreened blood transfusions should also be avoided.

Plague: Most cases are reported from the drier northern and eastern states from Bahia and Ceara south to Minas Gerais. Thirty five to 150 cases are reported annually. Travelers to these regions should avoid close contact with rodents (which may be carrying infective fleas). Prophylaxis with tetracycline may be protective.

Rabies: High risk, relative to other South American countries. Sixty to 120 human cases are reported annually, usually transmitted by stray dogs. Most cases occur in the northeastern states, but cases are also reported countrywide from both urban and rural areas. Pre-exposure vaccination against rabies (3 doses) is recommended for long-term travelers to this country and for travelers going to remote rural areas if they will be unable to receive antirabies treatment within 24 hours of exposure to a potentially rabid animal such as a dog, cat, or bat.

AIDS: The highest AIDS rate in South America occurs in Brazil. Most cases are reported from Rio de Janeiro and Sao Paulo. Causative factors are heterosexual promiscuity, prostitution, bisexuality, and IV drug use. Both HIV-1 and HIV-2 occur. Tropical spastic paraparesis, due to HTLV-1 (a sexually transmitted virus), is reported.

Other diseases: Angiostrongyliasis, brucellosis, cryptococcosis, cysticercosis, echinococcosis (in sheep-raising areas of the south), hemorrhagic fever with renal syndrome (transmitted by infective rodent urine or feces), leprosy (highly endemic in Recife area), leptospirosis, mansonellosis, measles, meningitis (epidemics reported from Sao Paulo; most cases due to serogroup B meningococci; current meningitis vaccine is not protective against this serogroup), trachoma, toxocariasis, tuberculosis (a serious public health problem; 25% of children in some areas may be infected), strongyloidiasis and other helminthic infections (e.g., hookworm, roundworm).

CHILE

Santiago ... GMT -4 hrs

Entry Requirements

- Passport/Visa: A valid passport is required.
- AIDS Test: Not required.
- Vaccinations: No vaccinations are required to enter this country.

Telephone Country Code: 56   **AT&T:** 00-0312   **MCI:** 00-0316

Electricity/Plugs: AC 50 Hz, 220 volts; plug type B, C. Adaptors and transformer necessary for U.S.-made appliances.

American Express: Turismo Cocha, Agustinas 1173. Santiago; Tel. (2) 698-2164.

Embassies/Consulates: U.S. Embassy, Santiago. Codina Building, Agustinas 1343; Tel. (2) 710-133. Canadian Embassy, Santiago. Ahumada 11, 10th Floor; Tel. (2) 696-2256.

Hospitals/Doctors: Jose Joaquin Aguirre Hospital (1,700 beds); general medical/surgical facility; Clinica las Condes, Santiago; Tel. (2) 211-1002; Guillermo H. Ugarte, M.D. Tel. (2) 225-5054.

Health Advisory

Malaria: There is no risk of malaria in Chile.

Yellow fever: There is no risk of yellow fever in Chile. Although a vaccination is not required to enter Chile, yellow fever vaccination may be required or recommended for travel to other countries in South America. Travelers should carefully review their itinerary.

Cholera: This disease is active in this country. Although cholera vaccination is not required for entry if arriving directly from the U.S. or Canada, it may be required if arriving from a cholera-infected area, or required for on-going travel to other countries in Latin America, Africa, the Middle East, or Asia. Travelers should consider vaccination (one dose) or a doctor's letter of exemption from vaccination. The risk to travelers of acquiring cholera is considered low. Prevention consists primarily in adhering to safe food and drink guidelines.

Travelers' diarrhea: High risk in most areas, especially outside resort areas and first-class hotels. Water supplies in Santiago are considered potable but breakdowns in the system can occur and travelers are advised to drink only boiled, bottled, or treated water. All water outside Santiago should be considered contaminated. Food and drink in first-class hotels in Santiago, Valparaiso, Valdiva, and Antofagasta are generally considered safe, but travelers should use caution. A quinolone antibiotic is recommended for the treatment of acute diarrhea. Diarrhea not responding to antibiotic treatment may be due to a parasitic disease such as giardiasis or amebiasis.

Typhoid fever: There is a high incidence of typhoid fever in this country, due primarily to transmission from chronic carriers of the typhoid bacteria. Vaccination is recommended for travelers venturing off the usual tourist routes and/or staying longer than 2 weeks in-country. All travelers should adhere to safe food and drink guidelines.

Hepatitis: All susceptible travelers should receive immune globulin or hepatitis A vaccine prior to visiting this country. The hepatitis B carrier rate in the general population is estimated at 1%. Vaccination against hepatitis B is recommended for all healthcare workers. Sporadic hepatitis E has been reported.

Chagas' disease: Reported in the rural and suburban areas in the northern half of this country. Transmission of Chagas' disease occurs primarily in rural areas where there are adobe-style huts and houses that often harbor the night-biting triatomid (assassin) bugs. Travelers sleeping in such structures should take precautions against nighttime bites. Precautions include sleeping under a mosquito net (well tucked in), sleeping away from walls, and spraying sleeping quarters with an insecticide (such as RAID Flying Insect Spray) prior to retiring. Unscreened blood transfusions are also a potential source of infection. The rate of contaminated blood reported by Chilean blood banks is in the 1.9%–6.5% range.

Rabies: Low risk. No human cases have been reported in this country since 1972. All travelers, nevertheless, should avoid contact with stray dogs. Any unprovoked attack by an animal should be considered a medical emergency and immediate medical care sought to evaluate the possible risk of rabies.

AIDS: Relatively low rates of HIV infection are reported, but the incidence is increasing, especially in urban areas. Seventy two percent of cases of AIDS are currently due to homo- and bisexual transmission. Cases due to heterosexual transmission are increasing.

Climate-related illness: Severe air pollution exists in Santiago and to a lesser extent in the Chilean countryside. Travelers with emphysema, asthma, and bronchitis may experience an increase in respiratory symptoms.

Other diseases/hazards: Brucellosis (rare cases are associated with contact with cattle), echinococcosis, meningitis (due to Group B meningococci; vaccine not protective), plague, taeniasis (pork and beef tapeworm disease), tuberculosis (a serious public health problem), strongyloidiasis and other helminthic infections. Insect-borne diseases are relatively unimportant in Chile. Animal hazards include black widow and brown widow spiders. There are no venomous land snakes on the mainland of Chile. Portuguese man-of-war, sea wasps, and several species of stingrays are found in the country's coastal waters and are potential hazards to swimmers.

COLOMBIA
Bogota ... GMT -5 hrs

Entry Requirements
- Passport/Visa: A valid passport is required for entry.
- AIDS Test: Not required.
- Vaccinations: No vaccinations are required for entry.

Telephone Country Code: 57   **AT&T:** 980-11-0010   **MCI:** 980-16-0001

Electricity/Plugs: AC 60 Hz, 110/220 volts; plug types A and B.

American Express: Tierra Mar Aire Ltd. Calle 92, 15-63. Bogota; Tel. (1) 218-5666.

Embassies/Consulates: U.S. Embassy, Bogota; Calle 38, 8-31; Tel. (1) 285-1300. U.S. Consulate, Barranquilla; Calle 77 Carrera 68, Centro Comercial Mayorista; Tel. (5) 45-7088. Canadian Embassy, Bogota; Calle 76, 11-52; Tel. (1) 23-0446.

Hospitals/Doctors: Hospital Militar Central, Bogota (800 beds); all specialties; ambulance service; Tel. (1) 285-2520. Clinic Marly, (100 beds); Tel. (1) 287-1020, 236-1503. In Cartagena: Simon Haydar, M.D. Tel. (59) 959-51112/42591.

Health Advisory

Yellow fever: This disease is active in this country. No cases officially reported since 1988. Vaccination, however, is strongly recommended, especially for travel to infected areas in the middle valley of the Magdalena River, eastern and western foothills of the Cordillera Oriental from the frontier with Ecuador to that with Venezuela, Uraba, foothills of the Sierra Nevada, eastern plains (Orinoquia) and Amazonia. This country is in the Yellow Fever Endemic Zone. Although yellow fever vaccination is not required for entry into this country, it may be required for on-going travel to other countries in Latin America, Africa, the Middle East, or Asia. Travelers should carefully check their itinerary.

Cholera: This disease is active in this country. Although cholera vaccination is not required for entry if arriving directly from the U.S. or Canada, it may be required if arriving from a cholera-infected area, or required for on-going travel to other countries in Latin America, Africa, the Middle East, or Asia. Travelers should consider vaccination (one dose) or a doctor's letter of exemption from vaccination. The risk to travelers of acquiring cholera is considered low. Prevention consists primarily in adhering to safe food and drink guidelines.

Malaria: This disease is highly endemic year-round below 800 meters elevation in rural areas of Uraba (Antioquia Dept.), Bajo Cauca-Nechi (Cauca and Antioquia Depts.), Magdalena Medio, Caqueta (Caqueta Intendencia), Sarare (Arauca Intendencia), Catatumbo (Norte de Santander Dept.), Pacifico Central and Sur, Putumayo (Putumayo Intendencia), Ariari (Meta Dept.), Alto Vaupes (Vaupes Comisaria), and Amazonas. There is no risk of malaria in Bogota Department and the major urban areas. The islands of San Andres and Providencia are also risk free. Falciparum malaria accounts for 34% of cases; the remainder are vivax. Chloroquine-resistant malaria is reported in all malarious areas. Widespread Fansidar resistance is reported in Amazonia, Orinoquia, and the Caribbean regions and the Cauca River Valley. Unconfirmed mefloquine resistance has been reported in the Amazonian region. Mefloquine or doxycycline prophylaxis is currently recommended when traveling to risk areas.

Travelers' diarrhea: Tap water is generally considered safe in large Colombian cities (Bogota, Medellin, and Cali), but all other water sources should be considered contaminated. Travelers should follow food and drink precautions. A quinolone antibiotic is recommended for the treatment of diarrhea. Diarrhea not responding to antibiotic treatment may be due to a parasitic disease such as giardiasis or amebiasis—or an intestinal virus.

Hepatitis: All susceptible travelers should receive immune globulin or hepatitis A vaccine prior to visiting this country. The hepatitis B carrier rate in the general population is estimated to be 2.8% and as high as 20% in high-risk groups (e.g., prostitutes, drug addicts). Vaccination against hepatitis B is recommended for all healthcare workers and should be considered by anyone planning an extended visit to this country.

Dengue fever: Risk is present and major outbreaks have previously occurred in this country. Most recent outbreaks of dengue are reported from Cali. A few cases of dengue hemorrhagic fever have been reported. Dengue occurs throughout Latin America. The aedes mosquitoes, which transmit dengue fever, bite primarily during the daytime and are present in populous urban areas as well as resort and rural areas. All travelers are advised to take measures to prevent mosquito bites.

Leishmaniasis: Risk of cutaneous leishmaniasis occurs primarily in the Pacific coastal region and in jungle and highland areas up to 1450 meters elevation. About 95% of reported cases are due to the cutaneous form. Visceral leishmaniasis is uncommon but at least one focus exists below 900 meters elevation in the Magdalena River valley in southern Cundinamarca County. Travelers to these areas should take measures to prevent insect (sandfly) bites.

Chagas' disease: Widely distributed below 2,500 meters elevation in central Colombia where up to 33% of the population may be sero-positive. Risk of transmission occurs primarily in those rural-agricultural areas where there are adobe-style huts and houses that often harbor the night-biting triatomid (assassin) bugs. Travelers sleeping in such structures should take precautions against nighttime bites.

Bartonellosis (Oroya fever): This severe bacterial disease is transmitted by sand flies between 800 and 3,000 meters elevation in the Andean mountain valleys of Colombia, Ecuador, and Peru. Prevention consists of avoiding insect (sandfly) bites.

Rabies: A relatively minor health threat in this country, but incidence may increase. Travelers should seek immediate treatment of any animal bite, especially from a dog. Rabies vaccination is indicated following the unprovoked bite of a dog, cat, bat, or monkey. Bites by other animals should be considered on an individual basis. Pre-exposure vaccination against rabies (3 doses) should be considered prior to long-term travel in this country.

AIDS: HIV screening of blood donors shows about 0.1% to be sero-positive. HIV prevalence estimated at 21% of homosexual males. All travelers are cautioned against unsafe sex, unsterile medical or dental injections, and unnecessary blood transfusions.

Altitude sickness (Acute mountain sickness-AMS): Risk is present for those arriving in Bogota (altitude 2,600 meters) or traveling to the Central Highlands where the elevation exceeds 3,000 meters in many areas. Travelers should consider acetazolamide prophylaxis and gradual acclimatization. The best treatment of moderate to severe AMS is immediate descent to a lower altitude.

Other diseases/hazards: Brucellosis (increased incidence in Uraba region of Antioquia Department), coccidiomycosis, echinococcosis, filariasis (mosquito-borne; a small focus is reported near Cartegena), onchocerciasis (black-fly-borne; isolated foci reported in the extreme west central area bordering Ecuador), tropical spastic paraparesis (due to HTLV-1, a sexually transmitted virus; reported near Tumaco on the South Pacific coast), tuberculosis (a serious public health problem), typhoid fever, viral encephalitis (mosquito-transmitted), and strongyloidiasis and other helminthic infections are reported. Animal hazards include snakes (vipers, coral snakes), centipedes, scorpions, and spiders (black widow, brown recluse, banana, wolf). Caimans and crocodiles are abundant and electric eels and poisonous frogs are found in the country's freshwaters. Pumas, jaguars, wild boar, and large tropical rodents also occur in Colombia. Sea wasps, Portuguese man-of-war, sea wasps, and stingrays are found in the coastal waters of Colombia and could be a hazard to swimmers.

ECUADOR

Quito ... GMT -5 hrs

Entry Requirements

- Passport/Visa: A valid passport is required.
- AIDS Test: Testing may be required for students or long-term visitors. Travelers should contact the Ecuadorian Embassy in Washington, D.C., for details; Tel: 202-234-7200.
- Vaccinations: A yellow fever vaccination certificate is required from travelers older than 1 year of age arriving from yellow fever infected areas.

Telephone Country Code: 593   **AT&T:** 119   **MCI:** 170

Electricity/Plugs: AC 60 Hz, 120/208, 127/220 volts; plug types A and C. Adaptors and transformer may be necessary for U.S.-made appliances.

American Express: Equadorian Tours, S.A. Amazonas 339, Quito; Tel. (2) 560-488.

Embassies/Consulates: U.S. Embassy, Quito; 120 Avenida Patria; Tel. (2) 562-890. U.S. Consulate, Guayaquil; 9 de Octobre y Garcia Moreno; Tel. (4) 323-570. Canadian Consulate, Guayaquil; Contact U.S. Consulate.

Hospitals/Doctors: Hospital Militar (450 beds), Quito; military hospital; most specialty services; helipad; Tel. (2) 529-355. Clinica Adventista; Tel. (2) 234-471. Quito Hospital Villalengue (278 beds); private hospital; emergency services. Jaime Beltran, M.D. Tel. (2) 564-064. Luis G. Fuenzalida, M.D. Tel. (2) 234-117.

Health Advisory

Yellow fever: This disease is active in this country. Vaccination is recommended for travel outside rural areas. Areas reported infected are Morona-Santiago Province, Napo Province, Pastaza Province, Zamora Chinchipe Province. This country is in the Yellow Fever Endemic Zone. Although yellow fever vaccination is not required for entry into this country if arriving from the United States or Canada, it may be required for on-going travel to other countries in Latin America, Africa, the Middle East, or Asia.

Cholera: This disease is active in this country. Although cholera vaccination is not required for entry if arriving directly from the U.S. or Canada, it may be required if arriving from a cholera-infected area, or required for on-going travel to other countries in Latin America, Africa, the Middle East, or Asia. Travelers should consider vaccination (one dose) or a doctor's letter of exemption from vaccination. The risk to tourists of acquiring cholera is considered low. Prevention of cholera consists primarily in adhering to safe food and drink guidelines.

Malaria: There is no risk of malaria in Quito and vicinity, Cuenca, the central highland tourist areas, and the Galapagos Islands. Elsewhere, risk is present countrywide year-round at altitudes below 1,500 meters. The disease is focally endemic with highly variable levels. Increased risk is found throughout all provinces along the eastern border and on the coastline, including urban areas. Risk of malaria may be elevated from February through August. Provinces where malaria occurs are Esmeraldas, El Oro, Guayas (including Guayaquil), Los Rios, Manabi, Morona-Santiago, Napo, Pastaza, Pichincha, and Zamora-Chinchipe Provinces. Most malaria cases in Ecuador occur in Esmeraldas Province on the north coast. Seventy to 75% of malaria is vivax, 25% to 30% is falciparum. Chloroquine-resistant *P. falciparum* is reported in all malarious areas. Mefloquine or doxycycline prophylaxis is advised for travel to malarious areas.

Travelers' diarrhea: High risk. Contaminated water is a major problem throughout Ecuador. Even the two largest cities, Quito and Guayaquil, do not have reliable sources of safe, potable water. Travelers should follow food and drink precautions. A quinolone antibiotic is recommended for the treatment of diarrhea. Diarrhea not responding to antibiotic treatment may be due to a parasitic disease such as giardiasis or amebiasis—or an intestinal virus.

Hepatitis: All susceptible travelers should receive immune globulin or hepatitis A vaccine prior to visiting this country. The hepatitis B carrier rate in the general population is estimated at 2%. Vaccination against hepatitis B is recommended for all healthcare workers and should be considered by anyone planning an extended visit to this country.

Dengue fever: The greatest risk of infection occurs in the coastal urban areas of this country, but some risk is also present in resort and rural areas. The *Aedes aegypti* mosquitoes, which transmit dengue fever, bite primarily during the daytime. All travelers are advised to take precautions against insect and mosquito bites.

Typhoid fever: Focal outbreaks occur throughout the country. Large outbreaks have occurred in Quito. Vaccination is recommended for travel exceeding 2–4 weeks. Prevention, however, consists primarily in following safe food and drink guidelines.

Leishmaniasis: Occurs in the tropical and subtropical Pacific coastal areas, the Andean plains, and the eastern Amazon regions. Leishmaniasis is considered a major public health problem, particularly in Imbabura and Pichincha Provinces. Increased risk occurs in areas under 1,000 meters elevation, but risk is present as high as 2,500 meters elevation. Ninety three percent of cases are cutaneous, the rest are due to the mucocutaneous form. All travelers should take precautions against insect (sandfly) bites.

Onchocerciasis: This disease occurs primarily along rivers in the Esmeralda Province. Outbreaks, however, are reported spreading from Esmeralda Province to other parts of the country. All travelers to rural areas with fast flowing rivers should take measures to prevent insect (black fly) bites.

Chagas' disease: Widely distributed in rural areas, but more common in the coastal region. Risk of transmission occurs in rural-agricultural areas where there are adobe-style huts and houses that potentially harbor the night-biting triatomid (assassin) bugs. Travelers sleeping in such structures should take measures to prevent nighttime bites. Unscreened blood transfusions are also a potential source of infection.

Rabies: Relatively low risk—about 15 human cases a year are reported. Human cases have been reported countrywide from both urban and rural areas. Pre-exposure vaccination against rabies (3 doses) is recommended for long-term travelers to this country and for travelers going to remote rural areas if they will be unable to receive antirabies treatment within 24 hours of exposure to a potentially rabid animal such as a dog, cat, or monkey.

Altitude sickness: Extreme variations in altitude occur in this country. Risk of altitude sickness is present for tourists arriving in Quito (altitude 3,000 meters) and other high-altitude destinations. Travelers to high altitudes should consider Diamox prophylaxis as well as gradual acclimatization prior to further ascent to higher altitudes.

AIDS: Incidence of HIV infection appears relatively low at the present time.

Other diseases/hazards: Brucellosis, bartonellosis (also known as Oroyo fever), cysticercosis, leprosy (endemic, particularly in Bolivar, El Oro, Loja, and Los Rios Provinces), plague, tuberculosis (a serious public health problem, especially in the Amazon region), and strongyloidiasis and other intestinal helminthic infections. Animal hazards include snakes (vipers, coral snakes), centipedes, scorpions, black widow spiders, brown recluse spiders, banana spiders, and wolf spiders. Electric eels and piranha may be found in the country's fresh waters. Vampire bats are also present in this country. Portuguese man-of war, sea wasps, and stingrays are found in the coastal waters of Ecuador and could be a hazard to swimmers.

FRENCH GUIANA
Cayenne ... GMT -3 hrs

Entry Requirements
- Passport/Visa: Visa not required.
- AIDS Test: Not required.
- Vaccinations: A yellow fever vaccination certificate is required from all travelers over 1 year of age arriving from ALL countries.

Telephone Country Code: 594

Electricity/Plugs: AC 50 Hz, 220 volts; plug types C, D, and E. Adaptors and transformer necessary for U.S.-made appliances.

Embassies/Consulates: The United States maintains no representation in French Guiana, which is an overseas department of the France. The department is within the following consular district: US Consulate General, 14 Rue Blanc, 97206, Fort-de-France CEDEX, Martinique, F.W.I. Local tel: 63-13-03.

Doctors/Hospitals: Clinique Saint Paul, Cayenne (81 beds); general medical/surgical facility; ob/gyn; cardiology; pediatrics. Clinic Veronique (230 beds); medical/surgical facility; ob/gyn.

Health Advisory

Yellow fever: No cases were reported during the 1980s but one case was reported in 1990. A yellow fever vaccination certificate is required for entry to this country. This country is in the Yellow Fever Endemic Zone and yellow fever vaccination may also be required for on-going travel to other countries in Latin America, Africa, the Middle East, or Asia. Travelers should check their itinerary carefully.

Cholera: This disease is active in this country. Although cholera vaccination is not required for entry if arriving directly from the U.S. or Canada, it may be required if arriving from a cholera-infected area, or required for on-going travel to other countries in Latin America, Africa, the Middle East, or Asia. Travelers should consider vaccination (one dose) or a doctor's letter of exemption from vaccination. The risk to travelers of acquiring cholera is considered low. Prevention consists primarily in adhering to safe food and drink guidelines.

Malaria: Risk is present in all areas of this country year-round. A high incidence of malaria occurs near the borders with Brazil and Suriname. Falciparum malaria accounts for 70% of cases and chloroquine-resistant falciparum malaria is reported. Quinine-resistant falciparum malaria may also occur. The risk of falciparum malaria is greatest in the western areas bordering Suriname. The risk of vivax malaria is greatest in the east and along the coast. Chemoprophylaxis with mefloquine (Lariam) or doxycycline is currently recommended. Alternative malaria regimes should be discussed with a travel medicine or infectious disease specialist. All travelers should take measures to prevent mosquito bites.

Travelers' diarrhea: Water in Cayenne is considered generally safe for consumption. Travelers should follow food and drink precautions, especially outside first-class hotels and resorts. A quinolone antibiotic (Cipro or Floxin) is recommended for the treatment of diarrhea. Diarrhea not responding to antibiotic treatment may be due to a parasitic disease such as giardiasis or amebiasis—or an intestinal virus.

Hepatitis: Immune globulin or hepatitis A vaccine is recommended for all susceptible travelers. The hepatitis B carrier rate in the population is 2%–13% with the higher rates in some rural areas. Vaccination against hepatitis B is recommended for healthcare workers and should be considered by long-term visitors to this country.

Leishmaniasis: This disease has become a public health problem among people in contact with the forest. Most cases of leishmaniasis are either cutaneous or mucocutaneous. Transmission occurs primarily from November through May with the highest risk of transmission during periods of lowest rainfall, October–December. Most cases of leishmaniasis occur in the eastern half of the country. Attack rates up to 78% have been reported in military units operating in jungle environments. Travelers to forested areas (where transmission is highest) should take protective measures against sand flies, which bite from dusk to dawn.

Schistosomiasis: Currently not reported, but may occur just across the border near Albina, in Suriname.

Dengue fever: Risk is present; a major epidemic of dengue hemorrhagic fever occurred in 1991–1992. All travelers should take measures to prevent mosquito bites.

Rabies: An outbreak of rabies occurred in 1984. Dogs are the primary source of infection although rabid vampire bats have also transmitted the disease. Travelers should especially avoid stray dogs and seek immediate treatment of any wild animal bite. Rabies vaccination is usually indicated following the unprovoked bite of a dog, cat, vampire bat, monkey, or other animal. Pre-exposure vaccination is recommended for long-term travelers to this country and for travelers going to remote rural areas if they will be unable to receive antirabies treatment within 24 hours of exposure to a potentially rabid animal.

AIDS: The highest officially reported HIV prevalence in the Americas. The primary risk factor for HIV infection is multiple heterosexual contacts, with HIV seropositivity highest among Haitian immigrants.

Other diseases: Bancroftian filariasis (occurs in coastal urban areas), Chagas' disease (widely distributed in rural areas), leptospirosis, leprosy (highly endemic, with countrywide prevalence), syphilis, tuberculosis (a serious public health problem), tungiasis, typhoid fever, strongyloidiasis and other helminthic infections are reported.Animal hazards include snakes (vipers), centipedes, scorpions, black widow spiders, brown recluse spiders, banana spiders, pruning spiders, and wolf spiders. Electric eels and various carnivorous fish (including piranha) may be found in the country's fresh waters. Vampire bats are also present in this country. Portuguese man-of-war, sea wasps, and stingrays are found in the coastal waters and could be a hazard to swimmers.

GUYANA
Georgetown ... GMT -3 hrs

Entry Requirements
- Passport/Visa: A valid passport and visa are required.
- AIDS Test: Not required.
- Vaccinations: A yellow fever vaccination certificate is required from travelers arriving from infected areas or from any country in the yellow fever endemic zones of Central and South America and Africa. Travelers arriving from Belize, Bolivia, Brazil, Colombia, Costa Rica, Ecuador, French Guiana, Guatemala, Honduras, Nicaragua, Panama, Suriname, and Venezuela are required to have a valid certificate. The *HealthGuide* recommends that any traveler arriving from any country in sub-Saharan Africa be in possession of a valid yellow fever certificate.

Telephone Country Code: 592   **AT&T:** 165

American Express: Guyana Stores Ltd. 19 Water Street, Georgetown; Tel. (2) 68-17.

Embassies/Consulates: U.S. Embassy, Georgetown. 31 Main Street; Tel. (2) 54-900. Canadian High Commission, Georgetown. High & Young Streets; Tel. (2) 72-081/5.

Hospitals/Doctors: St. Joseph Mercy Hospital, Georgetown (105 beds); care is below U.S. standards but adequate; hospital used by embassy personnel. Davis Memorial Georgetown (54 beds); used by embassy personnel. Georgetown Hospital (991 beds); government hospital; used for paramedical training. Frank Williams, M.D., 265 Thomas Street, Georgetown; Tel: (2) 65175 or 65979. Regional Hospital, New Amsterdam (250 beds); government hospital; general medical facility.

Health Advisory
Yellow fever: No recent cases have been reported. There were unconfirmed reports of cases occurring in 1983 in the extreme south near the Brazil border. This country is in the Yellow Fever Endemic Zone. Although yellow fever vaccination may not be required for entry into this country, it may be required for on-going travel to other countries in Latin America, Africa, the Middle East, or Asia.

Cholera: This disease is active in this country. Although cholera vaccination is not required for entry if arriving directly from the U.S. or Canada, it may be required if arriving from a cholera-infected area, or required for on-going travel to other countries in Latin America, Africa, the Middle East, or Asia. Travelers should consider vaccination (one dose) or a doctor's letter of exemption from vaccination.

Malaria: Risk is present year-round for all areas below 900 meters elevation beyond the coastal plain. Malaria is seasonal in the coastal plain, including the outskirts of Georgetown, with increased transmission associated with the rainy seasons (May through mid-August and November through January). Malaria risk is found especially in rural areas in the southern interior and the northwest coast, i.e., Rupununi and the North West Regions. Falciparum malaria accounts for 70% of cases, vivax 30%. Limited studies report some falciparum malaria highly resistant to chloroquine and Fansidar. Prophylaxis with mefloquine (Lariam) or doxycycline is currently recommended in malarious areas.

Traveler's diarrhea: High risk outside of first-class hotels and resorts. Travelers are advised to drink only bottled, boiled, filtered, or treated water, and consume only well-cooked food. A quinolone antibiotic is recommended for the treatment of acute diarrhea. Diarrhea not responding to antibiotic treatment may be due to a parasitic disease such as giardiasis or amebiasis—or an intestinal virus.

Hepatitis: All susceptible travelers should receive immune globulin or hepatitis A vaccine prior to visiting this country. The hepatitis B carrier rate in the general population is less than 5%. Vaccination against hepatitis B is recommended for all healthcare workers and should be considered by anyone planning an extended visit to this country.

Leishmaniasis: Outbreaks of cutaneous leishmaniasis have occurred in military personnel. Most cases are acquired in the interior forests and savannah areas. Travelers to these areas should take measures to prevent insect (sandfly) bites.

Filariasis: Bancroftian filariasis is endemic in Georgetown and other cities in the coastal plain, with up to 10% of the population infected. Travelers should take standard precautions to prevent mosquito bites.

Other diseases/hazards: Chagas' disease (very low prevalence in the north west district), mansonellosis, meningitis (6–15 cases annually), syphilis, AIDS (specific information not available), rabies, tuberculosis (incidence increased in the 1980s), typhoid fever, strongyloidiasis and other helminthic infections are reported. Animal hazards include snakes (vipers), centipedes, scorpions, black widow spiders, brown recluse spiders, banana spiders, pruning spiders, and wolf spiders. Electric eels and various carnivorous fish (including piranha) may be found in this country's fresh waters. Portuguese man-of-war, sea wasps, and stingrays are found in the coastal waters and could be a hazard to swimmers.

PARAGUAY

Asuncion ... GMT -4 hrs

Entry Requirements
- Passport/Visa: A valid passport is required.
- AIDS Test: Not required.
- Vaccinations: Yellow fever. No certificate is required to enter this country. A yellow fever vaccination certificate is required from travelers leaving Paraguay destined to countries in the Yellow Fever Endemic Zones. Travelers to this country should carefully consult their itinerary.

Telephone Country Code: 595
Electricity/Plugs: AC 50 Hz, 220 volts, plug type C.
American Express: Inter-Express, S.R.L. 690 Inter-Express Bldg., Asuncion; Tel. (21) 90111.
Embassies/Consulates: U.S. Embassy, Asuncion. 1776 M. Lopez Avenue; Tel. (21) 201-041.
Hospitals/Doctors: Adventist Hospital, Asunscion (35 beds); general medical; emergency and ICU units; physicians on 24-hr call. Tel. (21) 222-11/222-12. Migone Hospital, Asuncion (30 beds); general medical facility; emergency and ICU units; physicians on 24-hr call. Tel. (21) 205-016. Instituto Paraguayo de Diagnostico. Tel. (21) 930-21/930-22; Miguel Gonzalez Oddone, M.D. Tel: (21) 943-79/200-471.

Health Advisory

Yellow fever: No risk.

Malaria: Risk is present in rural areas bordering Brazil. Malaria risk occurs primarily from October through May in rural areas of Amambay, Canendiyu, and Alto Parana Departments. Urban areas and the Iguassu Falls vicinity are risk free. Vivax malaria is the most common variety. Chloroquine prophylaxis is recommended for travel to rural malarious areas.

Travelers' diarrhea: Moderate risk. In ten large urban areas, including the capital city of Asuncion, piped water is supplied and is considered safe for consumption. Travelers, nevertheless, should carefully follow food and drink precautions, especially outside urban areas. A quinolone antibiotic (Cipro or Floxin) is recommended for the treatment of diarrhea. Diarrhea not responding to treatment with an antibiotic may be due to a parasitic disease such as giardiasis or amebiasis. All cases of diarrhea should be treated with adequate fluid replacement.

Hepatitis: There is a lower risk of acute viral hepatitis A than in neighboring Brazil or Uruguay, but all susceptible travelers should consider immune globulin prophylaxis or hepatitis A vaccine prior to visiting this country. The hepatitis B carrier rate in the general population is estimated at less than 1%. Vaccination against hepatitis B is recommended for all healthcare workers and should be considered by anyone planning an extended visit to this country.

Leishmaniasis: Highly endemic in rural areas in the departments of Alto Parana, Amambay, Caaguazu, Caazapa, Canendiyu, Guaira, and San Pedro. The highest incidence occurs in Caaguaza Department. Seventy-five percent of cases are cutaneous, the remainder mucocutaneous. Travelers should take measures to prevent insect (sandfly) bites.

Schistosomiasis: This disease is not reported in Paraguay, but exists in adjacent areas of Brazil along the Parana River.

Dengue fever: Risk occurs during the warmer months (November–April), primarily in urban areas. An outbreak occurred in Asuncion in 1989. No cases of dengue hemorrhagic fever have been reported. Precautions against mosquito bites are advised.

Chagas' disease: Widely distributed in nearly all rural areas. Risk occurs primarily in Conception, San Pedro, Cordillera, and Paraguari Departments in areas where there are adobe-style huts and houses. These structures often harbor the night-biting triatomid (assassin) bugs which are responsible for transmitting Chagas' disease. Travelers sleeping in such structures should take precautions against nighttime bites. Unscreened blood transfusions are also a source of infection and should be avoided.

AIDS: Relatively low prevalence of HIV in the general population. 26% of male prostitutes are reported HIV positive.

Other diseases: Anthrax, brucellosis, coccidiomycosis, leptospirosis, measles, rabies (a relatively minor public health problem; about 4 human deaths annually are reported), tuberculosis (relatively high incidence, especially among Amerindian children), strongyloidiasis and other helminthic infections are reported. Animal hazards include snakes (vipers, coral snakes), centipedes, scorpions, black widow spiders, brown recluse spiders, banana spiders, and wolf spiders. Species of carnivorous fish occur in the freshwaters of Paraguay.

PERU

Lima ... GMT -5 hrs

Entry Requirements

- Passport/Visa: A valid passport is required.
- AIDS Test: Not required.
- Vaccinations: A yellow fever vaccination certificate is required of travelers 6 months or older arriving from infected areas. Peru recommends vaccination for those who intend to visit any rural area of the country.

Telephone Country Code: 51   **AT&T:** 191   **MCI:** 001-190

Electricity/Plugs: AC 50 Hz, 220 volts; plug type A.

American Express: Lima Tours, S.A., Belen 1040, Lima; Tel. (14) 27-6624.

Embassies/Consulates: U.S. Embassy, Lima. 346 Grimaldo Del Solar, Miraflores; Tel. (14) 44-3621/3921. U.S. Consulate, Miraflores. Grimaldo Del Solar 346; Tel. (14) 44-3621. Canadian Embassy, Lima. Federico Gerdes, Miraflores; Tel. (14) 44-4015.

Hospitals/Doctors: British American Hospital, Lima (100 beds); general medical/surgical facility; ambulance service; Tel. (14) 403-570 or 41-7570. Juan E. Dyer, M.D. Tel. 417-946.

Travel Advisory

Additional travel information is available through the South American Explorers' Club. They can be contacted in the United States at 800-274-0568. In Lima: Avenida Portugal 146, Brena (suburb of Lima); Telephone (14) 314480. Or write to South American Explorers' Club, Casilla #3714, Lima 100, Peru.

Health Advisory

Yellow fever: This disease is active in this country. Vaccination is recommended for all travelers. Infected areas are found in the Departments of Ayacucho, Cuzco, Huanuco, Junin, Loreto, Madre de Dios, and San Martin. Most cases occur at elevations of 400 to 1,000 meters, with increased risk December–June. This country is in the Yellow Fever Endemic Zone. Although yellow fever vaccination may not be required for entry into this country, it may be required for on-going travel to other countries in Latin America, Africa, the Middle East, or Asia.

Cholera: This disease is active in this country. Although cholera vaccination is not required for entry if arriving directly from the U.S. or Canada, it may be required if arriving from a cholera-infected area, or required for on-going travel to other countries in Latin America, Africa, the Middle East, or Asia. Travelers should consider vaccination or a doctor's letter of exemption from vaccination. The risk to travelers of acquiring cholera is considered low. Prevention consists primarily in adhering to safe food and drink guidelines.

Malaria: There is no risk to travelers who will only visit Lima and vicinity, the coastal areas south of Lima, or the highland tourist areas (Cuzco, Machu Picchu, Lake Titacaca). Malaria is highly endemic in rural areas below 1,500 meters elevation in northwestern, northeastern, and eastern Peru, especially along the border with Ecuador. Risk areas include rural areas of Departments of Amazonas, Cajamarca (except Hualgayoc Province), La Libertad (except Otuzco, Santiago de Chuco Provinces), Lambayeque, Loreto, Piura (except Talara Province), San Martin and Tumbes, Provinces of Santa (Ancash Dept.); parts of La Convension (Cuzco Dept.), Tayacaja (Huancavelica Dept.), Satipo (Junin Dept.). Most risk of malaria occurs in Piura Department. Falciparum malaria may account for 20% of cases in the northwest portion of the country and chloroquine-resistant *P. falciparum* is endemic in the regions bordering Brazil. Malaria infection rates may exceed 25% in some areas along the Peru-Ecuador border. Chemoprophylaxis with mefloquine or doxycycline is recommended for travelers going to the rural malarious areas of the northwest provinces bordering Brazil and Ecuador. For travelers to other parts of Peru, chemoprophylaxis with chloroquine is currently recommended. All travelers to rural areas should take measures to prevent mosquito bites.

Travelers' diarrhea: High risk, especially outside first-class hotels and resorts. Travelers should observe strict food and drink precautions. This includes consuming only bottled, boiled, or chemically treated water consumed without ice. All foods should be thoroughly cooked and consumed while still hot. All fruit should be peeled by the traveler. Because of the potential risk of cholera, travelers should strictly avoid raw or undercooked fish or shellfish, especially ceviche. All vegetables should be well cooked. Travelers should avoid salads. A quinolone antibiotic is recommended for the treatment of diarrhea. Diarrhea not responding to treatment with an antibiotic may be due to a parasitic disease such as giardiasis or amebiasis.

Hepatitis: All susceptible travelers to this country should receive immune globulin or hepatitis A vaccine. The hepatitis B carrier rate in the general population is approximately 1.4%. Lowest risk of hepatitis B occurs in the coastal areas. Risk of hepatitis B is increased in the Amazon Basin and the southern Andes where the carrier rate of the virus is as high as 6%. Vaccination against hepatitis B is recommended for all healthcare workers and should be considered by long-term visitors to this country.

Typhoid fever: The risk of typhoid is higher than in most other Latin American countries. Typhoid vaccination is recommended for persons who will travel off the usual tourist itineraries or will have an extended stay in this country.

Dengue fever: Occurs year-round in coastal and lowland urban areas. Reported also from the Amazon Basin region. All travelers are advised to take measures to prevent mosquito bites.

Leishmaniasis: Incidence of both cutaneous and mucocutaneous leishmaniasis (espundia) reportedly is increasing in the northeast lowlands but confirmatory evidence is not readily available. A form of cutaneous leishmaniasis called "uta" appears restricted to the western slopes and valleys of the Andean region between 600 and 3,000 meters elevation. Diffuse cutaneous leishmaniasis is rare. All travelers to high forested areas are advised to take measures to prevent insect (sandfly) bites.

Chagas' disease: Widely distributed in rural areas. Forty percent of Peruvians are considered at risk. Chagas' disease occurs primarily in rural-agricultural areas where there are adobe-style huts and houses. These structures often harbor the night-biting triatomid (assassin) bugs which are responsible for transmitting Chagas' disease. Travelers sleeping in such structures should take precautions against nighttime bites. Unscreened blood transfusions are also a source of infection and should be avoided.

Rabies: High risk, relative to other South American countries. Cases of human rabies, transmitted by dogs, has increased but the exact incidence of human rabies is not known. Two outbreaks of rabies, transmitted by vampire bats, claimed 40 lives in 1989-90. Vaccination against rabies is recommended for long-term travelers to this country and for travelers going to remote rural areas if they will be unable to receive antirabies treatment within 24 hours of exposure to a potentially rabid animal such as a dog, cat, or bat.

AIDS: Lower incidence than in other Latin American countries, such as Brazil. Prevalence of HIV in the blood donor population is 0.1% to 1.2%. Homosexual males have a prevalence estimated at 4.4%. An increasing number of HIV infections are associated with heterosexual activity.

Altitude sickness: Risk is present in the Sierra region of central Peru which contains the Andes mountain ranges (average elevations 2,743 meters to 5,791 meters). The city of Cuzco is at 3,500 meters elevation. Travelers to high elevations should consider Diamox prophylaxis to reduce their risk of acute mountain sickness. Travelers arriving at high altitudes should spend several days acclimatizing and restricting strenuous activity.

Other diseases/hazards: Anthrax, brucellosis, bartonellosis (Oroyo fever), coccidiomycosis (endemic in the Amazonian lowlands), cysticercosis (residents of rural, endemic areas of Peru have a disease prevalence of 8%), echinococcosis, leptospirosis, plague (flea-borne; primary focus in Piura Dept.), tuberculosis (a serious public health problem), strongyloidiasis and other helminthic infections, and typhus (flea- and louse-borne) are reported. Animal hazards include snakes (vipers), centipedes, scorpions, black widow spiders, brown recluse spiders, banana spiders, and wolf spiders. Nearly all snakes in Peru are found in the Montana region. Electric eels and piranha may be found in the country's fresh waters. Crocodiles and alligators are abundant. Portuguese man-of-war, sea wasps, and stingrays are found in the coastal waters of Peru and could be a hazard to swimmers.

SURINAME

Paramaribo ... GMT -3 hrs

Entry Requirements

- Passport/Visa: A valid passport and visa are required.
- AIDS Test: Not required.
- Vaccinations: A yellow fever vaccination certificate is required of all travelers arriving from infected areas.

Telephone Country Code: 597　　　　**AT&T:** 156

Electricity/Plugs: AC 60 Hz, 127/220 volts; plug types C and F.

American Express: Travel Bureau C. Kersten & Co. N.V. Hotel Krasnapolsky. Domineestraat 39. Paramaribo; Tel. 74448.

Embassies/Consulates: U.S. Embassy, Paramaribo. Dr. Sophie Redmondstraat 129; Tel. 72900/77881. Canadian Embassy (Guyana); Tel. (592) (2) 72081/5.

Hospitals/Doctors: St. Vincentius, Paramaribo (320 beds); private hospital; 4-bed ICU. University Hospital (425 beds); government hospital; 5-bed ICU. Medical Clinic, Paramaribo; Tel. 72-653. F. J. C. Fung, M.D. Tel. 99-158.

Health Advisory

Yellow fever: Vaccination is recommended for all travelers. This country is in the Yellow Fever Endemic Zone. A valid yellow fever certificate may be required for on-going travel to certain other countries in Latin America, Africa, the Middle East, and Asia.

Cholera: This disease is active in this country. Although cholera vaccination is not required for entry if arriving directly from the U.S. or Canada, it may be required if arriving from a cholera-infected area, or required for on-going travel to other countries in Latin America, Africa, the Middle East, or Asia. Travelers should consider vaccination or a doctor's letter of exemption from vaccination. The risk to travelers of acquiring cholera is considered low. Prevention consists primarily in adhering to safe food and drink guidelines.

Malaria: Risk is present year-round in nearly all parts of the country. Only the city of Paramaribo, a narrow strip along the Atlantic coast, and areas of the interior above 1,300 meters elevation are considered risk-free. Falciparum malaria accounts for 80–90% of cases, the remainder being due to *P. vivax*. Chloroquine- and Fansidar-resistant falciparum malaria are reported. Chemoprophylaxis with mefloquine or doxycycline is currently recommended in malarious areas.

Travelers' diarrhea: High risk. All water sources outside of Paramaribo should be considered contaminated. Travelers should strictly observe food and drink precautions. A quinolone antibiotic (Cipro or Floxin) is recommended for the treatment of acute diarrhea. Diarrhea not responding to treatment with an antibiotic may be due to a parasitic disease such as giardiasis or amebiasis—or an intestinal virus.

Hepatitis: All susceptible travelers should receive immune globulin or hepatitis A vaccine prior to visiting this country. The hepatitis B carrier rate in the general population is estimated at 2%–3%. Vaccination against hepatitis B is recommended for all healthcare workers and should be considered by anyone planning an extended visit to this country.

Dengue fever: Limited dengue transmission occurs, primarily in the Paramaribo area. The *Aedes* mosquitoes, which transmit dengue fever, bite primarily during the daytime and are present in populous urban areas as well as resort and rural areas. All travelers are advised to take precautions against mosquito bites.

Arboviral encephalitis: At least six distinct viruses causing encephalitis have been detected in Suriname. The area of greatest risk occurs in the savanna region located 20 to 40 km inland from the coastal strip. All travelers to these inland regions should take measures to prevent mosquito bites.

Leishmaniasis: Risk of cutaneous leishmaniasis ("bush yaws") or mucocutaneous leishmaniasis occurs, primarily in the forested areas of the interior. Travelers should take measures to prevent insect (sandfly) bites.

Schistosomiasis: Risk is present year-round, but elevated during the height of the rainy season (May–June). Infected areas are found in the northern coastal strip from the Commewijne

River west to the Nickerie River, with risk of infection apparently highest in Suriname and Saramacca Districts. Travelers should avoid swimming in freshwater lakes, ponds, or streams.

Rabies: Reported in animals, but no human rabies cases have been reported since the mid-1970s. Travelers, however, should seek immediate treatment of any animal bite. Rabies vaccination is usually indicated following the unprovoked bite of a dog, cat, bat, or monkey. Bites by other animals should be considered on an individual basis.

Other diseases/hazards: Bancroftian filariasis, brucellosis, Chagas' disease (incidence data lacking), fungal infections (e.g., histoplasmosis, coccidiomycosis), leprosy (high incidence, but incidence is declining), leptospirosis, AIDS (incidence data lacking due to inadequate surveillance), tuberculosis (moderately endemic), and strongyloidiasis and other helminthic infections. (Incidence of hookworm is reported as high as 40%.) Animal hazards include snakes (vipers), centipedes, scorpions, black widow spiders, brown recluse spiders, banana spiders, and wolf spiders. Electric eels and piranha may be found in the country's fresh waters. Portuguese man-of-war, sea wasps, and stingrays are found in the coastal waters of Suriname and could be a hazard to swimmers.

URUGUAY

Montevideo ... GMT -3 hrs

Entry Requirements

- Passport/Visa: A valid passport is required.
- AIDS Test: Not required.
- Vaccinations: None required.

Telephone Country Code: 598   **AT&T:** 00-0410

Electricity/Plugs: AC 50 Hz, 220 volts; plug types C and I.

American Express: Turisport Ltd. Mercedes 942. P.O. Box 6447, Montevideo. Tel. (2) 900474.

Embassies/Consulates: U.S. Embassy, Montevideo. Lauro Muller No. 1776. Tel. 40-90-51 or 40-91-26. Canadian Embassy (Argentina). Tel. 54 (1) 312-9081/88.

Hospitals/Doctors: Hospital Britanico, Montevideo (120 beds); commonly used by U.S. Embassy personnel; Tel. (2) 800-020/800-909. Jorge E. Stanham, M.D., Tel: (2) 800-857.

Health Advisory

Yellow fever: No risk.

Cholera: Not reported.

Malaria: No risk.

Travelers' diarrhea: Low to moderate risk. All water sources outside of Montevideo should be considered potentially contaminated. Beaches close to Montevideo may be contaminated by sewage. Travelers should observe food and drink precautions. A quinolone antibiotic (Cipro or Floxin) is recommended for the treatment of diarrhea. Diarrhea not responding to treatment with an antibiotic may be due to a parasitic disease such as giardiasis or amebiasis and treatment with metronidazole (Flagyl) or tinidazole (Fasigyn) should be considered.

Hepatitis: High risk of hepatitis A. All travelers should receive immune globulin prophylaxis. The carrier rate of the hepatitis B virus in the general population is under 1% and hepatitis B vaccination is not routinely recommended.

Dengue fever: Not currently reported. The risk to travelers appears minimal.

Chagas' disease: Reported in all rural areas of Uruguay except the Atlantic coast areas. Areas with high incidence include the Departments of Artigas, Rivera, Salto, and Tacuarembo. Risk occurs in those rural-agricultural areas where there are adobe-style huts and houses that potentially harbor the night-biting triatomid (assassin) bugs. Travelers sleeping in such structures should take precautions against nighttime bites.

Rabies: There is no risk of rabies in Uruguay.

Other diseases: Anthrax (human cases are reported frequently), brucellosis, echinococcosis, syphilis, AIDS (fewer than 200 cases reported), measles (extensive outbreaks reported), meningitis (sporadic outbreaks occur), tuberculosis (relatively low incidence), strongyloidiasis and other helminthic infections, and trichinosis (3% of the population infected).

VENEZUELA

Consulate: 212-826-1660   *Caracas*   *GMT -4 hrs*

Entry Requirements
- Passport/Visa: Valid passport/tourist card required.
- AIDS Test: Not required.
- Vaccinations: No vaccinations are required to visit this country.

Telephone Country Code: 58   **AT&T:** 80-011-120   **MCI:** 800-1114-0

Electricity/Plugs: AC 60 Hz, 120/240 volts; plug types I and J. Adaptors and transformer necessary for U.S.-made appliances.

American Express: Turismo Consolidado Turisol C.A. CCCT-Nivel C-2; Local 53F-07. Caracas; Tel. (2) 959-1011.

Embassies/Consulates: U.S. Embassy, Caracas. Avenida Francisco de Miranda &Avenida Princepal de la Floresta; Tel. (2) 284-7111/-6111. U.S. Consulate, Maracaibo. Edificio Sofimara, Piso 3 Calle 77 Con Avenida 13; Tel. (61) 84-252, 83-504/5. Canadian Embassy, Caracas; Tel. (2) 951-6166.

Hospitals/Doctors: Centro Medico La Floresta, Caracas (40+ beds); modern, high-quality private facility; some specialties; ICU and emergency services; Tel. (2) 284-8111. Hospital Universitario de Caracas (1,200 beds); most specialties; emergency services. Nissim M. Abecasis, M.D., Tel. (2) 529-603.

Health Advisory

Yellow fever: Only a few cases have been officially reported since 1980. Vaccination is recommended for all travelers, especially those who visit rural areas. Venezuela is in the Yellow Fever Endemic Zone. Although a vaccination certificate is not required to enter this country, one may be required for on-going travel to other countries in Latin America, Africa, the Middle East, and Asia.

Cholera: This disease is active in this country. Although cholera vaccination is not required for entry if arriving directly from the U.S. or Canada, it may be required if arriving from a cholera-infected area, or required for on-going travel to other countries in Latin America, Africa, the Middle East, or Asia. Travelers to this country should consider vaccination (one dose) or a doctor's letter of exemption from vaccination. The risk to travelers of acquiring cholera is considered to be low. Cholera is transmitted mainly in areas with inadequate sewage disposal and unsafe water supplies such as urban slums and rural areas. Prevention consists primarily in adhering to safe food and drink guidelines.

Malaria: Risk is present throughout this country year-round in rural areas of all border states and territories and the states of Barinas, Merida, and Portuguesa. Risk of malaria is highest near the western, southern, and eastern borders. There is no malaria risk in the cities and resorts of northern Venezuela, but limited risk may occur in northern rural areas below 600 meters elevation. Nationwide, *P. falciparum* accounts for 35% of cases, but incidence of *P. falciparum* varies between 1% (Sucre State) to 60% (Bolivar State). *P. vivax* causes almost all remaining cases of malaria, but a few cases caused by *P. malariae* also occur. Chloroquine-resistant falciparum malaria probably occurs in most malarious areas. Mefloquine or doxycycline prophylaxis is currently recommended for travel to malarious areas. All travelers to malarious areas should take special precautions to prevent insect bites.

Travelers' diarrhea: High risk outside of Merida, Caracas, Maracaibo, and resort areas. Water supplies in most urban areas are filtered and chlorinated, but may be contaminated within the distribution system. Travelers should follow food and drink precautions. A quinolone antibiotic (Cipro or Floxin) is recommended for the treatment of acute diarrhea. Diarrhea not responding to antibiotic treatment may be due to amebiasis or giardiasis. Amebiasis is estimated to cause 4% of all cases of diarrhea.

Hepatitis: All susceptible travelers should receive immune globulin or hepatitis A vaccine prior to visiting this country. The carrier rate of the hepatitis B virus in the general population is estimated at 2% to 3%, but rates as high as 31% have been found in some aboriginal populations (e.g., the Yucpa Indians in Zulia State). Vaccination against hepatitis B is recommended for all healthcare workers and should be considered by anyone planning an extended visit to this country.

Dengue fever: Outbreaks of dengue have recently occurred in central and northern Venezuela, including Caracas. The *Aedes aegypti* mosquitoes, which transmit dengue fever, bite primarily during the daytime and are present in populous urban areas as well as resort and rural areas. All travelers should take protective measures against mosquito bites.

Venezuelan equine encephalitis: Mosquito-borne; highest risk area located between the Guajira Peninsula and the Catatumbo River. All travelers should take protective measures against mosquito bites to prevent transmission of this viral disease.

Leishmaniasis: Widespread incidence, especially in rural areas. Most leishmaniasis is transmitted by sand flies at lower elevations, but transmission has been reported at elevations as high as 1,800 meters in the Andes. Most cases of leishmaniasis are of the cutaneous or mucocutaneous type, but some cases of visceral leishmaniasis have also been reported. All travelers to risk areas should take measures to prevent insect (sandfly) bites, especially at night.

Onchocerciasis: Risk occurs along fast flowing rivers at elevations up to 1,000 meters in the northcentral, northeast, and southern regions. Up to 90% of the population is infected in some southern regions. Travelers to these areas should take measures to prevent insect (black fly) bites.

Filariasis: Limited risk of mosquito-transmitted Bancroftian filariasis in coastal areas. Mansonellosis, another type of filariasis, transmitted by black flies, is endemic in Amazonas Federal Territory. Travelers to these regions should take measures to prevent insect bites.

Schistosomiasis: Risk is present year-round. Risk areas are limited to the central part of northern Venezuela, including the Federal District (but not Caracas) and the surrounding states of Aragua, Carabobo, Guarico, and Miranda. Travelers should avoid swimming in freshwater lakes, ponds, or streams that may harbor infective snails.

Chagas' disease: This disease is endemic to rural areas in the northern half of Venezuela. An extensive outbreak occurred in Guarico State in 1986. In some areas up to 50% of the population has been exposed. Risk occurs in those rural-agricultural areas where there are adobe-style huts and houses that potentially harbor the night-biting triatomid (assassin) bugs. Travelers sleeping in such structures should take precautions against nighttime bites. Unscreened blood transfusions are also a source of infection and should be avoided.

Rabies: Relatively low risk. About 10 human cases of rabies are reported annually in Venezuela. Travelers should especially avoid stray dogs and seek immediate treatment of any animal bite. Rabies vaccination is indicated following the unprovoked bite of a dog, cat, vampire bat, or monkey. Bites by other animals should be evaluated on an individual basis. Pre-exposure vaccination against rabies is recommended for long-term travelers to this country and for travelers going to remote rural areas if they will be unable to receive antirabies treatment within 24 hours of exposure to a potentially rabid animal.

Other diseases/hazards: Brucellosis, babesiosis (tick-borne), echinococcosis, plague (no human cases reported for several years), syphilis, AIDS, tuberculosis, typhoid fever, and helminthic diseases (due to hookworm, roundworm, whipworm and strongyloides) are reported. Animal hazards include snakes (vipers), centipedes, scorpions, black widow spiders, brown recluse spiders, banana spiders, and wolf spiders. Portuguese man-of-war, sea wasps, and stingrays are found in the coastal waters of Venezuela and could be a hazard to swimmers.

DISEASE RISK SUMMARY
Europe, Russia, CIS

Malaria: There is no risk of malaria in western or eastern Europe. (Vivax malaria may occur in parts of southern Bulgaria, but these reports are not substantiated.)

Travelers' diarrhea: Low risk in most western European countries. Higher risk occurs in Spain, Greece, the Balkans, and eastern Europe, especially Bulgaria, Hungary, and Romania. Travelers to higher risk areas should drink only bottled, boiled, or treated water and avoid undercooked food. A quinolone antibiotic (Cipro or Floxin) is recommended for the treatment of acute diarrhea. Diarrhea not responding to antibiotic treatment may be due to a parasitic disease such as giardiasis—or an intestinal virus.

Hepatitis: All susceptible travelers should receive immune globulin or hepatitis A vaccine prior to visiting Spain, Greece, Yugoslavia and the Balkan States, and the eastern European countries, especially Bulgaria, Hungary, and Romania. The hepatitis B carrier rate in the general population of Europe is variable, but is less than 1% in most western European countries. The hepatitis B carrier rate increases to 1%–4% in Spain, Greece, and Eastern Europe. Vaccination against hepatitis B is routinely recommended for healthcare workers and should be considered by anyone planning an extended visit to visit Spain, Greece, the Balkan States, and the eastern European countries, especially Bulgaria, Hungary, and Romania.

Typhoid fever: Persons traveling extensively in Spain, Greece, Yugoslavia and the Balkan States, or the eastern European countries, especially Bulgaria, Hungary, and Romania, should consider typhoid vaccination.

Lyme disease: Risk of transmission occurs throughout Europe in rural brushy, wooded, and forested areas up to 1,500 meters elevation, especially in Scandinavia, Austria, Switzerland, and southern Germany. The ticks that transmit Lyme disease (*Ixodes ricinus* or *I. persulcatus*) are most abundant and active April through September.

Leishmaniasis: Cutaneous and visceral leishmaniasis is present in the countries bordering the Mediterranean. Risk areas include Portugal, Spain, southern France, Majorca, the suburbs of Athens, and the Greek Isles. Travelers to these areas should take measures to prevent sandfly bites.

Mediterranean spotted fever (boutonneuse fever): Occurs in southern France and in the coastal regions of other Mediterranean countries, and also along the Black Sea coast, in brushy and/or forested areas below 1,000 meters elevation. Peak transmission period is July through September. Disease may be acquired in and around tick-infested houses and terrain, but more than 95% of cases are associated with contact with tick-carrying dogs.

European tickborne encephalitis (TBE): The tick vector for this disease, *Ixodes ricinus* (the same tick that transmits Lyme disease), is widely distributed in brushy and forested areas at elevations up to 1,500 meters. Travelers to rural areas of Europe should take measures to prevent tick bites.

Crimean-Congo hemorrhagic fever: This is a viral encephalitis transmitted by *Hyalomma marginatum* ticks. These ticks are most active from April until August, reaching peak feeding activity April through May. Hemorrhagic fever with renal syndrome (HFRS): Cases of severe illness (due to Hantaan virus) are reported in Slovenia and in eastern Europe. A milder form of HFRS (caused by Puumala virus) occurs in Scandinavia, other European countries, and European Russia. Travelers should avoid contact with rodent urine or rodent feces, which may transmit the virus.

Rabies: Occurs primarily in wild animals, especially foxes, in many rural areas of Europe. Human cases are infrequent. There is no risk of rabies in Finland, Iceland, Ireland, Sweden, the United Kingdom, Gibraltar, Malta, Monaco, Portugal, and Spain.

AIDS: Increased cases reported especially from eastern Europe (mainly Romania and Bulgaria) and Russia. Infected blood and contaminated needles and syringes are important sources of infection in these countries. Travelers should consider carrying sterile needles and syringes and should avoid, if possible, blood transfusions and medical injections in these countries. Blood supplies are reportedly screened in Czechoslovakia, Hungary, and Poland, but lack of public health funding may hamper complete screening for AIDS and hepatitis B

and C viruses. Travelers should consider evacuation to a European medical facility when acute medical or surgical care, or blood transfusion, may be needed.

In western Europe, intravenous drug users and homosexual males account for 70% of the AIDS cases in Denmark, Germany, the Netherlands, Norway, and the United Kingdom. In Italy and Spain, intravenous drug use accounts for the majority of cases.

Road safety: Pedestrians should use extra caution when crossing the street in countries where there is left-sided traffic. There is a higher incidence of motor vehicle fatalities in Spain, Portugal, Yugoslavia, Greece, and eastern Europe. Seat belts should be worn at all times. All drivers should be familiar with traffic laws and road signs.

Other illnesses/hazards: Anthrax (sporadic human cases from exposure to livestock in rural areas), brucellosis (risk associated with agricultural work and consumption of raw dairy products), echinococcosis (southern Europe), Legionnaire's disease (legionellosis; outbreaks have been reported in tourists on package tours to Spain and Naples, Italy; contaminated water probable source), leptospirosis, listeriosis (from contaminated soft cheeses and meat), tick-borne relapsing fever (risk in rocky, rural livestock areas), murine typhus (flea-borne; probably occurs), and soil-transmitted helminthic infections (roundworm, hookworm, and whipworm infections; reported occasionally in southern Europe).

ALBANIA

Tirane ... GMT +1 hr

Entry Requirements
- Passport/Visa: Passport, visa, and birth certificate are required.
- AIDS Test: Not required.
- Vaccinations: A vaccination certificate is required from travelers older than 1 year of age arriving from infected areas.

Telephone Country Code: 355

Electricity/Plugs: AC 50 Hz, 220 volts; plug types C and F.

Embassies/Consulates: The United States does not maintain diplomatic or consular relations with Albania. Canadian Embassy: Travelers should contact the Canadian Embassy in Yugoslavia for assistance; Tel. [38] (11) 644-666.

Doctors/Hospitals: Tirane Clinical Hospital #2 (900 beds); general medical/surgical facility; best treatment facility in Albania. Durres District Hospital (300 beds); general medical/surgical facility. Shkoder District Hospital (350 beds); general medical/surgical facility.

Health Advisory

Travelers' diarrhea: Tirane has a fairly well-developed municipal water system for offices; urban homes, however, are not connected. There is a high risk of travelers' diarrhea outside of first-class hotels and resorts. Travelers are advised to drink only bottled, boiled, filtered, or treated water and consume only well-cooked food. A quinolone antibiotic is recommended for the treatment of acute diarrhea. Diarrhea not responding to antibiotic treatment may be due to a parasitic disease such as giardiasis or amebiasis—or an intestinal virus.

Hepatitis: Immune globulin or hepatitis A vaccine is recommended for all susceptible travelers. The hepatitis B carrier rate in the general population is estimated at 3%–4%. Vaccination against hepatitis B is recommended for healthcare workers and should be considered by long-term visitors to this country.

Leishmaniasis: Cases of cutaneous and visceral leishmaniasis are reported sporadically. Travelers should take measures to prevent sandfly bites, especially May through October, when most transmission occurs.

Hemorrhagic fever with renal syndrome: Presumed transmission is via aerolization of Hantaan virus in dried rodent excreta. Most cases reported in rural mountainous regions. Shepherds and outdoorsmen are at greatest risk.

Crimean-Congo hemorrhagic fever (CCHF): Viral illness transmitted by ticks. Sporadic cases occur throughout the summer. Travelers should take measures to prevent tick bites.

Other illnesses/hazards: Anthrax (sporadic human cases), brucellosis, boutonneuse fever (may occur along the coast in bushy or forested areas), echinococcosis, leptospirosis, rabies (cases most common in stray dogs and cats, jackals, foxes, and wolves; rare in humans), tick-borne relapsing fever (risk in rocky, rural livestock areas), murine typhus (probably occurs), and helminthic infections (roundworm, hookworm, and whipworm).

AZORES (PORTUGAL)

GMT -1 hr

Entry Requirements

Telephone Country Code: 351

- Passport/Visa: Passport required.
- AIDS Test: Not required.
- Vaccinations: A yellow fever vaccination certificate is required of all travelers arriving from infected areas. Transit passengers at Funchal, Porto, Santo, and Santa Maria do not need a certificate.

Embassies/Consulates: U.S. Consulate, Ponta Delgada, Avenida D. Henrique; Tel. 22216. Canadian Embassy (Portugal); Tel. [351] (1) 56-3821.

Health Advisory

Malaria: No risk.

AUSTRIA
Vienna ... GMT +1 hr

Entry Requirements
- Passport/Visa: A valid passport is required.
- AIDS Test: Testing is required of foreign workers applying for residence permits.
- Vaccinations: None required.

Telephone Country Code: 43   **AT&T:** 022-903-011   **MCI:** 022-903-012

Electricity/Plugs: AC 50 Hz, 220 volts; plug type F.

American Express: American Express Travel Service. Kaerntnerstrasse 21/23, Vienna; Tel. (222) 51540.

Embassies/Consulates: U.S. Embassy, Vienna. Boltzmanngasse 16; Tel. (222) 31-5511. Canadian Embassy, Vienna. Dr. Karl Luegerring 10; Tel. (222) 533-3691.

Hospitals/Doctors: Vienna Municipal General Hospital (2,460 beds); major teaching facility; all specialties. For a physician referral in Vienna, contact the American Medical Society of Vienna, Tel: (222) 424-568, or the Doctor's Board of Vienna-Service Department for Foreign Patients, Weihburggasse 10 - 12, Vienna, Tel. (1) 40-144. The Doctor's Board also provides 24-hour physician referral throughout Austria. English spoken.

Health Advisory

Travelers' diarrhea: Low risk. Tap water supplied by municipal water systems is potable. In urban and resort areas, the hotels and restaurants serve safe food and beverages.

Hepatitis: Susceptible travelers should consider immune globulin or hepatitis A vaccination. The hepatitis B carrier rate in the general population is less than 1%. Except for healthcare workers, hepatitis B vaccination is not routinely recommended. Hepatitis E is not currently reported.

Lyme disease: The tick vector (*Ixodes ricinus*) is found in broad-leaf forests (usually oak forests) at elevations below 1,000 meters, especially in the Danube River basin of eastern Austria. Tick activity is high from March through September, but peaks in April and May.

Tick-borne encephalitis (TBE): This is a viral disease transmitted by Ixodes ticks, of which about 1% to 2% are infective. Risk is present in forested areas of southern, eastern, and northern Austria, particularly in areas around Klagenfurt, Graz, Wiener Neustadt, and Linz, and in some areas of the Danube River valley west of Vienna. Travelers to risk areas should take precautions against tick bites. Vaccination against TBE should be considered by people who expect significant long-term exposure to ticks.

Rabies: No human cases have been reported recently, but rabies is enzootic in foxes.

Other illnesses: Echinococcosis, leptospirosis (associated to exposure to livestock or swimming in lakes/streams), trichinosis (from wild swine), and tularemia (usually reported in outdoorsmen after contact with the meat of killed game).

BELGIUM
Brussels ... GMT +1 hr

Entry Requirements
- Passport/Visa: A valid passport is required.
- AIDS Test: Not required.
- Vaccinations: None required.

Telephone Country Code: 32   **AT&T:** 0800-100-10   **MCI:** 0800-100-12

Electricity/Plugs: AC 50 Hz, 220 volts; plug types C and E; a grounding wire is required in the electrical cord attached to appliances.

American Express Travel Service: 2 Place Louise, Brussels; Tel. (2) 512-1740.

Embassies/Consulates: U.S. Embassy, Brussels. 27 Boulevard du Regent; Tel. (2) 513-3830.

Hospitals/Doctors: Hospital Universitaire St. Pierre, Brussels (567 beds); all specialties; emergency room; burn unit; considered one of Belgium's best hospitals; Tel. (2) 535-3111.

Health Advisory

Travelers' diarrhea: Low risk. Municipal water of good quality and safe for drinking.
Hepatitis: Low risk; annual incidence (6 cases/100,000) among the lowest in Europe.
Lyme disease: Peak tick activity March through September; risk of disease transmission occurs primarily in the southeastern forested areas and the Ardennes.

BULGARIA

Embassy: 202-387-7969   *Sofia*   *GMT +1 hr*

Entry Requirements
- Passport/Visa: Passport required. A visa is required only if travel exceeds 30 days.
- AIDS Test: Testing required for all foreigners staying longer than one month for purpose of study or work.
- Vaccinations: None required.

Telephone Country Code: 359

Electricity/Plugs: AC 50 Hz, 220 volts; plug types C and F. Adaptors and transformer necessary for U.S.-made appliances.

American Express: Balkantourist. 1 Vitosha Boulevard, Sofia

Embassies/Consulates: U.S. Embassy, Sofia. 1 Alex. Stambolinsky Blvd; Tel. 88-48-01.

Hospitals/Doctors: Institute of Traumatology and Orthopedics, Sofia (400 beds); specialized treatment center for entire country.

Health Advisory

Malaria: Although Bulgaria has been officially "malaria free" since the 1970s, cases have been rising (over 2,500 reported in 1990). Many of these cases may be imported, but indigenous malaria cannot be excluded. Risk appears to be limited to the southern regions (bordering Greece and Turkey) and the southeastern coastal areas. Indigenous malaria most likely is vivax, but 50% of imported malaria may be due to *P. falciparum*. Travelers to the southern regions are advised to take precautions against mosquito bites and seek medical attention of any sudden illness with fever.

Travelers' diarrhea: High risk outside of first-class hotels and resorts. Piped water is potable in most cities but travelers are advised to drink only bottled, boiled, filtered, or treated water and consume only well-cooked food. A quinolone antibiotic (Floxin or Cipro) is recommended for the treatment of acute diarrhea. Diarrhea not responding to antibiotic treatment may be due to a parasitic disease such as giardiasis—or an intestinal virus.

Hepatitis: Bulgaria has among the highest rates of hepatitis A in Europe (200 cases/100,000). Immune globulin or hepatitis A vaccine is recommended for all susceptible travelers. The hepatitis B carrier rate in the general population is estimated at 3.5%. Vaccination against hepatitis B is recommended for healthcare workers and should be considered by long-term visitors to this country.

Lyme disease: Occurs focally in rural forested areas up to 1,500 meters elevation. Vector ticks (*Ixodes ricinus* or *I. persulcatus*) are most abundant and active from April through September.

Mediterranean spotted fever (boutonneuse fever): Endemic in eastern regions and along the Black Sea coast in brushy and/or forested areas.

European tick-borne encephalitis (TBE): Low apparent risk. The tick vector for this disease, *Ixodes ricinus* (the same tick that transmits Lyme disease), is widely distributed in brushy and forested areas at elevations up to 1,000 meters.

Crimean-Congo hemorrhagic fever: This is a viral encephalitis transmitted by ticks (*Hyalomma marginatum*). Ticks are most active from April until August, reaching peak feeding activity in April and May. Main risk areas are the southern provinces of Kurdzhali and Khaskovo and the southeastern provinces of Yambol and Burgas.

Other illnesses/hazards: Anthrax (sporadic human cases; exposure to livestock in rural areas), brucellosis (risk associated with consumption of raw dairy products), echinococcosis, leptospirosis, rabies (cases may occur in stray dogs and cats, jackals, foxes, and wolves; rare in humans; country officially "rabies free"), tick-borne relapsing fever (risk in rocky, rural livestock areas), murine typhus (probably occurs), and soil-transmitted helminthic infections (roundworm, hookworm, and whipworm infections reported occasionally).

CZECH REPUBLIC

Embassy: 202-363-6315   *Prague*   *GMT +1 hr*

Entry Requirements
- Passport/Visa: Passport required. A visa is not required for U.S. passport holders.
- AIDS Test: Not required.
- Vaccinations: None required.

Telephone Country Code: 42   **AT&T:** 00-420-00101   **MCI:** 00-42-000112

Electricity/Plugs: AC 50 Hz, 220 volts; plug type E.

American Express: Cedok, Foreign Travel Div., Na Prikope 18, Prague; Tel. (2) 22-4251.

Embassies/Consulates: U.S. Embassy, Prague. Trziste 15-12548 Praha; Tel. (2) 53-6641/8. Canadian Embassy, Prague. Mickiewiczova 6, 125 33 Prague 6; Tel. (2) 32-6941.

Hospitals/Doctors: Motol University Hospital, Prague (1,000 beds); most medical specialties; ICU. Contact the American or Canadian Embassy for physician referral.

Health Advisory (includes the Slovak Republic)

Travelers' diarrhea: Medium risk. Water supplies in urban areas are usually potable.

Hepatitis: Low to medium risk; immune globulin or hepatitis A vaccine is recommended for all susceptible travelers.

Tick-borne diseases: Both Central European tick-borne encephalitis (TBE) and Lyme disease occur in the lowland forested areas. Higher risk areas for TBE are south of Prague in the Vlatva River basin, north of Brno, the vicinity of Plzen, and in the Danube River basin near Bratislava. In the Slovak Republic there are widely distributed foci of tick-borne encepahalitis in western Slovakia, in central Slovakia, (including the Krupin Hills), and in eastern Slovakia (including the Slovak karst and Slanske hills). Risk of Lyme disease occurs primarily April through October in forests throughout these countries.

Other illnesses: Brucellosis, echinococcosis, leptospirosis, cysticercosis, rabies (moderately enzootic, with foxes serving as primary zoonotic reservoir; approximately 60% of domestic animal rabies occurs in stray cats), tularemia, and intestinal helminthic infections.

DENMARK

Copenhagen ... GMT +1 hr

Entry Requirements
- Passport/Visa: Passport required.
- AIDS Test: Not required.
- Vaccinations: None required.

Telephone Country Code: 45   **AT&T:** 8001-0010   **MCI:** 8001-0022

American Express: American Express Travel Service. Amagertorv 18 (Stroget), Copenhagen; Tel. (1) 33122301.

Embassies/Consulates: U.S. Embassy, Copenhagen. Dag Hammarskjolds Alie 24; Tel.(1) 42-31-44. Canadian Embassy, Copenhagen. K. R. Bernikowsgade 1; Tel.(1)12-2229.

Hospitals/Doctors: Bispebjerb Hospital, Copenhagen (1,150 beds); emergency room and trauma unit; Tel. 3531-3531. Jorgen Kelstrup, MD, Copenhagen; Tel. 3138-7828.

Health Advisory

Travelers' diarrhea: Low risk; potable water is available throughout the country.

Hepatitis: Low risk; incidence of hepatitis A in this country is among the lowest in Europe. Hepatitis B causes about 40% of acute viral hepatitis cases in this country. Carrier rate of the hepatitis B virus in the general population is less than one percent.

Lyme disease: Up to 20% of ticks in forested areas throughout the country are infected. Peak tick density occurs in April and May. Most cases of Lyme disease occur in the summer months and peak in July and August. Travelers to brushy or forested areas should take measures to prevent tick bites (Chapter 6).

FINLAND

Helsinki... GMT +2 hrs

Entry Requirements

- Passport/Visa – A valid passport is required.
- AIDS Test – Not required.
- Vaccinations – None required.

Telephone Country Code: 358   **AT&T:** 9800-100-10   **MCI:** 9800-102-80

Electricity/Plugs: AC 50 Hz, 220 volts; plug types C and F.

American Express: Travek Travel Bureau, Katajanokan Pohjoisranta 9-13, Helsinki; Tel. (0) 901-2511.

Embassies/Consulates: U.S. Embassy, Helsinki; Itainen Puistotie 14A; Tel. (0) 171-931; Canadian Embassy, Helsinki; P. Esplanadi 25B; Tel. (0) 171141.

Doctors/Hospitals

Helsinki Health Center (1,350 beds); most specialties, including critical care.

Antti Huunan-Seppala, M.D. Tel. (0) 434-1414/698-4765 (home). Eira Hospital, Helsinki; Tel. (0) 659-944.

Health Advisory

Lyme disease: Travelers should take tick bite precautions in brushy and broad-leaf forest (usually oak forest) areas in the southern coastal areas at elevations below 1,500 meters.

Tick-borne encephalitis: Rare cases are transmitted by *Ixodes ricinus* ticks found in brush and wooded areas. Most cases reported in forested areas along the coast of the Gulf of Finland from Kotka to the border with Russia, and all the islands south of Turku including the Aland islands.

Pagosta disease: Viral illness with encephalitis transmitted by mosquitoes (Culex sp.) especially in the mid-eastern region of Finland. Travelers should avoid mosquito bites.

FRANCE

Embassy: 202-944-6000   *Paris*   *GMT +1 hr*

Entry Requirements

- Passport/Visa: Valid passport required to visit France, Andorra, Monaco, Corsica, and French Polynesia. Visas not required for tourist/business stay up to 3 months (1 month in Polynesia).
- AIDS Test: Not required for tourists.
- Vaccinations: None required.

Telephone Country Code: 33   **AT&T:** 19-0011   **MCI:** 19-00-19

Electricity/Plugs: AC 50 Hz, 220 volts.

American Express: American Express Travel Service. 11 Rue Scribe, Paris; Tel. (1) 42-66-09-99.

U.S. Embassy: Paris. 2 Avenue Gabriel; Tel. (1) 42-96-12-02.

Hospitals/Doctors (Paris): The American Hospital, Paris; 63 Blvd. Victor Hugo, Neuilly-sur-Seine; most specialties; many American-trained physicians on staff; emergency room open 24 hours. Tel. (1) 46-41-25-25.

Hospital Pitie-Salpetriere, Paris (2,437 beds); most specialties including orthopedics and traumatology; cardiology; emergency medicine; Tel. (1) 45-70-21-12.

S.O.S. Doctors on Duty; will go to hotels or residences; Tel. (1) 47-07-77-77.

Medical Emergencies in Paris; Tel. (1) 48-28-40-04.

Clinic S. I. O.U; internal medicine; on call 24 hours; Tel. (1) 45-53-53-40.

Guy Viterbo, M.D.; pediatrics; will take emergency calls; on staff of American Hospital; Tel. (1) 47-34-68-09.

John Barthelmy, M.D.; pediatrics; will take emergency calls; on staff of American Hospital; Tel. (1) 46-51-88-55.

Diane Winaver, M.D.; gynecology; on staff of Hospital Salpetriere; Tel. (1) 45-51-82-32.
Stephen Wilson, M.D.; general practice; hours 8:00 to 20:00; Tel. (1)-45-67-26-53.
Marc Arrata, M.D. ophthalmology; Tel. (1) 42-72-35-76.
Pierre Marois, D.M.D.; Chief of dental dept., American Hospital; Tel. (1) 47-70-81-81.
Ambulance de la Tour Eiffel; ground ambulance transport; Tel. (1) 45-75-08-38.
NOTE: In case of emergency, travelers can dial 15 on almost any French telephone, and the nearest hospital will dispatch a medical unit.

Health Advisory

Travelers' diarrhea: Low risk. The domestic water supplies in urban areas are generally safe for drinking.

Hepatitis: There is a low risk of hepatitis A. Immune globulin is not considered necessary for routine travel to France. The carrier rate of the hepatitis B virus in the general population is less than 1%.

Lyme disease: Low risk of transmission occurs throughout the country in wooded, brushy areas or in broad-leaf (oak) forests. Travelers to rural areas countrywide should take measures to avoid tick bites.

Boutonneuse fever (Mediterranean spotted fever): Occurs in southern France in regions below 1,000 meters elevation. Peak transmission occurs July through September. The primary endemic areas are the southern Mediterranean coast (especially the vicinity of Marseille) and the island of Corsica. Disease may be acquired in and around tick-infested houses and terrain, but more than 95% of cases are associated with contact with tick-carrying dogs.

Leishmaniasis: Low risk, but visceral and cutaneous leishmaniasis do occur in rural areas of southern France, primarily in the departments of Bouche-de-Rhone, Provence, and Alpes-Maritimes, and on Corsica. Transmission occurs between May and November, peaking in July and August. Travelers should take measures to prevent insect (sandfly) bites.

Listeriosis: Outbreaks of listeriosis, caused by consumption of unpasteurized dairy products, especially soft cheeses, such as Brie, are reported. Some cases have been fatal. Young children, pregnant women, and travelers with compromised immunity should avoid soft cheese products.

Rabies: No human cases reported, but rabies reported enzootic in the fox population in the northeast and east.

Other diseases: Brucellosis, echinococcosis, giardiasis, hemorrhagic fever with renal syndrome, trichinosis (outbreaks associated with consumption of contaminated horsemeat have occurred), and typhoid fever.

GERMANY

Embassy: 202-298-4000   **Berlin**   *GMT +1 hr*

Entry Requirements

- Passport/Visa: A valid passport is required.
- AIDS Test: Testing is required for those applying for residence permits (Bavaria only). Travelers should contact the German Embassy in Washington for further details.
- Vaccinations: None required.

Telephone Country Code: 49   **AT&T:** 0130-0010   **MCI:** 0130-0012

Electricity/Plugs: AC 50 Hz, 220 volts; plug type F.

American Express: American Express Travel Service: Kurfuerstendamm 11, Berlin; Tel. (30) 882-7575.

Embassies/Consulates: U.S. Embassy, Berlin. Neustaedtische Kirchstrasse 4-5; Tel. (30) 220-2741. Canadian Embassy, Berlin. Europa, D-100 Berlin 30; Tel. (30) 261-1161.

Hospitals/Doctors: Universitatklinik, Bonn (1,774 beds); private hospital with all specialties. Universitatklinik, Cologne (1,800 beds); private hospital; all specialties.

Health Advisory

Travelers' diarrhea: In western Germany, drinking water in urban areas is safe, but well water in rural areas may be contaminated. In the new states of the former East Germany, advanced water treatment systems that reduce contamination from industrial solvents, pesticides, heavy metals, and other pollutants may be lacking. Water is safe to drink only in major cities and at the better hotels and restaurants. To be safe, travelers to eastern Germany are advised to drink only carbonated or commercially bottled water or other safe beverages. A quinolone antibiotic is recommended for the treatment of acute diarrhea.

Hepatitis: Low risk. The incidence of hepatitis A in western Germany is among the lowest in Europe. Susceptible travelers to the eastern regions, however, should consider receiving immune globulin or hepatitis A vaccine. The hepatitis B carrier rate in the general population is estimated at less than 1%. Vaccination against hepatitis B is recommended for healthcare workers and should be considered by long-term visitors to this country.

Lyme disease: This disease is reported, primarily in the south (in the state of Bayern). Up to 33% of ticks in some endemic areas are infected. The ticks that transmit Lyme disease (*Ixodes ricinus*) are found in brushy, wooded areas and broad-leaf (mostly oak) forests under 1,000 meters elevation. Travelers to rural areas should take precautions against tick bites.

Tick-borne encephalitis: Focally endemic in the southern lowland forests where the tick vector, *Ixodes ricinus*, is found. Most cases found in the region of the Bavarian Forest, Baden-Wurttemburg, the Main, and the Saar. Travelers should take measures to prevent tick bites. A vaccine is available for people at high risk of exposure.

Rabies: No human cases have been officially reported for several years. Wild foxes are the primary reservoir of the disease. Animal rabies has been declining in the west, but there is potential risk of transmission to humans, especially in the eastern regions. Travelers should seek immediate medical evaluation and treatment of any wild animal bite.

AIDS: Most cases are reported from the western regions. Primary risk groups include homosexual males and intravenous drug users.

Other diseases: Brucellosis, boutonneuse fever (low risk; reported from a region southeast of Frankfurt in the 1980s), hemorrhagic fever with renal syndrome (transmitted by infective rodent excreta; 14 cases reported in an outbreak in soldiers in 1989), echinococcosis (risk greatest in Swabbian uplands of central Wurttemberg State), legionellosis, and leptospirosis (risk may be elevated in the south).

GREECE

Embassy: 202-667-3168   *Athens*   *GMT +1.5 hrs*

Entry Requirements

- Passport/Visa: A valid passport is required.
- AIDS Test: Testing required for students on scholarship, performing artists. Travelers should contact the Greek Embassy in Washington for details.
- Vaccinations: A yellow fever vaccination certificate is required from all travelers older than 6 months arriving from infected or endemic areas.

Telephone Country Code: 30   **AT&T:** 00-800--1311   **MCI:** 00-800-1211

Electricity/Plugs: AC 50 Hz, 220 volts; plug types C, D, and F.

American Express: American Express Travel Service. 2 Hermou Street, Constitution Square, Athens; Tel. (1) 324-4975.

Embassies/Consulates: U.S. Embassy, Athens. 91 Vasilissis Sophias Boulevard; Tel. (1) 721-2951/-8401. Canadian Embassy, Athens. 4 Ioannou Ghemmadiou Street &Ypsilantou Street; Tel. (1) 723-9511.

Hospitals/Doctors: The Diagnostic and Therapeutic Center of Athens, "HYGEIA" (350 beds); well-equipped modern facility; Tel. (1) 682-7940. Apostolos Accident Hospital, Athens (1,000 beds); orthopedics; trauma care.

Health Advisory

Malaria: No apparent risk. Greece declared malaria-free in 1986.

Travelers' diarrhea: Low- to medium-risk for acute diarrheal disease due to bacteria (mainly *E. Coli*, salmonella, shigella, campylobacter), parasites, and viruses. Multi-drug resistance common among salmonella and shigella bacteria. Amebiasis, usually seen in adults, is more common in Greece than in most other parts of Europe. Tap water in small urban areas and rural areas is not considered safe. Travelers are advised to drink only bottled, boiled, filtered, or chemically treated water and consume only well-cooked food. All fruit should be peeled prior to consumption. A quinolone antibiotic is recommended for the treatment of acute diarrhea. Diarrhea not responding to antibiotic treatment may be due to a parasitic disease such as giardiasis or amebiasis—or an intestinal virus.

Hepatitis: Higher risk than in other western European countries. Immune globulin or hepatitis A vaccine is recommended for all susceptible travelers to this country. The hepatitis B carrier rate in the general population of Greece is estimated at 1%–4%. Vaccination against hepatitis B is recommended for healthcare workers and should be considered by long-term visitors. Sixty to 70% of cases of acute viral hepatitis in adults are caused by the hepatitis B virus.

Leishmaniasis: Risk of transmission is highest between May and October. Cutaneous leishmaniasis occurs only sporadically, with the highest prevalence on the Ionian Islands. Visceral leishmaniasis occurs focally on the mainland, including the Athens area, and on the islands, especially Crete. Travelers to these regions should take measures to avoid sandfly bites.

Tick-borne encephalitis (TBE): Low apparent risk; some cases of TBE occur in northern Greece where the tick vector *Ixodes ricinus* is present.

Crimean-Congo hemorrhagic fever (tick-borne): May be endemic in northeastern Greece near the border with Bulgaria.

Hemorrhagic fever with renal syndrome: Most cases are reported in the rural mountain regions in northern and northwestern Greece. Also reported on Crete and the Ionian Islands, including Corfu. Transmission is apparently via aerosolized dried rodent excreta.

Other illnesses/hazards: Anthrax (sporadic human cases; exposure to livestock in rural areas), boutonneuse fever (tick-borne), brucellosis echinococcosis, legionellosis (reported sporadically, usually in summer tourists), rabies (country now officially "rabies-free." Rabies occurs primarily in jackals, foxes, and wolves, with some dog and cat rabies. Rare in humans; most cases in the northeast and Peloponnese), sandfly fever, tick-borne relapsing fever (risk in rocky, rural livestock areas), murine typhus (probably occurs), helminthic infections (roundworm, hookworm, and whipworm infections reported occasionally from rural areas), and trichinosis.

Air pollution: Severe air-quality problems occur in Athens.

HUNGARY

Budapest ... GMT +1 hr

Entry Requirements
- Passport/Visa: A valid passport is required. A tourist visa is no longer required.
- AIDS Test: Not required.
- Vaccinations: None required.

Telephone Country Code: 36   **AT&T:** 00-800-01111   **MCI:** 00-800-01411

American Express: Ibusz Travel, Petofi Ter 3 opposite Intercontinental Hotel, Budapest; Tel. (1) 118-7680.

Embassies/Consulates: U.S. Embassy, Budapest. V. Szabadsag Ter 12; Tel. (1) 112-6450.

Hospitals/Doctors: Trauma Hospital (Orszagos Traumatologiai Intezet); handles all major accidents. May Korhaz Central Railroad Hospital, Budapest (1,200 beds); general medical services available. Institute for Advanced Medical Training, Budapest (2,500 beds); most specialties, including cardiology; pediatrics.

Health Advisory

Travelers' diarrhea: Low to moderate risk. Ninety percent of the population has access to piped, treated water supplies. In urban and resort areas, the hotels and restaurants generally serve reliable food and potable water. Elsewhere, especially in rural areas, travelers should observe all food and drink safety precautions. A quinolone antibiotic is recommended for the treatment of acute diarrhea. Diarrhea not responding to antibiotic treatment may be due to a parasitic disease such as giardiasis or amebiasis.

Hepatitis: There is a lower risk of hepatitis A in Hungary than in other eastern European countries. Immune globulin or hepatitis A vaccine, however, is recommended for all susceptible travelers. The hepatitis B carrier rate in the general population is estimated at 1%. Vaccination against hepatitis B is recommended for healthcare workers and should be considered by long-term visitors to this country.

Tick-borne diseases: Both European tick-borne encephalitis (TBE) and Lyme disease are reported, especially in the lowland forests where the tick vector, *Ixodes ricinus*, is most abundant. The highest incidence of TBE in Hungary occurs in forested areas of the three western counties neighboring Austria and Slovenia and in the northern Komarom County bordering Czechoslovakia. Most adult cases occur among male forestry workers. A vaccine is available to prevent TBE and should be considered by those who expect extended exposure to ticks.

Lyme disease: 58 confirmed cases were reported in 1986. To prevent Lyme disease (as well as TBE), all travelers should take measures to prevent tick bites, especially during the peak transmission period, March through September.

Rabies: Risk is present, but human cases have not been reported recently. Foxes are the main reservoir of the virus. Travelers should avoid wild animals, especially foxes and raccoons, in rural areas.

Other diseases: Anthrax (from exposure to livestock), brucellosis (from consuming unpasteurized dairy products), Crimean-Congo hemorrhagic fever, cysticercosis, hemorrhagic fever with renal syndrome (sporadic cases and outbreaks), leptospirosis (from swimming or bathing in water contaminated by animal urine), tularemia, and intestinal helminthic infections (hookworm disease, strongyloidiasis, ascariasis, and trichuriasis).

ITALY

Rome ... GMT +1 hr

Entry Requirements
- Passport/Visa: Passport required.
- AIDS Test: Not required.
- Vaccinations: None required.

Telephone Country Code: 39   **AT&T:** 172-1011   **MCI:** 172-1022

Electricity/Plugs: AC 50 Hz, 220 volts; plug types C and F.

American Express: American Express Travel Service. Piazza Di Spagna 38, Rome; Tel. (6) 67641.

Embassies/Consulates: U.S. Embassy, Rome. Via Veneto 119/A; Tel. (6) 46741.

Hospitals/Doctors: Ospedale S. Camillo de Lellis, Rome (3,461 beds); all specialties available. Medical Diagnostic Center, Rome; Tel. (6) 481-8429/481-8502. Luigi Cardi, M.D., Tel. 6) 861-434/499-7294/499-7459. Ospedale Maggiore di Milano, Milan; all specialties; 24-hour emergency; Tel. 8820. Aldo Curatolo, M.D., Milan; Tel. 215-651/261-955. Larry Burdick, M.D., Milan; Tel. 546-2917 or 279-167.

Health Advisory

Travelers' diarrhea: Low risk in major cities, such as Rome, Milan, and Verona, where the water supplies are adequately treated. Higher risk exists in the south and on the islands of Sicily and Sardinia. A quinolone antibiotic is recommended for the treatment of acute diarrhea. Diarrhea not responding to antibiotic treatment may be due to a parasitic disease such as giardiasis—or an intestinal virus. Amebiasis is uncommon in Italy.

Hepatitis: Increased risk of hepatitis A occurs in the south and on the islands of Sicily and Sardinia. Immune globulin or hepatitis A vaccine is recommended for all susceptible travelers to these areas. The hepatitis B carrier rate in the general population is estimated at 1%–2%. Hepatitis E may occur, but has not been reported.

Tick-borne diseases: Lyme disease, tick-borne encephalitis (TBE), and boutonneuse fever (Mediterranean spotted fever) are reported. Lyme disease has been reported along the Ligurian coast south of Genoa and along the Adriatic coast, Trieste to Rimini. TBE has been reported sporadically around Florence. Boutonneuse fever (transmitted by the brown dog tick) occurs primarily along the Ligurian coast and the islands of Sicily and Sardinia. Travelers to these regions should take measures to prevent tick bites.

Leishmaniasis: Cutaneous leishmaniasis and visceral leishmaniasis have been reported from rural areas in Tuscany, Calabria and Campania, and on the Islands of Sicily and Sardinia. Peak transmission occurs May through November. Travelers to these areas should take measures to prevent insect (sandfly) bites.

Legionnaire's disease: Six cases of Legionnaire's disease occurred in tourists who visited the Island of Ischia (near Naples) in 1989 and 1990. Source of the bacteria was thought to be contaminated water supplied by three hotels; municipal thermal baths were another possible source of infection. Travelers to southern Italy are advised to consume only bottled, boiled, or commercially treated water.

Rabies: No human cases have recently been reported, but animal rabies occurs in the fox population near the Austrian border. Travelers bitten by a wild animal, or sustaining an unprovoked bite by a dog or cat, should seek emergency medical treatment.

Other illnesses: Anthrax, brucellosis, echinococcosis, hemorrhagic fever with renal syndrome, listeriosis, leptospirosis, Q fever, typhoid fever, tularemia (exposure to wild boar meat and uncooked pork), and tuberculosis.

IRELAND
Dublin ... GMT 0 hrs

Entry Requirements
- Passport/Visa: Passport required.
- AIDS Test: Not required.
- Vaccinations: None required.

Telephone Country Code: 353   **AT&T:** 1-800-550-000   **MCI:** 1-800-55-1001

Electricity/Plugs: AC 50 Hz, 220 volts; plug types F and G.

American Express: American Express Travel Service. 116 Grafton Street, Dublin; Tel. (1) 772-874.

Embassies/Consulates: U.S. Embassy, Dublin. 42 Elgin Road, Ballsbridge; Tel. (1) 688-777. Canadian Embassy; Tel. (1) 781-988.

Hospitals/Doctors: Our Lady's Hospital for Sick Children, Dublin (pediatrics); Tel. 558-511 or 800-365. Consultant's Clinic, Dublin (OB/GYN); Tel. 544-506.

St. Jane's Hospital, Dublin (595 beds); all specialties; 4-bed ICU unit. Tel. 532-867/8.

W.A. Ryan M.D., Dublin; Tel. (1) 2691-581. Blackrock Clinic, Rock Road, Blackrock Co. Dublin; Tel. 883-364. Charlemont Clinic, Dublin (Professor Risteard Mulcahy, cardiology); Tel. 784-277.

Health Advisory

Travelers' diarrhea: Low risk. Water throughout Ireland is potable. Cryptosporidiosis and giardiasis are endemic at low levels. Incidence of amebiasis is not known but presumed low.

Hepatitis: Low risk. Immune globulin prophylaxis against hepatitis A is not routinely recommended. The carrier rate of the hepatitis B virus in the general population is less than 0.5 percent. Hepatitis E has not been reported.

Lyme disease: Endemic level undetermined but clinical cases reportedly occur among all age groups, usually during the summer months. *Ixodes ricinus* tick population peaks in May and September. Travelers to rural areas should take measures to prevent tick bites, especially in brushy, wooded, and forested areas.

Other diseases: Hemorrhagic fever with renal syndrome (no cases currently reported although virus appears to be circulating in the rodent population of Ireland), leptospirosis (acquired through contact with infective animal urine, often when swimming in polluted water), leptspirosis (human infection from exposure to livestock), and Q fever (rare cases in humans).

MALTA
Valletta ... GMT +1 hr

Entry Requirements
- Passport/Visa: Passport required.
- AIDS Test: Not required.
- Vaccinations: A yellow fever vaccination certificate is required for all travelers older than 6 months arriving from infected areas.

Telephone Country Code: 356

American Express: A & V Von Brockdorff Ltd., 4 Zachary Street, Valletta; Tel. 232-141.

Embassies/Consulates: U.S. Embassy, Valletta; Development House, 2nd Floor, St. Anne Street; Tel. 623-653/620-424. Canadian Embassy, Valletta. Demajo House, 103 Archbishop Street; Tel. 233-121/6.

Hospitals/Doctors: Travelers should contact the U.S. Embassy for physician and hospital referrals.

Health Advisory

Traveler's diarrhea: Medium to high risk outside of first-class hotels and resorts. Travelers are advised to drink only bottled, boiled, filtered, or treated water and consume only well-cooked food. All fruit should be peeled prior to consumption. A quinolone antibiotic (Floxin or Cipro) is recommended for the treatment of acute diarrhea. Diarrhea not responding to antibiotic treatment may be due to a parasitic disease such as giardiasis—or an intestinal virus.

Hepatitis: Immune globulin or hepatitis A vaccine is recommended for all susceptible travelers. The hepatitis B carrier rate in the general population is estimated at 1%–2%. Vaccination against hepatitis B is recommended for healthcare workers and should be considered by long-term visitors to this country.

NETHERLANDS
The Hague ... GMT +1 hr

Entry Requirements
- Passport/Visa: Passport required.
- AIDS Test: Not required.
- Vaccinations: None required.

Telephone Country Code: 31   **AT&T:** 06-022-9111   **MCI:** 06-022-9122

Electricity/Plugs: AC 50 Hz, 220 volts; plug types C and F.

American Express: American Express Travel Service. Venestraat 20, The Hague; Tel. (70) 469-515.

Embassies/Consulates: U. S. Embassy, The Hague. Lange Voorhout 102; Tel. (70) 624-911. Canadian Embassy, The Hague. Sophialaan 7; Tel. (70) 614-111.

Hospitals/Doctors: Wilhelmina Gasthuis/Zinnan Gasthuis, Amsterdam (923 beds); coronary care; ICU; emergency unit; first aid. I. C.C. Delprat, M.D., Amsterdam; Tel. (020) 662-6886. Academish Ziekenhuis, Rotterdam (1,004 beds); general medical/surgical facility; OB/GYN; pediatrics; trauma team; all major medical specialties. Academish Zeikenhuis, Utrecht (1,074 beds); all medical specialties including OB/GYN; pediatrics; emergency room; hemodialysis; trauma team. Bronovo Hospital, The Hague; Tel. (070) 124-141.

Health Advisory

Travelers' diarrhea: Low risk. Water is safe throughout this country.

Hepatitis: Low risk. Hepatitis B accounts for about 20% of all cases of acute viral hepatitis in this country.

Lyme disease: Reported from southern and eastern parts of the country. Travelers should take precautions to avoid tick bites in brushy or wooded areas.

NORWAY

Embassy: 202-333-6000   **Oslo**   **GMT +1 hr**

Entry Requirements
- Passport/Visa: Passport required.
- AIDS Test: Not required.
- Vaccinations: None required.

Telephone Country Code: 47   **AT&T:** 800-190-11   **MCI:** 800-199-12

American Express: Winge Reisebureau. Karl Johansgt. 33/35, Oslo; Tel. (2) 412-030.

Embassies/Consulates: U.S. Embassy, Oslo. Drammensveien 18; Tel. (2) 448-550. Canadian Embassy, Oslo. Oscar's Gate 20; Tel. (2) 466-955.

Hospitals/Doctors: Riks Hospital, Oslo (1,185 beds); all specialties; Tel. (2) 867-010. Ullevaal Hospital, Oslo; all specialties. Tel. (2) 118-080.

Health Advisory

Travelers' diarrhea: Low risk.

Tickborne diseases: Tickborne encephalitis occurs in scattered areas around Bergin. Lyme disease is transmitted by ticks found in brushy areas and forests in the southern coastal areas at elevations below 1,500 meters.

POLAND

Embassy: 202-234-3800   **Warsaw**   **GMT +1 hr**

Entry Requirements
- Passport/Visa: Passport and visa required.
- AIDS Test: Testing required for foreign students intending to remain in Poland more than a few weeks; U.S. test results not accepted.
- Vaccinations: None required.

Telephone Country Code: 48   **AT&T:** 0-010-480-0111   **MCI:** 0-01-04-800-222

American Express: Orbis Travel. Marszalkowska 142, Warsaw; Tel. (22) 267-501.

Embassies/Consulates: U.S. Embassy, Warsaw. Aleje Ujazdowskle 29/31; Tel. (22) 283-041.

Hospitals/Doctors: State Hospital #1, Warsaw (1,500 beds); most major specialties; ICU; staff includes 200 physicians. Medical Academy, Gdansk (1,000 beds); most specialties; ICU. Krakow City Hospital (1,200 beds); most major specialties; ICU. Tel. (22) 298-051.

Health Advisory

Travelers' diarrhea: Only 1% of the country's drinking water is considered suitable for drinking. Surface water is polluted with organic, industrial, and agricultural waste/run-off. Travelers should avoid tap water. All drinking water should preferably be bottled, boiled, filtered, or chemically treated. A quinolone antibiotic is recommended for the treatment of acute diarrhea. Diarrhea not responding to treatment with an antibiotic may be due to a parasitic disease such as giardiasis. (Giardiasis rate among the highest in Europe, especially in children.)

Hepatitis: Immune globulin or hepatitis A vaccine is recommended for all susceptible travelers. The hepatitis B carrier rate in the general population is estimated at 0.2% to 1.2% (up to 3% in the extreme northeast). Vaccination against hepatitis B is recommended for healthcare workers and should be considered by long-term visitors to this country.

Tick-borne diseases: Lyme disease and central European tick-borne encephalitis (TBE) are reported. Lyme disease is reported sporadically, and the incidence of TBE is low, about 50 cases a year. The tick vector, *Ixodes ricinus* (the European castor bean tick), is distributed widely in brushy, wooded areas throughout most of Poland. Increased risk is present in the northern forested areas around Gdansk south and eastward to the Russian border, including the areas around Bialystock. Other risk areas include the forested lands around Warsaw, Lodz, and Lukow, and along the border with Czechoslovakia south of Wroclaw.

Other illnesses/hazards: Anthrax, brucellosis (risk associated with consumption of raw dairy products), leptospirosis, rabies (enzootic in foxes; rare in humans), trichinosis (from raw or undercooked pork; elevated risk in eastern Poland), and typhoid fever.

Air pollution: Severe air pollution occurs in most industrial areas.

PORTUGAL

Embassy: 202-332-3007   *Lisbon*   *GMT 0 hrs*

Entry Requirements
- Passport/Visa: A valid passport is required.
- AIDS Test: Not required.
- Vaccinations: A yellow fever vaccination certificate is required from travelers more than 1 year of age coming from infected areas; this requirement applies only to travelers arriving in or destined for the Azores or Madeira Islands. However, no certificate is required from transit passengers on the islands of Funchal, Porto Santo, or Santa Maria.

Telephone Country Code: 351   **AT&T:** 05017-1-288   **MCI:** 05-017-1234

Electricity/Plugs: AC 50 Hz, 120/220 volts; plug types C and D.

American Express: Star Travel Service. Avda Sidonio, Pais 4-A, Lisbon; Tel. (1) 539-871.

Embassies/Consulates: U.S. Embassy, Lisbon. Avenida das Forcas Armadas; Tel. (1)726-6600 Canadian Embassy, Lisbon. Rua Rosa Araujo 2, 6th floor; Tel. (1)563-821.

Hospitals/Doctors: Santa Maria Hospital, Lisbon (1,384 beds); most medical specialties, including eye surgery and ENT; Tel. (1) 797-5171 or 797-8035. The British Hospital, Lisbon; Tel. (1) 602-020 or 678-161. Antonia Meyrelles do Souto, M.D., Lisbon; Tel. (1) 570-217.

Health Advisory

Malaria: There is no risk of malaria in Portugal.

Travelers'diarrhea: Medium risk; most sections of major cities have piped, potable water. In rural areas, water supplies may be contaminated. A quinolone antibiotic is recommended for the treatment of acute diarrhea.

Hepatitis: Immune globulin prophylaxis for hepatitis A is recommended for all susceptible travelers. The carrier rate of the hepatitis B virus in the general population is estimated at 1.3%—high for western Europe. Vaccination should be considered by long-term visitors.

Leishmaniasis: Cases of cutaneous leishmaniasis are rare but reported sporadically. Visceral leishmaniasis (VL) said to be increasing. Eighty percent of cases of VL occur in the Douro River Basin in the districts of Real, Braganca, Viseau, and Gaurda. Travelers should take measures to prevent sandfly bites.

Boutonneuse fever: Countrywide incidence below 1,000 meters elevation, especially in the Mediterranean coastal areas. Travelers should avoid close contact with dogs, which are carriers of the infective brown dog tick.

Rabies: No risk; Portugal is currently rabies free.

Other illnesses: Amebiasis and giardiasis (endemic), schistosomiasis (may occur in the Algarve Province in the extreme south), ehrlichiosis, echinococcosis, fascioliasis (infection rates of 2% to 7% reported from northern rural communities), leptospirosis, tick-borne relapsing fever, and typhoid fever.

MADEIRA (PORTUGAL)

GMT... 0 hrs

Entry Requirements
- Passport/Visa: A valid passport is required.
- AIDS Test: Not required.
- Vaccinations: A yellow fever vaccination certificate is required from all travelers older than 1 year arriving from infected areas.

Telephone Country Code: 351

Health Advisory

Travelers' diarrhea: Medium risk; giardiasis has been reported. Travelers should drink only bottled, boiled, or treated water and avoid undercooked food.

Hepatitis: Immune globulin prophylaxis is recommended.

RUSSIA

HEALTH ADVISORY ALSO INCLUDES: ARMENIA, AZERBAIJAN, THE BALTIC STATES, BELARUS, UKRAINE, GEORGIA, AND MOLDOVA

Embassy: 202-939-8916   *Moscow*   *GMT +3 hrs*

Entry Requirements

- Passport/Visa: A valid passport, visa, and exit permit required. Strict customs regulations may apply. For updated information for travel to Russia and the CIS, travelers should contact the Russian Embassy in Washington.
- AIDS Test: HIV testing is required for foreigners staying more than 3 months. U.S. test results acceptable.
- Vaccinations: None required.

Telephone Country Code: 7   **AT&T:** 155-5042   **MCI:** 8-10-800-497-7222

Electricity/Plugs: AC 50 Hz, 220 volts; plug types C and I.

American Express: 21-A Sadovo-Kudrinskaya Street, Moscow; Tel. (95) 254-4495.

Embassies/Consulates: U.S. Embassy, Moscow. Ulitsa Chaykovskogo 19/21/23; Tel. (95) 413-160 or 252-2451-59. Canadian Embassy. 23 Starokonyushenny Pereulok; Tel. (95) 413-401.

Hospitals/Doctors: Ambulance services: dial 03 countrywide. Kremlin Hospital, Moscow; all specialties; reportedly among the best in Russia.

Columbia-Presbyterian/Moscow Clinic. This is a joint venture between Columbia-Presbyterian Medical Center in New York City and Pepsico. The ambulatory care facility is located in the Medincentre Polyclinic (4th Dobryninsky Lane 4; Tel. [095] 974-2332) and is staffed by board-certified American physicians. Patients needing immediate hospital care are sent to an in-patient unit at the Central Clinical Hospital in Moscow or, if necessary, flown by air ambulance to London or New York. For membership information, travelers should contact Columbia-Presbyterian/Moscow's New York office at 212-305-5327. Resident memberships and 30-day travel memberships are available.

American Medical Center (Moscow and St. Petersburg). American-owned, western-quality health care clinics offer family practice and 24-hour emergency care. They primarily serve tourists, student groups, and corporate executives. In Moscow, Tel. (095) 259-7181/256-8378; in St. Petersburg, Tel. (812) 310-9611/371-7244. Membership plan is available. Travelers in the United States should call 203-327-0900 for information.

Travelers not receiving care at one of the above clinics should contact the U.S. Embassy in case of serious illness. Health care in Russia and the CIS is generally seriously deficient. All travelers should consider purchasing a travel insurance policy with telephone assistance and medical evacuation capabilities. Chapter 14 lists companies that offer assistance policies.

Health Advisory

Malaria: Risk is present in rural areas bordering Afghanistan, Turkey, and Iran, where vivax malaria predominates. Chloroquine prophylaxis is advised in risk areas. Drug-resistant falciparum malaria is not currently reported but travelers to risk areas should also consider carrying a treatment dose of Fansidar to take in the event of a possible malaria attack.

Travelers' diarrhea: High risk outside of first-class hotels. All water supplies in Russia are suspect, including municipal tap water, which may be untreated and grossly contaminated. Travelers should consume only bottled, boiled, or chemically treated water. Travelers should observe strict food and drink safety precautions. A quinolone antibiotic is recommended for the treatment of acute diarrhea. Diarrhea not responding to treatment with an antibiotic may be due to a parasitic disease, especially giardiasis, and treatment with metronidazole (Flagyl) or tinidazole (Fasigyn) should be considered. Amebiasis also occurs, but is common only in southern regions. Cryptosporidiosis has been reported from St. Petersburg (formerly Leningrad) and Moscow.

Cholera: At least 14 cases of cholera have been diagnosed in Moscow among visitors and new arrivals. Travelers are advised to avoid street vendor food, especially melons brought in from southern regions. Cholera outbreak has been reported in Dagestan, a republic within the Russian Federation and Moldava.

Hepatitis: All susceptible travelers should receive immune globulin or hepatitis A vaccine. The hepatitis B carrier rate in the general population of Russia is estimated at 8%. Vaccination against hepatitis B is recommended for all healthcare workers and should be considered by anyone planning an extended visit to this region. Hepatitis E accounts for up to 18% of hepatitis in the Volga Delta region, but less than 1% regionwide. Blood supplies may be contaminated with hepatitis B and C viruses.

Diphtheria: Over 700 cases of diphtheria and 24 deaths were reported in Moscow during 1992. Epidemic diphtheria is also reported from St. Petersburg and Kiev (Ukraine). All travelers to Russia and the CIS, including adults, should be fully immunized against this disease. Diphtheria vaccine is routinely administered in combination with tetanus toxoid vaccine.

Lyme disease: Occurs focally in rural forested areas from the Baltic region eastward, and north to 65 degrees north latitude. Up to 35% of ticks (*I. persulcatus*) tested in Estonia were infected with borrelia spirochetes. Vector ticks (*Ixodes ricinus* and *I. persulcatus*) are most abundant and active from May through August.

Tick-borne encephalitis (TBE): Tick-borne encephalitis is transmitted from the Baltics to the Crimea by Ixodes ticks (*Ixodes ricinus, Ixodes persulcatus*). Peak transmission period is April through June. Risk is present primarily in rural brushy and forested areas below 1,500 meters elevation—especially in suburban "forests" bordering large cities. TBE is usually known as "Central European tick-borne encephalitis" west of the Urals. Increased incidence reported in the Perm-Sverlovsk areas (central Urals) in the 1980s. Surveys in Latvia show 14%–27% of those tested were seropositive for TBE. Travelers to rural areas should take measures to prevent tick bites.

Crimean-Congo hemorrhagic fever: Also known as Central Asian hemorrhagic fever. Tickborne (*Hyalomma asiaticum, H. marginatum*). Reported mostly from southern areas, but outbreaks have occurred in some areas of Rostov Oblast (near the sea of Azov), April through November. Risk areas are rural steppe, savannah, semi-desert, and foothill/low mountain habitats below 2,000 meters elevation.

Arboviral diseases: Karelian fever (mosquito-borne; most cases occur July–September in the Karelian region); Tahjna virus fever (mosquito-borne; occurs sporadically from the Baltic region north to the Kolsky Peninsula); sandfly fever (sandfly-borne; limited to Moldova and the Crimea); dengue fever (mosquito-borne; cases previously reported from extreme southern regions); West Nile fever (mosquito-borne; virus reportedly circulates in the Volga Delta region from May–September); Sindbis virus fever (detected in the Volga Delta, July–August).

Leishmaniasis: Risk for cutaneous leishmaniasis primarily limited to southern regions, including portions of Georgia Republic and the southern Ukraine, below 1,300 meters elevation. Visceral leishmaniasis is confined to areas of the Transcaucasus. Travelers to these regions should take measures to prevent sandfly bites.

Other illnesses/hazards: Anthrax (sporadic human cases occur, related to exposure to livestock in rural areas, especially southern areas), boutonneuse fever (tick-borne; reported most commonly along the shores of the Black and Caspian Seas), brucellosis, echinococcosis (sheep and reindeer are hosts; dog feces are infective), legionellosis, leptospirosis (a particular problem in fish-breeding areas of Rostov Province; extensive outbreaks have occurred in east central areas), plague (flea-borne; usually occurs as isolated cases or small outbreaks in semi-arid areas of the southern republics of Azerbaijan, Armenia, and Georgia), rabies, rickettsialpox, tick-borne relapsing fever (may occur south of 55 degrees north latitude), trichinosis (greatest risk in western Belarus and the Ukraine), typhoid fever, tularemia ("rabbit fever"; risk may be elevated in the north), tuberculosis, and helminthic infections (roundworm, hookworm, and whipworm infections and strongyloidiasis) reported, especially from the Transcaucasus, especially Azerbaijan.

THE CAUCASUS, CENTRAL ASIA, SIBERIA, & FAR EAST REGIONS OF FORMER USSR

Health Advisory

Malaria: A few limited foci of vivax malaria reportedly exist in Kazakh, Tadzik, and Uzbek Republics. Chloroquine prophylaxis is advised in risk areas. Drug-resistant falciparum malaria is not currently reported.

Travelers' diarrhea: All water supplies are suspect, including municipal tap water, which may be untreated and grossly contaminated.

Hepatitis: All susceptible travelers should receive immune globulin or hepatitis A vaccine prior to visiting these regions. The hepatitis B carrier rate in the general population of these republics is estimated as high as 8%.

Lyme disease: Occurs focally in rural forested areas below 1,500 meters elevation.

Tick-borne encephalitis (TBE): Peak transmission period is April through June. Risk is present primarily in rural brushy and forested areas below 1,500 meters elevation. TBE is usually known as "Central European tick-borne encephalitis" or "Russian Spring-Summer encephalitis" west of the Urals.

Leishmaniasis: Risk for cutaneous leishmaniasis primarily limited to the Uzbek, Kazakh, and Turkmen Republics. Travelers to these regions should take measures to prevent sandfly bites.

Crimean-Congo hemorrhagic fever: Also known as Central Asian hemorrhagic fever. Risk areas are rural steppe, savannah, semi-desert, and foothill/low mountain habitats below 2,000 meters elevation. Outbreaks occurred in southcentral Kazakh Republic during 1989.

Arboviral diseases: Tahjna virus fever (mosquito-borne; virus circulates through much of the former USSR), sandfly fever (sandfly-borne; limited to regions of southern central Asia, April–October), dengue fever (mosquito-borne; no recent cases reported), West Nile fever (mosquito-borne; cases have occurred in the Tadzik Republic), North Asian tick fever (occurs wherever tick vectors are found).

Other illnesses/hazards: Boutonneuse fever (tick-borne; reported most commonly along the shores of the Black and Caspian Seas), brucellosis, echinococcosis (dog feces are infective), legionellosis, leptospirosis, rabies, rickettsialpox, tick-borne relapsing fever (reported from Kirghiz, Turkmen, and Uzbek Republics), trichinosis, typhoid fever, tularemia, tuberculosis, and soil-transmitted and helminthic infections (roundworm, hookworm, and whipworm infections and strongyloidiasis).

ROMANIA

Embassy: 202-232-4747   **Bucharest**   **GMT +2 hrs**

Entry Requirements

- Passport/Visa: Passport and visa required. Visa or tourist card obtained at border or from embassy before arrival. Travelers should call the Romanian Embassy for further information.
- AIDS Test: Not required.
- Vaccinations: None required.

Telephone Country Code: 40   **AT&T:** 01-800-4288   **MCI:** 01-800-1800

American Express: National Tourist Office, Carpati Boulevard Magheru NR. 7 Bucharest; Tel. (0) 145-16.

Embassies/Consulates: U.S. Embassy, Bucharest. Strada Tudor Arghezi 7-9; Tel. (0) 104-040. Canadian Embassy, Bucharest. 36 Nicolae Iorga; Tel. (0)506-580.

Hospitals/Doctors: Cantacuzina Hospital, Bucharest (1,200 beds); most specialties. Travelers should contact the U.S. Embassy for physician referrals.

Health Advisory

Travelers' diarrhea: High risk outside of first-class hotels and resorts. Water in the larger cities, but not rural areas, is generally potable. Travelers are advised to drink only bottled, boiled, filtered, or treated water and consume only well-cooked food. All fruit should be peeled prior to consumption. A quinolone antibiotic is recommended for the treatment of acute diarrhea. Diarrhea not responding to antibiotic treatment may be due to a parasitic disease such as giardiasis or amebiasis—or an intestinal virus.

Cholera: Sporadic cases are reported, especially from Tulcea, Braila, and Constanta counties and along the Danube River. Infections associated with the consumption of raw seafood have been reported along the Black Sea coast.

Hepatitis: All susceptible travelers should receive immune globulin or hepatitis A vaccine. The hepatitis B carrier rate in the general population is estimated at up to 9%—the highest in Europe. Vaccination against hepatitis B is recommended for all healthcare workers and should be considered by anyone planning an extended visit to this country. There is also increased risk of transmission of hepatitis B transmission from medical injections that are administered with unclean needles and syringes. Due to the possibility of contamination, blood transfusions should be avoided except in the most extreme emergency situation.

Tick-borne diseases: Lyme disease, tick-borne encephalitis, and boutonneuse fever are reported. The ticks that transmit these diseases (*Ixodes ricinus*) are found in brushy, wooded areas throughout the country. There is higher risk of tick-borne encephalitis in the Tulcea District and in Transylvania at the base of the Carpathian Mountains and Transylvanian Alps. Boutonneuse fever is endemic along the Black Sea coast.

AIDS: High incidence reported, especially in children and newborns—more cases, in fact, than have been reported cumulatively in all other European countries. Most cases occur in the Bucharest and Constanta areas. There is risk of transmission of HIV from unclean needles and syringes, as well as from contaminated blood transfusions. All travelers are cautioned against receiving unnecessary medical or dental injections and blood transfusions and travelers are advised to carry their own sterile needles and syringes in case a medical injection is necessary.

Other illnesses: Anthrax, brucellosis (enzootic at low levels, particularly in sheep, goats, and cattle; human cases usually due to consumption of unpasteurized milk or milk products), echinococcosis (stray dogs in urban and rural areas commonly infected; human cases reported sporadically), hemorrhagic fever with renal syndrome (similar to hantavirus syndrome; disease transmitted by rodent excreta), leptospirosis, rabies (enzootic in foxes, wolves, and wild canids; rare in humans), trichinosis (from raw or undercooked pork), tuberculosis (highest reported incidence in Europe), typhoid fever, typhus (murine and louse-borne), and helminthic infections (roundworm, hookworm, and whipworm infections, and strongyloidiasis).

SPAIN

Madrid ... GMT 0 hrs

Entry Requirements

- Passport/Visa: A valid passport is required.
- AIDS Test: Not required.
- Vaccinations: None required.

Telephone Country Code: 34   **AT&T:** 900-99-00-11   **MCI:** 900-99-0014

Electricity/Plugs: AC 50 Hz, 220 volts; plug types C and E.

American Express: American Express Travel Service, Plaza De Las Cortes 2, Madrid. Tel. (1) 429-5775.

Embassies/Consulates: U.S. Embassy, Madrid. Serrano 75. Tel. (1) 276-3400/-3600. Canadian Embassy, Madrid. Edificio Goya. Calle Nunez de Balboa 35. Tel. (1) 431-4300.

Hospitals/Doctors: Ciudad Sanitaria de la Paz, Madrid (2,346 beds); all specialties; Tel: (1)734-2600. Clinica Cuzco; Tel: 458-6143/234-5811. Unidad Medica Anglo-Americana; Tel: 431-2229/435-1595. Luis Fuentes, M.D., Madrid; Tel: 259-6262. Hospital Clinico y Provincal, Barcelona (1,001 beds); all specialties, including cardiology; Tel. (3) 451-5468/323-1414. Mary McCarthy, M.D., Barcelona; Tel. (3) 200-2924.

Health Advisory

Travelers' diarrhea: Medium risk. Urban water supplies are considered potable, but travelers are advised to consume only bottled, boiled, or treated water. Giardiasis, amebiasis, and cryptosporidiosis are endemic.

Hepatitis: Immune globulin or the hepatitis A vaccine is recommended prior to travel to this country. The hepatitis B carrier rate in the general population varies from approximately 1% in the northwest to more than 3% in the southeast Mediterranean areas. Vaccination against hepatitis B is not routinely recommended for travel to Spain.

Typhoid fever: Higher risk than in other major European countries. Risk may be elevated during summer months. Vaccination is recommended for visits exceeding 4 weeks, or for extensive travel in rural areas.

Lyme disease: First reported in Spain in 1986. About 500 cases/year are known. Travelers should take precautions against ticks in brushy, wooded areas throughout Spain.

Pneumococcal disease: Strains of penicillin-resistant *Streptococcus pneumoniae* bacteria are common in Spain. Resistance to chloramphenicol, TMP/SMX, and erythromycin also occurs. Pneumococcal polysaccharide vaccine is recommended for travelers with risk factors for serious pneumococcal infection. These risk factors include splenectomy, chronic heart and lung disease, diabetes, chronic renal failure, and immunosuppressive therapy. Travelers over age 65 should also be vaccinated.

Mediterranean spotted fever (Boutonneuse fever): Risk areas include the southern Mediterranean coast, central Spain (Salamanca, Madrid, and Toledo), and the Balearic Islands (Majorca, Menorca, and Ibiza). Ninety-five percent of cases result from contact with tick-carrying dogs.

Typhus: A fatal case of flea-borne typhus (also called endemic typhus or murine typhus; illness is caused by *Rickettsia typhi* organisms) reported in 1994 in a British tourist visiting the Costa del Sol. Infection with *Rickettsia typhi* is widespread in southern Europe but most cases are mild or subclinical. Typhus is controlled through elimination of rats near human habitation. Rats harbor the fleas that transmit the disease.

Leishmaniasis: Risk of cutaneous and visceral leishmaniasis occurs in rural areas of central Spain, the south (Andalucia), the east (Catalonia and Valencia), and the Balearic Islands. Travelers should take measures to prevent sandfly bites. Sand flies bite predominantly between dusk and dawn.

Rabies: Spain is currently rabies free.

Other diseases: Brucellosis, echinococcosis, legionellosis (outbreaks, often associated with resort hotels; reported in Granada and Majorca), trichinosis, tick-borne relapsing fever, tuberculosis, and intestinal helminth infections are reported.

SWITZERLAND

Bern ... GMT +1 hr

Entry Requirements

- Passport/Visa: A valid passport is required.
- AIDS Test: Not required.
- Vaccinations: None required.

Telephone Country Code: 41   **AT&T:** 155-00-11   **MCI:** 155-02-22

Electricity/Plugs: AC 50 Hz, 220 volts; plug types C and F. Adaptors and transformer necessary for U.S.-made appliances.

American Express: American Express Travel Service, Bubenbergplatz 11, Bern; Tel. (31) 229-401.

Embassies/Consulates: U.S. Embassy: Jubilaeumstrasse 93, Bern. Tel. (31) 437-255. U.S. Consulate, Geneva: 1–3 Ave. de la Paix. Tel. (22) 335-537. Canadian Embassy: 88 Kirchenfeldstrasse, Bern; Tel. (22) 44-63-81.

Hospitals/Doctors: University Hospital, Zurich (1,200 beds); all specialties; Tel: (1) 257-1111. Dr. B. Guertler, Zurich; Tel: (1) 281-0366. Canonal University Hospital, Geneva (1,800 beds); general medical/surgical; all specialties; Tel: (22) 469-211.

Health Advisory

Travelers' diarrhea: Low risk. More than 90% of the population is served by piped water. Tap water is considered safe in both urban and rural areas, but streams, lakes, and other sources of raw water may be contaminated. Bottled water is recommended in the Lugano/Locarno regions. Giardiasis and cryptosporidiosis have been reported from this country but the risk to the traveler is considered low. Salmonellosis (*S. typhimurium* or *S. enteritidis*) is the most common cause of acute diarrheal disease. Campylobacteriosis is the second most common cause of acute diarrheal disease. Shigellosis is less common, but is reported.

Lyme disease: The incidence of Lyme disease in Switzerland is among the highest in Europe, but the risk to the average traveler is low. Risk occurs primarily in wooded, forested areas below 1,500 meters elevation on the northern Swiss plateau. Approximately 20%–35% of the *Ixodes ricinus* ticks in this region are infected. Ticks are most active May–October. Travelers to rural areas should take precautions against tick bites while in endemic areas. A vaccine against Lyme disease is not available.

Tick-borne encephalitis (TBE): This viral illness is transmitted by the same tick (*Ixodes ricinus*) that transmits Lyme disease. Transmission occurs May–October, with the highest risk June–August. Ticks are found primarily in brushy and/or wooded areas of central and northern Switzerland. Most reported cases of TBE (40–50/year) occur in the vicinity of Zurich (especially to the north, in Schaffhausen) and Bern (Thun and Biel), and on the northern Swiss plateau. Prevention: Travelers to rural areas should take precautions against tick bites. A vaccine against TBE is available and is recommended for persons after prolonged exposure. Such persons include foresters and agricultural workers, as well as some hikers and campers.

Hepatitis A: Low risk. Immune globulin prophylaxis is not routinely recommended for travel to Switzerland.

Hepatitis B: The carrier rate of the hepatitis B virus in the general population is less than 1%. Vaccination against hepatitis B is not routinely recommended for travel to this country.

Rabies: No recent human cases have been reported. Rabies occurs primarily in the fox population in the northwest of this country, but the incidence is declining. Any traveler bitten by an animal should seek immediate medical care.

Acute mountain sickness (AMS): Travelers ascending rapidly to alpine elevations over 8,000 feet are subject to altitude sickness. Diamox (acetazolamide) may be useful for prevention or treatment, especially for persons who will be climbing and sleeping at high altitudes. Descent to a lower altitude is imperative if symptoms of AMS are severe.

Other illnesses: Brucellosis, listeriosis (may be transmitted by contaminated soft cheeses), leptospirosis, echinococcosis (risk may occur in the northwest), AIDS (highest rate in Europe), and legionellosis (sporadic cases).

SWEDEN
Stockholm ... GMT 0 hrs

Entry Requirements
- Passport/Visa: A valid passport is required.
- AIDS Test: Not required.
- Vaccinations: None required.

Telephone Country Code: 46   **AT&T:** 020-795-611   **MCI:** 020-795-922

American Express: American Express. Birger Jarlsgatan 1, Stockholm; Tel. (8) 240-200.

Embassies/Consulates: U.S. Embassy, Stockholm. Strandvagen 101; Tel. (8) 783-5300. Canadian High Commission, Stockholm. Tegelbacken 4, 7th Floor; Tel. (8) 237-920.

Hospitals/Doctors: Karolinska Hospital, Stockholm (1,654 beds); all specialties; Tel: (8) 729-2000. Sahlgrenska Hospital, Goteborg (1,979 beds); all specialties, Tel: (31) 60-1000.

Health Advisory

Travelers' diarrhea: Low risk. Piped water is potable. A quinolone antibiotic is recommended for the treatment of acute diarrhea. Diarrhea not responding to antibiotic treatment may be due to a parasitic disease such as amebiasis or giardiasis.

Hepatitis: Low risk. Nonimmune travelers, however, should consider immune globulin or hepatitis A vaccination. The hepatitis B carrier rate in the general population is less than 1%. Hepatitis B vaccination is not routinely recommended for travel to this country.

Lyme disease: Risk is present, especially in the forests of the southern coastal areas below 1,500 meters elevation. Travelers to rural areas during April-November should take measures to prevent tick bites.

Tick-borne encephalitis: Risk is present from the forested areas around Uppsala down to Kristianstad, including the islands of Gotland and Oland, and in the wooded areas around Goteborg.

Other illnesses: Hemorrhagic fever with renal syndrome (human cases usually in young adults exposed to dried or aerosolized rodent excreta), Karelian fever (mosquito-transmitted; endemic in rural areas of southern and coastal provinces), leptospirosis, and tularemia.

UNITED KINGDOM
London ... GMT 0 hrs

Entry Requirements
- Passport/Visa: A valid passport is required. Visa not required for U.S. citizens.
- AIDS Test: Not required.
- Vaccinations: None required.

Telephone Country Code: 44

American Express: American Express Travel Service. 6 Haymarket, London, SW1; Tel. (071) 930-4411.

Embassies/Consulates: U.S. Embassy, London. 24/31 Grosvenor Square, W1; Tel. (071)-499-9000. Canadian High Commission. Canada House, Trafalgar Square; Tel. (071) 629-9492.

Health Advisory

Travelers' diarrhea: Low risk. Piped water is potable. A quinolone antibiotic (Floxin or Cipro) is recommended for the treatment of acute diarrhea. Diarrhea not responding to antibiotic treatment may be due to a parasitic disease such as giardiasis—or an intestinal virus.

Hepatitis: Low risk. Nonimmune travelers, however, should consider immune globulin or hepatitis A vaccination. The hepatitis B carrier rate in the general population is less than 1%. Hepatitis B vaccination is not routinely recommended for travel to this country.

Traffic alert: Travelers should look to their right when crossing streets; traffic is left-sided and four to five pedestrian fatalities occur annually when tourists are struck by cars.

Lyme disease: Outbreaks have been reported in heavily forested rural areas and in parts of Scotland. Recently, the tick that transmits Lyme disease has been found in parks within the city of London.

Physicians and Hospitals in the Greater London Area

How the system works—There are significant differences between the American and British systems of health care delivery. For openers, drugstores are called "chemists" and a hospital emergency room is referred to as the "casualty department" or "casualty ward." Under the British National Health Care (NHS) system all medical care (except emergencies) is channeled through the general practitioner (GP), who is a specialist in family medicine. There are no pediatricians or internists. (These services are provided by general practitioners.) A GP's office hours are called "surgery hours." Under the NHS you cannot go directly to a specialist; you must be referred to one by a general practitioner. This may cause some resentment if the GP feels he or she is being contacted merely to pass your case along; therefore, if you do need a specialist, you may find it easier to contact one of the hospitals/clinics that have large staffs of private consultants/specialists. Two internationally known private hospitals are **The London Clinic** (071-935-444) and **The Harley St. Clinic**. A newer, very deluxe private hospital is the **Wellington Hospital** (071-722-7733).

Emergency care under the NHS is rendered free, but you should expect to pay for the treatment of any chronic, pre-existing condition. The interpretation of what constitutes free care, however, is left to the attending physician.

If you will be residing in Great Britain longer than 3 months, you can enroll in the NHS and qualify for free care. To contact a general practitioner, either for a referral or for treatment, refer to the list below. Hotels also maintain doctor on-call lists, as does the American Embassy and the Canadian High Commission.

General Practitioners/Clinics

Medical Express—117A Harley Street; Tel: (071) 499-1991. This is a private clinic, open Monday–Friday from 9:00am to 7:00pm, and 9:30am-2:00pm on Saturday. Initial consultation fee is £60.

Doctor's Call—Tel: (071) 351-5312. They will make house calls/hotels visits.

Dr. D.R. Rossdale—37 Montague Square; Tel: (071) 262-8229 (office)/624-0328 (H).

Dr. Michael S. Turner—The City Medical Center, 4th floor, St. Helen's Place; Tel: (071) 588-6503/638-4400. Appointments 9:00am–5:00pm only.

Drs. Peter Wheeler, John Hunt, MG Bushnell—82 Sloane Street; Tel: (071) 245-9333.

Dr. M. James Carne—7 Wood Lane, Highgate; Tel: (081) 883-3366.

Drs. Christine Ford and Owen Franklin—97 Brondesbury Road; Tel: (071) 328-0808.

Obstetricians/Gynecologists

Dr. Ruth E A Coles, FRCOG—28 Weymouth Street; Tel: (071) 580-1723.

Dr. Philip A F Chalk—90 Harley Street; Tel: (071) 486-2445.

Dr. Christopher H Naylor—116 Harley Street; Tel: (071) 935-6911/5411.

Dental Emergencies

Emergency Dental Service—Tel. (071) 499-0133.

Travel Medicine/Tropical Medicine

Travelers who suspect they have acquired a tropical disease such as malaria, or who require vaccinations or specialized travel medicines, should have a consultation with a travel medicine expert. Contact the Hospital for Tropical Disease Travelers' Clinic located at 180-182 Tottenham Court Road (1st floor, Queen's House); Tel: (071) 637-7793.

Hospital Casualty (Emergency) Departments

If you have an emergency medical problem, go directly to a hospital casualty department without waiting for a physician referral. In Great Britain, you can always locate the nearest teaching hospital with a 24-hour casualty department by dialing 999, the nationwide emergency telephone number.

North London: Royal Free Hospital—Pond Street; Tel: (071) 794-0500.

Central London: St. Thomas' Hospital—Lambeth Palace Road; Tel: (071) 928-9292.
University College Hospital—Gower Street; Tel: (071) 387-9300.
London Hospital—Whitechapel Road; Tel: (071) 377-7000.

East London: St. Bartholomew's Hospital—West Smithfield; Tel: (071) 601-8888.

West London: Charing Cross Hospital—Fulham Palace Road; Tel: (071) 745-2040.

South London: Guy's Hospital—St. Thomas Street; Tel: (071) 407-7600/955-5000.
King's College Hospital—Denmark Hill; Tel: (071) 274-6222.

YUGOSLAVIA, INCLUDING SLOVENIA AND CROATIA

Belgrade ... GMT +1 hr

Entry Requirements

- Passport/Visa: A valid passport and visa are required. Travelers should contact the Yugoslavian Embassy in Washington (202-462-3884) for details.
- AIDS Test: Not required.
- Vaccinations: None required.

Telephone Country Code: 38

American Express: Atlas Travel Agency. Zmaj Jovina 10, Belgrade; Tel. (11) 183-062.

Embassies/Consulates: U.S. Embassy, Belgrade. Kneza Milosa 50; Tel. (11) 645-655.

Hospitals/Doctors: Univerzitetski Klinicki Centar, Belgrade; Tel: 444-2222. University Hospital, Belgrade; ICU has latest equipment. Teaching Hospital, Zagreb; Tel. 276-693. Contact the U.S. Embassy for additional referrals and telephone numbers.

Health Advisory

Malaria: No risk. Yugoslavia was declared malaria free in 1974.

Travelers' diarrhea: High risk. Drinking water in Belgrade is considered safe, but water elsewhere should be considered contaminated, especially in smaller urban areas, and rural areas. A quinolone antibiotic is recommended for the treatment of acute diarrhea. Diarrhea not responding to treatment with an antibiotic, or chronic diarrhea, may be due to a parasitic disease such as giardiasis, amebiasis, or cryptosporidiosis.

Hepatitis: Immune globulin or hepatitis A vaccine is recommended for all susceptible travelers. The hepatitis B carrier rate in the general population is estimated at up to 4%. Vaccination against hepatitis B is recommended for healthcare and relief workers and should be considered by long-term visitors to this country.

Tick-borne diseases: Tick-borne viral encephalitis (TBE) occurs primarily in two forested areas: (1) In northern areas between the Sava and Drava Rivers (especially in Slovenia, in the Ljubljana area, and in northwest Croatia, north of Zagreb; and (2) in smaller pockets along the Adriatic coast, near Split and north of Dubrovnik. The tick vector that transmits TBE (*Ixodes ricinus*) also transmits Lyme disease. Ticks are abundant from March to September, with peak activity occurring in April and May. All travelers should take measures to prevent tick bites in these areas.

Leishmaniasis: Both cutaneous and visceral leishmaniasis are reported, but risk is low. Transmission of leishmaniasis occurs primarily May through October with the highest prevalence of cutaneous leishmaniasis on the islands and along the Dalmatian coast. Visceral leishmaniasis occurs more focally, especially in southeastern Serbia and also along the Dalmation coast. Travelers to these areas should take measures to prevent sandfly bites.

Sandfly fever: Risk period is primarily May through October along the Adriatic coast from Istria to Dubrovnik and from Mali Losinj to Korcula on the islands. Travelers to these areas should avoid sandfly bites. West Nile, Sindbis, and Tahnya virus fevers (mosquito-borne; reported in the border regions of Slovenia and Serbia).

Hemorrhagic fever with renal syndrome (HFRS): During the last seven years, more than 35 severe cases of HFRS have been identified in Slovenia. Transmission of the virus results from inhalation or contact with virus excreted or secreted in rodent urine, saliva, or feces. Exposure to virus can occur, e.g., when cleaning out a rodent-infested dwelling.

Rabies: Animal rabies occurs mostly in foxes, sporadically in dogs and cats; human cases occur, but are rare.

Other illnesses: Boutonneuse fever (infrequently reported), brucellosis (usually transmitted by raw goat/sheep milk), Crimean-Congo hemorrhagic fever (occurs especially in areas where ticks are found), echinococcosis (carried by stray dogs; reported sporadically, especially in southwestern areas—Montenegro, Dalmatia, Serbia), leptospirosis, relapsing fever (tick-borne), trichinosis, tuberculosis, tularemia (human cases are uncommon), typhoid fever (consider vaccination), typhus (louse-borne), and soil-transmitted helminthic infections (roundworm, hookworm, and whipworm) are common in rural areas.

DISEASE RISK SUMMARY
North Africa

Yellow fever: There is no risk of yellow fever in North Africa.

Malaria: This disease is not a major public health problem in North Africa. Malarious areas are found only in parts of Algeria and Egypt. *P. vivax* is the dominant species, but *P. falciparum* and *P. malariae* are also reported. There are no reports to date of chloroquine-resistant falciparum malaria. Chloroquine prophylaxis is recommended when traveling to malarious areas. All travelers to malarious areas should take personal protection measures against mosquito bites.

Travelers' diarrhea: High risk outside of resort areas and first-class hotels. Piped water supplies in this region are frequently untreated and may be grossly contaminated. Travelers should observe all food and drink safety precautions. A quinolone antibiotic (Cipro or Floxin) is recommended for the treatment of acute diarrhea. Diarrhea not responding to treatment with an antibiotic, or chronic diarrhea, may be due to a parasitic disease such as giardiasis or amebiasis—or an intestinal virus. Treatment with metronidazole (Flagyl) or tinidazole (Fasigyn) should be considered in cases of suspected parasitic disease.

Hepatitis: All susceptible travelers to North Africa should receive immune globulin or hepatitis A vaccine. The hepatitis B carrier rate in the general population of these countries is estimated at 4%–10%. Vaccination against hepatitis B is advised for healthcare workers and should be considered by all long-term travelers to this region.

Typhoid fever: Vaccination is recommended for extended travel outside the usual tourist routes of these countries.

Arboviral fevers: Few if any cases of dengue are reported from North Africa. Sandfly fever is widely distributed, especially in Egypt, Libya, and Tunisia. Rift Valley fever and West Nile fever are significant risks in Egypt. Crimean-Congo hemorrhagic fever and chikungunya fever: insufficient data are available to indicate whether or not these arboviral fevers have significant transmission in this region.

Mediterranean spotted fever (boutonneuse fever): Scattered cases are reported. Travelers are advised to avoid touching or petting dogs, which harbor dog ticks that transmit most cases of Mediterranean spotted fever.

Leishmaniasis: Both cutaneous and visceral leishmaniasis (kala azar) occur in North Africa. Most cases are reported from the central and/or northern areas of Morocco, Algeria, Libya, and Tunisia. In Egypt, risk areas include the eastern Nile Delta, the Suez Canal zone, and northern Sinai. Travelers to these areas should take measures to prevent insect (sandfly) bites.

Filariasis: Occurs focally in the Nile Delta. Travelers to this region should take measures to prevent mosquito bites.

Schistosomiasis: High risk occurs along the entire Nile River and in the Nile Delta region. Risk is present focally in Algeria (low risk), Libya, Tunisia, Morocco, and Western Sahara. Travelers to these countries should avoid swimming or wading in freshwater lakes, ponds, streams, or irrigation ditches.

Rabies: Animal rabies occurs in all countries. Human cases are also reported, usually from urban areas. Travelers should especially avoid contact with stray dogs and seek immediate treatment for any animal bite. Pre-exposure vaccination against rabies (3 doses) should be considered by anyone planning long-term travel to this region.

AIDS: There is a low prevalence of AIDS in North Africa.

Other illnesses: Brucellosis (usually transmitted by raw goat or sheep milk), echinococcosis (a major health problem in central Tunisia, and occurs elsewhere), meningitis (significant outbreaks have occurred in Egypt, involving Group A and C meningococci; vaccination is recommended for travelers who will have close contact with the indigenous population), relapsing fever (louse-borne and tick-borne; reported in northern Sahara and coastal areas), tuberculosis (common), helminthic infections (roundworm, hookworm, and whipworm) are common in rural areas; incidence is estimated at 5%.

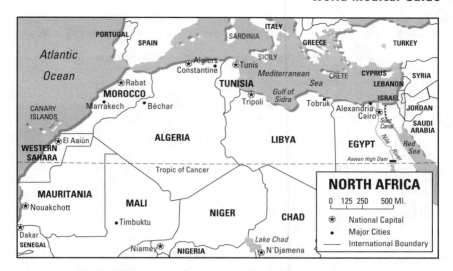

ALGERIA

Algiers ... GMT 0 hrs

Entry Requirements

- Passport/Visa: Valid passport and visa are required.
- AIDS Test: Not required.
- Vaccinations: A yellow fever vaccination certificate is required from all travelers older than 1 year arriving from infected areas.

Telephone Country Code: 213

Electricity/Plugs: AC 50 Hz, 127/220 volts; plug types C and F.

Embassies/Consulates: U.S. Embassy, Algiers. 4 Chemin Cheich Bachir Brahimi; Tel. (2) 601-425/-255/-186. U.S. Consulate, Oran; Tel: (6) 334-509. Canadian High Commission, Hydra. 27 Bis Rue Ali Massoudi; Tel. 606-611.

Hospitals/Doctors: University Hospital, Algiers (2,900 beds); all specialties. Institute Pasteur d'Algerie; Tel: 65-88-60. University Hospital, Oran (2,200 beds); general medical/surgical facility; all specialties.

Health Advisory

Malaria: Conflicting information indicates that a low malaria risk occurs primarily from November to March in the vicinities of Adrar and Ouargla, and from March to September/October in the vicinities of Tamanrasset and Djanet. Risk is limited primarily to the Sahara region, including Ouargla and other oases. *P. vivax* accounts for over 90% of cases. Less than 1% of cases are due to *P. falciparum*. Chloroquine prophylaxis is recommended in rural risk areas.

Travelers' diarrhea: High risk outside of first-class hotels and resorts. All water sources in Algeria should be considered potentially contaminated. An outbreak of cholera was reported in 1989 in Bouria Province, southeast of Algiers. Travelers should drink only bottled, boiled, or treated water. A quinolone antibiotic is recommended for the treatment of acute diarrhea. Diarrhea not responding to antibiotic treatment may be due to a parasitic disease such as giardiasis, amebiasis, or cryptosporidiosis—or an intestinal virus. Surveys indicate that 26% of the population harbor intestinal parasites.

Hepatitis: All susceptible travelers should receive immune globulin or hepatitis A vaccine prior to visiting this country. The hepatitis B carrier rate in the general population is estimated at 5%. Vaccination against hepatitis B is recommended for all healthcare workers and should be considered by anyone planning an extended visit to this country. Hepatitis E outbreaks have been reported. To prevent this type of hepatitis, travelers should drink only boiled, bottled, or treated water.

Mediterranean spotted fever (boutonneuse fever, African tick typhus): Occurs primarily in suburban coastal areas. Ninety percent of cases are transmitted by dog ticks. Travelers should avoid close contact with dogs.

Schistosomiasis: Risk is present year-round. Urinary schistosomiasis occurs in the north, primarily at Khemis El Khechna and El Harrach near Algiers. The disease has also been reported from Biskra and the Jdiouia Valley located east of Oran. Foci in the Sahara occur at Djanet and Iherir in the southeast, and from Aguedal-Anefid, south of Bechar. Travelers should avoid swimming or wading in freshwater lakes, ponds, or streams in these areas.

Leishmaniasis: Transmission occurs primarily from April to October, with peak sandfly densities occurring during late spring (April and May) and autumn (August and September). Cutaneous leishmaniasis is endemic in the semiarid steppe region of the northern part of the Algerian Sahara. Major risk areas include Biskra, Sidi Okba, Abadla, and M'sila. Visceral leishmaniasis (kala azar) occurs primarily in the less humid central and eastern parts of the northern coastal mountainous area; major foci are in the Grande Kabylie Region and in the vicinities of Constantine and Algiers.

Rabies: The State Department recommends vaccination prior to extended travel in this country. About 20 humans cases are reported yearly. Dogs, jackals, and foxes are the primary animal reservoirs.

Other diseases: Brucellosis (usually transmitted by raw goat or sheep milk), echinococcosis (a major health problem countrywide), relapsing fever (louse-borne and tick-borne), typhoid fever (outbreaks frequently reported), tuberculosis, and intestinal helminthic infections (roundworm, hookworm, and whipworm are common in rural areas).

EGYPT

Embassy: 202-232-5400   *Cairo*   *GMT +2 hrs*

Entry Requirements
- Passport/Visa: A valid passport and visa are required.
- AIDS Test: Testing is required for foreign contractors.
- Vaccinations: A yellow fever vaccination certificate is required from all travelers older than 1 year arriving from yellow fever–infected areas, or from any country in the Yellow Fever Endemic Zones. In addition, all travelers from the Sudan must possess a certificate stating that they have not been in that part of the Sudan south of 15 degrees N latitude within the preceding six days.
  NOTE: Travelers arriving from Sudan may also be required to show proof of vaccination against cholera, typhoid, and meningitis.

Telephone Country Code: 20

American Express: American Express Travel Service. 15 Sharia Kasr El Nil Street, Cairo; Tel. (2) 750-444.

Embassies/Consulates: U.S. Embassy, Cairo. 5 Sharia Latin America; Tel. (2) 354-7371, 354-8211. Canadian High Commission, Garden City. Mohamed Fahmy el Sayed; Tel. 354-3110.

Hospitals/Doctors: al-Salam Hospital, Cairo (300 beds); civilian; private hospital; quality of care probably Egypt's best; most major specialties; ambulance service; Tel: (2) 636-278. El Nasr City Medical Center, Cairo (600 beds); government hospital; sophisticated diagnostics and most medical specialties; ambulance service. Kamal Wahby, M.D., Cairo; Tel: (2) 340-4631 or 225-964 (home).

Health Advisory

Malaria: Risk is present in focal rural areas of the Nile Delta, El Faiyum Governate, and scattered oases (Bahariya and Farafra oases, however, may be risk-free). Possible risk exists along the Suez Canal, the northern Red Sea Coast, and part of southern Egypt, including Luxor and Karnak, and rural areas outside Aswan. There is no risk of malaria in urban areas, including

Cairo and Alexandria. Vivax malaria accounts for the majority of cases. Falciparum malaria is endemic only in the El Faiyum Governate. Chloroquine resistance has not been reported. Chloroquine prophylaxis is recommended for travel to malaria risk areas.

Travelers' diarrhea: High risk outside of first-class hotels. Bacteria commonly causing diarrhea include *E. coli*, salmonella, and shigella. Resistance to trimethoprim/sulfamethoxazole is widespread. A quinolone antibiotic is recommended for the treatment of acute diarrhea. Diarrhea not responding to antibiotic treatment may be due to a parasitic disease such as amebiasis, giardiasis, or cryptosporidiosis.

Hepatitis: High risk of hepatitis A in nonimmune travelers. All susceptible travelers should receive immune globulin or hepatitis A vaccine prior to arrival. Healthcare workers and long-term visitors and their families should be vaccinated against hepatitis B. An estimated 4%–10% of the Egyptian population are chronic carriers of the hepatitis B virus. The hepatitis C virus is hyperendemic in Egypt, with seroprevalence rates 9.7% to 37.5%. Travelers should be advised not to received transfusions of blood unscreened for hepatitis B or C virus.

Arboviral fevers: West Nile fever, Rift Valley fever, and sandfly fever are regularly reported. Highest transmission rates are June–October. There appears to be negligible risk of dengue fever in Egypt. All travelers to this country, particularly to the Nile Valley and Nile Delta, should take measures to prevent insect (mosquito and sandfly) bites. Human cases of Crimean-Congo hemorrhagic fever (a viral tick-borne illness) have not been reported.

Leishmaniasis: Cutaneous leishmaniasis is focally distributed countrywide in rural and periurban areas, including Cairo. Primary risk areas include the eastern Nile Delta, Suez Canal zone, and throughout the Sinai Peninsula. Travelers should take measures to prevent insect (sandfly) bites. Sand flies bite predominantly between dusk and dawn.

Filariasis: Reported primarily from the eastern Nile Delta. Up to 15% of surveyed individuals are infected. All travelers to this region should take precautions against insect (mosquito) bites.

Schistosomiasis: This disease is widespread in Egypt. Fifty percent of the rural population is infected. Urinary and intestinal schistosomiasis are found in the Nile Delta and the Nile Valley. Areas above the Aswan Dam are heavily infected due to a high freshwater snail population. Travelers should avoid swimming or wading in freshwater lakes, streams, or irrigated areas. Chlorinated swimming pools, however, are safe.

Intestinal helminthic infections: Fascioliasis is common in Cairo and the Nile Delta. Uncooked aquatic plants (e.g., wild watercress) are a source of infection, but the disease can also be transmitted by undercooked sheep and goat livers. Fascioliasis is suspected in travelers suffering from fever, enlarged liver, and eosinophilia. Treatment with bithional is effective. Prevention is primarily through avoiding watercress salad and thoroughly cooking sheep and goat livers. Eating Fessikh (salted raw fish) puts the traveler at risk for acquiring heterophyiasis, an intestinal infection of tiny flukes. Ascariasis (roundworm infection), ancylostomiasis (hookworm disease), trichuriasis (whipworm infection), and taeniasis (pork tapeworm disease) are common in rural areas of the Nile Delta and Valley.

Meningitis: Significant outbreaks have occurred in Egypt, involving primarily Group A meningococci. Up to 2,000 cases officially are reported annually with most risk in the Al-Jizah and Al-Sharqiyah Governates. Vaccination is recommended for travelers expecting to have extended contact with the indigenous population of this country.

Rabies: Primarily a risk in urban areas, including Cairo. Stray dogs are the primary source of human exposure, but jackals are also a reservoir of infection. Long-term visitors should consider rabies vaccination.

Other diseases/hazards: AIDS (low prevalence), Mediterranean spotted fever (low prevalence; also known as boutonneuse fever and African tick typhus; reported from Ghiza and the Sharqiya and Aswan Governates; transmitted primarily by dog ticks, often in suburban areas), brucellosis (risk from raw goat/sheep milk and cheese), cholera (sporadic outbreaks occur), echinococcosis. filariasis (endemic in eastern Nile Delta and possibly in Asyut Governate), flea-borne typhus (widespread in the Nile Delta, port cities, Nile Valley, northeast Sinai Peninsula, and along the Suez Canal; reported in Cairo and Alexandria), leprosy, leptospirosis, toxoplasmosis (infection rates as high as 20%–30%), trachoma, tuberculosis, typhoid fever (common; vaccination is advisable), murine typhus (flea-borne). Animal hazards include snakes (cobras, vipers), scorpions, and black widow spiders.

LIBYA
Tripoli ... GMT +1 hr

Entry Requirements

- Passport/Visa: A visa is required. U.S. passports no longer valid for travel to Libya without special validation from the State Dept. U.S. citizens should contact:
  U.S. Department of State (Att: Mr. Harry Coburn)
  1425 K Street, N.W.
  Washington, D.C. 20522-1705
- AIDS Test: Testing is required for those seeking residence permits. Short-term visitors are exempt. U.S. test results are accepted.
- Vaccinations: A yellow fever vaccination certificate is required for all travelers older than one year arriving from infected areas.

Telephone Country Code: 218

Electricity/Plugs: AC 50 Hz, 220 volts; plug type D. Adaptors and transformer necessary for U.S.-made appliances.

Hospitals/Doctors: Tripoli Central Hospital (1,200 beds); general medical/surgical facility; emergency services; ICU.

In Tunis: Kasbi Kamel, M.D., Tel. (1) 254-3355/225-964.

In Benghazi: Central Hospital (1,200 beds); general medical/surgical facility.

Health Advisory

Malaria: Very low risk is present from February to August in the valleys and isolated oases in the southwest (Fezzan). There is no malaria risk in urban areas. Most cases of malaria are now due to *P. vivax*; *P. falciparum* was the principal species in the south prior to the 1970s.

Travelers' diarrhea: Moderate to high risk outside of first-class hotels and resorts. Travelers are advised to drink only bottled, boiled, filtered, or treated water and consume only well-cooked food. Most large urban areas have piped water, but supplies are intermittent and delivery systems are subject to contamination. A quinolone antibiotic is recommended for the treatment of acute diarrhea. Diarrhea not responding to antibiotic treatment may be due to a parasitic disease such as giardiasis or amebiasis—or an intestinal virus.

Hepatitis: Immune globulin or hepatitis A vaccine is recommended for all susceptible travelers. The hepatitis B carrier rate in the general population is estimated at 5%. Vaccination is recommended for all long-term visitors. Hepatitis E is reported.

Leishmaniasis: Low risk of cutaneous leishmaniasis is present. Sporadic cases have been reported from rural villages in the northwest, in the semiarid area extending from Tripoli to the Tunisian border, and from the coast to the plateau of the Jebel Nefusa. No cases have been reported from Tripoli. Visceral leishmaniasis (kala azar) has been reported from the Benghazi region and the northeastern coastal areas. Visceral leishmaniasis tends to be associated with settlements, with dogs as the primary reservoir. Travelers to these regions should take measures to prevent sandfly bites.

Sandfly fever: Significant potential risk is present. Transmission occurs primarily April–October throughout the coastal regions. Travelers to these regions should take measures to prevent sandfly bites.

Schistosomiasis: Risk is present in widespread areas of the southwest, including valleys in the central Fezzan and the Ghat district on the Algerian border. Transmission also occurs in Darnah on the northeastern coast. Cases also reported from Taourga, an oasis located 240 km east of Tripoli. Travelers should avoid swimming or wading in freshwater lakes, irrigation systems, ponds, or streams.

Rabies: Animal rabies occurs throughout this country. Foxes, jackals, and hyenas are the principal animal reservoirs.

Other illnesses: Boutonneuse fever (occurs primarily in coastal areas; contracted from dog ticks, often in suburban areas), brucellosis (risk from raw goat/sheep milk and cheese), echinococcosis (10% of the children in Benghazi infected), plague (outbreaks have occurred near Tobruk), relapsing fever (tick-borne and louse-borne), toxoplasmosis (infection rates as high as 52%), tuberculosis, typhus, and helminthic infections (e.g., roundworm, hookworm disease).

MOROCCO
Rabat ... GMT 0 hrs

Entry Requirements
- Passport/Visa: Valid passport is required. Visa not required.
- AIDS Test: Not required.
- Vaccinations: None required.

Telephone Country Code: 212

Electricity/Plugs: AC 50 Hz, 220 volts; plug types C and E. Adaptors and transformer necessary for U.S.-made appliances.

American Express: Voyages Schwartz S.A., Casablanca. 112 Rue Prince Moulay Abdellah; Tel. 273-133. Voyages Schwarz, Tangier. 54 Blvd. Pasteur; Tel. (9) 334-59.

Embassies/Consulates: U.S. Consulate, Rabat; 8 Blvd. Moulay Yousefef. Tel. (7) 622-65. U.S. Consulate, Casablanca; Tel. 25-45-50. U.S. Consulate, Tangier; Tel. 359-04.

Hospitals/Doctors: Avicenne Hospital, Rabat (850 beds); general medical/surgical facility; blood bank. Clinique Beausejour, Rabat; Tel. (7) 806-67/813-13. Averroes Hospital, Casablanca (1,603 beds); general medical/surgical facility; neurosurgery. Croissant Rouge Marocain (Red Cross); Tel. 25-25-21. Dr. A. El Kouhen, Casablanca. Tel: 27-53-43. Dr. Ahmed Mansouri, Marrakesh. Tel. 43-07-54. Clinique California, Tangier; Tel: 388-24/387-22. Hopital Al Kortobi, Tangier; open 24 hours daily for medical emergencies. Tel. 310-73. Joseph Hirt, M.D., Tangier; well-known physician who will make hotel calls. Tel. 357-29.

Health Advisory

Malaria: There is limited risk in the rural areas of the coastal and inland provinces located north and west of a line extending from Marrakesh to Azilal to Taza. The majority of cases are reported from Beni Mellal, El Kelaa des Srarhna, Khemisset, Larache, Settat, Tanger, Taounate, Fes, Chaouen, Meknes, and Khouribga Provinces. No cases of malaria reported from urban areas. Vivax malaria accounts for 99% of cases. Chloroquine prophylaxis is recommended in risk areas.

Travelers' diarrhea: Water sources in Morocco should be considered potentially contaminated. In urban and resort areas, the first-class hotels and restaurants generally serve reliable food and potable water. Elsewhere, travelers should observe all food and drink safety precautions. A quinolone antibiotic is recommended for the treatment of acute diarrhea. Diarrhea not responding to antibiotic treatment may be due to a parasitic disease such as giardiasis, amebiasis, or cryptosporidiosis.

Hepatitis: Immune globulin or hepatitis A vaccine is recommended for all susceptible travelers. The hepatitis B carrier rate in the general population is estimated at 1%–6%. Vaccination against hepatitis B is recommended for healthcare workers and should be considered by long-term visitors to this country.

Leishmaniasis: Cutaneous leishmaniasis occurs primarily in rural semiarid areas, including the Fes vicinity and the oases of the southeast. Visceral leishmaniasis (kala-azar) is focally distributed throughout Morocco, including Fes, Marrakech, and the southwest Atlas region. All travelers should take precautions against sandfly bites in these areas.

Schistosomiasis: Year-round risk, with highest incidence in the summer. Urinary schistosomiasis is the principal variety and occurs in the south central areas (Saharan slopes of the Atlas mountains), southwestern areas (Agadir, Tiznit), Marrakech vicinity, northwestern, and northeastern areas. Travelers should avoid swimming in freshwater ponds, lakes, streams, or irrigation ditches.

African tick typhus (boutonneuse fever): Risk occurs primarily in coastal urban-suburban areas. Disease is transmitted by dog ticks.

Rabies: Human cases have been reported primarily from the populated northern areas. Rabies vaccination is recommended for long-term travel to this country.

Other illnesses: Brucellosis (risk from raw goat/sheep milk and cheese), cholera, echinococcosis (over 50% of stray dogs infected in some areas), leprosy, leptospirosis, relapsing fever (tick- and louse-borne), sandfly fever, typhus, toxoplasmosis (infection rates as high as 52%), tuberculosis (a major public health problem), typhus (flea-borne), and intestinal helminthic infections (especially roundworm) are common in rural areas.

TUNISIA

Tunis ... GMT +1 hr

Entry Requirements
- Passport/Visa: Passport is required.
- AIDS Test: Not required.
- Vaccinations: A yellow fever vaccination certificate is required from all travelers arriving from infected areas.

Telephone Country Code: 216

Electricity/Plugs: AC 50 Hz, 220 volts; plug types C, E, F, K, and L. Adaptors and transformer necessary for U.S.-made appliances.

American Express: Carthage Tours. 59 Avenue Bourguiba, Tunis; Tel: (1) 254-304.

Embassies/Consulates: U.S. Embassy, Tunis. 144 Avenue de la Liberte; Tel: (1) 782-566. Canadian High Commission, Tunis. 3 Rue de Senegal, Place Palestine; Tel: (1) 286-577.

Hospitals/Doctors: Charles Nicolle Hospital, Tunis (756 beds); general medical/surgical facility; Habib Thameur Hospital (555 beds); general medical/surgical facility; Hadi Chakar Hospital, Tunis (870 beds); general medical/surgical facility; Kasbi Kamel, M.D., Tunis; Tel: (1) 254-4335 or 225-964 (home).

Health Advisory

Malaria: Low risk. Indigenous malaria has not occurred since 1978 but foci of vivax malaria activity may still exist. Travelers should take measures to prevent mosquito bites and seek medical attention for any unexplained illness accompanied by chills, fever, and headache.

Travelers' diarrhea: High risk. Piped water in Tunis is not consistently potable. In most other large urban areas, and all rural areas, water supplies are not considered potable. Travelers should observe food and drink safety precautions. A quinolone antibiotic (Cipro or Floxin) is recommended for the treatment of acute diarrhea. Diarrhea not responding to treatment with an antibiotic, or chronic diarrhea, may be due to a parasitic disease such as giardiasis or amebiasis—or an intestinal virus.

Hepatitis: Immune globulin or hepatitis A vaccine is recommended for all susceptible travelers. The hepatitis B carrier rate in the general population is estimated at 4.6%. Vaccination against hepatitis B is recommended for healthcare workers and should be considered by long-term visitors to this country.

Sandfly fever: Disease risk is present in the northern, central, and southeastern areas of the country. Transmission occurs primarily April–October, when sandfly activity is highest.

Leishmaniasis: Cutaneous leishmaniasis is reported from northern, central (primarily Qafsah, Sidi Bu Zayd, and Safaqis Governorates), and the southeastern areas. Visceral leishmaniasis (kala-azar) occurs in the northern half of Tunisia, primarily northeast, including the outskirts of Tunis. All travelers should take protective measures to prevent insect (sandfly) bites.

Schistosomiasis: Low risk. Foci include oases in Qafsah and Qabis Governorates and in the village of Hadjeb El Aioun, 120 miles south of Tunis. Travelers should avoid swimming or wading in freshwater lakes, ponds, irrigation ditches, or streams in these areas.

Rabies: Human cases reported year-round. Vaccination is recommended for long-term travelers to this country, especially children. Wild animal reservoir of rabies virus is primarily foxes, jackals, and hyenas.

Other illnesses: Boutonneuse fever (African tick typhus; distribution is widespread; contracted from dog ticks, often in suburban areas), brucellosis (risk from raw goat/sheep milk and cheese), echinococcosis (a major health problem in central Tunisia), leptospirosis, trachoma, tuberculosis, typhoid fever, soil-transmitted helminthic infections (roundworm, hookworm) are common in rural areas.

DISEASE RISK SUMMARY
Sub-Saharan Africa

Yellow fever: This disease is currently reported active in nine countries—Angola, Cameroon, Gambia, Guinea, Kenya, Mali, Nigeria, Sudan, and Zaire. A vaccination certificate is absolutely required for entry to Benin, Burkina Fasso, Cameroon, Cote d'Ivoire (Ivory Coast), Gabon, Ghana, Liberia, Mali, Mauritania, Niger, Senegal, Sao Tome & Principe, and Togo, even if arriving directly from the United States or Canada. Travelers to Cape Verde Islands, Equatorial Guinea, Gambia, Guinea-Bissau, Nigeria, and Sierra Leone will need a vaccination certificate if arriving from any "infected" or yellow fever endemic countries in Africa or Latin America.

Cholera: This disease is reported active in many countries. Although cholera vaccination is not required for entry if arriving directly from the U.S. or Canada, it may be required for on-going travel to other countries in Africa, the Middle East, Asia, or Oceania. Travelers who plan to visit several countries should consider vaccination (one dose) or a doctor's letter of exemption from vaccination. Cholera occurs in areas with inadequate sanitation, such as urban slums and rural areas. The risk to tourists of acquiring cholera is considered low, but may be increased in travelers who are using anti-ulcer medication or antacids, or who will be living in less than sanitary conditions in areas of high cholera activity. These travelers should also consider vaccination. Prevention consists primarily in adhering to safe food and drink guidelines.

Malaria: High risk in most countries, including urban areas. Transmission of disease is greater during and just after the rainy seasons when the mosquito population increases. Highest malaria attack rates for tourists are reported from East Africa, Ghana, Nigeria, and Malawi. Most malaria in sub-Saharan Africa is caused by *P. falciparum*, but *P. vivax* occurs in Ethiopia, Somalia, and Sudan. There is widespread occurrence of chloroquine-resistant *P. falciparum* throughout sub-Saharan Africa. Chemoprophylaxis with mefloquine (Lariam) or doxycycline is currently advised for people who travel to malarious areas, but travelers should be aware that cases of mefloquine-resistant *P. falciparum* have been reported and that no prophylactic drug is guaranteed to provide 100% protection against all species of malaria. For this reason, travelers should also take careful measures to prevent mosquito bites. These measures include the frequent application of a deet-containing insect repellent, the wearing of permethrin-treated clothing, and, if necessary, the use of permethrin-treated mosquito bed nets. Travelers should seek immediate medical consultation for a suspected attack of malaria, even if they have been taking prophylactic drugs.

Note: Risk of malaria is low or absent in Nairobi, the Ethiopian highlands, or on the islands of Cape Verde, Mauritius, Reunion, and the Seychelles.

Travelers' diarrhea: High risk in all countries outside first-class hotels and resorts. Most water sources should be considered potentially contaminated. Travelers should strictly observe safe food and drink precautions. A quinolone antibiotic (Cipro or Floxin) is recommended for the treatment of acute diarrhea. Trimethoprim/sulfamethoxazole (Bactrim, Septra), or furazolidone (Furoxone) is recommended for treating children with diarrhea. Diarrhea not responding to treatment with an antibiotic, or chronic diarrhea, may be due to a parasitic disease such as giardiasis or amebiasis, and treatment with metronidazole (Flagyl) or tinidazole (Fasigyn) should be considered. All cases of diarrhea should be treated with adequate fluid replacement.

Typhoid fever: Vaccination is recommended for persons traveling off the usual tourist routes and/or on working assignments whose duration of travel exceeds 3–4 weeks.

Hepatitis: All susceptible travelers should be immunized with immune globulin or hepatitis A vaccine prior to traveling to Africa. The hepatitis B virus carrier rate in the countries of sub-Saharan Africa is estimated to exceed 10%. Vaccination against hepatitis B is recommended for all healthcare workers and should be considered by anyone planning an extended visit to this region.

Amebiasis: There is a high incidence of amebiasis in West and South Africa, where up to 50% of the high-risk population may be infected with *E. histolytica* parasites. To avoid ame-

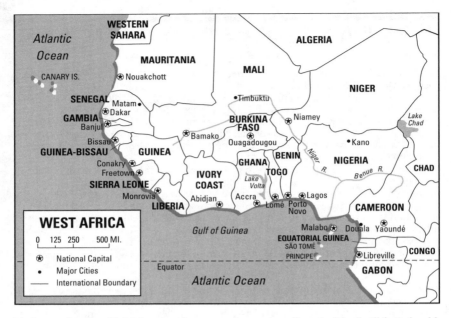

WEST AFRICA

0   125   250   500 MI.

⊛   National Capital
•   Major Cities
—   International Boundary

biasis, travelers should drink only safe water and eat only well-cooked food. All fruit should be peeled before eating.

Dengue fever: Low risk. Although the *Aedes aegypti* mosquito that transmits dengue is found in most countries of Africa, cases of dengue appear to be rare. Sporadic outbreaks have been reported most recently in Burkina Fasso, Cote d'Ivoire, Guinea, Nigeria, and Senegal. All travelers should take personal protection measures against mosquito bites to prevent this and other mosquito-borne diseases.

Leishmaniasis: Epidemics of visceral leishmaniasis (kala azar) have occurred in East Africa, Ethiopia, and Sudan, but sporadic cases also have been reported in Chad, Burkina Fasso, Central African Republic, Uganda, Zaire, and Zambia. Cutaneous leishmaniasis (Oriental sore) is widespread in Mali, Mauritania, Chad, the Central African Republic and is present, but less active, elsewhere, especially in the drier areas. To prevent leishmaniasis, travelers should take measures to prevent insect (sandfly) bites.

Schistosomiasis: Risk is present in all countries except for Cape Verde, Reunion, and the Seychelles. Travelers should avoid swimming, bathing, or wading in freshwater lakes, ponds, or streams.

Onchocerciasis: Widespread incidence in West and Central Africa, extending into Uganda, Sudan, and the Ethiopian highlands. Western Kenya is risk free. Travelers to risk areas should take measures to prevent blackfly bites. The black fly is a daytime biter and is rarely found indoors.

Filariasis: Mosquito-borne Bancroftian filariasis is widespread in all countries, except southern Africa. Advanced disease (very rare) causes a condition called elephantiasis. To prevent filariasis, travelers should take measures to prevent mosquito bites.

Loiasis: This form of filariasis is common in equatorial Africa, especially West and Central Africa. It is transmitted by the biting fly (Chrysops). Travelers should take protective measures against insect (fly) bites.

Meningitis: Travelers (especially teachers, relief workers, missionaries, etc.) planning an extended visit to sub-Saharan Africa should be vaccinated against meningococcal meningitis. There is an increased incidence of type A serogroup meningitis in Burundi, Kenya, and Tanzania and vaccination is recommended for travel to these countries, although the risk to tourists is deemed to be low.

African sleeping sickness (trypanosomiasis): This disease occurs in several countries of central and East Africa. Most risk to tourists occurs when visiting game parks. Travelers to rural areas should take measures to prevent insect (tsetse fly) bites.

West Nile fever, Chickungunya fever, Rift Valley fever: These mosquito-transmitted diseases are avoided by taking personal protection measures against insect bites.

Lassa fever: Low risk to tourists. Lassa fever occurs primarily in West Africa (from Nigeria to Guinea). The virus of Lassa fever is thought to be spread by infective rat and rodent urine. Travelers can reduce exposure by avoiding bush areas and the interiors of thatch huts.

Rabies: Animal rabies has been reported from all countries. Most human cases are transmitted by dog bites, with risk occurring in both urban and rural areas. Jackals and mongooses should also be considered potentially rabid. Travelers should seek emergency treatment of any animal bite, especially if the bite was unprovoked. Pre-exposure rabies vaccination is recommended for all travelers (especially children) planning an extended visit or extensive travel in sub-Saharan Africa.

AIDS: Widespread incidence of HIV infection in the countries of central and eastern Africa, where up to 30% of the urban population is HIV-1 positive. In West Africa, HIV-2 is endemic and up to 10% of the urban population is serologically positive. Travelers should avoid unsafe sexual contact, injections with unsterile needles and syringes, and unscreened blood transfusions. Travelers should consider carrying sterile needles and syringes in case an emergency medical injection is required.

Helminthic infections: There is widespread occurrence of hookworm, roundworm, and whipworm infections. Strongyloides infection is also prevalent. Travelers can prevent these infections by wearing shoes to prevent skin penetration by infectious worm larvae (hookworm, strongyloidiasis), and cook food thoroughly to destroy infectious roundworm and whipworm eggs. Paragonimiasis (lung fluke disease) occurs in West Africa and is transmitted by the consumption of raw crustaceans.

Other diseases: African tick typhus (transmitted primarily by dog ticks), anthrax, brucellosis, Crimean-Congo hemorrhagic fever (a tick-borne viral disease; occurs throughout Africa), cysticercosis and pork tapeworm disease, echinococcosis, leprosy, syphilis, trachoma (widespread), tuberculosis (a major health problem in many countries), typhus (louseborne), and acute hemorrhagic conjunctivitis are reported.

BENIN
Porto-Novo ... GMT +1 hr

Entry Requirements
- Passport/Visa: Valid passport and visa are required.
- AIDS Test: Not required.
- Vaccinations: A yellow fever vaccination certificate is required from all travelers arriving from ALL COUNTRIES, including the United States and Canada. Benin is in the yellow fever endemic zone.

Telephone Country Code: 229

Electricity/Plugs: AC 50 Hz, 220 volts; plug type D.

Embassies/Consulates: U.S. Embassy, Contonou. Rue Caporal Anani Bernard; Tel. 30-06-50/30-17-92.

Hospitals/Doctors: General Hospital, Porto-Novo; general medical/surgical facility; ENT, pediatrics. General Hospital, Cotonou (350 beds); general medical/surgical facility; teaching hospital. Clinique "Les Graces"; Tel. 32-11-70. Centre Hospitalier Universitaire; Tel. 30-01-55/20-06-56.

Health Advisory
Yellow fever: Although no outbreaks have recently been reported, this country is in the Yellow Fever Endemic Zone. A valid yellow fever vaccination certificate may be required for persons who leave this country and travel to other countries in South America, Africa, the Middle East, or Asia.

Cholera: This disease is active in this country. Although cholera vaccination is not required for entry if arriving directly from the U.S. or Canada, it may be required if arriving from a cholera-infected area, or required for on-going travel to other countries in Latin America, Africa, the Middle East, or Asia. Travelers should consider vaccination (one dose) or a doctor's letter of exemption. The risk to travelers of acquiring cholera is considered low. Prevention consists primarily in adhering to safe food and drink guidelines.

Malaria: Risk is present throughout this country, including urban areas. Falciparum malaria accounts for 85% of cases. Chloroquine-resistant falciparum malaria is common. Mefloquine resistance has been reported from the southern provinces of Zou and the Cotonou region. Prophylaxis with mefloquine or doxycycline is currently recommended when traveling to malarious areas.

Travelers' diarrhea: High risk in most areas. Although larger cities have piped water systems, all water supplies should be considered potentially contaminated. Travelers should observe all food and drink safety precautions. A quinolone antibiotic is recommended for the treatment of acute diarrhea. Diarrhea not responding to treatment with an antibiotic, or chronic diarrhea, may be due to a parasitic disease such as giardiasis or amebiasis—or an intestinal virus.

Hepatitis: All susceptible travelers should receive immune globulin or hepatitis A vaccine. The hepatitis B carrier rate in the general population is estimated at 16%. Vaccination against hepatitis B is recommended for healthcare workers and all long-term visitors to this country.

Schistosomiasis: Urinary schistosomiasis is focally distributed. Highest rate of disease is found in Mono Province, followed by Atakora and Borgou Provinces. Lowest rate in Oueme Province. Intestinal schistosomiasis appears limited to an area 30 km west of Cotonou. Travelers should avoid wading or swimming in freshwater streams, lakes, or ponds.

Trypanosomiasis (African sleeping sickness): Sporadic cases reported. Tsetse fly vectors are found in the northern areas, particularly in Atakora Province. Take personal protective measures against fly and insect bites.

Meningitis: Benin lies within the sub-Saharan meningitis belt, and there is a high incidence of Group A meningococcal meningitis. Vaccination is recommended for travelers staying in this country longer than 4 weeks, especially those who will have close contact with the indigenous population.

AIDS: Heterosexual contact is the predominate mode of transmission. HIV-1 prevalence estimated at 4.5% of the high-risk urban population. HIV-2 prevalence is estimated at 3.7% of high-risk individuals. All travelers are cautioned against unsafe sex, unsterile medical or dental injections, and unnecessary blood transfusions.

Other illnesses/hazards: African tick typhus, brucellosis (from consumption of raw dairy products), Bancroftian filariasis (mosquito-borne), Lassa fever, leishmaniasis (low apparent risk; sporadic cases have previously been reported), leprosy (overall prevalence 2 cases/1,000 population), onchocerciasis (black-fly-borne; transmitted near fast-flowing rivers; high incidence in coastal areas), rabies (transmitted primarily by stray dogs), toxoplasmosis, syphilis, tuberculosis (a major health problem), typhoid fever, and intestinal worms (very common). Animal hazards include snakes (boomslangs, cobras, vipers), centipedes, scorpions, and brown and black widow spiders.

BURKINA FASO
Ouagadougou ... GMT 0 hrs

Entry Requirements
- Passport/Visa: Valid passport and visa are required.
- AIDS Test: Not required.
- Vaccinations: A yellow fever vaccination certificate is required from all travelers arriving from ALL COUNTRIES, including the United States and Canada.

Electricity/Plugs: AC 50 Hz, 220 volts; plug types C and E.

Embassies/Consulates: U.S. Embassy, Ouagadougou. Tel. 306-723 or 333-422. Canadian Embassy (Ivory Coast). Tel. [225] 322-009.

Health Advisory

Yellow fever: There have been no recent reports of this disease. Vaccination is required for all travelers entering this country. This country is in the Yellow Fever Endemic Zone. A valid yellow fever vaccination certificate may also be required for on-going travel to other countries in South America, Africa, the Middle East, Asia, or Oceania.

Cholera: This disease is active in this country. Although cholera vaccination is not required for entry if arriving directly from the U.S. or Canada, it may be required if arriving from a cholera-infected area, or required for on-going travel to other countries in Latin America, Africa, the Middle East, or Asia. Travelers should consider vaccination (one dose) or a doctor's letter of exemption from vaccination. The risk to travelers of acquiring cholera is low. Prevention consists primarily in adhering to safe food and drink guidelines.

Malaria: Risk is present throughout this country year-round, including urban areas. Increased risk occurs June–September, after the rainy season. Falciparum malaria (caused by *P. falciparum*) accounts for 85%–95% of cases. Other cases of malaria are due to *P. ovale*, *P. malariae*, rarely *P. vivax*. Multidrug-resistant falciparum malaria is reported. Chemoprophylaxis with mefloquine or doxycycline is currently recommended.

Travelers' diarrhea: High risk. All surface water sources should be considered potentially contaminated. Water from deep wells is usually free of bacterial contamination, but may contain high levels of minerals and sediment. Travelers should observe all food and drink precautions. A quinolone antibiotic (Cipro or Floxin) is recommended for the treatment of acute diarrhea. Diarrhea not responding to treatment with an antibiotic may be due to a parasitic disease such as giardiasis or amebiasis.

Hepatitis: All susceptible travelers should receive immune globulin or hepatitis A vaccine. The hepatitis B carrier rate in the general population exceeds 10%. Vaccination against hepatitis B is recommended for all healthcare workers and long-term visitors to this country.

Schistosomiasis: Urinary schistosomiasis is widely distributed throughout this country, with foci in all major river basins. Intestinal schistosomiasis is widely distributed in the southwest, with scattered foci in other areas. Travelers should avoid swimming, wading, or bathing in freshwater lakes, ponds, or streams.

Leishmaniasis: Low apparent risk. Cutaneous leishmaniasis has been reported in the western and eastern areas, and a focus was identified north of Arabinda in 1986. Sporadic cases of visceral leishmaniasis have occurred. Travelers should take precautions against insect (sandfly) bites.

Trypanosomiasis (African sleeping sickness): Undetermined risk. Disease activity apparently has been reported in the vicinities of Banfora and Bobo Diolasso in the southwest, and the Koudougou vicinity west of Ouagadougou. Travelers to these regions should take protective measures against insect (tsetse fly) bites.

Onchocerciasis: May be transmitted near fast flowing rivers. Incidence is declining, due to control programs. Travelers should take measures to prevent black fly bites.

Filariasis: Bancroftian filariasis is reported. Travelers should take measures to prevent mosquito bites.

Meningitis: This country lies within the sub-Saharan meningitis belt, and there is a high incidence of Group A and C meningococcal meningitis. Vaccination is recommended for travelers staying in this country longer than 4 weeks, especially those who will have close contact with the indigenous population.

Rabies: Pre-exposure vaccination (3 doses) is recommended for long-term travel (more than 4 weeks) to this country, especially for travelers going to remote rural areas who will be unable to receive antirabies treatment within 24 hours of exposure to a potentially rabid animal.

AIDS: Heterosexual contact is the predominate mode of transmission. HIV-1 prevalence estimated at 17% of the high-risk urban population. HIV-2 prevalence estimated at 23% of the high-risk urban population. All travelers are cautioned against unsafe sex, unsterile medical or dental injections, and unnecessary blood transfusions.

Other diseases: African tick typhus (transmitted by dog ticks and bush ticks), anthrax, brucellosis, dengue (low risk; no recent reports), leprosy (overall prevalence 2 cases/1,000 population), rabies, tuberculosis (a major health problem), intestinal worms (common), and typhoid fever are reported. Lassa fever probably occurs but the incidence is not known.

THE GAMBIA
Banjul ... GMT 0 hrs

Entry Requirements
- Passport/Visa: Valid passport and visa are required.
- AIDS Test: Not required.
- Vaccinations: A yellow fever vaccination certificate is required from travelers older than 1 year arriving from infected areas or from any country in the Yellow Fever Endemic Zones.

Telephone Country Code: 220

Electricity/Plugs: AC 50 Hz, 220 volts; plug type G.

Embassies/Consulates: U.S. Embassy, Banjul. Fajara, Kairaba Avenue, P. M. B. No. 19; Tel. 92856 or 92858.

Hospitals/Doctors: Royal Victoria Hospital (255 beds), Banjul; general medical and surgical facility.

Health Advisory

Yellow fever: This disease is active in this country, with the Upper River Division considered "infected" by the WHO. No cases of yellow fever have been reported recently. Vaccination is recommended for travel to this country. This country is in the Yellow Fever Endemic Zone. A valid yellow fever vaccination certificate may be required for travel to other countries in South America, Africa, the Middle East, or Asia.

Cholera: No cases recently reported, but travelers should consider vaccination (one dose) or getting a doctor's letter of exemption from vaccination. Cholera vaccine gives only brief, incomplete protection and is not routinely recommended for travelers in good health. Prevention consists primarily in adhering to safe food and drink guidelines.

Malaria: Risk is present year-round throughout this country, including urban areas. Risk is elevated during and immediately after the rainy season, June–October. Falciparum malaria accounts for approximately 85% of cases. Other cases of malaria are due primarily to the *P. malariae* species. Chloroquine-resistant falciparum malaria is reported. Prophylaxis with mefloquine or doxycycline is currently recommended when traveling to malarious areas.

Travelers' diarrhea: Water in Banjul is treated and distributed through a piped system; nevertheless, all water sources should be considered potentially contaminated. Travelers should observe all food and drink precautions. A quinolone antibiotic is recommended for the treatment of acute diarrhea. Diarrhea not responding to treatment with an antibiotic may be due to a parasitic disease such as giardiasis, amebiasis, or cryptosporidiosis.

Hepatitis: High risk. All travelers should receive immune globulin or hepatitis A vaccine (when available). The hepatitis B carrier rate in the general population is 10%–35%. Hepatitis B vaccination is recommended for all healthcare workers and long-term residents and their families.

Leishmaniasis: Risk undetermined. Sporadic cases of cutaneous and visceral leishmaniasis were reported in the early 1980s in the Farafenni and Banjul vicinities. Current data not available. Travelers should take measures to prevent insect (sandfly) bites.

Schistosomiasis: Risk of urinary schistosomiasis is distributed along the Gambia River. Intestinal schistosomiasis has been reported in the extreme southwestern corner of the Gambia, including the Banjul vicinity. All travelers should avoid swimming, bathing, or wading in freshwater lakes, ponds, or streams.

AIDS: Heterosexual contact is the predominate mode of transmission. HIV-1 and HIV-2 prevalence estimated at 1.7% and 25.6% of the high-risk urban population, respectively. All travelers are cautioned against unsafe sex, unsterile medical or dental injections, and unnecessary blood transfusions.

Other illnesses/hazards: African tick typhus (contracted from dog ticks, often in urban areas, and bush ticks), anthrax, brucellosis (from consumption of raw dairy products), Bancroftian filariasis (mosquito-borne), Crimean-Congo hemorrhagic fever, leprosy (up to 0.8 cases/1,000 population), leptospirosis, onchocerciasis (black-fly-borne; transmitted near fast-flowing rivers), rabies, syphilis, trachoma, tuberculosis (a major health problem), typhoid fever, and intestinal worms (very common).

GHANA
Accra ... GMT 0 hrs

Entry Requirements
- Passport/Visa: Valid passport and visa are required for entry.
- AIDS Test: Not required.
- Vaccinations: A yellow fever vaccination certificate is required from all travelers arriving from ALL COUNTRIES, including the United States and Canada.

Telephone Country Code: 233

Electricity/Plugs: AC 50 Hz, 220 volts; frequency not stable; plug types D and G. Adaptors and transformer necessary for U.S.-made appliances.

American Express: Scantravel, High Street, Accra. Tel. (21) 63134.

Embassies/Consulates: U.S. Embassy, Accra. Ring Road, East. Tel. (21) 775-347. Canadian High Commission, Accra. Tel. (21) 228-555.

Hospitals/Doctors: Police Hospital, Accra; used by U.S. Embassy personnel. Nyaho Hospital, Accra; used by U.S. Embassy personnel. Korle Bu Central Hospital, Accra (1,500 beds); general medical/surgical facility and cardiothoracic center. Tudu Clinic, Accra. Tel. 224-833.

Health Advisory

Yellow fever: This disease is currently active in the Upper West Region. An outbreak of yellow fever previously occurred along Lake Volta in the Eastern Region during late 1987. Vaccination is required for entry to this country. Ghana is in the Yellow Fever Endemic Zone. A valid yellow fever vaccination certificate may be required for travel to other countries in South America, Africa, the Middle East, or Asia.

Cholera: This disease is reported active in this country. Most cases are occurring in the Accra Region. Although cholera vaccination is not required for entry if arriving directly from the U.S. or Canada, it may be required for on-going travel to other countries in Africa, the Middle East, or Asia. Travelers should consider vaccination (one dose) or getting a doctor's letter of exemption from vaccination. Cholera occurs in areas with inadequate sewage disposal and unsafe water supplies such as urban slums and rural areas. The risk to travelers of acquiring cholera is considered low. Prevention consists primarily in adhering to safe food and drink guidelines.

Malaria: Risk is present throughout this country year-round, including urban areas. Falciparum malaria (caused by *Plasmodium falciparum*) accounts for 85% of cases. Other cases of malaria are due to *P. ovale, P. malariae,* or *P. vivax.* Multidrug-resistant falciparum malaria is reported. Mefloquine chemoprophylaxis is currently recommended.

Travelers' diarrhea: Large urban areas have treated, piped water which is subject to recontamination during distribution. All water sources should be considered potentially contaminated. Travelers should observe food and drink precautions. A quinolone antibiotic (Cipro or Floxin) is recommended for the treatment of acute diarrhea. Diarrhea not responding to treatment with an antibiotic may be due to a parasitic disease such as giardiasis or amebiasis, and treatment with metronidazole (Flagyl) or tinidazole (Fasigyn) should be considered. All cases of diarrhea should be treated with adequate fluid replacement.

Hepatitis: High risk. All susceptible travelers should receive immune globulin or hepatitis A vaccine. The hepatitis B carrier rate in the general population is estimated to exceed 10%. Vaccination against hepatitis B is recommended for healthcare workers and all long-term visitors to this country.

Schistosomiasis: Swimming or bathing is unsafe in any of Ghana's bodies of freshwater. Urinary schistosomiasis is widely distributed. Many cases occur in the northeast, including the southern shores of Lake Volta, the area below the Akosombo dam, and the Accra vicinity. Limited foci of intestinal schistosomiasis are distributed sporadically, occurring in the extreme north, the southwest, (Tarkwa), and along the lower Volta. Acute infection (Katayama fever) has resulted from swimming in the estuary of the Volta.

Leishmaniasis: Low risk. Cases of cutaneous and visceral leishmaniasis have been reported from neighboring countries. Travelers should take precautions against insect (sandfly) bites.

Onchocerciasis: Widely distributed along fast-flowing rivers, but incidence has declined due to black fly control programs. Travelers should take precautions against insect (fly) bites.

Filariasis: Bancroftian filariasis is reported. Travelers should take measures to prevent mosquito bites.

African sleeping sickness (trypanosomiasis): Low risk, but cases were reported in the early 1980s. Travelers should avoid tsetse fly bites.

Meningitis: Northern Ghana lies in the sub-Saharan meningitis belt, but cases have also been reported from the central regions of this country. Vaccination is recommended for travelers who will have close, prolonged contact with the indigenous population.

Rabies: High incidence of dog rabies with many human cases reported. Travelers should seek immediate treatment of any animal bite. Pre-exposure vaccination against rabies (3 doses) should be considered for long-term travel to this country. This is especially true for travelers going to remote rural areas if they will be unable to receive antirabies treatment within 24 hours of exposure to a potentially rabid animal.

AIDS: HIV-1 prevalence is estimated at 2% of low-risk urban population and 25%–30% high-risk urban population, including prostitutes. HIV-2 prevalence estimated at 0.6% among low-risk urban population.

Other diseases: Brucellosis (from consumption of raw dairy products), African tick typhus (transmitted by dog ticks, often in urban areas, and bush ticks), anthrax, leprosy, leptospirosis (39% of agricultural workers have been exposed), tuberculosis (a major health problem), and intestinal worms (very common) are reported.

GUINEA

Conakry ... GMT 0 hrs

Entry Requirements

- Passport/Visa: Valid passport and visa are required.
- AIDS Test: Not required.
- Vaccinations: A yellow fever vaccination certificate is required from all travelers older than 1 year arriving from infected areas.

Telephone Country Code: 224

Electricity/Plugs: AC 50 Hz, 220 volts; plug types C, F, and K. Adaptors and transformer necessary for U.S.-made appliances.

Embassies/Consulates: U.S. Embassy, Conakry. 2nd Boulevard & 9th Avenue. Tel. (4) 441-520/21/23/24.

Hospitals/Doctors: Donka Hospital Center, Conakry (400 beds); general medical/surgical facility. Centre Hospitalier Universitaire. Tel. 442-018/461-326.

Health Advisory

Yellow fever: This disease is active in this country, with cases reported in the northeastern region of Siguiri in mid-1991. Vaccination is recommended for travel to this country. This country is in the Yellow Fever Endemic Zone.

Cholera: This disease is active in this country. Although cholera vaccination is not required for entry if arriving directly from the U.S. or Canada, it may be required if arriving from a cholera-infected area, or required for on-going travel to other countries in Latin America, Africa, the Middle East, or Asia. Travelers to this country should consider vaccination (one dose) or a doctor's letter of exemption from vaccination. The risk to travelers of acquiring cholera is considered low. Prevention consists primarily in adhering to safe food and drink guidelines.

Malaria: Risk is present throughout this country year-round, including urban areas. Falciparum malaria accounts for approximately 90% of cases. Other cases of malaria are primarily due to the *P. malariae* or *P. ovale*. Multidrug-resistant falciparum malaria is reported. Prophylaxis with mefloquine or doxycycline is currently recommended.

Travelers' diarrhea: High risk outside of first-class hotels and resorts. All water sources should be considered potentially contaminated. Travelers should observe food and drink precautions. A quinolone antibiotic (Cipro or Floxin) is recommended for the treatment of acute diarrhea. Diarrhea not responding to treatment with an antibiotic, or chronic diarrhea, may be due to a parasitic disease such as giardiasis or amebiasis, and treatment with metronidazole (Flagyl) or tinidazole (Fasigyn) should be considered.

Hepatitis: All susceptible travelers should receive immune globulin or hepatitis A vaccine. The hepatitis B carrier rate in the general population is reported as high as 18%. Hepatitis B vaccination is recommended for all healthcare workers and long-term residents, and their families.

Onchocerciasis: Widely distributed along fast-flowing rivers in northern and central areas, particularly Faranah and Dinguiraye, and also in the southeast and the southwest. Travelers should take measures to prevent black fly bites.

Schistosomiasis: Risk is present year-round throughout Guinea except for the coastal plain, where only Forecariah Region near the Sierra Leone border is infected. Highest infection rates occur in the regions of Gueckedou, Macenta, Faranah, and Nzerekore. Travelers should avoid swimming, bathing, or wading in freshwater lakes, ponds, or streams.

Meningitis: Officially reported outbreaks of meningococcal meningitis last occurred in 1987. Vaccination is recommended for long-term travelers who anticipate close contact with the indigenous population of this country or surrounding regions.

Trypanosomiasis (African sleeping sickness): Sporadic cases during the 1980s indicate persistent low-level transmission. Travelers should take precautions to prevent tsetse fly bites.

AIDS: Heterosexual transmission is the predominate means of transmission. Both HIV-1 and HIV-2 occur. Current infection rates of high-risk groups is presently not available.

Other illnesses/hazards: African tick typhus, anthrax, brucellosis, dengue (low apparent risk), Bancroftian filariasis, leishmaniasis (risk undetermined; sporadic cases of cutaneous leishmaniasis were reported in the 1970s from the western areas), leprosy (up to 2 cases/1,000 population), rabies, toxoplasmosis, syphilis, tuberculosis (a major health problem), typhoid fever, and intestinal worms (very common).

GUINEA-BISSAU

Bissau ... GMT 0 hrs

Entry Requirements

- Passport/Visa: Valid passport and visa are required.
- AIDS Test: Not required.
- Vaccinations: A yellow fever vaccination certificate is required from all travelers arriving from infected areas and from all countries in the Yellow Fever Endemic Zones, including Cape Verde, Djibouti, Madagascar, and Mozambique.

Electricity/Plugs: AC 50 Hz, 220 volts; plug types C, D, and F. Adaptors and transformer necessary for U.S.-made appliances.

Embassies/Consulates: U.S. Embassy, Bissau. Avenida Domingos Ramos. Tel. 21-2816, 21-3674. Canadian Embassy (Senegal). Tel. [221] 21-0290.

Doctors/Hospitals: Simao Mendes National Hospital, Bissau (100 beds); general medical/surgical facility; orthopedics, emergency services.

Health Advisory

Yellow fever: Vaccination is recommended. No cases recently reported, but yellow fever is active in neighboring Guinea. This country is in the Yellow Fever Endemic Zone. Although a vaccination certificate may not be required for entry to this country, one may be required for on-going travel to other countries in Africa, the Middle East, and Asia.

Cholera: This disease may be active. An extensive outbreak occurred in 1987. Although cholera vaccination is not required for entry if arriving directly from the U.S. or Canada, it may be required if arriving from a cholera-infected area, or required for on-going travel to other countries in Africa, the Middle East, or Asia. Travelers should consider vaccination (one dose) or getting a doctor's letter of exemption from vaccination. The risk to travelers of acquiring cholera is considered low. Prevention consists primarily in adhering to safe food and drink guidelines.

Malaria: Risk is present year-round throughout this country, including urban areas. Falciparum malaria accounts for approximately 90% of cases. Other cases of malaria are due primarily to the *P. malariae* species. Chloroquine-resistant falciparum malaria is reported. Prophylaxis with mefloquine or doxycycline is currently recommended when traveling to malarious areas. Alternative malaria regimes should be discussed with a travel medicine or infectious disease specialist.

Travelers' diarrhea: High risk. All water sources should be considered potentially contaminated. Potable water is accessible to only 30%–40% of the population. Travelers should observe all food and drink precautions. A quinolone antibiotic (Cipro or Floxin) is recommended for the treatment of acute diarrhea. Diarrhea not responding to treatment with an antibiotic may be due to a parasitic disease such as giardiasis or amebiasis, and treatment with metronidazole (Flagyl) or tinidazole (Fasigyn) should be considered. All cases of diarrhea should be treated with adequate fluid replacement.

Hepatitis: High risk. All susceptible travelers should receive immune globulin prophylaxis or hepatitis A vaccine. The hepatitis B carrier rate in the general population exceeds 10%. Vaccination against hepatitis B is recommended for healthcare workers and all long-term residents and their families.

Onchocerciasis: Reported to occur in the eastern Corubal and Geba River basins. Travelers should take precautions against insect (black fly) bites.

Schistosomiasis: Urinary schistosomiasis occurs in the northern half of Guinea Bissau, extending from the coastal region of Cacheau to the border with Guinea, including the valleys of the Cacheau and Geba River Basins. Travelers should avoid swimming, bathing, or wading in freshwater streams, lakes, or ponds.

Trypanosomiasis (African sleeping sickness): Sporadic cases were reported in the 1980s. Low-level transmission probably occurs in the coastal and northcentral areas. Travelers should take measures to avoid insect (tsetse) fly bites.

Rabies: Human cases have been reported countrywide from both urban and rural areas, but exact incidence is not known. Pre-exposure vaccination (3 doses) is recommended for long-term travel (more than 4 weeks) to this country, especially for travelers going to remote rural areas who will be unable to receive antirabies treatment within 24 hours of exposure to a potentially rabid animal.

AIDS: Heterosexual contact is the predominate mode of transmission. HIV-2 is currently the predominate infection with up to 10% of the urban population being seropositive. Highest seroprevalence rates are found in high-risk groups, such as female prostitutes. All travelers are cautioned against unsafe sex, or receiving unsterile medical or dental injections.

Other diseases: African tick typhus (transmitted by dog ticks, often in urban areas, and bush ticks), brucellosis (from consumption of raw dairy products), lassa fever (risk undetermined), leprosy, tuberculosis (a major health problem), typhoid fever, and intestinal worms (very common). There is low, but undetermined, risk of dengue, leishmaniasis, and filariasis. Potentially harmful marine animals found in the coastal waters of Guinea-Bissau include Black Sea urchin, jellyfish, Portuguese man-of-war, sea wasp, and stinging hydroid.

IVORY COAST (COTE D'IVOIRE)
Abidjan ... GMT

Entry Requirements
- Passport/Visa: Valid passport and visa are required.
- AIDS Test: Not required.
- Vaccinations: A yellow fever vaccination certificate is required from all travelers more than one year of age arriving from ALL COUNTRIES.

Telephone Country Code: 225

Electricity/Plugs: AC 50 Hz, 220 volts; plug type C. Adaptors and transformer necessary for U.S.-made appliances.

American Express: Socopao Voyages, Avenue Chardy, Abidjan; Tel. 32-35-54.

Embassies/Consulates: U.S. Embassy, Abidjan. 5 Rue Jesse Owens; Tel. 21-09-79. Canadian Embassy. Edifice Trade Center; Tel. 32-20-09.

Hospitals/Doctors: Treichville University Hospital, Abidjan (1,500 beds); general medical/surgical facility; most specialties. Polyclinic International St. Ann Marie, Cocody (300 beds); general medical/surgical facility; emergency room; dialysis; heliport. Travelers should contact the U.S. Embassy for additional healthcare referrals.

Health Advisory
Yellow fever: Vaccination is required. This country is in the Yellow Fever Endemic Zone. A valid yellow fever vaccination certificate may also be required for travel to other countries in South America, Africa, the Middle East, or Asia.

Cholera: This disease is active in this country. Although cholera vaccination is not required for entry if arriving directly from the U.S. or Canada, it may be required if arriving from a cholera-infected area, or required for on-going travel to other countries in Latin America, Africa, the Middle East, or Asia. Travelers should consider vaccination (one dose) or a doctor's letter of exemption from vaccination. The risk to travelers of acquiring cholera is considered low. Prevention consists primarily in adhering to safe food and drink guidelines.

Malaria: Risk is present year-round throughout this country, including urban areas. Falciparum malaria accounts for approximately 90% of cases. Other cases of malaria are due primarily to the *P. malariae* species, rarely *P. ovale*. Chloroquine-resistant falciparum malaria is reported. Prophylaxis with mefloquine or doxycycline is currently recommended when traveling to malarious areas. Alternative malaria regimes should be discussed with a travel medicine or infectious disease specialist.

Travelers' diarrhea: Piped water supplies may be contaminated. Surface water sources may be contaminated or contain excess total dissolved solids (salts). Travelers should observe all food and drink safety precautions. A quinolone antibiotic (Cipro or Floxin) is recommended for the treatment of acute diarrhea. Diarrhea not responding to treatment with an antibiotic, or chronic diarrhea, may be due to a parasitic disease such as giardiasis or amebiasis, and treatment with metronidazole (Flagyl) or tinidazole (Fasigyn) should be considered. All cases of diarrhea should be treated with adequate fluid replacement.

Hepatitis: High risk. All susceptible travelers should receive immune globulin prophylaxis or hepatitis A vaccine. The hepatitis B carrier rate in the general population is estimated to exceed 10%. Vaccination against hepatitis B is recommended for healthcare workers and all long-term visitors to this country.

Onchocerciasis: Focally distributed along fast-flowing rivers. Travelers should take measures to prevent black fly bites.

Schistosomiasis: Urinary schistosomiasis is widely distributed. Major activity occurs in the southeastern (Abidjan, Adzope), central (shores of Lake Kossou), western (Man, Danane), and the northern (Korhogo) areas. Intestinal schistosomiasis is less common and is distributed in the same areas. Travelers should avoid swimming, bathing, or wading in freshwater lakes or streams.

Trypanosomiasis (African sleeping sickness): Risk occurs in central and central eastern regions, including Dalao, Vavoua, Bouafle, and Abengoura. Travelers should take measures to prevent insect (tsetse fly) bites.

Meningitis: Northern Ivory Coast borders the sub-Saharan meningitis belt. There is a high incidence of Group A and C meningococcal meningitis. Most recent outbreak occurred in Korhogo vicinity in 1984. Vaccination recommended for travelers having close contact with the indigenous population.

Rabies: Sporadic cases reported countrywide, with increased risk in southeastern department of Abengourou.

AIDS: Heterosexual contact is the predominate mode of transmission. Prevalence of HIV-1 is estimated at 24% in the high-risk urban population. HIV-2 prevalence estimated at 17%. All travelers are cautioned against unsafe sex, unsterile medical or dental injections, and unnecessary blood transfusions.

Other diseases: African tick typhus (transmitted by dog ticks, often in urban areas, and bush ticks), anthrax, brucellosis (from consumption of raw dairy products), dengue (low risk; human incidence not known), filariasis (presumably endemic; incidence not known), Lassa fever (virus is present but risk of disease indeterminate), toxoplasmosis, tuberculosis (a major health problem), typhoid fever, and intestinal worms (very common) are reported.

LIBERIA

Monrovia ... GMT 0 hrs

Entry Requirements
- Passport/Visa: Valid passport and visa are required. An exit permit is required.
- AIDS Test: Not required
- Vaccinations: A yellow fever vaccination certificate is required from all travelers older than 1 year arriving from ALL COUNTRIES.

Telephone Country Code: 231

Electricity/Plugs: AC 60 Hz, 120/240 volts; plug type A and G. Adaptors and transformer may be necessary for U.S.-made appliances.

American Express: Doukor Travel Agency, Chase Manhattan Plaza, Randall Street. Tel. (22) 1104/4209.

Embassies/Consulates: U.S. Embassy, Monrovia. 111 United Nations Drive. Tel. 222-991/2/3/4. Canadian Consulate, Monrovia. EXCHEM Compound. Tel. 223-903.

Hospitals/Doctors: ELWA Mission Hospital, Monrovia (45 beds); 24-hour emergency services. JFK Memorial Hospital, Monrovia (337 beds); general medical/surgical facility. Firestone Plantation Hospital, Monrovia (200 beds); general medical/surgical facility; emergency services. Travelers should contact the U.S. Embassy for physician referrals.

Health Advisory

Yellow fever: No cases have been reported recently. Yellow fever vaccination is required for entry to Liberia. This country is in the Yellow Fever Endemic Zone. A valid yellow fever vaccination certificate may be required for persons who leave this country and travel to other countries in South America, Africa, the Middle East, or Asia.

Cholera: This disease is active in this country. Although cholera vaccination is not required for entry if arriving directly from the U.S. or Canada, it may be required if arriving from a cholera-infected area, or required for on-going travel to other countries in Latin America,

Africa, the Middle East, or Asia. Travelers should consider vaccination (one dose) or a doctor's letter of exemption from vaccination. The risk to travelers of acquiring cholera is considered low. Prevention consists primarily in adhering to safe food and drink guidelines.

Malaria: Transmission occurs year-round throughout this country, including urban areas. Falciparum malaria accounts for approximately 90% of cases. Other cases are due to the *P. malariae* species, or *P. ovale*. Chloroquine-resistant falciparum malaria has been reported from the northwest (Zorzor) and other areas. Resistance to Fansidar and mefloquine (Lariam) is also reported. Prophylaxis with mefloquine or doxycycline is currently recommended when traveling to malarious areas. Alternative malaria regimes should be discussed with a travel medicine or infectious disease specialist.

Travelers' diarrhea: High risk. All water sources should be considered potentially contaminated. Travelers should observe all food and drink precautions. A quinolone antibiotic (Cipro or Floxin) is recommended for the treatment of acute diarrhea. Diarrhea not responding to treatment with an antibiotic may be due to a parasitic disease such as giardiasis or amebiasis, and treatment with metronidazole (Flagyl) or tinidazole (Fasigyn) should be considered. All cases of diarrhea should be treated with adequate fluid replacement.

Hepatitis: High risk. All susceptible travelers should receive immune globulin prophylaxis or hepatitis A vaccine. The hepatitis B carrier rate in the general population is estimated to exceed 10%. Vaccination against hepatitis B is recommended for healthcare workers and all long-term visitors to this country.

Leishmaniasis: Low risk is estimated. Sporadic cases of cutaneous and visceral leishmaniasis have been reported from neighboring countries. Travelers are advised to take general precautions against insect bites, especially during the night.

Filariasis (Bancroftian variety): Infection rates of up to 37% have been reported from coastal villages, with highest rates in the eastern county of Maryland. Travelers should take protective measures against mosquito bites.

Onchocerciasis: Highly endemic, with foci reported in the west along the St. Paul and Lofa Rivers. Travelers should take personal protection measures against black fly bites.

Schistosomiasis: Risk is present, primarily in the northwestern and northcentral counties of Lofa, Bong, and Nimba. No transmission occurs in the coastal areas. Travelers should avoid swimming, bathing, or wading in freshwater lakes, ponds, or streams.

Lassa fever: Most cases are reported in the northwest regions. Low risk for tourists, but up to 17% of indigenous patients hospitalized with a fever in the Zorzor district in the 1980s were possibly infected with the Lassa fever virus. The virus of Lassa fever is possibly transmitted through infective rodent urine that contaminates food or dust. Travelers can lessen their exposure by avoiding bush areas and the interiors of thatch huts.

Paragonimiasis (lung fluke): Travelers should avoid ingesting raw or pickled crabs and crayfish, which may harbor the infective fluke.

Trypanosomiasis (African sleeping sickness): Sporadic cases have been reported from the Bong area. Travelers should take personal protection measures against tsetse fly bites.

Meningitis: Liberia lies just west of the sub-Saharan meningitis belt. Vaccination is recommended for travelers who expect to have close, prolonged contact with the indigenous population.

Rabies: Human cases reported from Monrovia and countrywide, where there are large stray dog populations. Pre-exposure vaccination against rabies (3 doses) is recommended for long-term travelers to this country and for travelers going to remote rural areas if they will be unable to receive antirabies treatment within 24 hours of exposure to a potentially rabid animal such as a dog, cat, or monkey. Pre-exposure vaccination does not preclude the need for additional post-exposure treatment.

AIDS: Prevalence appears to be low, based on limited data.

Other illnesses/hazards: African tick typhus (contracted from dog ticks, often in urban areas, and bush ticks), anthrax, brucellosis, leprosy (up to 2 cases/1,000 population), syphilis, tuberculosis (a major health problem), typhoid fever, and intestinal worms (very common). Animal hazards include snakes (vipers, mambas, cobras), centipedes, scorpions, and black widow spiders. Potentially harmful marine animals found in the coastal waters of Liberia include Portuguese man-of-war, sea nettle, marine catfish, moonjelly, mauve stinger, marine catfish, eagle ray, scorpionfish, and weeverfish. Swimmers should take sensible precautions to avoid these hazards.

MALI

Bamako ... GMT 0 hrs

Entry Requirements

- Passport/Visa: A valid passport and visa are required.
- AIDS Test: Not required.
- Vaccinations: A yellow fever vaccination certificate is required from all travelers older than 1 year of age arriving from ALL COUNTRIES.

Telephone Country Code: 223

Electricity/Plugs: AC 50 Hz, 220 volts; plug types C and E. Adaptors and transformer necessary for U.S.-made appliances.

Embassies/Consulates: U.S. Embassy, Rue Testard & Rue Mohammed, Bamako; Tel. (3) 224-835/225-476. Canadian Embassy , Koulkouro Road, Bamako; Tel. (3) 26-12-000.

Doctors/Hospitals: Point G Hospital, Bamako (550 beds); general medical/surgical facility. Centre Medical Interentreprise, Bamako; Tel. 22-25-54.

Health Advisory

Yellow fever: The Southwestern Region is considered officially infected by the WHO. The most recent outbreak of yellow fever occurred during late 1987 in the regions of Kayes and Koulikoro. Vaccination is presently required for entry to this country. Southern Mali is in the Yellow Fever Endemic Zone.

Cholera: This disease is active in this country. Although cholera vaccination is not required for entry if arriving directly from the U.S. or Canada, it may be required if arriving from a cholera-infected area, or required for on-going travel to other countries in Latin America, Africa, the Middle East, or Asia. Travelers should consider vaccination or a doctor's letter of exemption from vaccination. The risk to travelers of acquiring cholera is considered low. Prevention consists primarily in adhering to safe food and drink guidelines.

Malaria: Risk is present throughout this country, including urban areas. Risk is increased during and immediately following the rainy season (June–October). The highest risk of malaria occurs in southern Mali, particularly in the southern savanna and central Sahel zones. There is less risk in the northern Saharan region. Falciparum malaria accounts for approximately 85% of cases; *P. malariae* causes most other cases. Chloroquine-resistant falciparum malaria is prevalent, and mefloquine resistance has recently been reported. Chemoprophylaxis with either mefloquine or doxycycline is currently recommended.

Travelers' diarrhea: High risk. Surface water is almost always contaminated and ground water from deep wells commonly brackish. Piped water supplies are either untreated and often contaminated. Travelers should observe all food and drink precautions. A quinolone antibiotic (Cipro or Floxin) is recommended for the treatment of acute diarrhea. Diarrhea not responding to treatment with an antibiotic may be due to a parasitic disease such as giardiasis or amebiasis and treatment with metronidazole (Flagyl) or tinidazole (Fasigyn) should be considered. All cases of diarrhea should be treated with adequate fluid replacement.

Hepatitis: All susceptible travelers should receive immune globulin or hepatitis A vaccine. The hepatitis B carrier rate in the general population is estimated at 9%–18%. Vaccination against hepatitis B is recommended for healthcare workers and for those planning long-term residence (more than 4 weeks) in this country.

Leishmaniasis: Risk of cutaneous leishmaniasis occurs primarily in rural areas of the southern and central Sahel. Current incidence and distribution data are not available, but sporadic cases have been reported from semi-desert regions, with a major focus in the Nioro District of Kayes Region. Visceral leishmaniasis (kala azar) is currently not reported. All travelers to these regions should take measures to prevent sandfly bites.

Filariasis: Bancroftian filariasis is reported in southern areas. Travelers should take measures to prevent insect (mosquito) bites.

Onchocerciasis: Highly endemic foci are found in the Sikasso and Kayes Regions along rivers where black flies breed. Travelers should take measures to prevent insect (black fly) bites.

Schistosomiasis: Prevalence is particularly high in irrigated areas. Urinary schistosomiasis occurs throughout southern Mali, primarily in the upper reaches of the Niger River and the upper basin of the Senegal River. Intestinal schistosomiasis is almost as extensively distributed. A new focus of disease has recently been reported from the Bandiagara and Bankas Districts where the Dogon tribe is located. To prevent schistosomiasis, travelers should avoid swimming, bathing, or wading in freshwater lakes, ponds, or streams.

Trypanosomiasis (African sleeping sickness): There is a low risk of trypanosomiasis in Mali, primarily in the Koulikoro and Sikasso regions. Travelers to these regions should take precautions to prevent tsetse fly bites.

Meningitis: The southern half of Mali lies within the sub-Saharan meningitis belt. Periodic epidemics occur within this country. Most infections are caused by Group A organisms, but Type C also occurs. Vaccination is recommended for travelers who expect to have close, prolonged contact with the indigenous population.

Rabies: Human cases have been reported countrywide from both urban and rural areas. Pre-exposure vaccination against rabies is recommended for long-term travelers to this country and for travelers going to remote rural areas if they will be unable to receive antirabies treatment within 24 hours of exposure to a potentially rabid animal such as a dog, cat, jackal, or fox.

AIDS: HIV prevalence is apparently low in the general population but as high as 40% of surveyed prostitutes are infected.

Other illnesses/hazards: Anthrax (reported from Kati and Koulikoro Provinces), brucellosis (from consumption of raw dairy products), dracunculiasis (endemic at low levels), ehrlichiosis (tick-borne; single case reported in 1992 in a Canadian traveler), echinococcosis, hemorrhagic fever with renal syndrome (level of risk unclear; no human cases reported), Lassa fever, leprosy (4–7 cases/1,000 population in Bamako), Rift Valley fever, toxoplasmosis, tuberculosis (a major health problem), typhoid fever, and intestinal worms (very common). Animal hazards include snakes (vipers, cobras), centipedes, scorpions, and black widow spiders; crocodiles and hippopotamuses inhabit the rivers of Mali; lions and panthers are the major terrestrial hazards.

MAURITANIA
Nouakchott ... GMT 0 hrs

Entry Requirements
- Passport/Visa: Valid passport and visa are required.
- AIDS Test: Not required.
- Vaccinations: A yellow fever vaccination certificate is required from all travelers older than 1 year arriving from ALL COUNTRIES.

Telephone Country Code: 222

Electricity/Plugs: AC 50 Hz, 220 volts; plug type C. Adaptors and transformer necessary for U.S.-made appliances.

Embassies/Consulates: U.S. Embassy, Nouakchott; Tel. 52660. Canadian Embassy (Senegal); Tel. [221] 210-290.

Doctors/Hospitals: National Hospital, Nouakchott (460 beds); general medical/surgical facility; limited specialties.

Health Advisory
Yellow fever: Vaccination is recommended. Southern Mauritania borders the yellow fever endemic zone of Mali, considered "infected" by the World Health Organization.

Cholera: This disease is active in this country. Although cholera vaccination is not required for entry if arriving directly from the U.S. or Canada, it may be required if arriving from a cholera-infected area, or required for on-going travel to other countries in Latin America, Africa, the Middle East, or Asia. Travelers should consider vaccination (one dose) or a doctor's letter of exemption from vaccination. The risk to travelers of acquiring cholera is considered low. Prevention consists primarily in adhering to safe food and drink guidelines.

Malaria: Risk is present year-round in the south, including urban areas. Limited risk is present in the semi-desert/desert areas north of 20 degrees latitude, including the regions of Dahklet Nouadhibou, Inchiri, Adrar, and Tiris Zemmour. Vivax malaria accounts for 90%

of cases. Falciparum malaria reportedly accounts for less than 10% of cases. Chloroquine-resistant falciparum malaria presumably occurs. Mefloquine prophylaxis is recommended when traveling to malarious areas. Alternative malaria regimes (e.g., chloroquine with Fansidar standby) should be discussed with a travel medicine or infectious disease specialist.

Travelers' diarrhea: High risk. Ten urban areas receive water from a government utility; nevertheless, all water sources should be considered potentially contaminated. Travelers should observe food and drink safety precautions. A quinolone antibiotic (Cipro or Floxin) is recommended for the treatment of acute diarrhea. Diarrhea not responding to treatment with an antibiotic, or chronic diarrhea, may be due to a parasitic disease such as giardiasis or amebiasis, and treatment with metronidazole (Flagyl) or tinidazole (Fasigyn) should be considered. All cases of diarrhea should be treated with adequate fluid replacement.

Hepatitis: High risk. All susceptible travelers should receive immune globulin prophylaxis or hepatitis A vaccine. The hepatitis B carrier rate in the general population is estimated as high as 22%. Vaccination against hepatitis B is recommended for healthcare workers and all long-term visitors to this country.

Dengue fever: Undetermined risk, but probably low. Dengue virus is present in neighboring Senegal.

Leishmaniasis: Sporadic cases of cutaneous leishmaniasis have been reported along the border with Senegal and near the southern border with Mali. Travelers should take measures to prevent insect (sandfly) bites.

Schistosomiasis: Risk is greatest in the south along the Senegal River and extending into the southeast, and a smaller area farther north, around the Adrar mountain range in the vicinity of Atar, in central western Mauritania. Infection rates are highest in the south central border provinces of Asaba, Guidimaka, and Hodh El Gharbi. Travelers should avoid swimming, bathing, or wading in freshwater lakes, ponds, or streams.

Rabies: Vaccination is indicated following the unprovoked bite of a dog or other wild animal. Pre-exposure vaccination against rabies (3 doses) should be considered prior to long-term travel to this region. This is especially true for travelers going to remote rural areas if they will be unable to receive antirabies treatment within 24 hours of exposure to a potentially rabid animal. Pre-exposure vaccination does not preclude the need for post-exposure treatment.

AIDS: HIV prevalence appears to be low, based on limited data.

Other illnesses/hazards: African tick typhus, anthrax (incidence data lacking), brucellosis (from consumption of raw dairy products), meningitis, plague (human incidence data lacking), tuberculosis (a major health problem), typhoid fever, and intestinal worms (very common). Animal hazards include snakes (vipers, cobras, adders), centipedes, scorpions, and black widow spiders. Marine hazards include poisonous fishes (weever, scorpion, and toad fishes) and venomous marine invertebrates such as the Portuguese man-of-war, stinging corals, feather hydroids, and sea nettles, anemones, urchins, and sea cucumbers.

NIGER

Embassy: 202-483-4224   *Niamey*   *GMT +1 hr*

Entry Requirements

- Passport/Visa: Valid passport and visa are required.
- AIDS Test: Not required.
- Vaccinations: A yellow fever vaccination certificate is required from all travelers older than 1 year arriving from ALL COUNTRIES.

Telephone Country Code: 227

Electricity/Plugs: AC 50 Hz, 220 volts; plug types A, B, C, D, E, and F. Adaptors and transformer necessary for U.S.-made appliances.

Embassies/Consulates: U.S. Embassy, Niamey. B.P. 11201; Tel. 722-661. Canadian Embassy (Ivory Coast). Tel. [225] 322-009.

Hospitals/Doctors: Niamey Central Hospital (790 beds); general medical/surgical facility; some specialties. Gamkalley Hospital, Niamey (20 beds); basic emergency services only.

Health Advisory

Yellow fever: Vaccination is required for entry to this country. This country is in the Yellow Fever Endemic Zone. A vaccination certificate may also be required for on-going travel to other countries in Africa, the Middle East, and Asia.

Cholera: This disease is active in this country. Although cholera vaccination is not required for entry if arriving directly from the U.S. or Canada, it may be required if arriving from a cholera-infected area, or required for on-going travel to other countries in Latin America, Africa, the Middle East, or Asia. Travelers should consider vaccination (one dose) or a doctor's letter of exemption from vaccination. The risk to travelers of acquiring cholera is considered low. Prevention consists primarily in adhering to safe food and drink guidelines.

Malaria: Risk is present year-round throughout this country, including urban areas. Risk of malaria is higher in the south than in the northern Saharan areas. Falciparum malaria accounts for approximately 80% of cases. Other cases of malaria are due to the *P. ovale* and *P. malariae* species, rarely *P. vivax*. Chloroquine-resistant falciparum malaria is reported. Prophylaxis with mefloquine or doxycycline is currently recommended when traveling to malarious areas. Alternative malaria regimes should be discussed with a travel medicine or infectious disease specialist.

Travelers' diarrhea: High risk. Treated, piped water is available in some major areas, but water supplies are generally not potable. Niger River water is bacterially contaminated. The water in Lake Chad is highly saline. Travelers should observe all food and drink safety precautions. A quinolone antibiotic (Cipro or Floxin) is recommended for the treatment of acute diarrhea. Diarrhea not responding to treatment with an antibiotic, or chronic diarrhea, may be due to a parasitic disease such as giardiasis or amebiasis, and treatment with metronidazole (Flagyl) or tinidazole (Fasigyn) should be considered. All cases of diarrhea should be treated with adequate fluid replacement.

Hepatitis: High risk. All susceptible travelers should receive immune globulin prophylaxis or hepatitis A vaccine. The hepatitis B carrier rate in the general population is estimated at 16%–21%. Vaccination against hepatitis B is recommended for healthcare workers and all long-term visitors to this country.

Leishmaniasis: Foci of cutaneous leishmaniasis occur in the southwest and may be distributed throughout the southcentral and southeastern rural areas. Visceral leishmaniasis has been reported in the northwest. Travelers should take measures to prevent insect (sandfly) bites.

Schistosomiasis: Risk of urinary schistosomiasis is confined to areas below 15 degrees north latitude. Widely distributed in the Niger River Valley in the southwest with foci in southcentral Niger along the Nigerian border. Travelers should avoid swimming, bathing, or wading in freshwater lakes, ponds, or streams.

Trypanosomiasis (African sleeping sickness): Historically, cases have occurred on the border with Burkina Fasso, but no cases have been reported since 1980.

Meningitis: Southwestern and southern Niger lie within the sub-Saharan meningitis belt. Outbreaks are reported countrywide, usually during the dry season, November–May. There is increased risk in the southern regions. Vaccination is recommended for travelers who expect to have close contact with the indigenous population for extended periods of time (more than 2–4 weeks).

Rabies: Pre-exposure vaccination (3 doses) is recommended for long-term travel (more than 4 weeks) to this country, especially for travelers going to remote rural areas if they will be unable to receive antirabies treatment within 24 hours of exposure to a potentially rabid animal.

AIDS: Heterosexual contact is the predominate mode of transmission. HIV prevalence in the general population is estimated to be low, but up to 10% of surveyed prostitutes are HIV positive. All travelers are cautioned against unsafe sex, unsterile medical or dental injections, and unnecessary blood transfusions.

Other diseases/hazards: African tick typhus (transmitted by dog ticks, often in urban areas, and bush ticks), anthrax, brucellosis (from consumption of raw dairy products), filariasis (mosquito-borne; risk occurs in the rural southwest), leprosy (estimated prevalence of 1 case/ 1,000 population), leptospirosis, onchocerciasis (black-fly borne; endemic foci along rivers in the southwest), tuberculosis (a major health problem), and intestinal worms (very common) are reported. Animal hazards include snakes (vipers, cobras, puff adders), scorpions, and black widow spiders; hippopotamuses and crocodiles are found along the banks of the Niger River.

NIGERIA

Lagos ... GMT +1 hr

Entry Requirements
- Passport/Visa: Valid passport and visa are required. Must have sufficient funds.
- AIDS Test: Foreign nationals from countries that require HIV testing of Nigerians may be required to have an HIV test. Travelers should contact the closest Nigerian consulate or the Nigerian Embassy in Washington, D.C.
- Vaccinations: A yellow fever vaccination certificate is required from all travelers older than 1 year arriving from infected areas.

Telephone Country Code: 234

Electricity/Plugs: AC 50 Hz, 220 volts; plug types D and G. Adaptors and transformer necessary for U.S.-made appliances.

American Express: Mandilas Travel Ltd. 96/102 Broad Street, Lagos; Tel. (1) 663-333.

Embassies/Consulates: U.S. Embassy, Lagos. 2 Elleke Crescent; Tel. (1) 610-097. Canadian High Commission, Victoria Isle. 4 Idowa-Taylor Street; Tel. (1) 612-382.

Hospitals/Doctors: Lagos General Hospital (2,000 beds); some specialty clinics; ICU. University College Hospital, Lagos (822 beds); some specialty clinics. Lagos Clinic; Tel. 833-546. Kelu Specialist Clinic; Tel. 616-993. Baptist Mission Hospital, 120 km north of Ibadan; general medical/surgical facility.

Health Advisory

Yellow fever: This disease is active in this country. The following areas are considered infected: Anambra, Bauchi, Bendel, Benue, Cross River, Kaduna, Kwara, Lagos, Niger, Ogun, Ondo, Plateau State. Vaccination is recommended. This country is in the Yellow Fever Endemic Zone. A valid yellow fever vaccination certificate may be required for on-going travel to other countries in South America, Africa, the Middle East, or Asia.

Cholera: This disease is active in this country. Although cholera vaccination is not required for entry if arriving directly from the U.S. or Canada, it may be required if arriving from a cholera-infected area, or required for on-going travel to other countries in Latin America, Africa, the Middle East, or Asia. Travelers should consider vaccination or a doctor's letter of exemption from vaccination. The risk to travelers of acquiring cholera is considered low. Prevention consists primarily in adhering to safe food and drink guidelines.

Malaria: Risk is present year-round countrywide, including urban areas. Risk may be elevated during and just after the rainy seasons. Falciparum malaria accounts for approximately 95% of cases, followed by malaria due to *P. malariae*. Multidrug-resistant falciparum malaria has been reported. Mefloquine or doxycycline prophylaxis is currently recommended.

Travelers' diarrhea: High risk. Most of Nigeria's water sources are man-made lakes, rivers, streams, and wells, most of which are contaminated. The water supply in Lagos is pure at the source, but cross contamination with sewage may occur during distribution. Travelers should all observe food and drink safety precautions. A quinolone antibiotic is recommended for the treatment of acute diarrhea. Diarrhea not responding to treatment with an antibiotic, or chronic diarrhea, may be due to a parasitic disease such as giardiasis or amebiasis.

Hepatitis: High risk. All susceptible travelers should receive immune globulin prophylaxis or hepatitis A vaccine. The hepatitis B carrier rate in the general population is estimated at 15%. Vaccination against hepatitis B is recommended for healthcare workers and all long-term visitors to this country.

Arboviral fevers (mosquito-transmitted): Low risk of dengue (No cases recently reported). West Nile fever is endemic. Chikungunya fever occurs in outbreaks in rural populations.

Leishmaniasis: May occur in northern areas. Risk undetermined, but probably low.

Onchocerciasis: Widespread along fast-flowing rivers in both savanna and forest zones in parts of all states, except Lagos and Rivers. Travelers should take measures to prevent black fly bites.

Filariasis: Major area of Bancroftian filariasis in the south, including the Igwun Basin of Imo State, and the Niger Delta; infection rates up to 26% have been reported. Travelers should take measures to prevent mosquito bites.

Schistosomiasis: Risk is present, but infected areas are scattered. High risk areas include the Niger flood plain below Lake Kainji, Sokoto vicinity in the northwest, the central and northern highlands, around Lake Chad, and the southwest, including Lagos and Ibadan. Travelers should avoid swimming, bathing, or wading in freshwater lakes, ponds, or streams.

Trypanosomiasis (African sleeping sickness): Foci presumably exist in Gboko vicinity of Benue State (southeastern areas confluent with endemic areas of Cameroon), and the southwestern states of Edo and Delta. Extreme northern areas are tsetse free. Travelers should take measures to prevent tsetse fly bites.

Meningitis: Vaccination is recommended for travelers who expect to have close contact with the indigenous population for extended periods of time (more than 2–4 weeks).

Rabies: Considered a public health problem in many rural and urban areas, including Lagos; stray dogs are the primary cause of human infection. Travelers should seek immediate treatment of any animal bite. Pre-exposure vaccination against rabies (3 doses) should be considered for long-term travel to this country.

AIDS: HIV-1 and HIV-2 prevalences estimated at 1.7% and 0.9%, respectively, among high-risk urban populations.

Other diseases/hazards: African tick typhus, anthrax (sporadic human outbreaks), brucellosis, murine typhus (flea-borne), dracunculiasis (guinea worm disease—widely distributed), Lassa fever (sporadic outbreaks reported, most recently from south central states of Imo, Abia, Edo, and Delta), leprosy (highest prevalence in the southeast), leptospirosis, loiasis (deer-fly-borne; occurs in southern rain forests and swamp forests), paragonimiasis (19% infection rate in the Igwun Basin), tuberculosis (a major health problem), trachoma, and intestinal worms (very common). Animal hazards include snakes (vipers, cobras, puff adders, mambas), scorpions, brown recluse spider, and black widow spiders; potentially harmful marine animals which occur in the coastal waters of Nigeria include sea wasps, Portuguese man-of-war, rosy anemone, sea urchin, weeverfish, eagle ray, and sea nettle.

SAO TOME & PRINCIPE

Sao Tome ... GMT 0 hrs

Entry Requirements

- Passport/Visa: Valid passport and visa are required.
- AIDS Test: Not required.
- Vaccinations: A yellow fever vaccination certificate is required from all travelers older than 1 year arriving from ALL COUNTRIES. A yellow fever vaccination certificate is NOT required if arriving from a non-infected area and staying less than 2 weeks.

U.S. Embassy: The U.S. Ambassador based in Gabon is accredited to Sao Tome on a non-resident basis.

Health Advisory

Yellow fever: Vaccination is required for entry. No recent yellow fever cases are reported. This country is in the Yellow Fever Endemic Zone. A valid yellow fever vaccination certificate may be required for travel to other countries in South America, Africa, the Middle East, or Asia.

Cholera: This disease is active in this country. Although cholera vaccination is not required for entry if arriving directly from the U.S. or Canada, it may be required if arriving from a cholera-infected area, or required for on-going travel to other countries in Latin America, Africa, the Middle East, or Asia. Travelers should consider vaccination (one dose) or a doctor's letter of exemption from vaccination. The risk to travelers of acquiring cholera is considered low. Prevention consists primarily in adhering to safe food and drink guidelines.

Malaria: Risk is present year-round throughout this country, including urban areas. Falciparum malaria accounts for up to 90% of cases. Chloroquine-resistant falciparum malaria is reported. Prophylaxis with mefloquine or doxycycline is currently recommended when traveling to malarious areas of this country. Alternative malaria regimes should be discussed with a travel medicine or infectious disease specialist.

Travelers' diarrhea: High risk. Piped water supplies should be considered potentially contaminated. Travelers should observe all food and drink safety precautions. A quinolone antibiotic (Cipro or Floxin) is recommended for the treatment of acute diarrhea. Diarrhea not responding to treatment with an antibiotic, or chronic diarrhea, may be due to a parasitic disease such as giardiasis or amebiasis, and treatment with metronidazole (Flagyl) or tinidazole (Fasigyn) should be considered. All cases of diarrhea should be treated with adequate fluid replacement.

Hepatitis: High risk. All susceptible travelers should receive immune globulin prophylaxis or hepatitis A vaccine. The hepatitis B carrier rate in the general population is estimated to exceed 10%. Vaccination against hepatitis B is recommended for healthcare workers and all long-term visitors to this country.

Schistosomiasis: Widely distributed throughout the island of Sao Tome. The major risk area is in the northeast between the Rio Grande and Manuel Jorge Rivers, including the capital and environs, the surrounding Agua Grande District, and the adjacent part of Mezoxi District. Travelers should avoid swimming, bathing, or wading in freshwater lakes, ponds, or streams.

AIDS: Incidence is presumed low, but widespread surveys have not been done.

Other illnesses/hazards: Data on filariasis, onchocerciasis, leishmaniasis, tuberculosis, intestinal helminthic diseases, and rabies not available, but these diseases are presumed to occur.

SENEGAL

Dakar ... GMT 0 hrs

Entry Requirements
- Passport/Visa: Valid passport and visa are required.
- AIDS Test: Not required.
- Vaccinations: A yellow fever vaccination certificate is required from all travelers over 1 year of age arriving from any country any part of which is infected or from any country in the Yellow Fever Endemic Zones.

Telephone Country Code: 221

Electricity/Plugs: AC 50 Hz, 127/220 volts; plug types D, E, and K. Adaptors and transformer necessary for U.S.-made appliances.

American Express: Senegal Tours. 5 Place De L'Independance; Tel. 23-31-81.

Embassies/Consulates: U.S. Embassy, Dakar. Avenue Jean XXIII; Tel. 23-42-96 or 23-34-24. Canadian Embassy, Dakar. 45 Avenue De La Republique; Tel. 210-290.

Doctors/Hospitals: CTO Trauma Care Facility, Dakar (160 beds); general medical/surgical facility; trauma; orthopedics. Dantec Hospital, Dakar (190 beds); general medical/surgical facility; trauma. Hospitale Principale, Dakar (650 beds); cardiothoracic surgery; orthopedics. Majdi Kaouk, M.D., Dakar; Tel. 21-77-09 or 21-29-17 (home).

Health Advisory

Yellow fever: Vaccination is recommended. No cases have recently been reported. This country is in the Yellow Fever Endemic Zone.

Malaria: Risk is present year-round throughout this country, including Dakar and other urban areas. There is less risk in the Cap Vert vicinity January–June. Risk is highest in the central and southern areas of this country, but is also reported to be increasing in the north. Falciparum malaria accounts for approximately 90% of cases. Other cases of malaria are due to the *P. malariae* and *P. ovale* species, rarely *P. vivax*. Chloroquine-resistant falciparum malaria is reported. Prophylaxis with mefloquine or doxycycline is currently recommended when traveling to malarious areas. Alternative malaria regimes should be discussed with a travel medicine or infectious disease specialist.

Travelers' diarrhea: High risk. The towns of Dakar, Saint-Louis, Kaolack, Thies, and Ziguinchor have municipal water systems and public taps, but these systems may be contaminated. Travelers should observe all food and drink safety precautions. A quinolone antibiotic (Cipro or Floxin) is recommended for the treatment of acute diarrhea. Diarrhea not responding to treatment with an antibiotic, or chronic diarrhea, may be due to a parasitic disease such as giardiasis or amebiasis and treatment with metronidazole (Flagyl) or tinidazole (Fasigyn) should be considered. All cases of diarrhea should be treated with adequate fluid replacement.

Hepatitis: High risk. All susceptible travelers should receive immune globulin prophylaxis or hepatitis A vaccine. The hepatitis B carrier rate in the general population is estimated as high as 18%. Vaccination against hepatitis B is recommended for healthcare workers and all long-term visitors to this country.

Leishmaniasis: Risk of cutaneous leishmaniasis occurs in northwest (Keur Moussa in the Theis Region) and has been reported in the northeast along the Mauritanian border. Visceral leishmaniasis has not been reported. Travelers should take measures to prevent insect (sandfly) bites.

Schistosomiasis: Risk of urinary schistosomiasis is present in the Senegal River Valley, the west central region, and the southern region. Intestinal schistosomiasis occurs in scattered areas. Travelers should avoid swimming, bathing, or wading in freshwater lakes, ponds, or streams.

AIDS: Heterosexual contact is the predominate mode of transmission. HIV-1 prevalence estimated at 2.3% of the high-risk urban population. HIV-2 prevalence reported at 10% of the high-risk population. All travelers are cautioned against unsafe sex, unsterile medical or dental injections, and unnecessary blood transfusions.

Other diseases: African tick typhus (contracted from dog ticks and bush ticks), brucellosis (from consumption of raw dairy products and occupational exposure), chikungunya fever (endemic; reported in cyclic outbreaks), dengue (low risk; rarely reported), filariasis (mosquito-borne), leprosy, leptospirosis, meningitis, murine typhus (fleaborne), onchocerciasis (black-fly-borne; contracted near fast-flowing rivers), rabies (reported in both urban and rural areas), tick-borne relapsing fever, trypanosomiasis (no new cases of sleeping sickness since 1978), tuberculosis (a major health problem), and intestinal worms (very common) are reported.

SIERRA LEONE
Freetown ... GMT 0 hrs

Entry Requirements
- Passport/Visa: Valid passport and visa are required.
- AIDS Test: Not required.
- Vaccinations: A yellow fever vaccination certificate is required from all travelers over 1 year of age arriving from infected areas.

Telephone Country Code: 232

American Express: A. Yazbeck & Sons Agencies. 22 Siaka Stevens Street, Freetown; Tel. 24423.

Embassies/Consulates: U.S. Embassy, Freetown. Corner Walpole & Siaka Stevens; Tel. 26481. Canadian Embassy (Nigeria); Tel. [234] 612-382.

Hospitals/Doctors: Connaught Hospital, Freetown (240 beds); overcrowded, understaffed facility lacking modern equipment. Spiritus House, 8A Howe Street, Freetown; Tel. 26-671/31-746.

Health Advisory

Yellow fever: Vaccination is recommended. This country is in the Yellow Fever Endemic Zone. Although a vaccination certificate may not be required for entry to this country, one may be required for on-going travel to other countries in Africa, the Middle East, and Asia.

Malaria: Risk is present year-round throughout this country, including urban areas. Falciparum malaria accounts for 80% of cases. Other cases of malaria are due to the *P. malariae* and *P. ovale* species, rarely *P. vivax*. Chloroquine-resistant falciparum malaria is reported. Prophylaxis with mefloquine or doxycycline is currently recommended when traveling to malarious areas of this country.

Travelers' diarrhea: High risk outside of urban areas. In the Freetown area, chlorinated water from the Cuma Valley Dam is piped directly to the consumer. Piped water supplies, as well as all surface water, may be contaminated. Travelers should observe all food and drink safety precautions. A quinolone antibiotic (Cipro or Floxin) is recommended for the treatment of acute diarrhea. Diarrhea not responding to treatment with an antibiotic, or chronic diarrhea, may be due to a parasitic disease such as giardiasis or amebiasis, and treatment with metronidazole (Flagyl) or tinidazole (Fasigyn) should be considered. All cases of diarrhea should be treated with adequate fluid replacement.

Hepatitis: High risk. All susceptible travelers should receive immune globulin prophylaxis or hepatitis A vaccine. The hepatitis B carrier rate in the general population is estimated to exceed 10%. Vaccination against hepatitis B is recommended for healthcare workers and all long-term visitors to this country.

Leishmaniasis: Risk is undetermined, but probably is low.

Onchocerciasis: Widely distributed, except for the coastal plain and the Freetown peninsula. Travelers should take precautions to prevent insect (black fly) bites, especially near fast-flowing rivers, where black flies breed.

Schistosomiasis: Risk is present in eastern, central, and northern areas, but transmission reportedly does not occur within 100 km of the Atlantic coast. Travelers should avoid swimming, bathing, or wading in freshwater lakes, ponds, or streams.

Trypanosomiasis (African sleeping sickness): Current incidence and risk data are not available. Sporadic cases were reported during the early 1980s. Travelers should take precautions to prevent insect (tsetse fly) bites.

Lassa fever: Risk is countrywide (increased during the dry season, February–April), with most cases occurring in Eastern Province. Transmission of the virus is from contact with dust or food contaminated with infected rodent urine. Household sanitary measures and rodenticides should reduce or eliminate risk.

Rabies: Risk of exposure, especially from stray dogs, occurs in urban and rural areas. Pre-exposure vaccination against rabies (3 doses) should be considered for long-term travel to this region. This is especially true for travelers going to remote rural areas if they will be unable to receive antirabies treatment within 24 hours of exposure to a potentially rabid animal.

AIDS: Heterosexual contact is the predominate mode of transmission. HIV prevalence is estimated at 2%–3% of blood donors. Seropositivity of high-risk individuals not available. All travelers are cautioned against unsafe sex, unsterile medical or dental injections, and unnecessary blood transfusions.

Other diseases: African tick typhus (transmitted by dog ticks, often in urban areas, and bush ticks), anthrax, brucellosis (from consumption of raw dairy products), dengue (low risk), Bancroftian filariasis (mosquito-borne), leprosy (1 case/1,000 population), leptospirosis, tuberculosis (a major health problem), and intestinal helminths (very common) are reported.

TOGO

Lome ... GMT

Entry Requirements
- Passport/Visa: Travelers should possess valid passport. Visa not required.
- AIDS Test: Not required.
- Vaccinations: A yellow fever vaccination certificate is required from all travelers older than 1 year of age arriving from ALL COUNTRIES. Cholera: The State Department reports that a cholera vaccination certificate may also be required for entry into Togo.

Telephone Country Code: 228

Electricity/Plugs: AC 50 Hz, 220 volts; plug type C. Adaptors and transformer necessary for U.S.-made appliances.

American Express: S.T.M.P. Voyages. 2 Rue Du Commerce, Lome; Tel. 6190.

Embassies/Consulates: U.S. Embassy, Lome. Rue Pelletier Caventou & Rue Vouban; Tel. 2991. Canadian Embassy (Ghana); Tel. [233] 228-555.

Hospitals/Doctors: Tokoin National Hospital, Lome (650 beds); general medical/surgical facility; trauma unit; ENT. Hospital Baptiste Biblique Adeta; well-equipped medical/surgical facility. Travelers should contact the U.S. Embassy for additional physician referrals.

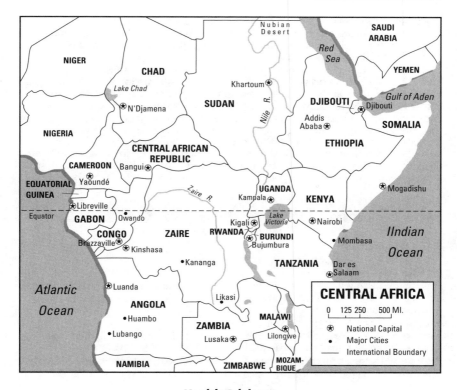

Health Advisory

Yellow fever: Vaccination is recommended for all travelers over 9 months of age who plan to travel outside urban areas. This country is in the Yellow Fever Endemic Zone and a valid yellow fever vaccination certificate may be required for entry to other countries.

Malaria: Risk is present throughout this country, including urban areas. Falciparum malaria accounts for approximately 85% of cases. Most other cases of malaria are due to the *P. malariae* and *P. ovale* species. Chloroquine-resistant falciparum malaria is reported. Mefloquine or doxycycline prophylaxis is currently recommended. Protection against mosquito bites is essential.

Travelers' diarrhea: High risk. Safe water is available in only a few urban areas where there are treatment plants and piped distribution systems. These systems are subject to contamination. Travelers should observe all food and drink safety precautions. A quinolone antibiotic (Cipro or Floxin) is recommended for the treatment of acute diarrhea. Diarrhea not responding to treatment with an antibiotic, or chronic diarrhea, may be due to a parasitic disease such as giardiasis or amebiasis, and treatment with metronidazole (Flagyl) or tinidazole (Fasigyn) should be considered. All cases of diarrhea should be treated with adequate fluid replacement.

Hepatitis: High risk. All susceptible travelers should receive immune globulin prophylaxis or hepatitis A vaccine. The hepatitis B carrier rate in the general population is estimated to exceed 10%. Vaccination against hepatitis B is recommended for healthcare workers and all long-term visitors to this country.

Schistosomiasis: Risk is present in eastern, central, and northern areas, but transmission reportedly does not occur within 100 km of the Atlantic coast. Travelers should avoid swimming or wading in freshwater lakes, ponds, or streams.

Meningitis: Togo lies within the sub-Saharan meningitis belt. Sporadic outbreaks of meningococcal meningitis occur, especially in the northern and central areas. Vaccination is recommended for travelers staying in these regions longer than 4 weeks who will have close contact with the indigenous population.

AIDS: Heterosexual transmission is the predominate means of transmission. Current infection rates of high-risk groups is presently not available. All travelers are cautioned against unsafe sex, unsterile medical or dental injections, and unnecessary blood transfusions.

Other illnesses/hazards: African tick typhus (contracted from dog ticks, often in urban areas, and bush ticks), anthrax, brucellosis (from consumption of raw dairy products), filariasis (mosquito-borne), Lassa fever, leishmaniasis (sporadic cases have previously been reported), leprosy (up to 1.3 cases/1,000 population), onchocerciasis (black-fly-borne; transmitted near fast-flowing rivers), toxoplasmosis, syphilis, tuberculosis (a major health problem), typhoid fever, and intestinal helminths (very common). Animal hazards include snakes (vipers, cobras), centipedes, scorpions, and black widow spiders.

ANGOLA

Luanda ... GMT +1 hr

Entry Requirements
- Passport/Visa: Valid passport and visa are required.
- AIDS Test: Not required.
- Vaccinations: A yellow fever vaccination certificate is required from all travelers older than 1 year arriving from infected countries.

Telephone Country Code: 263

Electricity/Plugs: AC 50 Hz, 220 volts; plug type C.

Embassies & Consulates: The United States does not presently maintain diplomatic relations with Angola. Canadian Embassy (Zimbabwe); Tel. [263] (4) 733-881.

Hospitals/Doctors: University Hospital, Luanda (500+ beds); Tel. 50-491 or 22-886. Americo Boavioa (600 beds); general medical/surgical facility.

Health Advisory

Yellow fever: This disease is active in this country. Risk is confined to the northeastern forested areas (Luanda and Bengo Provinces). Cases also reported in the capital city of Luanda in 1988. Yellow fever vaccination is recommended. This country is in the Yellow Fever Endemic Zone. A valid yellow fever vaccination certificate may be required for on-going travel to other countries in South America, Africa, the Middle East, or Asia.

Cholera: This disease is active in this country. Although cholera vaccination is not required for entry if arriving directly from the U.S. or Canada, it may be required if arriving from a cholera-infected area, or required for on-going travel to other countries in Latin America, Africa, the Middle East, or Asia. Travelers should consider vaccination (one dose) or a doctor's letter of exemption from vaccination. The risk to travelers of acquiring cholera is considered low. Prevention consists primarily in adhering to safe food and drink guidelines.

Malaria: Risk is present year-round throughout this country, including urban areas. Falciparum malaria accounts for 90% of cases. Most other cases of malaria are presumably caused by *P. malariae*, with even fewer cases due to *P. ovale* and *P. vivax*. Chloroquine-resistant falciparum malaria is reported. Prophylaxis with mefloquine or doxycycline is currently recommended when traveling to malarious areas of this country.

Travelers' diarrhea: High risk. Only major urban areas have access to public water systems, which serve primarily the former European sections. Water distribution systems may be damaged and contaminated. Travelers should all observe food and drink safety precautions. A quinolone antibiotic is recommended for the treatment of acute diarrhea. Diarrhea not responding to treatment with an antibiotic, or chronic diarrhea, may be due to a parasitic disease such as giardiasis or amebiasis.

Hepatitis: High risk. All susceptible travelers should receive immune globulin prophylaxis or hepatitis A vaccine. The hepatitis B carrier rate in the general population is estimated to exceed 10%. Vaccination against hepatitis B is recommended for healthcare workers and all long-term visitors to this country.

Dengue fever: Low risk. No recent cases have been reported.

Chikungunya fever: Mosquito-borne; human outbreaks have been reported in the Luanda area.

Rift Valley fever: Transmitted by culicine mosquitoes and also by contact with flesh of infected domestic animals. Low risk. Human outbreaks have occurred in this region.

Onchocerciasis: Transmitted by blackflies near fast-flowing rivers, primarily in the northern provinces, the plateau region of the central province of Bie, and the Cabinda exclave.

Schistosomiasis: Risk areas for urinary schistosomiasis are widely distributed except in the northeastern corner of the country and the southeastern area bordered by the Loangue Bongo River, the Cuito River, and the Zambian border. Intestinal schistosomiasis is endemic throughout Angola except for the southwest. Travelers should avoid swimming, bathing, or wading in freshwater ponds, lakes, or streams.

Trypanosomiasis (African sleeping sickness): Sporadic cases of the Rhodesian form of trypanosomiasis have been reported in the southeast. Foci of the Gambian form of trypanosomiasis have been detected in the northwestern provinces of Zaire, Uige, Luanda, and Cuanza Norte. Travelers should take measures to prevent insect (tsetse fly) bites.

Rabies: Considered a public health problem in many rural and urban areas; stray dogs are the primary cause of human infection. Travelers should seek immediate treatment of any animal bite. Pre-exposure vaccination against rabies should be considered prior to long-term travel (more than 4 weeks) to this country.

AIDS: Heterosexual transmission is the predominate means of transmission. HIV-1 and HIV-2 prevalences estimated at up to 14% of the urban population. Current infection rates of high-risk groups is presently not available. All travelers are cautioned against unsafe sex, unsterile medical or dental injections, and unnecessary blood transfusions.

Other illnesses/hazards: African tick typhus (contracted from dog ticks, often in urban areas, and bush ticks), brucellosis (from consumption of raw dairy products), Bancroftian filariasis (mosquito-borne; reported in the north, primarily Cabinda enclave and Zaire Province), leishmaniasis (low apparent risk; sporadic cases may have previously occurred), plague (flea-borne; human cases last reported from Benguela Province), relapsing fever (tick-borne and louse-borne), toxoplasmosis, syphilis, tuberculosis (a major health problem), typhoid fever, typhus (louse-borne and flea-borne), and intestinal worms (very common). Animal hazards include snakes (vipers, cobras, mambas), centipedes, scorpions, and black widow spiders. Sea wasps, Portuguese man-of-war, black sea urchins, weever fish, spiny dogfish are found in the coastal waters of Angola and could be a hazard to swimmers.

CENTRAL AFRICAN REPUBLIC
Bangui ... GMT +1 hr

Entry Requirements
- Passport/Visa: Valid passport and visa are required.
- AIDS Test: Not required.
- Vaccinations: A yellow fever vaccination certificate is required from all travelers older than 1 year of age arriving from ALL COUNTRIES.

Embassies/Consulates: U.S. Embassy, Bangui. Avenue President Dacko; Tel. 610-200/614-333. Canadian Embassy, Cameroon; Tel. [237] 221-090.

Hospitals/Doctors: National University Hospital Center, Bangui (700 beds); general medical/surgical facility; some French military medical officers on the staff. American Lutheran Church Missionary Hospital. Bouar (25 beds); general medical services. Clinicas las Condes, Bangui.

Health Advisory

Yellow fever: Vaccination is required of all travelers. This country is in the Yellow Fever Endemic Zone. A valid vaccination certificate may also be required for on-going travel to other countries.

Malaria: Risk is present year-round throughout this country, including urban areas. Falciparum malaria accounts for 85% of cases. Chloroquine-resistant falciparum malaria is reported. Mefloquine prophylaxis is currently advised.

Travelers' diarrhea: High risk. All water, including piped water from municipal treatment facilities, is considered contaminated. Travelers should observe all food and drink safety precautions. A quinolone antibiotic (Cipro or Floxin) is recommended for the treatment of acute diarrhea. Diarrhea not responding to treatment with an antibiotic, or chronic diarrhea, may be due to a parasitic disease such as giardiasis or amebiasis, and treatment with metronidazole (Flagyl) or tinidazole (Fasigyn) should be considered. All cases of diarrhea should be treated with adequate fluid replacement.

Hepatitis: High risk. All susceptible travelers should receive immune globulin prophylaxis or hepatitis A vaccine. The hepatitis B carrier rate in the general population is estimated at 10%–15%. Vaccination against hepatitis B is recommended for healthcare workers and all long-term visitors to this country.

Leishmaniasis: Risk undetermined. Sporadic cases of cutaneous leishmaniasis (in the northwest and southwest) and visceral leishmaniasis reportedly have occurred. Travelers should take measures to prevent insect (sandfly) bites.

Loiasis: Highly endemic focus in southwestern rain forest and swamp forest areas. Travelers should take measures to prevent insect (deer fly) bites.

Trypanosomiasis (African sleeping sickness): About 150 cases reported annually. Risk areas include the Ouham Valley, Nola vicinity, and the southeast. Travelers should take measures to prevent insect (tsetse fly) bites.

Meningitis: North Central African Republic lies within the sub-Saharan meningitis belt which has a high incidence of Group A meningococcal infections. Vaccination is recommended for travelers staying in this region longer than 4 weeks and having close contact with the indigenous population.

AIDS: Heterosexual transmission is the predominate means of transmission. HIV-1 prevalence estimated at 21% of the high-risk urban population. All travelers are cautioned against unsafe sex, unsterile medical or dental injections, and unnecessary blood transfusions.

Other illnesses/hazards: African tick typhus (contracted from dog ticks, often in urban areas, and bush ticks), brucellosis (from consumption of raw dairy products), Bancroftian filariasis (mosquito-borne; 1,000 cases reported during the 1980s), chikungunya fever (documented outbreak occurred in 1978), dengue (not reported), Lassa fever (low risk; current endemic status unclear), leprosy (up to 2.7 cases/1,000 population), rabies (transmitted primarily by dogs in urban and rural areas), syphilis, toxoplasmosis, tuberculosis (a major health problem), typhoid fever, and intestinal worms (very common). Animal hazards include snakes (boomslang, viper, cobra), centipedes, scorpions, and spiders (black widow, brown recluse).

CAMEROON
Yaounde ... GMT +1 hr

Entry Requirements
- Passport/Visa: Valid passport and visa are required.
- AIDS Test: Not required.
- Vaccinations: A yellow fever vaccination certificate is required from all travelers older than 1 year of age arriving from ALL COUNTRIES.

Telephone Country Code: 237

Electricity/Plugs: AC 50 Hz, 220 volts; plug types C, D, E, G, and K. Adaptors and transformer necessary for U.S.-made appliances.

American Express: Camvoyages. Imm. Socopao, "Vallee Tokoto." Descente Du Meridien, Douala; Tel. 422-544.

Embassies/Consulates: U.S. Embassy, Yaounde. Rue Nachtigal; Tel. 234-014. U.S. Consulate, Douala; 21 Avenue du General De Gaulle; Tel. 425-331. Canadian Embassy, Yaounde. Edifice Stamatiades, Place de l'Hotel; Tel. 221-090.

Hospitals/Doctors: University of Yaounde Medical Center; general medical services; radiology. Central Hospital, Yaounde (554 beds); general medical services; blood bank. Polyclinique Sende; Yaounde; general medical services. LaQuintinie Hospital, Douala (930 beds); general medical services; ICU; X-ray. Polyclinique de Douala; Tel. 424-289/420-547.

Health Advisory

Yellow fever: This disease is active in this country. Outbreaks were reported in late 1990 in Extreme-Nord Province. Yellow fever vaccination is required to enter this country. This country is in the Yellow Fever Endemic Zone. A valid yellow fever vaccination certificate may also be required for on-going travel to other countries.

Cholera: This disease is active in this country. Although cholera vaccination is not required for entry if arriving directly from the U.S. or Canada, it may be required if arriving from a cholera-infected area, or required for on-going travel to other countries in Latin America, Africa, the Middle East, or Asia. Travelers should consider vaccination (one dose) or a doctor's letter of exemption from vaccination. The risk to travelers of acquiring cholera is considered low. Prevention consists primarily in adhering to safe food and drink guidelines.

Malaria: Risk is present year-round throughout this country, including urban areas. Falciparum malaria accounts for approximately 85% of cases, followed by malaria due to *P. ovale* and *P. malariae*. Chloroquine-resistant falciparum malaria is prevalent throughout the country. Mefloquine- and quinine-resistant falciparum malaria has been reported in the northern regions. Prophylaxis with mefloquine or doxycycline is currently recommended. Alternative malaria regimes should be discussed with a travel medicine or infectious disease specialist.

Travelers' diarrhea: High risk. Several urban areas in the south, including Douala, Yaounde, and Mbalmayo, have treatment plants and piped water systems, but improper operation and poor maintenance of the plants allow bacterial recontamination. All water sources should be considered potentially contaminated. A quinolone antibiotic (Cipro or Floxin) is recommended for the treatment of acute diarrhea. Diarrhea not responding to treatment with an antibiotic, or chronic diarrhea, may be due to a parasitic disease such as giardiasis or amebiasis, and treatment with metronidazole (Flagyl) or tinidazole (Fasigyn) should be considered. All cases of diarrhea should be treated with adequate fluid replacement.

Hepatitis: High risk. All susceptible travelers should receive immune globulin prophylaxis or hepatitis A vaccine. The hepatitis B carrier rate in the general population is estimated at 10%–12%. Vaccination against hepatitis B is recommended for healthcare workers and all long-term visitors to this country.

Leishmaniasis: Undetermined risk; foci of disease presumably occur in the north, bordering Chad. Incidence data not currently available.

Onchocerciasis: Highly endemic foci presumably persist in the south and the southwest, and in the savanna area of northern Cameroon. All travelers should take measures to prevent insect (black fly) bites, especially in the vicinity of rivers.

Loiasis: Highly endemic foci presumably persist in southern rain forest and swamp forest areas. All travelers should take measures to prevent insect (deer fly) bites.

Schistosomiasis: Urinary and intestinal schistosomiasis are highly endemic in the north and in the southwest. Intestinal schistosomiasis, caused by *S. Mansoni*, is endemic in Nord Province and in Center-Sud Province. Areas also infested include Yaounde, Edea, and Douala. Travelers should avoid swimming, bathing, or wading in freshwater ponds, lakes, or streams.

Trypanosomiasis (African sleeping sickness): Most risk is found in the vicinities of Bafia (Mbam Division, Centre Province) and Fontem (Manyu/Fontem Division, Sud-Ouest Province). Mbam Division reports the most cases of sleeping sickness. Potential areas for recurrence include Extreme-Nord Province bordering Chad, and Est Province, bordering the Nola vicinity of the Central African Republic. Travelers to risk areas should take measures to prevent insect (tsetse fly) bites.

Meningitis: Northern Cameroon lies within the sub-Saharan meningitis belt. Outbreaks occurred in 1988 in the northern districts of Nord Province and in 1989 from Nord-Ouest Province. Vaccination is recommended for travelers who expect close, prolonged (more than 2–4 weeks) contact with the indigenous population.

Rabies: Last officially reported outbreak involving human cases occurred in the northwest in 1988. Pre-exposure vaccination (3 doses) is recommended for long-term travel (more than 4 weeks) to this country, especially for travelers going to remote rural areas who will be unable to receive antirabies treatment within 24 hours of exposure to a potentially rabid animal. Pre-exposure vaccination does not preclude the need for post-exposure treatment (2 additional doses of vaccine; rabies immune globulin not needed). Rabies post-exposure vaccination in previously unvaccinated travelers: 5 doses of vaccine, plus rabies immune globulin.

AIDS: Heterosexual transmission is the predominate means of transmission. HIV-1 prevalence estimated at 9% of the high-risk urban population. All travelers are cautioned against unsafe sex, unsterile medical or dental injections, and unnecessary blood transfusions.

Other illnesses/hazards: Brucellosis (from consumption of raw dairy products or occupational exposure), Bancroftian filariasis (mosquito-borne; over 7,000 cases reported in 1985), Lassa fever (current endemic status unclear), leprosy (up to 1.9 cases/1,000 population), toxoplasmosis, syphilis, tuberculosis (a major health problem), typhoid fever, and intestinal worms (very common). Animal hazards include snakes (vipers, mambas, cobras), centipedes, scorpions, and black widow spiders.

CHAD

Embassy: 202-462-4009   *N'Djamena*   *GMT +1 hr*

Entry Requirements

- Passport/Visa: Valid passport and visa are required.
- AIDS Test: Not required.
- Vaccinations: None required.

Telephone Country Code: 235

Electricity/Plugs: AC 50 Hz, 220 volts; plug types D, E, and F. Adaptors and transformer necessary for U.S.-made appliances.

Embassies/Consulates: U.S. Embassy, N'Djamena. Avenue Felix Eboue; Tel. (51) 62-18/32-69. Canadian Embassy (Cameroon); Tel. [237] 221-090.

Hospitals/Doctors: N'Djamena Central Hospital (620 beds); general medical services; some specialties. Sahr Hospital (325 beds); general medical facility. Travelers should contact the U.S. Embassy for physician referrals.

Health Advisory

Yellow fever: Vaccination is recommended for all travelers over age 9 months. No cases reported recently, but this country is in the Yellow Fever Endemic Zone. A valid vaccination certificate may be required for travel to other countries.

Cholera: This disease is active in this country. Although cholera vaccination is not required for entry if arriving directly from the U.S. or Canada, it may be required if arriving from a cholera-infected area, or required for on-going travel to other countries in Latin America, Africa, the Middle East, or Asia. Travelers should consider vaccination (one dose) or a doctor's letter of exemption from vaccination. The risk to travelers of acquiring cholera is considered low. Prevention consists primarily in adhering to safe food and drink guidelines.

Malaria: Risk is present year-round throughout this country, including urban areas. Malaria is moderately to highly endemic in southern and southwestern Chad, June through November (during and immediately following the rainy season). There is lower risk of malaria in the drier northern Saharan region. *P. falciparum* accounts for approximately 85% of cases, followed by *P. ovale* and *P. malariae*. Chloroquine-resistant falciparum malaria is reported. Low-level resistance to mefloquine presumably occurs. Prophylaxis with mefloquine or doxycycline is currently recommended

Travelers' diarrhea: High risk. The capital city and some other major urban areas are supplied with well water which, although treated, is consistently contaminated. Travelers should observe all food and drink safety precautions. A quinolone antibiotic is recommended for the treatment of acute diarrhea. Diarrhea not responding to treatment with an antibiotic, or chronic diarrhea, may be due to a parasitic disease such as giardiasis or amebiasis.

Hepatitis: High risk. All susceptible travelers should receive immune globulin prophylaxis or hepatitis A vaccine. The hepatitis B carrier rate in the general population is estimated at 15%, or higher. Vaccination against hepatitis B is recommended for healthcare workers and all long-term visitors to this country.

Leishmaniasis: Sporadic cases are reported and foci of infection probably occur throughout most of Chad. Visceral leishmaniasis occurs in the N'Djamena and Lake Chad areas, with foci extending eastward throughout southern Chad. Cutaneous leishmaniasis occurs in Chari-Baguirmi Prefecture (which also includes N'Djamena), along the Chari River in southcentral Chad, and in the neighboring western prefectures of Lac and Kanem Transmission occurs primarily from April through November. Travelers to these areas should take precautions against insect (sandfly) bites.

Filariasis (Bancroftian): Mosquito-borne; sporadic cases are reported in rural areas of southern Chad.

Onchocerciasis: Black-fly borne; moderate to highly endemic along most rivers in this country.

Loiasis: Deer fly-borne: Risk of transmission may occur in southwestern swamp forest areas.

Schistosomiasis: Transmission occurs year-round along Lake Chad and is endemic throughout the southern half of Chad, particularly in the Bol area. Infection rates for urinary schistosomiasis have exceeded 50% in highly endemic areas; prevalence has been much lower for intestinal schistosomiasis. Travelers should avoid swimming or wading in freshwater lakes, ponds, or streams.

Trypanosomiasis (sleeping sickness): Low risk. Sporadic cases reported in the Logone and Chari River valleys of the southwest, primarily in the prefectures of Logone Oriental (Gore sub-prefecture), Logone Occidental (Yapol prefecture), and Moyen-Chari (Moissala prefecture). Travelers to these areas should take measures to prevent insect (tsetse fly) bites.

Meningitis: Southern Chad lies within the sub-Saharan meningitis belt. Last outbreak involved 2,640 cases in 1988. Vaccination is recommended for travelers who will have close, prolonged contact with the indigenous population.

AIDS: HIV prevalence is estimated to be low, but incidence data are lacking. All travelers are cautioned against unsafe sex, unsterile medical or dental injections, and unnecessary blood transfusions.

Other illnesses/hazards: Anthrax, brucellosis, echinococcosis, leprosy (up to 2–4 cases/1,000 population), rabies, relapsing fever (louse-borne and tick-borne), syphilis, tuberculosis (a major health problem), typhoid fever, typhus (flea-borne and louse-borne), and intestinal helminths (very common). Animal hazards include snakes (adders, vipers, cobras), scorpions, and black widow spiders. Crocodiles and hippo inhabit Lake Chad.

CONGO

Brazzaville ... GMT +1 hr

Entry Requirements

- Passport/Visa: Valid passport and visa are required. Return or onward ticket required.
- AIDS Test: Not required.
- Vaccinations: A yellow fever vaccination certificate is required from all travelers older than 1 year of age arriving from ALL COUNTRIES.

Telephone Country Code: 242

Electricity/Plugs: AC 50 Hz, 220 volts; plug types C and E. Adaptors and transformer necessary for U.S.-made appliances.

Embassies/Consulates: U.S. Embassy, Brazzaville. Avenue Amilcar Cabral; Tel. 832-070/832-624. Canadian Embassy (Zaire); Tel. [243] (12) 27551.

Hospitals/Doctors: Brazzaville General Hospital (900 beds); general medical services. Travelers should contact the U.S. Embassy for physician referral.

Health Advisory

Yellow fever: No cases recently reported, but vaccination is recommended for those traveling outside urban areas. This country is in the Yellow Fever Endemic Zone. A valid vaccination certificate may be required for on-going travel to other countries.

Malaria: Risk is present year-round throughout this country, including urban areas. Risk may be elevated during and just after the rainy season (April through October north of the equator, October through May south of the equator). Falciparum malaria accounts for approximately 90% of cases. Chloroquine-resistant *P. falciparum* is reported. Prophylaxis with mefloquine or doxycycline is currently recommended when traveling to risk areas.

Travelers' diarrhea: High risk. Rural villages and towns obtain water from untreated sources. Brazzaville, Point Noire, and some other major cities have modern filtration and purification plants, but the water is subject to recontamination. Travelers should observe all food and drink safety precautions. A quinolone antibiotic is recommended for the treatment of acute diarrhea. Diarrhea not responding to treatment with an antibiotic, or chronic diarrhea, may be due to a parasitic disease such as giardiasis amebiasis, or cryptosporidiosis.

Hepatitis: High risk. All susceptible travelers should receive immune globulin or hepatitis A vaccine. The hepatitis B carrier rate in the general population is estimated at 7%–12%. Vaccination against hepatitis B is recommended for healthcare workers and all long-term visitors to this country.

Dengue fever: Not reported, although the mosquito vector, *Aedes aegypti*, is present in this country.

Leishmaniasis: Sporadic cases have been reported. Travelers should take personal protection measures against insect (sandfly) bites.

Onchocerciasis: High prevalence in two southwestern areas: the Djoue River basin and the bank region of the Congo River. Travelers should take personal protection measures against insect (black fly) bites.

Loiasis: Areas in the rain forest and villages in the Chaillu mountains are highly endemic. Travelers should take personal protection measures against biting deer flies.

Schistosomiasis: Risk of urinary schistosomiasis is present in the southwestern regions of Bouenza, Niari, and Kouilou, as well as the Brazzaville vicinity. Less risk occurs in the northern areas of the country, where the acidic soil is less conducive to the establishment of the freshwater snail intermediate hosts. Travelers should avoid swimming, bathing, or wading in freshwater lakes, ponds, or streams.

Trypanosomiasis (African sleeping sickness): Major risk areas include southern savanna of Niari and Bouenza Regions, along the Congo River north of Brazzaville to the vicinity of Mossaka, and in the extreme southwest of Cuvette Region (Okoyo vicinity); presumably occurs along the Lefini River. All travelers to these regions shoud take measures to prevent insect (tsetse fly) bites.

AIDS: Prevalence of HIV-1 estimated at 34% of the high-risk urban population. Heterosexual contact is the predominate mode of transmission. All travelers are cautioned against unsafe sex, unsterile medical or dental injections, and blood transfusions.

Other illnesses/hazards: Brucellosis (from consumption of raw dairy products or occupational exposure), mansonellosis (mosquito-borne form of filariasis), leprosy (up to 4 cases/1,000 population), rabies (usually transmitted by stray dogs), toxoplasmosis, tuberculosis (a major health problem), typhoid fever, and intestinal helminths (very common). Animal hazards include snakes (mambas, adders, vipers, cobras), centipedes, scorpions, and black widow spiders.

GABON

Embassy: 202-797-1000   **Libreville**   **GMT +1 hr**

Entry Requirements

- Passport/Visa: Valid passport and visa are required.
- AIDS Test: Not required.
- Vaccinations: A yellow fever vaccination certificate is required from all travelers older than 1 year of age arriving from ALL COUNTRIES.

Telephone Country Code: 241

Electricity/Plugs: AC 50 Hz, 220/380 volts; plug type C.

American Express: Eurafrique Voyages, Town Centre, Libreville; Tel. 762-787.

Embassies/Consulates: U.S. Embassy, Libreville. Boulevard de la Mer; Tel. 762-003, 743-492. Canadian Embassy, Libreville; Tel. 743-464.

Hospitals/Doctors: Libreville General Hospital (630 beds); general medical/surgical facility; maternity wing. The Albert Schweitzer Hospital, Lambarene. Bongolo Evangelical Hospital, La Bomba (80 beds); missionary hospital; emergency care available.

Health Advisory

Yellow fever: Vaccination is recommended for travel outside urban areas. No cases have been reported recently. This country is in the Yellow Fever Endemic Zone. A valid vaccination certificate may be required for on-going travel to other countries.

Malaria: Risk is present year-round, including urban areas. Risk is elevated during the rainy seasons (October-December, and February-April). Falciparum malaria accounts for approximately 95% of cases. Chloroquine-resistant falciparum malaria is reported. Prophylaxis with mefloquine or doxycycline is recommended when traveling to risk areas.

Travelers' diarrhea: High risk. Piped water supplies in Libreville, Port-Gentil, and Bata may be grossly contaminated. Travelers should observe all food and drink safety precautions. A quinolone antibiotic is recommended for the treatment of acute diarrhea. Diarrhea not responding to treatment with an antibiotic, or chronic diarrhea, may be due to a parasitic disease such as giardiasis, amebiasis, or cryptosporidiosis.

Hepatitis: High risk. All susceptible travelers should receive immune globulin or hepatitis A vaccine. The hepatitis B carrier rate in the general population is estimated at 7%– 12%. Vaccination against hepatitis B is recommended for healthcare workers and all long-term visitors to this country.

Onchocerciasis: Widely distributed, especially in Ndjole, Fougamou, Mimongo, Lebamba, Latoursville, and Makokou. Travelers should take measures to prevent insect (black fly) bites.

Loiasis: High risk present in the southeastern rain forest and swamp forest. Infection rate of 25% reported in the Franceville vicinity. Travelers should take measures to prevent insect (deer fly) bites.

Schistosomiasis: Foci of disease are scattered throughout all provinces, with a major focus in the Libreville area. Travelers should avoid swimming, bathing, or wading in freshwater lakes, ponds, or streams.

Other illnesses/hazards: African tick typhus, brucellosis (from consumption of raw dairy products), cholera, Chikungunya fever (mosquito-transmitted), dracunculiasis, Ebola-Marburg virus disease (endemic status unclear), echinococcosis, filariasis, Lassa fever (endemic status unclear), leprosy (up to 3 cases/1,000 population), rabies, paragonimiasis, sleeping sickness (risk areas persist along the coast, primarily the Komo estuary around Libreville, and the mouth of the Ogooue River near Port Gentil), toxoplasmosis, tuberculosis (a major health problem), trypanosomiasis (sporadic cases reported along the coast), typhoid fever, and intestinal helminths, particularly ancylostomiasis. Animal hazards include snakes (vipers, cobras), centipedes, scorpions, and black widow spiders.

MALAWI

Lilongwe ... GMT +2 hrs

Entry Requirements

- Passport/Visa: Travelers should possess valid passport. Visa not required.
- AIDS Test: Not required.
- Vaccinations: A yellow fever valid vaccination certificate is required from all travelers older than 1 year arriving from infected areas or from any country in the yellow fever endemic zones.

Telephone Country Code: 265

American Express: Manica Travel Services. City Centre Bureau, Lilongwe; Tel. 733-133.

Embassies/Consulates: U.S. Embassy, Lilongwe; Tel. 730-166. Canadian Embassy, (Zaire); Tel. [243] (12) 27551.

Hospitals/Doctors: Queen Elizabeth Central Hospital, Blantyre (640 beds); general medical/surgical facility. Malamulo Hospital, Blantyre; Tel. 620-399, 620-006. Likuni Mission Hospital, Lilongwe; recommended as the best local hospital. Adventist Health Centre, Blantyre; Tel. 731-819.

Health Advisory

Yellow fever: Vaccination is recommended for travel outside urban areas. This country is in the Yellow Fever Endemic Zone. A valid vaccination certificate may be required for on-going travel to other countries.

Cholera: This disease is reported active in this country. Although cholera vaccination is not required for entry if arriving directly from the U.S. or Canada, it may be required for on-going travel to other countries in Africa, the Middle East, or Asia. Travelers should consider vaccination (one dose) or getting a doctor's letter of exemption from vaccination. The risk to travelers of acquiring cholera is considered low. Prevention consists primarily in adhering to safe food and drink guidelines.

Malaria: Risk is present year-round throughout this country, including urban areas. Malaria risk is highest along the shores of Lake Malawi where the risk peaks at the end of the rainy season (November through April). Falciparum malaria accounts for approximately 90% of cases. Other cases of malaria are due to the *P. ovale* and *P. malariae* species, rarely *P. vivax*. Chloroquine-resistant falciparum malaria is reported. Prophylaxis with mefloquine or doxycycline is currently recommended when traveling to malarious areas.

Travelers' diarrhea: High risk. There are water treatment systems in some major urban areas, but even treated water should be considered potentially contaminated. Travelers should observe all food and drink safety precautions. A quinolone antibiotic is recommended for the treatment of acute diarrhea. Diarrhea not responding to treatment with an antibiotic, or chronic diarrhea, may be due to a parasitic disease such as giardiasis, amebiasis, or cryptosporidiosis.

Hepatitis: High risk. All susceptible travelers should receive immune globulin or hepatitis A vaccine. The hepatitis B carrier rate in the general population is estimated at 8%. Vaccination against hepatitis B is recommended for healthcare workers and all long-term visitors to this country.

Onchocerciasis: A focus of disease activity may exist in the southern Thyolo highlands. Travelers to this area should take measures to prevent insect (black fly) bites.

Schistosomiasis: An estimated 40%–50% of the population is infected. Risk areas are distributed country-wide. Travelers should avoid swimming, bathing, or wading in freshwater lakes, ponds, or streams.

Other illnesses/hazards: African tick typhus, brucellosis (from consumption of raw dairy products), dengue (low risk), echinococcosis, filariasis (may occur along the lower Shire River and along the shores of Lake Malawi), leishmaniasis (risk undetermined; sporadic cases may occur), leptospirosis, meningitis, plague, rabies (transmitted by dogs, hyenas, and jackals), toxoplasmosis, syphilis, tuberculosis (a major health problem), trypanosomiasis (reported from the Kasungu and Vwaza Game Reserves, near the Luangwa Valley of Zambia), trachoma, typhoid fever, and intestinal helminths (very common). Animal hazards include snakes (vipers, cobras), centipedes, scorpions, and black widow spiders.

ZAIRE

Embassy: 202-234-7690　　　　**Kinshasa**　　　　**GMT +2 hrs**

Entry Requirements

- Passport/Visa: Valid passport and visa are required. Proof of sufficient funds required.
- AIDS Test: Not required.
- Vaccinations: A yellow fever vaccination certificate is required from all travelers older than 1 year of age arriving from ALL COUNTRIES.

Telephone Country Code: 243

Electricity/Plugs: 220 volts; plug types C and D. Adaptors and transformer necessary for U.S.-made appliances.

Embassies/Consulates: U.S. Embassy, Kinshasa. 310 Avenue des Aviateures; Tel. (12) 25881/2/3. U.S. Consulte, Lubumbashi. 1029 Blvd. Kamanyola; Tel. (011) 222-324. Canadian Embassy, Kinshasa. 17 Avenue Pumbu Gombe; Tel. (12) 27551.

Hospitals/Doctors: Centre Medico-Chirurgical, Kinshasa; Tel. (12) 22-133/22-134. Mama Yemo Hospital (2,000 beds); general medical/surgical facility; some specialties.

Health Advisory

Yellow fever: This disease is considered active in this country, north of 10° south latitude. Yellow fever vaccination is recommended for all travelers. This country is in the Yellow Fever Endemic Zone. A valid vaccination certificate may be required for on-going travel to other countries.

Cholera: This disease active in this country. Although cholera vaccination is not officially required for entry, it may be unofficially required, or required for on-going travel to other countries in Africa, the Middle East, or Asia. Travelers should consider vaccination (one dose) or getting a doctor's letter of exemption from vaccination. The risk to travelers of acquiring cholera is considered low. Prevention consists primarily in adhering to safe food and drink guidelines.

Malaria: Risk is present year-round throughout this country, including urban areas. Falciparum malaria accounts for approximately 95% of cases. *P. malariae* species is the next most common cause of malaria. Other cases of malaria are due to the *P. ovale* and, rarely, the *P. vivax* species. Chloroquine-resistant falciparum malaria is reported. Prophylaxis with mefloquine or doxycycline is currently recommended when traveling to malarious areas. Alternative malaria regimes should be discussed with a travel medicine or infectious disease specialist.

Travelers' diarrhea: High risk. In urban areas, about 50% of the population has access to potable water. Piped water supplies may be contaminated. Travelers should observe all food and drink safety precautions. A quinolone antibiotic (Floxin or Cipro) is recommended for the treatment of acute diarrhea. Diarrhea not responding to treatment with an antibiotic, or chronic diarrhea, may be due to a parasitic disease such as giardiasis or amebiasis, and treatment with metronidazole (Flagyl) or tinidazole (Fasigyn) should be considered. All cases of diarrhea should be treated with adequate fluid replacement.

Hepatitis: High risk. All susceptible travelers should receive immune globulin prophylaxis or hepatitis A vaccine. The hepatitis B carrier rate in the general population is estimated at 13%. Vaccination against hepatitis B is recommended for healthcare workers and all long-term visitors to this country.

Leishmaniasis: Risk undetermined, but probably low. Sporadic cases of visceral leishmaniasis have been diagnosed in the northwest, on the fringe of the equatorial forest, and in the southeast, in the savanna belt. No cases of cutaneous leishmaniasis have recently been reported. Travelers should take personal protection measures against insect (sandfly) bites.

Onchocerciasis: Widespread risk, especially along fast-flowing rivers in the regions of Haut-Zaire, Kasai-Oriental, Kasai-Occidental, central and southern Equator, the forest zone of Maniema in Kivu, and western Bas-Zaire. Travelers to these regions should take measures to prevent insect (black fly) bites.

Schistosomiasis: High risk. Intestinal schistosomiasis occurs primarily in four geographical regions: the northern border along the Kibali-Uele Rivers and tributaries; the eastern border from Lake Mobuto to Lake Tanganyika; the Lualaba basin of Shaba region; and the area between Kinshasa and the Atlantic coast. High-risk area of urinary schistosomiasis occurs in the extreme southeast tip of Zaire. Travelers to these areas should avoid swimming, bathing, or wading in freshwater lakes or ponds.

Trypanosomiasis (sleeping sickness): Risk increased during the 1980s due to decreased tsetse fly control programs. Areas of disease risk (gambiense disease) include the western border region, the extreme northeast, and the southwest (including Bas Zaire Region), extending in a band across southcentral Zaire. High transmission levels exist along the Congo River. Foci of the Rhodesian form of sleeping sickness may occur in eastern Zaire. Travelers should take measures to prevent insect (tsetse fly) bites.

Plague: Outbreaks in 1987–1988 resulted in 843 human cases. Mahagi Administrative Zone of Haut-Zaire Region considered "infected" by the WHO. There has recently been an increase in the number of cases of plague in northeastern Zaire. Travelers should avoid close contact with rodents. Tetracycline or doxycycline are effective prophylactic antibiotics.

Rabies: Urban rabies, transmitted primarily by stray dogs, reported from Kinshasa and Lisala, and elsewhere. Pre-exposure vaccination (3 doses) is recommended for long-term travel (more than 4 weeks) to this country, especially for travelers going to remote rural areas who will be unable to receive antirabies treatment within 24 hours of exposure to a potentially rabid animal. Pre-exposure vaccination does not preclude the need for post-exposure treatment (2 additional doses of vaccine; rabies immune globulin not needed). Rabies post-exposure vaccination in previously unvaccinated travelers: 5 doses of vaccine, plus rabies immune globulin.

AIDS: Heterosexual contact is the predominate mode of transmission. HIV-1 prevalence estimated at 38% of the high-risk urban population. All travelers are cautioned against unsafe sex, unsterile medical or dental injections, and unnecessary blood transfusions.

Other illnesses/hazards: African tick typhus, brucellosis (from consumption of raw dairy products), Crimean-Congo hemorrhagic fever (tick-borne; sporadic cases of occur), Ebola-Marburg virus disease (low risk; last outbreak 1977–78), echinococcosis, filariasis (Bancroftian variety; mosquito-borne), loiasis (deer fly–borne), meningitis, toxoplasmosis, syphilis, tuberculosis (a major health problem), trachoma, typhoid fever, and intestinal helminths (very common). Animal hazards include snakes (vipers, cobras), centipedes, scorpions, and black widow spiders.

ZAMBIA

Embassy: 202-265-9717   *Lusaka*   *GMT +2 hrs*

Entry Requirements
- Passport/Visa: Valid passport and visa are required.
- AIDS Test: Not required.
- Vaccinations: No vaccinations are required.

Telephone Country Code: 260

Electricity/Plugs: AC 50 Hz, 220 volts; plug types C, D, and G. Adaptors and transformer necessary for U.S.-made appliances.

American Express: Eagle Travel Ltd. Findeco House, Cairo Road, Lusaka; Tel. (1) 214-916.

Embassies/Consulates: U.S. Embassy, Lusaka. Corner of Independence & United Nations Avenue; Tel. (1) 228-595, 228-601, 251-419. Canadian High Commission, Lusaka. Barclay's Bank, North End Branch, Cairo Roa; Tel. (1) 216-161.

Hospitals/Doctors: University Teaching Hospital, Lusaka (1,500 beds); Tel. (1) 254-468, 211-440.

Health Advisory

Yellow fever: Vaccination is recommended for travel outside urban areas. This country is in the Yellow Fever Endemic Zone. A valid vaccination certificate may be required for on-going travel to other countries.

Cholera: This disease is reported active in this country. Although cholera vaccination is not required for entry if arriving directly from the U.S. or Canada, it may be required for on-going travel to other countries in Africa, the Middle East, or Asia. Travelers should consider vaccination (one dose) or getting a doctor's letter of exemption from vaccination. Cholera vaccine gives only brief, incomplete protection and is not routinely recommended for travelers in good health. Cholera occurs in areas with inadequate sewage disposal and unsafe water supplies such as urban slums and rural areas. The risk to travelers of acquiring cholera is considered low. Prevention consists primarily in adhering to safe food and drink guidelines.

Malaria: Risk is present year-round throughout this country, including urban areas. Incidence has been increasing in Copperbelt Province and Southern Province. Falciparum malaria accounts for approximately 90% of cases. Other cases of malaria are due to the *P. ovale* and *P. malariae* species, and sometimes *P. vivax*. Chloroquine-resistant falciparum malaria is reported. Prophylaxis with mefloquine or doxycycline is currently recommended when traveling to malarious areas. Alternative malaria regimes should be discussed with a travel medicine or infectious disease specialist.

Travelers' diarrhea: Public water supplies are filtered and chlorinated. In Lusaka and Kabwe, water is obtained from deep bore holes and is treated. Water in these cities is considered potable. All other water sources in the country should be considered potentially contaminated. Travelers should observe all food and drink safety precautions. A quinolone antibiotic (Cipro or Floxin) is recommended for the treatment of acute diarrhea. Diarrhea not responding to treatment with an antibiotic, or chronic diarrhea, may be due to a parasitic disease such as giardiasis or amebiasis, and treatment with metronidazole (Flagyl) or tinidazole (Fasigyn) should be considered. All cases of diarrhea should be treated with adequate fluid replacement.

Hepatitis: High risk. All susceptible travelers should receive immune globulin prophylaxis or hepatitis A vaccine. The hepatitis B carrier rate in the general population is estimated at 13%–14%. Vaccination against hepatitis B is recommended for healthcare workers and all long-term visitors to this country.

Leishmaniasis: Low, but undetermined, risk. Cases of visceral leishmaniasis probably occur, but rarely. Travelers should take measures to prevent insect (sandfly) bites.

Onchocerciasis: Cases are reported near Choma in the Southern Province, perhaps the southernmost limit of transmission of this disease in Africa. Travelers should take precautions against insect (black fly) bites.

Filariasis (Bancroftian): Risk may occur in northern areas. Travelers should take precautions against mosquito bites.

Schistosomiasis: Urinary schistosomiasis is endemic in all provinces. Intestinal schistosomiasis is less widely distributed, with major foci in Northern Province, Luapula Province (including Lake Mweru vicinity), Lusaka vicinity, and Southern Province (including the shores of Lake Kariba). All travelers should avoid swimming, bathing, or wading in freshwater lakes, ponds, or streams.

Dengue and other arboviral fevers: Dengue has not been reported recently from this region. Human outbreaks of chikungunya fever have been reported from Zambia.

Trypanosomiasis (African sleeping sickness): Risk persists in the northern areas, particularly in the Luangwa Valley and Kafue National Park. One third of rural areas countrywide are infested with tsetse flies. Travelers should take personal protection measures against insect (tsetse fly) bites.

Rabies: Dogs are the primary source of human exposure. Outbreaks in cattle have been reported, primarily in the rural areas of Southern Province. Travelers should seek immediate treatment of any animal bite. Pre-exposure vaccination against rabies (3 doses) should be considered for long-term travel to this region. This is especially true for travelers going to remote rural areas if they will be unable to receive antirabies treatment within 24 hours of exposure to a potentially rabid animal. Pre-exposure vaccination does not preclude the need for post-exposure treatment.

AIDS: Heterosexual transmission is the predominate means of transmission. HIV-1 prevalence estimated at 54% of the high-risk urban population. All travelers are cautioned against unsafe sex, unsterile medical or dental injections, and unnecessary blood transfusions.

Other illnesses/hazards: African tick typhus (contracted from dog ticks, often in urban areas, and bush ticks), anthrax, brucellosis, leprosy (1.5 cases/1,000 population; incidence is decreasing), relapsing fever (tick-borne), toxoplasmosis, syphilis, tuberculosis (a major health problem), typhoid fever, and intestinal worms (very common). Animal hazards include snakes (vipers, cobras), centipedes, scorpions, and Black Widow spiders.

BURUNDI

Bujumbura ... GMT +2 hrs

Entry Requirements
- Passport/Visa: Valid passport and visa are required.
- AIDS Test: Not required.
- Vaccinations: Yellow fever: A yellow fever vaccination certificate is required for all travelers older than 1 year of age arriving from infected areas or from any country in the Yellow Fever Endemic Zones.

Electricity/Plugs: AC 50 Hz, 220 volts; frequency not stable; plug types C, E, and F. Adaptors and transformer necessary for U.S.-made appliances.

Embassies/Consulates: U.S. Embassy, Bujumbura. Avenue du Zaire; Tel. 234-54/55/56. Canadian Consulate, Bujumbura. Boulevard 1 Novembre; Tel. 22816.

Hospitals/Doctors: Hospital Prince Regent Charles; general medical/surgical facility; ICU. Clinique Prince Louis Rwagasore (13 beds). Travelers should contact the U.S. Embassy for physician referrals.

Health Advisory

Yellow fever: Vaccination is recommended. This country is in the Yellow Fever Endemic Zone. A valid vaccination certificate may be required for on-going travel to other countries.

Cholera: This disease is reported active in this country. Although cholera vaccination is not required for entry if arriving directly from the U.S. or Canada, it may be required for on-going travel to other countries in Africa, the Middle East, or Asia. Travelers should consider vaccination (one dose) or getting a doctor's letter of exemption from vaccination. The risk to travelers of acquiring cholera is considered low. Prevention consists primarily in adhering to safe food and drink guidelines.

Malaria: Risk is present year-round throughout this country, including urban areas. Falciparum malaria accounts for approximately 80% of cases. Other cases of malaria are due primarily to the *P. malariae* species. Chloroquine-resistant falciparum malaria is reported. Prophylaxis with mefloquine or doxycycline is currently recommended when traveling to malarious areas. Alternative malaria regimes should be discussed with a travel medicine or infectious disease specialist.

Travelers' diarrhea: High risk. Travelers should observe all food and drink safety precautions. A quinolone antibiotic (Floxin or Cipro) is recommended for the treatment of acute diarrhea. Diarrhea not responding to treatment with an antibiotic, or chronic diarrhea, may be due to a parasitic disease such as giardiasis or amebiasis, and treatment with metronidazole (Flagyl) or tinidazole (Fasigyn) should be considered. All cases of diarrhea should be treated with adequate fluid replacement.

Hepatitis: High risk. All susceptible travelers should receive immune globulin prophylaxis or hepatitis A vaccine. The hepatitis B carrier rate in the general population is estimated at 16%. Vaccination against hepatitis B is recommended for healthcare workers and all long-term visitors to this country.

Schistosomiasis: Risk is present mainly in two foci: the Imbo region (western lowlands extending across the Ruzizi plain and along the shores of Lake Tanganyika, including Bujumbura) and around Lake Cohoha in the northeast, along the Rwandan border. Travelers should avoid swimming, bathing, or wading in freshwater lakes, ponds, or streams.

Meningitis: Outbreaks of Group A meningococcal meningitis are occurring in this country. Over 2500 cases of meningitis were reported in 1992, but none apparently occurred in tourists. Vaccination is recommended for all travelers to this country, especially if they will be staying longer than 4 weeks, or will be having close contact with the indigenous population.

AIDS: Heterosexual contact is the predominate mode of transmission. HIV-1 prevalence estimated at 19% of the high-risk urban population. All travelers are cautioned against unsafe sex, unsterile medical or dental injections, and unnecessary blood transfusions.

Other illnesses/hazards: African tick typhus, brucellosis, filariasis, leishmaniasis (low risk), meningitis, rabies (transmitted primarily by dogs), toxoplasmosis, syphilis, tuberculosis (a major health problem), trachoma, typhoid fever, typhus (louse-borne; reported from the highlands), and intestinal worms (very common). Animal hazards include snakes (vipers, cobras), centipedes, scorpions, and black widow spiders.

DJIBOUTI

Djibouti ... GMT +3 hrs

Entry Requirements
- Passport/Visa: Valid passport and visa are required.
- AIDS Test: Not required.
- Vaccinations: A yellow fever vaccination certificate is required for all travelers older than 1 year of age arriving from infected areas.

Telephone Country Code: 253

Electricity/Plugs: AC 50 Hz, 220 volts; plug types C and E. Adaptors and transformer necessary for U.S.-made appliances.

Embassies/Consulates: U.S. Embassy, Djibouti. Villa Plateau du Serpent Boulevard; Tel. 353-849, 353-995, 352-916. Canadian Embassy (Ethiopia); Tel. [251] (1) 151-100.

Hospitals/Doctors: Peltier Hospital, Djibouti City (700 beds); limited emergency and surgical facilities; old and poorly maintained buildings.

Health Advisory

Malaria: Risk is present year-round throughout this country, including urban areas. Minimal risk is present in the city of Djibouti. Major outbreaks possibly occurred in 1989–1990 in the south, including the Dikhil District and the villages south of Djibouti City. Falciparum malaria accounts for approximately 80% of cases. Chloroquine-resistant falciparum malaria has not been reported, but may exist. Prophylaxis with mefloquine or doxycycline is currently recommended when traveling to malarious areas. Alternative malaria regimes should be discussed with a travel medicine or infectious disease specialist.

Travelers' diarrhea: Local tap water is potentially contaminated. Bottled water is recommended. A quinolone antibiotic (Cipro or Floxin) is recommended for the treatment of acute diarrhea. Diarrhea not responding to treatment with an antibiotic, or chronic diarrhea, may be due to a parasitic disease such as giardiasis or amebiasis, and treatment with metronidazole (Flagyl) or tinidazole (Fasigyn) should be considered. All cases of diarrhea should be treated with adequate fluid replacement.

Hepatitis: High risk. All susceptible travelers should receive immune globulin prophylaxis or hepatitis A vaccine. The hepatitis B carrier rate in the general population is estimated as high as 12%. Vaccination against hepatitis B is recommended for healthcare workers and all long-term visitors to this country.

Leishmaniasis: Sporadic cases of cutaneous and visceral leishmaniasis have been reported.

Rabies: Presumed present. Travelers should seek immediate treatment of any animal bite. Pre-exposure vaccination against rabies (3 doses) should be considered for long-term travel to this region.

AIDS: Low risk. Heterosexual transmission is the predominate means of transmission. HIV-1 prevalence estimated at 2.8% of the high-risk urban population (prostitutes). All travelers are cautioned against unsafe sex, unsterile medical or dental injections, and unnecessary blood transfusions.

Other illnesses/hazards: African tick typhus (contracted from dog ticks, often in urban areas, and bush ticks), anthrax, brucellosis, cholera (low risk), tuberculosis (a major health problem), typhoid fever, and intestinal worms.

ETHIOPIA

Embassy: 202-234-2281   *Addis Ababa*   *GMT +3 hrs*

Entry Requirements
- Passport/Visa: A valid passport and visa are required.
- AIDS Test: Not required.
- Vaccinations: A yellow fever vaccination certificate is required from all travelers older than 1 year of age arriving from yellow fever infected areas.

Telephone Country Code: 251

Electricity/Plugs: AC 50 Hz, 220 volts; plug type C. Adaptors and transformer necessary for U.S.-made appliances.

American Express: National Travel Agency. c/o The Hilton Hotel, Addis Ababa; Tel. (1) 144-8400.

Embassies/Consulates: U.S. Embassy, Addis Ababa. Entoto Street; Tel. (1)110-666/117/129. Canadian Embassy, Addis Ababa. African Solidarity Ins. Building. Unity Square; Tel. (1) 151-100/151-128.

Hospitals/Doctors: Empress Zauditu Memorial Hospital, Addis Ababa (207 beds); basic diagnostic and treatment services. Tikur Anbessa Hospital; Tel. (1) 151-211. Mekan Hiwet Hospital, Addis Ababa (750 beds); basic treatment and emergency services; surgical capabilities. Asrat Woldeyes, M.D., Addis Ababa; Tel. (1) 164-416.

Health Advisory

Yellow fever: Yellow fever not officially reported in this country, but epidemics occurred in the southwest in the 1960s. Yellow fever vaccination is recommended for all travelers. This country is in the Yellow Fever Endemic Zone. A valid vaccination certificate may be required for on-going travel to other countries.

Cholera: Although cholera vaccination is not required for entry if arriving directly from the U.S. or Canada, it may be required if arriving from a cholera-infected area, or required for on-going travel to other countries in Latin America, Africa, the Middle East, or Asia. Travelers to this country should consider vaccination (one dose) or a doctor's letter of exemption from vaccination. The risk to travelers of acquiring cholera is considered low. Prevention consists primarily in strictly adhering to safe food and drink guidelines.

Malaria: Transmission occurs year-round below 2,000 meters elevation, including urban areas. There is no malaria in Addis Ababa (elevation 2,450 meters) or the Ethiopian highlands. *P. falciparum* causes 80%–90% of human infections, followed by *P. vivax* and *P. malariae* species. Chloroquine-resistant *P. falciparum* is reported, primarily along the southern and western borders. Prophylaxis with mefloquine or doxycycline is currently recommended when traveling to malarious areas.

Travelers' diarrhea: High risk. Most rural water supplies consist of unprotected wells, streams, or natural springs. Large-scale international aid has improved rural wells and reservoirs. In urban areas, piped water is commonly available at public distribution points. Piped water supplies may be contaminated. Travelers should observe all food and drink safety precautions. A quinolone antibiotic is recommended for the treatment of acute diarrhea. Diarrhea not responding to treatment with an antibiotic, or chronic diarrhea, may be due to a parasitic disease such as giardiasis, amebiasis, or cryptosporidiosis. Rotavirus is a common cause of diarrhea in children.

Hepatitis: High risk. All susceptible travelers should receive immune globulin or hepatitis A vaccine. The hepatitis B carrier rate in the general population is estimated at 11%. Vaccination against hepatitis B is recommended for healthcare workers and all long-term visitors to this country.

Dengue and other arboviral fevers: Dengue (mosquito-borne) is reported in the coastal regions. Sandfly fever, West Nile fever, Chikungunya fever, Sindbis fever, and Rift Valley fever may occur.

Leishmaniasis: Widespread incidence, with focal distribution countrywide. Cutaneous leishmaniasis occurs in most areas of the Ethiopian highland plateau (elevation 1,500–2,500 meters), including Addis Ababa. Areas of risk for visceral leishmaniasis (kala azar) include the northwestern, southwestern, and southern lowlands. Risk also occurs in the northeastern low-lying arid areas along the Red Sea coast. Travelers to these areas should take measures to prevent insect (sandfly) bites.

Schistosomiasis: Peak transmission occurs during the dry season. Intestinal schistosomiasis is widely distributed in highland areas, primarily occurring in agricultural communities along streams between 1,300 and 2,000 meters elevation. Limited areas of urinary schistosomiasis are confined to warmer lowland areas (below 800 meters elevation), including the middle and lower Awash Valley, the lower Wabi Shebele Valley near the Somali border, and western Welega near the Sudan border. Travelers to these areas should avoid swimming, bathing, or wading in freshwater lakes, ponds, or streams.

Trypanosomiasis (African sleeping sickness): Areas of transmission occur in the southwestern administrative regions of Ilubabor and Kefa. Travelers to this area should take measures to prevent insect (tsetse fly) bites.

Meningitis: Ethiopia, excepting the southeast, lies within the sub-Saharan meningitis belt. Major meningococcal meningitis outbreaks (Group A usually predominates, but Group C also occurs) were reported in 1988–1989. Vaccination is advised for those travelers expecting to have close, extended (more than 4 weeks) contact with the indigenous population of this country.

Rabies: Higher than average risk. There is a large stray dog population, especially in Addis Ababa. Travelers should seek immediate treatment of any animal bite. Pre-exposure vaccination against rabies should be considered for long-term travel to this region. This is especially true for travelers going to remote rural areas if they will be unable to receive antirabies treatment within 24 hours of exposure to a potentially rabid animal.

Other illnesses/hazards: African tick typhus, anthrax (in Gonder region), brucellosis, cholera, echinococcosis (high prevalence among nomadic pastoralists in the southwest), filariasis (endemic focus of Bancroftian filariasis at Gambela), leptospirosis, onchocerciasis (black fly-borne; focally endemic along rivers where black flies breed; risk occurs primarily in the southwest and in the northwestern region of Gonder), relapsing fever (tick-borne and louse-borne; epidemics of louse-borne disease reported in prisoner-of-war transit camps in Bahr Dar and Mekele), toxoplasmosis, syphilis, tuberculosis (a major health problem), trachoma (up to one-half of the population infected), typhoid fever, typhus (louse-borne and flea-borne; endemic in highlands), and intestinal helminthic infections (very common). Animal hazards include snakes (vipers, cobras, mambas), centipedes, scorpions, and black widow spiders.

KENYA

Embassy: 202-387-6101   *Nairobi*   *GMT +3 hrs*

Entry Requirements
- Passport/Visa: Valid passport and visa are required.
- AIDS Test: Not required.
- Vaccinations: A yellow fever vaccination certificate is required from all travelers older than 1 year of age arriving from infected areas or from any country in the Yellow Fever Endemic Zones.
  Cholera: A validated vaccination certificate against cholera may be required if a traveler leaves Kenya and tries to enter a country where cholera is endemic. Such countries include Tanzania, Uganda, and other countries in Africa, the Middle East, India, Asia, and Oceania.

Telephone Country Code: 254

Electricity/Plugs: AC 50 Hz, 220 volts; plug types D and G.

American Express: Bruce House, Standard Street, Nairobi; Tel: (2) 334-722.

Embassies/Consulates: U.S. Embassy, Nairobi. Moi/Haile Selassie Avenue; Tel: (2) 334-141.

Hospitals/Doctors: The best medical care in Kenya is found in Nairobi, Mombasa, and Kisumu.

Nairobi: Nairobi Hospital, Argwings Kodhen Rd; private hospital; most major specialties; Tel: 722-160. Aga Khan Jubilee Hospital (183 beds); 3rd Parklands Ave; private hospital; most major specialties, including neurosurgery; Tel: 742-531. Kenyatta National Hospital, Nairobi (1,716 beds); all major specialties; overcrowded; inadequate supplies. Not recommended for routine use.

Private practioners (Nairobi): Maurice Wambani, M.D., Stanbank House, 1st floor; Tel: (2) 340-640 or 62-850 (home) Manuel D'Cruz, M.D.; Tel: 747-083. Dr. Colin Forbes (pediatrician); Jabuva Road; Tel: (2) 722-800.

Mombasa: Aga Khan Hospital, Vanga Rd; Tel: 312-953. Mombasa Medical Practice; Tel: 315-661.

Kisumu: Aga Khan Hospital, Otieno Oyoo St; Tel: 43516.

Air ambulance services: Flying Doctors Society of Africa, Nairobi; Tel: (2) 501-280; tourist membership available covering emergency air ambulance services. African Air Rescue, Wilson Airport, Nairobi; provides emergency evacuation services throughout East Africa. Tel: (2) 216-842/3/5.

Health Advisory

Yellow fever: This disease was reported active in 1993 with cases occurring in the Rift Valley (Lake Baringo and Elgeyo Marakwet Districts). The State Department recommends yellow fever vaccination for anyone traveling outside the city of Nairobi. This country is in the Yellow Fever Endemic Zone. A valid vaccination certificate may be required for on-going travel to other countries.

Cholera: This disease is active, especially in southern areas. Although cholera vaccination is not required for entry if arriving directly from the U.S. or Canada, it may be required if arriving from a cholera-infected area, or required for on-going travel to other countries in Latin America, Africa, the Middle East, or Asia. Travelers to this country should consider vaccination (one dose) or a doctor's letter of exemption from vaccination. The risk to travelers of acquiring cholera is low. Prevention consists primarily in strictly adhering to safe food and drink guidelines.

Malaria: This disease is highly endemic year-round in Mombasa and other coastal areas, the Tana River valley, and in western Kenya, especially near Lake Victoria. Seasonal malaria occurs in the game parks along the border with Tanzania, and in the Rift Valley, with the highest malaria transmission rates during and just after the semiannual rainy seasons, April through June and October through December. Malaria may occur in the highland areas (above 1,600 meters elevation) during and just after periods of exceptionally heavy rainfall. No malaria is reported in highland areas above 2,500 meters elevation (e.g., the Aberdare

Range, Mt. Kenya, Mt. Elgon), or in Nairobi. *P. falciparum* causes approximately 85% of malaria cases. The remainder are due to *P. malariae,* and sometimes *P. ovale.* Malaria due to *P. vivax* is rare. Chloroquine-resistant falciparum malaria is prevalent, especially in the coastal areas and in western Kenya. Fansidar- and mefloquine-resistant falciparum malaria has also been reported. Antimalarial prophylaxis with either mefloquine or doxycycline is recommended when traveling to this country. Alternative prophylaxis regimes (such as chloroquine plus proguanil) should be discussed with a travel medicine specialist. Compliance with antimalarial medication is extremely important. Most importantly, all travelers to malarious areas should take stringent measures to prevent mosquito bites, especially after sunset when anopheles mosquito activity is highest.

Travelers' diarrhea: Moderate to high risk outside of first-class hotels and resorts. The public water supply in Nairobi is considered potable, but bottled water is recommended for consumption. All water sources outside of major hotels and resorts should be considered potentially contaminated. Travelers should observe food and drink safety precautions. A quinolone antibiotic is recommended for the treatment of acute diarrhea. Diarrhea not responding to antibiotic treatment may be caused by a parasitic disease such as giardiasis or amebiasis—or an intestinal virus.

Hepatitis: All susceptible travelers should receive immune globulin or hepatitis A vaccine. The hepatitis B carrier rate in the general population is estimated to exceed 15%. Vaccination against hepatitis B is recommended for healthcare workers and all long-term visitors to this country.

Dengue fever: The risk of dengue is considered to be low but dengue may occur in irregular epidemics in coastal areas.

Chikungunya, West Nile, Rift Valley, and O'nyongnyong fevers: These mosquito-transmitted viral illnesses are reported mainly from the coast and in the Lake Victoria vicinity. The risk to tourists is low.

Leishmaniasis: Cutaneous leishmaniasis is reported from the highland areas, including the eastern slopes of Mt. Elgon, and the Aberdare Range. Risk areas for visceral leishmaniasis (kala azar) include Baringo, West Potok, and Turkana districts in Rift Valley Province and the Machakos, Kitue, and Meru districts in Eastern Province. All travelers to these areas should take measures to prevent sandfly bites.

Schistosomiasis: Urinary schistosomiasis is widely distributed, including the areas along the coastal plain, the Taveta region near Lake Jipe, the lower Valley of the Tana River, the Kitui district in Eastern Province, and in isolated foci in Nyanza Province bordering Lake Victoria. Intestinal schistosomiasis occurs primarily east of Nairobi, in the Taveta region bordering Tanzania, in the Nyanza Province bordering Lake Victoria, and on the islands of Rusinga and Mfangano.

Trypanosomiasis (African sleeping sickness): Sporadic cases are reported, with occasional outbreaks. Disease transmission restricted to Western and Nyanza Provinces, with a persistent focus in the Lambwe Valley, near Lake Victoria. Travelers to these areas should take measures to prevent tsetse fly bites.

Meningitis (meningococcal): Outbreaks of meningitis have occurred in Nairobi, Central, and Eastern Provinces in 1989, and in Kericho District and the southwestern Rift Valley Province in 1990–1991. Vaccination is recommended for all travelers visiting Kenya.

Rabies: Risk is increasing in urban areas, including Nairobi. Stray dogs are the main source of rabies transmission. Pre-exposure vaccination is recommended for long-term travel (more than 4 weeks) to this country, especially for travelers going to remote rural areas.

Altitude sickness: Climbers ascending Mt. Kilimanjaro and Mt. Kenya are at risk and should consider slow ascent and prophylaxis with acetazolamide (Diamox). Descent is the treatment of choice for moderate to severe altitude sickness.

AIDS: Heterosexual transmission is the predominate means of transmission. HIV-1 prevalence estimated at up to 90% of the high-risk urban population. All travelers are cautioned against unsafe sex, unsterile medical or dental injections, and blood transfusions.

Other illnesses/hazards: African tick typhus (contracted from dog ticks, often in urban areas, and bush ticks), anthrax, brucellosis, echinococcosis (highest known prevalence in the world occurs in the Turkana population in northwest Kenya), filariasis (mosquito-borne;

endemic in the coastal zone and along the Sabaki River), leptospirosis (associated with rodent-infected areas; reportedly widespread around Kisumu and along the coast), onchocerciasis (black fly-borne; last remaining focus was located on southwestern slopes of Mt. Elgon), plague (outbreak occurred in 1990 in Nairobi's Embakasi area), toxoplasmosis, syphilis, trachoma, tuberculosis (a major health problem), typhoid fever, and intestinal worms (very common).

Animal hazards: Snakes (vipers, cobras, black mambas, puff adders) are primarily found in the large arid regions of northern Kenya. Other animal hazards include centipedes, scorpions, and black widow spiders. Sea cones, sea urchins, and anemones inhabit the shallow coastal waters of Kenya and may pose a threat to swimmers.

RWANDA
Kigali ... GMT +2 hrs

Entry Requirements
- Passport/Visa: Valid passport and visa are required.
- AIDS Test: Not required.
- Vaccinations: A yellow fever vaccination certificate is required from all travelers older than 1 year of age arriving from ALL COUNTRIES.
  Cholera: Vaccination is not officially required, but is advised.

Telephone Country Code: 250

Electricity/Plugs: AC 50 Hz, 220 volts; plug types C and E.

Embassies/Consulates: U.S. Embassy, Kigali. Boulevard de la Revolution; Tel. 75601, 72126. Canadian Embassy (Zaire); Tel. [243] (12) 27551.

Hospitals/Doctors: Kigali Central Hospital (450 beds); general medical services. Dr. Ataullah Taaid, Kigali; Tel. 5677.

Health Advisory

Yellow fever: Vaccination is required for entry. This country is in the Yellow Fever Endemic Zone.

Cholera: This disease is reported active in this country. Cholera vaccination certificate may be required if arriving from an infected area or for on-going travel to other countries. Travelers should consider vaccination or obtaining a doctor's letter of exemption from vaccination. Due to resistant strains, furazolidone or a quinolone may be the antibiotics of choice for treatment.

Malaria: Risk is present throughout this country, including urban areas. Risk may be less in the northwest prefecture of Ruhengeri. *P. falciparum* accounts for approximately 90% of cases. Remainder of cases are due to the *P. ovale* and *P. malariae* species, rarely *P. vivax*. Chloroquine-resistant falciparum malaria is reported. Prophylaxis with mefloquine or doxycycline is currently recommended.

Travelers' diarrhea: High risk. Water supplies, even in Kigali, may be contaminated. Travelers should observe all food and drink safety precautions. A quinolone antibiotic is recommended for the treatment of acute diarrhea.

Hepatitis: High risk. All susceptible travelers should receive immune globulin or hepatitis A vaccine. The hepatitis B carrier rate in the general population is estimated to exceed 10%. Vaccination is recommended for healthcare and relief workers.

Schistosomiasis: Intestinal schistosomiasis occurs along Lake Kivu and in the northwest around Lakes Bulera and Ruhondu, with risk also in Byumba, Kigali, and Butare prefectures. Travelers to these regions should avoid swimming, bathing, or wading in freshwater lakes, ponds, or streams.

Trypanosomiasis (African sleeping sickness): Sporadic cases occur; risk areas include Akagera Game Park, in the northeast, and Nasho Lake vicinity (east of Kigali).

Other illnesses/hazards: AIDS, African tick typhus (contracted from dog ticks and bush ticks), brucellosis, dengue (not active), echinococcosis, filariasis, leishmaniasis (transmission occurs year-round), meningitis, plague, rabies (transmitted primarily by dogs), louse-borne relapsing fever and typhus fevers (primarily in highlands), Rift Valley fever, tuberculosis (a major health problem), trachoma, typhoid fever, and intestinal worms.

SOMALIA

Mogadishu ... GMT +3 hrs

Entry Requirements

- Passport/Visa: Valid passport and visa are required.
- AIDS Test: Not required.
- Vaccinations: A yellow fever vaccination certificate is required from all travelers arriving from infected areas.
  Cholera: A vaccination certificate is required if arriving from infected areas.

Electricity/Plugs: AC 50 Hz, 220 volts; plug types C and D.

Embassies/Consulates: U.S. Embassy, Mogadishu. Corso Primo Luglio; Tel. 20811.

Doctors/Hospitals: The local medical facilities are inadequate. The State Department recommends evacuating personnel to Nairobi, Kenya, in lieu of using Somali hospitals.

Health Advisory

Yellow fever: This country lies within the Yellow Fever Endemic Zone. Although yellow fever has not been reported, vaccination is recommended.

Cholera: Although cholera vaccination is not officially required for entry if arriving directly from the U.S. or Canada, it may be required unofficially, or be required for on-going travel to other countries in Africa, the Middle East, Asia, or Latin America. Travelers to this country should consider vaccination or getting a doctor's letter of exemption from vaccination. The risk to travelers of acquiring cholera is considered to be low.

Malaria: Risk is present year-round throughout this country, including urban areas. Risk of transmission is highest in July and December, after the semiannual rains. The risk of malaria is greater in the south, particularly along the Shabeelle and Juba River valleys. There is limited malaria risk in the city center of Mogadishu. Falciparum malaria accounts for 95% of cases countrywide, but in 106 US Marines returning from Somalia in 1993 *P. vivax* accounted for 87% of cases. Prophylaxis with mefloquine or doxycycline is currently recommended when traveling to malarious areas. (Note: 2 cases of mefloquine-resistant *P. falciparum* malaria were reported in U.S. troops stationed in Somalia.)

Travelers' diarrhea: High risk. All water supplies are potentially contaminated. Travelers should observe all food and drink safety precautions. A quinolone antibiotic is recommended for the treatment of acute diarrhea. Diarrhea not responding to antibiotic treatment may be due to a parasitic disease such as giardiasis or amebiasis.

Hepatitis: High risk. All susceptible travelers should receive immune globulin or hepatitis A vaccine. The hepatitis B carrier rate in the general population is estimated as high as 19%. Vaccination against hepatitis B is recommended for healthcare workers and all long-term visitors to this country. Hepatitis E outbreaks have been reported in refugee camps and is a hazard to healthcare and relief workers.

Leishmaniasis: A hyperendemic focus of visceral leishmaniasis (kala azar) persists along the Shabeelle River in the Giohar District in southern Somalia. Cutaneous leishmaniasis has not been reported but may occur in southern Somalia near the borders with Kenya and Ethiopia.

Schistosomiasis: Year-round risk of urinary schistosomiasis, primarily in the valleys of the Giuba and Shabeelle Rivers in southern Somalia. Travelers to these areas should avoid bathing, wading, or swimming in freshwater lakes, ponds, or streams.

Dengue fever: Moderate risk. Thirty-three cases of dengue were reported in American personnel in Somalia in 1992; the virus is estimated to have caused 17% of febrile illness in U.S. troops previously stationed in this country.

Arboviral fevers: Chikungunya fever, Rift Valley fever, West Nile fever, and sandfly fever may occur.

Other illnesses/hazards: African tick typhus brucellosis, echinococcosis, filariasis (occurs in southern Somalia, in the area between Kenya and the Indian Ocean), histoplasmosis (common), leptospirosis (high incidence), meningitis, Q fever, rabies (transmitted primarily by dogs but also by foxes, cats, camels, donkeys, hyenas, badgers, and jackals), tick-borne relapsing fever (endemic), tuberculosis (a major health problem), trachoma, typhoid fever, epidemic typhus (louse-borne; increased risk in those having contact with refugees), murine typhus (flea-borne), and intestinal worms.

SUDAN

Embassy: 202-466-6280   *Khartoum*   *GMT +2 hrs*

Entry Requirements
- Passport/Visa: A valid passport and visa are required.
- AIDS test: Not required.
- Vaccinations: A valid yellow fever vaccination certificate is required from all travelers older than 1 year of age arriving from infected areas or from any country in the Yellow Fever Endemic Zones. A vaccination certificate may also be required to leave Sudan.
  Cholera: A cholera vaccination certificate may be required of travelers arriving from infected areas.

Telephone Country Code: Operator-assisted calls only.

Electricity/Plugs: AC 50 Hz, 220 volts; plug types C, F, and G. Adaptors and transformer necessary for U.S.-made appliances.

American Express: Contomichalos Travel & Tourism. Al Barlman Street, Khartoum; Tel. (11) 70929.

Embassies/Consulates: U.S. Embassy/Khartoum. Sharia Ali Abdul Latif; Tel. (11) 74700. Canadian Embassy (Ethiopia); Tel. [251] (1) 151-100.

Hospitals/Doctors: Khartoum Civil Hospital (795 beds); general medical facility; some specialty services.

Health Advisory

Yellow fever: This disease is active in this country (south of 12° north latitude). Vaccination is recommended for all travelers. Sudan is in the Yellow Fever Endemic Zone. A valid vaccination certificate may be required for on-going travel to other countries.

Cholera: This disease is active in this country, but not officially reported. Although cholera vaccination is not officially required for entry if arriving directly from the U.S. or Canada, it may be unofficially required for entry, or required for on-going travel to other countries in Africa, the Middle East, or Asia. Travelers should consider vaccination or getting a doctor's letter of exemption from vaccination.

Malaria: Risk is present year-round throughout this country, including all urban areas. Increased risk occurs during, and after the rainy season, June through October, especially in southern Sudan. There is less malaria risk in the desert areas of the extreme north and northwest. Falciparum malaria accounts for approximately 84% of cases. Other cases of malaria are due to the *P. vivax* (9%–20%) and *P. malariae* species (7%), rarely *P. ovale*. Chloroquine-resistant falciparum malaria is reported. Prophylaxis with mefloquine or doxycycline is currently recommended when traveling to malarious areas.

Travelers' diarrhea: High risk. Water supplies are frequently untreated and may be bacterially contaminated. Travelers should observe all food and drink safety precautions. A quinolone antibiotic is recommended for the treatment of acute diarrhea. Diarrhea not responding to antibiotic treatment, or chronic diarrhea, may be due to a parasitic disease such as giardiasis, amebiasis, or cryptosporidiosis. Amebiasis is common and the giardia carrier rate in children is reported as high as 69%. Rotavirus is also a common cause of diarrhea in children.

Hepatitis: High risk. All susceptible travelers should receive immune globulin or hepatitis A vaccine. The hepatitis B carrier rate in the general population is estimated at 12%–19%. Vaccination against hepatitis B is recommended. Hepatitis E outbreaks have been reported from Khartoum, and elsewhere.

Dengue fever: Mosquito-borne. Reported primarily from the coastal regions. Other arboviral infections include sandfly fever (widespread), Rift Valley fever, Crimean-Congo hemorrhagic fever (tick-borne), and West Nile fever.

Leishmaniasis: An epidemic of visceral leishmaniasis (kala azar) is afflicting the Nuer and Dinka tribes in southern Sudan. Kala azar also reported from the Upper Blue Nile, Blue Nile, and Kassala Provinces, and Eastern Equatoria, Darfur, and Kordofan Districts. Outbreaks have also occurred north of Khartoum along the Nile River.

Cutaneous leishmaniasis: Risk is widespread. Endemic areas for cutaneous leishmaniasis include Darfur, Kordofan, and other provinces of central Sudan, and north of Khartoum, along the Nile River. Visceral leishmaniasis (kala azar) also occurs, especially in southern Sudan. Travelers to all regions should take measures to prevent insect (sandfly) bites.

Schistosomiasis: Risk is widespread, especially in the major irrigation systems in the Gezira area between the Blue and White Nile Rivers. Travelers should avoid swimming, bathing, or wading in freshwater lakes, ponds, or streams.

Trypanosomiasis (African sleeping sickness): The Gambian form of this illness occurs in southern Sudan, primarily in Western and Equatoria Provinces. Rhodesian sleeping sickness may occur in areas adjacent to Ethiopia and in areas adjacent to Uganda. Increased risk occurs during the dry season. Travelers should take measures to prevent tsetse fly bites.

Meningitis: Sudan lies within the sub-Saharan meningitis belt. Increased risk in central and southern regions. Vaccination is recommended for travelers who will have close, prolonged contact with the indigenous population.

Rabies: Risk of dog-transmitted rabies in Khartoum and elsewhere, including rural areas. Rabies vaccination is recommended prior to long-term travel (more than 4 weeks) to this country.

Other illnesses/hazards: AIDS (low prevalence), African tick typhus, brucellosis, dracunculiasis, Ebola-Marburg virus disease (risk may be elevated in southern areas), echinococcosis (high prevalence in the south), filariasis (mosquito-borne; reported from the Nuba Mountains around Kadogli in Kurdufan Province), loiasis (deer-fly-borne; confined to rain forests and nearby savanna of Western Equatoria Province in the southwest), leprosy (high incidence in the Nuba Mountains and the provinces of Southern Darfur, Bahr el Ghazal, Western and Eastern Equatoria), leptospirosis, onchocerciasis (high prevalence along rivers in southwestern Sudan), relapsing fever (louse-borne and tick-borne), toxoplasmosis, tuberculosis (a major health problem), trachoma, typhoid fever, typhus (flea-borne and louse-borne), and helminthic infections (intestinal worms; very common). Animal hazards include snakes (vipers, cobras), centipedes, scorpions, and black widow spiders.

TANZANIA

Dar es Salaam ... GMT +3 hrs

Entry Requirements
- Passport/Visa: Valid passport and visa are required.
- AIDS Test: Not required.
- Vaccinations: Yellow fever. A vaccination certificate is required from all travelers older than 1 year of age arriving from infected areas or from any country in the Yellow Fever Endemic Zones. This includes travelers arriving from Kenya and Uganda.
  Cholera: A vaccination certificate may be required for entry if arriving from an endemic area.

Telephone Country Code: 255

Electricity/Plugs: AC 50 Hz, 220/400 volts; plug types D and G.

Embassies/Consulates: U.S. Embassy, Dar es Salaam. 36 Laibon Road (off Bagamoyo Road); Tel. (51) 37501 to 4. Canadian High Commission. Pan African Insurance Building, Samora Avenue; Tel. (51) 20651.

Doctors/Hospitals: Muhimbili Hospital, Dar es Salaam (1,000 beds); general medical/surgical facility; orthopedics. S. DaSilva, M.D., Dar es Salaam; Tel. (51) 689-65/670-63 (home).

Health Advisory

Yellow fever: Vaccination recommended. No cases reported recently, but this country is in the Yellow Fever Endemic Zone. A valid yellow fever vaccination certificate may be required for persons who leave this country and travel to other countries in Africa, the Middle East, Asia, or Latin America.

Cholera: This disease is active in this country. Although cholera vaccination is not required for entry if arriving directly from the U.S. or Canada, it may be required if arriving from a cholera-infected area, or required for on-going travel to other countries in Latin America, Africa, the Middle East, or Asia. Travelers to this country should consider vaccination or a doctor's letter of exemption from vaccination.

Malaria: High risk is present throughout this country, including urban areas, the highland areas below 2,000 meters elevation, and the islands of Zanzibar and Pemba. Risk of malaria is increased during and just after the rainy seasons (November through December and March through May). Risk has also been increasing in high plateau areas, previously considered areas of limited risk. *P. falciparum* accounts for approximately 90% of cases. Other cases of malaria are due to the *P. malariae* (up to 10%), *P. ovale* (1%), and (rarely) *P. vivax.* Chloroquine-resistant *P. falciparum* is prevalent. Antimalarial prophylaxis with either mefloquine or doxycycline is recommended. All travelers to Tanzania should also take stringent measures to prevent mosquito bites, especially in the evening when mosquito activity is highest.

Travelers' diarrhea: High potential risk in all areas. Dar es Salaam reported an outbreak of multidrug-resistant shigellosis which continued throughout the mid-1980s. Several cities have water treatment facilities, but piped water supplies are frequently untreated and may be contaminated. Travelers should observe food and drink safety precautions. A quinolone antibiotic (Floxin or Cipro) is recommended for the treatment of acute diarrhea. Diarrhea not responding to antibiotic treatment may be due to a parasitic disease such as giardiasis, amebiasis, or cryptosporidiosis.

Hepatitis: High risk. All susceptible travelers should receive immune globulin or hepatitis A vaccine. The hepatitis B carrier rate in the general population is estimated at 10%. Vaccination against hepatitis B is recommended for healthcare workers and all long-term visitors to this country.

Leishmaniasis: Risk undetermined, but is estimated to be low. A focus of cutaneous leishmaniasis presumably persists south of Lake Victoria.

Filariasis: Bancroftian filariasis (mosquito-borne) is reported along the coast, including Pemba and Zanzibar, and also reported south of Lake Victoria, and north of Lake Nyasa.

Onchocerciasis: Black-fly borne; risk area extends from the Usambara mountains in the northeast to Lake Nyasa in the south. Travelers to these areas should take measures to prevent insect (black fly) bites.

Schistosomiasis: Risk areas include the shores of Lake Victoria, Tanga and Kigoma Districts, and the Lake Rukwa area. Urban transmission occurs in Dar es Salaam. Urinary schistosomiasis is transmitted on Zanzibar and Pemba Islands. Travelers should avoid swimming or wading in freshwater lakes, ponds, or streams.

Trypanosomiasis (African sleeping sickness): No current data on disease incidence are available. Cases of the Rhodesian form of the disease were reported in 1984 from the Kigoma and Arusha regions (northeast). Travelers to these areas should take protective measures against insect bites.

Meningitis: Outbreaks of Group A meningococcal meningitis are reported. Higher risk areas include the northern part of the Arusha Region (bordering Kenya), and the northern and central regions (including Mwanza, Mara, Arusha, Kilimanjaro, Tanga, Dar es Salaam, Morogoro, Dodoma, and Tabora). Over 4500 cases of meningitis reported during 1992, but none occurred in travelers. Vaccination, however, is recommended for all travelers to this country, especially if they will be staying longer than 4 weeks, or will be having close contact with the indigenous population.

Rabies: There is a large population of stray dogs in both rural and urban areas that can potentially transmit rabies. Pre-exposure vaccination is recommended for long-term travel (more than 4–6 weeks) to this country.

AIDS: Heterosexual transmission is the predominate means of transmission. HIV-1 prevalence estimated at 39% of the high-risk urban population. All travelers are cautioned against unsafe sex, unsterile medical or dental injections, and blood transfusions.

Other illnesses/hazards: African tick typhus, brucellosis, Chikungunya fever (mosquito-borne), dengue (no recent reports), echinococcosis (high incidence in the Masai of northern areas), filariasis (transmission may occur along the coast and south of Lake Victoria), leptospirosis, Lyme disease (risk unclear; one case reported in Peace Corps volunteer), onchocerciasis (black-fly-borne; from Usambara Mountains south to Lake Nyasa and Ruvuma Region), plague (flea-borne; 450 cases reported annually, mostly from the Lushoto District), relapsing fever (louse- and tick-borne), toxoplasmosis, tuberculosis (a major health problem), trachoma, typhoid fever, and intestinal worms (very common). Animal hazards include snakes (vipers, cobras), centipedes, scorpions, and black widow spiders.

UGANDA
Kampala ... GMT +3 hrs

Entry Requirements
- Passport/Visa: Valid passport and visa are required.
- AIDS Test: Not required.
- Vaccinations: A yellow fever vaccination certificate is required from all travelers older than 1 year arriving from infected areas or from any country in the Yellow Fever Endemic Zones. Cholera: Vaccination recommended to avoid possible delays at the border.

Telephone Country Code: 256

Embassies/Consulates: U.S. Embassy, Kampala. Parliament Avenue; Tel. (41) 259-791/2/3/5. Canadian High Commission (Kenya); Tel. [254] (2) 334-033.

Hospitals/Doctors: Mulago General Hospital, Kampala (1,080 beds); general medical facility; no anesthesiology. Nsambya Hospital, Kampala (370 beds); general medical/surgical facility. E.R. Gibbons, M.D. , Kampala. 12A Oboto Ave; Tel. (41) 650-03/42554 (home).

Health Advisory

Yellow fever: Vaccination is recommended. No cases have been reported recently, but this country is in the Yellow Fever Endemic Zone. A valid yellow fever vaccination certificate will be required if arriving from Kenya (where yellow fever is active).

Cholera: This disease is active in this country. Although cholera vaccination is not required for entry if arriving directly from the U.S. or Canada, it may be required if arriving from a cholera-infected area, or required for on-going travel to other countries in Latin America, Africa, the Middle East, or Asia. Travelers to this country should consider vaccination (one dose) or a doctor's letter of exemption from vaccination. The risk to travelers of acquiring cholera is considered low. Prevention consists primarily in following strict adherence to safe food and drink guidelines.

Malaria: Risk is present year-round throughout this country, including urban areas. Falciparum malaria accounts for approximately 80% of cases. Other cases of malaria are due to the *P. malariae* species, followed by *P. ovale* and (rarely) *P. vivax.* Chloroquine-resistant falciparum malaria is reported. Prophylaxis with mefloquine or doxycycline is currently recommended for travel to this country.

Travelers' diarrhea: High risk. Supplies of potable water are inadequate to meet the needs of the population. Piped water supplies may be grossly contaminated. Travelers should observe food and drink safety precautions. A quinolone antibiotic (Floxin or Cipro) is recommended for the treatment of acute diarrhea. Diarrhea not responding to treatment with an antibiotic, or chronic diarrhea, may be due to a parasitic disease such as giardiasis or amebiasis, and treatment with metronidazole (Flagyl) or tinidazole (Fasigyn) should be considered.

Hepatitis: High risk. All susceptible travelers should receive immune globulin prophylaxis or hepatitis A vaccine. The hepatitis B carrier rate in the general population is estimated at 10%. Vaccination against hepatitis B is recommended for healthcare workers and all long-term visitors to this country.

Schistosomiasis: Intestinal schistosomiasis occurs primarily in the northwest and along the northern shore of Lake Victoria. Urinary schistosomiasis is confined to northern central Uganda, north of Lake Kyoga. Travelers should avoid swimming or wading in freshwater lakes, ponds, or streams.

Filariasis, onchocerciasis, loiasis: Sporadic cases are reported. Travelers to this country are advised to take protective measures against black flies.

Leishmaniasis: Visceral leishmaniasis occurs in the northeast province of Karamoja. Sporadic cases of cutaneous leishmaniasis are reported from the Mt. Elgon vicinity. Travelers should take protective measures against insect (sandfly) bites.

Trypanosomiasis (African sleeping sickness): Prevalent in scattered areas countrywide. Major risk of disease presumably persists in the southeast (extending from the northern shore of Lake Victoria and Lake Kyoga), with foci of gambiense disease primarily in northwestern and north central areas (along the White Nile and the Sudanese border). All travelers to these regions should take measures to prevent tsetse fly bites.

Meningitis: Risk is present. An outbreak of meningococcal meningitis began in Kampala in 1989 and extended to other provinces. Vaccination against meningococcal disease is advised, especially for those who expect close, prolonged contact with the indigenous population.

Rabies: Increased incidence of rabies was reported in Kampala and Karamoja Province in 1986. Rabies vaccination is recommended for persons planning an extended stay in this country.

Plague: Three hundred cases were reported from Nebbi District in Western Province in 1986. Vaccination against plague should be considered by persons who may be occupationally exposed to wild rodents. Prophylaxis with tetracycline or doxycycline can be considered in lieu of vaccination.

AIDS: Promiscuous heterosexual contact is the predominate mode of transmission. HIV-1 prevalence is estimated at up to 86% of the high-risk urban population. All travelers are cautioned against unsafe sex, unsterile medical or dental injections, and unnecessary blood transfusions.

Other illnesses/hazards: African tick typhus (contracted from dog ticks—often in urban areas—and from bush ticks), brucellosis, chikungunya fever, Crimean-Congo hemorrhagic fever (cases reported from Entebbe), dengue (not reported recently), echinococcosis, leprosy, leptospirosis, louse-borne typhus, toxoplasmosis, syphilis, tuberculosis (a major health problem), trachoma, typhoid fever, and intestinal worms (very common). Animal hazards include snakes (vipers, cobras), centipedes, scorpions, and black widow spiders.

BOTSWANA
Gaborone ... GMT +2 hrs

Entry Requirements
- Passport/Visa: Travelers should possess a valid passport and tourist card.
- AIDS Test: Not required.
- Vaccinations: None required.

Telephone Country Code: 267

Electricity/Plugs: AC 50 Hz, 220 volts; plug types D and G. Adaptors and transformer necessary for U.S.-made appliances.

American Express: Manica Travel Services. Botsalano House, The Mall, Gaborone; Tel. (31) 352-021.

Embassies/Consulates: U.S. Embassy, Gaborone. The Mall; Tel. (31) 353-982. Canadian Embassy (Zimbabwe); Tel. [263] (4) 733-881.

Hospitals/Doctors: Princess Marina Hospital, Gaborone (237 beds); general medical and surgical services. A. E. Bhoola, M.D., Gaborone; Tel. 352-221/312-610.

Health Advisory

Malaria: Moderate seasonal risk in northern areas. Transmission is unstable, closely associated with seasonal rainfall. During the rainy season, malaria is moderately endemic in the north (including Boteti, Chobe, Ngamiland, Okavango, and Tutume districts/subdivisions), with sporadic cases reported along the southeastern border with South Africa. Gaborone is essentially risk free, except in years with very heavy rainfall. *P. falciparum* accounts for 95% of cases. Sporadic cases due to *P. malariae* have been reported. Chloroquine-resistant falciparum malaria has been confirmed. Prophylaxis with mefloquine or doxycycline is currently advised.

Travelers' diarrhea: High risk. Water from deep boreholes may be unpalatable due to high salinity. Indiscriminate disposal of human waste causes serious contamination of ground water in many villages, and in some towns. Piped water is available to 90% of the urban population but the water systems are often poorly maintained and are frequently contaminated. Travelers should observe all food and drink safety precautions. A quinolone antibiotic is recommended for the treatment of acute diarrhea. Diarrhea not responding to treatment with an antibiotic, or chronic diarrhea, may be due to a parasitic disease such as giardiasis or

amebiasis. Infection rates of 14% for both giardiasis and amebiasis among preschool children has been reported in rural southeastern areas.

Hepatitis: High risk. All susceptible travelers should receive immune globulin prophylaxis or hepatitis A vaccine. The hepatitis B carrier rate in the general population is estimated at 14%. Vaccination against hepatitis B is recommended for healthcare workers and all long-term visitors to this country.

Leishmaniasis: Low risk. Sporadic cases have been reported in the medical literature.

Schistosomiasis: Risk areas of urinary schistosomiasis are widely distributed along the eastern border from Francistown to Lobatse, with scattered foci in the north. Risk areas for intestinal schistosomiasis are confined to the Okavango marshlands in the northwest district of Ngamiland and the northeastern Chobe drainage system. Travelers to these areas should avoid swimming, bathing, or wading in freshwater ponds, lakes, or streams.

Plague: An outbreak in Central District, near Lake Xau, was reported in 1989–1990, with 164 human cases and 12 fatalities. Vaccination is recommended only if travelers expect to have close contact with rodents (e.g., field biologists, military personnel, etc.).

African sleeping sickness: Black-fly borne. Sporadic cases have been reported, mainly from the Okavango Swamps in the northwest district of Ngamiland. All travelers should take measures to prevent insect (tsetse fly) bites.

Rabies: Dogs are the primary source of human infection. Rabid jackals are also a potential threat, especially in the rural eastern areas, where an outbreak of wild animal rabies was reported in 1987. Travelers should seek immediate treatment of any animal bite. Rabies vaccination should be considered prior to long-term travel (more than 4 weeks) to this country.

AIDS: Heterosexual contact is the predominate mode of transmission. HIV-1 prevalence estimated at 1.2% of the high-risk urban population. All travelers are cautioned against unsafe sex, unsterile medical or dental injections, and unnecessary blood transfusions.

Other illnesses/hazards: African tick typhus (contracted from dog ticks, often in urban areas; disease also transmitted by bush ticks), arboviral fevers (mosquito-transmitted; West Nile, chikungunya, and Rift Valley fever may occur), brucellosis, dengue (not reported recently), syphilis, tuberculosis (a major health problem), trachoma, typhoid fever, and intestinal helminthic infections (very common). Animal hazards include snakes (vipers, cobras), centipedes, scorpions, and black widow spiders.

COMOROS ISLANDS
Moroni ... GMT +3 hrs

Entry Requirements
- Passport/Visa: Valid passport and visa are required.
- AIDS Test: Not required.
- Vaccinations: None required.

Health Advisory
Malaria: Risk is present throughout this country, including urban areas. Prophylaxis with mefloquine or doxycycline is currently recommended. All travelers should take precautions against mosquito bites.

Travelers' diarrhea: High risk. Travelers should observe all food and drink safety precautions. A quinolone antibiotic (Cipro or Floxin) is recommended for the treatment of acute diarrhea. Diarrhea not responding to treatment with an antibiotic, or chronic diarrhea, may be due to a parasitic disease such as giardiasis or amebiasis and treatment with metronidazole (Flagyl) or tinidazole (Fasigyn) should be considered. All cases of diarrhea should be treated with adequate fluid replacement.

Hepatitis: High risk. All susceptible travelers should receive immune globulin prophylaxis or hepatitis A vaccine. The hepatitis B carrier rate in the general population is estimated to exceed 10%. Vaccination against hepatitis B is recommended for healthcare workers and all long-term visitors to this country.

LESOTHO
Maseru ... GMT +2 hrs

Entry Requirements
- Passport/Visa: Travelers should possess valid passport. Visa not required.
- AIDS Test: Not required.
- Vaccinations: A yellow fever vaccination certificate is required from all travelers older than 1 year arriving from infected areas.

Telephone Country Code: 266

American Express: Manica Freight Services Travel. Kingsway, Maseru; Tel. 22554.

Embassies/Consulates: U.S. Embassy, Maseru; Tel. 312-666/7. Canadian Embassy (South Africa); Tel. [27] 287-062.

Health Advisory
Malaria: Transmission of malaria reportedly does not occur in Lesotho. Risk areas in surrounding South Africa are north of Lesotho.

Travelers' diarrhea: Travelers should observe all food and drink safety precautions. A quinolone antibiotic (Cipro or Floxin) is recommended for the treatment of acute diarrhea. Diarrhea not responding to treatment with an antibiotic, or chronic diarrhea, may be due to a parasitic disease such as giardiasis or amebiasis, and treatment with metronidazole (Flagyl) or tinidazole (Fasigyn) should be considered. All cases of diarrhea should be treated with adequate fluid replacement.

Hepatitis: All susceptible travelers should receive immune globulin prophylaxis or hepatitis A vaccine. The hepatitis B carrier rate in the general population is estimated at 8%. Vaccination against hepatitis B is recommended for healthcare workers and all long-term visitors to this country.

Schistosomiasis: No infected areas are reported in Lesotho. Both urinary and intestinal schistosomiasis, however, occur in eastern and northern regions of neighboring Natal Province of South Africa.

Other illnesses/hazards: AIDS (low incidence; HIV prevalence estimated at less than 1%), African tick typhus (contracted from dog ticks—often in urban areas—and from bush ticks), brucellosis, tuberculosis (a major health problem), typhoid fever, and intestinal worms (uncommon).

MADAGASCAR
Antananarivo ... GMT +3 hrs

Entry Requirements
- Passport/Visa: Valid passport and visa are required.
- AIDS Test: Not required.
- Vaccinations: A yellow fever vaccination certificate is required from all travelers arriving from, or transitting, infected areas.

Telephone: Operator assistance required.

American Express: Madagascar Airtours. Galerie Marchande, Hilton Hotel, Antananarivo; Tel. 24192.

Embassies/Consulates: U.S. Embassy, Antananarivo. 14 & 16 Rue Rainitovo; Tel. 212-57/209-56.

Canadian Consulate, Antananarivo. 20 Avenue de l'Independance; Tel. 29442.

Hospitals/Doctors: Hospital Befelatnana, Antananarivo (1,300 beds); general medical/surgical facility; Tel. 223-84. Fort Dauphin Hospital, Faradofay (80 beds); American Lutheran hospital.

Health Advisory

Malaria: Risk is present year-round throughout this country, including urban areas. There is minimal risk of malaria, however, in Antananarivo; minimal risk in towns of Antsirabe, Manjakandriana, and Andramasina. Highest risk of malaria occurs in the eastern coastal areas. Malaria now occurs on the high plateau, formerly risk free. Falciparum malaria accounts for approximately 90% of cases. Other cases of malaria are due to the *P. vivax* (approx. 10% of cases). Chloroquine-resistant *P. falciparum* is reported. Prophylaxis with mefloquine or doxycycline is currently recommended when traveling to malarious areas.

Travelers' diarrhea: High risk. Water distribution systems are found only in major urban areas and are old and in poor repair. Piped water supplies are frequently contaminated. Travelers should observe all food and drink safety precautions. A quinolone antibiotic (Cipro or Floxin) is recommended for the treatment of acute diarrhea. Diarrhea not responding to treatment with an antibiotic, or chronic diarrhea, may be due to a parasitic disease such as giardiasis or amebiasis, and treatment with metronidazole (Flagyl) or tinidazole (Fasigyn) should be considered. All cases of diarrhea should be treated with adequate fluid replacement.

Hepatitis: All susceptible travelers should receive immune globulin prophylaxis or hepatitis A vaccine. The hepatitis B carrier rate in the general population is estimated at 5%–10%. Vaccination against hepatitis B is recommended for healthcare workers and all long-term visitors to this country.

Leishmaniasis: Low risk. Incidence status undetermined.

Schistosomiasis: Widely distributed. Urinary schistosomiasis predominates on the west coast and in the northern regions, while intestinal schistosomiasis predominates in the central and southern coastal zone of Toamasina Province; the coastal zone of Fianarantsoa Province, and inland, in areas at moderate elevations to the south of the central highlands. Risk-free areas include the vicinities of Antsiranana and Antananarivo, and the Presquile Peninsula, including Maroantsetra and Antalaha.

Plague: Human cases are reported annually. Travelers should avoid contact with wild rodents (and their fleas) or patients with the pneumonic form of the disease. Doxycycline or tetracycline can be used prophylactically if exposure occurs.

AIDS: HIV prevalence is still extremely low, even in the high-risk urban population.

Other illnesses/hazards: Brucellosis, filariasis (mosquito-borne; reportedly occurs, but specific data are lacking), leprosy (prevalence of 2.5 cases/1,000 population), syphilis, tuberculosis (a major health problem in lower socio-economic groups), trachoma, typhoid fever, and intestinal worms (very common). Animal hazards include centipedes, scorpions, and black widow spiders. Portuguese man-of-war, sea nettles, sea wasps, stingrays, and several species of poisonous fish are common in the country's coastal waters and are potential hazards to unprotected swimmers.

MAURITIUS

Port Louis ... GMT +4 hrs

Entry Requirements

- Passport/Visa: Travelers should possess valid passport. Visa not required.
- AIDS Test: Not required.
- Vaccinations: A yellow fever vaccination certificate is required from all travelers older than 1 year arriving from infected areas and also from any country in the Yellow Fever Endemic Zones.

Telephone Country Code: 230

American Express: M.T.T.B. Ltd. Corner Sir William Newton & Royal Roads, Port Louis; Tel. (8) 2041.

Embassies/Consulates: U.S. Embassy, Port Louis. Rogers Building, 4th Floor, John Kennedy Street; Tel. (8) 082-347.

Hospitals/Doctors: R. Rivalland, M.D., Medical & Surgical Centre; Tel. (86) 1477/78 or 1096 (eve).

Health Advisory

Malaria: Risk is present between January and May in rural areas of Pamplemousse, Plaines Wilhelmes, Riviere du Ramparts, Grand Port, and Port Louis Districts. There is no malaria on the island of Rodriguez. Chloroquine-resistant falciparum malaria is reported. Prophylaxis with mefloquine or doxycycline is currently recommended when traveling to malarious areas. Alternative malaria regimes should be discussed with a travel medicine or infectious disease specialist.

Travelers' diarrhea: High risk. A quinolone antibiotic (Cipro or Floxin) is recommended for the treatment of acute diarrhea. Diarrhea not responding to treatment with an antibiotic, or chronic diarrhea, may be due to a parasitic disease such as giardiasis or amebiasis, and treatment with metronidazole (Flagyl) or tinidazole (Fasigyn) should be considered. All cases of diarrhea should be treated with adequate fluid replacement.

Hepatitis: All susceptible travelers should receive immune globulin prophylaxis or hepatitis A vaccine. The hepatitis B carrier rate in the general population is estimated to exceed 10%. Vaccination against hepatitis B is recommended for healthcare workers and all long-term visitors to this country.

Leishmaniasis: Both cutaneous and visceral leishmaniasis are reported. Travelers should take measures to prevent insect (sandfly) bites.

Filariasis: Risk is present throughout this country. Travelers should take measures to prevent insect (mosquito) bites.

Schistosomiasis: Risk is present throughout this country, including urban areas. Travelers should avoid swimming, bathing, or wading in freshwater lakes, ponds, or streams.

Other diseases/health threats: Echinococcosis, leprosy (highly endemic), rabies, tick-borne typhus, syphilis, tuberculosis (highly endemic), and soil-transmitted helminthic disease (ascariasis, hookworm disease, strongyloidiasis) are reported. Animal hazards include snakes (cobras, vipers), spiders (black and brown widow), crocodiles, and leeches. Stingrays, jellyfish, and several species of poisonous fish are common in the country's coastal waters and are potential hazards to unprotected swimmers.

MOZAMBIQUE
Maputo ... GMT +2 hrs

Entry Requirements
- Passport/Visa: Valid passport and visa are required.
- AIDS Test: Not required.
- Vaccinations: A yellow fever vaccination certificate is required from all travelers older than 1 year arriving from infected areas.

Telephone Country Code: 258
Electricity/Plugs: AC 50 Hz, 220 volts; plug types C and F.
Embassies/Consulates: U.S. Embassy, Maputo. Avenida Kaunda 193; Tel. 742-79/743-167/744-163. Canadian Embassy (Zimbabwe); Tel. [263] (4) 733-881.
Hospitals/Doctors: Travelers should contact the U.S. Embassy for physician referrals.

Health Advisory
Yellow fever: Vaccination recommended. No cases currently reported.
Cholera: This disease is active in this country.
Malaria: Very high risk is present throughout this country, including urban areas. There is increased malaria risk along the coast and in the lower Zambezi Valley. Outbreaks are reported in Xai-Xai and Maputo. Falciparum malaria accounts for up to 95% of cases. Other cases of malaria are due to the *P. malariae* species, rarely *P. ovale* and *P. vivax*. Chloroquine-resistant falciparum malaria is reported. Prophylaxis with mefloquine or doxycycline is currently recommended when traveling to malarious areas.
Travelers' diarrhea: High risk. Potable water is often in critically short supply. Piped water supplies in urban areas may be grossly contaminated. Travelers should observe all food and drink safety precautions. A quinolone antibiotic is recommended for the treatment of acute diarrhea.
Hepatitis: High risk. All susceptible travelers should receive immune globulin prophylaxis or hepatitis A vaccine. The hepatitis B carrier rate in the general population is estimated at 11%. Vaccination against hepatitis B is recommended for healthcare workers and all long-term visitors to this country.
Schistosomiasis: Risk of urinary schistosomiasis is reported from all provinces. Intestinal schistosomiasis appears almost as widely distributed, with major risk along the southern coastal plain, the Zambezi Valley, and the vicinity of Lake Malawi. All travelers should avoid swimming, bathing, or wading in freshwater lakes, ponds, or streams.
Trypanosomiasis (sleeping sickness): During the 1980s, approximately 75 cases were reported annually, mostly from Tete Province. All travelers should take precautions against insect (tsetse fly) bites.
Meningitis: Group C meningococcal meningitis outbreak occurred in Maputo in late 1989. Vaccination is recommended for those travelers staying in this country longer than 4 weeks, and those who will have close contact with the indigenous population.
Rabies: Occurs in rural and urban areas, including Maputo. Dogs are the primary source of human infections. Pre-exposure vaccination is recommended for long-term travel (more than 4 weeks) to this country, especially for travelers going to remote areas who will be unable to receive antirabies treatment within 24 hours of exposure to a potentially rabid animal.
AIDS: Heterosexual contact is the predominate mode of transmission. Lower risk compared to other countries in sub-Saharan Africa. HIV-1 prevalence estimated at 2.6% of the high-risk urban population. All travelers are cautioned against unsafe sex, unsterile medical or dental injections, and unnecessary blood transfusions.
Other illnesses/hazards: African tick typhus (contracted from dog ticks—often in urban areas—and from bush ticks), brucellosis, Bancroftian filariasis (presumably occurs in northern coastal areas and along the Zambezi River), leprosy, plague (no human cases reported since 1978), tuberculosis (a major health problem), trachoma, typhoid fever, and intestinal worms. Animal hazards include snakes (vipers, cobras, mambas), centipedes, scorpions, and black widow spiders. Stingrays, jellyfish, moon jelly, sea wasps, blue cones, octopi, bat rays and eagle rays, and several species of poisonous fish are common in the country's coastal waters and are potential hazards to unprotected swimmers.

NAMIBIA

Windhoek ... GMT +2 hrs

Entry Requirements

- Passport/Visa: Valid passport and visa are required.
- AIDS Test: Not required.
- Vaccinations: A yellow fever vaccination certificate is required from all travelers older than 1 year arriving from infected areas and also from any country in the Yellow Fever Endemic Zones.

Telephone Country Code: 264

Electricity/Plugs: AC 50 Hz, 220 volts; plug type D.

Embassies/Consulates: The United States maintains no permanent diplomatic relations in Namibia. The nearest U.S. Consulate is located in Capetown, South Africa.

Doctors/Hospitals: State Hospital, Windhoek (440 beds); general medical/surgical facility; limited burn treatment; emergency services, ICU.

Health Advisory

Malaria: Risk is present primarily from November to May–June, during and just after the rainy season, in northern rural regions along the borders with Angola, Zambia, and Botswana, including the Ovamboland, which borders Angola, and the Caprivi strip. Malaria risk has recently extended somewhat into the central plateau and eastern semiarid areas, but not the coastal desert. Major outbreaks in 1988 affected all areas except the coastal regions. Falciparum malaria accounts for up to 98% of cases countrywide. Chloroquine-resistant falciparum malaria is widespread. Prophylaxis with mefloquine or doxycycline is currently recommended when traveling to malarious areas.

Travelers' diarrhea: The water in major urban areas is treated, and in Swakopund, Walvis Bay, and Windhoek, the major hotels and restaurants serve generally safe food and drink. Outside of these areas, all water sources should be considered potentially contaminated. Some surface water in shallow lakes contains dangerously high concentrations of minerals and nitrites, and is unsafe for consumption. Bottled water is recommended. Travelers should observe all food and drink safety precautions. A quinolone antibiotic is recommended for the treatment of acute diarrhea.

Hepatitis: High risk. All susceptible travelers should receive immune globulin or hepatitis A vaccine. The hepatitis B carrier rate in the general population is estimated at 15%. Vaccination against hepatitis B is recommended for healthcare workers and all long-term visitors to this country.

Leishmaniasis: Sporadic cases of cutaneous leishmaniasis have been reported, primarily from the southern Keetmanshoop-Karasburg-Bethanie vicinity, and also from the central and more northern areas of the inland plateau and escarpment. Travelers should take measures to prevent sandfly bites. Visceral leishmaniasis is not reported.

Schistosomiasis: Risk is present in the northeast along the Angolan border, extending into the Caprivi Strip. Travelers should avoid swimming, bathing, or wading in freshwater lakes, ponds, or streams.

Trypanosomiasis (African sleeping sickness): Sporadic cases have been reported. Travelers should take personal protection measures against insect (tsetse fly) bites, especially in the Okavango area of the Caprivi Strip.

Poliomyelitis: An outbreak of 27 cases reported in the southern region 1993-1994.

Plague: Flea-borne; at least 80 cases were reported in late 1990, most from northern areas, particularly the Oshakati/Onandjokwe vicinity of Owambo District.

Rabies: Urban rabies, with dogs the primary source of human infection, occurs mainly in northern areas. Jackals may also be a source of rabies. Travelers should avoid stray dogs and wild animals, and seek immediate treatment of any animal bite.

Other illnesses/hazards: African tick typhus, brucellosis, dengue (not reported), relapsing fever (tick-borne; sandy floors of village mud huts provide favorable habitat for these ticks), tuberculosis (a major health problem), trachoma, typhoid fever, and intestinal worms (very common). Animal hazards include snakes (mambas, adders, vipers, cobras, coral snakes), scorpions, sac spiders, brown widow and black widow spiders.

SOUTH AFRICA

Embassy: 202-337-3452   *Pretoria*   *GMT +2 hrs*

Entry Requirements

- Passport/Visa: Passport and visa required.
- AIDS Test: HIV-positive travelers "prohibited." Travelers should contact the South African Embassy in Washington for details.
- Vaccinations: A yellow fever vaccination certificate is required from all travelers older than 1 year of age arriving from infected areas or from any country in the Yellow Fever Endemic Zone. Children under 1 year of age may be subject to surveillance. They may not proceed to Natal or to the Lowveld of the Transvaal within 6 days of leaving an infected area. Passengers arriving on charter aircraft at airports not used by scheduled airlines are required to have a valid vaccination certificate.

Telephone Country Code: 27   **AT&T Access:** 0-800-99-0123

Electricity/Plugs: AC 50 Hz, 220 volts; plug type D. Adaptors and transformer necessary for U.S.-made appliances.

Embassies/Consulates: U.S. Embassy, Pretoria. 225 Pretorious Street; Tel. (12) 284-266. U.S. Consulate, Johannesburg; Tel. (11) 331-1681. U.S. Consulate, Cape Town; Tel; (21) 214-280. Canadian Embassy, Pretoria; Church & Beatrix Streets; Tel. (12) 287-062.

Hospitals/Doctors: Gu Rankuwa Hospital, Pretoria (2,000 beds); all specialties, including hemodialysis capability. Groote Schuur Hospital, Capetown (1,350 beds); all specialties, including cardiovascular surgery, hemodialysis. Barabwanath Hospital, Johannesburg (2,640 beds); all specialties, including neurosurgery, hemodialysis, ICU. Dr. Joseph Teeger, Johannesburg; Tel. 287-711 or 728-4298.

Health Advisory

Malaria: Risk is present year-round, primarily in the northeastern areas of Transvaal Province bordering Botswana, Mozambique, and Zimbabwe, including the game parks. Malaria risk is also present along, and inland from, the Natal coast north of 29 degrees south latitude (Tugela River). Peak transmission occurs March through May. During the late 1980s, risk areas have extended south of the Tugela River in Natal Province, and malaria may occur in northern Cape Province along sections of the Orange and Molopo Rivers following extreme flooding. Malaria risk is present in Kruger National Park. Falciparum malaria accounts for up to 99% of cases. Chloroquine-resistant *P. falciparum* is reported in coastal areas north of Richard's Bay and in the northern Transvaal. Prophylaxis with mefloquine or doxycycline is currently recommended when traveling to malarious areas.

Travelers' diarrhea: Low risk in urban areas. Cities and towns have municipal water systems which supply treated, potable water to hotels and homes. Travelers outside urban areas should observe food and drink safety precautions. A quinolone antibiotic is recommended for the treatment of acute diarrhea. Diarrhea not responding to antibiotic treatment may be due to a parasitic disease such as giardiasis or amebiasis, or cryptosporidiosis.

Hepatitis: All susceptible travelers should receive immune globulin or hepatitis A vaccine. The hepatitis B carrier rate in the general population is estimated at 6%–15%. Vaccination against hepatitis B is recommended for healthcare workers and all long-term visitors to this country.

West Nile, Sindbis, and Chikungunya fevers: Sporadic outbreaks occur, primarily in Central Cape Province, and eastern and southern Transvaal during warmer months. Travelers should take measures to prevent insect (mosquito) bites.

Dengue fever: Low risk; currently not endemic.

Crimean-Congo hemorrhagic fever: Sporadic human cases reported. Viral infection may occur following exposure to infective ticks, animals, or humans.

Schistosomiasis: Risk is present primarily in the warmer months (October–April) in the northeast and east. Foci of urinary schistosomiasis extend from the Limpo River Basin southward, including most of northern Transvaal, northern and eastern Natal, and the coastal areas of Eastern Cape as far south as Port Elizabeth vicinity. Foci of intestinal schistosomiasis extend from the extreme northeast (Messina vicinity) southward, including northeastern

Transvaal and eastern Natal as far south as Durban. Travelers to these areas should avoid swimming, bathing, or wading in freshwater lakes, ponds, or streams.

Plague: No human cases have been reported since 1982. Vaccination against plague is recommended only for persons who may be occupationally exposed to wild rodents (anthropologists, archaeologists, medical personnel, and missionaries).

Meningitis: Low risk. South Africa is south of the sub-Saharan meningitis belt. Long-term visitors who expect to have close contact with the indigenous population should consider vaccination.

Rabies: Nearly all cases occur in the coastal region of Natal, including Durban, and is attributed to an increasing stray and wild dog population. Vaccination should be considered for prolonged travel (more than 3–4 weeks) to these areas.

AIDS: Previously, homosexual contact was the predominate mode of transmission. Heterosexual contact is now the predominate mode of transmission. HIV-1 prevalence estimated at 3.2% of the high-risk urban population. All travelers are cautioned against unsafe sex, unsterile medical or dental injections, and unnecessary blood transfusions.

Other diseases/health threats: African tick typhus (focally distributed, including periurban areas near Johannesburg; cases reported among travelers; contracted from dog ticks and bush ticks), brucellosis, leishmaniasis (low risk), leptospirosis, trachoma (high incidence in northern Transvaal), tuberculosis (highly endemic in Western Cape), and helminthic disease (ascariasis, hookworm disease, strongyloidiasis in lower socioeconomic populations) are reported. Animal hazards include snakes (cobras, mambas, adders, vipers), spiders (black and brown widow); Stingrays, jellyfish, and several species of poisonous fish are common in the country's coastal waters and are potential hazards to unprotected swimmers.

SWAZILAND
Mbabane ... GMT +2 hrs

Entry Requirements
- Passport/Visa: Travelers should possess valid passport. Tourist card, visa, or transit visa should be obtained upon arrival. Travelers must register with immigration within 48 hours.
- AIDS Test: Not required.
- Vaccinations: A yellow fever vaccination certificate is required of travelers arriving from endemic areas.

Telephone Country Code: 268

American Express: Manica Freight Services Travel, Allister Miller Street, Mbabane; Tel. 42298.

Embassies/Consulates: U.S. Embassy, Mbabane. Central Bank Building; Tel. 464-41. Canadian Embassy (South Africa): Tel. [27] 287-062.

Hospitals/Doctors: Mbabane Clinic (26 beds); general medical facility; x-ray and small laboratory. Tel. 2425 or 2886.

Health Advisory

Cholera: This disease is active in this country. Although cholera vaccination is not required for entry if arriving directly from the U.S. or Canada, it may be required if arriving from a cholera-infected area, or required for on-going travel to other countries in Africa, the Middle East, Asia, or Latin America. Travelers to this country should consider vaccination (one dose) or a doctor's letter of exemption from vaccination. The risk to travelers of acquiring cholera is very low. Prevention consists primarily in following strict adherence to safe food and drink guidelines.

Malaria: Malaria is absent in most of the country. Risk is present in the northern and eastern grassland and plain areas of Bordergate, Lomahasha, Mhlume, and Tshaneni. Falciparum malaria accounts for 99% of cases. Because chloroquine- and Fansidar resistant falciparum malaria are widespread in these areas, mefloquine or doxycycline prophylaxis is recommended.

Travelers' diarrhea: High risk. Piped water supplies are frequently untreated and may be grossly contaminated. Travelers should observe food and drink safety precautions. A quinolone antibiotic (Cipro or Floxin) is recommended for the treatment of acute diarrhea. Diarrhea not responding to treatment with an antibiotic, or chronic diarrhea, may be due to a parasitic disease such as giardiasis or amebiasis, and treatment with metronidazole (Flagyl) or tinidazole (Fasigyn) should be considered. All cases of diarrhea should be treated with adequate fluid replacement.

Hepatitis: High risk. All susceptible travelers should receive immune globulin prophylaxis or hepatitis A vaccine. The hepatitis B carrier rate in the general population is estimated at 14%. Vaccination against hepatitis B is recommended for healthcare workers and all long-term visitors to this country.

Schistosomiasis: Risk areas for urinary schistosomiasis are primarily in middleveld and lowveld areas. Intestinal schistosomiasis is found only in lowveld areas. Travelers are advised to avoid swimming or wading in freshwater ponds, lakes, or streams in these areas.

Other illnesses/hazards: African tick typhus (contracted from dog ticks—often in urban areas—and from bush ticks), brucellosis, leprosy, syphilis, tuberculosis (a major health problem), trachoma, typhoid fever, and intestinal worms (very common). Animal hazards include snakes (vipers, cobras), centipedes, scorpions, and black widow spiders.

ZIMBABWE
Harare ... GMT +2 hrs

Entry Requirements
- Passport/Visa: Travelers should possess valid passport. Visa not required. Must have proof of sufficient funds, a firm itinerary, and return ticket.
- AIDS Test: Not required.
- Vaccinations: A yellow fever vaccination certificate is required from all travelers older than 1 year arriving from infected or endemic areas.

Telephone Country Code: 263

Electricity/Plugs: AC 50 Hz, 220 volts; plug types D and G.

American Express: Manica Travel Services Travel Centre, 2nd Floor, Stanley Avenue, Harare; Tel. (4) 703-42.

Embassies/Consulates: U.S. Embassy, Harare. 172 Rhodes Avenue; Tel. (4) 794-521. Canadian High Commission, Harare. 45 Baines Avenue; Tel. (4) 733-881.

Hospitals/Doctors: Parirenyatwa Hospital, Harare (900 beds); emergency services; intensive care and burn units. Mpilo Central Hospital. Bulawayo (600 beds); general medical facility. The Avenues Clinic, Harare; Tel. (4) 732-055. Eric Cohen, M.D., Bulawayo; Tel. (9) 70-709.

Health Advisory

Cholera: This disease is active in this country. Although cholera vaccination is not required for entry if arriving directly from the U.S. or Canada, it may be required if arriving from a cholera-infected area, or required for on-going travel to other countries in Africa, the Middle East, Asia, or Latin America. Travelers to this country should consider vaccination or a doctor's letter of exemption from vaccination.

Malaria: Year-round transmission occurs in the low-lying areas of the Zambezi Valley in the north (border area with Zambia) and the Sabi-Limpopo system in the south, but transmission is seasonal in the rest of the country below 1,200 meters elevation, occurring primarily from November through June (during and just after the warm wet months of November and March). The central plateau (stretching from the southwest to the northeast, with elevations from 1,200 to 1,500 meters, including Harare City) is essentially risk free. Epidemics have occurred in the Matabeleland North and northern Midlands Provinces. Falciparum malaria accounts for approximately 98% of cases countrywide. Other cases of malaria are usually due to the *P. malariae*. Chloroquine-resistant falciparum malaria is reported. Prophylaxis with mefloquine or doxycycline is currently recommended when traveling to malarious areas. Malaria prophylaxis is especially recommended for travel to Victoria Falls.

Travelers' diarrhea: Water in major urban systems is chlorinated and checked for potability. In Harare, water is chemically treated with flocculents and clarifiers and is sand-filtered. Outside major urban areas, travelers should observe all food and drink safety precautions. A quinolone antibiotic is recommended for the treatment of acute diarrhea. Diarrhea not responding to treatment with an antibiotic, or chronic diarrhea, may be due to a parasitic disease such as giardiasis or amebiasis.

Hepatitis: High risk. All susceptible travelers should receive immune globulin or hepatitis A vaccine. Hepatitis E has been reported, but incidence data are not available. The hepatitis B carrier rate in the general population is estimated at 8%. Vaccination against hepatitis B is recommended for healthcare workers and all long-term visitors to this country.

Chikungunya fever, West Nile fever, Rift Valley fever: These viral, mosquito-transmitted illnesses occur in this geographical region. Dengue fever is not reported. All travelers should take measures to prevent insect bites.

Schistosomiasis: Peak transmission of urinary schistosomiasis occurs in the northeast during the hot, dry season (September–October). Transmission is year-round in the Zambezi Valley, the shores of Lake Kariba and the southeast lowveld. Intestinal schistosomiasis occurs primarily in the north and east. Travelers are advised to avoid swimming or wading in freshwater lakes, ponds, or streams.

Meningitis: Low risk. Zimbabwe is south of the sub-Saharan meningitis belt. Long-term visitors who expect to have close contact with the indigenous population should, however, consider vaccination.

Trypanosomiasis (African sleeping sickness): Low risk of infection among tourists. Outbreaks along the border with Mozambique were reported in the 1980s. Travelers should take measures to prevent insect (tsetse fly) bites.

Plague: Sporadic cases have occurred in the northwest, and north of Harare. Vaccination against plague is recommended only for persons who may be occupationally exposed to wild rodents (anthropologists, archaeologists, medical personnel, and missionaries).

Rabies: Sporadic human cases are reported, with dogs and jackals as the primary source of exposure. Most cases occur in Matabeleland North and South Provinces, which have been declared "rabies areas." Rabies vaccination is recommended for persons planning an extended stay (more than 4 weeks).

Other illnesses/hazards: African tick typhus (contracted from dog ticks—often in urban areas—and bush ticks), brucellosis (from consumption of raw dairy products), Crimean-Congo hemorrhagic fever (tick-borne), leishmaniasis (low risk), leptospirosis, tuberculosis (a major health problem), typhoid fever, and intestinal worms (very common). Animal hazards include snakes (vipers, cobras), centipedes, scorpions, and black widow spiders.

D I S E A S E   R I S K   S U M M A R Y
The Middle East

Malaria: The risk of malaria is low in this region. There is no malaria in Kuwait, Bahrain, Cyprus, Israel, Jordan, Lebanon, or Qatar. Vivax malaria is found in the northern third of Iraq below 1,500 meters elevation. In Saudi Arabia, malaria is confined to the extreme southwest, about 500 km south of Jeddah. The highest risk of malaria in the Middle East occurs during the rainy season, from December through March. Falciparum malaria accounts for 50%–70% of cases, vivax the remainder. Chloroquine-resistant falciparum is reported in Yemen and Iran, and may occur in Oman and Saudi Arabia; mefloquine prophylaxis should be considered for travel to malarious areas of these countries. In other malarious regions, chloroquine prophylaxis is recommended. Personal protection measures against mosquito bites, including permethrin-impregnated bed nets, should be used by all travelers.

Travelers' diarrhea: Medium to high risk throughout this region. Travelers should drink only bottled, boiled, or chemically treated water, especially in rural areas. All food should be well cooked. Fruit should be peeled. Increased resistance (up to 93% of bacteria tested) of Shigella and *E. coli* to trimethoprim/sulfamethoxazole (Bactrim, Septra) has been reported. A quinolone antibiotic (Cipro or Floxin) is recommended for the treatment of acute diarrhea. Diarrhea not responding to treatment with an antibiotic, or chronic diarrhea, may be due to a parasitic disease such as giardiasis or amebiasis, and treatment with metronidazole (Flagyl) or tinidazole (Fasigyn) should be considered. Diarrhea due to cryptosporidiosis usually does not require antibiotic treatment. All cases of diarrhea should be treated with adequate fluid replacement.

Hepatitis: High risk. All susceptible travelers should receive immune globulin prophylaxis or hepatitis A vaccine. The hepatitis B carrier rate in the general population of this region is estimated at 2%–10%. Vaccination against hepatitis B is recommended for healthcare workers and all long-term visitors to this region. Hepatitis E is prevalent among guest workers in these countries and may possibly be a threat to travelers. Prevention of hepatitis E requires avoiding the consumption of contaminated water since immune globulin is not protective against this illness.

Cutaneous leishmaniasis: Risk is low, but this sandfly-transmitted disease is reported throughout the Middle East. Travelers should take protective measures to prevent insect (sandfly) bites.

Visceral leishmaniasis (kala azar): Cases are reported throughout the region, especially from rural areas. Twenty cases of kala azar occurred in U.S. Desert Storm troops stationed in Saudi Arabia. All travelers to the Middle East are advised to take protective measures against insect (sandfly) bites.

Schistosomiasis: Risk is present in Yemen, Oman, Jordan, Iraq, Saudi Arabia, and Syria. Travelers should avoid swimming, bathing, or wading in freshwater lakes, ponds, streams, or irrigated areas in these regions.

Rabies: Animal rabies, mainly in dogs and foxes, is a problem in most countries, but human cases occur infrequently. Travelers should consider rabies vaccination if they will be in remote or rural areas for extended periods and unable to obtain prompt medical care after being bitten by a dog or wild animal.

Other diseases: Epidemic typhus, murine typhus, Q fever, sandfly fever (a viral illness transmitted by sandflies), Congo-Crimean hemorrhagic fever (a viral illness transmitted by ticks), brucellosis (transmitted by unpasteurized dairy products), echinococcosis, typhoid fever (most cases occur in the summer and early fall; multidrug-resistant strains salmonella bacteria are reported; treatment drugs of choice are the quinolones and third generation cephalosporins), tapeworm and hookworm disease, and tuberculosis are reported from many areas. Meningitis occurs in sporadic epidemics in Saudi Arabia, especially among travelers to Mecca. Plague has not been reported in the Middle East for 15 years. A case of human dirofilariasis has recently been reported from Kuwait.

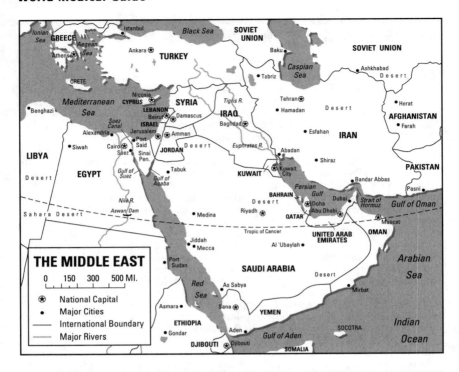

BAHRAIN
Manama ... GMT +3 hrs

Entry Requirements
- Passport/Visa: Passport required. Travelers should obtain visa or tourist card on arrival.
- AIDS Test: Not required.
- Vaccinations: A yellow fever vaccination certificate required of travelers arriving from infected areas.

Telephone Country Code: 973   **AT&T:** 800-001   **MCI:** 800-002

Electricity/Plugs: AC 50/60 Hz, 220 volts; plugs are types D and G. A grounding conductor is required in the electrical cord attached to appliances. Adaptors and transformer necessary for U.S.-made appliances.

American Express: Kanoo Travel Agency. Al Khalifa Rd., Manama; Tel. 254-081.

Embassies/Consulates: American Embassy. Shaikh Rd., Manama; Tel. 714-151.

Hospitals/Doctors: International Hospital, Bahrain (300 beds); new civilian facility; most specialty services; emergency and surgical capabilities. Al-Salmaniyah Medical Center, Manama (620 beds); government teaching facility; all specialty services except neurosurgery.

Health Advisory

Malaria: There is no risk of malaria in this country.

Travelers' diarrhea: Low to medium risk. Travelers should drink only bottled or treated water. All food should be well-cooked.

Hepatitis: Immune globulin prophylaxis is recommended. The hepatitis B carrier rate in the general population is 2 percent. Vaccination is not necessary for routine travel.

CYPRUS

Nicosia ... GMT +2 hrs

Entry Requirements
- Passport/Visa: A valid passport is required.
- AIDS Test: Foreign entertainers may be required to have test. Contact the Cyprus Embassy in Washington (202-462-5772) for further details.
- Vaccinations: None required.

Telephone Country Code: 357   **AT&T:** 080-90010   **MCI:** 080-90000

American Express: A.L. Mantovani & Sons, Ltd. 35–37 Evagoras A Avenue, Nicosia; Tel. (2) 443777.

Embassies/Consulates: American Embassy. Therissos St. and Dositheos St., Nicosia; Tel. (2) 465-151. Canadian Embassy. 3 Thermistocles St., Tel. (2) 451-630.

Hospitals/Doctors: Nicosia General Hospital (485 beds); ICU; emergency room; neurosurgery. Lanarca General Hospital (225 beds); government-operated civilian facility; five surgical suites. George Partelides, M.D., 28 Sofoules St., Nicosia; Tel: (2) 444-633 or 474-812 (home).

Health Advisory

Malaria: There is no malaria on Cyprus.

Travelers' diarrhea: Low to moderate risk. In urban and resort areas, the hotels and restaurants generally serve reliable food and potable water. Major cities have piped, potable water. Elsewhere, travelers should observe all food and drink safety precautions. A quinolone antibiotic (Floxin or Cipro) is recommended for the treatment of acute diarrhea. Diarrhea not responding to antibiotic treatment may be due to a parasitic disease such as giardiasis or amebiasis.

Hepatitis: Immune globulin or hepatitis A vaccine is recommended for all susceptible travelers. The hepatitis B carrier rate in the general population is estimated at 1%. Vaccination against hepatitis B is recommended for healthcare workers and should be considered by long-term visitors to this country.

Leishmaniasis: Cutaneous leishmaniasis is not reported on Cyprus. There have been a few reports of visceral leishmaniasis in tourists, but the risk is deemed to be low.

IRAN

Tehran ... GMT +3½ hrs

Entry Requirements
- Passport/Visa: A valid passport and visa required.
- AIDS Test: Not required.
- Vaccinations: No vaccinations are required.

Telephone Country Code: 98

Electricity/Plugs: AC 50 Hz, 220 volts; no information is currently available about plugs. Adaptors and transformer necessary for U.S.-made appliances.

Embassies/Consulates: The U.S. government does not maintain diplomatic relations with Iran. American interests are represented by the Swedish Embassy; Tel. 675-011 or 675-020.

Hospitals/Doctors: Local medical facilities are substantially below Western standards and should be used by U.S. citizens only in the case of emergency.

Health Advisory

Malaria: Risk is present in various areas. Transmission occurs year-round in the southwest, south, and southeast, but only during the summer in the north and northeast. Malaria is endemic in approximately one-third of the land area of Iran, in the southwest and south (along the Persian Gulf, south of the Zagros mountains), in the southeast (Sistan-Baluchistan), and in the north and northeast (along the Caspian sea and south of the border with the former USSR). Malaria transmission occurs in rural areas at elevations up to 1,500 meters. Transmission may occur in urban areas in the south and southwest. Other urban areas (including

Tehran) are risk free. The majority of malaria cases occur in the southwest, south, and southeast (Baluchestan, va Sistan, Kerman, and Hormozgan Provinces). Falciparum malaria accounts for 25% of the cases in the southeast and 5% to 10% of the cases in the southwest and south. Vivax malaria accounts for the rest of the cases. Chloroquine-resistant falciparum malaria is reported. Prophylaxis with mefloquine or doxycycline is currently recommended when traveling to malarious areas.

Hepatitis: All susceptible travelers should receive immune globulin or hepatitis A vaccine prior to visiting this country. The hepatitis B carrier rate in the general population is estimated at 4%. Vaccination against hepatitis B is recommended for all healthcare workers and should be considered by anyone planning an extended visit to this country.

Leishmaniasis: Cutaneous leishmaniasis occurs throughout Iran in the rural and semirural areas at the margins of deserts throughout the country. Visceral leishmaniasis (kala azar) is widespread (except for the arid zones in the southeast and deserts), particularly in Fars, Azarbbayjan-e Khavari, and the northeastern Khorasan provinces. Travelers to these areas should take protective measures against sandfly bites.

Filariasis: Reported in the southeastern province of Baluchistan-Sistan where the mosquito vector is present. Travelers to these areas should take measures to prevent mosquito bites.

Schistosomiasis: Transmission occurs year-round and increases in the spring rainy seasons, March to May. Distribution is focal along a branch of the Rud-e Karun River, between Ahvaz and Dezful, in the western province of Khuzestan. Travelers to these areas should avoid swimming or wading in freshwater ponds, lakes, or streams.

Rabies: Animal rabies is common in the wolf and stray dog population. Twenty to 50 human rabies cases occur annually, usually in rural villages.

Other illnesses: Brucellosis, Crimean-Congo hemorrhagic fever (tick-transmitted; most cases reported from East Azerbajian and areas near the Caspian Sea), echinococcosis, north Asian tick typhus, flea-borne typhus, tick-borne relapsing fever, tuberculosis, and helminthic infections.

IRAQ
Baghdad ... GMT +3 hrs

Entry Requirements
- Passport/Visa: Valid passport and visa required. Tourist visas not issued.
- AIDS Test: Testing required for visits lasting 5 days or more. Contact the Iraqi Embassy in Washington (202-483-7500) for details.
- Vaccinations: A yellow fever vaccination certificate is required of travelers arriving from infected areas.

Telephone Country Code: 964
Operator-assisted calls only
Electricity/Plugs: AC 50 Hz, 220 volts; plugs are types C, D, and G. A grounding conductor is required in the electrical cord of appliances.
Embassies/Consulates: American Embassy, Baghdad. Opposite Foreign Ministry Club (Masbah Quarter); Tel. (1) 719-6138/9. Canadian Embassy; Tel. (1) 542-1459.

Health Advisory
Malaria: Occurs in northern Iraq. Risk areas include rural and urban areas in the northern provinces of Dahuk, Ninawa, Irbil, Tamin, and As Sulaymaniyah below 1,500 meters elevation. Small, scattered, sporadic outbreaks probably occur in the southern and central areas from the Tigris-Euphrates River basin to the border with Iran. Nearly all cases of malaria in Iraq are currently of the vivax variety. Chloroquine-resistant falciparum malaria has not been reported. There is no malaria in Baghdad. Travelers to risk areas are advised to take weekly chloroquine and avoid mosquito bites.

Travelers' diarrhea: High risk. There is a high incidence of shigellosis and salmonellosis in this country. Travelers should drink only bottled, boiled, or treated water. All food should be well cooked. A quinolone antibiotic is recommended for the treatment of acute diarrhea.

Diarrhea not improving with antibiotic treatment may be due to a parasitic disease such as amebiasis or giardiasis.

Hepatitis: All susceptible travelers should receive immune globulin or hepatitis A vaccine prior to visiting this country. The hepatitis B carrier rate in the general population is estimated at 4%. Vaccination against hepatitis B is recommended for anyone planning an extended visit to this country.

Leishmaniasis: Cutaneous leishmaniasis occurs commonly in the central regions, sporadically in the north, and is rare in the south. Visceral leishmaniasis (kala azar) occurs in the central region, with most cases reported from December through March. Travelers to these areas should take measures to prevent insect (sandfly) bites.

Schistosomiasis: Risk occurs near the Tigris and Euphrates Rivers, especially in the central regions. No transmission occurs south of Basra. Travelers should avoid swimming or wading in freshwater ponds, lakes, or streams in risk areas.

Other illnesses: Boutonneuse fever (infrequently reported), brucellosis (usually transmitted by raw goat or camel milk), Crimean-Congo hemorrhagic fever (tick-borne; the virus is also transmitted through exposure to livestock), dengue fever (may occur in southern regions), echinococcosis (carried by stray dogs; reported sporadically from rural and urban areas), rabies (transmitted by jackals, foxes, and dogs), relapsing fever (louse-borne; endemic in northern Iraq), sandfly fever (risk may be limited to the southwestern border with Saudi Arabia), trachoma, tuberculosis, typhus (flea-borne; sporadic cases in southern areas), typhoid fever, and helminthic infections (roundworm, hookworm, and whipworm infections are common).

ISRAEL

Embassy: 202-364-5500   **Jerusalem**   **GMT +2 hrs**

Entry Requirements
- Passport/Visa: A valid passport is required.
- AIDS Test: Testing not required of tourists staying less than 3 months.
- Vaccinations: None required.

Telephone Country Code: 972   **AT&T:** 177-100-2727   **MCI:** 177-150-2727

Electricity/Plugs: AC 50 Hz, 220 volts, frequency stable; plug types C and H.

American Express: Meditrad Ltd. 16 Ben Yehuda St., Tel. (3) 294-654.

Embassies/Consulates: American Embassy, Tel Aviv. 71 Hayarkon St., Tel. (3) 654-338. Canadian Embassy, Tel Aviv. 220 Hayarkon St., Tel. 228-122.

Hospitals/ Doctors: Herzliya Medical Centers, Haifa and Tel Aviv. Official referral hospitals for the Multinational Forces in Sinai; the Haifa facility can do open heart procedures; both of these prestigious private hospitals also accept Blue Cross/Blue Shield payments; in Haifa, Tel. (4) 305-222; in Tel Aviv, Tel. (9) 592-554/5; Chaim Sheba Medical Center, Tel Aviv (1,500 beds); all specialties; emergency room; Tel. (3) 530-530. Ichilov Municipal Hospital, Tel Aviv (public hospital; 500 beds); all specialties; emergency room; Tel. (3) 697-4444. Hadassah-Hebrew Medical Center, Jerusalem (680 beds); Tel. (2)427-427. Rothschild Hadassah University Hospital, Jerusalem (680 beds); all specialties. Rambam Medical Center, Haifa (850 beds); all specialties; Soroka University Hospital, Beer-Sheva (700 beds); Tel. 660-485.

Health Advisory

Malaria: No risk.

Cholera: Reported active in the Gaza Strip.

Travelers' diarrhea: Medium risk. Although the risk of bacterial gastroenteritis is lower than in the neighboring Arab countries, it is markedly higher than in Europe. Shigellosis both occurs sporadically and in large outbreaks, the most recent being in Haifa, when 10,000 cases occurred. Amebiasis occurs infrequently. Travelers are advised to drink only bottled, filtered, or treated water and consume only well-cooked food. In urban and resort areas, the hotels and restaurants generally serve reliable food and potable water. A quinolone antibiotic is recommended for the treatment of acute diarrhea. Diarrhea not responding to antibiotic treatment may be due to a parasitic disease such as giardiasis, amebiasis, or cryptosporidiosis.

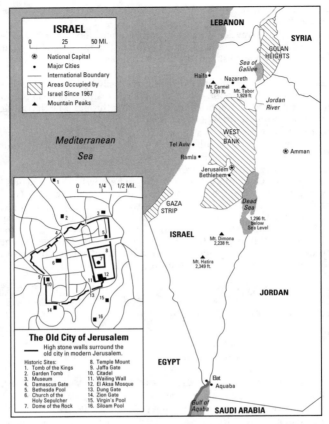

Hepatitis: All susceptible travelers should receive immune globulin or hepatitis A vaccine prior to visiting this country. The hepatitis B carrier rate in the general population is estimated at less than 1%. Vaccination against hepatitis B is recommended for all healthcare workers and should be considered by anyone planning an extended visit to this country.

Mediterranean spotted fever: Occurs countrywide in rural areas. Highest risk of transmission is in southern Israel, especially the northwest part of the Negev desert and the coastal plain area. This rickettsial disease (caused by *R. conorii*) is transmitted by the brown dog tick and has emerged as the most common insect-borne disease in Israel. Travelers, especially to rural areas, should avoid dogs (as well as sheep and goats), which harbor the infective ticks. Infective ticks are also found on grass and around hay stacks, and along wild animal paths.

Relapsing (cave) fever: Cave fever, caused by the spirochete *Borrelia persica*, is transmitted in rural areas by soft ticks that inhabit animal burrows, cracks in boulders, archeological sites, and especially caves. Ten percent of the caves in Israel are infested by ticks (55% infested in the lower Galilee). Risk areas include the Negev, the West Bank, the coastal plain, and the northern areas. Treatment, as well as prophylaxis, with tetracycline, is effective.

Leishmaniasis: Low risk. Cutaneous leishmaniasis is present in the Jordan Valley, especially around Jericho and the Dead Sea, and in the wadis of the Negev Desert (including Keziot), the Arava Valley, and Samaria. Visceral leishmaniasis may occur in Western Galilee. Peak transmission of leishmaniasis occurs between April and October. The best treatment is prevention. Travelers should take measures to prevent insect (sandfly) bites.

Schistosomiasis: This disease is apparently no longer a threat in Israel. Urinary schistosomiasis was once endemic in the Jordan River, but no recent indigenous cases have been reported.

Rabies: Incidence of rabies in animals, especially foxes, is increasing, but no recent human cases of rabies have been reported. Travelers should seek immediate medical attention for any dog or wild animal bite.

Other illnesses: Anthrax, brucellosis (usually transmitted by raw goat/sheep milk; common cause of fever in humans), echinococcosis (carried by a small percentage of rural dogs; low incidence in humans), leptospirosis (low incidence), tuberculosis, typhoid fever, West Nile fever, and helminthic infections (due to roundworms, hookworms, and whipworms; low incidence).

JORDAN

Amman ... GMT +2 hrs

Entry Requirements

- Passport/Visa: A valid passport and visa are required. Visa will not be issued if travelers have an Israeli visa on their passport.
- AIDS Test: Not required.
- Vaccinations: None required.

Telephone Country Code: 962

Electricity/Plugs: AC 50 Hz, 220 volts; plugs are types C, F, and G. A grounding conductor is required in the electrical cord of appliances.

American Express: International Traders. King Hussein Street; Tel. (6) 666-1014.

Embassies/Consulates: U.S. Embassy, Amman; Tel. (6) 644-371.

Hospitals/Doctors: Ashrifiyah Hospital, Amman (520 beds); most medical specialties; burn unit. King Hussein Medical Center, Amman (600 beds); all specialties; latest state-of-the-art Western medical and surgical equipment.University of Jordan Hospital (400 beds); teaching facility; all specialties.

Health Advisory

Malaria: There is no risk of malaria in this country.

Travelers' diarrhea: High risk. Piped water supplies are unreliable and may be contaminated. Travelers should observe food and drink safety precautions. Bottled mineral water is available locally. A quinolone antibiotic is recommended for the treatment of acute diarrhea. Diarrhea not responding to treatment with an antibiotic, or chronic diarrhea, may be due to a parasitic disease such as giardiasis, amebiasis, or cryptosporidiosis.

Hepatitis: Immune globulin or hepatitis A vaccine is recommended for all susceptible travelers. The hepatitis B carrier rate in the general population is estimated at 10%. Vaccination against hepatitis B is recommended for healthcare workers and should be considered by long-term visitors to this country.

Leishmaniasis: There is a low risk of cutaneous leishmaniasis in the northern foothills of Jordan, as well as in the middle and lower Jordan Valley. Visceral leishmaniasis has not been reported since the 1950s. Travelers to Jordan should take measures to prevent insect (sandfly) bites.

Schistosomiasis: Twenty-four cases of schistosomiasis were reported in 1984. A larger outbreak occurred in 1988. Irrigation projects have increased the transmission of this disease. Risk areas include the Jordan River and east Ghor canal, Wadi Al Hasa, and the Zarqa River (including the King Talal Dam). Travelers should avoid swimming or wading in freshwater rivers, ponds, streams, or irrigated areas.

Other illnesses: Mediterranean spotted fever (infrequently reported), brucellosis, dengue (historically reported from the Jordan Valley but current data not available), echinococcosis (carried by stray dogs; reported sporadically, especially in northern areas), meningitis (cyclic outbreaks; Group A predominates; Group W-135 increasing), rabies (most cases of animal rabies occur in foxes, with spillover into the dog population; occurs sporadically in humans), relapsing fever (tick-borne), sandfly fever, tuberculosis, murine typhus (flea-borne), typhoid fever, and helminthic infections (roundworm, hookworm, and whipworm infections are common in rural areas; incidence is estimated at 5%).

LEBANON

Beirut ... GMT +2 hrs

Entry Requirements

- Passport/Visa: U.S. passports are invalid for travel to Lebanon. Passport validation requests should be forwarded to Mr. Harry L. Coburn, U.S. Dept. of State, 1425 K Street, Room 300, Washington, DC 20522-1705.
- AIDS Test: Not required.
- Vaccinations: A yellow fever vaccination certificate is required from all travelers older than 1 year arriving from infected areas.

Telephone Country Code: 965   **AT&T:** 426-801

Electricity/Plugs: AC 50, 110/190, 220/380 volts, frequency not stable; plug types A, B, C, D, and G.

Embassies/Consulates: The U.S. Embassy is closed. Canadian citizens should contact the Canadian Embassy in Damascus, Syria.

OMAN

Muscat ... GMT +4 hrs

Entry Requirements

- Passport/Visa: Valid passport and visa required of all travelers.
- AIDS Test: Not required.
- Vaccinations: A yellow fever vaccination certificate is required from all travelers older than 1 year arriving from infected areas.

Telephone Country Code: 968

Electricity/Plugs: AC 50 Hz, 220 volts; plugs are types D and G. Adaptors and transformer necessary for U.S.-made appliances.

American Express: Zubair Travel & Service Bureau. Oman International Bank Building; Tel. 677-7390.

Embassies & Consulates: American Embassy, Muscat; Tel. 738-231 or 738-006.

Health Advisory

Malaria: Risk is present year-round below 2,000 meters elevation in the inland mountainous village areas of north-central Oman, especially around Nazwa. Malaria also occurs along the Batinah coastal plain north of the Seeb International Airport, to the northern border with the United Arab Emirates. The capital area around Muscat and the southern Dhofar region are risk free. Falciparum malaria accounts for 80% of cases, vivax 20%. Two cases of chloroquine-resistant falciparum malaria were reported from the Ibri district in 1989. Travelers to risk areas should consider mefloquine prophylaxis. Alternative malaria regimes should be discussed with a travel medicine or infectious disease specialist.

Travelers' diarrhea: First-class hotels and restaurants in Muscat generally serve reliable food and potable water. Travelers are advised to drink only bottled, boiled, or treated water and consume only well-cooked food. All fruit should be peeled prior to consumption.A quinolone antibiotic (Floxin or Cipro) is recommended for the treatment of acute diarrhea. Diarrhea not responding to antibiotic treatment may be due to a parasitic disease such as giardiasis or amebiasis.

Hepatitis: Immune globulin or hepatitis A vaccine is recommended for all susceptible travelers. The hepatitis B carrier rate in the general population is about 3 percent. Vaccination is recommended for healthcare workers and others expecting close contact with the indigenous population.

Leishmaniasis: There is a low risk of cutaneous leishmaniasis. Visceral leishmaniasis (kala azar) occurs rarely and has been reported from several northeastern mountain villages. Travelers to country should take protective measures against sandfly bites.

Schistosomiasis: Risk areas include the southern Dhofar region, in the vicinity of Salalah (in the coastal wadis). Travelers should avoid swimming or wading in freshwater rivers, ponds, streams, or irrigated areas in these areas.

Rabies: Occurs very sporadically in stray dogs, usually in the mountainous inland villages of northeastern Oman; rarely reported in humans. Most cases of animal rabies occur in foxes.

Other illnesses/hazards: Brucellosis (usually transmitted by raw goat/sheep milk, especially in the southern Dhofar region), echinococcosis (carried by stray dogs; reported sporadically, especially in northern areas), relapsing fever (tick-borne), tuberculosis, soil-transmitted helminthic infections (roundworm, hookworm, and whipworm infections are common in rural areas; incidence is estimated at 5%). Centipedes, scorpions, black widow spiders inhabit the dry, interior regions of Oman. Sea urchins and marine rays inhabit the coastal waters of Oman and could pose a hazard to swimmers.

QATAR

Doha ... GMT +3 hrs

Entry Requirements
- Passport/Visa: Passport required. No tourist visas are issued for this country.
- AIDS Test: Test required for work or study. Travelers should contact Qatar Embassy in Washington (202-338-0111) for further details.
- Vaccinations: A yellow fever vaccination certificate is required from all travelers arriving from infected areas.

Telephone Country Code: 974   **AT&T:** 0800-011-77   **MCI:** 0800-012-77

Electricity/Plugs: AC 50 Hz, 220 volts; plugs types D and G. Adaptors and transformer necessary for U.S.-made appliances.

American Express: Darwish Travel Bureau, Doha; Tel. 418-666.

Embassies/Consulates: U.S. Embassy, Doha; Fariq Bin, Omran; Tel. 864-701/2/3. Canadian Embassy (Kuwait); Tel. [965] 251-1451.

Hospitals/Doctors: Hamad Hospital, Doha (600 beds); major referral center; all specialties; well-equipped and staffed.

Health Advisory
Malaria: There is no risk of malaria in this country.

Travelers' diarrhea: First-class hotels and restaurants generally serve reliable food and drink. Tap water is reported to be potable. Water is obtained almost exclusively from desalination plants. The high mineral content of underground water makes it unsuitable for drinking. A quinolone antibiotic (Floxin or Cipro) is recommended for the treatment of acute diarrhea. Diarrhea not responding to antibiotic treatment may be due to a parasitic disease such as giardiasis or amebiasis.

Hepatitis: Immune globulin or hepatitis A vaccine is recommended for all susceptible travelers. The hepatitis B carrier rate in the general population is estimated at 2%. Vaccination against hepatitis B is recommended for healthcare workers and should be considered by long-term visitors to this country.

Other illnesses: Brucellosis (usually transmitted by raw dairy products), rabies (occurs rarely in stray dogs), trachoma, tuberculosis (low incidence), typhoid fever, soil-transmitted helminthic infections (roundworm, hookworm, and whipworm infections are common in rural areas; incidence is estimated at less than 5%).

SAUDI ARABIA

Riyadh ... GMT +3 hrs

Entry Requirements
- Passport/Visa: A valid passport is required. No tourist visas are issued.
- AIDS Test: Test required for applicants for work visas. Travelers should contact the Saudi Embassy (202-342-3800) for further details.
- Vaccinations: A yellow fever vaccination certificate is required from all travelers arriving from, or transiting through, any country any part of which is infected with yellow fever. Meningococcal meningitis: A vaccination certificate issued within the past 2 years is required. This certificate must be issued no less than 3 weeks before the date of arrival.

World Medical Guide

Telephone Country Code: 966   **AT&T:** 1-800-10   **MCI:** 1-800-11

Electricity/Plugs: AC 50/60 Hz, 127/220, 220/380, volts; plugs are types A, B, C, D, E, F, G, H, I, and J.

American Express: Ace Travel. Olaya Main Street, Riyadh; Tel. (1) 464-8810.

Embassies/Consulates: U.S. Embassy, Riyadh. Diplomatic Quarter; Tel. (1) 488-3800. Canadian Embassy, Riyadh. Diplomatic Quarter; Tel. (1) 488-2288.

Hospitals/Doctors: King Faisal Specialist Hospital, Riyadh (400 beds); all specialties; ambulance service and helipad; rated best medical facility in Saudi Arabia. Aramco Hospital, Dhahran (361 beds); private accredited hospital; most specialties; one of the best medical facilities in the country. Ebbe Hartelius, M.D., Transad Medical Clinic, Riyadh; Tel. (3) 864-0270/864-4435. Larry Fout, M.D., Dhahran; Tel. (3) 966-874-8121 or 873-8068.

Health Advisory

Malaria: Transmission of this disease occurs year-round in the southern areas, with increased risk October through April. Risk exists up to 2,000 meters elevation in rural and urban areas of the Tihama coastal region, and the Asir highlands in the southwest (Jizan, Asir, and Al Bahah provinces). Risk in the western provinces (Makkah and Al Madinah) is limited to rural valley foci in the Hijaz mountains, and along the Red Sea coast. Urban areas in the western provinces are risk free, as are all other parts of the country (Ar'ar, Al Jawf, Al Qurayyah, Riyadh, Tabuk, At Taif). There is no malaria in the urban areas of Jedda, Mecca, Medina, and Al Qatif.

The most intense malaria transmission occurs in the southern provinces where *P. falciparum* accounts for over 80% of the cases; *P. vivax* accounts for the remainder. A low level of chloroquine-resistant falciparum malaria is suspected in the southwest. (Chloroquine resistance has been confirmed in adjacent areas in Yemen.) Prophylaxis with chloroquine or mefloquine is currently recommended when traveling to malarious areas of this country. Malaria prophylaxis regimes should be discussed with a travel medicine or infectious disease specialist.

Travelers' diarrhea: Water is supplied via potable water distribution systems in all major urban areas of Saudi Arabia and is safe for drinking. Outside of major urban areas all travelers should drink only boiled, bottled, or treated/filtered water. All food should be well cooked. A quinolone antibiotic (Floxin or Cipro) is recommended for the treatment of acute diarrhea. Diarrhea not responding to antibiotic treatment may be due to a parasitic disease such as giardiasis or amebiasis—or an intestinal virus.

Hepatitis: Immune globulin or hepatitis A vaccine is recommended for all susceptible travelers. The hepatitis B carrier rate in the general population is estimated at 8%. Vaccination against hepatitis B is recommended for healthcare workers and should be considered by long-term visitors to this country.

Dengue fever: Low risk of potential disease in the eastern coastal areas where the *Aedes* mosquito is found. No current data available. Travelers to this area should take measures to prevent mosquito bites.

Meningitis: Sporadic cases occur, as well as small outbreaks, usually related to pilgrimages to Mecca where crowded conditions promote disease transmission. The CDC recommends that all travelers be vaccinated against meningococcal meningitis at least 21 days prior to departure for this country.

Leishmaniasis: Transmission of cutaneous leishmaniasis occurs year-round in the oases of the eastern and central provinces and the mountains of the western provinces. Transmission of visceral leishmaniasis (kala azar) occurs year-round and is restricted to the southwestern provinces. Travelers should take measures to prevent sandfly bites.

Schistosomiasis: Risk is present in the western (in wadis and cisterns) and central (in oases) provinces. Intestinal schistosomiasis foci occur in the central (Hail, Riyadh), northern (Al Jawf), northwestern (Tabuk, Medina), midwestern (Makkah, Al Bahah), and the highlands of the southwestern (Jiazan) and midwestern (Makkah) provinces. In these areas, all travelers should avoid swimming or wading in freshwater ponds, lakes, streams, or irrigated areas.

Crimean-Congo hemorrhagic fever: Virus circulates in rural agricultural areas. A small number of human cases are reported sporadically. This disease is usually transmitted by infective ticks, and occasionally by exposure to infected animals (usually sheep, goats, or cattle that have been slaughtered). Low risk to most travelers. All travelers should take precautions to prevent tick bites or exposure to freshly slaughtered meat.

Rabies: Human cases are very sporadic, usually in the northern and eastern rural areas. Most animal rabies are in foxes with spillover into the stray dog population. Travelers should seek immediate treatment of any animal bite. Rabies vaccination is indicated following the unprovoked bite of a dog or fox. Bites by other animals should be considered on an individual basis.

Other illnesses: AIDS (very low prevalence), anthrax (occurs primarily in sheep, goats, cattle, and camels; human cases usually involve exposure to sheep), brucellosis (usually transmitted by raw goat or camel milk, or milk products), echinococcosis (carried by stray dogs, especially in rural and agricultural areas), onchocerciasis (black-fly-borne; confined to the southwestern Arabian peninsula in focally endemic area), plague (flea-borne; no cases reported recently, but enzootic foci exist in the Asir region of the southwestern Arabian peninsula and along the Tigris-Euphrates river extending to Kuwait), Q fever, sandfly fever, trachoma (highly endemic), tuberculosis (moderate prevalence in rural areas among lower socio-economic groups), typhoid fever, flea-borne typhus (sporadic cases occur in eastern areas), soil-transmitted helminthic infections (roundworm, hookworm, and whipworm) infections (moderate prevalence in rural areas).

SYRIA (SYRIAN ARAB REPUBLIC)

Damascus ... GMT +2 hrs

Entry Requirements

- Passport/Visa: Valid passport and visa required.
- AIDS Test: Testing required for students and anyone staying more than 1 year. Contact the Syrian Embassy (202-232-6313) for further details.
- Vaccinations: A yellow fever vaccination certificate is required from all travelers arriving from infected areas.

Telephone Country Code: 963

Electricity/Plugs: AC 50 Hz, 220 volts, frequency not stable; plug types C, E, and L.

American Express: Chami Travel, Rue Fardous, Mouradi Building, Damascus. Tel. (11) 211-652.

Embassies/Consulates: U.S. Embassy , Damascus. Abu Rumaneh, Al Mansur Street, No. 2; Tel. (11) 333-052/332-557. Canadian Embassy, Damascus. Sheraton Hotel; Tel. (11) 229-300.

Doctors/Hospitals: Mu'assat University Hospital, Damascus (850 beds); all specialties; emergency and trauma services. Social Insurance Foundation Hospital, Damascus (400 beds); specializes in emergency, trauma, and occupational medicine. National Hospital, Aleppo (482 beds); general medical facility.

Health Advisory

Malaria: This disease occurs at elevations below 1,100 meters in rural areas of the northeast (Tigris-Euphrates River and the Orontes River valley, north of Hanah). Epidemics may occur in wet years. Ninety-nine percent of malaria cases are vivax, 1% falciparum. Chloroquine prophylaxis is recommended for travel to the lower river valleys of northeast Syria.

Travelers' diarrhea: Medium-high risk outside of first-class hotels. Water distribution systems may be contaminated. Travelers should drink only bottled, boiled, or treated water. All food should be well cooked. Shigellosis is common in this country. Cases of amebiasis and giardiasis occur, even among the higher socio-economic classes. A quinolone antibiotic (Floxin or Cipro) is recommended for the treatment of acute diarrhea. Diarrhea not responding to antibiotic treatment may be due to a parasitic disease such as giardiasis or amebiasis—or an intestinal virus.

Hepatitis: Immune globulin or hepatitis A vaccine is recommended for all susceptible travelers. The hepatitis B carrier rate in the general population is estimated at 3%–4%. Vaccination against hepatitis B is recommended for healthcare workers and should be considered by long-term visitors to this country.

Leishmaniasis: Cases of cutaneous leishmaniasis occur in the steppe region, which is the transitional area between the fertile river valleys and the southeastern desert area. There is no apparent risk of visceral leishmaniasis. Travelers to this country should take measures to prevent insect (sandfly) bites.

Schistosomiasis: Urinary schistosomiasis is found in the basins of the Euphrates and Bolikh Rivers, to the Iraqi border in the northeast. Travelers should avoid swimming or wading in freshwater streams, ponds, or irrigated areas.

Rabies: Human cases occur sporadically (about 10 cases per year). Foxes, jackals, and stray dogs constitute the main animal reservoir of rabies in this country. Travelers should avoid stray animals and seek immediate medical attention of any animal bite.

Other illnesses: Anthrax (related to livestock exposure), boutonneuse fever (may occur, but is not reported), brucellosis (usually transmitted by raw goat or sheep dairy products), echinococcosis (carried by stray dogs; reported sporadically), relapsing fever (tick-borne; reported frequently), trachoma, tuberculosis, typhoid fever, soil-transmitted helminthic infections (roundworm, hookworm, and whipworm infections are common in rural areas; estimated prevalence is low).

TURKEY

Ankara ... GMT +2 hrs

Entry Requirements

- Passport/Visa: A valid passport is required.
- AIDS Test: There is no formal testing requirement, but 75 centers, most of them located at border checkpoints and tourist areas, have been established to conduct HIV screening tests.
- Vaccinations: None required.

Telephone Country Code: 90   **AT&T:** 00-800-12277   **MCI:** 00-8001-1177

Electricity/Plugs: AC 50 Hz; 220 volts; plug type B. Adaptors and transformer necessary for U.S.-made appliances.

American Express: Turk Ekspres. Cinnah Cad. 9/4. Cankaya; Ankara; Tel. (4) 167-7334.

Embassies/Consulates: U.S. Embassy, Ankara. 110 Ataturk Boulevard; Tel. (4) 126-5470. Canadian Embassy, Ankara. 75 Gaziosmanpasa; Tel. (4) 136-1275.

Hospitals/Doctors: Ankara University Hospital (1,280 beds); most medical specialties; one of the country's most modern hospitals. Cankaya Hospital, Ankara; private; most medical specialties. Admiral Bristol Hospital, Istanbul; Tel. (1) 133-0754.

Health Advisory

Malaria: Risk is present between February and November, and peaks in June and July. Transmission occurs up to 1,500 meters elevation in risk areas. Principal risk areas include southeast Anatolia (particularly along the Mediterranean coast and river basins in Antalya, Icel, Adana, and Hatay Provinces) and the regions bordering Syria, Iraq, and Iran. Low-level transmission may occur in other areas of Turkey. There is no risk of malaria in the major cities such as Istanbul and Ankara. Vivax malaria accounts for 100% of cases. Chloroquine prophylaxis is recommended in risk areas.

Travelers' diarrhea: High risk outside of resorts and first-class hotels. Contamination of existing municipal water systems is common. A quinolone antibiotic is recommended for the treatment of acute diarrhea.

Hepatitis: Immune globulin or hepatitis A vaccine is recommended for all susceptible travelers. The hepatitis B carrier rate in the general population is estimated at 6%–10%. Vaccination against hepatitis B is recommended for healthcare workers and long-term visitors to this country.

Leishmaniasis: Cutaneous leishmaniasis is common in the southeastern region of Turkey and the Tigris-Euphrates Basin. Visceral leishmaniasis (kala azar) occurs along the Aegean coast, the Mediterranean coast, the Sea of Marmara coast, and the Black Sea coast. Travelers should take measures to prevent insect (sandfly) bites.

Schistosomiasis: Transmission occurs in the southern-most areas of the Belikh branch of the Euphrates River (near the Syrian border). Risk is deemed to be low.

Rabies: Human cases frequently reported are usually due to contact with rabid stray dogs. Travelers should seek immediate treatment following the unprovoked bite of a dog, cat, or fox. Bites by other animals should be considered on an individual basis.

Other illnesses: Anthrax, brucellosis, Mediterranean spotted fever (boutonneuse fever; tick-borne; occurs in the western and southern regions), brucellosis (usually transmitted by raw goat or sheep milk), cholera, echinococcosis (human cases reported sporadically, especially in northern and northeastern areas), viral encephalitis (tick-borne; sporadic cases reported; presumed risk in brushy, forested western and northern regions), leprosy (low prevalence), plague (flea-borne; low risk of transmission may exist in the southeast near Syria and Iraq, in the northeast near Iran, and in central Anatolia), murine typhus (flea-borne), North Asian tick typhus (in areas bordering the former Soviet Union), tuberculosis, and helminthic infections (roundworm, hookworm, and whipworm) infections are common in rural areas.

UNITED ARAB EMIRATES
Abu Dhabi ... GMT +4 hrs

Entry Requirements
* Passport/Visa: Valid passport and visa are required. No tourist visas are issued.
* AIDS Test: Applicants for work and residence (more than 30 days) are tested upon arrival. Contact the UAE Embassy (202-338-6500) for further details.
* Vaccinations: A yellow fever vaccination certificate is required of all travelers arriving from infected areas.

Telephone Country Code: 971   **AT&T:** 800-121   **MCI:** 800-111

Electricity/Plugs: AC 50 Hz, 220 volts; plugs are types D and G.

American Express: Al Masaood Travel & Services. Al Nasr Street, Abu Dhabi; Tel. (2) 212-100.

Embassies/Consulates: U.S. Embassy, Abu Dhabi. Al Sudan Street; Tel. (2) 336-691. Canadian Embassy (Saudi Arabia); Tel. [966] (1) 488-2288.

Hospitals/Doctors: Mafraq, Abu Dhabi (520 beds); most specialties; burn unit; ambulance service; helipad. Dubai Hospital (635 beds); major referral facility; ambulance service; helipad. Raship Hospital, Dubai (500 beds); emergency/trauma facility; ambulance; helipad. Fuhair Abu Risheh, M.D. ADCO/ADMA Clinic, Abu Dhabi; Tel. (2) 361-359 or 361-929 (H).

Health Advisory
Malaria: Transmission occurs at the inland oasis of Al Ayn, and on the east coast along the Gulf of Oman. Cases are reported year-round, and the incidence increases from May to July. Most of the country (Dubai, Sharjah, Ajman, Umm al Qaiwan, the Emirate of Abu Dhabi, and the west coast) is malaria free. Vivax malaria accounts for virtually all cases. Travelers should take weekly chloroquine in malarious areas.

Travelers' diarrhea: Moderate risk. Viral cases of diarrhea increase from December through March, bacterial cases from June to October. A quinolone antibiotic is recommended for the treatment of acute diarrhea.

Hepatitis A: Low risk in Abu Dhabi and Dubai due to improved levels of sanitation. Immune globulin or hepatitis A vaccine is recommended for all susceptible travelers to this country. The hepatitis B carrier rate in the general population is estimated at 2%. Vaccination against hepatitis B is recommended for healthcare workers.

Rabies: Animal rabies occurs mostly in foxes and sporadically in stray dogs. There have been no recently reported cases of rabies in humans.

Other illnesses: Brucellosis (usually transmitted by unpasteurized goat/sheep milk), meningitis, tuberculosis (prevalence is low), typhoid fever, helminthic infections (roundworm, hookworm, and whipworm) are reported; incidence is very low.

YEMEN (YEMEN ARAB REPUBLIC)

Sanaa ... GMT +3 hrs

Entry Requirements

- Passport/Visa: Valid passport and visa are required.
- AIDS Test: Not required.
- Vaccinations: A yellow fever vaccination certificate is required of all travelers arriving from infected areas.

Telephone Country Code: 967

Electricity/Plugs: AC 50 Hz, 220 volts; plugs are types C and D.

American Express: Marib Travel & Tourism, Sanaa; Tel. (2) 71741.

Embassies/Consulates: U.S. Embassy, Sanaa; Tel. (2) 271-950/1/2/3/4.

Hospitals/Doctors: Caution—Travelers should use hospitals for emergency situations only; care is well below Western standards.

Health Advisory

Malaria: Transmission occurs in all areas (including urban areas) in the foothills and coastal areas. In the highlands, malaria occurs only in rural areas. The northeastern provinces of Hajjah and Sa'dah (which includes Sanaa) are risk-free. *P. falciparum* causes 95% of cases. There are a few sporadic reports of chloroquine-resistant falciparum malaria. Mefloquine or doxycycline prophylaxis is recommended for travel to malarious areas.

Travelers' diarrhea: High risk. Well water usually is contaminated. Water supplies in Aden are limited. Piped water supplies are potentially contaminated. Bottled water or carbonated soft drinks are available and thought to be safe. Travelers should observe food and drink safety precautions. A quinolone antibiotic is recommended for the treatment of acute diarrhea.

Hepatitis: Immune globulin or hepatitis A vaccine is recommended for all susceptible travelers. The hepatitis B carrier rate in the general population is estimated at 10%–15%. Vaccination against hepatitis B is recommended for healthcare workers as well as long-term visitors to this country.

Leishmaniasis: Cutaneous leishmaniasis commonly occurs in semirural villages of the Asir mountains. Visceral leishmaniasis occurs sporadically in rural areas, usually in the foothills region or the Asir mountains, at elevations between 400 and 1,500 meters. Travelers to these areas should take measures to prevent insect (sandfly) bites.

Onchocerciasis: Blackfly-borne. Probably occurs throughout the length of Yemen, in wadis flowing into the Gulf of Aden and the Red Sea; known to be endemic in all westward-flowing permanent streams (wadis) between the northern Wadi Surdud (Al Hudaydah Province) and the southern Wadi Ghayl (Taiz Province) at elevations of 300 to 1,200 meters; cases have been reported from Al Hudafdah to Taiz, mostly in Al Barh between Mokha and Taiz. All travelers to these regions should take measures to prevent insect (black fly) bites.

Schistosomiasis: Transmission occurs year-round. Focally distributed (commonly associated with wadis, oases, aqueducts, cisterns, and irrigation canals) in urban and rural locales, particularly in foothill and highland areas; only Marib and Al Bayda are risk-free. Primary recognized risk areas occur in Ibb, Taiz, and Sanaa Provinces.

Rabies: High potential risk due to large population of stray dogs. Human cases are reported frequently. Travelers should seek immediate treatment of any animal bite. Rabies vaccination is indicated following the unprovoked bite of a dog, cat, jackal, or fox. Bites by other animals should be considered on an individual basis.

Other illnesses: Anthrax (human cases usually involve agricultural exposure), Bancroftian filariasis (mosquito-borne; sporadically reported), brucellosis (human cases usually related to exposure to unpasteurized dairy products, especially raw goat/sheep milk or milk products), dracunculiasis (endemic in Al Hudaydah Province, with cases reported from Sadah Province), echinococcosis (reported sporadically in humans), plague (flea-borne; last outbreak in 1969 Sadah Province; cases were also reported in the 1980s), flea-borne typhus, louse-borne typhus, and louse-borne relapsing fever, and tick-borne rickettsioses (may occur), trachoma, tuberculosis, and helminthic infections (roundworm, hookworm, and whipworm—common in rural areas).

D I S E A S E   R I S K   S U M M A R Y
China and the Indian Subcontinent

(Afghanistan, Bangladesh, Bhutan, India, Nepal, Pakistan, Sri Lanka)

Malaria: There is risk of vivax malaria and as well as chloroquine-resistant falciparum malaria in southern China and other parts of the Indian subcontinent. Mefloquine prophylaxis is recommended in most malarious areas. Alternately, some travelers may wish to consult with their physician about taking chloroquine weekly and carrying a treatment dose of Fansidar. All travelers should take measures to prevent mosquito bites by using a combination of a skin repellent and permethrin. Anti-mosquito measures will also have the effect of reducing the risk of contracting other diseases, such as dengue and viral encephalitis.

Yellow fever: This disease does not occur in Asia, but many countries require a vaccination certificate from travelers arriving from infected or endemic areas. Travelers should carefully check their itineraries to determine the necessity for this vaccination.

Cholera: This disease is reported active in India, Bhutan, and Nepal. India and Pakistan may require a certificate from travelers arriving from cholera-infected countries. Other countries in Africa, the Middle East, Asia, and Latin America may also require a certificate from travelers arriving from cholera-infected areas. Travelers who transit between cholera-infected countries should consider vaccination (one dose needed to validate certificate) or a doctor's letter of exemption from vaccination. The risk to tourists of acquiring cholera is considered low. Prevention consists primarily in adhering to safe food and drink guidelines. Travelers to countries where cholera is active should eat only well-cooked food and drink only bottled, boiled, or treated water. An antibiotic (tetracycline or doxycycline preferred) and oral fluids are recommended for the immediate treatment of severe cholera. Travelers who develop watery diarrhea causing dehydration need hospital treatment.

Travelers' diarrhea: High risk outside of resort areas and first-class hotels. Travelers should follow safe food and drink guidelines. All food should be well cooked. Raw fish, crayfish, and crabs should be strictly avoided. Travelers should drink only bottled, boiled, or treated water. A quinolone antibiotic is recommended for the treatment of acute diarrhea. Diarrhea not responding to antibiotics may be due to a parasitic diseases such as giardiasis, amebiasis, or cryptosporidiosis—or an intestinal virus.

Typhoid fever: Vaccination is recommended for travel outside the usual tourist routes.

Amebiasis: There is a high incidence of amebiasis in India, where up to 50% of the high-risk population may be infected with *E. histolytica* parasites. Variable risk elsewhere. To avoid amebiasis, travelers should drink only safe water and eat only well-cooked food. All fruit should be peeled before eating.

Hepatitis A: High risk. Susceptible travelers to this region should receive immune globulin or hepatitis A vaccine.

Hepatitis E: High risk, especially in India, Nepal and Pakistan. This viral illness is similar to hepatitis A and is transmitted primarily by sewage-contaminated water. Travelers should drink only water that is bottled, boiled, or treated to eliminate viruses.

Hepatitis B: A high percentage (10%–20%) of the general population of these countries are chronic carriers of the hepatitis B virus. Vaccination is recommended for healthcare workers, relief workers, corporate employees, and others who will have prolonged contact (more than 4 weeks) with the indigenous population of these countries.

Dengue fever: Epidemics, as well as sporadic cases, occur in India, Pakistan, Bangladesh, and Sri Lanka. In China, dengue occurs in frequent, often widespread outbreaks. There is no risk of dengue in Afghanistan and Nepal. The *Aedes aegypti* mosquitoes, which transmit dengue, bite during the daytime and are present in populous urban areas as well as resort and rural areas. Prevention consists of taking protective measures against mosquito bites.

Japanese encephalitis: This mosquito-transmitted viral disease is widespread in China, southern Nepal, India, Bhutan, Burma, Bangladesh, and Sri Lanka. Vaccination against Japanese encephalitis is recommended for travelers who will be staying in rural-agricultural endemic areas for long periods (more than 4 weeks) during the transmission season. In addition, all travelers should take personal protection measures against mosquito bites, especially in the evening.

Leishmaniasis: Visceral leishmaniasis (kala azar) is found in China and India. Cutaneous leishmaniasis is present in northwestern India, Afghanistan, and Pakistan. Travelers to these areas should take protective measures against sandfly bites.

Filariasis: Bancroftian filariasis, transmitted by mosquitoes, is widespread in India, China, Bhutan, Bangladesh, and southern Nepal. Travelers to these areas should take measures to prevent mosquito bites.

Schistosomiasis: Risk is present throughout southern China, as well as eastern China, along the entire Yangtze River and its tributaries. There is no schistosomiasis in the other countries of this region. Travelers to risk areas in China should avoid swimming or wading in freshwater ponds, streams, or irrigated areas.

Lyme disease: Low risk. Cases of Lyme disease have been reported only from the northeastern coastal provinces of China.

Rabies: A high prevalence of animal rabies exists throughout Asia with many human cases reported, especially in India. Travelers should seek emergency treatment of any animal bite, especially from a dog, or a wolf. Bites from other animals should be evaluated on an individual basis. Individual need for pre-exposure rabies vaccination should be evaluated on the duration of travel, especially to rural areas, and availability of rabies vaccine and rabies immune globulin in the areas to be visited. Vaccination is recommended for all travelers who will spend extended periods of time in rural areas, away from medical care. Pre-exposure vaccination does not eliminate the need for additional inoculations should potential rabies exposure occur.

Meningitis: Outbreaks reported in New Delhi, India, and Nepal. Vaccination is recommended for travelers and trekkers to these countries who expect to have close contact with the indigenous population.

Plague: An epidemic of primarily pneumonic plague broke out in western India in August 1994. There are no reports of tourists being infected and this disease, which is primarily a disease of poverty, is not considered to be a significant threat to travelers.

Helminthic infections: Hookworm and whipworm are common, especially in rural areas. Travelers should wear shoes to prevent transmission of these diseases. Ascariasis, caused by the ingestion of food contaminated with the eggs of roundworms, can be prevented by adequate cooking. Other helminthic diseases (paragonimiasis, clonorchiasis, fasciolopsiasis) are moderately endemic in China. Pork tapeworm disease is prevalent and can be avoided by thorough cooking of meat.

AIDS: The AIDS virus appears to be spreading most rapidly in India, where 20%–30% of the prostitutes in the major cities are now HIV positive, up from 1% in 1987. A lower incidence of AIDS is found in the other countries of this region. Travelers should avoid unsafe sex and consider carrying a supply of sterile needles and syringes.

Animal hazards: Snakes common to this region include the Indian krait, king cobra, king snake, Russell's viper, and beaked sea snake. Spiders common to this region include the black and brown widow spiders, black scorpion, and spotted house scorpion. Large leeches, which are not poisonous but inflict slow-healing and easily infected bites, are abundant in the streams, marshes, and jungles of these countries. Crocodiles; pythons; poisonous frogs and toads; large, aggressive lizards; tigers; leopards; and bears may also present a hazard in certain areas. Stingrays, jellyfish, sea wasps, and several species of invertebrates (cones, nettles, cucumbers, urchins, anemones, and starfish) may be found in the estuarial and coastal waters of these countries.

Plant hazards: Bamboo, rattan, and large palm- or fernlike trees, which can cause serious puncture wounds and slow-healing lacerations, are widespread in the forested areas of these countries. Regas are large forest trees whose black resinous sap can cause a potent poison ivy-type skin reaction. Stinging nettles, small thorny trees, and many species of euphorbia can also cause skin eruptions.

AFGHANISTAN
Kabul ... GMT +4½ hrs

Entry Requirements
- Passport/Visa: Passport required. No tourist visas are issued.
- AIDS Test: Not required.
- Vaccinations: A yellow fever vaccination certificate is required of travelers arriving from infected areas.

Electricity/Plugs: AC 50 Hz, 220 volts; plugs are type D. Adaptors and transformer necessary for U.S.-made appliances.

Embassies/Consulates: There is no American or Canadian representation at this time.

Hospitals/Doctors: Local medical facilities are below Western standards and should be considered for use only in an extreme emergency.

Health Advisory

Malaria: Occurs between June and November, with peak transmission in August and September, when mosquitoes are most active. There is risk of malaria in the provinces in the east (Konarha, Laghan, and Nangarhar), in the north-northeast (Kunduz, Takhar, and Badakhshan), and in the south (Helmand, Qandahar). Malaria transmission occurs in rural areas of these provinces below 2,000 meters elevation. There is no malaria risk in Kabul. There may be malaria risk, however, in the urban areas in the south. Vivax malaria accounts for 90%–95% of cases, the remainder of cases being due to *P. falciparum.* Most cases of falciparum malaria have occurred in the eastern area along the border with Pakistan. Chloroquine-resistant falciparum malaria is reported, and apparently occurs, at this time, only along the border area with Pakistan. In addition to taking measures to prevent mosquito bites, travelers who visit malarious areas are advised to take a prophylactic drug. Mefloquine or doxycycline is recommended for those travelers visiting rural areas where falciparum malaria is prevalent. In other areas, travelers should take weekly chloroquine and carry a treatment dose of Fansidar.

Travelers' diarrhea: High risk. Shigellosis is a major problem in this country. Cases of amebiasis and giardiasis are also common. Only bottled, boiled, or treated water should be consumed. All food should be well cooked. A quinolone antibiotic is recommended for the treatment of diarrhea. Diarrhea not improving with antibiotic treatment may be due to a parasitic infection—or an intestinal virus.

Hepatitis: All susceptible travelers should receive immune globulin or hepatitis A vaccine prior to visiting this country. The hepatitis B carrier rate in the general population is estimated as high as 5%. Vaccination against hepatitis B is recommended for all healthcare workers and should be considered by anyone planning an extended visit to this country.

Hepatitis E: High risk. This disease is widespread in rural areas. Prevention consists of treating all drinking water to eliminate viruses. A vaccine is not available.

Japanese encephalitis: Low risk; historically occurs along the eastern borders.

Leishmaniasis: Cutaneous leishmaniasis occurs in rural and semirural areas, especially in the northern parts of the country at elevations between 400 and 800 meters. Major risk areas include the northern Afghan plains and the outskirts of Kabul. Other risk areas include Qandahar in the south and Herat in the west. There are sporadic cases of visceral leishmaniasis. There is no apparent focal distribution. All travelers to risk areas should take measures to prevent insect (sandfly) bites.

Rabies: Human cases occur sporadically in rural villages. Travelers who will stay for extended periods (more than 4 weeks) in remote, rural areas should consider pre-exposure rabies vaccination.

Other illnesses: Brucellosis, cholera, echinococcosis, leptospirosis, louse-borne typhus, sandfly fever (mosquito-transmitted), Siberian tick typhus, tick-borne relapsing fever, typhoid fever (highly endemic), tuberculosis, and intestinal helminthic infections.

BANGLADESH

Embassy: 202-342-8372   ***Dhaka***   ***GMT +6 hrs***

Entry Requirements
- Passport/Visa: Valid passport and visa are required.
- AIDS Test: Not required.
- Vaccinations: A yellow fever vaccination certificate is required from all travelers arriving from, or transiting through, any country any part of which is infected. A certificate is required if arriving from any country in the Yellow Fever Endemic Zones or from Botswana, Malawi, Mauritania, Belize, Costa Rica, Guatemala, Honduras, or Nicaragua.

Telephone Country Code: 880

Electricity/Plugs: AC 50 Hz, 220 volts; frequency not stable; plug types C and D.

American Express: American Express Travel Service, Alko Building, 18-20 Motijheel, Dhaka; Tel. (2) 238-351.

Embassies/Consulates: U.S. Embassy, Dhaka. Diplomatic Enclave, Mandani Avenue, Baridhara Model Town; Tel. (2) 608-170 or 235-081.

Hospitals/Doctors: Holy Family Hospital, Dhaka (286 beds); minimally equipped facility; should be used only for emergency stabilization. H. Rahman, M.D. Tel. 400-011.

Health Advisory

Malaria: Risk is present year-round throughout this country. There is risk of malaria in all urban areas. The most intense transmission of malaria occurs along the eastern border in the forested hills of the Chittagong Hill Tracts. Falciparum malaria accounts for 50%–75% of malaria cases in this country, vivax the remainder. Chloroquine-resistant falciparum malaria is confirmed in the eastern and northeastern regions. Mefloquine or doxycycline prophylaxis is advised for travel to these regions.

Cholera: Occurs year-round, although not reported "active" by the World Health Organization. The risk to tourists of acquiring cholera is low. To prevent cholera, travelers should follow safe food and drink guidelines.

Travelers' diarrhea: High risk. Water supplies in Bangladesh are obtained from ditches, ponds, and streams in rural areas and from canals and ponds in urban areas of the country. Generally, water sources are contaminated with human and animal waste. In addition to waste, the mineral content of the water is high. Piped water supplies may be contaminated. Travelers should observe strict food and drink guidelines. A quinolone antibiotic is recommended for the treatment of acute diarrhea. Diarrhea not responding to treatment with an antibiotic, or chronic diarrhea, may be due to a parasitic disease such as giardiasis or amebiasis.

Hepatitis: High risk. All susceptible travelers should receive immune globulin or hepatitis A vaccine prior to visiting this country. The hepatitis B carrier rate in the general population is estimated at 10%. Hepatitis B vaccination is recommended for all healthcare workers and should be considered by anyone planning an extended visit to this country.

Japanese encephalitis: Risk of transmission is greatest from June through October in rural agricultural areas. Sporadic cases occur year-round. Last report of disease was in 1977 during an outbreak in the central district of Tangail. Vaccination against Japanese encephalitis is recommended for travelers who will be staying in rural-agricultural endemic areas for long periods (more than several weeks). In addition, all travelers should take measures to prevent mosquito bites, especially in the evening.

Dengue fever: Low apparent risk. Last cases were officially reported in 1964, although there were unconfirmed reports of dengue in 1988. All travelers should take measures to prevent mosquito bites.

Leishmaniasis: Transmission occurs year-round under 600 meters elevation. Visceral leishmaniasis (kala azar) is transmitted countrywide, including urban areas, with an increased incidence in the central delta districts of Mymensingh and Pabna. Travelers should take measures to prevent insect (sandfly) bites, especially in rural areas.

Filariasis: Bancroftian filariasis is reported, with 10% of the population infected. The prevalence is highest in the northern and central districts. Travelers should take measures to prevent mosquito bites.

Rabies: Over 2,000 deaths occur annually. Most rabies in Bangladesh is transmitted by stray dogs. Pre-exposure rabies vaccination should be considered by travelers to this country.

Other illnesses/hazards: Anthrax, leprosy (affects a small percentage of the population), scabies, tuberculosis (a major health problem), typhoid fever, and intestinal worms (whipworms, roundworms, hookworms) are reported. Animal hazards include snakes (kraits, cobras, vipers), centipedes, scorpions, and black widow spiders, brown recluse spiders, and large leeches (not poisonous, but can cause slow-healing ulcers). Other possible hazards include crocodiles, pythons, poisonous frogs and toads, lizards, tigers, leopards, and bears (sloth, Himalayan black, and Malayan sun).

BHUTAN
Thimphu ... GMT +5½ hrs

Entry Requirements
- Passport/Visa: Valid passport and visa are required.
- AIDS Test: Not required.
- Vaccinations: A yellow fever vaccination certificate is required from all travelers arriving from infected areas.

Telephone Country Code: 975

Embassies/Consulates: No formal diplomatic relations exist between the United States and Bhutan. The U.S. Embassy in New Delhi should be contacted.

Health Advisory

Malaria: Highly endemic. Risk is present year-round in the south and southeastern districts bordering India, including urban areas. (Risk generally limited to the Duars Plain and the mountain valleys of the Lesser Himalayas up to 1,700 meters elevation in the Samchi, Chirang, Gaylegphug, Shemgang, and Samdrup Jongkhar Districts.) Risk may be elevated during the rainy season, May through mid-October. Thimbu is risk free. *P. falciparum* causes 60% of cases. Mefloquine or doxycycline prophylaxis is advised in risk areas.

Cholera: This disease is active in this country. Although cholera vaccination is not required for entry if arriving directly from the U.S. or Canada, it may be required if arriving from a cholera-infected area, or required for on-going travel to other countries in Latin America, Africa, the Middle East, or Asia. Travelers should consider vaccination or a doctor's letter of exemption from vaccination. The risk to travelers of acquiring cholera is considered low. Prevention consists primarily in following safe food and drink guidelines.

Travelers' diarrhea: High risk. Water supplies in Bhutan are frequently contaminated as a result of substandard sanitary conditions. Prevention of diarrhea consists primarily in following strict adherence to safe food and drink guidelines. A quinolone antibiotic is recommended for the treatment of acute diarrhea. Diarrhea not responding to treatment with an antibiotic, or chronic diarrhea, may be due to a parasitic disease such as giardiasis or amebiasis.

Hepatitis: All susceptible travelers should receive immune globulin or hepatitis A vaccine prior to visiting this country. The hepatitis B carrier rate in the general population is estimated at 4%. Vaccination against hepatitis B is recommended for anyone planning an extended visit to this country. Hepatitis E is the predominant cause of acute hepatitis in Bhutan, usually occurring in adults. Sporadic outbreaks as well as large epidemics occur. Transmission is primarily through sewage-contaminated water. Travelers should drink only water that has been boiled, bottled, or chemically treated.

Japanese encephalitis: Presumably endemic; not officially reported but is believed to occur in the southern (terai) foothill districts.

Rabies: Highly prevalent. Stray dogs are the main source of infection. Pre-exposure rabies vaccination should be considered prior to travel to this country.

Other illnesses/hazards: Brucellosis (reported in low numbers), dengue (presumably endemic), filariasis, leprosy (highly prevalent; an estimated 5–10 cases/1,000 population), scabies, murine and scrub typhus, trachoma, tuberculosis (a major health problem), typhoid fever, and intestinal worms (whipworms, roundworms, hookworms) are reported.

CHINA, PEOPLE'S REPUBLIC OF

Embassy: 202-328-2500   *Beijing*   **GMT +8 hrs**

Entry Requirements

- Passport/Visa: Valid passport and visa are required.
- AIDS Test: Test required for those staying 6 months or more. For further details, travelers should contact the Chinese Consulate in Washington at 202-328-2517.
- Vaccinations: A valid yellow fever vaccination certificate is required from all travelers arriving from infected areas.

Telephone Country Code: 86   **AT&T:** 10811

Electricity/Plugs: AC 50 Hz, 220 volts; plug types A, D, and I; adaptors and transformer necessary for U.S.-made appliances.

American Express Travel Service: Beijing-Toronto Hotel, Shop A3 Jianguo Men; Tel. (1) 500-2266.

Embassies/Consulates: U.S. Embassy, Beijing. Xiu Shui Bei Jie 3; Tel. (1) 532-831. U.S. Consulate, Shanghai; Tel. 379-880. U.S. Consulate, Chengdu; Tel. 28-24481. U.S. Consulate, Guangzhou; Tel. 668-800. Canadian Embassy, Beijing. 10 San Li Tun Road. Chao Yang District; Tel. (1) 532-3536.

Hospitals/Doctors: Beijing Airport Health Quarantine Bureau (contact Professor Hua Xu), 20 Hepinglibeijie, Beijing 100013; Tel: (1) 456-2801. Beijing Union Medical College Hospital (1,200 beds); sophisticated diagnostic services; emergency services; Tel. 512-7733, ext. 372. The Sino-German Clinic, Beijing (located in the Landmark Building); staffed by Chinese, German, and U.S. physicians; open 24 hours a day. In Shanghai: Shanghai Medical University, Zhong Shan Hospital; Tel. 310-400.

Health Advisory

Cholera: This disease is active. Although cholera vaccination is not required for entry to this country if arriving directly from the United States or Canada, it may be required if arriving from cholera-infected areas—or required for on-going travel from China to other countries in Latin America, Africa, the Middle East, or Asia. Travelers should carefully check their itinerary and consider cholera vaccination (one dose) or a doctor's letter of exemption from vaccination. The risk to travelers of acquiring cholera is considered low. Prevention consists in adhering to safe food and drink guidelines.

Malaria: Occurs countrywide in rural areas below 1,500 meters elevation, except for the risk-free northern areas bordering Mongolia and the western provinces of Heilungkiang, Kirin, Ningsia Hui Tibet, and Tsinghai. Most cases of malaria occur in southern and eastern China, with the highest incidence occurring in Hainan and Andhui Provinces, Hainan Island, and the areas bordering Laos, Vietnam, and Burma (Myanmar). Year-round risk of malaria is present in the tropical provinces (Guangdang, Guangxi, Yunnan) and Hainan Island.

In northern and central malarious areas, *P. vivax* predominates, while on southern China *P. falciparum* predominates and mixed infections are common. Sporadic cases of *P. malariae* are reported. Although malaria is transmitted in rural lowland areas during the warmer months, the risk to travelers appears to be very low. Travelers to most central and northern areas within China who venture into the countryside (including trips by car or train, river cruises, and bicycle tours) should take weekly chloroquine prophylaxis. In southern China, however, multidrug-resistant falciparum malaria is reported in areas bordering Burma, Laos, Vietnam, the Gulf of Tonkin, and the areas southwest of Canton, including Hainan Island. Mefloquine or doxycycline prophylaxis is recommended for travel to these southern regions, especially Yunnan and Guangxi Provinces. Travelers visiting only cities and popular rural tourist sites, or taking only daytime trips to the countryside, are not deemed to be at significant risk and malaria prophylaxis is not routinely recommended. Travelers on special scientific, educational, or recreational visits should check whether their itineraries include evening or nighttime exposure in areas of risk, or in areas of chloroquine resistance.

Travelers' diarrhea: Moderate to high risk. In most large urban areas, inefficient treatment and inadequate distribution systems provide piped water, which is commonly contaminated. In urban and resort areas, most hotels have generally safe restaurants and potable water. Trav-

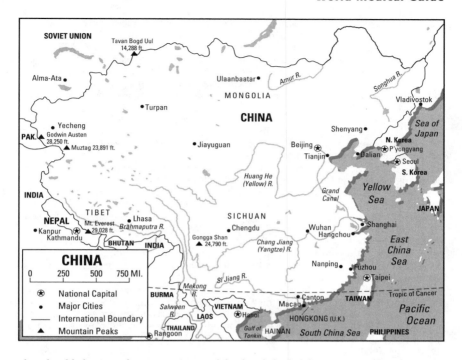

elers should observe safety precautions and drink only boiled, bottled, or chemically treated water and consume only well-cooked food. Raw fish and shellfish, and undercooked aquatic plants (e.g., watercress salad), should specifically be avoided. A quinolone antibiotic is recommended for the treatment of acute diarrhea. Diarrhea not responding to antibiotic treatment may be due to a parasitic disease such as giardiasis, amebiasis, or cryptosporidiosis. The giardiasis infection rate in the general population is about 1%. Amebiasis infection rate is about 0.4%. Up to 8% of diarrhea may be caused by cryptosporidiosis.

Hepatitis A, B & C: There is a high risk of hepatitis A in this country. All susceptible travelers should receive immune globulin or hepatitis A vaccine. The hepatitis B carrier rate in the general population is 9%–11%. Vaccination is recommended for all healthcare workers and long-term visitors. Travelers should avoid acupuncture treatments unless assured that all needles have been heat sterilized or are of the disposable variety. Hepatitis C virus is endemic.

Hepatitis E: This is a leading cause of sporadic acute viral hepatitis in China. High incidence is reported in rural areas. Transmission is primarily by water from contaminated pools and canals. To avoid hepatitis E, all travelers, especially to rural areas, should drink only boiled, bottled, or chemically treated water.

Typhoid fever: Moderate risk. Vaccination is recommended for extended travel outside of tourist areas. The highest incidence of typhoid fever is reported from the Xianjiang Autonomous Region.

Dengue fever: Occurs as frequent, often widespread outbreaks. Highest risk occurs in southeastern China, primarily the coastal urban areas south of 30 degrees north latitude. Most disease transmission occurs during the summer months; in the tropical provinces, however, the transmission period extends from March through November. The Aedes mosquitoes, which transmit dengue, bite during the daytime and are present in populous urban areas as well as resort and rural areas. Prevention of dengue fever consists of taking protective measures against mosquito bites. A vaccine is not available.

Japanese encephalitis: Disease is present in all regions except in Qinghai Province, Xinjiang, and Xizang Autonomous Region. Risk is greatest in rural pig-breeding agricultural areas of central and eastern China during warm, rainy months (June–October). Risk of JE is year-round in the tropical southern provinces. There is some risk of transmission in the suburban areas of major cities. Vaccination against Japanese encephalitis (3 doses) is recommended for travelers who will be staying in rural-agricultural endemic areas for extended periods (more than 4 weeks). In addition, all travelers should take measures to prevent mosquito bites.

Schistosomiasis: This disease occurs primarily in rural areas, especially in lowland and eastern coastal areas. Highest risk occurs from April to November, but year-round risk occurs in the southern tropical provinces. All travelers should avoid swimming, wading, or bathing in freshwater lakes, ponds, or streams.

Leishmaniasis: Visceral leishmaniasis (kala azar) occurs in the temperate central and northeastern provinces, mainly Gansu, Shanxi, and the Shaanxi, with a western focus in Xinjiang Autonomous Region. Risk of disease transmission is elevated from May through October, when sand flies are more active. Cutaneous leishmaniasis has been reported from the Xinjiang Autonomous Region. All travelers to these areas should avoid sandfly bites when visiting these areas.

Filariasis: Both the Bancroftian and Malayan forms are reported in the southwestern provinces. Travelers to these areas should take measures to prevent mosquito bites.

Lyme disease: Reported among agricultural workers in the northeastern coastal provinces. Travelers should take precautions against tick bites.

Rabies: Higher than average incidence reported in urban and rural areas, with stray dogs the main threat. Travelers should seek immediate treatment of any unprovoked animal bite. Rabies vaccination is indicated following the unprovoked bite of a dog, cat, bat, or monkey. Bites by other animals should be considered on an individual basis. Pre-exposure vaccination against rabies should be considered for long-term travel to this country.

Helminthic diseases: Moderately to highly endemic in rural and urban areas. Diseases caused by soil-transmitted helminths (hookworm disease, strongyloidiasis) can be prevented by wearing shoes and not walking barefoot outside. Food-transmitted roundworm infections (ascariasis, trichuriasis) can be prevented by washing salads and/or vegetables or thoroughly cooking food to destroy infective eggs. Lung fluke and liver fluke disease (paragonimiasis, clonorchiasis) can be prevented by not eating raw freshwater crabs, crayfish, or fish.Fasciolopsiasis (large intestinal fluke disease) and fascioliasis (sheep liver fluke disease) can be prevented by not eating undercooked or raw water plants, such as watercress and other aquatic vegetables. Anisakiasis can be avoided by not eating raw saltwater fish, including raw octopus and squid; capillariasis can be prevented by avoiding raw or undercooked freshwater fish.

Echinococcosis: Human alveolar echinococcosis, a potentially fatal disease caused by *E. multilocularis*, occurs in northern Xinjiang Autonomous Region and central China. This disease, caused by the larval stage of the fox tapeworm, is spread to humans by close contact with infected domesticated dogs or by contact with fox/canine feces. Cystic hydatid disease, caused by *E. granulosus*, is common throughout western and northwestern China.

Air pollution: Harsh conditions exist in Beijing, where the air is severely polluted. Pollutants include windblown dust and dirt, soot from coal burning stoves, and exhaust from vehicles.

Influenza: Vaccination is recommended for travelers visiting China from October to May.

Other diseases/health threats: Anthrax, brucellosis (high incidence), Crimean-Congo hemorrhagic fever (low endemicity; in Xinjiang Province only), leptospirosis, melioidosis (endemic in Guangdong and Hainan Provinces, and Guangxi Autonomous Region); plague (reported sporadically from the western provinces), Russian spring-summer encephalitis (presumably occurs in northern China, especially Inner Mongolia), syphilis, AIDS (intensifying among IV drug users in Yunnan Province), scrub typhus (most risk in temperate provinces of southeastern China, tuberculosis (highly endemic), trachoma (widespread), typhoid fever, and typhus (low risk of murine typhus and epidemic typhus). Stingrays, jellyfish, sea anemones, poisonous fish (stone, puffer, scorpion, and zebra), sea cucumbers, and spiny sea urchins inhabit the coastal waters of China and are potential hazards to swimmers.

HONG KONG (U.K.)

Trade Mission: 202-331-8947　　　*Hong Kong*　　　*GMT +8 hrs*

Entry Requirements

- Passport/Visa: Travelers should possess valid passport. A visa is not required.
- AIDS Test: Not required.
- Vaccinations: None required.

Telephone Country Code: 852

American Express: American Express Travel Service, New World Tower Building, G/F 16-18 Queen's Road Central, Hong Kong; Tel. (5) 844-8668.

Embassies/Consulates: U.S. Embassy, Hong Kong. 26 Garden Road; Tel. (5) 239-011.

Hospitals/Doctors: George T.F. Tong, M.D., Manning House, 38 Queen's Road Central; Tel. (5) 238-295 or 813-0375 (H). Hong Kong Adventist Hospital; 24-hr. emergency service; Tel. (5) 574-6211. TST Medical Clinic, Kowloon; Tel. (3) 723-1199.

Health Advisory

Malaria: The urban area of Hong Kong is risk free. Malaria has been reported in rural northern border areas. Travelers to the northern border areas should take weekly doses of chloroquine. Chloroquine-resistant falciparum malaria has not been reported.

Travelers' diarrhea: All drinking water in Hong Kong is purified and chlorinated. In urban and resort areas, the hotels and restaurants serve reliable food and potable water. Elsewhere, travelers should observe food and drink safety precautions. Raw shellfish should be avoided. A quinolone antibiotic (Floxin or Cipro) is recommended for the treatment of acute diarrhea. Diarrhea not responding to antibiotic treatment may be due to a parasitic disease such as giardiasis or amebiasis.

Hepatitis: Outbreaks of hepatitis A usually occur every 2–3 years in Hong Kong, but the incidence of hepatitis A has declined during the past decade. The commonest source of hepatitis A in Hong Kong is improperly cooked or raw shellfish, oysters in particular. (These are often bred in sewage-contaminated sea-beds.) To prevent hepatitis A, all susceptible travelers should receive immune globulin or hepatitis A vaccine, and avoid raw shellfish. The hepatitis B carrier rate in the general population is estimated at 9%–11%. Vaccination against hepatitis B is recommended for healthcare workers, corporate employees, expatriates, teachers, and others (including family members) who will have close, prolonged contact with the indigenous population. Hepatitis E is present in Hong Kong, but no major outbreaks have been reported.

Typhoid fever: Vaccination is recommended for those traveling more than four weeks outside of tourist or resort areas.

Dengue fever: Risk is present and outbreaks have previously occurred. The *Aedes* mosquitoes, which transmit dengue, bite primarily during the daytime and are present in periurban areas as well as resort and rural areas. All travelers are advised to take measures to prevent mosquito bites.

Japanese encephalitis: Sporadic cases are reported year-round. Vaccination (now available again in the United States, as well as Canada) is recommended for extended travel in this region. Travelers to Hong Kong should also take measures to prevent mosquito bites.

Helminthic diseases:

INDIA

Embassy: 202-939-7000   *New Delhi*   *GMT +5½ hrs*

Entry Requirements

- Passport/Visa: A valid passport and visa are required.
- AIDS Test: Test required for foreign students over 18 years of age and those staying beyond 1 year. Travelers should contact the Indian Embassy for further information.
- Vaccinations: A yellow fever vaccination certificate is required from all travelers arriving from any country any part of which is infected, or from any country in the Yellow Fever Endemic Zones, including Trinidad & Tobago. The *HealthGuide* recommends that all travelers arriving from any country in sub-Saharan Africa or from Latin America have a valid yellow fever vaccination certificate in their possession.

  Cholera: This disease is active at this time. A valid certificate of vaccination against cholera (or a letter of exemption from vaccination) is recommended for all travelers to India who will be proceeding to other countries in Asia, Africa, or the Middle East.

Telephone Country Code: 91   **AT&T:** 000-117

Electricity/Plugs: AC 50 Hz, 220 volts; plug types C and D.

American Express: American Express Bank Ltd. TRS. Wenger House, A Block, Connaught Place, New Delhi; Tel. (11) 332-4119.

Embassies/Consulates: U.S. Embassy, New Delhi. Shanti Path, Chanakyapuri; Tel. (11) 600-651. American Consulates: Bombay; Tel. (022) 822-3611. Calcutta; Tel. (033) 44-3611/6. Madras; Tel. (44) 477-552.

Hospitals/Doctors: Irwin Hospital, New Delhi (1,173 beds); most specialties; Tel. 275-071. East-West Medical Center, New Delhi; Tel. 623-738. J.J. Hospital, Bombay (1,272 beds); most specialties, including orthopedics. The Bombay Hospital Centre; Tel. 297-100. National Medical College Hospital, Calcutta (803 beds); most specialties; infectious diseases. The East India Clinic, Calcutta; Tel. 45-3951.

Health Advisory

Yellow fever: No risk.

Cholera: This disease is active in this country. Although cholera vaccination is not required for entry to India if arriving directly from the U.S. or Canada, it may be required if arriving from infected countries, or required for on-going travel to other countries in Latin America, Africa, the Middle East, or Asia. Depending upon their itinerary, travelers should consider vaccination or a doctor's letter of exemption from vaccination. The risk to travelers of acquiring cholera is low. Prevention consists in adhering to safe food and drink guidelines.

NOTE: A new strain of epidemic cholera has appeared in the Bay of Bengal. It is not prevented by the cholera vaccine in current use.

Malaria: Risk of malaria is present countrywide below 2,000 meters elevation, including cities and urban areas. Risk is elevated during warm and wet months, June through October. Incidence has increased recently in Delhi, Tamil Nadu State, and Haryana State. No malaria is reported in Himachal Pradesh, Jammu, Kashmir, and Sikkim. The most intense malaria transmission in India occurs in the eastern and northeastern states. In these areas, *P. falciparum* causes 60%–70% of cases. Elsewhere, *P. falciparum* accounts for up to 35% of cases with *P. vivax* accounting for most of the remainder, followed by *P. malariae.* Isolated cases of *P. ovale* have been reported from Orissa State. Chloroquine-resistant falciparum malaria is reported countrywide but is especially prevalent in the eastern and northeastern states. Mefloquine prophylaxis is recommended for travel to the eastern states and northeastern states. Travelers to the southern and western states, where there is less risk of chloroquine-resistant *P. falciparum,* have the option of taking either weekly mefloquine or taking weekly chloroquine and carrying a self-treatment dose of halofantrine or Fansidar.

Travelers' diarrhea: High risk year-round, countrywide. Risk is higher in rural villages where water supplies are frequently obtained from wells which commonly are contaminated. Untreated sewage, industrial wastes, and agricultural runoffs contaminate most of India's rivers. Piped water supplies throughout India are quite limited and all water should be considered nonpotable. Travelers should observe food and drink safety precautions, especially outside major hotels and resorts. A quinolone antibiotic is recommended for the treatment of

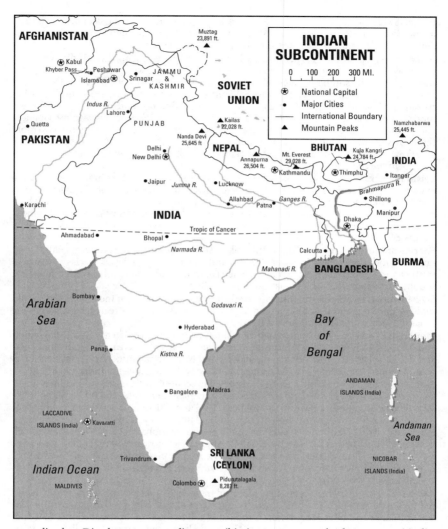

acute diarrhea. Diarrhea not responding to antibiotic treatment may be due to a parasitic disease such as giardiasis or amebiasis. Amebiasis infection rates up to 84% have been reported in northern India and amebic liver abscess is a serious problem in many areas. Giardiasis infection rates of 21%–62% are reported in this country.

Hepatitis: There is a high risk of hepatitis A in nonimmune travelers. All susceptible travelers should receive immune globulin or hepatitis A vaccine. The hepatitis B carrier rate in the general population is estimated at 5%. Vaccination against hepatitis B is recommended for all healthcare workers and should be considered by anyone planning an extended visit to this country. Hepatitis E: This is the most common form of acute viral hepatitis in adults in this country. Most cases are transmitted by sewage-contaminated water in rural areas. A vaccine against hepatitis E is not available. Travelers can reduce their risk of illness by drinking only boiled, bottled, or chemically treated water. This disease has a 15%–20% mortality rate in pregnant women.

Typhoid fever: Highly endemic. Vaccination is recommended for travel exceeding two weeks.

Dengue fever: Periodic epidemics occur in urban and semi-rural areas countrywide below 1,000 meters elevation, with most outbreaks occurring in the north-central states. Relatively few cases are reported from the western states. In southern areas, the of risk of dengue is year-round. In the northern states, the risk is elevated from April through October. To prevent dengue, travelers should take measures to prevent mosquito bites.

Japanese encephalitis: This disease occurs year-round, except in northern India, where the risk is primarily April through November. The risk is low in the western states. Only sporadic cases occur in the southern states. Most Japanese encephalitis risk is present in the eastern and northeastern states, where explosive epidemics have occurred. Since 1978, the disease has spread into Uttar Pradesh, with yearly epidemics. The *Culex* mosquito transmits this disease, mostly in rural areas below 1,000 meters elevation. Vaccination (3 doses) against Japanese encephalitis is recommended for travelers who will be staying or traveling extensively (more than 4 weeks) in rural-agricultural endemic areas during the peak transmission period. In addition, all travelers should take personal protection measures against mosquito bites, especially in the evening.

Leishmaniasis: Cases of visceral leishmaniasis occur in large numbers in rural areas of the eastern states, but this disease is rarely reported from other regions. Sporadic cases of cutaneous leishmaniasis have been reported in the western states along the Pakistani-Indian border. Most cases of cutaneous leishmaniasis occur in adults in urban or periurban hutment areas (slums). Travelers should take measures to prevent insect (sandfly) bites, especially in the eastern states.

Filariasis: Mosquito-borne. Bancroftian filariasis is widespread in southern, central, and northern India, especially in Uttar Pradesh and Bihar States. Malayan filariasis occurs in southern India, especially Kerala State. The risk to tourists is low. All travelers, however, should take standard measures to prevent mosquito bites.

Schistosomiasis: There is minimal risk of schistosomiasis in southern India. Travelers should avoid swimming, wading, or bathing in freshwater lakes, ponds, or streams, especially in the states of Andhra Pradesh or Maharashtra.

Meningitis: Increased risk of meningococcal meningitis is reported in the New Delhi region and adjacent southern areas (Madhya Pradesh State). There is increased risk in rural areas and urban slums. Because sporadic meningitis outbreaks occur countrywide, vaccination is recommended for all travelers planning residence or extended travel in India.

Plague: Outbreaks of plague have been reported in western India in several localities north and east of Bombay, particularly the cities of Surat, in Gujarat state, and Bir, in Maharashta state. Plague has also been confirmed in New Delhi and Calcutta in persons traveling from Surat. These outbreaks involve both the bubonic and pneumonic forms of the disease. Plague is primarily a disease of poverty and the risk to the international traveler is extremely small, if not negligible (per CDC, November 1994). Any traveler, however, who has had close contact (e.g., face to face contact) with a suspected pneumonic plague patient should receive prophylactic antibiotic therapy for 7 days with tetracycline, doxycycline, or trimethoprim/sulfamethoxazole (Bactrim).

Rabies: This country has the highest reported incidence of dog rabies in the world. More than 25,000 human cases occur annually. Travelers should seek immediate treatment of any animal bite. Rabies vaccination is indicated following the unprovoked bite of a dog, cat, bat, or monkey. Bites by other animals should be considered on an individual basis. Pre-exposure rabies vaccination is recommended for anyone planning long-term travel to this country.

Other diseases/health threats: Brucellosis (uncommon in humans), Crimean-Congo hemorrhagic fever (tick-borne), cysticercosis (neurocysticercosis causes 2% of epileptic seizures in this country), echinococcosis, Kyasanur Forest disease (tick-borne; risk elevated during the dry season, Nov.–May), leprosy (widespread among lower socioeconomic groups and in rural areas), leptospirosis, Indian tick typhus (reported in southern India), helminthic infections (ascariasis, ancylostomiasis, trichuriasis, and strongyloidiasis are highly prevalent), scabies (widespread), AIDS (spreading rapidly, with heterosexual transmission increasingly predominant), trachoma (widespread in rural areas), tuberculosis (highly endemic), and typhus (both murine and scrub typhus occur). Animal hazards to consider include snakes (kraits, cobras, coral snakes, vipers), scorpions, spiders, and leeches (abundant in the streams, marshes, and jungles). Stingrays, sea wasps, cones, jellyfish, urchins, and anemones are common in India's coastal waters and are potential hazards to unprotected swimmers.

NEPAL

Embassy: 202-667-4550   *Kathmandu*   *GMT +5¾ hrs*

Entry Requirements
- Passport/Visa: Valid passport and visa are required.
- AIDS Test: Not required.
- Vaccinations: A yellow fever vaccination certificate is required from all travelers older than 1 year arriving from infected areas. The *HealthGuide* recommends vaccination if arriving from any country in the Yellow Fever Endemic Zones.

Telephone Country Code: 977
Electricity/Plugs: AC 50 Hz, 220 volts; plug type D.
American Express: Yeti Travels Pvt. Ltd. Hotel Mayalu, Jamal Tole, Durbar Marg, P.O. Box 76, Kathmandu; Tel. 221-234.
Embassies/Consulates: U.S. Embassy, Kathmandu. Pani Pokhari; Tel. 411-179 or 412-718. Canadian Embassy (India); Tel. [91] (11) 601-161.
Hospitals/Doctors: Kalimati Clinic, Kathmandu. This facility can supply Japanese encephalitis vaccine; Tel. 214-743. CIWEC Clinic, Kathmandu; offers inoculations and emergency treatment to travelers; rabies vaccine available; Tel. 228-531. Patan Hospital; 24-hour emergency department; Tel. 522-278. United Mission Hospital (100 beds); general medical and surgical facility. Bir Hospital (300 beds); general medical and surgical facility; blood bank.

Health Advisory

Cholera: This disease is active in this country. Although cholera vaccination is not required for entry if arriving directly from the U.S. or Canada, it may be required if arriving from a cholera-infected area, or required for on-going travel to other countries in Latin America, Africa, the Middle East, or Asia. Travelers should consider vaccination (one dose) or a doctor's letter of exemption from vaccination. The risk to travelers of acquiring cholera is considered low. Prevention consists primarily in following safe food and drink guidelines.

Malaria: Risk is year-round in the southern (terai) area, including urban areas, up to 2,100 meters elevation. Increased transmission occurs during the monsoon season (usually July through mid-October). The most intense malaria transmission occurs in the lowland southwestern districts, especially Kanchanpur and Kailali. Kathmandu and the northern Himalayan districts are risk free. *P. vivax* accounts for 92% of malaria cases countrywide, with *P. falciparum* accounting for the remainder. Chloroquine-resistant *P. falciparum* has been reported, particularly near the Indian border. Mefloquine prophylaxis is recommended when traveling to malarious areas.

Travelers' diarrhea: In Kathmandu, the food and drink in first-class restaurants and hotels are considered generally safe. Elsewhere, the risk of travelers' diarrhea is higher. Piped water supplies countrywide are frequently untreated and may be grossly contaminated. Travelers should observe food and drink safety precautions. A quinolone antibiotic is recommended for the treatment of acute diarrhea. Diarrhea not responding to treatment with an antibiotic, or chronic diarrhea, may be due to a parasitic disease such as giardiasis, amebiasis, or cryptosporidiosis.

Hepatitis: Immune globulin or hepatitis A vaccination is recommended for all susceptible travelers. The carrier rate of the hepatitis B virus in the general population is 1%–2%. Hepatitis B vaccination should be considered by healthcare workers and others having close, prolonged contact with the indigenous population of this country. Hepatitis E is widespread in Nepal and is usually transmitted by sewage-contaminated ground water. Hepatitis E accounts for the majority (86%) of cases of acute viral hepatitis in adults in Nepal. To reduce the risk of disease, travelers should drink only boiled, bottled, or chemically treated water.

Typhoid fever: Highly endemic. Vaccination is recommended for extended travel outside of tourist areas.

Meningitis: Occurs countrywide, with recent epidemics confirmed in the Kathmandu Valley. There is increased risk November through February. Vaccination is recommended for all trekkers, long-term visitors, or those traveling outside of tourist areas.

Japanese encephalitis: Highly endemic within the Terai plain and inner Terai zone. Yearly epidemics occur in the southern agricultural areas bordering India, at elevations below 1,000 meters. All travelers to endemic areas should take precautions to prevent insect bites. Vaccination is recommended for extended travel (more than 3 to 4 weeks) June through November in rural-agricultural rice-growing regions of the southern terai. Japanese encephalitis vaccine is available at the Kalimati Clinic in Kathmandu, from the Thai Red Cross Society in Bangkok, and from most travel clinics in the United States and Canada.

Dengue fever: Low apparent risk. Although there have been epidemics in neighboring districts of India, dengue is not currently reported in Nepal. Travelers, however, should still take sensible antimosquito precautions.

Leishmaniasis: Visceral leishmaniasis (kala azar) occurs, primarily in small villages and towns of the eastern region of the terai (foothills) at elevations below 1,000 meters. Travelers to this region should take measures to prevent insect (sandfly) bites.

Rabies: This disease is prevalent. Approximately 100 human fatalities are reported annually. Infective (rabid) dogs are the main threat. Trekkers and travelers (including children) should consider pre-exposure rabies vaccination if they will be potentially unable to receive prompt anti-rabies treatment (available in Kathmandu). All animal bites, especially those by a dog, should be examined as soon as possible by a physician.

Altitude sickness: Risk is present above 2,200 meters. Trekkers to higher altitudes should follow precautions (e.g., gradual ascent, acclimatization) to reduce the risk of acute altitude sickness. Travelers should consider prophylaxis with the drug acetazolamide (Diamox) and remember that descent is the best treatment for moderate to severe altitude sickness.

Other diseases/health threats: Cysticercosis (due to larval stages of the pork tapeworm), filariasis (occurs primarily in the southern terai), leprosy (highly prevalent), hookworm disease and other helminthic infections (very common), syphilis (60% seropositivity in women of the Badi tribe in northwest Nepal), AIDS (low incidence; reported primarily in prostitutes who become infected in India), scabies, trachoma (second leading cause of blindness in Nepal), tuberculosis (highly prevalent; a serious public health problem), and typhus (transmitted by ticks, fleas, and mites).

PAKISTAN

Embassy: 203-939-6200   *Islamabad*   *GMT +5 hrs*

Entry Requirements

- Passport/Visa: Valid passport and visa are required.
- AIDS Test: Test required if staying more than 1 year. Travelers should contact the Pakistani Embassy for further details.
- Vaccinations: A yellow fever vaccination certificate is required from all travelers older than 1 year arriving from any country any part of which is infected. A certificate is also required if arriving from any country in the Yellow Fever Endemic Zones.

    Cholera: A vaccination certificate is required if arriving from any country any part of which is infected.

Telephone Country Code: 92

Electricity/Plugs: AC 50 Hz, 220 volts; plug types C and D. Adaptors and transformer necessary for U.S.-made appliances.

American Express: American Express Bank Ltd. Ali Plaza, 1-E, Shahrah-E-Quaid-E-Azam, Islamabad; Tel. (51) 829-422/5.

Embassies/Consulates: U.S. Embassy, Islamabad, Diplomatic Enclave, Ramna 5; Tel. (51) 826-161, extension 2418/2519/2430. Canadian Embassy, Islamabad. Diplomatic Enclave 5; Tel. (51) 821-101.

Hospitals/Doctors: Jinnah Central Hospital, Karachi (800 beds); government hospital; all specialties. Seventh Day Adventist Hospital, Karachi (120 beds); private hospital; most specialties; Tel. 718-080. United Christian Hospital, Lahore; Tel. 881-961. Khyber Medical Center, Peshawar; Tel. 40-952.

World Medical Guide

Health Advisory

Cholera: This disease is active in this country. The vaccine-resistant Bengal strain of cholera has been reported. Although cholera vaccination is not required for entry if arriving directly from the U.S. or Canada, it may be required if arriving from a cholera-infected area, or required for on-going travel to other countries in Latin America, Africa, the Middle East, or Asia. Travelers should consider vaccination (one dose) or a doctor's letter of exemption from vaccination. The risk to travelers of acquiring cholera is considered low. Prevention consists primarily in adhering to safe food and drink guidelines.

Malaria: Malaria is endemic throughout the Indus Basin (Punjab in the east, Sind in the south), along the Gulf of Oman (Baluchistan), and in the Northwest Frontier Province. Punjab is the most malarious area. Transmission occurs in rural areas up to 2,000 meters elevation and in the valleys up to 3,500 meters in the Gilgit Agency in the north. Transmission also occurs in the urban areas in the south (including the perimeter of Karachi). Urban areas in the north (Islamabad) and the east (Lahore) are at much lower risk, but not risk free, since transmission occurs at the fringes. *P. falciparum* causes 77% of malaria in Baluchistan and Sind Province, 33% in Punjab Province, and 15% in NW Frontier Province; *P. vivax* causes the remainder. Chloroquine-resistant *P. falciparum* has been reported in Punjab. Mefloquine or doxycycline prophylaxis is recommended when traveling to risk areas.

Travelers' diarrhea: High risk. Although urban areas usually have water treatment facilities, central distribution systems, and public taps, none of the water in Pakistan should be considered potable. Piped water supplies are frequently untreated and may be grossly contaminated. Travelers should observe food and drink safety precautions. A quinolone antibiotic (Floxin or Cipro) is recommended for the treatment of acute diarrhea. Diarrhea not responding to treatment with an antibiotic, or chronic diarrhea, may be due to a parasitic disease such as giardiasis or amebiasis—or an intestinal virus.

Hepatitis: High risk of hepatitis A. All nonimmune travelers should receive immune globulin or hepatitis A vaccine. The hepatitis B carrier rate in the general population is estimated at 5%–8%. Hepatitis B vaccination is recommended for healthcare workers and others who will have close contact with the indigenous population (schoolteachers, relief workers, Peace Corps volunteers, etc.). There is a very high incidence of hepatitis E in this country. All travelers should avoid drinking water that may be virus-contaminated (e.g., untreated well water, tap water, or ground water).

Typhoid fever: Highly endemic. Risk is elevated June–August, especially in urban areas. Vaccination is recommended for people traveling extensively outside of tourist areas.

Japanese encephalitis: Low risk. A few cases have been reported near Karachi.

Dengue fever: Low risk. This disease may no longer be active to a significant degree.

Leishmaniasis: Cutaneous leishmaniasis occurs sporadically in the urban and semirural areas at the margin of the deserts, especially in the west, in Baluchistan. In Baluchistan and Baltistan, 25% of the population has leishmaniasis scars. Visceral leishmaniasis occurs sporadically in the northern areas (Baltistan, Azad Kashmir) at elevations between 2,000 and 6,000 meters. Travelers should protect themselves against sandfly bites.

Rabies: Human cases (more than 100 per year) usually occurs sporadically in rural villages or on the outskirts of larger cities. Travelers should seek immediate treatment of any animal bite, especially by a dog. Pre-exposure vaccination against rabies (3 doses) should be considered prior to long-term travel to this region.

Other diseases/health threats: Anthrax, brucellosis (human cases associated with occupational exposure to livestock), Crimean-Congo hemorrhagic fever (sporadic outbreaks; transmitted by ticks), dracunculiasis (focally endemic in NW Frontier, Punjab, Sind Provinces), echinococcosis, filariasis (Bancroftian filariasis occurs in the southern Indus delta), leprosy (widespread among lower socioeconomic groups), leptospirosis (rare in humans), Indian tick typhus (boutonneuse fever, reported sporadically), sandfly fever (highly endemic below 1,800 meters elevation; risk is higher in nondesert areas of Pakistan), West Nile fever (mosquito-transmitted; absent during winter), soil-transmitted intestinal worms (ascarid and hookworm widespread, especially in rural areas), syphilis (moderate incidence), AIDS (spreading rapidly), trachoma (widespread in western rural areas), tuberculosis (highly endemic in rural areas), typhoid fever, West Nile fever, and typhus (both murine and scrub typhus occur).

389

SRI LANKA

Embassy: 202-483-4025   *Colombo*   *GMT +5½ hrs*

Entry Requirements
- Passport/Visa: Valid passport and tourist card are required. Visa not required.
- AIDS Test: Not required.
- Vaccinations: A yellow fever vaccination certificate is required from all travelers older than 1 year arriving from infected areas.

Telephone Country Code: 94

Electricity/Plugs: AC 50 Hz, 220 volts; plug type D.

American Express: MacKinnons Travels Ltd. 4 Leyden Bastian Road, Colombo; Tel. (1) 29881.

Embassies/Consulates: U.S. Embassy, Colombo. 210 Galle Road; Tel. (1) 548-007. Canadian High Commission, Colombo. 6 Gregory's Road, Cinnamon Gardens; Tel. (1) 595-841.

Hospitals/Doctors: Sri Jayewardhanapura Hospital, Colombo (1,001 beds); ICU; emergency services. Lakeside Medical Center, Kandy; Tel. 23-466.

Health Advisory

Cholera: This disease is active in this country. The risk to travelers of acquiring cholera is very low. Prevention consists primarily in following strict adherence to safe food and drink guidelines.

Malaria: Malaria occurs countrywide, including urban areas. Areas above 800 meters are risk free. Colombo is also free of malaria. The northwest and central areas are highly malarious, especially around Anuradhapura. Malaria is less common in the Jaffna Peninsula or the southwestern areas because mosquito breeding sites are scarce. Falciparum malaria accounts for 30%–40% of cases, vivax the rest. Chloroquine- and Fansidar-resistant falciparum malaria reported. Mefloquine (Lariam) or doxycycline prophylaxis is recommended in malarious areas.

Travelers' diarrhea: High risk. All water supplies in Sri Lanka, including piped city water supplies, are potentially contaminated. Travelers should observe strict food and drink safety precautions. A quinolone antibiotic (Cipro or Floxin) is recommended for the treatment of acute diarrhea.

Hepatitis: Immune globulin prophylaxis or hepatitis A vaccination is recommended for all susceptible travelers. The carrier rate of the hepatitis B virus in the general population is estimated at 1%—lower than other countries in Asia. Vaccination against hepatitis B is recommended for healthcare workers and should be considered by long-term visitors to this country. No outbreaks of hepatitis E have been reported.

Japanese encephalitis: Sporadic cases occur year-round, but there have also been recent explosive epidemics in the region around Anuradhapura, due to increased mosquito breeding sites. JE vaccination is recommended for extended travel (more than 4 weeks) in rural-agricultural areas. All travelers should take measures to prevent mosquito bites.

Dengue fever: Risk is year-round below 1,000 meters elevation, including urban areas. The *Aedes* mosquitoes, which transmit dengue fever, bite during the daytime. Prevention of dengue consists of taking measures to prevent mosquito bites.

Leishmaniasis: This disease is not a threat in Sri Lanka.

Filariasis: Bancroftian filariasis is endemic in both urban and rural areas of the southwestern coast. All travelers should take measures to prevent mosquito bites.

Rabies: Risk is present, but declining. Stray dogs transmit most cases of human rabies. Preexposure rabies vaccination should be considered prior to extended travel in this country.

Other diseases/health threats: Anthrax, echinococcosis, leptospirosis, syphilis, tuberculosis (moderately endemic), typhoid fever, and soil-transmitted helminthic infections (due to roundworms, hookworms, and whipworms) are reported. Animal hazards include snakes (kraits, cobras, coral snakes, vipers), spiders (black widow and red-backed), leopards, bears, and wild pigs. Stingrays, sea wasps, starfish, and marine invertebrates (cones, jellyfish, nettles, urchins, anemones) are common in the country's coastal waters and are potential hazards to unprotected swimmers.

DISEASE   RISK   SUMMARY
Southeast Asia

Yellow fever: This disease does not occur in Asia, but many countries require a certificate of vaccination from travelers arriving from yellow fever-infected countries or from countries in the Yellow Fever Endemic Zones.

Cholera: Sporadic disease activity is reported in many SE Asian countries. Although cholera vaccination is not required for entry to any country if arriving directly from the U.S. or Canada, it may be required if arriving from a cholera-infected country, or required for on-going travel to other countries in Asia, Africa, the Middle East, or Latin America. (Indonesia and Malaysia, e.g., may require a valid cholera vaccination certificate if a traveler is departing for a cholera-endemic area.) To avoid possible entry problems, travelers should consider cholera vaccination (one dose) or a doctor's letter of exemption from vaccination. Cholera vaccine gives only brief, incomplete protection and is not routinely recommended for travelers in good health. Cholera occurs primarily in areas with inadequate sewage disposal and unsafe water supplies such as urban slums and rural areas. The risk to travelers of acquiring cholera is considered low. Prevention consists in strict adherence to safe food and drink guidelines.

Malaria: Both vivax and falciparum malaria occur in SE Asia. The falciparum-vivax ratio is usually about 2:1 in most areas, but may vary. Malaria caused by *P. malariae* accounts for 2%–5% of cases. Chloroquine- and multidrug-resistant *P. falciparum* is reported. In Indonesia and Irian Jaya, chloroquine-resistant *P. vivax* has been reported. Mefloquine or doxycycline prophylaxis is recommended when traveling to rural risk areas. Alternative malaria regimes should be discussed with a travel medicine or infectious disease specialist. All travelers to malarious areas should take measures to prevent insect bites. These measures include applying a DEET-containing skin repellent, wearing permethrin-treated clothing, and utilizing, as needed, a mosquito bed net, also treated with permethrin.

Travelers' diarrhea: High risk in many areas, but some major cities (e.g., Singapore, Bangkok) in SE Asia are much safer than others. It is recommended that travelers to SE Asia drink only bottled, boiled, or treated water and consume only well-cooked food. Raw fish, crayfish, and crabs, as well as uncooked aquatic plants (e.g., watercress), should be strictly avoided. Travelers should carry a quinolone antibiotic (Cipro or Floxin) with which to treat acute diarrhea. Diarrhea not responding to antibiotic treatment, or diarrhea that becomes chronic, may be due to a parasitic disease such as giardiasis or amebiasis, and treatment with metronidazole (Flagyl) or tinidazole (Fasigyn) should be considered. All cases of diarrhea should be treated with adequate fluid replacement.

Hepatitis: All susceptible travelers should receive immune globulin or hepatitis A vaccine prior to visiting SE Asia. The hepatitis B carrier rate in the general population of SE Asia is estimated at 10% to 20%. Vaccination against hepatitis B is recommended for all healthcare workers, overseas corporate employees, expatriates, relief workers, teachers, and others who will have extended (more than 4 weeks) contact with the indigenous populations of the countries in this region.

Typhoid fever: Vaccination is recommended for extended travel outside tourist areas.

Japanese encephalitis (JE): This disease is widespread throughout SE Asia. Japanese encephalitis may be transmitted seasonally, or year-round (in tropical regions). Vaccination against JE (3 doses) is recommended for travelers who will be staying in, or visiting (longer than 30 days), rural-agricultural rice-growing endemic areas during the peak transmission season. Depending upon the epidemic circumstances, vaccine should be considered for persons spending less than 30 days whose activities, such as extensive outdoor activities in rural areas, place them at particularly high risk for exposure. Travelers can inquire from the nearest U.S. consulate about the local availability of JE vaccine. This vaccine is now again available in the United States. All travelers to risk areas should also take measures to prevent mosquito bites.

Dengue fever: This disease is widespread throughout SE Asia in both sporadic and epidemic form and in both urban and rural areas. There is a high incidence of dengue hemorrhagic

fever in Bangkok. The *Aedes* mosquitoes, which transmit dengue, are most active during the daytime. Travelers should also take measures to prevent mosquito bites.

Leishmaniasis: Low risk. Leishmaniasis is reported in only Burma (Myanmar). Travelers there should take measures to avoid insect (sandfly) bites.

Filariasis: The Bancroftian and Malayan forms are widespread in SE Asia. Filariasis is transmitted by four different species of mosquitoes. Insect precautions are recommended for rural travel. Travelers should apply a DEET-containing skin repellent and a permethrin clothing spray, and a mosquito bed net (permethrin treated) should be used to prevent bites while sleeping.

Schistosomiasis: There is low risk of schistosomiasis in most countries of SE Asia. Risk is present in the Philippines and in central Sulawesi (Indonesia) and also occurs in small foci in the Mekong Delta of Vietnam. There are several small foci among the aboriginal Malays in Perak and Pahang States in Malaysia. Travelers should avoid swimming or wading in freshwater lakes, ponds, or streams in these areas.

Scrub typhus: This chigger mite–transmitted disease is reported from many SE Asian countries. Chigger mites commonly inhabit second-growth forest, fruit, oil palm, or rubber plantations where there is tall grass. People who walk through tropical brush should inspect their skin for the presence of mites or ticks. Repellents and permethrin clothing spray should also be used in these areas.

Helminthic infections: Hookworm, roundworm, whipworm, and strongyloides are highly prevalent in most rural areas of SE Asia. Travelers should wear shoes to prevent the hookworm and strongyloides larvae from penetrating the skin of the foot, and food should be thoroughly washed and/or cooked to destroy roundworm and whipworm eggs.

Helminthic infections (flukes): Oriental lung fluke disease (paragonimiasis) and liver fluke diseases (clonorchiasis, fascioliasis) are prevalent in the Indochina peninsula and the Philippines. Travelers should avoid eating raw, salted, or wine-soaked crustacea such as freshwater crabs or crayfish (which can transmit clonorchiasis and paragonimiasis) and also avoid uncooked aquatic vegetables, such as watercress, which can transmit fascioliasis. Fasciolopsiasis (large intestinal fluke disease) can also be acquired through eating undercooked aquatic plants such as water chestnuts, bamboo shoots, and caltrops. These, too, should be avoided, if uncooked. Anisakiasis and capillariasis are other intestinal infections acquired through eating raw or undercooked fish (including fresh catch, crab, or squid). Cases have been reported from the Philippines, Thailand, Taiwan, and, recently, Indonesia.

Rabies: Animal rabies has been reported from all countries in SE Asia. The highest risk occurs in Thailand. All travelers, especially children, should avoid touching or petting stray dogs. Travelers should seek immediate treatment of any animal bite. Rabies vaccination is indicated following the unprovoked bite of a dog, cat, bat, or monkey. Bites by other animals, including livestock, should be individually assessed. Pre-exposure vaccination against rabies (3 doses) should be considered prior to long-term travel to this region. This is especially true for travelers going to remote rural areas who will be unable to receive rabies vaccination treatment within 24 hours of exposure. Pre-exposure vaccination does not preclude the need for additional post-exposure vaccinations.

AIDS: Although the AIDS virus was only recently introduced to SE Asia, it is spreading with alarming speed. Thailand has the highest incidence. The virus initially affected mostly homosexuals, but then spread quickly to IV drug users (IVDU). By 1992, almost 50% of IVDU in Bangkok were HIV positive. The third wave of the epidemic now involves prostitutes and their heterosexual partners. Up to 70% of prostitutes in some rural areas of Thailand are now seropositive, and contact with infected prostitutes is spreading AIDS into the general population. In the Philippines, Malaysia, Singapore, Taiwan, Korea, and Indonesia, the HIV infection rate among prostitutes and the indigenous population is still relatively low. The potential for the eventual spread of AIDS in these areas, however, is considered high.

Other diseases/hazards: Other illnesses reported with varying frequency include anthrax, brucellosis, leprosy, leptospirosis, melioidosis, meningococcal meningitis, plague, toxoplasmosis, yaws, and tuberculosis. There is low risk to the average traveler of acquiring these illnesses. Stingrays, poisonous fish, sea anemones, the Indo-China man-o'-war, and the very dangerous sea wasp are found along the coral reefs that fringe the countries of SE Asia. Swimmers should take sensible precautions to avoid these hazards.

Plant hazards: Bamboo, rattan, and large palm- or fern-like trees, which can cause serious puncture wounds and slow-healing lacerations, are widespread in the forested areas of these countries. Also common are Regas, which are large forest trees whose black resinous sap can cause a potent poison ivy–type skin reaction. Stinging nettles, small thorny trees, and many species of euphorbs can also cause skin reactions.

BRUNEI DARUSSALAM

Embassy: 202-342-0159   *Bandar Seri Begawan*   *GMT +8 hrs*

Entry Requirements

- Passport/Visa: A valid passport, visa, and tourist card are required.
- AIDS Test: Not required.
- Vaccinations: A valid yellow fever vaccination certificate is required of all travelers older than one year coming from infected areas or coming from or transiting through any country in the Yellow Fever Endemic Zones within the previous 6 days.

Telephone Country Code: 673

Embassies/Consulates: U.S. Embassy, Bandar Seri Begawan; Tel. (2) 29670. Canadian Embassy (Malaysia); Tel. [60] (3) 261-2000.

Health Advisory

Malaria: There is no risk of malaria within this country.

Cholera: Not reported active, but sporadic cases occur.

Travelers' diarrhea: The food and drink in first-class restaurants and hotels are considered generally safe. Elsewhere, travelers should observe food and drink safety precautions. A quinolone antibiotic (Cipro or Floxin) is recommended for the treatment of acute diarrhea. Diarrhea not responding to treatment with an antibiotic, or chronic diarrhea, may be due to a parasitic disease such as giardiasis or amebiasis, and treatment with metronidazole (Flagyl) or tinidazole (Fasigyn) should be considered. All cases of diarrhea should be treated with adequate fluid replacement.

Hepatitis: All travelers should receive immune globulin or hepatitis A vaccine. The hepatitis B carrier rate in the general population is estimated at 10%–12%. Vaccination against hepatitis B is recommended for all healthcare workers and should be considered by anyone planning an extended visit to this country.

Dengue fever: There is risk of both dengue and dengue hemorrhagic fever. The *Aedes* mosquitoes, which transmit dengue, bite primarily during the daytime and are present in populous urban areas as well as resort and rural areas. To prevent dengue, all travelers are advised to take precautions against mosquito bites.

Japanese encephalitis: Vaccination against Japanese encephalitis is recommended for travelers who will be staying in rural-agricultural areas for extended periods (more than 4 weeks). In addition, all travelers should take precautions against mosquito bites, especially in the evening.

Other disease/risks: Fasciolopsiasis (giant intestinal fluke), helminthic infections (e.g., hookworm, roundworm), filariasis (transmitted by mosquitoes), mite-borne typhus, melioidosis, rabies, and typhoid fever are reported. Other possible hazards include snake bites and leeches.

BURMA (MYANMAR)

Rangoon ... GMT +6½ hrs

Entry Requirements

- Passport/Visa: A valid passport and visa required. Rangoon only port of entry. Overland travel in and out of Burma not permitted. Group travel only is permitted.
- AIDS Test: Not required.
- Vaccinations: A yellow fever vaccination certificate is required of all travelers arriving from infected areas. A certificate is also required of nationals and residents of Myanmar departing for an infected area.

Electricity/Plugs: AC 50 Hz, 220 volts; plug types D & G.

American Express: A.E. Liaison Office, 148 Sule Pagoda Road, Rangoon; Tel. 31937/75361.

Embassies/Consulates: U.S. Embassy, Rangoon. 581 Merchant Street; Tel. 82055/82181. Canadian Embassy (Bangladesh); Tel. [880] (2) 607-071.

Hospitals/Doctors: JICA Hospital, Rangoon (220 beds); general medical/surgical facility; ICU. Travelers should be aware that the U.S. Embassy evacuates its personnel to Bangkok, Thailand, in lieu of using local Burmese hospitals.

Health Advisory

Malaria: Occurs countrywide with the greatest risk of transmission April through December. Malaria is most prevalent in mountainous and rural areas below 1,000 meters elevation. There is less malaria in the plains and urban areas. Malaria risk is present in all cities except Rangoon and the urban centers of Mandalay, Magwe, Pegu, and Sagaing. Falciparum malaria accounts for approximately 85% of cases. There is widespread occurrence of chloroquine-resistant falciparum malaria in this country. Mefloquine or doxycycline prophylaxis is recommended for travel to rural areas. Multidrug-resistant malaria is reported along the Thai-Burmese border. Doxycycline prophylaxis is recommended for those traveling to border areas adjacent to Thailand.

Travelers' diarrhea: High risk. Potable water is almost nonexistent in Burma. Rural water supplies usually are grossly contaminated and urban water supplies invariably are subject to contamination. Local dairy products are considered unsafe. Local fruits and vegetables should be scrubbed and soaked in a chlorine or iodine solution before consumption. The local restaurants do not maintain Western standards of sanitation. Travelers should observe all food and drink safety precautions. A quinolone antibiotic is recommended for the treatment of acute diarrhea. Diarrhea not responding to treatment with an antibiotic, or chronic diarrhea, may be due to a parasitic disease such as giardiasis or amebiasis.

Hepatitis: Hepatitis A is highly endemic. All susceptible travelers should receive immune globulin or hepatitis A vaccine. The hepatitis B carrier rate in the general population is estimated at 10%. Vaccination against hepatitis B is recommended for all healthcare workers, expatriates, relief workers, teachers, and others (including family members) who will have prolonged (more than 4 weeks) contact with the indigenous population of this country. There is a high incidence of hepatitis E in this country. Explosive outbreaks occur, most commonly due to the consumption of sewage-contaminated water. All travelers, especially pregnant women, should follow safe drinking water guidelines.

Typhoid fever: Vaccination is recommended for those traveling outside tourist areas.

Dengue fever: Highly endemic. The peak infection rate usually occurs in the late monsoon season. Dengue occurs countrywide, but predominates in urban areas. Dengue hemorrhagic fever (a severe form of the disease) often occurs in persons who have had one or more previous dengue infections. The *Aedes* mosquitoes transmitting dengue bite during the daytime. A vaccine is not available. Prevention consists of taking personal protection measures against mosquito bites.

Japanese encephalitis: Both rural and urban areas may experience epidemics of Japanese encephalitis. Sporadic cases occur year-round. Peak of transmission occurs during, and shortly after, the monsoon season. Vaccination against Japanese encephalitis is recommended for travelers who will be staying in rural-agricultural areas longer than 4 weeks. In addition, all travelers to endemic areas should take personal protection measures against mosquito bites, especially in the evening.

Filariasis: Bancroftian and Malayan filariasis (mosquito-borne) are highly endemic in rural and urban areas. All travelers should take measures to prevent insect (mosquito) bites.

Other illnesses/hazards: Anthrax, brucellosis (low incidence), helminthic infections (ascariasis and hookworm disease are highly endemic in urban and rural areas), paragonimiasis (lung fluke disease; presumed endemic in small foci in rural areas), echinococcosis, leishmaniasis (low risk; sand-fly-borne, probably visceral type, reported historically), leprosy (highly endemic), rabies, epidemic typhus (louse-borne; may occur in northern upland provinces), murine typhus (flea-borne), scrub typhus (mite-borne; risk elevated in grassy rural areas), tuberculosis (highly endemic), and trachoma (highly endemic). Animal hazards include snakes (vipers, cobras), centipedes, scorpions, and black widow spiders. Other possible hazards include crocodiles, pythons, and large, aggressive lizards, all abundant in and near Burma's swamps and rivers, and leopards, wildcats, and bears, all found in the hilly regions of the country. Stingrays, sea wasps, cones, jellyfish, spiny sea urchins, and anemones are common in the country's coastal waters and are potentially hazardous to unprotected or careless swimmers.

CAMBODIA (KAMPUCHEA)

Phnom Penh ... GMT +7 hrs

Entry Requirements

- Passport/Visa: A passport and visa are required.
- AIDS Test: Visa applicants must present a medical certificate. Enforcement of this requirement is inconsistent.
- Vaccinations: A yellow fever vaccination certificate is required of all travelers arriving from infected areas.

Electricity/Plugs: AC 50 Hz, 220 volts; no information on plug types and adapter availability.

Embassies/Consulates: The U.S. government does not maintain diplomatic relations with Cambodia. U.S. passports are valid for travel to this country. Canadian Embassy (Thailand); Tel. [66] (2) 234-1561/8.

Hospitals/Doctors: 7 Jan 1979 Hospital, Phnom Penh (500 beds); some specialties; emergency services; may be best hospital in country. Battambang Provincial Hospital (325 beds); some specialty services.

Health Advisory

Cholera: This disease is active in this country. Although cholera vaccination is not required for entry if arriving directly from the U.S. or Canada, it may be required if arriving from a cholera-infected area, or required for on-going travel to other countries in Latin America, Africa, the Middle East, or Asia. Travelers should consider vaccination (one dose) or a doctor's letter of exemption from vaccination.

Malaria: Risk is present year-round throughout this country, including urban areas. There is increased risk in mountainous and rural areas. Falciparum malaria accounts for an estimated 75% of cases, vivax the remainder. Multidrug-resistant falciparum malaria is common, especially near the Thai-Cambodian border. Doxycycline prophylaxis is recommended for travel to malarious areas.

Travelers' diarrhea: High risk. All water sources should be considered biologically contaminated. Travelers should observe strict food and drink safety precautions. A quinolone antibiotic (Cipro or Floxin) is recommended for the treatment of acute diarrhea. Diarrhea not responding to treatment with an antibiotic, or chronic diarrhea, may be due to a parasitic disease such as giardiasis or amebiasis—or an intestinal virus.

Hepatitis: There is a high risk of hepatitis A in this country. All susceptible travelers should receive immune globulin or hepatitis A vaccine. Hepatitis E is also reported, but data not available. The hepatitis B carrier rate in the general population is estimated to exceed 10%. Vaccination against hepatitis B is recommended for healthcare workers and long-term visitors.

Dengue fever: There is risk of dengue year-round. The *Aedes* mosquitoes, which transmit dengue, bite primarily during the daytime and are present in populous urban areas as well as resort and rural areas. All travelers are advised to take precautions against mosquito bites.

Japanese encephalitis: Sporadic cases occur throughout the year, primarily in rural areas, but occasionally near or within urban areas. Vaccination is recommended for travelers planning an extended stay (more than 3–4 weeks) in rural-agricultural areas during the peak transmission season, June through October.

Schistosomiasis: Risk is present year-round, especially along the Mekong and Mun Rivers and in Battambang Province. Travelers should avoid swimming, bathing, or wading in freshwater lakes, ponds, or streams.

Other diseases/health threats: Anthrax (associated with eating buffalo meat), echinococcosis, filariasis (highly endemic in urban and rural areas), leprosy (highly endemic), leptospirosis, plague, rabies, scrub typhus, syphilis, tuberculosis (highly endemic), typhoid fever, soil-transmitted helminthic diseases (ascariasis, hookworm disease, strongyloidiasis), and other helminthic infections (fasciolopsiasis, opisthorchiasis, and clonorchiasis) are reported. Animal hazards include snakes (cobras, vipers), spiders (black and brown widow), crocodiles, and leeches. Stingrays, jellyfish, and several species of poisonous fish are common in the country's coastal waters and are potential hazards to unprotected swimmers.

INDONESIA

Embassy: 202-775-5200　　　*Jakarta*　　　*GMT +7 to +9 hrs*

Entry Requirements

- Passport/Visa: A valid passport is required.
- AIDS Test: Not required.
- Vaccinations: A yellow fever vaccination certificate is required of all travelers arriving from infected areas or from any country in the Yellow Fever Endemic Zones.

  Cholera: a vaccination certificate may be required of a traveler who is departing Indonesia for a country where cholera is reported active.

Telephone Country Code: 62

Electricity/Plugs: AC 50 Hz, 220 volts; plug types C, E, and F. Adaptors and transformer necessary for U.S.-made appliances.

American Express: Pacto Ltd., Arthaloka Building, Jakarta; Tel. (21) 570-3310.

Embassies/Consulates: U.S. Embassy, Jakarta. Medan Merdeka Selatan 5; Tel. (21) 360-360. U.S. Consulate, Surabaya; Tel. 69287/8. U.S. Consulate, Medan; Tel. 322-200. Canadian Embassy, Jakarta. Wisma Metropolitan 1, Jalan Jendral Sudirman; Tel. (21) 510-709.

Hospitals/Doctors: St. Carolus Hospital, Jakarta (645 beds); most specialties, 24-hour emergency service, ICU, ambulance service; Local Tel. (21) 883-091. Pertamina Hospital, Jakarta (300 beds); ICU, burn unit; limited 24-hour emergency service; local Tel. 707-1/9; ambulance: 707-211. University Hospital, Jakarta (1,335 beds); general medical services; coronary care unit; Tel. 334-030. Kediri Baptist Hospital. Tel. (21) 41-172.

Health Advisory

Cholera: This disease is reported active by the World Health Organization. Although cholera vaccination is not required for entry to Indonesia if arriving directly from the U.S. or Canada, it may be required if arriving from cholera-infected countries. Anyone who plans on-going travel from Indonesia to other countries in Asia, Oceania, Africa, the Middle East, or Latin America should also consider cholera vaccination (one dose) or a doctor's letter of exemption from vaccination. Cholera vaccine gives only brief, incomplete protection and is not routinely recommended for travelers in good health. Cholera occurs in areas with inadequate sewage disposal and unsafe water supplies such as urban slums and rural areas. The risk to travelers of acquiring cholera is considered low. Prevention consists primarily in adhering to safe food and drink guidelines.

Malaria: This disease is transmitted by the bite of various species of the female *Anopheles* mosquito, whose abundance and distribution vary widely from island to island. *Anopheles* mosquitoes (there are nine infective species) reside in nearly every type of habitat, including coastal brackish waters, mountain stream pools below 1,600 meters elevation, and ground pools in periurban areas. The is no risk of malaria in the big cities and the main resort areas of Java and Bali. Malaria risk is primarily in rural areas below 1,200 meters elevation. The highest rates of malaria are in Irian Jaya (the western half of the island of New Guinea), Sulawesi, Sumatra, Flores, and northern coastal Java. In some malarious areas, the infection rate approaches 75% of the populace. Falciparum malaria predominates 2:1 over vivax malaria in mountainous regions. Vivax malaria, however, is more common in low-lying rice-growing areas. *P. malariae* may cause 2%–5% of cases on some islands. Chloroquine- and Fansidar-resistant *P. falciparum* is widespread. Chloroquine-resistant *P. vivax* has been reported from Sumatra and Irian Jaya. The recommended drug prophylaxis for adult travelers going to malarious areas is mefloquine, 250 mg weekly, or doxycycline, 100 mg daily. In addition, all travelers to Indonesia, especially those going to malarious areas, should take precautions against mosquito bites. These precautions include applying a deet-containing skin repellent (e.g., Ultrathon), wearing permethrin-treated clothing, and if necessary, sleeping under a mosquito net which has also been treated (sprayed or impregnated) with permethrin.

Travelers' diarrhea: In resort areas, the hotels and restaurants generally serve reliable food and potable water. Elsewhere, travelers should strictly observe food and drink safety precautions. A quinolone antibiotic is recommended for the treatment of acute diarrhea. Diarrhea not responding to treatment with an antibiotic, or chronic diarrhea, may be due to a parasitic disease such as giardiasis or amebiasis, and treatment with metronidazole (Flagyl) or tinidazole (Fasigyn) should be considered. All cases of diarrhea should be treated with adequate fluid replacement.

Hepatitis: There is a high risk of hepatitis A in this country. All susceptible travelers should receive immune globulin or hepatitis A vaccine. Hepatitis E: Outbreaks are reported in West Kalimantan. The hepatitis B carrier rate in the general population is estimated to exceed 15%. Vaccination against hepatitis B is recommended for healthcare workers, corporate employees, expatriates, relief workers, teachers, and others who will have close contact with the indigenous population.

Typhoid fever: There is a relatively high risk of typhoid fever in Indonesia. Vaccination is recommended for all travelers staying in this country longer than 3–4 weeks, or traveling outside the usual tourist sites or resorts. All travelers should meticulously follow safe food and drink guidelines.

Dengue fever: Year-round risk, elevated from November through May–June. Risk is higher in urban and peri-urban areas. Outbreaks in peak years have involved millions of people. Dengue hemorrhagic fever (a severe form of the disease, usually associated with sequential infection by different dengue virus serotypes) is common. Dengue is transmitted by the bite of infective *Aedes* mosquitoes. Two species of *Aedes* mosquito can carry the virus—*Ae. aegypti* and *Ae. albopictus* (the Asian tiger mosquito). These mosquitoes are daytime biters with a short flight range. Prevention of dengue fever consists of taking protection measures against mosquito bites.

Japanese encephalitis: Cases of Japanese encephalitis occur throughout the Indonesian archipelago, but the risk of illness is generally low. The peak transmission period is from November through May or June (the monsoon season). Vaccination against Japanese encephalitis is recommended for travelers who will be staying in rural-agricultural endemic areas below 1,000 meters elevation for periods exceeding 4 weeks during the peak transmission season. In addition, all travelers should take personal protection measures against mosquito bites, especially in the evening when *Culex* mosquitoes, which transmit Japanese encephalitis, are most active.

Filariasis: Highly endemic. The Bancroftian and Malayan varieties of this disease are transmitted in both urban and rural environments. Travelers should take measures to prevent mosquito bites.

Schistosomiasis: Risk is present year-round in the Lindu and Napu Valleys of Sulawesi. Travelers to these areas should avoid swimming, bathing, or wading in freshwater lakes, ponds, or streams.

Rabies: Significant risk occurs in rural as well as urban areas of this country. All animal bites, but especially dog bites, should be considered a medical emergency. Pre-exposure vaccination against rabies (3 doses) is recommended for long-term travel to this country. This is especially true for travelers going to remote rural areas if they will be unable to receive antirabies treatment within 24 hours of exposure to a potentially rabid animal. Pre-exposure vaccination does not preclude the need for post-exposure treatment.

AIDS: Cases have been reported, but HIV testing is erratic, and HIV seroprevalence data are generally lacking.

Other diseases/health threats: Anthrax (usually associated with eating contaminated buffalo meat), brucellosis, capillariasis (from eating raw fish, especially fresh catch, crab, squid), echinococcosis, influenza (occurs countrywide; risk elevated in cities; vaccination advised for travelers over age 65), leprosy (highly endemic), leptospirosis, rabies, relapsing fever (tick-borne), scrub typhus (year-round in grassy, rural areas), syphilis, tuberculosis (highly endemic), soil-transmitted helminthic disease (ascariasis, trichuriasis, hookworm disease, strongyloidiasis), and yaws (decreasing, but still significant in Sumatra, Kalimantan, and Irian Jaya) are reported.

Animal hazards include snakes (kraits, cobras, pit vipers), spiders, scorpions, tarantulas, crocodiles, panthers, bears, wild pigs, and wild cattle. Stingrays, jellyfish, sea wasps, poisonous fish (multiple species), and the Indo-Pacific man-of-war are common in the country's coastal waters and are potential hazards to careless or unprotected swimmers.

LAOS

Vientiane ... GMT +7 hrs

Entry Requirements

- Passport/Visa: Passport and visa required. No tourist visas issued.
- AIDS Test: Not required.
- Vaccinations: A yellow fever vaccination certificate is required from all travelers arriving from infected areas or Endemic Zones.

  Cholera: The government of Laos may require a valid cholera vaccination certificate for entry. It is recommended that travelers have a cholera vaccination (1 dose) or a doctor's letter of exemption from vaccination.

Electricity/Plugs: AC 50 Hz, 220 volts; plug types A and C. Adaptors and transformer necessary for U.S.-made appliances.

Embassies/Consulates: U.S. Embassy, Vientiane. Rue Bartholonie; Tel. 2220/2357/2384. Canadian Embassy (Thailand); Tel. [66] (2) 234-1561.

Doctors/Hospitals: Mahosot Hospital, Vientiane (220 beds); capabilities well below Western standards.

Clinique Diplomatique. Tel. 3113/2390. Pakse Provincial Hospital (160 beds); capabilities well below Western standards.

Health Advisory

Note: Medical and dental capabilities in Laos are extremely limited; pharmaceuticals are in very short supply; water supplies are grossly contaminated in most areas.

Malaria: Risk is present countrywide, but is more prevalent in mountainous and rural areas than in the lowland plains or urban areas. There is no risk of malaria in Vientiane. *P. falciparum* accounts for up to 75% of cases in the mountainous and hilly areas. *P. vivax* accounts for most cases in the plains and peri-urban areas. Multidrug-resistant falciparum malaria is reported, especially near the border with Thailand. Mefloquine or doxycycline prophylaxis is recommended when traveling to malarious areas. Malaria prophylaxis and treatment regimes should be discussed with a travel medicine or infectious disease specialist.

Travelers' diarrhea: Piped water supplies countrywide are frequently untreated and may be grossly contaminated. Travelers should observe all food and drink safety precautions. A quinolone antibiotic (Cipro or Floxin) is recommended for the treatment of acute diarrhea. Diarrhea not responding to treatment with an antibiotic, or chronic diarrhea, may be due to a parasitic disease such as giardiasis or amebiasis—or an intestinal virus.

Hepatitis: There is a high risk of hepatitis A in this country. All susceptible travelers should receive immune globulin or hepatitis A vaccine. The hepatitis B carrier rate in the general population is estimated to exceed 10%. Vaccination against hepatitis B is recommended for healthcare workers, corporate employees, expatriates, relief workers, teachers, and others (including family members) who plan an extended visit to this country.

Typhoid fever: High endemicity. Vaccination is recommended.

Dengue fever: Peak infection rates occur in the late monsoon season. The *Aedes* mosquitoes, which transmit dengue fever, are more active during the daytime and are present in populous urban areas as well as rural areas. Prevention of dengue consists of taking protective measures against mosquito bites.

Japanese encephalitis: Sporadic cases occur throughout the year, except at high elevations. Vaccination is recommended for travelers planning an extended stay (more than 3–4 weeks) in rural-agricultural areas during the peak transmission season, June through October. Travelers should also take measures against mosquito bites.

Filariasis: Both the Bancroftian and Malayan varieties are highly endemic in rural and urban areas. Travelers should take personal protection measures against mosquito bites.

Schistosomiasis: Risk is present year-round. Focal distribution occurs along the Mekong River (including Vientiane), and in Louangphrabang and Champasak Provinces. Travelers should avoid swimming, bathing, or wading in freshwater rivers, lakes, ponds, or streams.

Helminthic infections: Soil-transmitted infections (caused by hookworms, roundworms, whipworms, strongyloides) are highly prevalent in most rural areas. Travelers should wear shoes (to prevent the hookworm and strongyloides larvae from penetrating the skin) and food should be thoroughly washed/cooked (to destroy roundworm and whipworm eggs).

Helminthic infections (flukes): Oriental lung fluke disease (paragonimiasis), and liver fluke diseases (clonorchiasis, fascioliasis) are prevalent. Travelers should avoid eating raw, salted, or wine-soaked crustacea (freshwater crabs or crayfish), or undercooked water vegetables and plants, such as watercress.

AIDS: HIV probably present, but not officially reported as of February 1991.

Other diseases/health threats: Anthrax, echinococcosis, leprosy (highly endemic), leptospirosis, melioidosis, plague, rabies, scrub typhus (mite-borne), syphilis, tuberculosis (highly endemic) are reported. Animal hazards include snakes (cobras, vipers), spiders (black and brown widow), tigers, leopards, and large leeches. Plant hazards: Bamboo, rattan, and large palm- or fern-like trees, which can cause serious puncture wounds and slow-healing lacerations, are widespread in the forested areas of the country. Regas are large forest trees whose black resinous sap can cause a potent poison ivy–type skin reaction. Stinging nettles, small thorny trees, and many species of euphorbs can also cause skin reactions.

MALAYSIA
Kuala Lumpur ... GMT +8 hrs

Entry Requirements
- Passport/Visa: A valid passport is required.
- AIDS Test: Not presently required.
- Vaccinations: A yellow fever vaccination certificate is required from all travelers older than 1 year arriving from infected areas. A certificate also required of any traveler arriving from any country in the Yellow Fever Endemic Zones.
  Cholera: a vaccination certificate may be required for travelers departing Malaysia for any country where cholera is endemic.

Telephone Country Code: 60

Electricity/Plugs: AC 50 Hz, 220 volts; frequency stable; plug type G. Adaptors and transformer necessary for U.S.-made appliances.

American Express: Mayflower Acme Tours. Mas Building, 5th Floor; Jln Sultan Ismail, Kuala Lumpur; Tel. (3) 248-9011.

Embassies/Consulates: U.S. Embassy, Kuala Lumpur. 376 Jalan Tun Razak; Tel. (3) 248-9011. Canadian High Commission, Kuala Lumpur. Plaza MBF, 7th Floor, 172 Jalan Ampang; Tel. (3) 261-2000.

Hospitals/Doctors: Subang Jaya Hospital, Kuala Lumpur (244 beds); some specialties; ICU; 24-hour emergency services; used by U.S. Embassy personnel; Tel. 734-1212. Tawakal Hospital; 24-hour emergency service; used by U.S. Embassy personnel. General Hospital, Kuala Lumpur (2,400 beds); used by U.S. Embassy only as an alternate to Subang or Tawakal Hospitals. David C. Williams, M.D., Kuala Lumpur; Tel. (3) 756-8496. Penang Adventist Hospital (400 beds); general medical/surgical facility; ICU; local Tel. (4) 373-344.

Health Advisory
Cholera: This disease is active. Endemic areas include Sabah, Penang, and Sarawak. Although cholera vaccination is not required for entry if arriving directly from the U.S. or Canada, it may be required if arriving from a cholera-infected area, or required for on-going travel to other countries in Latin America, Africa, the Middle East, or Asia. Travelers should consider vaccination (one dose) or a doctor's letter of exemption from vaccination. The risk to travelers of acquiring cholera is considered low. Prevention consists primarily in adhering to safe food and drink guidelines.

Malaria: Year-round risk, but the highest risk of transmission is from March through June–July in Sabah and Sarawak, and from October through December–January in peninsular Malaysia. Malaria risk is country-wide below 1,700 meters elevation, but is more prevalent in mountainous and rural areas than in lowland regions. Major foci include Perak and Pahang States (peninsular Malaysia) and Sabah and Sarawak States. Major metropolitan areas are considered malaria free. Falciparum malaria cases outnumber vivax malaria cases 2:1. Chloroquine- and Fansidar-resistant falciparum malaria reported. The recommended prophylaxis for adult travelers is mefloquine, 250 mg weekly, or doxycycline, 100 mg daily.

Hepatitis: All susceptible travelers should receive immune globulin or hepatitis A vaccine prior to visiting this country. The hepatitis B carrier rate in the general population is estimated at 5%. Vaccination against hepatitis B is recommended for all healthcare workers and should be considered by anyone planning an extended visit to this country. About 40% of cases of acute hepatitis are due to hepatitis C.

Japanese encephalitis: Sporadic cases occur throughout the year. Nearly all cases are in rural areas. Long-term travelers to rural areas should be vaccinated. All travelers should take personal protection measures against insect bites.

Dengue fever: Peak infection rates occur in the late monsoon season. Dengue hemorrhagic fever (a severe form of the disease) reported in those who have had one or more previous dengue infections. The *Aedes* mosquitoes transmitting dengue fever bite during the daytime and are present in populous urban areas as well as resort and rural areas. Prevention of dengue consists of preventing mosquito bites.

Filariasis: Malayan and Bancroftian filariasis occur. Moderate risk in rural areas. Travelers should take measures to prevent mosquito bites.

Schistosomiasis: Risk is present year-round in areas among the aboriginal Malays in Perak and Pahang States. Travelers to this area should avoid swimming or wading in snail-infested freshwater lakes, ponds, or streams in risk areas.

Other illnesses/hazards: Intestinal helminthic infections (ascariasis and hookworm disease are moderately endemic in urban and rural areas, especially in children), clonorchiasis and paragonimiasis, leptospirosis (countrywide risk, except in urban areas), rabies (presumably endemic; last reported in 1985), scrub typhus (mite-borne; risk elevated in grassy rural areas), tuberculosis (highly endemic), typhoid fever, and trachoma (highly endemic). Animal hazards include snakes (kraits, vipers, cobras), centipedes, scorpions, and black widow spiders. Other possible hazards include tigers, bears, and wild pigs.

Stingrays, sea wasps, cones, jellyfish, the Indo-Pacific man-of-war, spiny sea urchins, and anemones are common in the country's coastal waters and are potentially hazardous to unprotected or careless swimmers.

PHILIPPINES

Embassy: 202-483-1414　　　　*Manila*　　　　　　*GMT +8 hrs*

Entry Requirements

- Passport/Visa: A valid passport is required.
- AIDS Test: Applicants for permanent residence must be tested. Travelers should contact the Philippine Embassy for details.
- Vaccinations: A yellow fever vaccination certificate is required from all travelers older than 1 year arriving from infected areas or from any country in the Yellow Fever Endemic Zones.
  Cholera: A valid vaccination certificate may be required if arriving from an infected area.

Telephone Country Code: 63

Electricity/Plugs: AC 60 Hz, 110/220 volts; plug types A, B, C, D, and J.

American Express: PCI Travel Corporation. Philamlife Building, Ground Floor, Manila; Tel. (2) 521-9492.

Embassies/Consulates: U.S. Embassy, Manila. 1201 Roxas Boulevard; Tel. (2) 521-7116. U.S. Consulate, Cebu; Tel: 734-86. Canadian Embassy, Manila. Allied Bank Centre, 9th Floor; Tel. (2) 63676.

Hospitals/Doctors: Makati Medical Center, Manila (300 beds); most specialties; 24-hour ambulance and emergency services and ICU; Tel. (2) 853-311 or 853-344. University of Santo Tomas Hospital, Manila. Tel. (2) 269-116. Paulo C. Campos, M.D. (Int. Med.); Tel: 596-773/853-311/505-133.

Health Advisory

Cholera: This disease is active in this country. Travelers to this country should consider vaccination or a doctor's letter of exemption from vaccination.

Malaria: Year-round risk; highest malaria risk is on Luzon, Palawan, and Mindanao. Basilan, Mindoro, and Sulu Archipelago are also malarious areas. Risk may be elevated in foothill areas. Malaria is found only below 1,000 meters of elevation and is mostly transmitted in rural areas rarely visited by tourists. Most risk occurs during and just after the monsoon season, May through November. *P. falciparum* accounts for up to 63% of malaria. Chloroquine-resistant falciparum malaria is common. Mefloquine prophylaxis is advised for travel to risk areas. There is no malaria in Bohol, Catanduanes, Cebu, Leyte, the plains of the islands of Negros and Panay, the city of Manila, or other urban centers.

Travelers' diarrhea: High risk outside of first-class hotels and resorts. Metropolitan water supplies are erratic and may be contaminated. Travelers are advised to drink only bottled, boiled, filtered or treated water and consume only well-cooked food. All fruit should be peeled prior to consumption. A quinolone antibiotic (Floxin or Cipro) is recommended for the treatment of acute diarrhea. Diarrhea not responding to antibiotic treatment may be due to a parasitic disease such as giardiasis or amebiasis.

Hepatitis: Immune globulin or hepatitis A vaccine is recommended for all susceptible travelers. The hepatitis B carrier rate in the general population is estimated at 10%–12%. Vaccination against hepatitis B is recommended for healthcare workers and should be considered by long-term visitors to this country.

Japanese encephalitis: Moderate risk is present in Luzon and Mindanao, with high endemicity in extreme southern Luzon, Negros, Cebu, and the Catanduanes Island. Peak incidence is in the monsoon season. Vaccination against Japanese encephalitis is recommended for travelers who will be staying in rural-agricultural endemic areas for long periods (more than 4 weeks). In addition, all travelers should take personal protection measures against mosquito bites, especially in the evening.

Dengue fever: Occurs year-round; risk increased in urban areas. Peak infection rates occur during the monsoon season, June through December. The *Aedes* mosquitoes, which transmit dengue, bite during the daytime and are present in populous urban areas as well as resort and rural areas. Prevention of dengue consists of taking daytime protective measures against mosquito bites.

Filariasis: Bancroftian and Malayan forms of the disease are transmitted by mosquitoes in rural areas. Disease is endemic on Luzon, Leyte, Mindoro, Palawan, Samar, Mindanao, and Sulu. Travelers to these islands should take measures to prevent insect bites.

Schistosomiasis: Risk exists year-round. *S. japonicum* is distributed widely in southern Luzon, Leyte, Samar, Mindanao, and the east coast of Mindanao and Bohol Islands. All travelers to these areas should avoid swimming in freshwater lakes, ponds, or streams.

Rabies: About 200 human rabies cases a year are reported. Travelers should seek immediate treatment of any animal bite, especially those inflicted by a dog. Pre-exposure vaccination against rabies (3 doses) should be considered prior to long-term travel to this region.

Helminthic infections: Soil-transmitted infections (caused by hookworms, roundworms, strongyloides) are prevalent in most rural areas. Travelers should wear shoes (to prevent the hookworm and strongyloides larvae from penetrating the skin) and food should be thoroughly washed/cooked (to destroy roundworm eggs).

Other helminthic infections: Paragonimiasis (oriental lung fluke disease), fascioliasis, clonorchiasis (liver fluke disease), and gnathostomiasis are prevalent. Capillariasis and opisthorchiasis are endemic. Travelers should avoid eating raw freshwater fish and shellfish, wild watercress salad, or aquatic plants.

Other illnesses/hazards: Leptospirosis, Chikungunya fever, murine typhus (flea-borne), scrub typhus (mite-borne; risk elevated in grassy rural areas), tuberculosis (highly endemic), and typhoid fever. Animal hazards include snakes (cobras), centipedes, scorpions, and black widow spiders. Stingrays, jellyfish, nettles, sea cucumbers, sea wasps (potentially fatal), urchins, anemones, and the Indo-Pacific man-of-war are common in the country's coastal waters and are potentially hazardous to unprotected or careless swimmers.

SINGAPORE
Singapore ... GMT +8 hrs

Entry Requirements
- Passport/Visa: A valid passport is required. Travelers must have sufficient funds.
- AIDS Test: Not required.
- Vaccinations: A yellow fever vaccination certificate is required from all travelers older than 1 year arriving from any country any part of which is infected. A certificate is also required of any traveler arriving from countries in the Yellow Fever Endemic Zones.

Telephone Country Code: 65

Electricity/Plugs: AC 50 Hz, 220 volts; plug types C and G. Adaptors and transformer necessary for U.S.-made appliances.

American Express: American Express Travel Service. U01 Building, 96 Somerset Road, Singapore; Tel. 235-8133.

Embassies/Consulates: U.S. Embassy, Singapore. 30 Hill Street; Tel. 338-0251. Canadian High Commission, Singapore. 80 Anson Road; Tel. 255-6363.

Hospitals/Doctors: Mt. Elizabeth Hospital (485 beds); all specialties; emergency, burn, trauma units; considered one of the best hospitals in SE Asia; Tel. 737-2666.

Gleneagles Hospital (125 beds); some specialties; used by U.S. Embassy personnel; Tel. 63-7222. G. Caldwell, M.D. (general practice); Tel. 734-0618. Michael Yap, M.D. (neurology); Tel. 737-7066 or 469-0615 (home). Eddie Chang, M.D. (surgery); 235-8650 or 535-8833 (evenings).

Health Advisory

Cholera: This disease is active in this country. Although cholera vaccination is not required for entry if arriving directly from the U.S. or Canada, it may be required if arriving from a cholera-infected area, or required for on-going travel to other countries in Latin America, Africa, the Middle East, or Asia. Travelers should consider vaccination (one dose) or a doctor's letter of exemption from vaccination. The risk to travelers of acquiring cholera is low. Prevention consists primarily in adhering to safe food and drink guidelines.

Malaria: There is no risk of malaria in Singapore.

Travelers' diarrhea: Low risk. Tap water in Singapore is potable. A quinolone antibiotic is recommended for the treatment of acute diarrhea. Diarrhea not responding to antibiotic treatment may be due to a parasitic disease such as giardiasis or amebiasis—or an intestinal virus.

Hepatitis: Immune globulin or hepatitis A vaccine is recommended for all susceptible travelers. The hepatitis B carrier rate in the general population is estimated at 5%. Vaccination against hepatitis B is recommended for healthcare workers and should be considered by long-term visitors to this country.

Japanese encephalitis: Low risk, due to absence of breeding areas for the *Culex* mosquitoes. Vaccination against Japanese encephalitis is recommended only for travelers who will be staying in rural-agricultural endemic areas for long periods (more than 2-3 weeks). All travelers should take personal protection measures against mosquito bites, especially in the evening.

Dengue fever: Moderately endemic with seasonal outbreaks. Risk elevated from May through September, countrywide The disease is more common in urban areas where the *Aedes* mosquitoes breed in discarded containers. All persons should take daytime protective measures against mosquito bites. A vaccine is not available.

Filariasis: Both the Bancroftian and Malayan forms occur and are transmitted by a variety of mosquitoes. Travelers should take protective measures against insect bites.

Other diseases/hazards: Leptospirosis (low risk), helminthic infections (ascariasis, ancylostomiasis, hookworm, clonorchiasis, opisthorchiasis, and taeniasis; low endemicity), hemorrhagic fever with renal syndrome (a few cases reported), melioidosis (rare), and tuberculosis. Stingrays, poisonous fish, sea anemones, the Indo-China man-o'-war, and the very dangerous sea wasp are found along the coral reefs that fringe Singapore. Swimmers should take sensible precautions to avoid these hazards.

THAILAND

Entry Requirements

- Passport/Visa: A valid passport is required. Travelers must have evidence of sufficient funds.
- AIDS Test: "Those suspected of carrying AIDS" may be denied entry. Travelers should contact the Thai Embassy in Washington for further information and advice.
- Vaccinations: A yellow fever vaccination certificate is required of all travelers arriving from infected areas or from countries in the Yellow Fever Endemic Zones in Africa and South America.

Telephone Country Code: 66

Electricity/Plugs: AC 50 Hz, 220 volts; frequency stable; plug types A and C.

American Express: Sea Tours Company Ltd. 965 Ramal Road, Suite 413-414, Bangkok; Tel. (2) 251-4862.

Embassies/Consulates: U.S. Embassy, Bangkok. 95 Wireless Road; Tel. (2) 252-5040/5171. The American Embassy Regional Medical can assist with physician referrals. Canadian Embassy, Bangkok. Boonmitr Building, 11th Floor, 138 Silom Road; Tel. (2) 234-1561/8.

Hospitals/Doctors: Bangkok General Hospital & Heart Institute; most specialties; 24-hour physician-staffed emergency room; ICU; Tel. (2) 318-0066 to 0077. Ambulance. Tel. 318-0066. Phyathai Hospital (110 beds); 24-hour physician-staffed emergency services; often used by expatriates; Tel. 245-2621-8. Siriraj University Hospital, Bangkok (1,500 beds); extensive neurosurgical, cardiovascular, and trauma capability; Tel. 411-0241. Bumrungrad Medical Center (near Grace Hotel). This facility is fully equipped with CT, MRI, and lithotripser; Tel. 252-0570. Samitivej Hospital. This is a luxurious hospital located in an expatriate neighborhood; Tel. 392-0010 to 0011. McCormick Hospital, Chiang Mai; English spoken; hospital well set up to treat foreigners; Tel. 241-107.

Health Advisory

Malaria: This disease rarely occurs in people visiting the usual tourist sites in Thailand. There is no risk of malaria in Bangkok and other major urban areas (Chiangmai, Chiangrai) or the large coastal resort cities (Phuket, Pattaya, Haadya, and Sonkhla). Malaria is mostly eradicated from urban areas and the plains, but there is risk of malaria in the forested foothill areas, rubber plantations, and fruit orchards. The highest incidence of malaria has been reported from the border provinces (Mae Hong Son, Tak, Kanchanaburi, Trat, Chanthaburi, Rayong, Chumphon, Ratchaburi, Krabi, and Yala). There is no malaria in the rain forests immediately adjacent to Chiangmai, but trekkers venturing deeper into the foothills and rain forest or staying overnight in huts of hill tribes should take antimalarial prophylaxis and protect themselves against mosquito bites, especially between dusk and dawn when mosquito activity is highest. Major malaria risk areas include eastern and northeastern Thailand along the Thai-Cambodian border, and western and northwestern Thailand along the Thai-Burmese border. *Plasmodium falciparum* causes about 65% of malaria, *P. vivax* about 34%. *P. malariae* causes less than 1% of cases. There is a high incidence of multidrug-resistant falciparum malaria, especially in the forested border areas. *P. falciparum* resistance to standard treatment doses of mefloquine and halofantrine runs as high as 35%. Travelers to malarious areas should take doxycycline, 100 mg daily. The best alternative prophylactic regimen is proguanil, 200 mg daily, plus sulfisoxazole (Gantrisan), 2 gm daily. The current treatment of choice of falciparum malaria acquired in Thailand is a 7-day course of quinine plus tetracycline or clindamycin.

Travelers' diarrhea: Low to moderate risk. In urban and resort areas, the hotels and restaurants generally serve reliable food and potable water. Elsewhere, travelers should observe all food and drink safety precautions. A quinolone antibiotic is recommended for the treatment of acute diarrhea. Diarrhea not responding to antibiotic treatment may be due to a parasitic disease such as giardiasis or amebiasis—or an intestinal virus.

Hepatitis: Immune globulin or hepatitis A vaccine is recommended for all susceptible travelers. Hepatitis E is presumably endemic. The hepatitis B carrier rate in the general population is estimated at 10%. Vaccination against hepatitis B is recommended for healthcare workers as well as long-term visitors to this country.

Dengue fever: Highly endemic; peak infection rates occur in the late monsoon season. Dengue occurs more commonly in urban than in rural areas. Epidemics of this disease occur and dengue hemorrhagic fever is a protracted problem in Bangkok. The *Aedes* mosquitoes, which transmit dengue, bite during the daytime. Prevention of dengue consists of taking protective measures against mosquito bites.

Filariasis: Both the Malayan and Bancroftian varieties occur and are transmitted by mosquitoes. Filariasis is moderately endemic in rural areas.

Japanese encephalitis: Highly endemic, especially in the central and northern provinces; sporadic cases occur in the south. Elevated risk occurs in rural and periurban areas where pig farming and mosquito-breeding sites coexist. There is also risk of infection in the suburban areas of major cities. Vaccination against Japanese encephalitis is recommended for travelers who will be staying in rural-agricultural endemic areas longer than 2–3 weeks during the peak transmission season. In addition, all travelers should take personal protection measures against mosquito bites, especially in the evening. The Regional Medical Officer of the American Embassy currently recommends JE vaccination for all expatriate Americans.

Schistosomiasis: There is risk of schistosomiasis, albeit minimal. To be safe, travelers should avoid swimming or wading in freshwater lakes, ponds, or streams.

Rabies: There is a high incidence of dog rabies in Thailand and human cases are reported frequently. Rabies, however, is rare among tourists—but there is risk. Rabid, stray dogs are common in Bangkok as well as other urban and rural areas. No one should pet or pick up stray animals, especially dogs and cats. All children should avoid contact with unknown animals. Travelers to remote rural areas should be vaccinated if they will be unable to receive antirabies treatment within 24 hours of exposure to a potentially rabid animal such as a dog, a cat, or a monkey. The State Department recommends vaccination for all expatriate corporate employees and their families, especially the children. A rabies clinic is operated by the Queen Saovabha Institute/Thai Red Cross Society Hospital in Bangkok. Tel: (2) 252-6117.

AIDS: An explosive increase of HIV infection has occurred among prostitutes, of whom 20% or more are now seropositive. HIV is now being passed with much greater frequency into the heterosexual population and Thailand now has the highest AIDS rate in Southeast Asia. Blood used for transfusion in Thailand is checked for the AIDS virus. O-negative blood, however, is in short supply for travelers in need of an emergency transfusion.

Other illnesses/hazards: Anthrax (low endemicity; occurs in rural areas), capillariasis (associated with eating raw fish), Chikungunya fever (rare but intense, focal outbreaks occur; last outbreak in northeastern Thailand during 1988), gnathostomiasis (human cases associated with eating raw fish or poultry), helminthic infections (ascariasis, hookworm disease, and strongyloidiasis are highly endemic in urban and rural areas), leptospirosis, melioidosis, opisthorchiasis and clonorchiasis (liver fluke diseases; transmitted by raw seafood; travelers should especially avoid "Koi Pla"—uncooked freshwater fish), paragonimiasis (lung fluke disease; endemic in northern Thailand; travelers should avoid raw freshwater crabs), murine typhus (flea-borne), scrub typhus (mite-borne; risk elevated in brushy rural areas, but also reported from Bangkok; drug-resistant scrub typhus reported near Changmai), toxoplasmosis, tuberculosis (highly endemic), and typhoid fever. Animal hazards include snakes (kraits, vipers, cobras), centipedes, scorpions, and black widow spiders. Other possible hazards include tigers, leopards, crocodiles, pythons, poisonous toads and frogs, and large, aggressive lizards. Stingrays, jellyfish, and several species of poisonous fish (puffer, goblin, stone, toad, scorpion, pig, porcupine, and box fish) are common in the country's coastal waters and are potentially hazardous to unprotected or careless swimmers.

Accidents: Bangkok is sometimes called "the gridlock city" because of its chaotic traffic. The traffic is left hand (as in England) and there is a high incidence of accidents and pedestrian injury. All drivers should be alert, and seat belts should be worn at all times.

VIETNAM
Hanoi ... GMT +7 hrs

Entry Requirements
- Passport/Visa: Passport and visa are required.
- AIDS Test: Not required.
- Vaccinations: A yellow fever vaccination certificate is required of all travelers older than 1 year arriving from infected areas.

Electricity/Plugs: AC 50 Hz, 220 volts; frequency not stable, plug types unknown.

Embassies/Consulates: The U.S. government does not maintain diplomatic relations with Vietnam. U.S. passports are valid for travel to this country. Canadian High Commission (Thailand); Tel. [66] (2) 234-1561/8.

Doctors/Hospitals: Bach Mai Hospital, Hanoi (1,200 beds); general medical facility. Ho Chi Minh City Hospital (Saigon). Cho Ray Hospital. Czech Friendship Hospital, Haiphong.

Health Advisory
Cholera: This disease is active in this country. Although cholera vaccination is not required for entry if arriving directly from the U.S. or Canada, it may be required if arriving from a cholera-infected area, or required for on-going travel to other countries in Asia, Africa, Latin America, or the Middle East. Travelers to this country should consider vaccination or a doctor's letter of exemption from vaccination.

Malaria: Countrywide distribution, with attack rates highest in rural mountainous areas, followed by the central plains and the lowland deltas, respectively. Elevated risk occurs during the rainy season, May through October. Malaria risk in urban areas is low. *P. falciparum* causes 80% of cases. Vivax malaria is common in the delta and lowland regions of coastal and southern Vietnam. Chloroquine- and mefloquine-resistant falciparum malaria are reported. Mefloquine or doxycycline prophylaxis advised for travelers visiting malarious areas.

Travelers' diarrhea: All water supplies should be considered potentially contaminated. Travelers should observe food and drink safety precautions. A quinolone antibiotic is recommended for the treatment of diarrhea. Diarrhea not responding to treatment with an antibiotic, or chronic diarrhea, may be due to a parasitic disease such as giardiasis or amebiasis—or an intestinal virus.

Hepatitis: All susceptible travelers should receive immune globulin or hepatitis A vaccine prior to visiting this country. The hepatitis B carrier rate in the general population is estimated to exceed 10%. Hepatitis E presumably occurs but has not been reported.

Dengue fever: Occurs year-round, presumably countrywide, with peak transmission in the rainy season, May through October. Elevated risk occurs in urban areas. All travelers are advised to take precautions against mosquito bites.

Japanese encephalitis: Risk is present in rural and periurban lowland areas countrywide, with peak transmission during the monsoon season, especially June and July. Risk is year-round in the south. Travelers to rural areas should consider vaccination.

Schistosomiasis: Endemic status unknown. Risk may occur in rural, lowland, and delta areas. Travelers to these regions should avoid swimming or wading in freshwater lakes, ponds, streams, or irrigation ditches.

Other illnesses/hazards: Angiostrongyliasis (associated with ingestion of raw snails, slugs, or vegetables), helminthic infections (ascariasis, hookworm disease, strongyloidiasis); other helminthic infections (clonorchiasis, fasciolopsiasis, and paragonimiasis), filariasis (mosquito-borne; low to moderate risk), leptospirosis, leprosy (moderately high levels), melioidosis, plague (reported annually, especially from the central highlands), rabies (transmitted by feral dogs; highly enzootic in rural and urban areas), typhus (louse-borne and flea-borne), scrub typhus (mite-borne; risk elevated in grassy rural areas), tuberculosis (highly endemic), typhoid fever, and trachoma (widespread). Animal hazards include snakes (vipers, cobras, kraits), centipedes, scorpions, and black widow spiders. Other hazards include crocodiles, pythons, large, aggressive lizards, and poisonous frogs and toads, all abundant in and near swamps and rivers; tigers, leopards, bears, and wild pigs are found in the forested and hilly regions of the country. Stingrays, jellyfish, and several species of poisonous fish are common in the country's coastal waters and are potentially hazardous to swimmers.

DISEASE RISK SUMMARY
Japan, Korea, and Taiwan

Malaria: There is no risk of malaria in these countries.

Travelers' diarrhea: Low risk in Japan. Medium to high risk in Korea and Taiwan, especially in rural areas. In urban and resort areas, the first-class hotels and restaurants generally serve reliable food and potable water. Elsewhere, travelers should observe all food and drink safety precautions. A quinolone antibiotic (Floxin or Cipro) is recommended for the treatment of acute diarrhea. Diarrhea not responding to antibiotic treatment may be due to a parasitic disease such as giardiasis or amebiasis—or an intestinal virus.

Hepatitis: All susceptible travelers to these countries should receive immune globulin or hepatitis A vaccine. The hepatitis B carrier rate in the population of Japan is estimated at 2%. In Korea and Taiwan the hepatitis B carrier rate is much higher, 9%–20%. Vaccination against hepatitis B is recommended for all healthcare workers and is recommended for anyone planning an extended visit to these countries, especially Taiwan or Korea.

Dengue fever: A large outbreak of dengue occurred in Taiwan in 1987 after a 40-year absence. Ten thousand more cases were reported in 1988. There is minimal risk of dengue in Japan and Korea. The *Aedes* mosquitoes, which transmit dengue, bite primarily during the daytime and are present in populous urban areas as well as resort and rural areas. All travelers are advised to take precautions against mosquito bites. These precautions include applying a deet-containing skin repellent, wearing permethrin-treated clothing and, if necessary, sleeping under a mosquito bed net, also treated with permethrin.

Japanese encephalitis (JE): Low level of disease activity occurs in rural and peri-urban areas of Taiwan. Unvaccinated travelers to rural rice-growing areas of Japan and Korea may also be at slight risk. No cases of JE have been reported from Seoul, Korea. Vaccination against Japanese encephalitis is recommended for travelers who will be staying in rural-agricultural endemic areas longer than 2–3 weeks during the peak JE transmission season. In addition, all travelers to risk areas should take measures to prevent mosquito bites.

Filariasis: There is a low risk of filariasis in Korea. Travelers to the southern provinces should take measures to prevent mosquito bites.

Helminths: Paragonimiasis (oriental lung fluke disease), clonorchiasis and fascioliasis (liver fluke diseases), and fasciolopsiasis (giant intestinal fluke disease) occur in these countries. Capillariasis is reported from Taiwan. To prevent these diseases, travelers should avoid eating uncooked aquatic plants, such as watercress and water chestnuts, and avoid raw or undercooked fish, crabs, crayfish or other shellfish. (Ke Jang, raw crab in soy sauce, is a common source of paragonimiasis in Korea.) Other helminthic infections (ascariasis, trichuriasis, hookworm disease) may occur in rural areas.

Other illnesses/hazards: Angiostrongyliasis, anisakiasis (transmitted by raw fish; widely distributed in Japan), hemorrhagic fever with renal syndrome (low risk; transmission of hantavirus through airborne dust particles contaminated with rodent excreta is presumed; farmers and outdoor workers at higher risk), viral influenza ("flu" shot recommended), Kawasaki disease (Japan, Korea), Lyme disease (cases reported from Japan), leptospirosis, echinococcosis, rabies (occasional cases reported from Korea), murine typhus (flea-borne; reported rarely in Korea), scrub typhus (mite-borne; risk present in grassy rural areas), tuberculosis (higher rates in Korea), typhoid fever, and trachoma (highly endemic). Portuguese man-of-war, octopuses, stingrays, jellyfish, sea cones, sea wasps, occur in the coastal waters of Japan and, to some extent, Taiwan. Many species of poisonous fish (rabbit fish, peacock sole, scorpion fish, zebrafish, Japanese stingfish, spiny dogfish, sturgeonfish, and puffer fish) can inflict painful stings and even fatalities and pose a potential threat to careless or unprotected swimmers. Sea nettles, cucumbers, bristleworms, and urchins are also potential hazards.

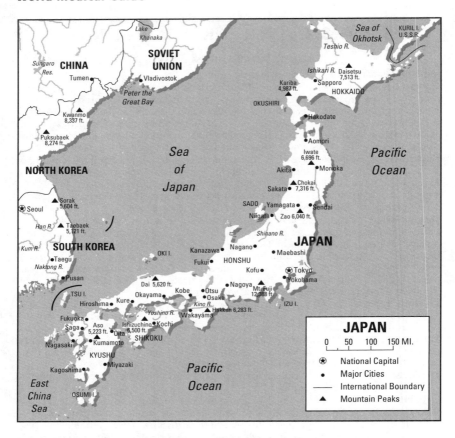

JAPAN

Embassy: 202-939-6800   *Tokyo*   ***GMT +9 hrs***

Entry Requirements
- Passport/Visa: A passport is required. Travelers should obtain tourist card or visa prior to arrival.
- AIDS Test: A 1988 AIDS prevention measure barred entry of HIV-infected foreigners and authorized mandatory testing of those seeking entry who are suspected of being HIV positive.
- Vaccinations: None required.

Telephone Country Code: 81

Electricity/Plugs: AC 50, 60 Hz, 100/200 volts; plug types A, B, and I.

American Express: American Express Travel Service: Ginza 4-Star Building: 4-1 Ginza 4-Chome, Tokyo; Tel. (3) 564-4381.

Embassies/Consulates: U.S. Embassy, Tokyo. 10-1 Alaska 1-Chome; Tel. (33) 224-5000. U.S. Consulate, Osaka; Tel. (6) 315-5900. U.S. Consulate, Sapporo; Tel. (11) 641-1115. U. S. Consulate, Fukuoka; Tel. (092) 751-9331. Canadian Embassy, Tokyo. 3-38 Akasaka, 7-Chome; Tel. (33) 408-2101.

Hospitals/Doctors:
National Hospital Medical Center, Tokyo (1,000 beds); all specialties; 24-hour emergency services; Tel. (03) 202-7181.

St. Luke's International Hospital, Tokyo (359 beds); primary facility for foreign tourists; Tel. (3) 541-5151.
National Nagoya Hospital; most specialties; Tel. (052) 951-1111.
Osaka University Hospital (1,011 beds); most specialties; Tel. (6) 451-0051.
Alan Fair, M.D., John Marshall, M.D., Tokyo Med. & Surg. Clinic; Tel. (33) 436-3028.
Shiun Dong Hsieh, M.D., Tokyo; Tel. (33) 583-2675 or 833-1452 (H).
Beverly Tucker, M.D., Kyoto; Tel. (75) 231-5663.
Sakabe International Clinic, Kyoto; Tel. (075) 231-1624.
Kobe Kasai Hospital; Tel. (078) 871-5201.

Health Advisory

Malaria: There is no risk of malaria in Japan.

Travelers' diarrhea: Low risk. Nearly all areas of Japan are supplied with potable water. Many water treatment facilities, however, are in need of modernization. Travelers should drink bottled or treated water unless sure of the potability of water from a particular source. A quinolone antibiotic (Cipro or Floxin) is recommended for the treatment of diarrhea. Diarrhea not responding to antibiotic treatment may be due to a parasitic disease such as giardiasis or amebiasis—or an intestinal virus.

Hepatitis: There is a generally low risk of hepatitis A, which affects less than 1% of people under 25 years of age. All susceptible travelers, however, should consider receiving immune globulin or the hepatitis A vaccine. The hepatitis B carrier rate in the general population is estimated at 2%. Vaccination is recommended for healthcare workers and people planning an extended stay in this country.

Japanese encephalitis: Due to a widespread vaccination program in Japan and modernization of agricultural methods, this disease is under control. Fewer than 100 cases/year are reported. Unvaccinated foreigners, however, are at potential risk of illness in rural-agricultural pig farming areas where infective *Culex* mosquitoes are active. Vaccination against Japanese encephalitis is recommended for persons who will be staying in rural-agricultural endemic areas for 2–3 weeks, or longer, during the peak transmission period, May through September. Unvaccinated travelers to rural areas should take personal protection measures against mosquito bites, especially in the evening.

Schistosomiasis: Low risk; a small focus of transmission exists in the Obitsu River Basin of the central Bosu peninsula. Schistosomiasis is not reported elsewhere.

Lyme disease: This disease is present countrywide in Japan, but the incidence is low. Hikers and forest workers, however, are frequently bitten by ticks. The dominant species of ticks are *Ixodes persulcatus* and *Ixodes ovatus*. The prevalence of Lyme disease spirochetes (*Borrelia burgdorferi*) in these tick species is estimated at 16.6% and 23.6%, respectively. Travelers to wooded, brushy, or forested areas should take measures to prevent tick bites.

Helminthic diseases: Paragonimiasis (lung fluke disease) is reported. To prevent this disease, all travelers should avoid eating raw crab or crayfish or the juice of raw crabs or crayfish. Clonorchiasis (an infection of the biliary tract by the Chinese liver fluke) occurs in this country. Clonorchiasis is transmitted by raw fish, such as sashimi, and pickled fish in vinegar (sunomono). Prevention is through thorough cooking or freezing of all freshwater fish prior to consumption. Fasciolopsiasis (giant intestinal fluke disease) is reported in Japan. Prevention is through the thorough cooking of all aquatic plants and vegetables prior to consumption. Raw fish, consumed as sushi or sashimi, is a potential source of intestinal parasites, including fish tapeworms and fish roundworms. Fish such as cod, haddock, herring, and salmon are the most common sources of these worms. Consumption of raw fish, or fish that has been insufficiently cooked, smoked, salted, or marinated, may lead to one of several conditions involving infection of the intestine. One such disease, anisakiasis, is transmitted most often by contaminated raw salmon or Pacific red snapper. Although the sushi bars in Japan are strictly regulated, consumption of raw fish is not without some risk. Each traveler must decide to what extent they wish to be exposed to this potential risk.

Other illnesses/hazards: Angiostrongyliasis (occurs mostly in the southwest islands, including Kyushu), soil-transmitted intestinal helminthic infections (trichuriasis; low endemicity in rural areas), echinococcosis (reported in Hokkaido), Kawasaki disease, scrub typhus (mite-borne; risk elevated in grassy rural areas), tuberculosis (endemic), and typhoid fever.

NORTH KOREA

Pyongyang ... GMT +9 hrs

Entry Requirements

- Passport/Visa: Passport and visa are required. Travelers should contact the Treasury Department in Washington at 202-376-0236 for travel information. Dual nationals should contact the Office of Citizens Consular Affairs at 202-647-3675. The United States does not maintain diplomatic, consular, or trade relations with North Korea. No third country represents U.S. interests in North Korea.
- AIDS Test: Not required.
- Vaccinations: None required.

SOUTH KOREA

Embassy: 202-939-5600   *Seoul*   **GMT +9 hrs**

Entry Requirements

- Passport/Visa: Passport required. Tourist card and visa can be obtained on arrival.
- AIDS Test: Required for stays over 90 days by foreigners working as entertainers.
- Vaccinations: None required.

Telephone Country Code: 82

Electricity/Plugs: AC 60 Hz, 220 volts; frequency stable; plug types A and F.

American Express: Global Tours Han. Young Building, 57-9 Seosomun-Dong, Chung-Ku, Seoul; Tel. (2) 323-0131.

Embassies/Consulates: U.S. Embassy, Seoul. 82 Chongro-Ku; Tel. (2) 732-2601/8.

Hospitals/Doctors: International Clinic, Seoul. Tel. (2) 796-1871. Catholic Medical Center; Tel. (2) 593-6121 or 593-7349.

Health Advisory

Travelers' diarrhea: Medium to high risk outside of first-class hotels and resorts. Travelers are advised to drink only bottled, boiled, filtered, or treated water and consume only well-cooked food. All fruit should be peeled prior to consumption. A quinolone antibiotic is recommended for the treatment of acute diarrhea. Diarrhea not responding to antibiotic treatment may be due to a parasitic disease such as giardiasis or amebiasis.

Hepatitis: All susceptible travelers should receive immune globulin or hepatitis A vaccine prior to visiting this country. The hepatitis B carrier rate in the general population is estimated at 6%–9%. Vaccination against hepatitis B is recommended for all healthcare workers and should be considered by anyone planning an extended visit to this country.

Dengue fever: Low apparent risk. The *Aedes* mosquitoes, which transmit dengue, bite primarily during the daytime and are present in populous urban areas, as well as resort and rural areas. Travelers should take protective measures against mosquito bites.

Japanese encephalitis (JE): Risk is present, but at very low levels. There is no risk of JE in Seoul. Cases of Japanese encephalitis have been reported in the southwest, during the transmission season, June through October. Vaccination is recommended for travelers who will be staying in rural-agricultural endemic areas longer than 2–3 weeks during the peak transmission season. All travelers to rural areas should take measures to prevent mosquito bites.

Helminthic infections: Ascariasis and hookworm disease are endemic in urban and rural areas. Fascioliasis, fasciolopsiasis, paragonimiasis, and clonorchiasis are also prevalent. Travelers should avoid eating uncooked water plants and raw or undercooked seafood and shellfish, including Ke Jang (raw crab in soy sauce).

Other illnesses/hazards: Anthrax (occurs sporadically in rural areas), filariasis (Malayan variety; mosquito-borne; moderately endemic in southern provinces), Kawasaki disease, leptospirosis, rabies (occurs infrequently), murine typhus (flea-borne), scrub typhus (mite-borne; risk elevated in grassy rural areas), tuberculosis (highly endemic), typhoid fever, and acute hemorrhagic conjunctivitis. Animal hazards include centipedes and black widow spiders. Tigers, leopards, lynxes, bears, and wild boars may be encountered in remote areas.

TAIWAN

Taipei ... GMT +8 hrs

Entry Requirements

- Passport/Visa: A valid passport is required. A visa is no longer necessary.
- AIDS Test: Required for those staying more than 3 months.
- Vaccinations: A yellow fever vaccination certificate is required from all travelers older than 1 year arriving from infected or endemic areas.

Telephone Country Code: 886

Electricity/Plugs: AC 60 Hz, 120 volts; frequency stable; plug types A, B, and I.

American Express: American Express Travel Service. Tun Hwa Financial Building, 214 Tun Hua North Road, Taipei; Tel. (2) 719-0808.

Embassies/Consulates: The American Institute (embassy). Hsin Yi Road, Section 3, Taipei; Tel. (2) 708-4151.

Hospitals/Doctors: Taiwan Adventist Hospital, Taipei; used by American Institute (Embassy) personnel; Tel. 771-8151. National Taiwan University Hospital, Taipei (1,000 beds); general medical/surgical facility; Tel. 312-3456.

Health Advisory

Malaria: There is no risk of malaria on Taiwan.

Travelers' diarrhea: Medium to high risk outside of first-class hotels and resorts. Travelers are advised to drink only bottled, boiled, filtered, or treated water, and consume only well-cooked food. All fruit should be peeled prior to consumption. A quinolone antibiotic is recommended for the treatment of acute diarrhea. Diarrhea not responding to antibiotic treatment may be due to a parasitic disease such as giardiasis, amebiasis or cryptosporidiosis.

Hepatitis: All susceptible travelers should receive immune globulin or hepatitis A vaccine prior to visiting this country. The hepatitis B carrier rate in the general population is estimated at 15%–20%. Vaccination against hepatitis B is recommended for all healthcare workers and anyone planning an extended visit to this country.

Dengue fever: Large outbreak reported in 1988, and sporadic cases continue to occur. The incidence of dengue is higher in the southern and eastern parts of Taiwan, especially in Kaohsiung County and Kao-hsiung City. The *Aedes* mosquitoes which transmit dengue fever are most active during the daytime in populous urban areas, as well as resort and rural areas. Prevention of dengue consists of taking protective measures against mosquito bites.

Japanese encephalitis (JE): Risk is present at low levels in rural and peri-urban areas. Peak transmission period of Japanese encephalitis is May through October. Vaccination is recommended for travelers who will be staying in rural-agricultural endemic areas longer than 3–4 weeks, especially during the peak transmission season. In addition, all travelers should take measures to prevent mosquito bites.

Helminthic diseases: Fasciolopsiasis, paragonimiasis, and clonorchiasis are reported. Travelers should avoid eating uncooked water plants and raw or undercooked freshwater fish and shellfish.

Other illnesses/hazards: Angiostrongyliasis (associated with ingesting raw seafood, snails, vegetables), filariasis (endemic on the Pescadores, Kinmen, and Matsu Islands), hookworm disease, scrub typhus (mite-borne; risk is countrywide; transmitted primarily in mountainous wooded or grassy areas and the Pescadores Islands), tuberculosis (highly endemic), typhoid fever, and acute hemorrhagic conjunctivitis. Animal hazards include snakes (coral, krait, viper), centipedes, scorpions, and black widow spiders. Several species of poisonous fishes (stone, puffer, scorpion, zebra), as well as jellyfish, anemones, nettles, urchins, and sea cucumbers are found in the coastal waters around Taiwan and are potential hazards to swimmers.

DISEASE RISK SUMMARY

Australia, New Zealand, Papua N. Guinea & Oceania

(Oceania = The Islands of Polynesia, Micronesia, and Melanesia)

Malaria: This disease occurs only in Papua New Guinea, the Solomon Islands, and Vanuatu. Falciparum malaria predominates over vivax approximately 2:1. Chloroquine- and multi-drug-resistant *P. falciparum* malaria occurs. The recommended antimalarial prophylaxis for adult travelers is mefloquine, 250 mg weekly, except in Papua New Guinea where doxycycline, 100 mg daily, is recommended. Chloroquine-resistant *P. vivax* has been reported from Papua New Guinea. There is no risk of malaria in Australia, New Zealand, or the other islands of Polynesia, Micronesia, or Melanesia.

Cholera: Reported active in Tuvalu. Although cholera vaccination is not required for entry if arriving directly from the U.S. or Canada, it may be required if arriving from a cholera-infected area, or required for on-going travel to other countries in Latin America, Africa, the Middle East, or Asia. Travelers to this country should consider vaccination (one dose) or a doctor's letter of exemption from vaccination. The risk to travelers of acquiring cholera is considered low. Prevention consists primarily in following safe food and drink guidelines.

Travelers' diarrhea: Low risk in Australia and New Zealand. Moderate risk in French Polynesia. Higher risk in the Solomon Islands, Vanuatu, and Micronesia. Most risk occurs outside of first-class hotels and resorts. Travelers are best advised to drink only bottled, boiled, filtered, or treated water and consume only well-cooked food. All fruit should be peeled prior to consumption. A quinolone antibiotic is recommended for the treatment of acute diarrhea. Diarrhea not responding to antibiotic treatment may be due to a parasitic disease such as giardiasis or amebiasis—or an intestinal virus. Amebiasis and giardiasis are more common to the Solomon Islands, Kiribati, Vanuatu, and Micronesia, and less common in Fiji and the French Territories.

Hepatitis: All travelers to Papua New Guinea and Oceania who may be susceptible to hepatitis A should receive immune globulin or hepatitis A vaccine. The hepatitis B carrier rate in Oceania is estimated as high as 15%. Vaccination against hepatitis B is recommended for healthcare workers and should be considered by others planning an extended visit to Papua New Guinea or Oceania. There is a low risk of hepatitis in Australia and vaccination is not routinely recommended.

Typhoid fever: Typhoid outbreaks occurred in Vanuatu in 1987 and in Fiji in 1985. Travelers should consider typhoid vaccination prior to travel to these countries. Typhoid vaccination is also advised when traveling to any area with sub-standard sanitation outside the usual tourist routes. Typhoid is best prevented by strict adherence to safe food and drink guidelines.

Dengue fever: Sporadic cases and epidemics occur in nearly all of the island groups of the South Pacific. Dengue is also reported in Northern Queensland (Australia). Peak infection rates occur during the rainy season months, December–January and May–June. Prevention of dengue consists of taking protective measures against mosquito bites.

Filariasis: Bancroftian filariasis occurs in the Solomon Islands and Vanuatu; aperiodic Malayan filariasis is widespread in the rest of Oceania. Up to 19% prevalence has been reported in French Polynesia. Travelers should take personal protection measures against mosquito bites.

AIDS: A small number of AIDS cases and HIV infections have been reported from various areas. At the present, AIDS is not considered a major public health problem in Australia, New Zealand, or Oceania.

Other illnesses/hazards: Angiostrongyliasis, brucellosis, and echinococcosis occur at low levels; scrub typhus occurs in the Solomon Islands and Vanuatu. Hookworm disease, round-worm disease, strongyloidiasis, and other helminthic infections are reported throughout Oceania. Tuberculosis (moderately endemic), trachoma, and yaws are reported (Oceania). Corals, jelly fish, poisonous fish, sharks, and sea snakes are a potential hazard to bathers.

AUSTRALIA

Entry Requirements

- Passport/Visa: Passport required.
- AIDS Test: Required of all applicants for permanent residence age 15 or over. All other applicants who require medical examinations are tested if it is indicated on clinical grounds. Testing may be required of long-term temporary residents who are deemed at high risk of HIV infections.
- Vaccinations: A yellow fever vaccination certificate is required if arriving from any country any part of which is infected, or has been infected, during the past 10 years.

Telephone Country Code: 61

Electricity/Plugs: AC 50 Hz, 220 volts; frequency stable; plug type I. Adaptors and transformer necessary for U.S.-made appliances.

American Express: American Express Travel Service. Centre Point, GPOB 153, City Walk & Petrie Plaza, Canberra; Tel. (62) 47-2333.

Embassies/Consulates: U.S. Embassy, Canberra. Moonah Place; Tel. (62) 70-5000. U.S. Consulate, Sydney; Tel. 264-7044. U.S. Consulate, Melbourne; Tel. 699-2244. U.S. Consulate, Perth; Tel. 322-4466. U.S. Consulate, Brisbane; Tel. 839-8955. Canadian High Commission, Canberra. Commonwealth Avenue; Tel. (62) 73-3844.

Doctors/Hospitals: Royal Melbourne Hospital (702 beds); most specialties and diagnostic capabilities; emergency services; Tel. (03) 347-7111. Traveller's Medical and Vaccination Centre, Melbourne; Tel. 650-7600. Royal Prince Alfred Hospital, Sydney (1,532 beds); most specialties and diagnostic capabilities; emergency services; ICU; Tel. (02) 516-6111. Traveller's Medical and Vaccination Centre, Sydney; Tel. 221-7133. Royal Darwin Hospital (648 beds); most specialties and diagnostic capabilities; emergency services. Royal Perth Hospital (1,072 beds); ICU, CCU, burn unit; 24-hour emergency; ambulance service; Tel. (09) 325-0101. Traveller's Medical and Vaccination Centre, Perth; Tel. (09) 321-1977. Queen Elizabeth Hospital, Adelaide (Travel Clinic); Tel. 347-0296. Princess Alexandra Hospital, Brisbane (1,104 beds); many specialties; emergency and ambulance services; Tel. (07) 240-2111.

Health Advisory

Malaria: No risk.

Yellow fever: No risk. To avoid entry delays, vaccination is recommended if any traveler arriving from any country in the Yellow Fever Endemic Zones.

Travelers' diarrhea: Low risk. Water in major cities and urban areas is potable. Hotels and restaurants generally serve reliable food and potable water. Water in rural areas and settlements may be of lower quality and may not meet strict standards of purification. A quinolone antibiotic (Floxin or Cipro) is recommended for the treatment of acute diarrhea.

Hepatitis A: Low risk. Susceptible travelers should consider immune globulin or hepatitis A vaccination. Immune globulin prophylaxis is not routinely recommended.

Hepatitis B: Low risk. The carrier rate of the hepatitis B virus in the general population is 0.05–0.1 percent. Vaccination against hepatitis B is not routinely recommended.

Dengue fever: Reported in parts of Northern Queensland and Torres Strait Islands. Areas of greatest risk are along the coast from Cornavon to Port Darwin to Townsville. Peak infection rates occur during October to March–April. The *Aedes* mosquitoes, which transmit dengue fever, bite during the daytime and are present in populous urban areas as well as resort and rural areas. Prevention of dengue consists of taking protective measures against mosquito bites.

Viral encephalitis: Outbreaks of Ross River fever and Australian encephalitis (caused by the Murray Valley encephalitis virus) occur annually. Highest attack rates occur in the summer and fall (November–May), especially after periods of heavy rainfall. Most cases reported from Western Australia (tropical Kimberly region in the north of Western Australia), Victoria, and South Australia. A small number of cases occur in the Northern Territory. Viral encephalitis is transmitted by *Culex* and *Aedes* mosquitoes. Travelers should take mosquito bite precautions to reduce the risk of illness.

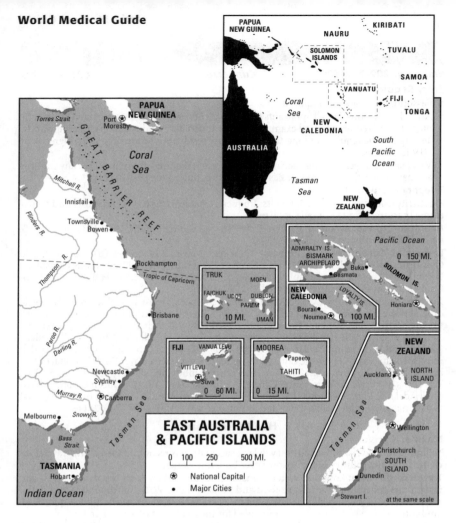

Other illnesses/hazards: Brucellosis (from consumption of raw dairy products; low ende-micity in rural areas), Barmah forest disease (mosquito-borne viral disease; occurs rarely, mostly in wet years), AIDS (1–5% of prostitutes in Sydney are HIV positive), leptospirosis, Q fever (associated with occupational animal contact), scrub typhus (occurs in northeast Queensland in rain forest areas of high humidity; a new focus has been reported in Litchfield Park in the Northern Territory), and helminthic infections (especially hookworm disease). Animal hazards include snakes (death adder, Australian copperhead, Australian coral, and others), centipedes and scorpions, and spiders (red back, northern funnel-web, mouse, and brown recluse). Fresh- and saltwater crocodiles occur in Australia, but only the saltwater va-riety has been known to attack humans. Male platypuses can inflict painful puncture wounds and should be avoided. Rogue scrub cattle (domestic animals gone wild) are particularly dan-gerous terrestrial animals and have been known to attack humans and vehicles without provocation. The box jellyfish, the most dangerous jellyfish in the world, and also the sea wasp, are found in northern coastal waters. Four other varieties of jellyfish (jimble, irukandji, mauve stinger, and hairy stinger) should also be avoided. Other hazards including sharks, stingrays, and poisonous cone shells are potential hazards in the coastal waters surrounding Australia. Swimmers should take sensible precautions to avoid these hazards.

CHRISTMAS ISLAND (AUSTRALIA)

GMT +7 hrs

Entry Requirements

- Passport/Visa: A passport is required.
- Vaccinations: Same requirements as Australia.
- AIDS tests: Same requirements as Australia.

Health Advisory

Malaria: No risk.

Travelers' diarrhea: Low risk, but travelers advised to drink bottled or treated water. A quinolone antibiotic (Cipro or Floxin) is recommended for the treatment of diarrhea. Diarrhea not responding to antibiotic treatment may be due to a parasitic disease such as giardiasis or amebiasis—or a virus.

Dengue fever: Low risk. Prevention of dengue consists of taking protective measures against mosquito bites.

COOK ISLANDS (NEW ZEALAND)

Avarua, Rorotonga ... GMT -10½ hrs

Entry Requirements

- Passport/Visa: Passport required.
- AIDS Test: Not required.
- Vaccinations: None required.

Telephone Country Code: 682

Electricity/Plugs: AC 50 Hz, 230 volts; plug type I. Adaptors and transformer necessary for U.S.-made appliances.

Embassies/Consulates: There are no local embassies. The U.S. Embassy in Wellington, New Zealand, has jurisdiction.

Hospitals/Doctors: General Hospital (89 beds); general medical facility; x-ray, laboratory, pharmacy; Tel. 22-664. Tupapa Outpatient Clinic, Avarua. Hours are 8am-4pm Mon-Fri and 8-11am on Saturday.

Health Advisory

Malaria: No risk.

Travelers' diarrhea: Low to medium risk. Tap water on Rarotonga is generally safe to drink. (Most hotels have filtration systems.) Tap water on Aitutaki is not considered safe and travelers are advised to consume only bottled, boiled, or treated water. All fruit should be peeled prior to consumption. A quinolone antibiotic (Floxin or Cipro) is recommended for the treatment of acute diarrhea. Diarrhea not responding to antibiotic treatment may be due to a parasitic disease such as giardiasis or amebiasis—or an intestinal virus.

Hepatitis: Immune globulin or hepatitis A vaccine is recommended for all susceptible travelers. The hepatitis B carrier rate in the general population is estimated at 10%. Vaccination against hepatitis B is recommended for healthcare workers and should be considered by long-term visitors to this country.

Dengue fever: This disease is active. The mosquitoes that transmit dengue (*Aedes aegypti*) bite primarily during the daytime. All travelers should take measures to prevent insect bites.

Ross River fever: This mosquito-transmitted viral illness occurs in periodic epidemics. Travelers should take protective measures against insect bites.

Filariasis: The Malayan variety of filariasis is reported. Travelers should take protective measures against mosquito bites.

Japanese encephalitis: Vaccination against Japanese encephalitis is recommended for travelers who will be staying in rural-agricultural endemic areas for long periods (more than several weeks). All travelers should take protective measures against mosquito bites, especially in the evening.

FIJI
Suva

Entry Requirements
- Passport/Visa: Travelers can obtain visa or tourist card on arrival. Travelers must have sufficient funds for stay.
- AIDS Test: Not required.
- Vaccinations: A yellow fever vaccination certificate is required of travelers arriving from infected or endemic areas.

Telephone Country Code: 679

Electricity/Plugs: AC 50 Hz, 240 volts; plug type I. Adaptors and transformer necessary for U.S.-made appliances.

American Express: Tapa Intl. Ltd. ANZ building. 25 Victoria Parade, Suva; Tel. 302-333.

Embassies/Consulates: U.S. Embassy, Suva. 31 Loftus St; Tel. 314-466, 314-069. Canadian Consulate, Suva. 50 Thompson Street; Tel. 311-844.

Hospitals/Doctors: Gordon Street Medical Center, Suva; Tel. 313-131 or 313-355.
Colonial War Memorial Hospital, Suva (376 beds); emergency room, x-ray, pharmacy; Tel. 31-3444. Dr. Ram Raju, Nadi; Tel. 599-765. Dr. Joel Taoi, Savusavu; Tel. 850346.

Health Advisory

Travelers' diarrhea: Urban areas of Fiji have some water treatment facilities, but most water should be considered potentially contaminated. Travelers are advised to drink only bottled or treated water. Food and milk are considered safe. A quinolone antibiotic (Cipro or Floxin) is recommended for the treatment of acute diarrhea.

Hepatitis: Immune globulin or hepatitis A vaccine is recommended for all susceptible travelers. The hepatitis B carrier rate in the general population is estimated at 10%. Vaccination against hepatitis B is recommended for healthcare workers and should be considered by long-term visitors to this country.

Typhoid fever: An outbreak occurred in 1985. Vaccination is recommended for those travelers on extended visit (more than 4 weeks) to this country.

Dengue fever: Increased risk during the rainy season months, December-January and May-June. Travelers should take precautions to avoid mosquito bites.

Ross River fever: Mosquito-transmitted viral illness occurs in periodic epidemics.

Filariasis: Malayan filariasis occurs year-round. Travelers should take precautions against mosquito bites.

FRENCH POLYNESIA
Papeete ... GMT -10 hrs

Entry Requirements
- Passport/Visa: Valid passport required. Visas are issued on arrival.
- AIDS Test: Not required.
- Vaccinations: A yellow fever vaccination certificate is required of travelers arriving from infected areas.

Telephone Country Code: 689

Electricity/Plugs: AC 50 Hz, 220 volts. Adaptors and transformer necessary for U.S.-made appliances.

American Express: Tahiti Tours. Rue Jeanne d'Arc, Papeete; Tel. 427-870.

Embassies/Consulates: The nearest U.S. embassy is in Auckland, New Zealand.

Hospitals/Doctors: Mamao Territory Hospital (400 beds); emergency room; x-ray. Jean Prince Hospital (140 beds); emergency room; burn unit; ambulance service. Clinique Cardella, Rue Anne Marie Javouhey; Tel. 428-010. Clinique Paofai, Blvd. Pomare; Tel. 437-700. Dr. Christian Joinville, Pao Pao, Moorea; Tel. 561-104.

Health Advisory

Malaria: No risk.

Travelers' diarrhea: Low to medium risk. The tap water on most of the main islands is generally safe, but travelers are advised to drink bottled, boiled, or treated water. Food and milk are considered safe, but food should be eaten well cooked. All fruit should be peeled prior to consumption. A quinolone antibiotic (Floxin or Cipro) is recommended for the treatment of acute diarrhea. Diarrhea not responding to antibiotic treatment may be due to a parasitic disease such as giardiasis or amebiasis—or an intestinal virus. (Amoebic dysentery has been reported.)

Hepatitis: Immune globulin or hepatitis A vaccine is recommended for all susceptible travelers. The hepatitis B carrier rate in the general population of Oceania is estimated at 5.5%–15%. Vaccination against hepatitis B is recommended for healthcare workers and should be considered by long-term visitors to this country.

Typhoid fever: Outbreak of typhoid fever was reported in 1983, but the incidence of this illness is low. Travelers should follow safe food and drink guidelines. Vaccination is recommended only for long-term travelers to this country.

Dengue fever: This disease is reported. Most risk occurs during the rainy season months. Travelers should take protective measures against mosquito bites.

Filariasis: Moderately high rates (up to 19%) of Malayan filariasis reported in the general population. Travelers should take protective measures against mosquito bites.

AIDS: A small number of AIDS cases and HIV infections have been reported. The hospital blood supply is screened for HIV and is considered safe.

GUAM (U.S. TERRITORY)

Agana ... GMT +10 hrs

Entry Requirements
- Passport/Visa: Not required for U.S. citizens.
- AIDS Test: Not required.
- Vaccinations: None required.

Telephone Country Code: 671

American Express: Travel Pacificana, 117 Martyr Street, Agana; Tel. (472) 8884.

Health Advisory

Travelers' diarrhea: Food and water are safe in the major hotels. A quinolone antibiotic (Floxin or Cipro) is recommended for the treatment of acute diarrhea. Diarrhea not responding to antibiotic treatment may be due to a parasitic disease such as giardiasis or amebiasis—or an intestinal virus.

Hepatitis: Immune globulin or hepatitis A vaccine is recommended for all susceptible travelers. The hepatitis B carrier rate in the general population of Oceania is estimated at 5.5%–15%. Vaccination against hepatitis B is recommended for healthcare workers and should be considered by long-term visitors to this country.

Tropical diseases: Filariasis, dengue fever, and Japanese encephalitis are reported. To avoid these illnesses, all travelers should take measures to prevent mosquito bites.

KIRIBATI

Tarawa ... GMT +12 hrs

Entry Requirements
- Passport/Visa: Passport is required.
- AIDS Test: Not required.
- Vaccinations: A yellow fever vaccination certificate is required of travelers arriving from infected areas.

Telephone Country Code: 686

Embassies/Consulates: This country consists of 33 atolls and one island scattered over five million square km. Formerly the Gilberts of the British Gilbert and Ellice Islands Colony, it became the Republic of Kiribati in 1979.

Hospitals/Doctors: Tungaru Central Referral Hospital (140 beds); general medical facility. Betio Hospital (10 beds); general medical facility.

MICRONESIA (FEDERATED STATES OF)

Palikir ... GMT +11 hrs

Entry Requirements

- Passport/visa: Passport required. Micronesia is self-governing in free association with the United States. The 600 islands and atolls were formerly part of the U.S. Trust Territory of the Pacific.
- AIDS Test: Required of anyone staying over one year.
- Vaccinations: None required.

Telephone Country Code: 691

Health Advisory

Travelers' diarrhea: Low to moderate risk. In urban and resort areas, the hotels and restaurants generally serve reliable food and potable water. Elsewhere, travelers should observe all food and drink safety precautions. A quinolone antibiotic (Floxin or Cipro) is recommended for the treatment of acute diarrhea. Diarrhea not responding to antibiotic treatment may be due to a parasitic disease such as giardiasis or amebiasis—or an intestinal virus. A cholera outbreak occurred in 1982, but there have been no recent reports of this disease.

Hepatitis: Immune globulin or hepatitis A vaccine is recommended for all susceptible travelers. The hepatitis B carrier rate in parts of Oceania is as high as 15%. Vaccination against hepatitis B is recommended for healthcare workers and should be considered by long-term visitors to this country.

Filariasis, Japanese encephalitis, dengue fever: Sporadic cases and outbreaks are reported. Travelers should take protective measures against mosquito bites.

NAURU

Yaren ... GMT +12 hrs

Entry Requirements

- Passport/Visa: Passport is required.
- AIDS Test: Not required.
- Vaccinations: A yellow fever vaccination certificate is required of travelers arriving from infected areas.

Telephone Country Code: 674

Health Advisory

Travelers' diarrhea: Low to moderate risk. First-class hotels and restaurants generally serve reliable food and potable water. Elsewhere, travelers should observe all food and drink safety precautions. A quinolone antibiotic (Floxin or Cipro) is recommended for the treatment of acute diarrhea. Diarrhea not responding to antibiotic treatment may be due to a parasitic disease such as giardiasis or amebiasis.

Hepatitis: Immune globulin or hepatitis A vaccine is recommended for all susceptible travelers. The hepatitis B carrier rate in the general population of Oceania is estimated at 5.5%–15%. Vaccination against hepatitis B is recommended for healthcare workers and should be considered by long-term visitors to this country.

Filariasis, Japanese encephalitis, dengue fever: Sporadic cases are reported. Travelers should take protective measures against mosquito bites.

NEW ZEALAND
Wellington ... GMT +12 hrs

Entry Requirements
- Passport/Visa: Passport required.
- AIDS Test: Not required.
- Vaccinations: None required.

Telephone Country Code: 64

American Express: Century 21 Travel. 276 Lambton Quay, Wellington; Tel: (4) 731-221.

Embassies/Consulates: U.S. Embassy, Wellington. 29 Fitzherbert Terrace; Tel. (4) 722-068.

Hospitals/Doctors: Wellington Hospital (959 beds); Tel: (4) 385-5999. Greenlane Hospital (565 beds), Auckland; Tel: (9) 604-106. Christchurch Public Hospital (408 beds); Tel: (3) 640-640. Epsom Medical Center, Aukland; Tel. (9) 794-540. Harold Gray, M.D., Wellington; Tel. (4) 849-675 or 862-124.

Health Advisory

Travelers' diarrhea: Low risk. Tap water is considered potable countrywide. A quinolone antibiotic (Floxin or Cipro) is recommended for the treatment of acute diarrhea. Diarrhea not responding to antibiotic treatment may be due to a parasitic disease such as giardiasis or amebiasis—or an intestinal virus.

Hepatitis: Low risk to tourists. Susceptible travelers should consider immune globulin or hepatitis A vaccination. There is a high carrier rate of the hepatitis B virus among the Maori tribe and Asian/Polynesian residents.

NORTHERN MARIANA ISLANDS (U.S.)
SAIPAN, TINIAN, AND ROTA
GMT +11 hrs

Entry Requirements
- Passport/Visa: Not required by U.S. citizens.
- AIDS Test: Not required.
- Vaccinations: None required

Embassies/Consulates

These islands are a self-governing U.S. territory since 1986.

Health Advisory

Malaria: No risk.

Traveler's diarrhea: Medium risk outside of first-class hotels and resorts. A quinolone antibiotic (Floxin or Cipro) is recommended for the treatment of acute diarrhea. Diarrhea not responding to antibiotic treatment may be due to a parasitic disease such as giardiasis or amebiasis—or an intestinal virus.

Hepatitis: All susceptible travelers should receive immune globulin or hepatitis A vaccine. The hepatitis B carrier rate in the general population is estimated at 10%. Vaccination against hepatitis B is recommended for all healthcare workers and long-term visitors.

Filariasis, Japanese encephalitis, dengue fever: Sporadic cases and outbreaks are reported. Travelers to this region should take protective measures against mosquito bites.

PALAU
Koror ... GMT +9 hrs

Entry Requirements
- Passport/Visa: Not required for U.S. citizens. U.S. Embassy, Palau; Tel: (680) 920-990.
- AIDS Test: Not required.
- Vaccinations: None required.

Health Advisory

Malaria: No risk.

Travelers' diarrhea: Medium risk. A quinolone antibiotic (Cipro or Floxin) is recommended for the treatment of diarrhea.

Hepatitis: All travelers should receive immune globulin prophylaxis against hepatitis A. The hepatitis B carrier rate in the general population is approximately 15 percent. Vaccination against hepatitis B is recommended for all healthcare workers and long-term visitors.

Filariasis, Japanese encephalitis, dengue fever: Sporadic cases and outbreaks are reported. Travelers should take protective measures against mosquito bites.

PAPUA NEW GUINEA

Embassy: 202-659-0856   **Port Moresby**   **GMT +10 hrs**

Entry Requirements
- Passport/Visa: Passport and visa required. Sufficient funds required.
- AIDS Test: Test required for foreign workers or anyone seeking residency.
- Vaccinations: A yellow fever vaccination certificate is required from all travelers older than 1 year arriving from infected areas.

Telephone Country Code: 675

American Express: Coral Sea Travel Services. P.N.G.B.C. Building, Musgrave & Douglas Streets, Port Moresby; Tel. 214-422.

Embassies/Consulates: U.S. Embassy, Port Moresby. Armit Street; Tel. 211-4554. Canadian High Commission (Australia); Tel. [61] (62) 733-844.

Hospitals/Doctors: Port Moresby General Hospital (700 beds); Jacobi Medical Center, Port Moresby; Tel. 255-355. General Hospital, Madanng (280 beds); general medical facility; x-ray, laboratory. Base Hospital, Lae (297 beds); x-ray, pharmacy, laboratory.

Health Advisory

Malaria: Highly endemic. Risk is present countrywide (including urban areas) year-round at elevations below 1,800 meters; elevated risk occurs along coastal areas and in the lowlands. *P. falciparum* accounts for 77% of cases, followed by *P. vivax*. Up to 5% of malaria cases are caused by *P. malariae*. Chloroquine- and Fansidar-resistant falciparum malaria is widespread, and mefloquine-resistant *P. falciparum* has been reported. The recommended antimalarial prophylaxis for adult travelers is doxycycline, 100 mg daily, or mefloquine, 250 mg weekly.

Travelers' diarrhea: Medium to high risk outside of first-class hotels and resorts. Travelers are advised to drink only bottled, boiled, filtered, or treated water and consume only well-cooked food. All fruit should be peeled prior to consumption. A quinolone antibiotic is recommended for the treatment of acute diarrhea. Diarrhea not responding to antibiotic treatment may be due to a parasitic disease such as giardiasis, amebiasis, or cryptosporidiosis. These parasitic diseases are commonly reported.

Hepatitis: Immune globulin or hepatitis A vaccine is recommended for all susceptible travelers. The hepatitis B carrier rate in the general population is estimated at as high as 15%. Vaccination against hepatitis B is recommended for healthcare workers and should be considered by long-term visitors to this country.

Dengue fever: Countrywide risk except for the deep mountain interior over 1,000 meters elevation. Urban areas and low-lying rural areas are considered at high risk from October through May. The *Aedes* mosquito, which transmits dengue, bites during the daytime and is present in populous urban areas as well as resort and rural areas. Prevention of dengue consists of taking protective measures against mosquito bites.

Filariasis: Bancroftian filariasis is highly endemic in coastal and low-lying regions and some islands off the mainland. All travelers should take measures to avoid mosquito bites.

Japanese encephalitis: Endemic status uncertain, but this disease occurs in neighboring Irian Jaya. Vaccination against Japanese encephalitis is recommended for travelers who will be staying in rural-agricultural endemic areas more than several weeks during the peak transmission season. All travelers should take protective measures against mosquito bites, especially in the evening.

Rabies: There is no rabies reported from Papua New Guinea.

Other illnesses/hazards: Angiostrongyliasis, brucellosis (low incidence), hydatid disease, helminthic infections (ascariasis, hookworm disease, strongyloidiasis are highly endemic in urban and rural areas), paragonimiasis, leprosy (highly endemic), melioidosis, Ross River fever (mosquito-borne; low incidence), epidemic typhus (louse-borne; low endemicity), scrub typhus (mite-borne; risk elevated in grassy rural areas; low endemicity), tuberculosis (highly endemic), typhoid fever, and yaws. Animal hazards include snakes (various species of adders), centipedes, scorpions, red back spiders, mouse spiders. Other possible hazards include crocodiles, tigers, panthers, bears, wild pigs, and wild cattle. Large leeches, which are not poisonous but inflict slow-healing, easily infected bites, are abundant in the swamps and streams of this country. Stingrays, sea wasps, the Indo-Pacific man-of-war, and poisonous sea cones are common in the country's coastal waters and are potentially hazardous to unprotected or careless swimmers.

AMERICAN SAMOA
Pago Pago

Entry Requirements
- Passport/Visa: Passport required. American Samoa consists of seven islands and atolls that are a U.S. territory.
- AIDS Test: Not required.
- Vaccinations: A yellow fever vaccination certificate is required from travelers over 6 months of age coming from infected or endemic areas.

Telephone Country Code: 684

Health Advisory

Malaria: No risk.

Travelers' diarrhea: Low to moderate risk. In urban and resort areas, the hotels and restaurants generally serve reliable food and potable water. Elsewhere, travelers should observe all food and drink safety precautions. A quinolone antibiotic (Floxin or Cipro) is recommended for the treatment of acute diarrhea. Diarrhea not responding to antibiotic treatment may be due to a parasitic disease such as giardiasis or amebiasis—or an intestinal virus.

Hepatitis: All susceptible travelers should receive immune globulin prophylaxis or hepatitis A vaccine prior to visiting this country. The hepatitis B carrier rate in the general population is estimated at 5.5%. Vaccination against hepatitis B is recommended for all healthcare workers and should be considered by anyone planning an extended visit to this country.

Filariasis, Japanese encephalitis, dengue fever: Sporadic cases and outbreaks are reported. Travelers should take protective measures against mosquito bites.

SAMOA (WESTERN)
Apia ... GMT -11 hrs

Entry Requirements
- Passport/Visa: Passport required.
- AIDS Test: Not required.
- Vaccinations: A yellow fever vaccination certificate is required from travelers over 6 months of age coming from infected or endemic areas.

Telephone Country Code: 685
Hospitals/Doctors: National Hospital (335 beds); general medical facility; emergency room.
Embassies & Consulates: U.S. Embassy, Apia; Tel: 21631.

Health Advisory

Malaria: No risk.
Travelers' diarrhea: Moderate risk outside of first-class hotels and resorts. Travelers should drink only bottled, boiled, or treated water. Food should be eaten well cooked. A quinolone antibiotic (Floxin or Cipro) is recommended for the treatment of acute diarrhea. Diarrhea not responding to antibiotic treatment may be due to a parasitic disease such as giardiasis or amebiasis—or an intestinal virus.
Hepatitis: Immune globulin or hepatitis A vaccine is recommended for all susceptible travelers. The hepatitis B carrier rate in the general population is estimated at 10%. Vaccination against hepatitis B is recommended for healthcare workers and should be considered by long-term visitors to this country.
Dengue fever: Most risk occurs during rainy season months. Travelers should take protective measures against mosquito bites.
Filariasis: Malayan filariasis occurs in this country. Travelers should take protective measures against mosquito bites.

SOLOMON ISLANDS
Honiara ... GMT +11 hrs

Entry Requirements
- Passport/Visa: Passport and visa required. The Solomon Islands are an independent member since 1978 of the British Commonwealth of Nations.
- AIDS Test: Not required.
- Vaccination: A yellow fever vaccination certificate is required from travelers over 1 year of age arriving from infected or endemic areas.

Telephone Country Code: 677
Electricity/Plugs: AC 50 Hz, 230 volts; plug types H, I; adaptors and transformer necessary for U.S.-made appliances. (Three hotels in Honiara have 110 volts for shavers.)
Embassies/Consulates: U.S. Embassy, Honiara. Mud Alley; Tel. 23890.
Hospitals/Doctors: Island Medical Clinic, Honiara. Tel: 23-139/23-277. Central Hospital (158 beds); general medical facility; x-ray, pharmacy, laboratory. Tel. 23600. Ambulance; Tel. 22200. Ato'ifi Adventist Hospital (91 beds); general medical facility; x-ray, pharmacy. The U.S. Peace Corps (Tel. 21612) or embassy can also be contacted for a physician recommendation.

Health Advisory

Malaria: Risk is present countrywide, including urban areas. Falciparum malaria predominates 2:1 over vivax malaria. Multidrug-resistant falciparum malaria occurs, and chloroquine- and Fansidar-resistant falciparum malaria is widespread. The recommended prophylaxis for adult travelers is mefloquine, 250 mg weekly, or doxycycline, 100 mg daily.
Travelers' diarrhea: Medium risk. All tap water should be considered unsafe. Travelers are advised to drink only bottled, boiled, or treated water. A quinolone antibiotic (Cipro or Floxin) is recommended for the treatment of acute diarrhea.

Hepatitis: All susceptible travelers should receive immune globulin or hepatitis A vaccine prior to visiting this country. The hepatitis B carrier rate in the general population is estimated to exceed 10%. Vaccination against hepatitis B is recommended for all healthcare workers and should be considered by anyone planning an extended visit to this country.

Filariasis, Japanese encephalitis: Bancroftian filariasis is endemic. Sporadic cases and outbreaks of Japanese encephalitis are reported. All travelers should take protective measures against mosquito bites.

Dengue fever: Urban areas and low-lying rural areas are considered at high risk of dengue outbreaks during the rainy season months, December-January to May-June. The Aedes mosquito, which transmits dengue, bites during the daytime and is present in populous urban areas as well as resort and rural areas. Prevention of dengue consists of taking protective measures against mosquito bites.

Other diseases/health hazards: Hookworm is endemic. Travelers are advised to wear shoes/sandals to prevent transmission of the hookworm larvae through the soles of the feet. There is a low risk of scrub typhus during the rainy seasons. Travelers walking through grassy areas should protect themselves from chigger mites. Centipedes, scorpions, and large black ants may be encountered by hikers and "bush walkers."

TONGA
Nuku'alofa ... GMT +13 hrs

Entry Requirements
- Passport/Visa: A visa is required only for visits exceeding 30 days.
- AIDS Test: Not required.
- Vaccinations: A yellow fever vaccination certificate is required from all travelers coming from infected or endemic areas.

Telephone Country Code: 676

Electricity/Plugs: AC 50 Hz, 220 volts; plug type I. Adaptors and transformer necessary for U.S.-made appliances.

Embassies/Consulates: The nearest U.S. embassy is in Suva, Fiji.

Hospitals/Doctors: Vaiola Hospital, Nuku'alofa (202 beds); general medical/surgical facility; emergency room. Tel. 21-200. Dr. Helga Schafer-Macdonald, Nuku'alofa. Tel. 22-736. Ngu Hospital, Neiafu (61 beds); limited medical and surgical services.

Health Advisory

Malaria: No risk.

Hepatitis: All travelers should receive immune globulin prophylaxis against hepatitis A. The hepatitis B carrier rate in the general population exceeds 10 percent. Vaccination against hepatitis B is recommended for all healthcare workers and long-term visitors.

Travelers' diarrhea: Low to medium risk: The tap water in Nuku'alofa is potable, but travelers are advised to consume only boiled or bottled water unless assured the water has been adequately treated. A quinolone antibiotic is recommended for the treatment of diarrhea.

Cholera: This water-borne diarrheal disease occurs sporadically in Oceania. Rare cases of cholera have occurred in this country but there is little, if any, danger to tourists.

Filariasis, Japanese encephalitis, Ross River fever, dengue fever: Sporadic cases and outbreaks are reported. Travelers should take protective measures against mosquito bites.

Animal hazards: Stingrays, poisonous fish, various sharks, sea anemones, corals and jellyfish are hazards to swimmers. Tropical centipedes can inflict painful stings if touched. Common sense is usually adequate to avoid these hazards.

TOKELAU (NEW ZEALAND)

Entry Requirements
- Passport/Visa: A visa is not required.
- AIDS Test: Not required.
- Vaccinations: None required.

Embassies/Consulates
The nearest U.S. embassy is in Aukland, New Zealand.

Health Advisory

Malaria: No risk.

Travelers' diarrhea: Medium-high risk outside of first-class hotels and resorts. Travelers are advised to drink only bottled, boiled, filtered, or treated water and consume only well-cooked food. A quinolone antibiotic (Floxin or Cipro) is recommended for the treatment of acute diarrhea. Diarrhea not responding to antibiotic treatment may be due to a parasitic disease such as giardiasis or amebiasis—or an intestinal virus.

Hepatitis: All travelers should receive immune globulin prophylaxis against hepatitis A. The hepatitis B carrier rate in the general population is approximately 10 percent. Vaccination against hepatitis B is recommended for all healthcare workers and long-term visitors.

Typhoid fever: Low risk to tourists. Vaccination should be considered by long-term visitors.

Filariasis, Japanese encephalitis, dengue fever: Sporadic cases and outbreaks are reported. Travelers should take protective measures against mosquito bites.

Marine hazards: Stingrays, poisonous fish, sea anemones, corals and jellyfish are potential hazards to swimmers.

TUVALU
Funafuti ... GMT +12 hrs

Entry Requirements
- Passport/visas: A visa is not required.
- AIDS Test: Not required.
- Vaccinations: None required.

Hospitals/Doctors
Princess Margaret Hospital, Funafuti. Tel: 752.

Health Advisory

Malaria: No risk.

Hepatitis: All travelers should receive immune globulin prophylaxis against hepatitis A. The hepatitis B carrier rate in the general population exceeds 10 percent. Vaccination against hepatitis B is recommended for all healthcare workers and long-term visitors.

Filariasis, Japanese encephalitis, dengue fever: Sporadic cases and outbreaks are reported. Travelers should take protective measures against mosquito bites.

Marine hazards: Stingrays, poisonous fish, sea anemones, corals and jellyfish are hazards to swimmers.

VANUATU
Port-Vila ... GMT +11–12 hrs

Entry Requirements
- Passport/Visa: Temporary 30-day visas are issued to travelers with an onward ticket and sufficient funds.
- AIDS Test: Not required.
- Vaccinations: None required.

Telephone Country Code: 678

Electricity/Plugs: AC 50 Hz, 220 volts; plug types H, I. Converter and adaptor necessary for U.S.-made appliances.

Embassies/Consulates: Vanuatu has been independent since 1980 and maintains diplomatic relations with the United States. The nearest U.S. embassy is in Honoria, Solomon Islands.

Hospitals/Doctors: Bougainville House, Port Villa. Tel: 3065. Jean Luc Bador, MD. Tel. 3065 or 2925. Dr. Ernest Finburg, Vila Medical Center. Tel. 22826 or 22565 (home). Vila Central Hospital (100 beds); X-ray, pharmacy, laboratory. Basic services only. Tel. 22100. Lenakel Hospital (50 beds); X-ray; small laboratory.

Health Advisory

Malaria: There is a generally high risk of malaria throughout this country, including urban areas. There is no malaria on Futuna Island. *P. falciparum* accounts for 80% of cases, *P. vivax* 20%. Chloroquine-resistant falciparum malaria is reported. Resistance to Fansidar is also reported. Resistance to quinine may also occur. Mefloquine or doxycycline prophylaxis is recommended for all travelers. All travelers should take personal protection measures against mosquito bites, especially between dusk and dawn—the time when the malaria-carrying *Anopheles* mosquitoes are most active. Anti-insect precautions are especially important in the northern islands, where mosquito activity is highest.

Travelers' diarrhea: Medium risk. The drinking water in this country is collected in ground catchment systems and water supplies should be considered potentially contaminated. All travelers are advised to drink only bottled, boiled, or treated water unless assured that the local tap water has been treated. (The tap water in Vila is considered safe.) Standard safe food precautions should also be observed. A quinolone antibiotic (Cipro or Floxin) is recommended for the treatment of acute diarrhea. Diarrheal illness not responding to antibiotic treatment may be due to giardiasis, which is moderately endemic in this country.

Typhoid fever: An outbreak of typhoid fever occurred in 1987. The risk of typhoid is low for tourists. Vaccination is recommended only for long-term visitors to this country. All travelers to this country should follow safe food and water guidelines. The risk of typhoid is increased during the rainy season, when ground water may become contaminated.

Hepatitis: Immune globulin or hepatitis A vaccine is recommended for all susceptible travelers. The hepatitis B carrier rate in the general population is estimated to exceed 10%. Vaccination against hepatitis B is recommended for healthcare workers and should be considered by long-term visitors to this country.

Insect-borne diseases: Filariasis, Japanese encephalitis, and dengue occur sporadically, with occasional outbreaks reported. Travelers should take personal protective measures against mosquito bites. Long-term visitors should consider vaccination against Japanese encephalitis.

Scrub typhus: There is a low incidence of scrub typhus reported from this country. Travelers walking through grassy areas should protect themselves from chigger mites by using a deet-containing skin repellent and permethrin-treated clothing.

WALLIS & FUTUNA (FRANCE)

GMT +12 hrs

Entry Requirements
- AIDS Test: Not required.
- Vaccinations: None required.

Hospitals/Doctors

Wallis Hospital (85 beds); general medical facility; pharmacy, x-ray, laboratory.

Health Advisory

Malaria: No risk.

Hepatitis: All susceptible travelers should receive immune globulin or hepatitis A vaccine. The hepatitis B carrier rate in the general population exceeds 10 percent. Vaccination against hepatitis B is recommended for all healthcare workers and long-term visitors to this country.

Travelers' diarrhea: Medium risk. Water supplies should be considered potentially contaminated and travelers are advised to drink only bottled, boiled, or treated water, unless assured that the local water is safe. Standard safe food precautions should also be observed.

Typhoid fever: Risk is low, but long-term travelers should consider vaccination. All travelers should observe safe food and water guidelines.

Insect-borne diseases: Filariasis, Japanese encephalitis, Ross River fever, and dengue are potential risks. All travelers should take personal protective measures against mosquito and insect bites. Long-term visitors should consider vaccination against Japanese encephalitis.

Appendix

Special Notice

The *International Travel HealthGuide* has compiled an extensive listing of over five hundred yellow fever vaccination centers and travel medicine specialists. The directory is provided solely for the convenience of our readers. We do not guarantee, nor are we responsible for, the capabilities and professional qualifications of those clinics and physicians listed below.

NOTE: Physicians or clinics identified with an asterisk (★) are members of the American Society of Tropical Medicine & Hygiene.

Travelers' Clinics in the United States & Canada

ALABAMA

Alabama Dept. of
Public Health
Immunization Division
206 State Office Building
Montgomery, AL 36130
205-261-5052

Montgomery County
Health Dept.
515 W. Jeff Davis Ave.
Montgomery, AL 36104
205-263-6671

David O. Freedman, MD
Travelers' Health Clinic
Univ. of Alabama
Division of Geographic
Medicine
1025 18th Street, Rm 240
Birmingham, AL 35205
205-934-4000
Acute illness: 205-934-1630
205-934-3411 (Evening)

Jefferson County Health Dept.
1400 Sixth Ave., South
Birmingham, AL 35233
205-933-9110 x1460

Mobile County Health Dept.
251 N. Bayou Ave.
Mobile, AL 36603
295-690-8157

Family Practice Center
4724 Airport Blvd.
Mobile, AL 36608
205-343-2044

Madison County Health Dept.
304 Eustis Ave.
Huntsville, AL 35801
205-539-3711

Houston County Health Dept.
2101 Cottonwood Road
Dothan, AL 36301
205-793-1911

Roger W. Boswell, MD
1810 Merchants Drive
Hoover, AL 35244
205-987-9133

ALASKA

Division of Public Health
Pouch H-06H
Juneau, AK 99811
907-465-3141

ARIZONA

Arizona Dept. of Health
1740 West Adams Street
Phoenix, AZ 85007
602-542-1000

Maricopa County
Health Dept.
1825 East Roosevelt
Phoenix, AZ 85006
602-258-6381

International Travel Clinic
Pima County Health Dept.
332 S. Lee Freeway
Tucson, AZ 85714
602-624-8328

Petersen, Eskild, MD
Univ. of Arizona School
of Medicine
1501 North Campbell Ave.
Tucson, AZ 85724
602-626-7900

Cordes, D.H., MD ★
Travelers' Clinic
Univ. of Arizona
Dept. of Family &
Community Medicine
Tucson, AZ 85724
602-626-7900

Peate, Wayne F., MD, MPH ★
Corporate Medical Center
2545 E. Adams Street
Tucson, AZ 85716
602-881-0050

Kuberski, Timothy, MD ★
5757 W. Thunderbird Rd.
Suite W212
Glendale, AZ 85306
602-439-0274

The Scottsdale Clinic
9220 E. Mountain View
Scottsdale, AZ 85258
602-391-1805

Medical Office Center
5127 W. Indian School Road
Phoenix, AZ 85031
602-245-0901

Medical Office Center
2740 S. Alma School Road
Mesa, AZ 85202
602-897-9781

Medical Office Center
940 East Baseline Road
Tempe, AZ 85283
602-820-9121

ARKANSAS

Arkansas Department
of Health
Communicable Disease Div.
4815 W. Markham
Little Rock, AR 72201
501-661-2352

N.W. Riegler, MD
1024 Scott
Little Rock, AR 72202
501-375-3326

James H. Arkins, MD
Bentonville Medical Clinic
306 NE Blake
Bentonville, AR 72712
501-273-9056

Charles Crawley, MD
328 Kittel Rd.
Forrest City, AR 72335
501-633-1425

Jim Citty, MD
2900 Hawkins Drive
Searcy, AR 72143
501-268-5364 ext. 130

J.E. Dorman, MD
Box 689
Springdale, AR 72764
501-755-6161

William Finfrock, MD
41 Kings Highway
Eureka Springs, AR 72632
501-253-9726

Jim Greene, MD
605 Lexington
Fort Smith, AR 72901
501-782-6081

Bill Harper, MD
425 Oak
El Dorado, AR 71730
501-863-5135

Karmen Hopkins, MD
209 W. Blake
Pine Bluff, AR 71601
501-536-6600

Kelly Meyer, MD
2504 W. Main
Russellville, AR 72801
501-968-3640

James Thomas, MD
605 SW Drive
Jonesboro, AR 72401
501-935-8510

Thomas H. Wortham, MD
813 Marshall Rd.
Jacksonville, AR 72076
501-982-2141

CALIFORNIA

Department of Health Services
Infectious Disease Branch
Berkeley, CA
415-540-2566

In California, each county health
department maintains a list of
physicians who can administer

the yellow fever vaccine. There
is no centralized office that
maintains a statewide listing of
travelers' clinics.

Bay Area
International Travel Clinic
5601 Norric Canyon Road
San Ramon, CA 94583
510-277-2050

Dr. James Seward
Cowell Hospital
University of California
Berkeley, CA 94720
415-642-5981

J. Gordon Frierson, MD, ★
Director
Dr. Charles Beal ★
Paul DeLay, MD, DTM&H ★
Goldsmith, Robert M., MD,
DTM&H ★
Markell, Edward, MD, PhD ★
Travelers' Clinic & Tropical
Diseases Laboratory
University of California
350 Parnassus Street
San Francisco, CA 94143
Travelers' Clinic
415-476-5787
Tropical Disease Lab
415-476-2166

Overseas Medical Center
10 California St.
San Francisco, CA 94111
415-982-8380

International Medical
311 California, 4th floor
San Francisco, CA 94111
415-398-5300

C. Allan Wall, MD
Sutter Medical Group
1154 Sutter Street at Polk
San Francisco, CA 94109
415-441-6930

Jerome Greenbaum, M.D,
2200 O'Farrell
San Francisco, CA 94115
415-929-4939

Readi-Care Clinic
100 Pine Street, Suite 900
San Francisco, CA 94111
415-391-6650

Lauren Smookler, MD
Airport Medical Facility
San Francisco Intl. Airport
Central Terminal Lower Level
San Francisco, CA 94128
415-877-0444

Eric L. Weiss, MD, DTM&H★
Stanford Travel Medicine
Service
Stanford University Hospital
300 Pasteur Drive
Stanford, CA 94305-5239
415-723-2600

Richard F. Thompson, M.D.
The Travel Clinic
Sunnyvale Medical Center
325 North Mathilda Avenue
Sunnyvale, CA 94086
408-733-4380

Bob Young, MD ★
Travel Immunization Clinic
40 East Alamar Ave.
Santa Barbara, CA 93101
805-682-8188

Travelers' Immunization Clinic
Arbor Medical Group
1300 E. Cypress St., #E
Santa Maria, CA 93454
805-925-2344

Partev Manasjan, MD
Medical Clinic
for Immunizations
7060 Hollywood Blvd.
Los Angeles, CA 90028
213-469-4334

Sylvester Sailes, MD
6200 Wilshire Blvd.
Los Angeles, CA 90048
213-937-1766

Bernard McNamara, MD
1462 N. Vine St.
Los Angeles, CA 90028
213-461-9355

Gary A. Tarshis, MD
Bay Shores Medical Group
502 Torrance Blvd.
Redondo Beach, CA 90277
213-316-0811

Claire B. Panosian, MD ★
UCLA Travelers' & Tropical
Medicine Clinic
UCLA Medical Center

10833 LeConte Ave.
Los Angeles, CA 90024
213-825-9711

Johnson, Byron L., MD
UCLA School of Medicine
32-220, CHS
Westwood & Le Conte
West Los Angeles, CA 90024
213-825-9711

Jonathan Rand, MD
213-821-9800
Irving Sobel, MD
213-821-7571
4644 Lincoln Blvd. Suite 507
Marina Del Ray, CA 90292

Travel Medicine
& Immunization Center
1450 10th Street, Suite 300
Santa Monica, CA
213-396-3241
INFO LINE 395-4598

Victor Kovner, MD ★
Travelers' Immunization Center
12311 Ventura Blvd.
Studio City, CA 91604
818-762-1167

James Novick, MD ★
725 South San Fernando Blvd.
Burbank, CA 91502
818-843-8555

Richard A. Foulon, MD
544 North Glendale Avenue
Glendale, CA 91206
818-241-4331

Delcarmen Medical Center
19234 Van Owen St.
Reseda, CA 91335
818-705-1115

Charles M. Jacobson, MD
Jacobsen Medical Group
21317 Devonshire St.
Chatsworth, CA 91311
818-998-3008

Gerald S. Rothman, MD
7301 Medical Center Drive
Canoga Park, CA 91307
818-346-9911

Samuel A. Wilson, MD
7301 Medical Center Drive
Canoga Park, CA 91307
818-347-2477

Jerome Adler, MD
Bruce Barnett, MD
Mark Schenkel, MD
14624 Sherman Way
Van Nuys, CA 91405
818-997-4561

Pasadena City Health Dept.
100 N. Garfield Ave.
Pasadena, CA 91109
818-405-4391

Norman F. Johnson, MD
Sierra Madre Medical Group
245 W. Sierra Madre Blvd.
Sierra Madre, CA 91024
818-355-3435

Huntington Medical Group
55 South Raymond, Suite 200
Alhambra, CA 91801
818-570-8005

Timothy V. Dalton, MD
10414 Vacco Street
South El Monte, CA 91733
818-443-3163

Community Health Projects
120 North Lang Ave.
West Covina, CA 91790
818-960-3064

Community Health Projects
354 E. Ervilla St.
Pomona, CA 91733
714-623-0539

Clinic for Infectious Diseases
11160 Warner Ave., Suite 323
Fountain Valley, CA 92708
714-751-7002

The Institute
of Travel Medicine
2617 E. Chapman,
Orange, CA 92669
714-744-5802

Scripps Clinic
& Research Foundation
10666 N. Torrey Pines Road
La Jolla, CA 92037
619-457-8620

Scripps Medical Arts Building
Dr. Herman Froeb
9844 Genessee, Suite 109
La Jolla, CA 92037
619-453-5366

Kaiser Hospital
(members only)
Nurses' Clinic, 2nd floor
4647 Zion Avenue
San Diego, CA 92120
619-563-2824

Coronado International
Travelers Clinic
230 Prospect Place, Suite 230
Coronado, CA 92118
619-435-7282

Sharp Rees-Stealy
Medical Group
16870 W. Bernardo Drive
San Diego, CA 92127
619-234-6261

Life Extension Institute
9620 Chesapeake Dr.
Suite 104
San Diego, CA 92123
619-560-0764

ElizabethBarrett-Connor, MD
Tropical Disease &
Travelers' Clinic
Family Medicine Clinic
UCSD Medical Center
225 West Dickinson
San Diego, CA 92103
619-543-5787/6222

COLORADO

Colorado Dept. of Health
4210 East 11th Street
Denver, CO 80220
303-320-6137

Denver Disease
Control Center
605 Bannock Street
Denver, CO 80204
303-893-6171

Dr. Stephen K. Mostow
International Health Pass
Rose Medical Center
4567 E. 9th Ave.
Denver, CO 80220
303-320-7277 or 2947

Travel Health Consultants
7401 N. Lowell Blvd.
Denver, CO 80030
303-428-7449

International Travelers' Service
University Hospital
4200 E. 9th Street
Denver, CO 80262
303-270-7006

Stapleton Airport Clinic
Stapleton Intl. Airport
3600 Circle Way
Denver, CO 80207
303-388-6491
(yellow fever only)

Presbyterian/St.Luke's
Healthcare Center
17200 E. Iliff Ave. Unit A-1
Aurora, CO 80013
303-755-4111

Peter Westenberger, MD ★
HealthONE Travelcare
Centennial HealthCare Plaza
14100 E. Arapahoe Road,
Suite 210
Englewood, CO 80112
303-699-3080

Larimer County Health Dept.
363 Jefferson Street
Ft. Collins, CO 80521
303-221-7460
(yellow fever only)

San Juan Basin Health Dept.
3803 Main Street
P.O. Box 140
Durango, CO 81302
303-247-5702

Boulder Medical Center
2750 Broadway
Boulder, CO 80302
303-440-310

Helios Health Center
4150 Darley Ave., Suite #6
Boulder, CO 80303
303-499-9224

El Paso County Health Dept.
501 N. Foote Ave.
Colorado Springs, CO 80903
303-578-3199

Mesa County Health Dept.
515 Patterson Ave.
Grand Junction, CO 81501
303-244-1743

CONNECTICUT

State of Connecticut Dept. of
Health Services
79 Elm Street
Hartford, CT 06106
203-566-4800
203-566-2279

Stamford Health Department
888 Washington Ave.
P.O. Box 10152
Stamford, CT 06905-2152
203-977-4399

Michelle Barry, MD ★
Tropical Medicine & Interna-
tional
Travelers' Clinic
Yale University School of
Medicine
20 York Street
New Haven, CT 06504
203-785-2476

Frank Bia, MD ★
Tropical Medicine
& International
Travelers' Clinic
Yale University School of
Medicine
20 York Street
New Haven, CT 06504
203-785-2476
After 5 PM 203-785-2471

Martin E. Gordon, MD ★
Gastroenterology &
Diseases of Travel
Yale School of Medicine
111 Sherman Ave.
New Haven, CT 06511
203-624-5850

Paul Iannini, MD
Danbury Hospital
24 Hospital Ave.
Danbury, CT 06810
203-797-7413

David R. Hill, MD ★
Infectious Disease Division
U CONN Health Center
263 Farmington Ave.
Farmington, CT 06030-3212
203-679-4225

Kenneth R. Dardick, MD ★
Mansfield Family Practice
Mansfield Professional Park
Storrs, CT 06268
203-487-0002

Dr. Richard Quintiliani
Primary Care Unit
Travelers' Clinic
Hartford Hospital
80 Seymour Street
Hartford, CT 06115
203-524-2878

The Immediate Care Center
2531 Albany Avenue
West Hartford, CT 06117
203-232-4891

The Immediate Care Center
940 Silver Lane
East Hartford, CT 06118
203-569-8800

The Immediate Care Center
263 W. Middle Turnpike
Manchester, CT 06040
203-646-8595

The Immediate Care Center
1100 Silas Deane Highway
Wethersfield, CT 06109
203-529-1100

Robert Levitz, MD
Travelers' Clinic
Meriden - Wallingford Hospital
181 Cook Ave.
Meriden, CT 06450
203-238-8221

Norwalk Health Department
(Ms. Laura Howell)
137-139 East Avenue
Norwalk, CT 06851
203-854-7900

DELAWARE

Division of Public Health
Capital Square
Dover, DE 19901
302-736-4624

DISTRICT OF COLUMBIA

D.C. Dept. of Human Services
1875 Connecticut Ave. N.W.
Washington, D.C. 20009
202-673-6738

Martin S. Wolfe, MD ★
Travelers' Medical Service
2141 K St.- Suite 408
Washington, D.C. 20037
202-466-8109

David Abramson, MD, FAAP,
FACEP
Farragut Medical & Travel Care
815 Connecticut Ave, NW
Washington, DC 20006

International Health Service
Georgetown University Hospital
3800 Resevoir Road, NW
Washington, D.C.
202-687-8672

David Parenti, MD ★
Travelers' Clinic
George Washington
University Hospital
Ambulatory Care Center
22nd & Eye Street
Washington, D.C. 20037
202-994-8466

FLORIDA

Department of Health
1317 Winewood Boulevard
Building 6, Room 276
Tallahassee, FL 32399-0700
904-488-2901

Dodson, David, MD
Carden, Alexander, MD
Krisko, Istvan, MD
Travelers' Medical Service
1411 N. Flagler Dr., Suite 7900
West Palm Beach, FL 33401
407-655-0506

MacCleod, Caroline, MD ★
Tropical Medicine &
Travelers' Clinic
3741 LeJeaune Road, SW
Miami, FL 33146-2809
305-663-9666

Dayton, Evelyn, MD
Travelers' Clinic
1529 South East 4th Ave.
Fort Lauderdale, FL 33316
305-525-4724

Port Medical Center
1701 S.E. 20th St.
Port Everglades, FL 33316
305-467-2140

Sunshine Medical Center
Port Everglades
1750 S.E. 32nd St.
P.O. Box 165464
Ft. Lauderdale, FL 3316
305-767-9999

Sunshine Medical Center
6341 Sunset Drive
South Miami, FL 33143
305-566-5971

Sunshine Medical Center
Port of Miami
907 S. America Way
Miami, FL 33132
305-372-1930

Ellen Melvin, MD
3675 20th Street, (RT. 60),
Vero Beach, FL 32960
407-569-6869

Reifsnyder, David N., MD
Travelers' Medicine
901 N. Hercules Ave., Suite C
Clearwater, FL 34625
813-446-3515

GEORGIA

Department of Human
Resources
2 Martin Luther King Jr. Drive
Atlanta, GA 30334

Travel Immunization Center
3250 Howell Mill Rd., N.W./205
Atlanta, GA 30327-4187
404-262-1414

The Travel Clinic
Piedmont Minor Emergency
Clinic
3115 Piedmont Rd., N.E.
Atlanta, GA 30305
404-237-1755

Ralph T. Bryan, MD ★
Division of Parasitic Diseases
Centers for Disease Control
Bldg. 23/Chamblee/F-13
Atlanta, GA 30333
404-488-4437

Daniel S. Blumenthal, MD ★
Morehouse Family
Practice Center
501 Fairburn Rd. SW
Atlanta, GA 30331
404-752-1624

Travel Well Clinic
Crawford Long Hospital
Phyllis Kozarsky, MD ★
20 Linden Ave., N.E.
Suite 101 - G
Atlanta, GA 30308
404-686-5885

Industrial Medicine, P.C.
1903 Abercorn Street
Savannah, GA 31401
912-232-5169

Chatham County Health Dept.
2011 Eisenhower Drive
Savannah, GA 31406
912-356-2108

DeKalb County Health Dept.
440 Winn Way
Decatur, GA 30031
404-294-3700

Infectious Disease Associates
6285 Don Hastings Drive
Riverdale, GA 30274
404-991-1500

Industrial Clinic, P.C.
3580 Atlantic Avenue
Hapeville, GA 30354
404-768-3351

Travel Clinic
University Health Service
University of Georgia
Athens, GA 30602
404-542-5575 or 542-1162

Family Practice Clinic
The Medical Center
Columbus, GA 31994
404-571-1145

GUAM

Dept. of Public Health & Social
Services
Government of Guam
Agana, Guam 96910
671-734-2951

HAWAII

State Department of Health
P.O. Box 3378
Honolulu, HI 96801
808-548-5886

Vernon Ansdell, MD, MRCP,
DTM&H ★
Travel Medicine Clinic
Kaiser Permanente Clinic
1010 Pensacola St.
Honolulu, HI 96814
808-591-2055
808-597-2394 (information)
808-834-5333 (Emergency
consult, evenings)

Michael Kusaka, MD
Straub Occupational Health
Services
839 S. Beretannia
Honolulu, HI 96813
808-522-3393

Steven Berman, MD
1380 Lusitania
Honolulu, HI 96813
808-524-0066

James S. Phillips, MD
Kaiser Travel Clinic
Hualai Medical Center
75-184 Hualai Road
Kualai-Kona, HI 96740
808-327-2900

IDAHO

Department of Health and
Welfare (Main center for
immunizations)
1455 North Orchard
Boise, ID 83706
208-375-5211 ext. 231

Thomas Coffman, MD
Kurt Stevenson, MD
125 East Idaho, Suite 203
Boise, ID 83712
208-342-4634

ILLINOIS

Illinois Department of
Public Health
535 West Jefferson
Springfield, IL 62761
217-785-2060

Evanston Hospital
Donald J. Carnow, MD, MPH
Travel Immunization Center
2650 Ridge Avenue
Evanston, IL 60201
708-570-2300

Glenbrook Hospital Donald J.
Carnow, MD, MPH
Travel Immunization Center
Ambulatory Care Suite
2100 Pfingsten Road
Glenview, IL 60025
708-657-5670

University of Chicago
Medical Center
University Health Services
5841 S. Maryland St.
Chicago, IL 60637
312-702-6840 (main clinic #)

Immunization Clinic
Northwestern Memorial
Hospital
251 East Chicago Ave., Rm.168
Chicago, IL 60611
312-908-3155

Southern Illinois Univ.
Student Health Services
115 Greek Row
Carbondale, IL 62901-6802
618-536-2391 (appointments)
For info: Contact Elizabeth
James, R.N.
618-453-4472

Dreyer Medical Clinic
David A. Lucks, M.D.
1870 West Galena Blvd.
Aurora, IL 60506
708-859-6910

David Fletcher, M. D.
1770 East Lake Shore Drive
Suite 200
Decatur, IL 62521
217-423-4300

Steven D. O' Marro, MD
Division of Infectious Diseases
& Travel Medicine
Springfield Clinic
1025 S. Seventh St.
Springfield, IL 62794-9248
217-528-7541

INDIANA

Indiana State Board of Health
1330 West Michigan Street
P.O. Box 1964
Indianapolis, IN 46206
317-633-0167

Methodist Hospital Travel
Clinic
1633 N. Capitol Ave., Suite 700
Indianapolis, IN 46202
317-929-7200

Fort Wayne-Allen County
Health Dept.
One East Main St.
Fort Wayne, IN 46802
219-428-7504

Gary Health Department
1145 W. 5th Ave.
Gary, IN 46407
219-882-5565

St. Joseph County
Health Department
County-City Building,
South Bend, IN 46601
219-284-9783

Lake County Health Dept.
2293 N. Main St.
Crown Point, IN 46307
219-738-2020 ext. 219

Elkhart County Health Dept.
315 S. 2nd Street
Elkhart, IN 46516
219-523-2259

Evansville-Vanderburgh
County Health Dept.
City-County Adm. Building
Room 129
Evansville, IN 47708
812-426-5692

IOWA

Immunization Division
State Department of Health
Lucas State Office Building
Des Moines, IA 50319
515-281-4917

Dale Anderson, MD
McFarland International
Travelers' Clinic
1215 Duff Ave.
Ames, Iowa 50010
515-239-4480

Polk County Health Dept.
1915 Hickman
Des Moines, Iowa 50314
515-286-3798

University Hospital
Student Health Service
Iowa City, Iowa 52242
319-335-8370

Siouxland District
Health Dept.
205 5th St.
Sioux City, Iowa 51101
712-279-6121

KANSAS

Kansas Dept. of Health
& Environment
Forbes Field, Building 321
Topeka, KS 66620
913-862-9360

Larry W. Rumans, MD ★
C. Michael West, MD
Institute of Infectious Diseases
631 Horne, Suite 420
Topeka, KS 66606
913-234-8405

Montgomery County
Health Dept.
604 Union
Coffeyville, KS 67337
316-251-4210

Kansas City-Wyandotte
County Health Dept.
619 Ann Avenue
Kansas City, KS 66101
913-321-4803

Kearney County Health Dept.
Courthouse
Lakin, KS 67860
316-355-6342

Lawrence-Douglas County
Health Dept.
336 Missouri - Suite 201
Lawrence, KS 66044
913-843-0721

Watkins Memorial Hospital
Student Health Service
University of Kansas
Lawrence, KS 66045
913-864-9500

Leavenworth County
Health Dept.
620 Olive
Leavenworth, KS 66048
913-682-0245

LaFene Student Health Center
University Hospital
Kansas State University
Manhattan, KS 66506
913-532-6544

Johnson County Health Dept.
6000 Lamar, Rm. 140
Mission, KS 66202
913-384-1100

Salina-Saline County
Health Department
300 West Ash
Salina, KS 67401
913-827-9376

Topeka-Shawnee County
Health Department
1615 West 8th Street
Topeka, KS 66606
913-233-5141

KENTUCKY

Louisville-Jefferson County
Health Department
400 East Gray
Louisville, KY 40202
502-625-6530

Lexington-Fayette County
Health Department
650 New Town Pike
Lexington, KY 40508
606-252-2371

LOUISIANA

Office of Health Services and
Environmental Quality
325 Loyola Avenue, Rm. 304
New Orleans, LA 70112
504-568-5413

Rodney C. Jung, MD, PhD ★
Consultant in
Tropical Medicine
3600 Chestnut St.
New Orleans, LA 70115
504-895-2007

W.A. Krotoski, MD, PhD, MPH ★
Consultant in
Tropical Medicine
11620 Rue de Tonti
Baton Rouge, LA 70810
504-769-7496

George Pankey, MD
The Ochsner Travelers' Clinic
1514 Jefferson Highway
Jefferson, LA 70121
504-838-4111

Carondelet Clinic
2223 Carondelet Street
New Orleans, LA 70130
504-524-1605

Comprehensive Health Clinic
Tulane Medical Center
1415 Tulane Ave.
New Orleans, LA 70112
504-588-5199

William A. Sodeman, Jr., MD★
Louisiana State University
School of Medicine
P.O. Box 33932
Schreveport, LA 71130-3932
318-674-5190

Westbank Surgical Clinic
4475 Westbank Expressway
Marrero, LA 70072
504-347-8471

Raul G. Reyes, MD
Int'l Maritime Medical Services
1527 Antonine St.
New Orleans, LA 70115
504-895-5216

Arthur Axelrod, MD
318 Baronne
New Orleans, LA 70112
504-561-1051

AMI Occupational Health
3640 Houma Blvd.
Metairie, LA 70006
504-456-9014

E. Baton Rouge Parish Health
353 N. 12th Street
Baton Rouge, LA 70821
504-342-1788

Whitley-Bourgeois Clinic
1122 8th St.
Morgan City, LA 70380
504-384-2260

Ouachita Parish Health Unit
2913 De Siard St.
Monroe, LA 71203
504-586-4497

New Orleans City Health Dept.
Room 1W07-City Hall
1300 Perdido St.
New Orleans, LA 70112
504-586-4497

Rapides Parish Health Unit
1200 Texas Ave.
Alexandria, LA 71301
318-487-5282

Lafayette Parish Health Unit
2100 Jefferson Street
Lafayette, LA 70505
318-254-5616

Family Health Network
1202 Monroe St.
Gretna, LA 70053
504-368-4524

MAINE

Department of Human Services
Bureau of Health
State House, Station #11
Augusta, ME 04333
707-298-2301

Mid-Maine Medical Center
Thayer Unit-Special Procedures
Waterville, ME 04901
207-872-1463

Martin's Point
Health Care Center
331 Veranda St.
Portland, ME 04103
207-774-5801

Robert P. Smith, MD ★
Spurwink Internal
Medicine Assoc.
155 Spurwink Ave.
Cape Elizabeth, ME 04107
207-767-2174

MARIANA ISLANDS

Department of Health Services
Trust Territory of the
Pacific Islands
Office of the High
Commissioner
Saipan, Mariana Islands 96950

MARYLAND

Maryland Dept. of Health &
Mental Hygiene
300 West Preston Street
Baltimore, MD 21201
301-383-2636

Michael Sauri, MD, MPH
&TM ★
Maryland Authorized
Immunization Ctr.
9715 Medical Ctr. Drive
Suite 201
Rockville, MD 20850
301-738-6420

Travelers' Health Service ★
Deirdre Herrington, MD
G. Thomas Strickland, MD
Univ. of Maryland Medical
Group
Univ. of Maryland Hospital
22 South Green St.
Baltimore, MD 21201
301-328-5196

Bradley Sack, MD, Sc.D ★
Johns Hopkins International
Medical Services
Division of Geographic
Medicine
The Johns Hopkins Hospital
550 N. Broadway, Rm. 107
Baltimore, MD 21205
301-955-8931

Alfred J. Saah, MD, MPH ★
NIAID, NIH Westwood
Building, Rm. 739
Bethesda, MD 20892
301-496-7065

Kenneth Wagner, Capt., MC,
USN ★
Infectious Diseases/Emporiatrics
Clinic
Naval Hospital
Bethesda, MD 20814-5011
202-295-4237
Active duty and retired military
and dependents

Leonard William Scheibel, MD,
FACP ★
Uniformed Services University
Division of Tropical Public
Health
4301 Jones Bridge Rd.
Bethesda, MD 20814-4799
202-295-3730

MASSACHUSETTS

Massachusetts Department of
Public Health
600 Washington Street
Boston, MA 02111
617-727-7170

Gary E. Tratt, MD
66 School Street
Hyannis, MA 02601
508-771-5300

Travelers' World
The Lahey Clinic
41 Mall Road
Burlington, MA 01805
800-643-4300
617-273-8000/8080

Andover Walk-In
Medical Center
Doctors' Park
138 Haverhill St.
Andover, MA 01810
508-475-1051

East Boston Logan
Health Associates
Logan International-Terminal D
Airport Clinic
Boston, MA 02128
617-569-8652

Travelers' Center
Tufts-New England
Medical Center
Boston, MA 02111
617-956-7001

David J. Wyler, MD ★
Division of Geographic
Medicine and
Infectious Diseases
New England Medical
Center Hospitals
750 Washington St. Box 041
Boston, MA 02111
617-956-7002

Donna Felsenstein, MD ★
Travelers' Advice &
Immunization Center
Wang ACC 037
Massachusetts General Hospital
7 Fruit St.
Boston, MA 02114
617-726-3906

John S. Wolfson, MD ★
Travelers' Advice &
Immunization Center
Wang ACC 428
Massachusetts General Hospital
7 Fruit St.
Boston, MA 02114
617-726-2748

Peter F. Weller, MD ★
Division of Infectious Diseases
Beth Israel Hospital
330 Brookline Ave.
Boston, MA 02215
617-735-3307

Cambridge Hospital
617-498-1552

Medical Care Affiliates
1 Boylston Place
Prudential Center
Boston, MA 02199
617-262-1500

K. McNulty, RN
Harvard University
Health Services
75 Mt. Auburn St.
Cambridge, MA 02138
617-495-4171

Dr. Joan Savitsky
Mount Auburn Hospital
330 Mt. Auburn Street
Cambridge, MA 02238
617-492-3500 ext. 1266

Wilson, Mary E., MD ★
Travelers' Clinic
Mount Auburn Hospital
330 Mt. Auburn Street
Cambridge, MA 02238
617- 499-5055

Leonnard Marcus, MD, DVM★
Travelers' Health &
Immunization Service
148 Highland Ave.
Newton, MA 02160
617-527-4003

Newton-Wellesley Hospital
Newton, MA
617-243-6146

Framingham Union Hospital
Framingham, MA
508-626-3564

Lawrence General Hospital
Lawrence, MA
508-683-4000, x2343

Lawrence Memorial Hospital
Lawrence, MA
508-396-9250, x1800

Board of Health
37 Lee St.
Worcester, MA 01602
508-799-8534

UMass Medical Center
Worcester, MA
508-856-2703

Hillcrest Hospital
International Travelers' Service
165 Tor Court
Pittsfield, MA 01201
413-443-4761 ext. 136

Berkshire Medical Center
Traveler's Clinic
Pittsfield, MA 01201
413-499-4161 ext. 2847

UMass Health Service
Amherst, MA
413-549-2671

Northampton Health Center
70 Main Street
Florence, MA 01060
413-586-8400

Stuart R. Rose, MD★
Noble Hospital Travelers' Clinic
115 W. Silver Street
Westfield, MA 01085
413-568-2811 ext. 5685

Michael Sands, MD
Travelers' Vaccination Service
Baystate Medical Center
759 Chestnut Street
Springfield, MA 01199
413-784-3689

MICHIGAN

Michigan Dept. of
Public Health
3500 North Logan
P.O. Box 30035
Lansing, MI 48909
517-373-9437

Louis Saravolatz, MD ★
Travel Health Clinic
Henry Ford Hospital
Clara Ford Pavillion, 1st Floor
2799 West Grand Blvd.
Detroit, MI 48202
313-876-2573

Evelyn J. Fisher, MD ★
Travel Health Clinic
Henry Ford Hospital
Clara Ford Pavillion, 1st Floor
2799 West Grand Blvd.
Detroit, MI 48202
313-876-2556

Dr. Jeffrey Band ★
INTERHEALTH - Health Care
for Int'l Travelers
William Beaumont Hospital
Medical Office Building-S. 707
3535 W. Thirteen Mile Rd.
Royal Oak, MI 48072
313-551-0496
313-288-2736

Travelers' Immunization Service
Marquette Family Health Center
1414 West Fair Ave.
Marquette, MI 49855
906-225-3864

Foreign Travel Medical Service
201 South Madison
Traverse City, MI 49684
616-946-7670

MINNESOTA

Minnesota Department
of Health
171 Delaware Street, S.E.
Minneapolis, MN 55440
612-623-5100

Airport Medical Clinic
7775 26th Ave. South
Minneapolis, MN 55450
612-726-1771

Boynton Health Services ★
University of Minnesota
410 Church St., S.E.
Minneapolis, MN 55455
612-625-3232

Occupational Medicine
Consultants, Ltd.
6500 Barrie Road
Edina, MN 55435
612-920-5663

The Duluth Clinic
400 East Third St.
Duluth, MN 55805
218-722-8364

The Mayo Clinic
Immunization Clinic
200 First St. S.W.
Rochester, MN 55901
507-284-8416 or 284-2511

St. Paul Ramsey Hospital
Infectious Disease Section
640 Jackson St.
St. Paul, MN 55101
612-221-8858

St. Paul Div. of Public Health
555 Cedar St.
St. Paul, MN 55101
612-292-7746

Park-Nicollet Medical Center
5000 W. 39th St.
St. Louis Park, MN 55416
612-927-1991

MISSISSIPPI

Mississippi Board of Health
Jackson, MS 39205
601-354-6680

MISSOURI

Missouri Division of Health
Jefferson City, MO 65102
314-751-2017

Mark D. Winton, MD
The Travel Clinic
200 St. Mary's Medical Center
Jefferson City, MO 65101
314-636-7183

The Health Information Center
for International Travel
6400 Prospect, Suite 142
Kansas City, MO 64132
816-822-8985

Helen Aff, MD
Travelers' Immunization Service
6065 Helen Ave.
Berkeley, MO 63134
314-522-6410

Travelers' Clinic
Family Medicine of St. Louis
Deaconess Medical Office Ctr

6125 Clayton Ave., Suite 101
St. Louis, MO 63139
314-768-3685

Gary J. Weil, MD ★
The Jewish Hospital at
Washington Univ. Medical Ctr.
Infectious Diseases Division
216 South Kings Highway
St. Louis, MO 63110
314-454-7782

Donald J. Krogstead, MD ★
Washington University
School of Medicine
660 S. Euclid Ave.
St. Louis, MO 63110
314-362-2998

MONTANA

Montana Dept. of Health
& Environmental Sciences
Cogswell Building
Helena, MT 59620
406-499-4740

Winship, M.J., MD ★
2825 Ft. Missoula Rd.
Missoula, MT 59501
406-549-4782

NEBRASKA

State of Nebraska
Dept. of Health
310 Centennial Mall
South Lincoln, NE 68509

Douglas County Health Dept.
Travelers' Clinic
4102 Woolworth Ave.
Omaha, NE 68105
402-444-7207

Univ. of Nebraska - Lincoln
Student Health Center
15th & U Streets
Lincoln, NE 68588
402-472-7460

Gary Settje, MD
908 N. Howard St., Suite 108
Grand Isle, NE 68801
308-381-0162

Walter Harvey, MD
1955 10th St.
Gering, NE 69341
308-436-4141

NEVADA

Department of Human
Resources
Room 200 King Street
Carson City, NV 89710
702-885-4740

Adult Medicine of
Southern Nevada
Intl. Travel &
Immunization Clinic
1641 E. Flamingo, Suite 10
Las Vegas, NV 89119
702-735-8887

NEW HAMPSHIRE

New Hampshire Division
of Public Health
Health and Welfare Building
Hazen Drive
Concord, NH 03301
603-271-4551

Betsy Eccles, RN
C. Fordham Von Reyn, MD
Dartmouth-Hitchcock Med. Ctr.
Dept. of Infectious Disease
Travelers' Clinic
Hanover, NH 03755
603-646-8840

Dr. George Idelkope
Hinsdale Family Health Ctr.
28 Brattleboro Road, Box 11
Hinsdale, NH 03451
603-336-5948

NEW JERSEY

New Jersey Dept. of Health
John Fitch Plaza, CN 364
Trenton, NJ 08625
609-292-4076

Dr. Jerome F. Levine
TravelCare
Hackensack Medical Center
Hackensack, NJ 07601
201-487-4088

Dr. Samuel Pietrandrea
215 Old Hook Rd.
WestWood, NJ 07675
201-664-3900

Company Medical Associates
160 Paris Ave.
Northvale, NJ 07647
201-767-8400

Urgent Care Associates
182 Kinderkamack
Park Ridge, NJ 07656
201-930-1700

EmergiMed
576 Anderson Ave,
Cliffside Park, NJ 07010
201-945-0491

Dr. Sheldon N. Fineberg
46 Orient Way
Rutherford, NJ 07070
201-896-0333

Dr. Patricia Ruggeri-Weigel
Medical Associates of Westfield
324 East South Ave.
Westfield, NJ 07090
908-233-1444

Newark Intl. Airport
Medical Dispensary
Bldg. 5, North Terminal
Newark, NJ 07114
201-961-2525

Rutgers University
Hurtado Health Center
11 Bishop Place
New Brunswick, NJ 08903
201-932-7401

EnviroCare
135 Raritan Center Parkway
Edison, NJ 08837
201-225-5454

Robert Wood Johnson
Medical School
1 Robert Wood Johnson Place
New Brunswick, NJ 08903
201-937-7709

Travel Med
Morristown Memorial Hospital
95 Mt. Kemble Ave.
Morristown, NJ 07960
201-285-4480

Chatham Family Practice
396 Main St.
Chatham, NJ 07928
201-635-2432

Overlook Family Practice
Overlook Hospital
Summit, NJ 07901
201-273-4700

ImmediCenter
1358 Broad St.
Clifton, NJ 07013
201-778-5566

John Nicollai Medical Center
219 Paterson Ave.
Little Falls, NJ 07424
201-890-0855

Isabelle McCosh Infirmary
(Yellow fever only.
Public accepted)
Princeton University
Princeton, NJ 08544
609-258-3129

Professional Emergency Services
of Lawrenceville
2500 Brunswick Pike
Lawrenceville, NJ 08648
609-771-6660

NEW MEXICO

Health and Environmental
Department
P.O. Box 968
Santa Fe, NM 87504
505-827-2623

Dr. Donald A. Romig
1482 C St. Francis Dr.
Santa Fe, NM 87501
505-984-1981

Occupational Medicine
and Sports Clinic
Lovelace Medical Center
5400 Gibson Blvd. S.E.
Albuquerque, NM 87108
505-262-7008

NEW YORK

New York State Health Dept.
Immunization Program
Corning Tower, Rm. 668
Empire State Plaza
Albany, NY 12237
518-473-4437

New York City area
Travel Health Services
Bradley A. Connor, MD ★
50 East 69th Street
New York, NY 10021
212-734-3000

International Health
Care Service
Warren Johnson, M.D.★
The New York Hospital-Cornell
Medical Center
440 E. 69th Street
New York, NY 10021
212-746-1601

Most, Harry, MD ★
New York University
Medical Center
341 E. 25th St.
New York, NY 10010
212-263-6764

Weiss, Louis M., MD ★
Whitner, Murray, MD ★
Tanowitz, Herbert B., MD ★
Albert Einstein College
of Medicine
1300 Morris Park Ave.
Bronx, NY 10461
212-430-2142

Hilton, Eileen, MD ★
Travel & Immunization Ctr.
Long Island Jewish
Medical Center
Rm. B202
Lakeville Road
New Hyde Park, NY 11042
718-470-7290 or 470-4415

Tropical Disease Center
Lenox Hill Hospital
130 E. 77th St.
New York, NY 10021
212-439-2345

Katz, Michael, MD ★
Director of Pediatrics
Babies Hospital Unit
Presbyterian Hospital
630 West 168th St.
New York, NY 10032
212-305-2500

Dr. John Frame
475 Riverside Dr., Rm. 649
New York , NY 10115
212-870-3053

Cunha, Bruce A., MD ★
International Travelers' Ctr.
Winthrop-University Hospital
259 First Ave.
Mineola, NY 11501
516-663-2505

Immediate Medical Care
116 W. 72 St.
New York, NY 10023
212-496-9620

The Executive Health Group
777 3rd Ave.
New York, NY 10017
212-303-1760
800-544-0681

Life Extension Institute, Inc.
437 Madison Ave.
New York, NY 10022
212-415-4747

Health Care Now
211 W. 71st Street
New York, NY 10023
212-226-3243

Metro Medical Downtown
5 Broadway
New York, NY
212-514-5750

Yorkville Medical Care
163 East 92nd St.
New York, NY 10128
212-410-5001

Medical Associates of Wall St.
135 William St.
New York, NY 10038
212-233-3040

Dr. Marvin Cooper
3 East 76th Street
New York, NY 10021
212-737-0324

New York Health Care
55 E. 34th St.
New York, NY 10016
212-683-1000

First Med Immediate
210 -17 Northern Blvd.
Bayside, NY 11361
718-224-5790

Kennedy Medical Office
Kennedy Airport
Building 198
Jamaica, Queens, NY
718-656-5344

International Travel Medicine
Service
865 Northern Blvd.
Great Neck, NY 11021
516-773-7650

Dr. Melvin Boskin
900 Straight Path
Babylon, NY 11704
516-957-0066

Island Medical Care
20 Veterans Highway
Commack, NY 11725
516-462-6644

Island Medical Care
4568 Sunrise Highway
Oakdale, NY 11769
516-567-3000

Island Health Care
1647 Route 112
Medford, NY 11763
516-758-2220

Westchester County Health
Dept. (7 locations)
85 Court Street
White Plains, NY 10601
914-285-5062

Rockland County Health Dept.
Sanatorium Road
Pomona, NY 10970
914-354-0200 ex. 2520

Horowitz, Harold, MD
International Travelers' Health
Service
New York Medical College
Room 209, Macy Pavillion S.E.
Valhalla, NY 10595
914-285-8867
914-993-4655

Rush, Thomas J., MD
Infectious Diseases
& Travel Health
141 North State Rd.
Briarcliff Manor, NY 10510
914-762-2276
or Middlebranch Offices
Rt. 6
Brewster, NY 10509
914-762-2276

Dutchess County Health Dept.
22 Market St.
Poughkeepsie, NY 12601
914-431-2015

Putnam County Health Dept.
110 Old Route 6 Center
Carmel, NY 10512
914-225-2115

Dr. Donald I. Philips
201 Homestead Ave.
Maybrook, NY 12543
914-427-2141

New York State Health Dept.
Immunization Program
Corning Tower, Rm. 668
Empire State Plaza
Albany, NY 12237
518-473-4437

Donald C. Blair, MD
Travel Health Services
SUNY Health Sciences Center
550 Harrison Center, Room 200
Syracuse, NY 13210
315-464-5815

Erie County Health Dept.
95 Franklin Street
Buffalo, NY
716-858-7714

Richard V. Lee, MD★
Department of Medicine
Children's Hospital of Buffalo
Buffalo, NY 14222
716-878-7751

Monroe County Health Dept.
111 Westfall Road
Rochester, NY 14620
716-274-6000

Group Health
Wilson Health Center
Immunization Service
800 Carter St.
Rochester, NY 14621
716-338-1400

Rochester Occupational Center
909 W. Main St. - Suite 203
Rochester, NY 14611
716-235-7520

NORTH CAROLINA

North Carolina Department of
Human Resources
P.O. Box 2091
Raleigh, NC 27602
919-733-7081
Immunization Program
919-733-7752

Wake County Health Dept.
3010 New Bern Ave.
P.O. Box 949
Raleigh, NC 27601
919-755-0761

UNC Hospitals Travelers'
Health Clinic
Family Medicine Building
Manning Drive at 15-501 Bypass
Chapel Hill, NC 27514
919-966-2491

Cushing Travel Clinic
Duke University Medical Center
Duke Hospital South, 3rd Floor
Durham, NC 27710
919-681-5420

Frothingham, Thomas E.,MD★
Durack, David T., MD
Duke University Medical Center
Durham, NC 27710
919-684-6832
919-684-8111 page I.D.#9704

Guilford County Health Dept.
301 N. Eugene St.
Greensboro, NC 27401
919-373-3256

New Hanover County
Health Dept.
2029 South 17th St.
Wilmington, NC 28406
919-763-2931

Maritime Industrial Clinic
2301 Delaney Ave.
Wilmington, NC 28403
919-763-0159

Ben Yue, MD
1810 Glen Meade Road
Wilmington, NC 28401
919-762-1730

Forsyth County Health Dept.
Reynolds Health Center
741 North Highland Ave.
Winston-Salem, NC 27102
919-727-8231

Park Medical Center
22 Park Plaza
Research Triangle Park,
NC 27709
919-549-9326

Salisbury Internal Medicine
319 Mocksville Ave.
Salisbury, NC 28144
704-637-3538

Jaars Center Clinic
Davis Road
Waxhaw, NC 28173
704-843-2185

NORTH DAKOTA

State Health Department
Capitol Building
Bismarck, ND 58505
701-224-2367

OHIO

Ohio Dept of Public Health
246 North High Street
Columbus, OH 43216
614-466-4626

Ohio State University
Family Practice Clinic
456 Clinic Drive, Room 1830
Columbus, OH 43210
614-293-8100

Ronald J. Bloomfield, MD
Travel Medicine Clinic
130 South Davis Ave., Suite 100
Columbus, OH 43222
614-228-2777

Dr. Tennyson Williams
456 Clinic Drive
Columbus, OH 43210
614-421-8007

Akron General Medical Center
400 Wabash Ave.
Akron, OH 44307
216-384-6326

Akron City Health Dept.
177 South Broadway
Akron, OH 44308
216-375-2960

Ohio University
Hudson Health Center
Athens, OH 45701
614-594-5521

Canton City Health Dept.
City Hall, 3rd floor
Canton, OH 44702
216-489-3231

Case Western Reserve
University
Division of Geographic
Medicine
University Hospital
Cleveland, OH 44106
216-589-9650 or
216-844-3295

Lutheran Medical Center
Downtown Health
Care Services
1313 Superior Ave.
Cleveland, OH 44114
216-589-9650

Mednet Intl Travel Clinic
18599 Lakeshore Blvd.
Euclid, OH 44119
216-383-6052

Cincinnati City Health Dept.
3101 Burnett Ave.
Cincinnati, OH 45229
513-352-3147

Montgomery County
Health Dept.
P.O. Box 972
451 West 3rd St.
Dayton, OH 45422
513-225-4550 or 225-4508

Miami University
Student Health Services
Wade-MacMillan Hall
Spring Street
Oxford, OH 45056
513-529-3333

Toledo City Health Dept.
Health Center
635 North Erie St.
Toledo, OH 43624
419-245-1710

Medical College of Ohio
West Campus
3000 Arlington Ave.
Toledo, OH 43699
419-381-4327

Mahoning County
Health Dept.
2801 Market St.
Youngstown, OH 44507
216-788-5011

PromptCare
17747 Chillicothe Road
Chagrin Falls, OH 44022
216-543-6728

OKLAHOMA

Oklahoma Dept. of Health
N.E. 10th & Stonewall
Oklahoma City, OK 73152
405-271-5601

OREGON

Deparment of Human
Resources
508 State Office Building
1400 S.E. 5th, P.O. Box 231
Portland, OR 97207
503-299-6760

Cherry Park Internal Medicine
1020 Southeast Main St., #12
Portland, OR 97216
503-253-1228

Oregon Health Sciences Univ.
3181 S.W. Sam Jackson Park
Portland, OR 97201
503-225-7735

Kaiser-Permanente
East Medical Office - Montana
3414 N. Kaiser Center Drive
Portland, OR 97227
503-249-8555

Dr. Thomas Olsen
Medical Clinic
4212 N.E. Broadway
Portland, OR 97213
503-249-8787

Metropolitan Clinic
265 N. Broadway
Portland, OR 97227
503-230-5381

Occupational Health Center
1313 N.W. 19th
Portland, OR 97209
503-226-6744

Portland Clinic
800 S.W. 13th Ave.
Portland, OR 97205
503-221-0161

Portland Occupational
Health Ctr.
3310 N.W. Yeon Ave.
Portland, OR 97210
503-227-7562

Dr. David Gilbert
4805 N.E. Glisan
Portland, OR
503-230-6086

Providence Medical Center
4806 N.E. Glisan
Portland, OR 97213
503-230-6153

Sylvan Medical Service, Inc.
5415 S.W. Westgate Drive
Portland, OR 97221
503-297-3371

Dr. AL Torres
2220 NW Pettygrove St.
Portland, OR 97210
503-224-0103

Dr. C.W. Dronkowski
818 W. 6th, Suite 4
The Dalles, OR 97058
503-296-1151

Washington County
Health Dept.
150 N. First St.
Hillsboro, OR 97123
503-648-8881

Benton County Health Dept.
530 N.W. 27th St.
Corvallis, OR 97330
503-757-6835

Oakridge Medical Center
4309 Oakridge Road
Lake Oswego, OR 97034
503-636-9687

North Bend Medical Center
1900 Woodland Drive
Coos Bay, OR 97420
503-267-5151

Douglas County
Health Center
621 W. Madrone
Roseburg, OR 97470
503-440-3500

Jackson County Public
Health Center
1313 Maple Grove Drive
Medford, OR 97501
503-776-7300

Lake County Health Office
700 S. J St.
Lakeview, OR 97630
503-947-2214 ext. 282

Dr. James C. Buie
132 E. Broadway, Suite 716
Eugene, OR 97401
503-484-5200

Dr. David White ★
2460 Willamette St.
Eugene, OR 97405
503-687-1163

Eugene Hospital & Clinic
Immunization Clinic
1162 Willamette
Eugene, OR 97401
503-687-6041

Dr. Robert A. Moffitt
1621 Centennial Blvd.
Springfield, OR 97477
503-746-4451

Westmoreland Medical Clinic
1650 Chambers St.
Eugene, OR 97402
503-686-1711

Dr. David L. White
2460 Willamette St.
Eugene, OR 97405
503-687-1163

Dr. John C. Girod
801 Mission St. S.E.
Salem, OR 97302
503-585-0777

Kaiser Permanente
2400 Lancaster Drive, N.E.
Salem, OR 97305
503-371-7703

PENNSYLVANIA

Pennsylvania Dept. of Health
P.O. Box 90
Harrisburg, PA 17108
717-787-5900

Pittsburgh Infectious
Diseases, Ltd. ★
1400 Locust St.
Pittsburgh, PA 15219
412-232-7398

International Travel Service ★
Montefiore Hospital
3459 Fifth Ave.
Pittsburgh, PA 15213
412-648-6410

Allegheny County Health Dept.
3441 Forbes Ave.
Pittsburgh, PA 15213
412-578-8060

Brookville Hospital
South Main St.
(Emergency Room)
Brookville, PA 15825
814-849-2312

Travelers' Clinic
Geisinger Medical Center
Danville, PA 17822
717-275-6401

Erie County Health Dept.
606 W. 2nd Street
Erie, PA 16507
814-451-6700

Centre Health Network
501 Rolling Ridge Dr., Suite 120
State College, PA 16801
814-865-6556

Ritenour Health Center
Pennsylvania State University
University Park, PA 16802
814-865-6556

International Travel Clinic
Hershey Medical Center ★
500 University Ave.
Hershey, PA 17033
717-531-8885

Dr. Harris Baderak
Community Hospital of
Lancaster
Travelers' Clinic
1100 East Orange St.
Lancaster, PA 17604
717-397-3711 ext. 545

St. Luke's Hospital
801 Ostrum St.
Bethlehem, PA 18015
215-691-4205/4206

Abington Memorial Hospital
1200 York Road - Suite 302
Abington, PA 19001
215-886-8075

Crozer Center for Occupational
Health
Division of Intl. Travel
One Medical Center Boulevard
Upland, PA 19013
215-447-2890

Travelers' Health Service
Haverford Medical Consultants,
Ltd.
5101 Township Line Road
Drexel Hill, PA 19026
610-446-5550

Delaware Valley Infectious
Disease Assoc.
Travel Health Center
Lankenau Medical Building East
Suite 467
Wynnewood, PA 19096
215-896-0210

Hospital of the University
of Pennsylvania
Ground Floor Silverstein
3400 Spruce Ave.
Philadelphia, PA 19104
215-662-2427

James C. Giuffre Med. Center
8th Street & Girard
Philadelphia, PA 19122
215-787-2473

Travelhealth Center
The Medical College
of Pennsylvania
3300 Henry Ave.
Philadelphia, PA 19129
215-842-6465/6969

Mercy Careport
Philadelphia Int'l. Airport
Concourse C
Philadelphia, PA 19153
215-492-2196

Drs. Levin & Mingroni
1439 E. Passyunk Avenue
Philadelphia, PA 19147
215-334-5656

Paoli Memorial Hospital
Occupational Health Dept.
Medical Office Building 1
Lancaster Ave.
Paoli, PA 19301
215-648-1430

Eugene A. Hildreth, M.D.★
TravelHealth Center
The Reading Hospital and
Medical Center
6th Ave. & Spruce St.
West Reading, PA 19611
610-378-6566

PUERTO RICO

Puerto Rico Department of
Health
San Juan, PR 00908

RHODE ISLAND

Rhode Island Dept. of Health
103 Cannon Building
75 Davis Street
Providence, RI 02908
401-277-2853

Wickford Internists, Inc.
Henry Sanders, MD
320 Phillips Street, Suite 201
Wickford, RI 02852
401-295-3120

Geographic Medicine Clinic
The Miriam Hospital
164 Summit Street
Providence, RI 02906
401-274-3700

SOUTH CAROLINA

South Carolina Department of
Health & Environmental
Control
2600 Bull Street
Columbia, SC 29201
803-758-5555

Lettau, Ludwig A., MD ★
Dept. of Internal Medicine
Greenville Memorial
Med. Center
701 Grove Road
Greenville, SC 29605
803-242-7889

SOUTH DAKOTA

State of South Dakota Health
Dept.
523 E. Capital
Pierre, SD 57501
605-773-3737

TENNESSEE

State Department of Health
State Office Building
Ben Alles Road
Nashville, TN 37216
615-741-7366

Schaffner, William, MD ★
Vanderbilt University Hospital
21st Ave. South
Nashville, TN 37232
615-322-2017

Metropolitan Health Dept.
311 23rd Ave., North
Nashville, TN 37203
615-291-5100

Washington County Health
Dept.
Att: Phyllis Taylor, RN
415 State of Franklin Road
Johnson City, TN 37601

Chattanooga-Hamilton County
Health Department
921 East 3rd Street
Chattanooga, TN 37403
615-757-2078/2082

Memphis-Shelby County
Health Department
Memphis, TN 38105
901-528-3911

Knox County Health Dept.
Cleveland Place
Knoxville, TN 37917
615-546-4606

Sullivan County Health Dept.
State Highway 26
Blountville, TN 37617
615-323-7131

TEXAS

Texas Department of Health
Immunization Section
1100 West 49th Street
Austin, TX 78756
512-458-7405

Foreign Travel Clinic
1936 Amelia Court
Dallas, TX 75235-7795
214-920-7899

The Samuel Clinic
5940 Forest Park Road
Dallas, TX 75235
214-350-4611

Keystone Medical Center
8702 B Spring Valley Road
Dallas, TX 75240
214-437-9090

The Boyd Clinic
703 McKinney Ave., Suite 200
Dallas, TX 75202
214-954-1717

Dallas County Health Dept.
1936 Amelia Court
Dallas, TX 75235
214-920-7900

Emergency Care Center
2001 W. Airport Freeway
Irving, TX 75062
214-659-1234

Hermann Hospital
Center for Travel Medicine
6411 Fannin, Room 8490
Houston, TX 77030
713-797-4686

Immunization Clinic
Kelsey-Seybold Clinic
909 Fannin St.
Houston, TX 77010
713-654-4401

Medical Clinic of Houston
1707 Sunset Blvd.
Houston, TX 77005
713-526-5511

International Medicine Center
Edward R. Rensimer, MD,
FACP, Director
902 Frostwood, Suite 171
Houston, TX
713-973-6078

International Medicine Center
7737 S.W. Freeway, Suite 840
Houston, TX 77074
713-777-4547

Dr. Paul Radelat
Diagnostic Clinic of Houston
6448 Fannin
Houston, TX 77030
713-797-9191

Milby Medical Group
215 Milby
Houston, TX 77003
713-225-0463

MacGregor Medical
Association
8100 Greenbriar
Houston, TX 77054
713-797-1466

Dr. Arthur Speck
4800 N.E. Stallings Dr.
Nacogdoches, TX 75961
409-569-9241

Dr. Howard Williams
Park Avenue Medical Center
1301 Park
Orange, TX 77630
409-886-1313

Dr. Robert Sullivan
421 South Oak
La Marque, TX 77568
409-935-2411

Austin Diagnostic Clinic
Travelers' Clinic
801 W. 34th
Austin, TX 78705
512-459-1111 (ext. 5553)

Austin Medicenter
6343 Cameron Road
Austin, TX 78723
512-467-2052

Austin Medicenter
9034 North IH 35
Austin, TX 78753
415-339-8114

Student Health Center
University of Texas
P.O. Box 7339
Austin, TX 78713
512-471-4955

Internal Medicine Associates
1420 Nix Medical Center
San Antonio, TX 78205
512-225-2551

Texas MedClinic
777 N.E. Loop 410
San Antonio, TX 78209
512-820-0377

Everhart Occupational Medicine
Clinic
4541 Everhart Road
Corpus Christi, TX 78411
512-852-8255

S. Texas Occupational Medicine
Clinic
1521 South Staples, Suite 102
Corpus Christi, TX 78404
512-881-9000

Dr. Wilbur Cleaves
3130 S. Alameda
Corpus Christi, TX 78404
512-882-3379

Edinburgh Medical Center
1200 South 10th St.
Edinburgh, TX 78539
512-838-2761

Hillcrest Medical Center
1110 South 10th
Edinburgh, TX 78539
512-383-3803

Huguley Industrial Clinic
11803 S. Freeway, Suite 101
Fort Worth, TX 76115
817-293-7311

Tarrant County Health Dept.
1800 University Drive
Fort Worth, TX 76107
817-870-7279

The Fort Worth Clinic
1221 West Lancaster Ave.
Fort Worth, TX 76102
817-336-7191

Texas College of Osteopathic
Medicine
Intl. Travel Medicine Clinic
3500 Camp Bowie Blvd.
Fort Worth, TX 76107-2690
817-735-2000

Dr. M.A. Caravageli
4420 Caduceus
Galveston, TX 77550
409-765-5991

Angelina County Health Dept.
202 South Bynum
Lufkin, TX 75901
409-632-1139

Care Plus Family Med. Center
1712 S.W. Parkway, Suite 105
College Station, TX 77840
409-696-0683

Family Practice Clinic
1512 Holleman
College Station, TX 77840
409-693-1510

STAT CARE
490 IH 10 North
Beaumont, TX 77702
409-839-4099

UTAH

Utah Department of Health
P.O. Box 2500
Salt Lake City, UT 84110
801-533-6120

Center for Infectious Diseases
Univ. of Utah School
of Medicine
Salt Lake City, UT 84132
801-581-8811

VERMONT

State Department of Health
60 Main Street
Burlington, VT 05401
802-862-5701 ext. 207

State Health Dept.
International Travel Clinic
1193 North Ave.
Burlington, VT 05402
802-863-7323

VIRGINIA

Virginia State Health Dept.
109 Governor Street, Rm. 100
Richmond, VA 23219
804-786-3551

Guerrant, Richard L., MD ★
Pearson, R.D., MD ★
Hewlett, E.L., MD
Petri, W.A., MD, PhD
Ravdin, J.I., MD
Travelers' Clinic
Division of Geographic
Medicine
Univ. of Virginia Hospital
Charlottesville, VA 22908
804-924-9677
804-924-0000 (beeper # 1369)
for urgent consultations

Thos. Jefferson Health District
1138 Rose Hill Drive
Charlottesville, VA 22906
804-972-6200

Montgomery County Health
Dept.
401 Depot St. S.W.
Christiansburg, VA 24073
703-382-6154

Fairfax County Health Dept.
4080 Chain Bridge Rd.
Fairfax, VA 22030
703-246-2000

Fairfax County Health Dept.
Immunization Clinic
3750 Old Lee Highway
Fairfax City, VA 22030
703-246-7100

Fairfax Country Health Dept.
Immunization Clinic
1850 Cameron Glen Drive
Reston, VA 22090
703-481-4242

Richmond City Health Dept.
500 N. 10th St.
Richmond, VA 23219
804-780-6855

Roanoke City Health Dept.
515 8th St., S.W.
P.O. Box 12926
Roanoke, VA 12926
703-981-2636

Dr. Padma Shukla
1130 Town Center Parkway
Reston, VA 22090
703-437-1100

VIRGIN ISLANDS

Virgin Islands Dept. of Health
P.O. Box 520, Christiansted,
St. Croix, U.S.V.I. 00820
809-773-1311

WASHINGTON

Immunization Section LP-19
Office of Disease
Prevention & Control
Division of Health
Olympia, WA 98504
206-753-5909

Auburn Health Center
Seattle-King County
Health Department
20 Auburn Ave.
Auburn, WA 98002
206-833-8400

Kent Medical Center
Kulendu G. Vasavda, M.D.
17700 S.E. 272nd St., Suite 240
Kent, WA 98042
206-859-6800

Dr. Elaine C. Jong ★
Dr. Russell McMullen ★
Travel & Tropical
Medicine Clinic
Univ. of Washington
School of Medicine
University Hospital RC - 02
1959 NE Pacific
Seattle, WA 98195
206-548-4226

Dr. Craig Karpilow ★
Travelers' Medical & Immunization Clinic
509 Olive Way - Suite 1201
Seattle, WA 98101
206-624-6933

Paul P. Roberts, MD, M.Sc. ★
The Polyclinic
1145 Broadway
Seattle, WA 98122
206-329-1760

Dr. Richard A. Miller ★
Travelers' Clinic
Pacific Medical Center
1200 -12th Ave. South
Seattle, WA 98144
206-326-4013

Kevin M. O'Keeffe, MD, MPH
Occupational
Health Resources
2203 Airport Way South -
Suite 210
Seattle, WA 98134
206-682-2234

Kaiser Permanente,Vancouver
Cascade Park Medical Office
12607 SE Mill Plain Blvd.
Vancouver, WA 98684

Vancouver-Clark County
Health Center
2000 Fort Vancouver Way
Vancouver, WA 98663
206-695-9215

Clallam County Health Dept.
223 East 4th St.
Port Angeles, WA 98362
206-452-7831

Chelan-Douglas County
Health Dept.
316 Washington St.
Wenatchee, WA 98801
509-664-5306

Federal Way Immunization
Clinic
1814 S. 324 Place
Federal Way, WA 98003
206-838-4557

Snohomish Health District
Courthouse
Everett, WA 98201
206-339-5200

Physicians Medical Center
1624 South "I" St., Suite 402
Tacoma, WA 98405
206-627-4123

Tacoma-Pierce County
Health Department
3629 South "D" St.
Tacoma, WA 98312
206-591-6452

Bremerton-Kitsap County
Health Department
109 Austin Drive
Bremerton, WA 98312
206-478-5235

Skagit County Health Dept.
Courthouse Administration
Building
205 West Kincaid St.
Mount Vernon, WA 98273
206-336-9380

Dr. E. Rezvani
1220 - 22nd Street
Anacortes, WA 98221
206-293-4518

Spokane County Health Dept.
West 1101 College Ave.
Spokane, WA 99201
509-456-3630

Rockwood Clinic
400 East Fifth Ave.
Spokane, WA 99202
509-838-2531

Thurston County Health Dept.
529 S.W. Fourth Ave.
Olympia, WA 98501
206-786-5581

Walla Wallla County
Health Dept.
310 West Poplar
Walla Walla, WA 99362
509-527-3290

Bellingham-Whatcom County
Health Department
509 Girard St.
Bellingham, WA 98227
206-676-6720

Yakima County
Health District
104 North First Street
Yakima, WA 98901
509-575-4040

WEST VIRGINIA

West Virginia Dept. of Health
1800 Washington Street
Charleston, WV 23505
304-348-0644

Walden, John B., MD ★
Travelers' Clinic
Marshall University
School of Medicine
1801 Sixth Avenue
Huntington, WV 25701
304-696-7046

WISCONSIN

Wisconsin Division of Health
P.O. Box 309
Madison, WI 53701-0309
608-266-2346

Jackson Clinic
345 W. Washington Ave.
Madison, WI 53703
608-252-8510

University of Wisconsin
Madison Health Service
1552 University Ave.
Madison, WI 53705
608-262-1388

Dean Medical Center
1313 Fish Hatchery Road
Madison, WI 53715
608-252-8109
608-252-8000

Occupational Health & Wellness
Center
Beloit Memorial Hospital
421 East Grand Ave.
Beloit, WI 53511
608-364-4666

Richland Medical Center
1313 Seminary St.
Richland Center, WI 53581
608-647-6161

Gundersen Clinic
1836 South Ave.
LaCrosse, WI 54601
608-782-7300

LaCrosse County Health Dept.
1707 Main Street
LaCrosse, WI 54601
608-785-9723

Manitwoc Clinic
601 Reed Avenue
Manitowoc, WI 54220
414-682-8841

Marshfield Clinic
1000 N. Oak Ave.
Marshfield, WI 54449
715-387-5511

Medical Assoc. Health Center
Town Hall Road
Menomonwa Falls, WI 53051
715-255-7020

Milwaukee Health Dept.
841 North Broadway, Rm. 102
Milwaukee, WI 53202
414-278-3624

International Travelers' Clinic
St. Luke's Hospital
2900 West Oklahoma
Milwaukee, WI 53215
414-649-6666

Gary P. Barnas, MD
Travelers' Clinic
Froedtert Hospital
9200 W. Wisconsin Ave.
Milwaukee, WI 53226
414-259-2712

Dr. Robert Dedmon
Kimberly Clark Health Center
2100 Winchester Road
Neenah, WI 54956
414-721-5994

Family Practice Center
1514 Ogden Street
Superior, WI 54880
715-394-5557

CANADA

Additional information on
travel clinics in Canada is
available through The Canadian
Society For International
Health, Division Of Tropical
Medicine, 1565 Carling Ave.,
Suite 400, Ottawa, Ontario K1Z
8R1; 613-725-3789

QUEBEC

MacLean, J.D. MD, FRCP
McGill University
Centre for Tropical Diseases
Montreal General Hospital
1650 Cedar Ave. - Rm. 787
Montreal, Quebec H3G 1A4
514-934-8049

Community Health Centre
Travel & Innoculation Clinic
CLSC des Coteaux
326, des Sagueneens
Chicoutimi, Quebec G7H 6J6
418-545-1262

Community Health Dept.
Saint-Sacrement Hospital
1050 Ste-Foy St.
Quebec City, Quebec G1S 4L8
418-688-3670

ONTARIO

Dr. David Lawee
Travel and Inoculation Unit
Toronto General Hospital
First Floor Eaton North,
Rm. 250
200 Elizabeth St.
Toronto, Ontario M5G 2C4
416-340-3670

Keystone, J.S., MD, FRCPC★
Travel Medicine Consulting
Director, Tropical Disease Unit
Toronto General Hospital
200 Elizabeth Street, en g-214
Toronto, Ontario M5G 2C4
416-340-3671

Dr. Kenneth Gamble
International Medical Services
4000 Leslie St.
North York, Ontario M2K 2R9
416-494-7512

Travel Counselling &
Immunization Service
St. Michael's Hospital
61 Queen Street, 3rd floor
Toronto, Ontario
416-864-6040

Yonge-Gerrard Travel Clinic
415 Yonge Street, Suite 101
Toronto, Ont., M5B 2E7
416-585-2322
(Open 365 days a year)

Tropical Disease Clinic
Ottawa Civic Hospital
1053 Carling Ave.
Ottawa, Ontario K1Y 4E9

International Association for
Medical Assistance for Travellers
(IAMAT)
1287 St. Clair Ave. West, Suite 1
Toronto, Ontario M6E 1B8
416-652-0137

International Travel Clinic
University Hospital
339 Windermere Road
London, Ontario N6A 5A5
519-663-3395

Dr. Douglas MacPherson
Tropical Disease &
Travelers' Clinic
McMaster University Med. Ctr
1200 Main St. West
Hamilton, Ontario L8N 3Z5
416-521-2100 ext. 5997

Dr. Mark Wise
The Travel Clinic
Bishops' Cross Medical Centre
2300 John St.
Thornhill, Ontario L3T 6G7
905-889-5777

Clinique du Voyage Int'l
Boutique Sante 2000
Carrefour de L'Estrie
3050 boul. Portland
Sherbrooke, Ontario J1L 1K1
819-564-1010

Medical Officer for Health
Sudbury & District Health Unit
1300 Paris Crescent
Sudbury, Ontario P3E 3A3
705-522-9200 ext. 202

Medical Officer for Health
Health Unit
835 Weller St.

Peterborough, Ontario
K9J 4Y1
705-743-1160

Thunder Bay District
Health Unit
999 Balmoral Street
Thunder Bay, Ontario
P7B 2W6
807-625-5900
807-625-5944

Medical Officer for Health
Porcuoine Health Unit
169 Pine Street South
Timmins, Ontario P4N 8B7
705-267-1181

Medical Officer for Health
Algoma Health Unit
99 Foster Drive
Sault Ste-Marie, Ontario
P6A 5X6
705-759-5287

Regional Niagara Health
Services
130 Lockhart Drive
St. Catherines, Ontario
P3E 3A3
416-688-3762

NEW BRUNSWICK

District Medical Health Officer
Region II
157 Duke St.
Saint John, NB E2L 3X1
506-658-2455

NEWFOUNDLAND

District Health Unit
Public Service Building
Forest Road
St. John's, NF A1C 5T7
709-576-3435

NOVA SCOTIA

Medical Services
3129 Kempt Road
Halifax, NS B3K 5N6
902-426-3998

Cape Breton Health Unit
Provincial Health Unit
Provincial Building
Prince Street
Sydney, NS B1P 5L1
902-564-4447 or 564-4448

PRINCE EDWARD
ISLAND

Department of Health
Sullivan Building
16 Fitzroy St.
Charlottetown, PEI C1A 7N8
902-892-5471

ALBERTA

International Travel Immunization Clinic
Health Sciences Center
3330 Hospital Drive N.W.
Calgary, Alberta T2N 4N1
403-220-4274

Central Health Clinic
10005 - 103 A Avenue
Edmonton, Alberta T5J 0K1
403-428-3444

MANITOBA

Medical Services
Health & Welfare Canada
303 Main St.
Winnepeg, Manitoba
R3C 0H4
204-949-4194

SASKATCHEWAN

City Health Department
1910 McIntyre
Regina, S4P 2R3
306-522-3621

Medical Health Officer
Saskatoon Community
Health Unit
350 - 3rd Ave.
Saskatoon, S7K 6G7
306-664-9627

BRITISH COLUMBIA

Dr. S. Boraston
Travelers' Clinic
Vancouver Health Dept.
Burrard Health Unit
1770 W. 7th Ave., 2nd floor
Vancouver, B. C., V6J 4Y6
604-736-9844

Northern Interior Health Unit
1444 Edmonton Street
Prince George, BC V2M 6W5
604-565-7311

Index

D

Dapsone
  treatment for leishmaniasis 116
Death
  government assistance 11
Decongestants
  during air flight 43
DEET 96
Dehydration
  during travel 37, 67
Delhi boil 115
Dengue fever 106
Dengue hemorrhagic fever 106
Denmark 277
Dexamethasone, for typhoid fever 126
DIA-PAK 30
Diabetes
  and air travel
    and insulin dosages 30
  Travel kits for diabetics 30
Diarrhea, chronic 58
Diethylcarbamazine, for filariasis 113
Dirofilariasis 361
Disease Risk Summaries
  Australia and Oceania 412
  Central America 219
  China and the Indian sub-
    Continent 375
  Europe and Russia 272
  Japan, Korea, and Taiwan 407
  Mexico 219
  North Africa 296
  South America 249
  Southeast Asia 391
  the Caribbean 219
  the Middle East 361
Diuretics 30
Divers Alert Network 20, 186
Diving accident emergency
  information 20
Djibouti 339
Dominica 237
Dominican Republic 237
Doxycycline
  for malaria 83
  for sexually transmitted
    diseases 160

Dramamine 40
Duranon 102
Dysentery 57

E

Ear infection, and flight 42
Ecuador 260
Eddie Bauer 18
Egypt 298
ELISA screening test
  for filariasis 113
Emergency dental kit 30
Encephalopathy
  due to Lyme disease 142
Engerix-B hep atitis vaccine 148
Entex LA 43
EpiPen 28
Erlichiosis 139
Ethiopia 340
Eustachian tube, during flight 41
Exercise and pregnancy 208
EZY DOSE syringe, for dehydration 71

F

Fansidar 85
Fascioliasis 133, 382, 393
Fasciolopsiasis 133, 382, 393
Fasigyn 122
Fever, causes of, in travelers 31
Fiji 416
Filariasis 112
Finland 278
First aid, books about 9
Flagyl
  for amebiasis 123
Floxin (ofloxacin)
for travelers' diarrhea 64
  Flu shot, for preventing
    meningitis 129
Flying Doctors Society 191
Flying, during pregnancy 210
Food-based oral hydration
  solutions 69
Foot care, for travel 30
Foreign hospitals
  assessing capabilities 176
Foreign physicians, capabilities of 176

International Road Signs

Left Bend
(Right if reversed)

Double Bend

Dangerous Bend

Crossroads

Dangerous Crossroad

Narrowing Road

Danger

Rough Road

School Crossing

Pedestrian Crossing

Men at Work

Railroad Crossing

Slippery Road

Loose Gravel

Falling Rocks

Light Signals

No Entry

No U Turn

Road Closed

No Passing

Speed Limit

Quiet Zone

Do Not Enter

No Turns
In Directions Indicated

Appears in red on actual signs